Quality Programming

Quality Programming

Developing and Testing Software With Statistical Quality Control

Chin-Kuei Cho, Ph.D.

Computa, Inc.

JOHN WILEY & SONS, INC.

New York · Chichester · Brisbane · Toronto · Singapore

This publication is designed to provide accurate and
authoritative information in regard to the subject
matter covered. It is sold with the understanding that
the publisher is not engaged in rendering legal, accounting,
or other professional service. If legal advice or other
expert assistance is required, the services of a competent
professional person should be sought. *From a Declaration
of Principles jointly adopted by a Committee of the
American Bar Association and a Committee of Publishers.*

Library of Congress Cataloging in Publication Data:

Cho, Chin-Kuei, 1937–
  Quality programming.

  Bibliography: p.
  1. Computer software—Quality control—Statistical methods. I. Title.
QA76.76.Q35C47 1987 005.1 87-2022
ISBN 0-471-84899-9

Printed in the United States of America

10 9 8 7 6 5 4 3 2 1

To

Yush-Chye
Mary
Jennifer

Foreword

When I first read C. K. Cho's book, *An Introduction to Software Quality Control* six years ago, I was surprised by the way he used a statistical approach to control the quality of software. It was refreshing to consider a program as a factory which processes raw materials (the inputs) into usable products (the outputs). The key concept in his book is the specification of the input domain of a software system by means of the "Symbolic Input Attribute Decomposition" (SIAD) tree. The SIAD tree enforces the development of well-defined requirements, and imposes disciplines in both design and implementation. Furthermore, a test plan based on the SIAD tree can be designed and implemented concurrently with the development. The quality control comes from the imposed discipline as well as from the systematic application of statistical sampling techniques using the SIAD tree.

Although much progress has been made in software technology during the past six years, the industry has progressed little. The application backlog has increased despite the introduction of new tools and methodologies, and the maintenance costs continue to escalate. The "software crises" have escalated and a jump into the new technology curve is considered absolutely necessary!

Over the past 10 years, several trends in software technology have emerged. Dijkstra's pioneering work in "Structured Programming" has stimulated major research efforts in program specification, abstract data type, and proof of program correctness. Of equal importance is the "object-oriented" approach originated by the programming language "Small-Talk," which paved the way for sophisticated graphical interfaces. More recently, there have been a number of people advocating the use of new paradigms for software evolution.

Amid all the progress in software technology I continue to hold Cho's statistical quality control a major contribution. Cho's approach not only is practical in the development of quality software but I believe his idea can scale up in the quality control of major software development centers. Therefore, I am delighted to see Cho's current book in which he has refined his techniques, reports many actual experiences, and introduces a number of new techniques. Software quality is not free. Cho's approach provides a practical way of achieving and controlling quality.

RAYMOND T. YEH

Austin, Texas
December 1986

Preface

In manufacturing industries,

Show credibility, show product warranty

has been a winning strategy in modern competitive markets. A warranty such as:

Five years or 50,000 miles: parts and labor free

is not uncommon in the automobile industry.

However, in the software industry,

Show credibility, show software warranty

is a dream seemingly unattainable to many software users and developers. A software warranty such as:

> **The program is sold "as is" without warranty of any kind, either expressed or implied, including, but not limited to the warranties of merchantability and fitness for your purpose. The entire risk as to the quality and performance of the program is with you. If the program is found to be defective, you (and not the developer or an authorized dealer) assume the entire cost of all necessary servicing, repair, or correction. ... This warranty gives you specific legal rights and you may also have other rights which vary from state to state.**
>
> **The developer does not warrant that the functions contained in the program will meet your requirements or that the operations of the software will be uninterrupted or error free. The developer does warrant as the only warranty provided to you, that the diskette(s) or cassette(s) on which the program is furnished will be free from defects in materials and workmanship under normal use for ninety (90) days from the date of purchase evidenced by your receipt.**

is common in the software industry.

Why are the warranties being offered in manufacturing industries and in the software industry so different? The answer is surprisingly simple: Statistical quality control is widely used in manufacturing industries, but not yet widely used in the software industry.

Statistical quality control, invented in the United States during World War II for procurement of quality military hardware, has been a proven, powerful, and widely used tool in manufacturing industries to ensure product quality for over 40 years in the United States and abroad. The Japanese have been using this technology so effectively that their products dominate the international competitive marketplace. As a result, statistical quality control has been called the third industrial revolution technology. Dr. W. Edwards Deming, who taught the Japanese how to use this technology for production of quality products, has been named the father of Japanese quality. In a recent article in *Parade* magazine, Deming was named the father of the third industrial revolution.[1]

Can statistical quality control be used in the software industry? A recent survey, conducted by Thayer, revealed that there are 20 problems existing in the industry.[2] These problems are in the areas of: requirements, success, project, cost, schedule, design, test, maintainability, warranty, control, organizing type, accountability, project manager, visibility, reliability, goodness, programmers, and tracing in software engineering and development. Although modern software technologies are being practiced, such as structured programming, structured analysis, structured design, and structured testing, these problems persist! What happens? Can continuing practices of these technologies solve any of these 20 problems? What could be the root of these problems? What could be the solutions? Questions like these are answered from the perspectives of statistical quality control in the book.

The software warranty problem mentioned earlier is a natural consequence of the 20 problems mentioned. Unless these problems are solved, demanding/delivering software warranty will remain an unattainable dream to software users/developers. Yes, statistical quality control can be used to solve many of the 20 problems that lead to the offering of warranty in the industry. The technology is now available and is discussed throughout this book.

A new software methodology called "Quality Programming,"[3] incorporating statistical quality control for development of high quality and cost effective software, is introduced and treated in great detail in this book. Emphases are placed on deployment of statistical quality control during every stage of the software life cycle, from modeling, requirements specification, concurrent software design and test design, concurrent implementation of software design and test design, test and integration, to software acceptance that leads to the offering of meaningful software warranty. It should be noted that the software user can now use this methodology to demand software warranty and the developer can use the same methodology to deliver software warranty in order to gain a competitive edge in their respective businesses. The software

[1] David Halberstam, "W. Edwards Deming, the Man Who Taught Japan about Quality, Believes: Yes We Can," *Parade*, Parade Publications, Inc., New York, July 8, 1984, pp. 4–7.

[2] R. H. Thayer, A. Pyster, and R. C. Wood, "The Challenge of Software Engineering Project Management," *IEEE Computer*, Vol. 13, No. 8, August 1980, pp. 51–59.

[3] C. K. Cho, *An Introduction to Software Quality Control*, Wiley, New York, 1980.

industry can now enjoy the same winning strategy

Show credibility, show software warranty

Since the publication of my first book,[3] courses under various titles such as Software Engineering and Quality Assurance have been taught by me at both the undergraduate and graduate levels in the Computer Science and the Electrical Engineering Departments at the University of Maryland and in the Department of Electrical Engineering and Computer Science at George Washington University, using my first book as a textbook. In addition, a one-week seminar on Software Engineering and Quality Assurance has been given more than 25 times worldwide since August 1980, also using the same book as a textbook. I have been invited to give professional presentations and tutorials at numerous conferences. Thousands of professionals, including project managers, software engineers, software quality assurance personnel, and company executives, have been exposed to the application of statistical quality control for software development and testing. Numerous companies have benefited from using this technology to gain their competitive edge. These invaluable experiences all go into this book.

The book is written to be used in three ways:

1. As a textbook for software engineering and software methodology courses at the undergraduate and graduate levels at colleges and universities (with ample background materials and exercises).
2. As a reference book for practicing professionals (with ample cross references).
3. As a software development and quality assurance plan for both software users and developers (with repeating details that serve as a checklist at each stage of the software development life cycle).

The Quality Programming methodology can be used for the development of scientific, business, batch, on-line, real-time, and large- or small-sized software.

Deming has conducted many four-day seminars to introduce top-management people, from large and small companies in many different industries, to the use of statistical quality control to increase quality and productivity. He pointed out 14 obligations of top management in any organization, as part of their responsibility to stockholders and to the general public. Ten of the fourteen obligations are applicable in the software industry and are discussed in this book. The materials given here fill in the need of software user/developer companies to win in the modern market.

I am deeply grateful to many of my friends and colleagues for their help, input, and suggestions, in particular, G. Gordon Schulmeyer, James I. McManus, James J. Holden III, Dr. Hui Chuan Chen, Dr. James Hsu, and Dr. Michael C. Chen. The opinions and views presented are solely the author's.

Dr. Raymond T. Yeh's foreword is an invaluable contribution to this book. His kindness is deeply appreciated. I am also indebted to the professionals at John Wiley & Sons for their help in creating a smooth transition as my manuscript was turned into a book. In particular I am thankful to John Mahaney, my editor, for assisting me throughout this process.

I am indebted to Jerry Ackerman for his valuable contributions to the preparation and editing of the manuscript. Its final quality was largely the result of his efforts.

CHIN-KUEI CHO

Rockville, Maryland
December 25, 1986

Acknowledgment

The following acknowledgment is reprinted from **American National Standard Programming Language COBOL, X3.23-1974**, published by the American National Standards Institute, Inc.

COBOL is an industry language and is not the property of any company or group of companies, or of any organization or group of organizations. No warranty, expressed or implied, is made by any contributor or by the CODASYL Programming Language Committee as to the accuracy and functioning of the programming system and language. Moreover, no responsibility is assumed by any contributor, or by the committee, in connection herewith. The authors and copyright holders of the copyrighted material used herein

FLOW-MATIC (trademark of Sperry Rand Corporation), Programming for the UNIVAC^{R} I and II, Data Automation Systems copyrighted 1958, 1959, by Sperry Rand Corporation; IBM Commercial Translator Form No. F 28-8013, copyright 1959 by IBM; FACT, DSI 27A5260-2760, copyrighted 1960 by Minneapolis-Honeywell

have specifically authorized the use of this material in whole or in part, in the COBOL specifications. Such authorization extends to the reproduction and use of COBOL specifications in programming manuals or similar publications.

How To Use This Book

As this book is a self-contained treatment intended for readers of different backgrounds, a guide to the readers is offered.

A. For scientific application readers:

a. If you have statistical and quality control background, then read:

Chapters 1, 4, 7, 8, 9, 10, 11, 12, 13, 14, 15

b. If you have statistical background only, then read:

Chapters 1, 4, 5, 6, 7, 8, 9, 10, 11, 12, 13, 14, 15

c. If you have no statistical and quality control background, then read:

Chapters 1, 2, 3, 4, 5, 6, 7, 8, 9, 10, 11, 12, 13, 14, 15

B. For commercial and data processing application readers:

a. If you have statistical and quality control background, then read:

Chapters 1, 4, 7, 8, 9, 10, 11, 12, 13, 15

b. If you have statistical background only, then read:

Chapters 1, 4, 5, 6, 7, 8, 9, 10, 11, 12, 13, 15

c. If you have no statistical and quality control background, then read:

Chapters 1, 2, 3, 4, 5, 6, 7, 8, 9, 10, 11, 12, 13, 15

Contents

Quality Programming

CHAPTER 1

Introduction

Quality and productivity are weapons that any enterprising organization must use to win dominance in the global, competitive markets of the information age. A company that can produce higher quality goods using fewer resources than other companies will have the competitive edge in any kind of market. Producers of poor or average quality products with low productivity, whatever their past market shares, will lose ground and will not be able to compete.

Any organization that wants to survive in the information age must recognize that the world is in the midst of a third wave of the industrial revolution. The first wave began with the invention of machinery-based factories, introduced by Eli Whitney. The second wave was assembly line mass production, initiated by Henry Ford. The third wave is now here, but it is not what many people think it is. Surprisingly, it is not the modern technology of computers, lasers, microelectronics, or telecommunications. The third wave of the industrial revolution is the use of statistical quality control, established by Dr. W. Edwards Deming [44]. Each wave transforms the marketplace and the workplace, drastically changing consumer expectations, how workers are treated, and the scale of business operations. Each wave results in a quantum jump in productivity—of thousands upon thousands of percent—and makes the old ways of doing business obsolete.

The world of the third wave of the industrial revolution presents an inescapable challenge to all businesses. Deming, considered the father of Japanese quality control, has taught how to produce quality goods using statistical quality control in Japan for more than 25 years. As a result, Japanese consumer goods have gained worldwide dominance in the marketplace, be it in automobiles, electronics, computer hardware, televisions, cameras, or VCRs. This quality invasion has been costly to the United States, causing the loss of millions of jobs alone. The situation is likely to become worse before it becomes better, even provided that everyone in the manufacturing industries is quality-conscious.

Ironically, statistical quality control was invented in the United States. It was developed during World War II for the procurement of hardware for the military, and since then, it has been used in manufacturing industries worldwide. The Japanese have used it to the fullest. Equally ironic, the computer software industry, with its image of being the ultimate in modern technology, is, perhaps, the last frontier where this powerful tool has not been used.

The ground for applying statistical quality control in the software industry has been broken by the publication of Cho [28] in 1980. Since then, the author has conducted more than 50 in-house training sessions and five-day seminars, courses, presentations, and tutorials for thousands of professionals. Numerous software companies have successfully used the statistical quality control tool in software development or are in the process of applying the tool to their software development environment. The references in Cho [31], Fultyn [40], Wohlwend [41], and Jump [42] are but a few current examples.

The materials in Cho [28], input from many of the professionals who have taken the author's seminars and courses, and the author's own 16 years of professional experience have gone into the writing of this book. It is sincerely hoped that this book will serve as a starting point for moving the software industry into the third wave of the industrial revolution.

1.1 SOFTWARE ENGINEERING GOALS AND PRINCIPLES (MURE AIMLUCCS)*

Software excellence begins with dedication to the goals of software engineering, recognized by the industry as the fundamental requirements

*Pronounced "more aim lucks."

of quality software. These goals are:

Modifiability
Understandability
Reliability
Efficiency

To achieve these goals, it is generally accepted that software must be developed in accordance with the following principles:

Abstract data typing
Information hiding
Modularization
Localization
Uniformity
Completeness
Confirmability
Statistical quality control

These goals and principles will be described in detail and discussed throughout this book. The reader may remember them by the mnemonic: MURE AIMLUCCS. It will be seen that wherever there is software quality, these software engineering goals and principles are in evidence.

1.2 THE PROBLEMS OF SOFTWARE WARRANTY

Almost universally, manufacturers pledge the quality of their products in the form of a warranty. Every consumer recognizes the key clauses at the heart of all warranties: "Satisfaction guaranteed or your money back," "Five years or 50,000 miles parts and labor free," and so on. A warranty is the manufacturer's legally binding promise to replace defective parts, and make repairs due to inferior workmanship, and so on at its own expense. A powerful warranty can mean a competitive edge. The sale may go to the company that can deliver the longest or most comprehensive warranty. Generally, the company that can best ensure quality and productivity will be able to offer the best warranty.

The purpose of a warranty is to protect the consumer. A manufacturer who must offer a warranty to stay competitive, but whose product is defective, can take serious losses, as happened to the automobile industry during the period of numerous "recalls" for defective parts in crucial safety systems of many automobiles.

This program is sold 'as is' without warranty of any kind, either expressed or implied, including, but not limited, to the warranties of merchantability and fitness for your purpose. The entire risk as to the quality and performance of the program is with you. If the program is found to be defective, you (and not the developer or an authorized dealer) assume the entire cost of all necessary servicing, repair, or correction.... This warranty gives you specific legal rights and you may also have other rights which vary from state to state.

The developer does not warrant that the functions contained in the program will meet your requirements or that the operation of the software will be uninterrupted or error-free. The developer does warrant as the only warranty provided to you, that the diskette(s) or cassette(s) on which the program is furnished will be free from defects in materials and workmanship under normal use for ninety (90) days from the date of purchase evidenced by your receipt.

Figure 1.1 A software "warranty."

If the reader brings his or her reasonable consumer expectations of meaningful warranty into a computer store, he or she is likely to be shocked at the kinds of warranties offered on software products. Figure 1.1 shows an example of the type of warranty given on a commercially available software package.

Why is the software industry so different than other manufacturing industries when it comes to warranty? The answer is that the software industry is struggling with problems that result in poor quality, cost overruns, late delivery, and dissatisfied users, and none of the modern software development methodologies—sometimes considered great advances—have solved these problems.

A survey conducted in the software industry revealed that methodologies such as structured programming, structured analysis, structured design technique, and so on contribute meagerly to developing good quality and cost-effective software. Thus it is natural that software developers cannot afford to offer warranties on their products. To do so, they would first have to start solving the major problems of software development.

1.3 THE 20 PROBLEMS OF THE CURRENT SOFTWARE INDUSTRY

When modern computers were first invented, software was treated as an integral part of the hardware. Not until recent years has the economic importance of software to the development and application of computer systems been recognized. Now software is viewed as reflected in *Webster's New World Dictionary*:

> Programming material, systems, etc., for a computer, as distinguished from the physical components (hardware) of the computer itself.

Unfortunately, what has made the impact of software more appreciated has been, to some extent, the problems of software development and the consequences of poor software quality. The high cost and low reliability of software gradually caught people's attention both inside and outside the software industry.

1.3.1 High Cost of Software

The high cost of software may be illustrated by the spending of the U.S. government. In 1978, the cost of software development, testing, and maintenance for the government was estimated at about $8 billion, including about $4 billion for defense applications. The Air Force alone spent about 80 to 90 percent systems procurement cost on software [23], compared with about 15 percent in 1955 [25]. The costs of many individual projects are also high. For example, in IBM OS/360 cost about $200 million; the SAGE (a military system), about $250 million; and the Manned Space Program, about $1 billion [25].

It is interesting to note the distribution of the cost in the conventional software development stages of program analysis and design (excluding system analysis), implementation, integration, and testing. Figure 1.2 shows the cost distributions for five large software projects [25]. The numbers are surprisingly close for each development stage of each project. The average cost distribution over the three stages of

Projects	Analysis and Design	Implementation	Integration and Testing
SAGE	0.39	0.14	0.47
NTDS	0.30	0.20	0.50
Gemini	0.36	0.17	0.47
Saturn V	0.32	0.24	0.44
OS/360	0.33	0.17	0.50
Average	0.34	0.184	0.476
TRW Survey	0.46	0.20	0.34

Figure 1.2 An example of software development cost distributions.

development are 0.34, 0.184, and 0.476, respectively. The comparison numbers reported in a TRW survey, also given in Figure 1.2, would appear to indicate that more effort spent in the earlier stages of development may dramatically reduce the cost of later stages.

1.3.2 Low Reliability of Software

Low reliability of software has been an equal source of concern. The existing software development situation regarding reliability may be summarized as follows [27]:

A. Development is often accomplished by amateurs (whether at universities, software houses, or hardware manufacturers), using tinkering (at the universities) or a human-wave ("million monkey") approach.

B. Developed software is often unreliable and requires permanent "maintenance" (here "maintenance" means correction of errors that are assumed to be present at the very beginning of development).

C. Existing software is often messy and lacks transparency and ease of improvement or extension.

1.3.3 The 20 Problems

As software products become more essential to an increasing number of applications, more attention has been focused on the problems areas of software development. High cost and low reliability now seem like the tip of the iceberg. Every aspect of software project management and programming practice is being evaluated. Figure 1.3 shows the results of a recent survey which identified at least 20 problems in the software industry that are urgently waiting for solutions [36].

The problems are so central to the theme of this book that they will be referred to repeatedly in later chapters as "the 20 problems stated in Figure 1.3." The reader is encouraged to refer to this figure frequently.

To date, the software industry has not been able to solve these problems. Attempts to apply existing software development methodologies have led to confusion. To the developer and user, a software development project often seems like the edifice in M. C. Escher's "Waterfall" (see Figure 1.4). For all of the available structured techniques, the system does not seem to work.

Planning

1. *Requirements:* Requirement specifications are frequently incomplete, ambiguous, inconsistent, and / or unmeasurable.

2. *Success:* Success criteria for a software development are frequently inappropriate, which result in "poor-quality" delivered software; that is, not maintainable, unreliable, difficult to use, relatively undocumented, and so on.

3. *Project:* Planning for software engineering projects is generally poor.

4. *Cost:* The ability to estimate accurately the resources required to accomplish a software development is poor.

5. *Schedule:* The ability to estimate accurately the delivery time on a software development is poor.

6. *Design:* Decision rules for use in selecting the correct software design techniques, equipment, and aids to be used in designing software in a software engineering project are not available.

7. *Test:* Decision rules for use in selecting the correct procedures, strategies, and tools to be used in testing software developed in a software engineering project are not available.

8. *Maintainability:* Procedures, techniques, and strategies for designing maintainable software are not available.

9. *Warranty:* Methods to guarantee or warranty that the delivered software will "work" for the user are not available.

10 *Control:* Procedures, methods, and techniques for designing a project control system that will enable project managers to successfully control their project are not readily available.

Organizing

11. *Type:* Decision rules for selecting the proper organizational structure, for example, project, matrix, function, are not available.

12. *Accountability:* The accountability structure in many software engineering projects is poor, leaving some question as to who is responsible for various project functions.

Staffing

13. *Project manager:* Procedures and techniques for the selection of project managers are poor.

Directing

14. *Techniques:* Decision rules for use in selecting the correct management techniques for software engineering project management are not available.

Controlling

15. *Visibility:* Procedures, techniques, strategies, and aids that will provide visibility of progress (not just resources used) to the project manager are not available.

16. *Reliability:* Measurements or indexes of reliability that can be used as an element of software design are not available and there is no way to predict software failure; that is, there is no practical way to show the delivered software meets a given reliability criteria.

17. *Maintainability:* Measurements or indexes of maintainability that can be used as an element of software design are not available; that is, there is no practical way to show that a given program is more maintainable than another.

18. *Goodness:* Measurements or indexes of "goodness" of code that can be used as an element of software design are not available; that is, there is no practical way to show that one program is better than another.

19. *Programmers:* Standards and techniques for measuring the quality of performance and the quantity of production expected from programmers and data processing analysts are not available.

20. *Tracing:* Techniques and aids that provide an acceptable means of tracing a software development from requirements to completed code are not generally available.

Figure 1.3 Twenty problems in software engineering project management. (Reproduced with permission from R. H. Thayer, A. Pyster, and R. C. Wood, "The Challenge of Software Engineering Project Management," IEEE *Computer*, Vol. 13, No. 8, August, 1980, pp. 51–59. © 1980 IEEE.)

Figure 1.4 Maurits C. Escher's "Waterfall" provides an example of insufficiency in using structured programming. The machine is well designed. The driver is powerful. The data flow is crystal clear. The system is well modularized and possesses excellent understandability. The "developer" is enjoying the bigness and beauty of the system while the user is urgently waiting for the data. Yet the entire system does not work at all. (Picture reproduced with permission from the collection of the Haags Gemeentemuseum, The Hague. © M. C. Escher Heirs, c/o Cordon Art-Baarn-Holland.)

At the root of these problems is a misconception of the nature of the software industry. The solutions to the problems of software development must begin with a change of perspective.

1.4 SOFTWARE DEVELOPMENT AS A MANUFACTURING INDUSTRY

Is software development a manufacturing industry? According to *Webster's New World Dictionary*, the word "manufacturing" is defined as "to work (wool, steel, etc.) into usable form." Thus software development is one of the manufacturing industries that works some raw material into usable form. The raw material in software development is the data input to a piece of software. The usable material is the data output by the program. The software itself is the factory that works the raw data into usable form. This analogy is illustrated in Figure 1.5.

Once software professionals can make this shift of perspective, they can leave behind the Escher like confusion of current software development and start applying the time-tested lessons of the other manufacturing industries.

First, almost without exception, modern manufacturing facilities are built after the products that are well-defined. For example, in the petroleum industry, a refinery process is established after definition of the product—gasoline. Similarly, in the automobile industry, a manufacturing plant is built after definition of the product—automobiles.

Second, the consumer of a product is concerned only with the quality of the product design and of the finished goods, and is not interested in

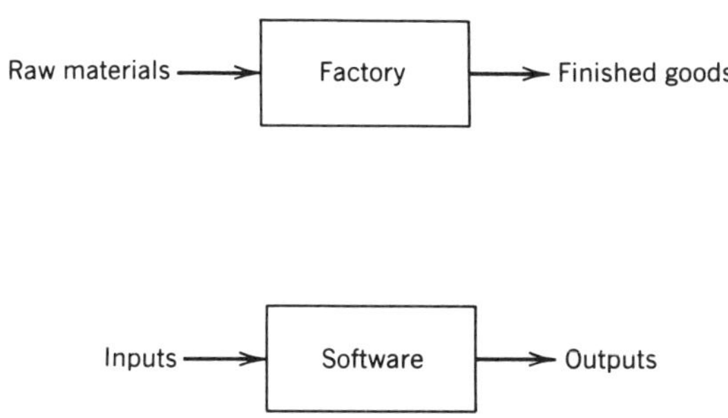

Figure 1.5 An analogy between a factory and a piece of software.

the quality or reliability of the factory. Therefore, manufacturers shape their activities completely around the goal of ensuring the quality of the product—from the inspection of raw materials, the precision of the tools used, the temperature and humidity of the machine shop, the variation of workmanship, and so on, to the inspection of the end product. Above all, there is one powerful tool widely relied on to help a manufacturer attain the goal of satisfying the consumer: statistical quality control.

It is inconceivable that a manufacturer would build a factory before the product is well-defined and designed, and expect a good quality product. Yet, current practice in the software industry appears to be doing just that. This is because the current software industry treats the software itself as the end product, and does not see that the user is interested in the quality of the software only as a means to an end: producing quality output for the user's application. This is evidenced by the lack of rigorous treatment of the input domain and the output, that is, product unit definition by almost all of the current software development methodologies.

The input domain is the source from which input data, analogous to the raw materials in manufacturing, are constructed for the software. If the input domain is not well-defined, the input data may not be properly constructed and may tend to be of poor quality. For any manufacturing industry, poor quality raw materials always lead to defective products, regardless of how correct or reliable the factory is. Product unit definition is the foundation for applying statistical quality control principles. A collection of product units becomes a population for which various statistics can be studied to ascertain the quality of the product. Without input domain and product unit definitions, it is hardly possible to control the quality of the data produced by a piece of software. Without using statistical quality control, it is doubtful that current practice will help produce cost-effective, usable data for the user.

1.5 THE NATURE OF QUALITY CONTROL

The purpose of using statistical quality control is to attain excellence in product quality. The statistical tool described in this book is part of a total commitment to quality that the manufacturing industries apply to every phase of the product life cycle. To begin to understand how and why quality control is an integral part of every manufacturing process, it is necessary to consider the definition of quality control and quality characteristics, the economics of quality control, and the set of basic quality control principles.

1.5.1 Definition of Quality Control

According to *Webster's New World Dictionary*, the term "quality" is defined as follows:

> (1) That which makes something what it is; characteristic element; attribute. (2) Basic nature; character; kind. (3) The degree of excellence which a thing possesses; hence, (4) excellence; superiority. . . .

The term "control" is defined as follows:

> (1) Originally to check or verify (payments, etc.) by comparison with a duplicate register; hence, (2) to regulate (financial affairs). (3) To verify, as an experiment, by comparison with a standard, or by other experiments. (4) To exercise authority over; direct; command; hence, (5) to curb, restrain; hold back. . . .

Thus, in general, quality control refers to a set of activities that helps attain something's characteristic excellence.

Quality control has a somewhat more specific meaning in the manufacturing industries. According to Juran, Seder, and Gryna [1], the term "quality" is defined as follows:

> (1) The degree to which a specific product satisfies the wants of a specific consumer. . . . This might be termed "marketplace quality." (2) The degree to which a specific product conforms to a design or specification. This is known as "quality of conformance."

The term "control" is defined as follows:

> (1) The act of direction, influence, restraint, or command over something. (2) The act of verification or correction of something. (3) A standard of comparison against which to check the results of an experiment.

Thus quality control may be defined as the act of directing, influencing, verifying, and correcting to ensure the conformance of a specific product to a design or specification.

1.5.2 Quality Characteristics

A quality characteristic is any property or element that can be used to define the nature of a product. Each characteristic can be a physical or chemical property such as size, weight, volume, color, or composition. For example, the characteristics of a ball bearing may be the inner and outer diameters, the shape of the bearings, the hardness of the bearings, and so on.

Each quality characteristic is closely associated with the manufacturing of a product. Figure 1.6 shows such a relationship [1]. A designer specifies the characteristics of the product and designs the product. An engineer specifies the process that will be used to realize the design and to manufacture the product.

The product cycle starts with product concept formulation, based on an understanding of the human needs that the product is intended to

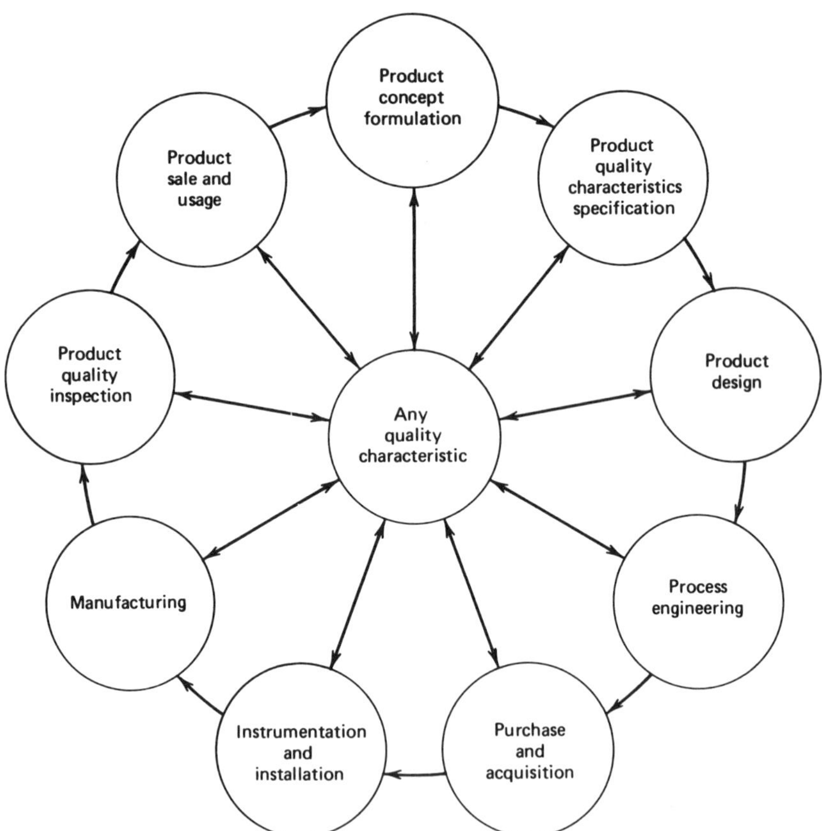

Figure 1.6 Relationship between product quality characteristics and product manufacturing cycle.

fulfill. The product concept is expressed in some representational media, such as engineering drawings, and the characteristics expected of the products are identified. The characteristics form a basis or standard of product design that, in turn, is used to plan manufacturing methods and process engineering. Materials and machinery are then purchased. Equipment and instruments are installed, and operators are trained. Finally, the manufacturing of the product takes place. The product units are then inspected to verify the conformance of the product units to the quality characteristics. Subsequently, consumers buy and use the product. Their experiences with the product are communicated as feedback to the manufacturer. Then the product cycle starts all over again.

The manufacturer is concerned with two aspects of product quality: quality of design and quality of conformance. Quality of design is the degree of excellence to which the product is designed. Quality of conformance is the degree of excellence to which the product conforms to the design. For example, black-and-white television sets and color television sets serve the same basic function, but it is generally accepted that color television offers a more satisfying experience to the user, and thus has a higher quality of design. A color set that shows no color because of defective parts, and a color set that shows color both have the same quality of design, but vary in quality of conformance.

All manufacturers know that, despite the most rigorous efforts to control product quality, the degree of quality of conformance achieved varies from one product unit to the next. Regardless of how refined and correct the manufacturing process, the variation in product quality is unavoidable. For this reason, the effectiveness of controlling product quality must be measured statistically. This is done by treating measurements made on each of the successive product units produced by the factory as if they were measurements sampled at random from a population having a mean and variance. (Mean and variance are statistical representations of the population discussed in Chapter 3.) Thus manufacturers determine product quality by statistical sampling.

1.5.3 Economics of Quality Control

Is quality control necessary? What justifies the commitment of time and resources to quality control activities? These questions may be answered by the diagram shown in Figure 1.7 [1].

In the figure, the x-axis represents the degree of quality control, and the y-axis shows the production cost. When the degree of quality control is low, then the cost associated with the activity is also low, as indicated

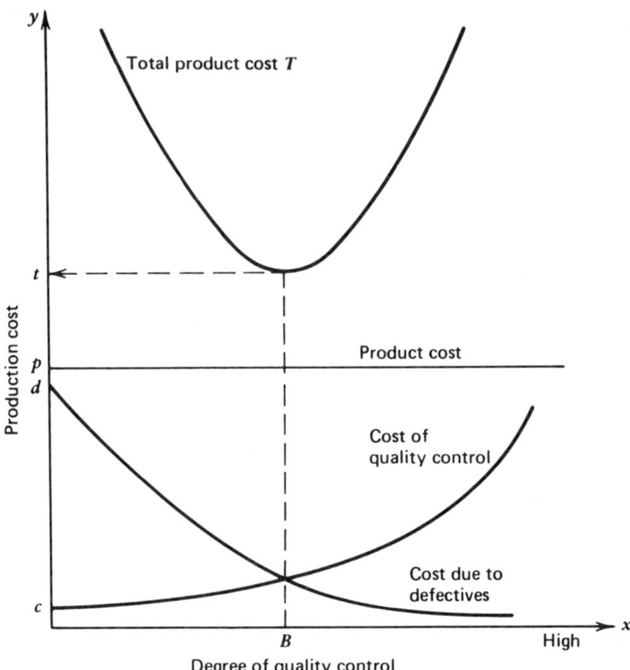

Figure 1.7 Economics of quality control.

by point c. But losses due to defective units, such as low sales volume or poor goodwill for the company, are high, as indicated by point d. As the degree of quality control (and its associated cost) increases, the losses due to defective units decreases. B is the break-even point at which gains and losses are equal. The product cost is indicated by point p. The total cost is represented by the curve T. The total cost at point B, which may be optimal, is represented by t. This indicates that quality control is necessary in order for a company to maintain its competitiveness. Quality control is also a must in manufacturing products such as aircraft, where the defectiveness of the product could cost human lives.

1.5.4 Quality Control Principles

Quality control activities in the manufacturing industries may be summarized by the following principles:

A. Set Quality Standards. For each quality characteristic, standard should be established as a product specification with which to compare the characteristic of the finished product. For example, the diameter and acceptable tolerance, that is, variation, of a steel ball to be used in a ball bearing should be specified, perhaps as 0.25 ± 0.001 inch. If the diameter of a finished ball is between 0.249 and 0.251 inch, the ball is considered acceptable. Otherwise, it is considered defective.

B. **Make a Plan to Attain the Quality Standards.** The achievement of product quality requires careful planning and engineering of the manufacturing process and equipment, acquisition of good quality materials, training operators, and so on.

C. **Determine Preventive Methods to Control the Manufacturing Process.** During the manufacturing process, all possible factors affecting the quality characteristics of the product must be carefully controlled. For example, the purity of raw materials, temperature, and pressure control can affect the diameter of a steel ball.

D. **Determine Quality of Conformance.** This determination includes:
Interpretation of the product quality standard
Random sampling of product units for inspection
Inspection and measurement of the sample product units
Comparison of the characteristics of each sampled product unit with the product quality standard
Evaluation of the quality of conformance of each product unit
Acceptance or rejection of the product population by statistical methods
Documentation of the inspection data

1.6 SOFTWARE QUALITY CONTROL

The statistical quality control tool is just as applicable to software development. However, this is considered to be a myth by many software professionals, particularly those who have no background in statistical quality control. It is not surprising, then, that a total commitment to product quality is lacking in the software industry. In fact, the conventional software life cycle is like the diagram in Figure 1.8. It can be observed that several steps of the cycle are missing—namely, product concept formulation, product quality characteristics specification, and product design. Without these steps, it is difficult to apply the statistical quality control tool to software development. However, the following

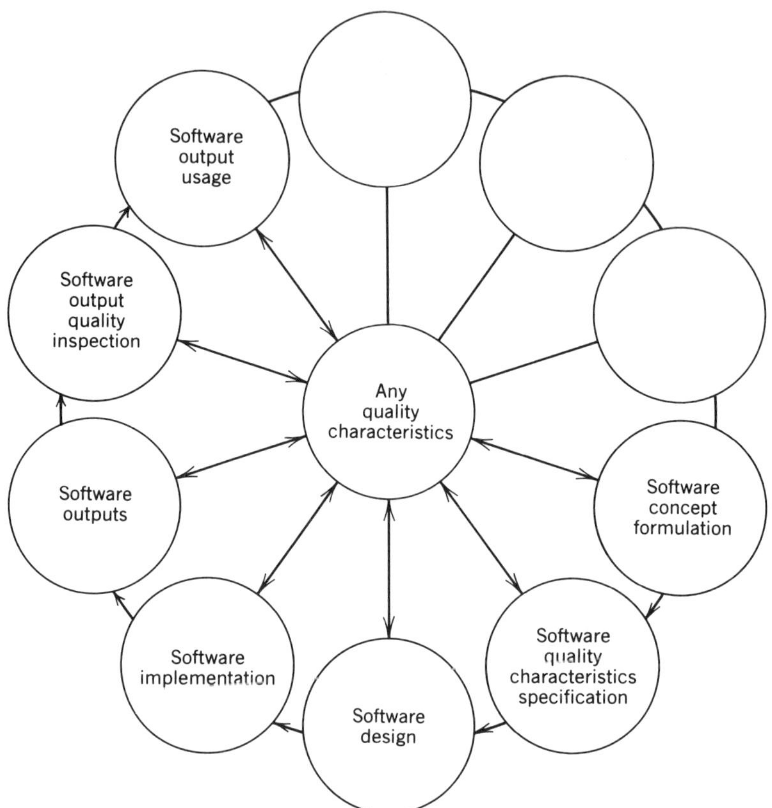

Figure 1.8 An incomplete software life cycle.

sections show how the quality control principles discussed in Section 1.5 are applicable to controlling software product quality.

1.6.1 Software Product Quality Characteristics

Like manufactured products, each product unit output by a piece of software has quality characteristics that are closely related to every phase of the product cycle. This relationship is shown in Figure 1.9. The quality characteristics of a software product unit can be defined as precisely as those of any manufactured product. The following are some of the dimensions that can be used to define the software product unit's

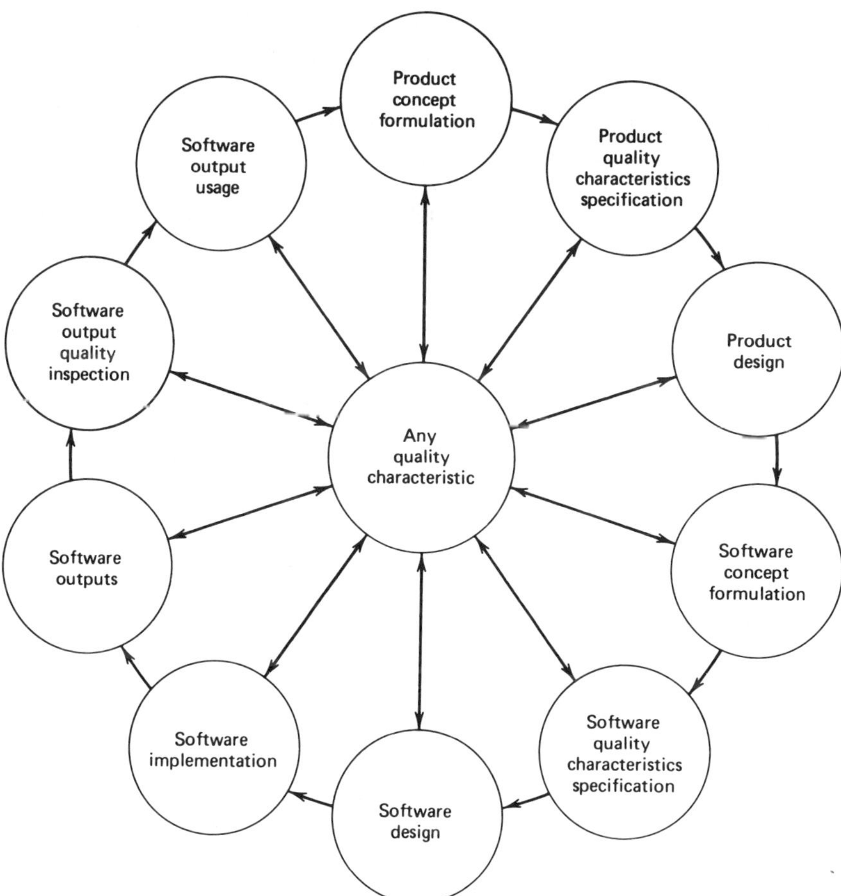

Figure 1.9 Relationship between product quality characteristics and software life cycle.

quality characteristics:

A. **Correctness.** The data contained in a product unit must be free of errors. For example, if the value of X in the product unit is required to be positive, but the actual value is negative, then the product contains errors and is defective.

B. **Accuracy.** This is the degree of exactness of the data contained in a product unit. For example, if the value of X is required to be within the tolerances of ± 0.00001, e.g., 1 ± 0.00001, in the product unit, then if the actual value of X falls within the limits, the product unit is accurate.

C. **Usability.** This is the quality of being usable. The data contained in a product unit may be correct and accurate, but may not be usable by the user. For example, if the value of X is required to be within the tolerance of ± 0.00000001, e.g., 1 ± 0.00000001, then the accurate value of X within the tolerance limits of ± 0.00001 may not be usable.

D. **Communicativeness.** Each product unit should be easy to interpret and understand. Contents and formats of the data should be self-explanatory.

1.6.2 Software System Quality Characteristics

In Figure 1.8 there is a step in the software life cycle called Software Quality Characteristics Specification. In conventional software development methodologies, this is where most of the efforts to ensure quality are placed. Some of the major software system characteristics that are considered desirable include:

A. **Reliability.** The system should be able to produce reliably quality product units under defined conditions.

B. **Understandability.** The system should be easy to read and understand. Variable names should be meaningful, redundant data avoided, comments brief and to the point, program constructs easy to follow, module interface and data flow among the modules easy to trace, and reference materials furnished.

C. **Efficiency.** The system should be able to accomplish its functions with minimum resources. It should not use any hardware components or peripheral equipment unnecessarily. Input and output operations should be reduced to a minimum. Redundant instructions should not be present in the code. For example, if the instruction $N = 1*(2**10 - 1)$ is to be executed many times, it should be coded as $N = 1*1023$.

D. **Structuredness.** The system should be organized using program constructs such as SEQUENCE, IF-THEN-ELSE, and DOWHILE for better readability.

E. **Consistency.** The system should be consistent in the use of notations, terminologies, and symbols. Code should be indented in a consistent manner.

F. **Robustness.** The system should be able to continue execution under certain imperfect conditions, such as input data out of order or part of the input data missing. It should generate error messages and continue to read and execute the next data set when these conditions occur.

G. **Testability.** The ability of the system to produce quality product units should be easily testable. Useful messages should be generated for testing and debugging purposes.

H. **Human Engineering.** The system should be easy to use and difficult to misuse. For example, instructions should be sequentially numbered, diagnostic messages self-explanatory, and documents easy to understand and error free.

I. **Modifiability.** Change and enhancement of the system should be easily implementable.

J. **Maintainability.** The system should be easy to keep up for its intended use. Changes for improving operational efficiency should be easy to implement. Failed operations should be easy to restore to satisfactory condition.

K. **Portability.** The system should be portable among people and among machines. Attainment of the other quality characteristics greatly facilitates portability.

Other software system characteristic that may be of use to the interested reader can be found in Boehm, Brown, Lipow, Macleod, and Merritt [15].

Although no one would deny the importance of these software system characteristics, it is necessary to realize that they may not be measurable and, therefore, may not provide a means for controlling the quality of the product, that is, the software output.

1.6.3 Economics of Software Quality Control

The economics of software quality control follow closely the relationships between degree of quality control, cost of quality control, and product cost shown in Figure 1.7. A discussion of this topic can be found in Alberts [22].

1.6.4 Software Quality Control Principles

The principles discussed in Section 1.5 are also applicable to controlling both software product quality and software system quality. However, as pointed out in Section 1.6.2, software system quality characteristics may not be measurable and their conformance to the user's requirements may require a subjective evaluation. On the contrary, the conformance of the software product to the user's needs is testable. The quality of a product unit can be examined. Each unit can be classified as either acceptable or defective. This inspection is equivalent to random sampling of a product unit from a population called the binomial distribution, which is discussed in Chapters 3 to 6.

At present, there is a large gap between the state of quality control as practiced in the manufacturing industries, and the state of software quality control. Since the success of software quality control also depends on random sampling of product units for quality inspection, the basis on which to apply sampling methods to software output must be developed. This author has developed a tool called the Symbolic Input Attribute Decomposition (SIAD) Tree, which is used to represent the input domain of a piece of software in a form that facilitates construction of random test input units for producing random product units for quality inspection. Thus, with this book, the software industry can begin to bridge the gap in quality control.

1.7 QUALITY PROGRAMMING

Quality Programming is a means to implement a complete software life cycle incorporating the principles of statistical quality control [28]. The process of Quality Programming is shown in Figure 1.10 [43]. As shown, the process is divided into the following stages:

Modeling
Requirements specification
Concurrent software design and test design

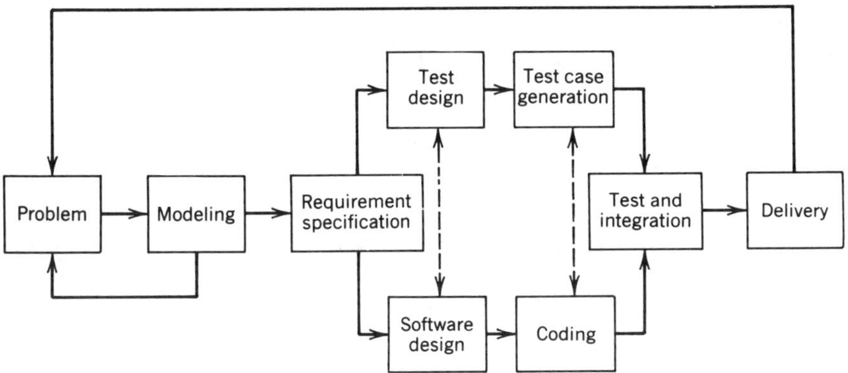

Figure 1.10 The quality programming process.

Concurrent implementation of software design and test design
Test and integration
Software acceptance

At each of these stages, quality control is an integral part of the software development activities.

1.7.1 Modeling

The modeling stage emulates the way that modeling is performed in the manufacturing industries. The result of the modeling activities is a document that represents a thorough understanding of the problem that the proposed software is intended to solve. This understanding of the problem is represented in terms that will support a quality software solution and allow the use of statistical quality control.

The modeling activity includes:

A. Modeling of Inputs and Outputs

This activity is analogous to the modeling of raw materials and final products in the manufacturing industries. Inputs are modeled in terms of types of input data, quality characteristics of each type of input, rules for constructing inputs, and sources of inputs. The modeling of output includes the crucial definitions of product unit and product unit defectiveness on which the design and testing of the software must be based. This part of the modeling includes output quality planning, in which sampling methods and parameters for software testing and the acceptance procedure are determined.

B. *Modeling of the Software*

This activity is analogous to the modeling of a factory. The software itself, as distinct from its output, is modeled in terms of the description of the process being automated, rules for using inputs, methods for producing outputs, data flows, process control, and methods for developing the software system.

1.7.2 Requirements Specification

Requirements specification is the activity of identifying all of the requirements necessary to develop the software and fulfill the user's needs. In conventional practice, this phase is conducted poorly and test requirements in terms of statistical quality control are not addressed at all. To apply the statistical quality control tool, requirements specification must include identification of the following requirements:

A. *Software Requirements*

Software requirements cover all input, processing, and output requirements. In particular, the input domain of the software, that is, the types of input, quality characteristics of each type of input, rules for using the input, and constraints on using the input, is identified from the modeling document and refined. Here, the SIAD tree is a powerful tool to represent the input domain in a convenient form. The author has developed four types of SIAD trees—regular, weighted, ruled, and "network"—for this crucial part of requirements specification.

The output requirements are specified for both the software system and for each module of the system, and include refinement of the product unit and product defectiveness definitions.

B. *Test Requirements*

The test requirements include specification of test methods, statistical sampling methods, statistical inference requirements, and software acceptance criteria. The test methods may be any combination of regular, weighted, boundary, invalid, and special tests. The test requirements also include specification of an important parameter, the defectiveness criterion, which will be used in the determination of the defectivness or nondefectiveness of each product unit.

C. *Documentation Requirements*

All documentation requirements may be specified. In the Quality Programming methodology, documents are developed as part of each software development activity, and used to help ensure the understandability and quality of the software.

1.7.3 Concurrent Software Design and Test Design

With well-prepared modeling and requirements specification documents, software design and test design can proceed concurrently. The concurrent development is advantageous because it allows cross-checking of the designs as early as possible and shortened considerably development time. In conventional practice, test design is sometimes delayed until the software has been implemented. Then it is too late to inspect the quality of the software. When test design is insufficiently developed before the software is put into operation, the result is costly maintenance. Also, when the software design and test design are developed concurrently, they can be cross-verified as an additional quality control check.

A. *Software Design*

Software design begins with a review of the modeling and requirements specification documents. The designer selects a design methodology or approach, reflecting either a function-oriented or an object-oriented design, but it is crucial that the design be organized in a top-down hierarchical structure that will facilitate definition of the input domain of each module.

B. *Test Design*

Test design begins with review of the requirements specification and, in particular, the product unit definition, product unit defectiveness definition, selected test methods, and sampling plans. An important task here is designing the test input units, using SIAD trees, for each test method. The regular, weighted, boundary, invalid, and special tests will be used to test different product unit populations which represent crucial aspects of the software output and operations. Test must be designed for both the software system and each module of the system.

1.7.4 Concurrent Implementation of Software Design and Test Design

Software design implementation and test design implementation are also concurrent activities. The advantage of concurrent implementation is that the test and integration stage can begin as soon as the design is ready. It also allows cross-verification of both implementation as a further quality control check.

Implementation of the software design is conducted with special attention to human factors—including man-machine interfaces, software portability, and programming support environments—and to the selection of a programming language that must have the features necessary to support the design constructs and a structured module interface scheme.

Implementation of the test design includes selection and testing of a random number generator to be used in constructing test input units during software testing and the acceptance procedure.

1.7.5 Test and Integration

Test and integration follows a "critical-modules-first" bottom-up approach. Since test design has been completed and implemented concurrently with the software design, each module can be tested using the statistical quality control tool as soon as it is ready, and the system can be built on a "secure-quality-part" basis.

Once the modules have been tested and integrated, the entire software system can be tested. The statistical quality control tool is used to estimate the defective rate of the output product unit population. If the defective rate is too big to satisfy test requirements, the software is not ready for delivery to the user.

1.7.6 Software Acceptance

Software acceptance takes place after the developer has conducted test and integration tasks and has estimated the defective rate of the software product unit population. The user may accept the software based on the test data provided by the developer, or may elect to conduct an acceptance procedure.

The acceptance procedure is also based on statistical quality control principles using random sampling techniques. Particular attention is paid to the statistically defined producer's risk, that is, the probability that the developer will have good software rejected; and to the user's risk, that is, the probability that the user will accept poor quality software.

1.8 HOW TO DEMAND / DELIVER SOFTWARE WARRANTY

The old saying "Nothing ventured, nothing gained" is very applicable in the matter of demanding/delivering software warranty. Both the developer and the user must be willing to allocate time and resources to the tasks that will make a meaningful software warranty possible. To demand a software warranty, the user has to do sufficient homework to be able to tell the developer what is required of the software. To deliver a warranty, the developer must know how to do it. Detailed guidelines for the user are given in Chapters 2 through 8. Guidelines to help the developer understand and apply software engineering (development) with statistical control to his or her product are given in Chapters 2 through 12.

Thus the way to demand/deliver software warranty is to learn from the manufacturing industries and develop the foundations that will make reliance on statistical evidence of product quality an integral part of the software industry.

1.9 OVERVIEW

A major goal of this book is aiming at proposing solutions to some of the 20 problems in Figure 1.3 using statistical quality control. Therefore, this book is divided into three major parts: statistical background for quality control (Chapters 2 through 6), good quality software through prevention (Chapters 7 through 10), and good quality software through promotion (Chapters 11 through 15).

Chapter 2 deals with basic probability concepts required for understanding statistical distributions. Major topics include repetitive operations, sample space, events, probability, permutation and combination, random variables, randomization, and random numbers.

Chapter 3 is concerned with important statistical distributions essential to the derivation of sampling plans for estimating software defectiveness and for software acceptance. The discussion is concentrated on the hypergeometric, binomial, Poisson, and normal distributions. These distributions are closely related. A binomial distribution can be derived from a hypergeometric distribution and can be approximated by a Poisson or a normal distribution. The normal distribution can be used as a convenience vehicle for statistical inference. The Poisson distribution is used for formulating acceptance sampling plans.

Chapter 4 examines methods of generating and testing of random numbers. The discussion serves as the modeling of a real world phenomenon and is used as an example for the selection of an automatic random number generator.

Chapter 5 explains two sampling techniques, simple random sampling and sequential random sampling, for estimating the defective rate of a product unit population.

Chapter 6 describes the formulation of product unit population acceptance sampling plans, including single sampling and sequential sampling. The acceptance plans are formulated using a set of common criteria agreed on by the producer and the user of the population.

Chapter 7 discusses modeling activities of a physical or conceptual phenomenon being considered for automation via a piece of software. It is shown that software modeling very closely resembles factory modeling before building the factory in a manufacturing industry. The discussions are given in terms of building a factory. What are required in order to apply statistical quality control discussed in Chapters 2 through 6 to enable the software user to demand, and the software developer to deliver, software warranty is addressed. This is just like a manufacturing industry in offering warranty on consumer goods. The modeling is to be done in many iterations to demonstrate as thoroughly as practical what the software is all about.

Chapter 8 gives a framework for generating software requirements specification in the four major areas: software engineering (development) goals and principles, software, test, and documentation. A new concept of a SIAD tree to represent input domains of a piece of software for systematic generation of software test input units is given. There are four types of SIAD trees: regular, weighted, ruled, and "network". It is pointed out that to assess properly software quality, five test methods must be considered: regular, weighted, boundary, invalid, and special tests. What are required, including meaningful numerical software acceptance criteria, in order to apply statistical quality control for software development are discussed in detail.

Chapter 9 shows that software design and test design are to be proceeded concurrently based on the requirement documents prepared according to the requirements framework given in Chapter 8. Although there are many software design methodologies being practiced in the software industry, it is pointed out that they can be classified into two classes: function-oriented and object-oriented design. Detailed discussions on these two classes of methodologies and their respective limitations are given. The software test design given in this chapter is unique in the software industry. The design is oriented toward the application of statistical quality control using the four types of SIAD trees for the five test methods introduced in Chapter 8. It is pointed out that requirements specification is insufficient or incomplete if software design and test design cannot be progressed concurrently. It is important at this point that requirements specification be redone. Otherwise costly consequences may result.

Chapter 10 shows concurrent implementations of software design and test design. Human factors, selection of software implementation languages, and strategies are pointed out for software implementation. In test design implementation, the error sources, strategies, and selection of random number generators are discussed. Cross-verification of the implementations serves as a crucial quality check to ready the software for test and integration.

Chapter 11 emphasizes software testing, integration, independent verification and validation, and debugging using statistical quality control. All activities are guided by the principles of statistical quality control from Chapters 7 through 11. Software success criteria, sampling process, software module and system test procedures, and debugging effectiveness measure using the defective rate of software product unit population, factors that must be examined in demanding and delivering software warranty by user and developer, respectively, are addressed. Three examples of different application types are given to illustrate the approaches discussed in this chapter.

On successful completion, software delivery takes place. The approaches to accepting a piece of software are shown so that software acceptance can be conducted using statistical quality control principles. The user has a tool to help accept or reject the software. The details are given in Chapter 12.

Chapter 13 uses a complete example to illustrate the stages of quality programming process shown in Figure 1.10. It also describes how to use the defective rate of a software product unit population to assess software quality, how to conclude the measure of software quality statistically. An example of software warranty based on statistical quality measures is given.

Currently, there are many software reliability models, based on hardware reliability models, being proposed for measuring software reliability. The merits and applicability of these models are addressed in Chapter 14. Three counterexamples are given to show that most of these models cannot be applied even in a very simple and small piece of software.

Deming, the father of Japanese quality and credited to be the initiator of the third industrial revolution, points out that there are 14 obligations the top management of any organization must do to survive in the modern, competitive market. These obligations are based on statistical quality control. It is also pointed out that 10 of the 14 obligations are applicable in the software industry. What are these obligations? How to fulfill it? Questions like these are discussed in Chapter 15.

The solutions to some of the 20 problems in Figure 1.3 are proposed and embedded in this book. It would be most beneficial to read the entire book to get the whole picture.

REFERENCES

1. J. M. Juran, L. A. Seder, and F. M. Gryna (Eds.), *Quality Control Handbook*, 2nd ed., McGraw-Hill, New York, 1962.
2. G. J. Myers, *Software Reliability Principles and Practices*, Wiley-Interscience, New York, 1976.
3. IEEE, *Program Testing Techniques*, IEEE Computer Society, New York, 1977.
4. R. T. Yeh (Ed.), *Current Trends in Programming Methodology*, Volumes 1 and 2, Prentice-Hall, Englewood Cliffs, New Jersey, 1977.
5. E. Horowitz (Ed.), *Practical Strategies for Developing Large Software Systems*, Addison-Wesley, Reading, Massachusetts, 1975.
6. E. Yourdon, *Techniques of Program Structure and Design*, Prentice-Hall, Englewood Cliffs, New Jersey, 1975.
7. IEEE, *Structured Programming*, IEEE Computer Society, New York, 1977.
8. A. Ralston and C. L. Meek (Eds.), *Encyclopedia of Computer Science*, Petrocelli/Charter, New York, 1976.
9. D. Bates (Ed.), *Structured Programming* (Infotech State-of-the-Art Report), Infotech International Ltd., Maidenhead, Berkshire, England, 1976.
10. O. J. Dahl, E. W. Dijkstra, and C. A. R. Hoare, *Structured Programming*, Academic, New York, 1972.
11. D. E. Knuth, "Structured Programming with GOTO Statements," *ACM Computing Surveys*, Vol. 6, No. 4, December 1974, pp. 261–302.
12. E. W. Dijkstra, "The Humble Programmer," *Communications of the ACM*, Vol. 15, No. 10, Oct. 1972, pp. 859–866.
13. P. J. Denning, "A Hard Look at Structured Programming," in *Structured Programming* (Infotech State-of-the-Art Report), Infotech International Ltd., Maidenhead, Berkshire, England, 1976, pp. 183–202.
14. B. W. Bohem, J. R. Brown, and M. Lipow, "Quantitative Evaluation of Software Quality," *Proceedings, 2nd International Conference on Software Engineering*, ACM, IEEE, and National Bureau of Standards, 1976, pp. 592–605.

15. B. W. Boehm, J. R. Brown, M. Lipow, G. J. Macleod, and M. J. Merritt, *Characteristics of Software Quality*, North-Holland, New York, 1978.

16. T. A. Thayer, M. Lipow, and E. C. Nelson, *Software Reliability, A Study of Large Project Reality*, North-Holland, New York, 1978.

17. E. W. Dijkstra, "Programming Considered as a Human Activity," in W. A. Kalenich, (Ed.), *Proceedings, IFIP Congress 65*, Spartan Books, Washington, D.C., 1965.

18. E. W. Dijkstra, "The GOTO Statement considered Harmful," *Communications of the ACM*, Vol. 11, No. 3, March 1968, pp. 147–148.

19. F. T. Baker, "Chief Programming Management of Production Programming," *IBM Systems Journal*, January 1971, pp. 56–73.

20. G. M. Weinberg, *The Psychology of Computer Programming*, Van Nostrand Reinhold, New York, 1971.

21. D. H. Harris, and F. B. Chaney, *Human Factors in Quality Assurance*, Wiley, New York, 1969.

22. D. S. Alberts, "The Economics of Software Quality Assurance," *Proceedings, National Computer Conference*, Vol. 45, AFIPS Press, Montvale, New Jersey, 1976, pp. 433–442.

23. W. Myers, "COMSAC 78 Wrap-Up," *Computer*, IEEE, New York, January 1979, pp. 62–70.

24. P. Freeman and A. I. Wasserman (Eds.), *Software Design Techniques*, 2nd ed., IEEE Computer Society, New York, 1977.

25. B. W. Boehm, "Software and Its Impact: A Quantitative Assessment," *Datamation*, May 1973, pp. 48–59.

26. B. W. Boehm, "Software Design and Structuring," in E. Horowitz (Ed.), *Practical Strategies for Developing Large Software Systems*, Addison-Wesley, Reading, Massachusetts, 1975, pp. 103–128.

27. F. L. Bauer, "Software Engineering," in A. Ralston and C. L. Meek (Eds.), *Encyclopedia of Computer Science*, Petrocelli/Charter, New York, 1976.

28. C. K. Cho, *An Introduction to Software Quality Control*, Wiley-Interscience, New York, 1980.

29. C. K. Cho, "Statistical Methods Applied to Software Quality Control," in G. Gordon Schulmeyer and J. McManus (Eds.), *Handbook of Software Quality Assurance*, Van Nostrand Reinhold, New York, 1987.

30. C. K. Cho, *High Quality Software—An Introduction*, (in Japanese), Translated and Published by Kindai Kagaku Sha, Tokyo, Japan, 1982.

31. C. K. Cho, *AERA (Automated En Route Air Traffic Control System) Package 1 Testbed Software Quality Assurance Tests of the Aircraft Data Manager*, Working Paper No. WP-81W00285, MITRE Corporation, McLean, Virginia, 1981.

32. C. K. Cho, *AERA (Automated En Route Air Traffic Control System) Horizontal Route Analysis Test Results*, Memo No. W41-M4782, MITRE Corporation, McLean, Virginia, 1980.

33. C. K. Cho, *AERA (Automated En Route Air Traffic Control System) Horizontal Route Analysis (HRA) and Horizontal Route Generation (HRG) Program Retest Results*, Memo No. W41-M4922, MITRE Corporation, McLean, Virginia, 1980.

34. C. K. Cho, *Performance Evaluation of the Aircraft Data Manager and Display Data Manager of the AERA (Automated En Route Air Traffic Control System) Build 1 System*, Memo No. W41-M5578, MITRE Corporation, McLean, Virginia, 1981.

35. W. Edwards Deming, *Quality, Productivity and Competitive Position*, Center for Advanced Engineering Study, Massachusetts Institute of Technology, Cambridge, Massachusetts, 1982.

36. R. H. Thayer, A. Pyster, and R. C. Wood, "The Challenge of Software Engineering Project Management," *IEEE Computer*, Vol. 13, No. 8, August 1980. pp. 51–59.

37. C. R. Vick and C. V. Ramamoorthy, *Handbook of Software Engineering*, Van Nostrand Reinhold, New York, 1984.

38. M. L. Martin, *Software Engineering Design, Reliability, and Management*, McGraw-Hill, New York, 1983.

39. G. Booch, *Software Engineering with Ada*, Benjamin/Cummings, Menlo Park, California, 1983.

40. R. V. Fultyn, *Computer Assisted Software Testing*, Digital Equipment Corporation, Maynard, Massachusetts, 1982.

41. H. Wohlwend, "An Application of Statistical Sampling to Software Quality Measurement," Presented in the National Conference on Software Quality and Productivity Sponsored by Department of Defense, National Security Industries Association, etc., Williamsburg, Virginia, 1985.

42. L. B. Jump, *Software Quality Control: A Case Study*, Applied Data Systems, Laurel, Maryland, 1983.

43. C. K. Cho, "Software Engineering and Quality Assurance, Continuing Engineering Education Course No. CE705LE Handouts," George Washington University, Washington, D.C., July 1986.

44. D. Halberstam, "W. Edwards Deming, the Man Who Taught Japan about Quality, Believes: Yes We Can!" *Parade*, Parade Publication, Inc., New York, July 8, 1984.

CHAPTER 2

Basic Concepts in Probability

The concept of performing a repetitive operation plays an important role in the study of probability. An outcome is the result of conducting the operation once. The set of all possible outcomes that can occur in performing the operation once is called the sample space of the performance. A set of outcomes is called an event. The term "probability" of a certain event to occur when a repetitive operation is conducted once is defined as a ratio of the number of outcomes in the event to the number of outcomes in the sample space. To find the probability of an event to occur often involves lengthy and tedious computation. The notation of permutation and combination is a useful tool to help simplify the computation. The notation is also helpful to the development of two important probability distributions: the hypergeometric and binomial distributions discussed in Chapter 3.

The concept of random variables is a basic idea for developing a probability function that, in turn, is used for devising a sampling plan for quality control. The formulation of such a plan is based on randomization, which can be realized by using random numbers.

2.1 REPETITIVE OPERATIONS

The concept of performing a repetitive operation is essential to the study of both theory and applications of statistics and probability. The purpose of performing the operation is to understand, with minimum effort, the characteristics of a phenomenon so that useful conclusions can be drawn for decision making.

The following are examples of a repetitive operation:

A. Tossing a coin once.
B. Tossing a coin twice.
C. Tossing a coin three times.
D. Throwing two dice once.
E. Drawing two balls randomly from a box of four balls.
F. Drawing three computer outputs from a lot of five outputs.
G. Testing the randomness of a set of 1000 numbers generated by a random number generator.

When each of the operations is performed once under same conditions, then the possible outcomes vary from one performance to another.

2.2 SAMPLE SPACE

When an operation is performed over and over again under the same conditions, the set of all possible outcomes is called the sample space of the performance.

The following are the sample spaces of the operations given in the last section:

A. When a coin is tossed once the possible outcome is either a head H or a tail T. The sample space is simply the set of H and T, denoted by $S = \{H, T\}$.
B. When a coin is tossed twice, the possible outcome is either HH, HT, TH, or TT. The sample space is $S = \{HH, HT, TH, TT\}$.
C. When a coin is tossed three times once, the sample space is $S = \{HHH, HHT, HTH, THH, HTT, THT, TTH, TTT\}$.
D. When a pair of dice is thrown once, the sample space is $S = \{11, 12, 13, 14, 15, 16, 21, 22, 23, 24, 25, 26, 31, 32, 33, 34, 35, 36, 41, 42, 43, 44, 45, 46, 51, 52, 53, 54, 55, 56, 61, 62, 63, 64, 65, 66\}$, where the first

digit of a number represents the number of points on one of the dice and the second digit represents that on the other.

E. When two balls are drawn from a box of four, the sample space is $S = \{12, 13, 14, 23, 24, 34\}$, where 1 represents ball 1, 2 represents ball 2, and so on.

F. When three computer outputs are drawn from a lot of five outputs, the sample space is $S = \{123, 124, 125, 134, 135, 145, 234, 235, 245, 345\}$, where 1 represents output 1, 2 represents output 2, and so on.

G. When the randomness of a set of 1000 numbers is tested once, the sample space is $S = \{R, N\}$, where R means random and N means nonrandom.

Each of the foregoing sample spaces contains a finite number of outcomes and is called a finite sample space. A sample space containing an infinite number of outcomes is called an infinite sample space. For example, the sample space of drawing a real number between 0 and 1 is infinite. Similarly, the sample space in testing a software system contains an infinite number of outcomes since an infinite number of test cases can be prepared for the test.

2.3 EVENTS

In the study of probability and statistics it is often necessary to know a set of outcomes possessing certain characteristics. The set of outcomes is called an event. By definition every outcome in an event is an outcome in the sample space. Therefore an event may be called a subset of the sample space. Symbolically, let A be an event and S be a sample space. Then $A \subseteq S$ means that A is a subset of S containing a less or equal number of outcomes in S. The symbol $B \subset S$ means that B is a subset of S containing fewer outcomes than S. (B is also called a proper subset of S.)

In the example of tossing a coin three times, the sample space S contains eight outcomes,

$$S = \{HHH, HHT, HTH, THH, HTT, THT, TTH, TTT\}$$

Let A be the event containing the same outcomes, then $A \subseteq S$. Let B be the event containing the outcomes HHT, HTH, HTT, namely $B = \{HHT, HTH, HTT\}$. Then $B \subset S$.

Sometimes it is of interest to know the relationship among different events. Such relationships may be represented by a diagram called the Venn diagram. Figure 2.1 shows an example of such a diagram.

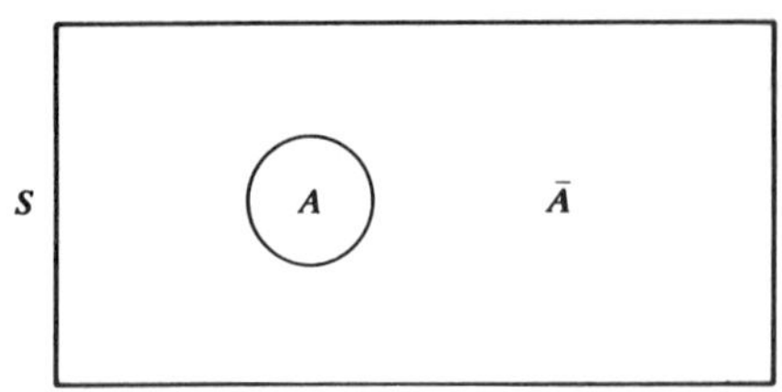

Figure 2.1 A Venn diagram.

The rectangle represents a sample space and the circle an event. The complement of A, denoted by $\overline{A}$, is the set containing outcomes of S not contained in A. For example, let

$$S = \{HHH, HHT, HTH, THH, HTT, THT, TTH, TTT\}$$
$$A = \{HHT, HTH, HTT\}$$
$$B = \{HHH, HHT, THH, TTT, THT, TTH\}$$

Then $\overline{A} = \{HHH, THH, THT, TTH, TTT\}$ and $\overline{B} = \{HTH, HTT\}$. It is seen that every outcome in S is either in A or B or both. The event that contains outcomes of A or B or both is called the union of A and B, written as $A \cup B$. By definition, $S = A \cup B$. Similarly, $S = A \cup \overline{A}$ in Figure 2.1.

An event C containing no outcome is called an empty set, denoted by ϕ. It is usually written as $C = \phi$.

In the preceding example, the outcome HHT is contained in both A and B, while all other outcomes are contained in either A or B but not both. The event that an outcome is contained in both A and B is called the intersection of A and B, denoted by $A \cap B$. From the example, $A \cap B = \{HHT\}$. Notice that $A \cap \overline{A} = \phi$. Figure 2.2 shows two Venn diagrams of S, $A \cup B$, and $A \cap B$.

If every outcome in G is an outcome in K and every outcome in K is an outcome of G, then G and K are called equal events, denoted by $G = K$. If a set of outcomes is in G but not in K, the set is called the difference between G and K, denoted by $G - K$.

If $A_1, A_2, \ldots, A_n$ are events in a sample space, then the event of all outcomes contained in A_i or A_j for some i and j, $1 \le i, j \le n$, is the union of $A_1, A_2, \ldots, A_n$, denoted by $A_1 \cup A_2 \ldots \cup A_n$ or

$$\bigcup_{i=1}^{n} A_i$$

Similarly, the event of all outcomes contained in all A_i, for $i = 1, 2, \ldots, n$, is the intersection of $A_1, A_2, \ldots, A_n$, denoted by $A_1 \cap$

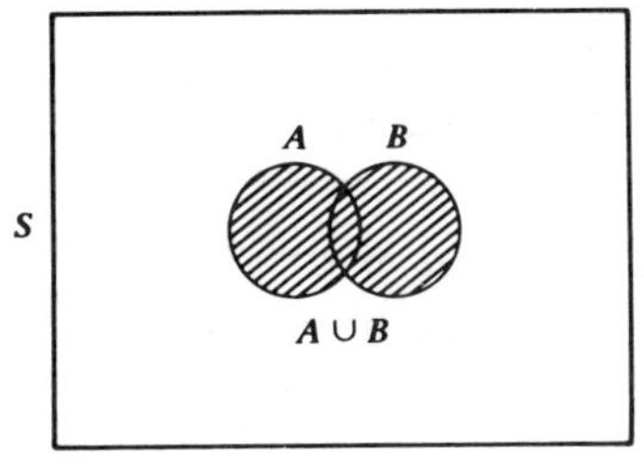

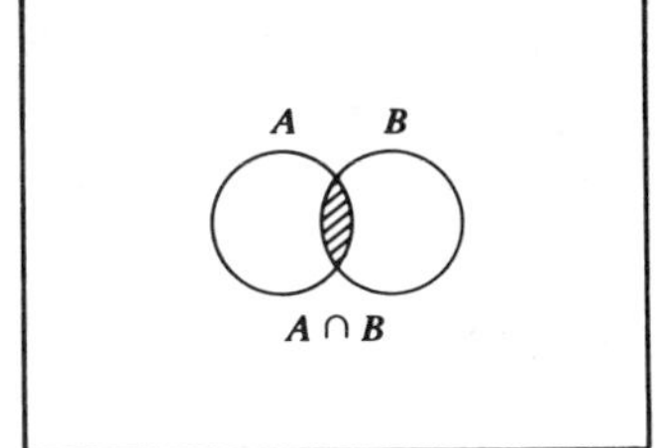

Figure 2.2 Venn diagrams illustrating S, $A \cup B$, and $A \cap B$.

$A_2 \ldots \cap A_n$ or

$$\bigcap_{i=1}^{n} A_i$$

If $A_i \cap A_j = \phi$, for all i and j, $1 \le i \le n$, and $1 \le j \le n$, then $A_1, A_2, \ldots, A_n$ are disjoint events.

It is often necessary to know the number of outcomes in an event. Let N_A, N_B, N_C be the number of outcomes in events A, B, and C, respectively; $N_{A \cap B}$, $N_{A \cap C}$, $N_{B \cap C}$, and $N_{A \cap B \cap C}$ be that in events $A \cap B$, $A \cap C$, $B \cap C$, and $A \cap B \cap C$ respectively. Then $N_{A \cup B} = N_A + N_B - N_{A \cap B}$. The computation can be verified by the Venn diagram of Figure 2.2. The number of outcomes in $A \cap B$ is counted twice in adding N_A and N_B. It must be substracted from the addition. Similarly, $N_{A \cup B \cup C} = N_A + N_B + N_C - N_{A \cap B} - N_{A \cap C} - N_{B \cap C} + N_{A \cap B \cap C}$.

In general, for n events $A_1, A_2, \ldots, A_n$,

$$N_{A_1 \cup A_2 \ldots \cup A_n} = \sum_{i=1}^{n} N_{A_i} - \sum_{j>i=1}^{n} N_{A_i \cap A_j} + \sum_{k>j>i=1}^{n} N_{A_i \cap A_j \cap A_k} + \ldots + (-1)^{n-1} N_{A_1 \cap A_2 \ldots \cap A_n} \quad (2.1)$$

The following is an example: A lot of 10,000 computer outputs is found containing

a. 100 outputs with I/O errors, denoted by type A errors.

b. 50 outputs with computational errors, denoted by type B errors.

c. 20 outputs with logical errors, denoted by type C errors.
d. 10 outputs with both I/O and computational errors.
e. 5 outputs with both I/O and logical errors.
f. 3 outputs with both computational and logical errors.
g. 2 outputs with I/O, computational, and logical errors.

It is seen that $N_A = 100$, $N_B = 50$, $N_C = 20$, $N_{A\cap B} = 10$, $N_{A\cap C} = 5$, $N_{B\cap C} = 3$, and $N_{A\cap B\cap C} = 2$. Thus the number of outputs having either I/O errors or computation errors is

$$N_{A\cup B} = N_A + N_B - N_{A\cap B} = 100 + 50 - 10 = 140$$

The number of outputs having at least one of the three types of errors is

$$\begin{aligned} N_{A\cup B\cup C} &= N_A + N_B + N_C - N_{A\cap B} - N_{A\cap C} - N_{B\cap C} + N_{A\cap B\cap C} \\ &= 100 + 50 + 20 - 10 - 5 - 3 + 2 = 154 \end{aligned}$$

The number of outputs having none of the errors is

$$N_{\bar{A}\cap\bar{B}\cap\bar{C}} = 10{,}000 - N_{A\cup B\cup C} = 10{,}000 - 154 = 9846$$

The number of outputs having only I/O errors is

$$\begin{aligned} N_{A\cap\bar{B}\cap\bar{C}} &= N_A - N_{A\cap B} - N_{A\cap C} + N_{A\cap B\cap C} \\ &= 100 - 10 - 5 + 2 = 87 \end{aligned}$$

The number of outputs having only computation errors is

$$\begin{aligned} N_{\bar{A}\cap B\cap\bar{C}} &= N_B - N_{A\cap B} - N_{B\cap C} + N_{A\cap B\cap C} \\ &= 50 - 10 - 3 + 2 = 39 \end{aligned}$$

The number of outputs having only logic errors is

$$\begin{aligned} N_{\bar{A}\cap\bar{B}\cap C} &= N_C - N_{A\cap C} - N_{B\cap C} + N_{A\cap B\cap C} \\ &= 20 - 5 - 3 + 2 = 14 \end{aligned}$$

The results can be verified by the Venn diagram of Figure 2.3.

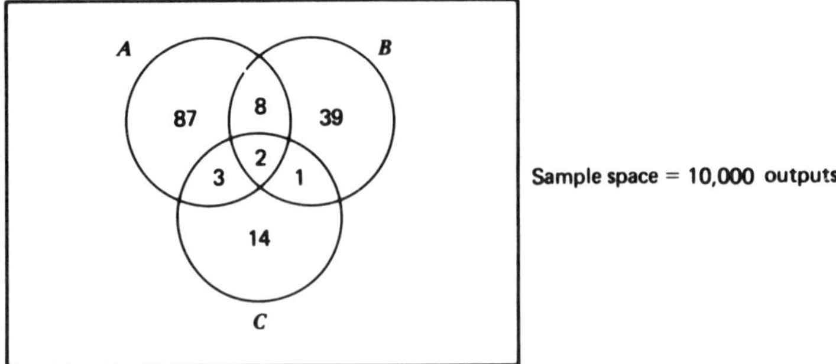

Figure 2.3 Venn diagram illustrating 10,000 computer outputs.

2.4 PROBABILITY

The term probability is associated with the study of the degree of expectancy of occurrence for an event when a repetitive operation is performed once. It is defined as the ratio of the number of outcomes in the event to the number of outcomes in the sample space. Let A be an event in S, N_A be the number of outcomes in A, and N_S be the number of outcomes in the sample space S. Then the probability of the event A to occur is simply $P(A) = N_A/N_S$.

The following discussions are based on the operation of tossing a coin three times: The sample space contains eight outcomes, namely, $S = \{HHH, HHT, HTH, THH, HTT, THT, TTH, TTT\}$. The probability of getting the outcome HH is 0 since, under normal conditions, throwing a coin three times results in three occurrences of H or T. The probability of the outcome HHH to occur is 1/8 while that of the outcomes HHT to occur is 1/8, and so on. The sum of the probabilities of the eight outcomes to occur is

$$P(HHH) + P(HHT) + P(HTH) + P(THH) + P(HTT) + P(THT) + P(TTH) + P(TTT) = 1$$

Let $A_1 = \{HHH, HHT, THH\}$ and $A_2 = \{TTH, HTH, TTT\}$. Then both of the events are disjoint, since they contain no outcome in common. Thus the probability of either A_1 or A_2 to occur is

$$P(A_1 \cup A_2) = P(A_1) + P(A_2) - P(A_1 \cap A_2) = \tfrac{3}{8} + \tfrac{3}{8} - 0 = \tfrac{6}{8}$$

Similarly, let $A_1 = \{HHH, HHT, THH\}$ and $A_2 = \{TTT, THH, THT\}$. Then both of the events contain the outcome THH. Thus the probability of either A_1 or A_2 to occur is

$$P(A_1 \cup A_2) = P(A_1) + P(A_2) - P(A_1 \cap A_2) = \tfrac{3}{8} + \tfrac{3}{8} - \tfrac{1}{8} = \tfrac{5}{8}$$

The probabilities of events in a finite sample space have several interesting characteristics:

A. If A is an event in S, then $0 < P(A) \leq 1$.

B. If S is the sample space of a repetitive operation, then $P(S) = 1$.

C. If $A_1, A_2, \ldots, A_n$ are events in S, then (referring to Equation (2.1))

$$P(A_1 \cup A_2 \cup \cdots \cup A_n) = \sum_{i=1}^{n} P(A_i) - \sum_{j>i=1}^{n} P(A_i \cap A_j) + \sum_{k>j>i=1}^{n} P(A_i \cap A_j \cap A_k) + \cdots + (-1)^{n-1} P(A_1 \cap A_2 \cdots A_n)$$

D. If $A_1, A_2, \ldots, A_n$ are disjoint events in S, then

a. $P(A_1 \cup A_2 \cup \cdots \cup A_n) = \sum_{i=1}^{n} P(A_i)$

b. $P(\bar{A}_1 \cap \bar{A}_2 \cap \cdots \cap \bar{A}_n) = 1 - P(A_1 \cup A_2 \cup \cdots \cup A_n)$

2.5 CONDITIONAL PROBABILITY

It is often necessary to find the probability that an event B occurs given that another event A has occurred. The probability $P(B|A)$ can be computed by

$$P(B|A) = \frac{P(A \cap B)}{P(A)}$$

By the definitions given in Section 2.4, the probability is given by

$$P(B|A) = \frac{(N_{A \cap B}/N_S)}{(N_A/N_S)} = \frac{N_{A \cap B}}{N_A}$$

The conditional probability is simply the ratio of the number of outcomes in the event $A \cap B$ to that in the event A.

In practice, the probability of any event to occur in an experiment without reference to some sample space is meaningless. Thus all probabilities are conditional probabilities. The probability $P(A|S)$ is usually written as $P(A)$ if the sample space is apparent and no confusion is likely to arise. The following is an example:

A box contains 1000 computer outputs: 100 contain type A(I/O) errors, 45 have type B (computational) errors, 5 contain both types A and B errors. An output is randomly taken from the box and is found having I/O errors. What is the probability that it also contains computational errors?

The probability is found by

$$P(B|A) = \frac{N_{A \cap B}}{N_A} = \frac{5}{100} = .05$$

One important concept in the study of probability is that of an independent event. Two events are independent if the occurrence of one has no effect on that of the other. More precisely, if $P(B|A) = P(B)$, then A and B are independent events. Since

$$P(B|A) = P(B) = \frac{P(A \cap B)}{P(A)}$$

Thus

$$P(A \cap B) = P(A)P(B)$$

which is called the multiplication rule of probability. For example, if a "true" coin is thrown n times, the probability of never getting a head is given by

$$P(A_1 \cap A_2 \cap \cdots \cap A_n) = P(A_1)P(A_2) \cdots P(A_n) = \left(\tfrac{1}{2}\right)^n$$

2.6 PERMUTATION AND COMBINATION

The computation of the probability of an event to occur when a repetitive operation is performed once often involves counting the outcomes in the event. Such counting can be tedious and cumbersome. However, it can be greatly simplified with the help of two important concepts: permutation and combination. Permutation is an arrangement of things in different order. Combination is a selection of things without regard to order.

The discussion of both permutation and combination involves an important notation called n factorial, denoted by $n!$, which means the product of n, $n-1$, $n-2, \ldots,$ and 1. Namely,

$$n! = n \times (n-1) \times (n-2) \times \ldots \times 2 \times 1$$

For example, $4! = 4 \times 3 \times 2 \times 1 = 24$, and $5! = 5 \times 4 \times 3 \times 2 \times 1 = 120$. Notice that in this notation 0! is defined to be 1.

A. *Permutation*

A set of k things taken from n things for arrangement in an order is called a permutation, denoted by $p(n, k)$. The value is computed by

$$p(n, k) = \frac{n!}{(n-k)!} = n \times (n-1) \times (n-2) \times \cdots \times (n-k+1) \tag{2.2}$$

For example, there are four positions, 1, 2, 3, and 4 to be filled by the letters A, B, C, and D. There are four choices of the letters to fill position 1. There are three remaining letters to be selected for position 2. And so on. Thus there are $4! = 24$ different ways to fill the positions with the letters.

B. *Combination*

A set of k things taken from n things without regard to order is called a combination, denoted by $\binom{n}{k}$. The concept of combination is closely related to that of permutation. A permutation may be viewed as a two-step process. First, k things are taken from n things. Second, k things are taken from these k things for arrangement in an order. The relationship between a permutation and a combination is given by

$$p(n, k) = \binom{n}{k} p(k, k) = \binom{n}{k} k!$$

Thus

$$\binom{n}{k} = \frac{p(n, k)}{k!} = \frac{n!}{(n - k)!k!} \tag{2.3}$$

For example, there are six possible combinations in taking two from the four letters A, B, C, and D. Namely, AB, AC, AD, BC, BD, and CD. (The order in which two letters are arranged is immaterial. The alphabetical order is given for convenience.) If enumeration is not done, then the total number of combinations can be computed by

$$\binom{4}{2} = \frac{4!}{(4 - 2)!2!} = \frac{4 \times 3 \times 2 \times 1}{2 \times 1 \times 2 \times 1} = 6$$

In the derivation of Equation (2.3), the n things are divided into two groups. One contains the selected k things and the other the remaining $n - k$ things. Let $k_1 = k$ and $k_2 = n - k$, then Equation (2.3) becomes

$$\binom{n}{k_1, k_2} = \frac{n!}{k_1!k_2!} \tag{2.4}$$

Similarly, if n things are divided into r groups, each containing k_i things, for $1 \leq i \leq r$ and $k_1 + k_2 + \cdots + k_r = n$, then Equation (2.4) becomes

$$\binom{n}{k_1, k_2, \ldots, k_r} = \frac{n!}{k_1!k_2! \cdots k_r!} \tag{2.5}$$

For example, the word COMBINATION contains eight groups of letters. Namely, one C, two O's, one M, one B, two I's, two N's, one A, and one T. The number of combinations that can be formed by the groups of letters can be computed as follows:

There are $\binom{11}{1}$ ways of selecting a position for the letter C to occupy. In each of the $\binom{11}{1}$ ways there are $\binom{11 - 1}{2}$ ways of selecting two positions from the remaining 10 positions for the two O's. Under each of the $\binom{11 - 1}{2}$ ways, there are $\binom{11 - 1 - 2}{1}$ ways of choosing one position from the remaining eight positions for the letter M, and so on.

Thus, a total of

$$\binom{11}{1}\binom{11-1}{2}\binom{11-1-2}{1}\cdots\binom{11-1-2-\cdots-1}{1} = \frac{11!}{1!2!1!1!2!2!1!1!}$$

combinations can be formed.

2.7 COMPUTATION OF PROBABILITY USING COMBINATIONS

The concept of combination is a powerful tool in the study of probability. It is used extensively in cases where sample spaces are finite.

For example, a box contains 100 computer outputs. Five of the outputs are defective having errors. Ten outputs are randomly drawn from the lot. The probability of getting exactly one defective in the sample is given as follows:

The sample space of this experiment contains $\binom{100}{10}$ outcomes. There are $\binom{5}{1}$ ways of getting a defective and $\binom{100-5}{10-1}$ ways of getting nondefectives. Thus the event contains $\binom{5}{1}\binom{95}{9}$ outcomes. The probability is simply the ratio

$$\frac{\binom{5}{1}\binom{95}{9}}{\binom{100}{10}}$$

2.8 RANDOM VARIABLES

In algebra the equation $y = f(x)$ means that y is a function of x. Assigning a real number to x will give a value to y according to the function f. This concept can be extended to cases where the independent variable x is not a real number. For example, the volume of a box is a function of its dimensions; the weight of an alloy is a function of its components.

In the study of probability, a (real and single valued) function X defined on each outcome in a sample space is called a random variable. A typical example is the number of points appearing when two dice are thrown once. The value of the random variable ranges from 2 to 12, which is defined on each of the 36 outcomes in the sample space.

Let $A_1, A_2, \ldots, A_n$ be the disjoint events in the sample space S such that their union is equal to S. Let $x_1, x_2, \ldots, x_n$ be all the values that can be assigned to X. Let A_i be the event $X = x_i$ with the probability $P(A_i) = P(X = x_i) = p(x_i)$ that A_i will occur, for $i = 1, 2, \ldots, n$. Since $A_1 \cup A_2 \ldots \cup A_n = S$, the equation

$$p(x_1) + p(x_2) + \ldots + p(x_n) = 1$$

holds. The function

$$P(X = x_i) = p(x_i) \qquad \text{for } i = 1, 2, \ldots, n$$

is called the probability function of the random variable X. The set of values $x_1, x_2, \ldots x_n$ is called the sample space of X.

In the example of throwing two dice once, the probability function can be represented by

x_i	2	3	4	5	6	7	8	9	10	11	12
$p(x_i)$	$\frac{1}{36}$	$\frac{2}{36}$	$\frac{3}{36}$	$\frac{4}{36}$	$\frac{5}{36}$	$\frac{6}{36}$	$\frac{5}{36}$	$\frac{4}{36}$	$\frac{3}{36}$	$\frac{2}{36}$	$\frac{1}{36}$

2.9 RANDOMIZATION AND RANDOM NUMBERS

The term probability is defined as the number of outcomes in an event to the number of outcomes in a sample space. This definition is valid only if every outcome in the sample space has an equal chance of occurring in an experiment. One way to ensure the equal chance is through randomization.

Randomization is a procedure of arranging things without careful choice. Many activities in human life involve randomization. For example, throwing a coin to determine action in a baseball game; drawing a number from a container in a bingo game; shuffling a poker card deck; and so on. These activities involve physical means trying to guarantee equal chances of winning. However, one common phenomenon in the physical randomization is that

A. It is time consuming.

B. It is performed a small number of times.

C. It can be biased resulting from some physical factors in the operation, such as a poker deck is insufficiently shuffled.

Randomization in the study of probability and statistics seldom uses a physical means. Some mechanism that is fast and can be used over and over again with a minimum bias is desirable. One approach is through the use of random numbers.

A set of numbers is called a set of random numbers if each number is put into the set without careful arrangement. In performing the repetitive operation of drawing a digit randomly from the digits 0, 1, 2, 3, 4, 5, 6, 7, 8, 9 once, each of the digits has an equal chance of being drawn. If the experiment is performed over and over again, then the set of numbers so drawn is a sequence of random numbers. For example,

7 2 2 4 8 1 5 9 6 3 5 9 3 7 6 7

is such a sequence. In practice there are many methods of generating the numbers. A detailed discussion of some methods is given in Chapter 4. Appendix 1 lists a set of 12,000 random digits produced by a computer.

One use of random numbers in statistical applications is a procedure involving randomization. For example, a box contains 100 computer outputs. Ten outputs are to be taken randomly from the box. The sampling can be done by the following steps:

A. Numbering the 100 outputs from 00 to 99.
B. Generating 10 two-digit random numbers.
C. Drawing the 10 outputs with numbers corresponding to the 10 random numbers.

Thus if 10 numbers are generated such as 16, 95, 05, 74, 56, 39, 82, 66, 26, 00, then the outputs with those numbers are taken from the box.

In practice the numbering of the objects need not be done physically. Any conceptual means suffices as long as there is a way to relate the objects of interest with the random numbers. For example, the objects can be arranged in an order, and a random number refers to a position in the order.

REFERENCES

1. W. Feller, *An Introduction to Probability Theory and Its Applications*, Vol. 1 and 2, Wiley, New York, 1968 and 1971.
2. J. D. Braverman and W. C. Stewart, *Statistics for Business and Economics*, Ronald, New York, 1973.
3. K. A. Brownlee, *Statistical Theory and Methodology in Science and Engineering*, Wiley, New York, 1960.
4. I. Guttman and S. S. Wilks, *Introductory Engineering Statistics*, Wiley, New York, 1965.
5. G. W. Snedecor and W. G. Cochran, *Statistical Methods*, 6th ed. The Iowa State University Press, Ames, Iowa, 1976.

6. G. W. Summers, W. S. Peters, and C. P. Armstrong, *Basic Statistics in Business and Economics*, 2nd ed., Wadsworth, Belmont, California, 1977.

EXERCISES

1. List five different repetitive operations and their sample spaces.

2. A lot of 10,000 outputs is found containing

   (a) 250 outputs with I/O errors.
   (b) 150 outputs with computational errors.
   (c) 60 outputs with logical errors.
   (d) 50 outputs with I/O and computational errors.
   (e) 30 outputs with I/O and logical errors.
   (f) 20 outputs with computational and logical errors.
   (g) 10 outputs with I/O, computational, and logical errors.

   How many outputs contain
   (a) I/O or computational errors?
   (b) At least one type of error?
   (c) Only I/O errors?
   (d) Only computational errors?
   (e) Only logical errors?

3. If a sample of 10 outputs is drawn at random from the lot given in Exercise 2, what is the probability that the sample contains

   (a) No errors.
   (b) Only computational errors.
   (c) At least one of the errors.
   (d) Either I/O, computational, or logical errors?

4. If the sample of Exercise 3 contains I/O errors, what is the probability that it also contains logical errors?

5. How many outcomes are there in the sample space of drawing 13 cards from a deck of 52 poker cards?

6. If four cards are drawn randomly from a deck of 52 poker cards, what is the probability of getting four Aces with replacement and without replacement?

7. What is the probability of getting two Aces if 13 cards are taken at random from a deck of 52 cards?

8. Two dice are rolled simultaneously, what is the probability that

   (a) no ones turn up?

   (b) the sum of dots turned up is odd?

9. Discuss how to select a bridge hand so that every hand has an equal probability of being drawn, using random numbers.

10. Describe how to select 1000 persons randomly from a telephone book.

CHAPTER 3

Important Statistical Distributions for Software Quality Control

The purpose of statistical study is to understand a phenomenon with a minimum effort. Associated with a phenomenon are certain characteristics expressed in the form of data such as length, weight, volume, and so on. Such data are the results of some observations or measurements. A set of data that consists of all possible measurements of the phenomenom is called a population. A set of data that consists of only a portion of the measurements is called a sample. The activity of taking a subset of data from the population is called sampling.

Basically, there are two kinds of population —finite population and infinite population. A finite population consists of a countably finite number of measurements. A lot of 1000 computer printouts, a box of 100 balls are examples of finite population. An infinite population consists of a limitless number of observations or measurements. The number of input cases in testing a program is an example of an infinite population.

The results or data are usually represented in different forms for analysis. Statistical distributions are common representations. Important distributions are introduced, including the hypergeometric distribution, the binomial distribution, the Poisson distribution, and the normal distribution.

The binomial distribution plays a central role in software quality control. It is derived from the hypergeometric distribution. There are occasions in which the application of the binomial distribution is tedious. The Poisson distribution and the normal distribution can be used to approximate the distribution as a convenient vehicle for discussion. The concepts developed in this chapter are important to the materials of Chapter 5.

3.1 FREQUENCY DISTRIBUTION

When two dice are thrown once, the sum of dots appearing on the faces is a random variable x having a value from 2 to 12. Figure 3.1 shows 108 sums in throwing the dice 108 times.

The values may be considered as a sample from a large population of values that could have appeared. If the dice are thrown another 108 times, another set of values will appear. The number 108 is called a sample size, which is the number of measurements in the sample.

The purpose of sampling is to understand the characteristics of the population through understanding of the characteristics of the sample, for economic reasons. The understanding of the sample requires manipulation of the measurements for easy analysis.

The values given in Figure 3.1 can be represented by a graph called the dot frequency diagram, as shown in Figure 3.2. Each of the values is indicated by a dot plotted above the number on the x-axis. The diagram gives a concise representation of the data for quick analysis. For example, the question of how many numbers are less than or equal

8	8	2	5	8	9	7	7	10	6	6	7	6	9	7	8
4	7	5	12	8	8	11	10	6	6	9	8	7	8	6	7
9	9	9	6	6	6	6	11	5	8	3	5	4	5	7	6
7	2	9	5	3	4	8	7	6	5	9	12	5	2	2	2
8	7	6	10	7	5	3	4	7	5	7	9	9	10	6	8
7	7	7	10	7	5	4	11	10	7	7	8	9	8	8	4
4	9	5	8	9	3	11	11	10	9	7	4				

Figure 3.1 Sums of dots appearing on faces when two dice are thrown 108 times.

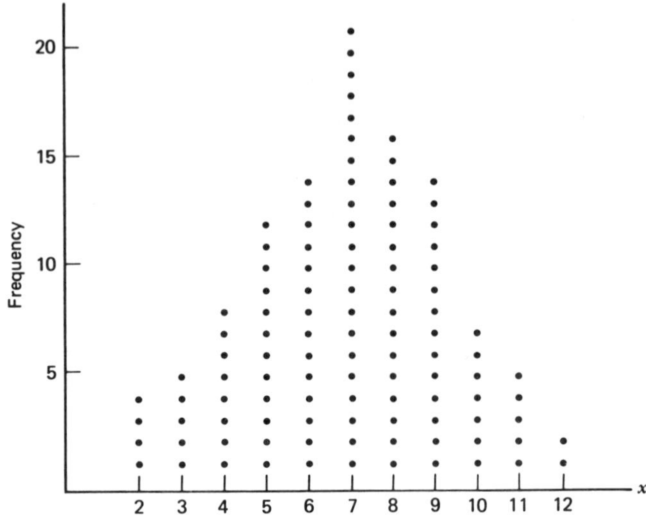

Figure 3.2 A dot frequency diagram of the values of Figure 3.1.

to 4 can be answered rapidly by counting the dots appearing on labels 2, 3, and 4, which are 17.

Another representation of the same data is a frequency table, as shown in Figure 3.3. Each of the numbers in Figure 3.1 is tallied in column 3. The cell boundaries in column 1 are given for later use. The total tallies are the frequencies in column 4. The frequencies in column 5 are obtained by dividing that in column 4 by 108. Columns 6 and 7 are frequencies in cumulative terms.

The frequencies of columns 4 and 5 in Figure 3.3 can also be represented by a graph called the frequency histogram, as shown in Figure 3.4. Two scales, frequency and percent frequency, are given in the figure. Similarly, the cumulative and percent frequencies can be represented by a graph called the cumulative polygon, as shown in Figure 3.5.

Many characteristics of the sample can be studied using the polygon. For example, the percent of cases lying between 4.5 and 9.5 can be determined by projecting the numbers vertically to the polygon and then horizontally to the percent cumulative frequency scale. The difference between the two points on the scale is the answer. Thus the result is 71%. The actual result is 71.3%.

The foregoing procedure of representing a sample can be generalized for any sample of any number of measurements. The details are left to the reader.

Cell Boundaries (1)	Cell Mid-Points (2)	Tallied Frequency (3)	Frequency (4)	Percent Frequency (5)	Cumulative Frequency (6)	Percent Cumulative Frequency (7)
1.5 - 2.5	2	////	4	0.037	4	0.037
2.5 - 3.5	3	~~////~~	5	0.046	9	0.083
3.5 - 4.5	4	~~////~~ ///	8	0.074	17	0.157
4.5 - 5.5	5	~~////~~ ~~////~~ //	12	0.111	29	0.268
5.5 - 6.5	6	~~////~~ ~~////~~ ////	14	0.130	43	0.398
6.5 - 7.5	7	~~////~~ ~~////~~ ~~////~~ ~~////~~ /	21	0.194	64	0.592
7.5 - 8.5	8	~~////~~ ~~////~~ ~~////~~ /	16	0.148	80	0.740
8.5 - 9.5	9	~~////~~ ~~////~~ ////	14	0.130	94	0.870
9.5 -10.5	10	~~////~~ //	7	0.065	101	0.935
10.5 -11.5	11	~~////~~	5	0.046	106	0.981
11.5 -12.5	12	//	2	0.019	108	1.000
Total			108	1.000		

Figure 3.3 A frequency table of the values of Figure 3.1.

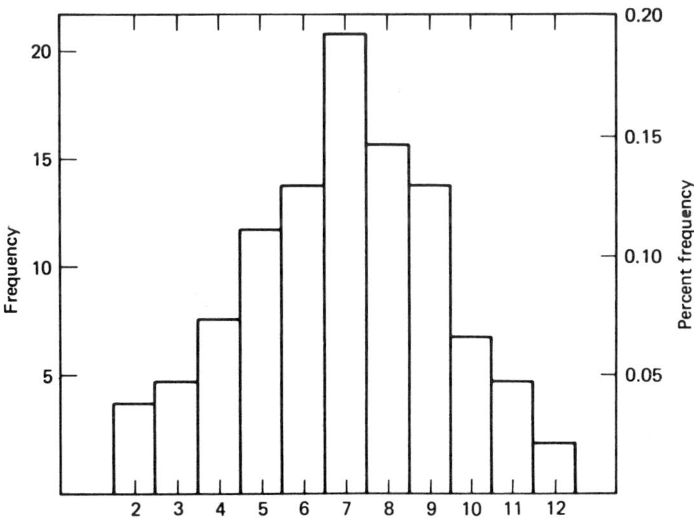

Figure 3.4 A histogram of the frequency and the percent frequency of Figure 3.3.

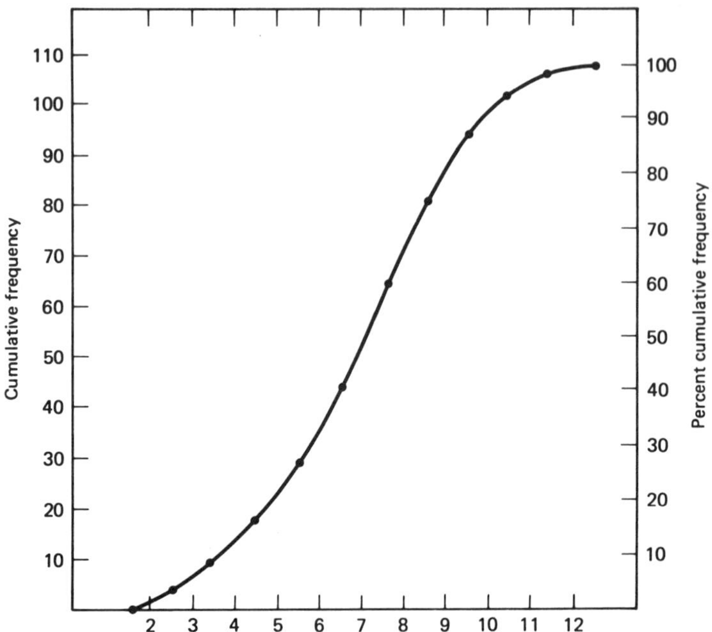

Figure 3.5 A cumulative polygon of the cumulative frequency and the percent cumulative frequency of Figure 3.3.

3.2 MEAN, STANDARD DEVIATION, AND DEGREE OF FREEDOM

In addition to the representation of a sample discussed in Section 3.1, there are two other important concepts or statistics associated with sample analysis. One is that of the mean and the other the standard deviation of the sample measurements. The sample mean is an indication of the middle of the distribution, whereas the sample standard deviation is that of the spread of the distribution.

A. *Sample Mean*

Let $x_1, x_2, \ldots, x_n$ be a sample of n measurements. The sample mean $\bar{x}$ can be computed by

$$\bar{x} = \frac{x_1 + x_2 + \cdots + x_n}{n} = \frac{\sum_{i=1}^{n} x_i}{n} \tag{3.1}$$

For example, the mean of the sample of Figure 3.1 is calculated as follows:

$$\bar{x} = \frac{(8 + 8 + 2 + \cdots + 7 + 4)}{108} = 6.9352$$

An interesting characteristic of the sample mean is that the sum of the differences between each measurement and the mean is 0. Namely,

$$(x_1 - \bar{x}) + (x_2 - \bar{x}) + \cdots + (x_n - \bar{x}) = \sum_{i=1}^{n} (x_i - \bar{x}) = 0$$

B. Sample Standard Deviation

The standard deviation, denoted by s, of a sample of n measurements is computed by

$$s^2 = \frac{\sum_{i=1}^{n} (x_i - \bar{x})^2}{(n - 1)} \tag{3.2}$$

The quantity s^2 is called the sample variance. For example, the standard deviation of the sample of Figure 3.1 is calculated as follows:

$$s^2 = \frac{(8 - 6.9352)^2 + (8 - 6.9352)^2 + \cdots + (4 - 6.9352)^2}{(108 - 1)} = 5.4069$$

Thus $s = 2.3253$. Note that the denominator in Equation (3.2) is $(n - 1)$, called the degrees of freedom, instead of the sample size n.

C. Degrees of Freedom

The degrees of freedom of a sample of n measurements is defined as n minus the number of linear dependence among the measurements. For example, in the computation of the standard deviation s, the terms $(x_i - \bar{x})$, for $i = 1, 2, \ldots, n$, are not independent of each other. They are constrained by the linear relation

$$\sum_{i=1}^{n} (x_i - \bar{x}) = 0$$

Only $n - 1$ of these terms are independent. Thus there are $n - 1$ degrees of freedom in this case. Hence the denominator of Equation (3.2) is $n - 1$. If n is large, then there is little difference in using n or $n - 1$.

3.3 THE HYPERGEOMETRIC DISTRIBUTION

The concept of sampling is closely related to that of combination. A sample is simply a combination of n things taken from N things. Thus there are $\binom{N}{n}$ possible combinations that are the number of outcomes in the sample space of the problem. The probability of each outcome of being drawn is considered as $1/\binom{N}{n}$.

The population of N things may be classified into two groups: defective and nondefective, according to certain attributes. If a sample is taken from the population without replacement, it is of interest to find the probability, denoted by $h(x)$, that x defective things are contained in the sample. The ratio x/n may be used to estimate the defective rate, denoted by θ, of the population. Namely, the ratio $\theta = K/N$ can be approximated by x/n if n is a fairly large number, where K is the number of defectives in the population.

Since there are $\binom{N_1}{x}$ ways of drawing x things from N_1 things and $\binom{N_2}{n-x}$ ways of taking $n - x$ things from the remaining N_2 things, the probability $h(x)$ can be computed by

$$h(x) = \frac{\binom{N_1}{x}\binom{N_2}{n-x}}{\binom{N}{n}} \tag{3.3}$$

Equation (3.3) is called the probability function of the hypergeometric distribution. Notice that the sampling is done without returning the drawn units to the population.

Equation (3.3) can be expressed for convenience as follows:

$$h(x) = \frac{\binom{N\theta}{x}\binom{N - N\theta}{n-x}}{\binom{N}{n}} \tag{3.4}$$

The mean μ and the variance σ^2 of the distribution are [1]

$$\mu = n\theta$$

$$\sigma^2 = \frac{N-n}{N-1} n\theta(1-\theta)$$

Example 3.1

A box contains 100 computer printouts. Five printouts are defective, having severe errors. A sample of 10 printouts are drawn at random from the box. What is the probability that the sample contains 0, 1, 2 defective printouts?

From Equation (3.3), the probability is computed as follow:

$$h(0) = \frac{\binom{5}{0}\binom{95}{10}}{\binom{100}{10}} = 0.5837$$

$$h(1) = \frac{\binom{5}{1}\binom{95}{9}}{\binom{100}{10}} = 0.3394$$

$$h(2) = \frac{\binom{5}{2}\binom{95}{8}}{\binom{100}{10}} = 0.072$$

3.4 THE BINOMIAL DISTRIBUTION

The preceding section discusses sampling from a finite population without replacement. There are cases in which (1) sampling from a finite population is done with replacement and (2) sampling is done from an infinite population with or without replacement. The hypergeometric distribution is not suitable for the application. The following distribution, called the binomial distribution, is used instead:

$$b(x) = \binom{n}{x}\theta^x(1-\theta)^{n-x} \tag{3.5}$$

Equation (3.5) can be derived from Equation (3.4) directly if the population size N is large [1].

The mean μ and the variance σ^2 of the binomial distribution are [1]

$$\mu = n\theta$$
$$\sigma^2 = n\theta(1-\theta)$$

Example 3.2

A lot contains 100,000 computer printouts, 5% of which are defective. A sample of 10 printouts is drawn from the lot. What is the probability that the sample contains 0, 1, 2 defective units?

The probability is given by

$$b(0) = \binom{10}{0} \times 0.05^0 \times 0.95^{10} = 0.5987$$

$$b(1) = \binom{10}{1} \times 0.05^1 \times 0.95^9 = 0.3151$$

$$b(2) = \binom{10}{2} \times 0.05^2 \times 0.95^8 = 0.0746$$

3.5 THE POISSON DISTRIBUTION

Sampling from an infinite population with small defective rate with or without replacement often involves a large sample size n. The computation of $\binom{n}{x}$ in the binomial distribution is tedious when n is large. The distribution can be approximated as follows by a distribution called the Poisson distribution, when $n \to \infty$, $\theta \to 0$, and $n\theta$ remains constant:

$$p(x) = \frac{(n\theta)^x e^{-n\theta}}{x!} \tag{3.6}$$

where $x = 0, 1, \ldots, n$ and $e = 2.71828\ldots$ Equation (3.6) can be derived from Equation (3.5) directly [1].

The mean μ and the variance σ^2 of the Poisson distribution are [1]

$$\mu = n\theta$$
$$\sigma^2 = n\theta$$

Example 3.3

The probability of getting 0, 1, 2 defective printouts in Example 3.2 can be computed by Equation (3.6) as follows:

$$p(0) = \frac{0.5^0 e^{-0.5}}{0!} = 0.6065$$

$$p(1) = \frac{0.5^1 e^{-0.5}}{1!} = 0.3033$$

$$p(2) = \frac{0.5^2 e^{-0.5}}{2!} = 0.0758$$

3.6 THE NORMAL DISTRIBUTION

The normal distribution is the basis of many important statistical techniques, such as sampling and statistical inference. It can be used to approximate the binomial distribution, which plays a central role in controlling software quality.

A. *The Distribution*

The function

$$f(x) = \frac{1}{\sigma\sqrt{2\pi}} e^{-(x-\mu)^2/2\sigma^2} \tag{3.7}$$

is called the normal distribution of the random variable x, $-\infty < x < \infty$, where $\pi = 3.14159\ldots$, and $e = 2.71828\ldots$. The mean and the variance of the distribution are μ and σ^2 respectively.

A curve representing the distribution is given in Figure 3.6. Given a value c for x, the probability from $-\infty$ to c can be found by

$$p(x \le c) = \int_{-\infty}^{c} f(x)\, dx \tag{3.8}$$

The curve is symmetric about the mean μ. It is interesting to note that the area under the curve, from $-\infty$ to ∞, is 1. The shaded area is about 0.02, which means about 2% of the measurements of the random variable x will fall in this region, from $\mu + 2\sigma$ to ∞. In general the area under the curve from c_1 to c_2 can be found by

$$p(c_1 < x \le c_2) = \int_{-\infty}^{c_2} f(x)\, dx - \int_{-\infty}^{c_1} f(x)\, dx$$

The computation of the probability is tedious, involving the evaluation of the integrals of the normal distribution. It can be simplified

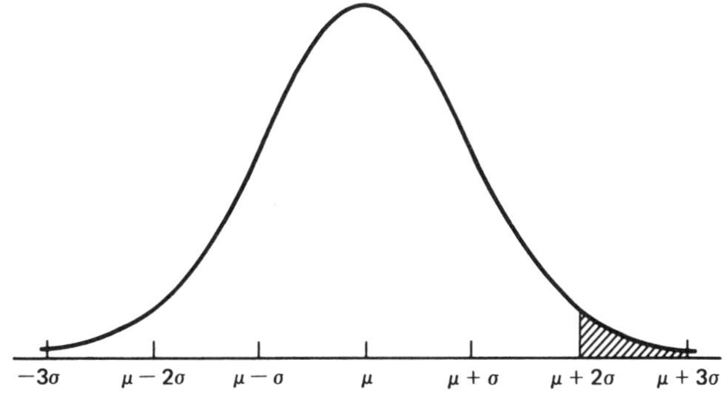

Figure 3.6 A curve of the normal distribution.

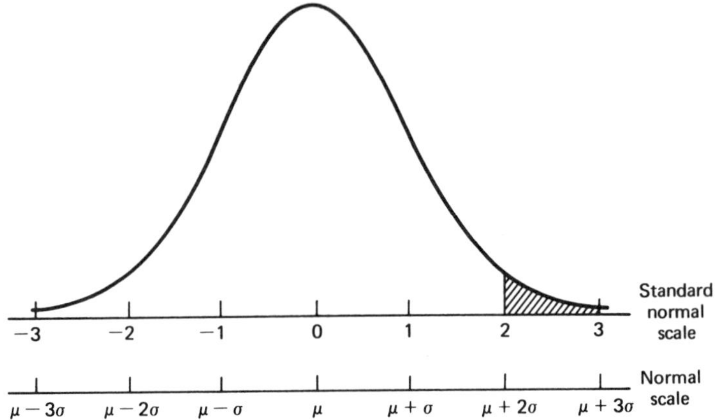

Figure 3.7 Relationship between the normal and the standard normal distribution.

through the following distribution, called the standard normal distribution:

$$\phi(z) = \frac{1}{\sqrt{2\pi}} e^{-z^2/2} \tag{3.9}$$

where $z = (x - \mu)/\sigma$ and $-\infty < z < \infty$. The variable z is called the standard normal variable and is used throughout this book.

A standardized normal distribution table is given in Appendix 5 for finding the value of

$$\Phi(z) = \int_{-\infty}^{z} \phi(y)\, dy$$

For example, the value of $\Phi(-2)$ is 0.02275 and that of $\Phi(2)$ is 0.97724. The probability under the normal curve between $z = -2$ and $z = 2$ is $0.97724 - 0.02275 = 0.95449$.

The difference between the normal and the standard normal distributions is that of the scaling, as shown in Figure 3.7. The variable z is sometimes called the standard deviation factor of the normal distribution.

Similar to Figure 3.5, a curve can also be plotted for the normal cumulative distribution, as shown in Figure 3.8, for rapid determination of the probability under the normal curve. To find the probability from $-\infty$ to c on the z-axis (or from $-\infty$ to c' on the x-axis), a line is projected vertically to the curve and then horizontally to the vertical scale. The number found on the scale is the desired probability. For example, the probability from $-\infty$ to 1 on the z-axis is 0.84.

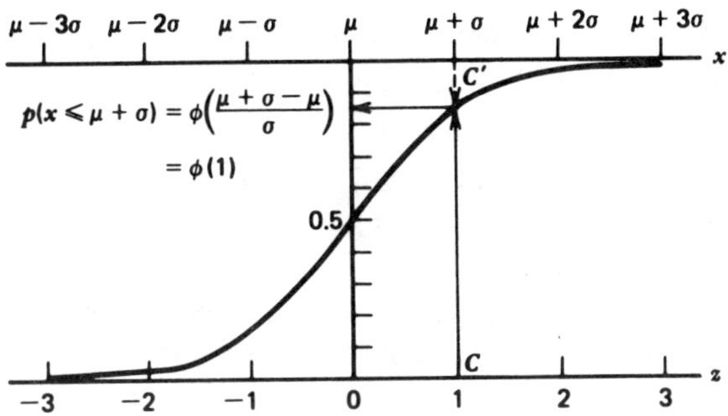

Figure 3.8 A cumulative normal distribution function defined by Equation (3.8).

Example 3.4

Two dice are thrown 108 times. What is the probability that the sum of dots x appearing is between 3.5 and 10.5?

The results and the associated histogram are given in Figures 3.1 and 3.4 respectively. The shape of the histogram appears approximately normal. The normal distribution may be used to solve the problem.

Figure 3.9 shows the conversion of the cell boundaries from the x-axis to z-axis. Column x is identical to column 1 of Figure 3.3. Since the mean and the standard deviation are 6.9352 and 2.3253 respectively, an entry in column $x - \bar{x}$ is the result of subtracting 6.9352 from the corresponding entry in column x. An entry in the last column is the result of dividing 2.3253 into the corresponding entry in column $x - \bar{x}$.

x	$x - \bar{x}$	$z = (x - \bar{x})/s$
1.5–2.5	−5.44– −4.44	−2.34– −1.91
2.5–3.5	−4.44– −3.44	−1.91– −1.48
3.5–4.5	−3.44– −2.44	−1.48– −1.05
4.5–5.5	−2.44– −1.44	−1.05– −0.62
5.5–6.5	−1.44– −0.44	−0.62– −0.19
6.5–7.5	−0.44–0.56	−0.19–0.24
7.5–8.5	0.56–1.56	0.24–0.67
8.5–9.5	1.56–2.56	0.67–1.10
9.5–10.5	2.56–3.56	1.10–1.53
10.5–11.5	3.56–4.56	1.53–1.96
11.5–12.5	4.56–5.56	1.96–2.39

Figure 3.9 Conversion of the cell boundaries of Figure 3.3 from the x-axis to the z-axis.

Thus the relationship $3.5 \leq x \leq 10.5$ is converted into $-1.48 \leq z \leq 1.53$. The probability is found to be

$$p(-1.48 \leq z \leq 1.53) = p(-\infty \leq z \leq 1.53) - p(-\infty \leq z \leq -1.48)$$
$$= 0.94 - 0.07 = 0.87$$

The true percent found in Figure 3.3 is 0.85.

One important application of the standard normal variable z is that of the significance points in statistical inference, which is discussed in Chapter 5. The concept is based on the following:

Let α be an arbitrary probability under the normal curve and z_α be the standard random variable such that

$$\alpha = \int_{z_\alpha}^{\infty} \phi(y)\, dy$$

or

$$1 - \alpha = \int_{-\infty}^{z_\alpha} \phi(y)\, dy$$

Then z_α is the 100 $(1 - \alpha)$ percentage point of the standard normal distribution. Owing to the symmetry of the distribution, $z_\alpha = -z_{1-\alpha}$. For example, $z_{0.05} = 1.645$, which is the 5% level of significance of the distribution.

B. Relationship between the Normal Distribution and the Binomial Distribution

The mean and the variance of the binomial distribution

$$b(x) = \binom{n}{x}\theta^x(1 - \theta)^x$$

is $\mu = n\theta$ and $\sigma^2 = n\theta(1 - \theta)$. The standard normal variable z in

$$z = \frac{x - \mu}{\sigma}$$

becomes

$$z = \frac{x - n\theta}{\sqrt{n\theta(1 - \theta)}}$$

after substituting μ by $n\theta$ and σ by $\sqrt{n\theta(1 - \theta)}$. The variable z has the normal distribution with mean equal to 0 and standard deviation equal to 1. In other words, the random variable x in the binomial distribution has approximately the normal distribution with mean $\mu = n\theta$ and $\sigma = n\theta(1 - \theta)$. This relationship greatly simplifies the computation of the probabilities given by the binomial distribution. The probabilities can be found with the standard normal distribution table given in Appendix 5.

Example 3.5

A lot contains 100,000 computer printouts, 10% of which are defective having errors. A sample of 100 units is taken randomly from the lot. What is the probability of getting x, $3 \leq x \leq 5$, defectives in the sample?

The probability of getting x defectives in the sample is given by

$$b(x) = \binom{100}{x} 0.1^x 0.9^{100-x}$$

Thus

$$b(3 \leq x \leq 5) = \sum_{x=3}^{5} \binom{100}{x} 0.1^x 0.9^{100-x}$$

which is tedious to compute. This probability can be approximated by the standard normal distribution

$$p(3 \leq x \leq 5) = p\left(\frac{2.5 - 10}{3} \leq \frac{x - 10}{3} \leq \frac{5.5 - 10}{3}\right)$$
$$= p(-2.5 \leq z \leq -1.50) = 0.06681 - 0.00621 = 0.0606$$

The probability computed by the binomial distribution is 0.05498, which is close to 0.0606.

The relationship between the binomial and the normal distribution is shown in Figure 3.10. The normal curve passes through the top center point of each rectangle. Each rectangle starts at the middle point between two numbers on the x-axis and stops at another. Thus the numbers 2.5 and 5.5, instead of 3 and 5, are used in computing the probability by the normal distribution. This is required to reduce the

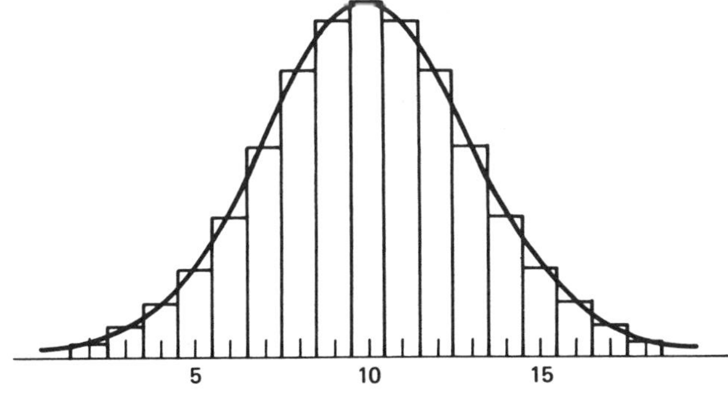

Figure 3.10 Approximation of the binomial distribution by the normal distribution of Example 3.5.

error. Otherwise half of the left and the right rectangles are omitted from the computation.

REFERENCES

1. I. Guttman and S. S. Wilks, *Introductory Engineering Statistics*, Wiley, New York, 1965.
2. W. Feller, *An Introduction to Probability Theory and Its Applications*, Vols. 1 and 2, Wiley, New York, 1968 and 1971.
3. G. W. Summers, W. S. Peters, and C. P. Armstrong, *Basic Statistics in Business and Economics*, 2nd ed., Wadsworth, Belmont, California, 1977.
4. J. E. Freund and F. J. Williams, *Elementary Business Statistics—The Modern Approach*, 3rd ed., Prentice-Hall, Englewood Cliffs, New Jersey, 1977.

EXERCISES

1. Two dice are thrown once. What is the probability of getting a sum between 5 and 7, inclusive?
2. A box contains 100 computer printouts, 10% of which are defective of computational errors. A sample of 20 units is taken at random from the box. What is the probability of getting less than 2 defectives in the sample, using the hypergeometric distribution?
3. Repeat Exercise 2, using the binomial distribution.
4. Repeat Exercise 2, using the Poisson Distribution.
5. Repeat Exercise 2, using the normal distribution.
6. A set of 100 digits is drawn randomly from the random numbers of Appendix 1. What is the probability that the sample contains twelve 0's?
7. Derive Equation (3.5) from Equation (3.4).
8. Derive Equation (3.6) from Equation (3.5).

CHAPTER **4**

Random Number Generation

Extensive discussions on software reliability and program testing have been given in the literature. However, most of them are narrative in nature with emphasis on what, instead of how, to do in controlling software quality. Quantitative approaches together with examples are scarce. It is difficult for a reader to get a clear understanding of how program testing should be conducted after reading an article.

Since random numbers play an important role in statistics and software quality control, methods and programs for generating such numbers are introduced here, as well as testing of the programs. Included in the discussion are (1) random number generation according to a uniform or a nonuniform distribution, (2) FORTRAN and COBOL generators given as examples, and (3) program testing using these generators. The randomness of numbers is tested using the chi-square goodness-of-fit test.

4.1 RANDOM NUMBERS

The word random means different things to people in different environments. It means undertaking without choice in speech and certain sciences and something closely related to probability in statistics. The most popular usage of the term in statistics is, perhaps, in random sampling where every object in a set of objects has an equal chance of being drawn from the set. To ensure randomness, the sampling must follow carefully chosen rules. Such rules vary from one application to another. For example, sizes and weights tend to bias the chance of a ball from being taken from a container. All balls must be carefully inspected in size and weight for such sampling purpose if randomness is gained by physically stirring the balls. The size and weight of a ball is immaterial if the sampling is done by using random numbers. Every ball in the container is identified by a number between 1 and N, where N is the total number of balls in the container. A random number between 1 and N is generated. The ball that corresponds to the number is drawn. In this sampling, the randomness of the numbers must be carefully analyzed to avoid introducing side effects to the results. The generation of such numbers is extremely important in modern statistical and scientific applications.

Four major characteristics must be considered in selecting a random number generator:

A. **Efficiency.** Random numbers are used in thousands or millions in practice. Generation of such numbers must be efficient and economical. A computer is usually used because of its power and speed.

B. **Reproducibility.** A sequence of random numbers should be reproducible by the original generator. This is useful in an application where other conditions can be varied while keeping the numbers static to understand a phenomenon.

C. **Long Period.** Some generators produce series of random numbers that repeat undesirably. The period of a generator is defined as the count of such numbers in the series. For example, a computer generator always produces such repeating series owing to fixed-length word arithmetic. For any meaningful application, the period must be reasonably long, that is, in a magnitude of millions or billions.

D. **Statistical Acceptability.** Random numbers can be generated according to a statistical distribution such as the normal distribution. The numbers must be investigated to determine its acceptability.

4.2 RANDOM NUMBER GENERATION

Random numbers can be generated by a computer using such different methods as the middle-square method, the multiplication method, or the congruence (or power residue) method [1]. The most commonly used is, perhaps, the congruence method. This method works as follows:

In algebra, the equation

$$Y = N X + R$$

is the same as

$$Y - R = N X \tag{4.1}$$

which reads $(Y - R)$ is divisible by N, where N is called the modulus and R the residue of the division.

Sometimes Equation (4.1) may be written as

$$Y \equiv R \pmod{N} \tag{4.2}$$

which is called a congruence relation in the study of number theory. Equation (4.2) is read as "Y is congruent to R modulo N." For example, let $Y = 375$, $N = 6$, then $375 - 3 = 6 \times 62$, or $375 \equiv 3 \pmod{6}$.

The following definitions are needed before further discussions:

A. **Relatively Prime Numbers.** A and B are relatively prime numbers if the greatest common divisor (GCD) of A and B is 1, written $(A, B) = 1$. For example, $(2, 13) = 1$.

B. **Power Residue.** The residue of the successive powers of a number M is divided by another number N. Namely, $R = M^i \pmod{N}$ for $i = 1, 2, 3, \ldots$. For example, let $M = 2$ and $N = 5$, then

$$2^1 \pmod{5} = 2$$
$$2^2 \pmod{5} = 4$$
$$2^3 \pmod{5} = 3$$
$$2^4 \pmod{5} = 1$$
$$2^5 \pmod{5} = 2$$
$$2^6 \pmod{5} = 4$$
$$2^7 \pmod{5} = 3$$
$$2^8 \pmod{5} = 1$$

The series of the power residues 2, 4, 3, 1 repeats for all powers of the number 2. The numbers 2, 4, 3, and 1 are random numbers generated by the power residue manipulation. The period is only 4.

The power residue method in generating random numbers is unsatisfactory since the period is too short. However, it can be modified as follows:

$$x_{i+1} = c\, x_i \pmod N, \qquad i = 0, 1, 2, \ldots \tag{4.3}$$

where c is a positive constant, x_0 is any positive number relatively prime to N, and N is $2{*}{*}b$ (b being the word size in bits of a computer).

Equation (4.3) is referred to as the congruence method. It has been shown in reference [1] that the maximum period of the generator is $2{*}{*}(b - 2)$ if c equals 3 (mod 8) or 5 (mod 8) and x_0 is a positive odd integer number. For example, the maximum period of the generator on a 16-bit mini computor with $c = 331$, where $331 = 3 \pmod 8$, is $2{*}{*}(16 - 2) = 16384$.

The numbers generated by Equation (4.3) are called uniform random numbers since every number between 0 and $2{*}{*}b$, exclusive, has an equal probability of being produced. These numbers can be transformed into a nonuniform distribution according to a statistical distribution. The transformation is left to the reader.

4.3 FORTRAN AND COBOL RANDOM NUMBER GENERATORS

Figures 4.1 and 4.2 show two random number generators implementing Equation (4.3) on an IBM 360 or 370 32-bit computer. The period of both generators is 2**30 which is 1,073,741,824—a number sufficient for most practical applications.

In addition, both generators are efficient and able to reproduce any sequence of numbers by submitting the same starting number for N.

```
SUBROUTINE RANDU (N, RN)
N = N*65539
IF(N.LT.0) N = N + 2147483647 + 1
RN = N
RN = RN/2147483647
RETURN
END
```

Figure 4.1 A FORTRAN random number generator on a 32-bit computer.

```
IDENTIFICATION DIVISION.
      PROGRAM-ID. RAND-U.
ENVIRONMENT DIVISION.
CONFIGURATION SECTION.
SOURCE-COMPUTER. IBM-370-145.
OBJECT-COMPUTER. IBM-370-145.
DATA DIVISION.
LINKAGE SECTION.
77    N PIC   S9(10) COMP SYNC.
77    RN   COMP-1   SYNC.
PROCEDURE DIVISION USING N, RN.
RAND-BEGIN.
      COMPUTE N = N * 65539.
      IF N IS LESS THAN 0 COMPUTE N = N + 2147483647 + 1.
      MOVE N TO RN.
      COMPUTE RN = RN / 2147483647.
RAND-RETURN.
      EXIT PROGRAM.
```

Figure 4.2 A COBOL random number generator on a 32-bit computer.

The only question about the generators is: Are the numbers produced random? The statistical acceptability of the numbers must be examined. This is explained in the next sections.

4.4 CHI-SQUARE GOODNESS-OF-FIT TEST

In statistical applications, it is often necessary to compare the observed with the expected frequencies of certain outcomes of an experiment. A vehicle called the chi-square goodness-of-fit test can be used for this purpose. The test is based on a statistical distribution called the multinomial distribution, which is derived from the binomial distribution.

The probability function of the binomial distribution is

$$b(x) = \binom{n}{x} p^x q^{n-x} = \frac{n!}{x!\,(n-x)!} p^x q^{n-x}$$

Let $x_1 = x$, $x_2 = (n - x)$, $p_1 = p$, and $p_2 = q$. Then $b(x)$ becomes

$$b(x) = G(x_1, x_2) = \frac{n!}{x_1!x_2!} p_1^{x_1} p_2^{x_2}$$

In general,

$$G(x_1, x_2, \ldots, x_k) = \frac{n!}{x_1!x_2! \cdots x_k!} p_1^{x_1} p_2^{x_2} \cdots p_k^{x_k} \tag{4.4}$$

where $x_1 + x_2 + \cdots + x_k = n$ and the expectation of x_i is np_i. Equation (4.4) is called the probability function of the multinomial distribution. It is useful in modeling independent trial processes under the conditions similar to those under which the binomial trial is modeled except that the number of possible outcomes in each trial is k, instead of 2.

For example, a box holds 1000 computer printed outputs of different contents in different formats. Twenty are defective containing severe errors. Fifty have don't-care errors. The remaining are of acceptable quality. A sample of 10 outputs is taken at random from the box. What is the probability that the sample contains one defective, one don't-care error, and eight acceptable outputs?

The rate of defective outputs is $p_1 = 20/1000 = 0.02$, that of outputs having don't-care errors is $p_2 = 50/1000 = 0.05$, and that of acceptable quality outputs is $p_3 = (1000 - 20 - 50)/1000 = 0.93$. Thus the probability can be computed by Equation (4.4) as follows:

$$G(1, 1, 8) = \frac{10!}{1!\,1!\,8!}(0.02)^1(0.05)^1(0.93)^8 = 0.05036$$

The foregoing sample represents an observed performance. The numbers 1, 1, and 8 are the observed frequencies of different outputs in the sample. The expected frequencies are $10 \times 0.02 = 0.2$, $10 \times 0.05 = 0.5$, and $10 \times 0.93 = 9.3$, respectively. An interesting consideration is whether or not the sample comes from the multinomial distribution with probabilities $P(O_i) = p_i$, for $i = 1, 2, \ldots, k$. (There are a number of factors affecting the results, such as use of poor random numbers.) The judgment can be done through comparing the observed and the expected frequencies of the outcomes as follows:

A. Form a hypothesis that the sample comes from the multinomial distribution.

B. Use the following equation as a statistic to test the hypothesis:

$$\chi^2 = \sum_{i=1}^{k} \frac{(x_i - np_i)^2}{np_i} \tag{4.5}$$

If $x_i = np_i$, for all i, then the value of χ^2 is 0, which means a perfect "fit" between the observed and the expected frequencies. The hypothesis is accepted. In general, the acceptability depends on the value of χ^2. The smaller the value, the better the acceptability.

The distribution of the χ^2 value computed by Equation (4.5) is approximately the chi-square distribution with $k - 1$ degrees of freedom for moderately large n. In practice, the value of n is usually selected so that $np_i \geq 5$ for all i. If this criterion is difficult to meet, then certain outcomes (such as O_1, O_2, and O_3) having the smallest probabilities (such as p_1, p_2, and p_3) may be combined into a single outcome with the probability p_c so that $np_c \geq 5$ (such as $p_c = p_1 + p_2 + p_3$).

Outcome O_i (No. of Points on Both Dice)	Observed Frequency (x_i)	Probability (p_i)	Expected Frequency (np_i)	$(x_i - np_i)^2$	$\frac{(x_i - np_i)^2}{np_i}$
2	4	1/36	3	0	0.000
3	5	2/36	6		
4	8	3/36	9	1	0.111
5	12	4/36	12	0	0.000
6	14	5/36	15	1	0.067
7	21	6/36	18	9	0.5
8	16	5/36	15	1	0.067
9	14	4/36	12	4	0.333
10	7	3/36	9	4	0.444
11	5	2/36	6		
12	2	1/36	3	4	0.444
Total	$n = 108$	36/36	108		$\chi^2 = 1.966$

Figure 4.3 Results and analysis of 108 throws of two dice of Figure 3.1.

The acceptability of the hypothesis is determined as follows: If $\chi^2 < \chi^2_{k-1,\alpha}$ then the hypothesis is accepted, where $\chi^2_{k-1,\alpha}$ is the expected χ^2 value found in Appendix 7 (with $k - 1$ degrees of freedom and at the $100\alpha\%$ level of significance). Otherwise, the hypothesis is rejected. For example, Figure 4.3 shows the computation of the χ^2 value for determining whether the dice are true. If the dice are true, then the probability of getting two points in throwing them once is 1/36; that of getting three points is 2/36; and so on. These probabilities are listed under p_i in the figure.

The first two outcomes are combined into one since the expected frequency of the first is $np_1 = 3$, which is less than 5. Similarly, the last two outcomes are combined into another one. The degrees of freedom for the test is $k - 2 - 1 = 11 - 3 = 8$. The computed χ^2 value is 1.966. The expected value is $\chi^2_{8,\,0.05} = 15.5073$ (from Appendix 7). Since $1.966 < 15.5073$, the hypothesis that the sample comes from the multinomial distribution is accepted at the 5% level of significance. In other words, the observed frequencies and the expected frequencies are not different at the 5% level of significance. Namely, it can be reasonably concluded that the dice behave like true dice.

4.5 TEST OF RANDOM NUMBERS

The random number generator of Figure 4.1 (and of Figure 4.2) presents a very special case of software testing. It is a correct program (as can be shown by both informal code examination and by the correctness proof in Chapter 11). But the generator may not be usable. The usability is judged by the randomness of the numbers it generates, not by the program correctness.

The testing of the generator requires extensive study of a user's application and requires the investigation of the randomness under consideration. The usability of the subroutine for one application does not necessarily mean that for another application. It must be examined on a case-by-case basis. The following sections are an example of testing the randomness of the numbers using the frequency, serial, poker, and gap methods. The discussion is based on a sequence of 1000 decimal digits produced by the generator, as shown in Figure 4.4 (The

```
95821 83466 63187 92943 09251 98094 55391 83576 36309 42365
10164 33176 26597 56242 67059 01728 90123 01497 24567 48907
28972 41977 90837 96315 20371 90670 10099 35849 89726 46631
00885 42047 43021 19347 63824 34010 53734 29501 09249 87629
74801 85448 12921 30716 25115 40649 57460 13498 13489 64531
84201 48778 99494 44289 65100 83685 68638 85573 70897 70222
77660 09285 73945 88492 83412 53037 95742 96749 42558 75039
17247 69728 73179 35299 88208 85461 33087 45019 66944 85828
97634 34579 11156 54996 09943 07378 87863 22220 16489 50273
96174 49490 04979 67720 04690 03767 99918 17353 10934 55072
83190 66399 62523 18749 17401 63843 16937 35172 33610 96399
38811 83468 17131 40639 41533 53247 83570 38857 63459 95473
71604 03629 55708 70586 64513 58415 22295 41770 68855 35332
13918 78832 14453 22099 38834 87984 74237 60621 11890 78129
07449 14861 32842 43201 62727 42951 05072 72314 64355 92834
46531 03692 41294 50743 97567 10921 43406 21536 45435 10350
01349 92539 71328 44909 68070 38877 25770 48164 66139 90677
98103 43110 36954 98012 20548 23424 55238 59382 51045 61640
05984 77972 92943 89846 22381 50091 15782 69458 32770 08189
70138 28250 12987 34880 18573 11153 01933 95878 44081 93418
```

Figure 4.4 A sequence of 1,000 random digits.

initial odd integer number x_0 is 751003. A digit is obtained by multiplying 10 by a uniform random number between 0 and 1, exclusive, and by truncating the result to the integer.)

4.5.1 The Frequency Test

This method examines the number of occurrences of each digit in the sequence of Figure 4.4. There are different ways of accomplishing this; for example, counting of a digit in the sequence. The discussion is based on a matrix called the frequency and serial test matrix, as shown in Figure 4.5. An entry a_{ij} in the figure is the frequency of the digit i followed by the digit j in the 1000 digits of Figure 4.4. For example, $a_{01} = 20$ means digit 0 is followed by digit 1 20 times in the sequence. Similarly, $a_{86} = 4$ means digit 8 is followed by digit 6 four times, and so on. To make the 1000 digits yield exactly 1000 pairs of i and j, the last digit, 8, is considered followed by the first digit, 9, to form the pair 89.

An entry in the TOTAL column r_i is the sum of the entries in row i. It is also the total number of occurrences of digit i in the sequence. For example, $r_0 = 96$ means there are 96 0's in the sequence. An entry in the TOTAL row c_j has a meaning similar to that in the TOTAL column, r_i. Notice that $r_i = c_i$.

The entry 1000, which appears in the lower right-hand corner of Figure 4.5, is the grand total of the row total (or that of the column

i \ j	0	1	2	3	4	5	6	7	8	9	Total
0	11	20	3	11	6	6	8	9	9	13	96
1	15	11	7	12	7	9	9	10	13	8	101
2	9	8	10	9	10	9	4	6	12	14	91
3	9	15	9	6	20	12	8	10	12	12	113
4	8	7	12	14	10	15	10	7	12	17	112
5	10	9	5	14	10	8	8	12	9	6	89
6	5	6	10	14	10	5	8	8	5	7	78
7	12	6	16	11	14	3	10	12	8	10	102
8	5	11	9	12	11	11	4	14	13	14	104
9	12	8	10	10	14	11	11	14	11	13	114
Total	96	101	91	113	112	89	78	102	104	114	1000

Figure 4.5 Frequency and serial test data of the sequence of 1,000 digits of Figure 4.4.

Outcome (O_i)	Observed Frequency (x_i)	Probability (p_i)	Expected Frequency (np_i)	$(x_i - np_i)^2$	$\frac{(x_i - np_i)^2}{np_i}$
0	96	0.1	100	16	0.16
1	101	0.1	100	1	0.01
2	91	0.1	100	81	0.81
3	113	0.1	100	169	1.69
4	112	0.1	100	144	1.44
5	89	0.1	100	121	1.21
6	78	0.1	100	484	4.84
7	102	0.1	100	4	0.04
8	104	0.1	100	16	0.16
9	114	0.1	100	196	1.96
Total	$n = 1000$		1000		$\chi^2 = 12.32$

Figure 4.6 Results and analysis of 1,000 random digits using the frequency test.

total). The row total and the column total serve as a cross-check.

The hypothesis to test is that the sample of outcomes of digits $0, 1, \ldots, 9$ comes from the multinomial distribution with $P(0) = 0.1$, $P(1) = 0.1, \ldots, P(9) = 0.1$. Equation (4.5) is used as the statistic for the test. The computation of the χ^2 value is shown in Figure 4.6.

From Appendix 7 the expected value of $\chi^2_{10-1,\,0.05}$ is 16.9190. The computed χ^2 value is 12.32, which is less than 16.9190. Thus it is concluded that the 1000 digits of Figure 4.4 passes the frequency test at the 5% level of significance.

4.5.2 The Serial Test

This method tests the number of occurrences of a digit followed by another. Namely, to compare the entry of a_{ij} of the matrix of Figure 4.5 with the theoretical number of 10.

The hypothesis is that the sample of the outcomes of $00, 01, \ldots, 98, 99$ comes from the multinomial distribution with $P(00) = 0.01$, $P(01) = 0.01, \ldots, P(98) = 0.01$, $P(99) = 0.01$. Equation (4.5) is used as the statistic for the test. The computation of the χ^2 value is shown in Figure 4.7.

Outcome (O_i)	Observed Frequency (x_i)	Probability (p_i)	Expected Frequency (np_i)	$(x_i - np_i)^2$	$\frac{(x_i - np_i)^2}{np_i}$
00	11	0.01	10	1	0.1
01	20	0.01	10	100	10.0
.	.	.	.	.	.
.	.	.	.	.	.
.	.	.	.	.	.
98	11	0.01	10	1	0.1
99	13	0.01	10	9	0.9
Total	$n = 1000$		1000		$\chi^2 = 111.8$

Figure 4.7 Results and analysis of 1,000 random digits using the serial test.

The number of degrees of freedom in this test is $k - 9 - 1 = 100 - 9 - 1 = 90$. (Since there are 10 linear constraints imposed by the condition that the totals of r_i and c_i are the same, but only nine are independent; and there is one constraint imposed by the grand total.) From Appendix 7, the expected value of $\chi^2_{90,\,0.05}$ is 113.145. The computed value of χ^2 is 111.8, which is less than 113.145. Thus it is concluded that the 1000 digits of Figure 4.4 pass the serial test at the 5% level of significance.

4.5.3 The Poker Test

If a sequence of random digits is partitioned into blocks of y digits, then each block can contain (1) y identical digits, (2) $y - 1$ identical digits, and so on. For example, if $y = 4$, then a block can contain (1) four identical digits, such as 2222, 5555, denoted by *aaaa*; (2) three identical digits, such as 2223, 4544, 8999, denoted by *aaab*; (3) two identical digits, such as 2234, 5699, 8335, denoted by *aabc*; (4) two identical digit pairs, such as 3535, 8778, 1010, denoted by *aabb*; and (5) all four digits are different, such as 1234, 7598, 0374, denoted by *abcd*.

The probability of each case to happen in a block, assuming uniform random digits, can be computed and can be used to test the randomness of the digits. The test is referred to as the poker test since it resembles the possible outcomes of the poker card game. The probability is computed as follows for a block of size 4:

The sample space is $10 \times 10 \times 10 \times 10 = 10{,}000$. The probability of each of the five cases to occur can be found by the reasoning:

A. **Case *aaaa*.** This case is the same as taking four positions out of four for combination. Since there are 10 digits that can fill the positions,

$$p_1 = \frac{10 \times \binom{4}{4}}{10{,}000} = 0.001$$

B. **Case *aaab*.** Three positions are taken out of four for combination. Once the three positions are filled by a digit, each of the remaining digits can sit in the other position. Thus

$$p_2 = \frac{10 \times 9 \times \binom{4}{3}}{10{,}000} = 0.036$$

C. **Case *aabc*.** Two positions are taken out of four for combination. Once a digit occupies the two positions, one of the remaining nine digits can fill in one of the other two positions. Once the "third" position is filled, one of the remaining eight digits can sit in the "fourth." Thus

$$p_3 = \frac{10 \times 9 \times 8 \times \binom{4}{2}}{10{,}000} = 0.432$$

D. **Case *aabb*.** Two out of four positions are taken for combination. Ten digits can fill in the selected positions. Each of the remaining nine digits can fill in both of the two remaining positions. Since each pair will be counted twice in this case (such as 2233 and 3322), the result of the computation must be reduced by half. Thus

$$p_4 = \frac{\left[10 \times 9 \times \binom{4}{2} \Big/ 2\right]}{10{,}000} = 0.027$$

E. **Case *abcd*.** The computation is straight forward.

$$p_5 = \frac{10 \times 9 \times 8 \times 7}{10{,}000} = 0.504$$

The hypothesis for the test is that the sample of the outcomes of *aaaa*, *aaab*, *aabc*, *aabb*, and *abcd* comes from the multinomial distribution with $P(aaaa) = 0.001$, $P(aaab) = 0.036$, $P(aabc) = 0.432$, $P(aabb) = 0.027$, and $P(abcd) = 0.504$. Equation (4.5) is used as the statistic for the test. The computation of the χ^2 value is shown in Figure 4.8.

Outcome (O_i)	Observed Frequency (x_i)	Probability (p_i)	Expected Frequency (np_i)	$(x_i - np_i)^2$	$\frac{(x_i - np_i)^2}{np_i}$
aaaa	0	0.001	0.25		
				1.5625	0.1689
aaab	8	0.036	9.00		
aabb	8	0.027	6.75	1.5625	0.2315
aabc	88	0.432	108.00	400.0000	3.7037
abcd	146	0.504	126.00	400.0000	3.1746
Total	$n = 250$		250.00		$\chi^2 = 7.2787$

Figure 4.8 Results and analysis of 1,000 random digits using the poker test.

Notice that the outcomes *aaaa* and *aaab* are combined into one in the computation of the χ^2 value. The number of degrees of freedom in this test is $k - 1 = (5 - 1) - 1 = 3$. From Appendix 7, the expected value of $\chi^2_{3,\,0.05}$ is 7.81473. The computed value of χ^2 is 7.2787, which is less than 7.81473. Thus it is concluded that the 1000 digits of Figure 4.4 pass the poker test at the 5% level of significance.

4.5.4 The Gap Test

A gap in a sequence of digits is defined as the number of digits between two identical digits. For example, the gap between the first two 6's in the sequence 63896546923 is 3 and that between the second and the third 6 is 2. Let d be the gap size. The probability of a gap equal to d can be computed by [1]

$$p_d = \left(1 - \frac{1}{h}\right)^d \frac{1}{h}, \qquad \text{for } d = 0, 1, 2, \ldots$$

where h is the base of number system of the digits in the sequence. For example, let $h = 10$. Then

$$p_0 = \left(1 - \tfrac{1}{10}\right)^0 \tfrac{1}{10} = 0.10$$

$$p_1 = \left(1 - \tfrac{1}{10}\right)^1 \tfrac{1}{10} = 0.09$$

The probabilities can also be used to test the randomness of random digits. Such a test is called the gap test. The hypothesis of the test is that the sample of the outcomes of gap sizes equal 0, 1, 2, . . . comes

Outcome (O_i)	Observed Frequency (x_i)	Probability (p_i)	Expected Frequency (np_i)	$(x_i - np_i)^2$	$\frac{(x_i - np_i)^2}{np_i}$
0	11	0.100	9.500		
1	6	0.090	8.550	22.515	0.875
2	4	0.081	7.695		
3	4	0.073	6.935		
4	5	0.066	6.270	14.516	0.772
5	6	0.059	5.605		
6	6	0.053	5.035		
7	7	0.048	4.560	5.3824	0.393
8	3	0.043	4.085		
9	5	0.039	3.705		
10	2	0.035	3.325	0.000	0.000
11	3	0.031	2.945		
12 and over	33	0.282	26.790	38.564	1.439
Total	95		95.000		$\chi^2 = 3.479$

Figure 4.9 Results and analysis of 1,000 random digits using the gap test.

from the multinomial distribution with $P(0) = 0.10$, $P(1) = 0.09$, $P(2) = 0.081, \ldots$ Equation (4.5) is used as the statistic for the test. The computation of χ^2 value is shown in Figure 4.9.

Notice that every three outcomes are combined into one in the computation of the χ^2 value, except the last entry of "12 and over." The number of degrees of freedom in this test is 4. From Appendix 7, the expected value of $\chi^2_{4,\,0.05}$ is 9.48773. The computed value of χ^2 is 3.479. Thus it is concluded that the 1000 digits of Figure 4.4 pass the gap test at the 5% level of significance.

REFERENCES

1. B. Jansson, *Random Number Generators*, Victor Pettersons Bokindustri Aktiebolag, Stockholm, Sweden, 1966.
2. International Business Machines Corporation, *Random Number Generation and Testing*, Reference Manual C20-8011, IBM, White Plains, New York, 1959.
3. A. Ralston and C. L. Meek (Eds.), *Encyclopedia of Computer Science*, Petrocelli/Charter, New York, 1976.

4. Rand Corporation, *A Million Random Digits with* 100,000 *Normal Deviates*, The Free Press, Glencoe, Illinois, 1955.
5. M. G. Kendall and B. B. Smith, "Randomness and Random Sampling Numbers," *Journal of the Royal Statistical Society*, Vol. 101, 1938, pp. 147–166.
6. International Business Machines Corporation, System/360 Scientific Subroutine Packages (360A-CM-03X), Version III, IBM, White Plains, New York, 1968.
7. I. Guttman and S. S. Wilks, *Introductory Engineering Statistics*, Wiley, New York, 1965.

EXERCISES

1. Write a random number generator in a language on a computer of your choice using Equation (4.3).
2. What is the maximum period of the generator of Exercise 1?
3. A box contains 10,000 computer printed outputs, some of which contain the following defects:

   (a) Computational errors, 5%.
   (b) I/O errors, 2%.
   (c) Format errors, 1%.
   (d) Incomplete results, 1%.

   A sample of nine outputs is taken at random from the box. What is the probability that the sample contains one output with computational errors, two with I/O errors, zero with format errors, and one with incomplete results?
4. Use the generator of Exercise 1 to produce a sequence of 800 digits similar to that of Figure 4.4.
5. Test the randomness of the sequence of Exercise 4, following the frequency, serial, poker, and gap methods discussed in this chapter.
6. If the sequence of Exercise 4 is partitioned into 160 blocks (each containing 5 digits), what are the combination cases that can happen in a block? Compute the probability for each case.

CHAPTER 5

Sampling Techniques And Statistical Inference

Sampling is a practical and economical method of gathering facts about any phenomenon under observation, such as about computer and software performance. Associated with a fact-finding process is some measurement work, such as measuring the busy-time and idle-time ratio of a computer under certain operating conditions. In every kind of measurement work there are always chances of making errors. An error can be minor or significant. Thus certain tolerance will be needed to accept a measurement with error. The gathered facts or measured data may be used to explain the phenomenon with some deviation. In other words, the facts may be used to explain the phenomenon with a certain level of confidence, such as 95% confident that the facts explain the phenomenon. In software quality control, a statement equivalent to this is "95% confident that the software is valid."

The phenomenon mentioned may be defined as a collection of objects which, in turn, may be called a population. Sampling is then the activity of taking some objects from the population.

There are two sampling techniques suitable for software testing and acceptance. One is simple random sampling and the other sequential sampling. Associated with the first is the determination of the number of objects, called the sample size, to be taken from the population so that the gathered facts are sufficient to explain the characteristics of the population. The explanation is done through statistical inference on sample data and through estimation of important parameters such as mean and variance of the population.

The second sampling technique is basically the same as the first except that a different approach is used. It requires no determination of sample size and may need a sample smaller than the first needs.

5.1 SIMPLE RANDOM SAMPLING

Simple random sampling is perhaps the most common sampling technique in statistical study. It involves drawing n objects, called a sample, from a set of N objects, called a population. There are $\binom{N}{n}$ ways of drawing the sample from the population. If each of the ways has an equal probability of being drawn, then the sampling is called simple random sampling.

The sampling procedure, the determination of sample size, and statistical inference principles including testing and estimating parameters of a population are discussed in detail in the following subsections. These concepts can be applied to the testing and acceptance of a software system.

5.1.1 Sampling Procedure

The total number of ways of drawing n units from a population of N units is $\binom{N}{n}$. If each of the ways has an equal probability of being chosen, then the set of n units is called a simple random sample from the population.

The following is a sampling procedure:

A. Conceptually number each unit from 1 to N in the population.

B. Generate a uniform random number R, $0 < R < 1$.

C. Compute the random number I by $I = [R \times N] + 1$, where $[R \times N]$ is the integer part of $R \times N$.

D. Draw the Ith unit from the population. If the unit has already been taken, then repeat **B** through **D**.

E. Repeat **B** through **D** n times, obtaining a sample of n units.

Notice that a unit selected is not returned to the population. Sampling of this kind is called simple random sampling without replacement. The same procedure is applicable to cases in which a selected unit is returned to the population before the next unit is drawn. This sampling is called simple random sampling with replacement. The following is an example.

Example 5.1

A box contains 100 light bulbs; 10 are to be taken randomly from the box. The sampling is done by the following process:

a. Each bulb is conceptually numbered between 1 and 100, inclusive.
b. A random number R is generated. For example, $R = 0.4729$.
c. The random number I is computed by $I = [0.4729 \times 100] + 1 = 48$.
d. The forty-eighth bulb is taken from the box. Recompute I if the bulb has been drawn.
e. Repeat **b** through **d** 10 times, getting 10 bulbs.

5.1.2 Sample Size Determination

The sample size is one important factor that affects the accuracy of inferencing population characteristics through sampling. In theory the exhaustive inspection of the population is the best approach to understanding such characteristics. It is hardly possible to do so in practice because of many considerations such as available resources and the nature of the population (e.g. the population may be infinite).

An alternative to exhaustive inspection is sampling inspection. A small number of objects is drawn from the population and analyzed. The results are used to understand the population. There is a problem associated with sampling—the number of objects to be drawn, which is dependent upon some parameter of the population. The problem can be solved by dynamic adjustment of the sample size during sampling. The determination of the size is based on three important concepts: the Chebychev's inequality, the central limit theorem, and the law of large numbers.

A. The Chebychev Inequality

In the study of statistics it is often necessary to find the probability in the tail regions of a probability function. For example, the probability represented by the shaded regions of the normal distribution in Figure

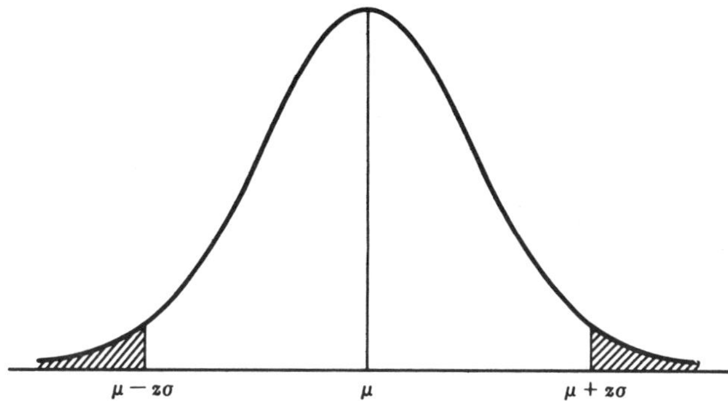

Figure 5.1 The normal distribution for computing an upper bound of probability lying in the shaded area.

5.1 can be of particular interest. Although such probability can be computed through the evaluation of the integrals of the function, such as using the standard normal distribution table in Appendix 5, it is desirable to approximate it. The inequality

$$p(|x - \mu| > z\sigma) \leq \frac{1}{z^2} \tag{5.1}$$

states that if x is a random variable having a probability function $f(x)$ with a finite mean μ and a finite variance σ^2, then the probability of interest is less than or equal to $1/z^2$. It gives the upper bound of the approximation and is sometimes referred to as the Chebychev's inequality.

Inequality 5.1 holds for any continuous probability function and for any discrete probability function such as the binomial distribution in Figure 3.10. Since a sample of measurements $x_1, x_2, \ldots, x_n$ with sample means $\bar{x}$ and sample variance s^2 forms a discrete distribution, the inequality is also applicable to the sample. In other words, the probability of the measurements lying in the intervals $(-\infty, \bar{x} - zs)$ and $(\bar{x} + zs, \infty)$ cannot be greater than $1/z^2$. The following is an example.

Example 5.2

A sample of size n is taken from a binomial population containing 5% defective units. What is the probability that the number of defectives d in the sample differs from $0.05n$ by more than $0.975\sqrt{n}$?

The mean and the variance of the binomial distribution are $\mu = n\theta$ and $\sigma^2 = n\theta(1 - \theta)$, respectively. Thus $\mu = 0.05n$ and

$\sigma = \sqrt{0.05n(1-0.05)} = \sqrt{0.0475n} = 0.218\sqrt{n}$. So $z = 4.472$ since $z\sigma = 0.218z\sqrt{n} = 0.975\sqrt{n}$. The probability is

$$p(|d - 0.05n| \geq 0.975\sqrt{n}) = \frac{1}{4.472^2} = 0.05$$

B. *The Central Limit Theorem*

There is a basic concept in statistics called the central limit theorem, which can be stated as follows:

> The distribution of the mean $\bar{x}$ of the sample from a continuous or discrete probability function having mean μ and variance σ^2 is the normal distribution with mean μ and variance σ^2/n if the sample size n is large.

This theorem justifies the application of the normal distribution to many problems including the approximation of the binomial distribution.

The sample size n in the theorem must be sufficiently large. However, it is difficult to determine the value of n in practice since the value is affected by the shape of the population. In general, unless the shape is skewed to either direction, $n = 30$ is considered sufficiently large. The following is an example.

Example 5.3

A sample of size 64 is taken from a population with an unknown mean μ and a known variance $\sigma^2 = 64$. What is the probability that the sample mean $\bar{x}$ differs from μ by less than or equal to two standard deviations?

The variance of the normal distribution is $\sigma^2/n = 64/64 = 1$. Thus the standard deviation is 1. Consulting Appendix 5, the probability that $|\bar{x} - \mu| \leq 2$ is $1 - 2 \times (1 - 0.97724) = 0.95448$.

C. *The Law of Large Numbers*

The purpose of taking samples from a population is to understand the characteristics of the population through the samples. Such characteristics are often associated with the mean μ and the variance σ^2 of the population. In practice, the mean and the variance are unknown and are estimated from the sample mean $\bar{x}$ and the sample variance s^2. The estimate can be biased resulting in error. It is desirable to reduce such error to a minimum. One way to achieve this is through the determination of the sample size n. In general the larger the n, the smaller the error. It is based on the following:

Since the Inequality 5.1 is applicable to any probability function, it also holds for the distribution of the sample mean $\bar{x}$. Thus

$$p\left(|\bar{x} - \mu| > \frac{z\sigma}{\sqrt{n}}\right) \leq \frac{1}{z^2}$$

Let $\varepsilon = z\sigma/\sqrt{n}$. Then $z = \varepsilon\sqrt{n}\,/\sigma$. Hence

$$p(|\bar{x} - \mu| > \varepsilon) \leq \frac{\sigma^2}{\varepsilon^2 n} \qquad (5.2)$$

The inequality is referred to as the (weak) law of large numbers. It states that given a small positive number ε and a desired probability p, there exists a sample size n such that the difference between the sample mean $\bar{x}$ and the population mean μ will not be greater than ε. The determination of the sample size plays an important role in sampling, statistical inference, and software quality control.

D. *The Determination of Sample Size*

The binomial distribution plays a central role in software quality control through random sampling. One important consideration in sampling study is the determination of the proper sample size n so that the mean μ and the variance σ^2 of the population can be estimated from the sample mean $\bar{x}$ and sample variance s^2 with sufficient accuracy. The existence of n is justified by Inequality 5.2 with desired p and ε.

Since μ and σ^2 of the binomial distribution are $\mu = n\theta$ and $\sigma^2 = n\theta(1 - \theta)$, the value of n may be approximated through the normal distribution as follows: If a sample is taken from the normal population, the distribution of the sample resembles closely that of the

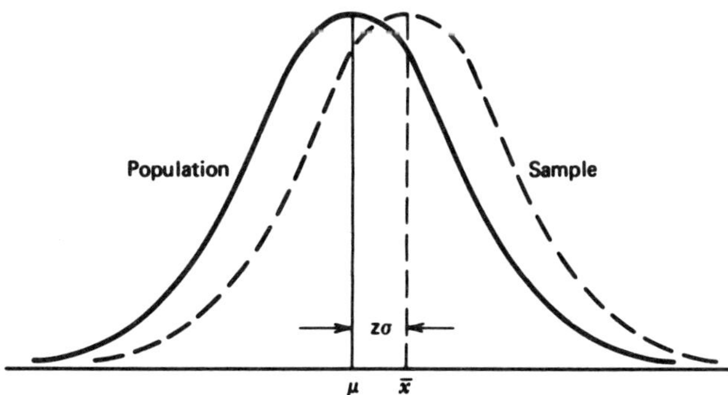

Figure 5.2 Distribution of the normal population and a sample from the population.

population, as shown in Figure 5.2. The difference between $\bar{x}$ and μ equals $z\sigma$. Namely,

$$\bar{x} - \mu = z\sigma$$

Thus

$$\bar{x} - n\theta = z\sqrt{n\theta(1 - \theta)}$$

Let θ° be the defective rate of the sample. Then $\bar{x}$ may be expressed as $\bar{x} = n\theta^\circ$. Consequently,

$$n\theta^\circ - n\theta = n(\theta^\circ - \theta) = z\sqrt{n\theta(1 - \theta)}$$

Let $\theta^\circ - \theta = a\theta$, where a is called the accuracy factor and $0 < a < 1$. Then

$$na\theta = z\sqrt{n\theta(1 - \theta)}$$

So

$$n = \frac{z^2(1 - \theta)}{a^2\theta} \tag{5.3}$$

Note that Equation 5.3 is derived from the relationship $\mu \leq \bar{x}$. It also holds with the relationship $\bar{x} \leq \mu$.

Example 5.4

A sample of size n is to be taken from the binomial distribution having a defective rate $\theta = 0.05$. Given the probability 0.95 that the sample mean differs from the population mean by not more than $0.1n\theta$, what is the sample size?

Since the probability is 0.95, z is found to be 1.96 from the standard normal table in Appendix 5 (0.025 on either tail of the distribution) and the accuracy factor a is 0.1, it follows that

$$n = \frac{1.96^2 \times (1 - 0.05)}{0.1^2 \times 0.05} = 7299$$

The value of n is a function of a, z, and θ in Equation 5.3. The value of a and z are assigned constants while that of θ is unknown and is to be estimated. Thus the determination of n requires dynamic adjustment during sampling. An adjustment procedure, which is iterative in nature, is given as follows:

A. Take an initial sample of small size k (e.g. 50) from the population.
B. Let $n_0 = k$ and θ_0° be the defective rate of the sample of size n_0.

C. Compute the sample size n_{i+1} by

$$n_{i+1} = \frac{z^2(1 - \theta_i^\circ)}{a^2\theta_i^\circ} \tag{5.3a}$$

where θ_i° is the defective rate of the sample already taken after ith computation, and $i = 0, 1, 2, \ldots$.

D. If $n_{i+1} > n_i$, then take $(n_{i+1} - n_i)$ additional units and repeat steps C and D.

E. Else stop. The sample taken is sufficient.

Example 5.5

A sample of size n is to be taken from the binomial distribution having an unknown defective rate θ. Given the probability 0.95 that the sample mean differs from the population mean by not more than $0.1n\theta$, determine the sample size.

Since the probability is 0.95, the standard deviation factor z is found to be 1.96 from Appendix 5. The determination of n is determined as follows:

a. An initial sample of 50 units is taken from the population.

b. Compute the sample defective rate θ°. The value is assumed 0.08 for discussion purpose.

c. Determine n_1 by

$$n_1 = \frac{1.96^2(1 - 0.08)}{0.1 \times 0.1 \times 0.08} = 4412$$

d. Since $n_1 > n_0$, $4412 - 50 = 4362$ additional units are needed if the population defective rate is indeed 0.08.

c. Determine n_2, after the additional units are sampled and θ_1° is decided (assumed to be 0.05), by

$$n_2 = \frac{1.96^2(1 - 0.05)}{0.1 \times 0.1 \times 0.05} = 7299$$

d. Because $n_2 > n_1$, a sample of $7299 - 4412$ or 2887 additional units is required if $\theta = 0.05$.

c. If θ_2° is found to be 0.051 after a total of 7299 units have been sampled, then

$$n_3 = \frac{1.96^2(1 - 0.051)}{0.1 \times 0.1 \times 0.051} = 7148$$

d. Since $n_3 < n_2$, the sample taken is sufficient.

5.1.3 Statistical Inference Principles

It is often necessary to test if a sample is taken from a population having a given mean or variance. For example, if a sample is drawn from a binomial distribution, it is desired to see whether the sample comes from a population having a mean μ^*. Or if two samples are taken from two binomial distributions, could the samples come from the populations having equal means. The test is done by inferring the statistics such as means and variances determined from the sample or samples.

There are three types of statistical inference important in software quality control: (1) testing the mean of a binomial distribution, (2) testing the variance of a binomial distribution, and (3) testing the difference of the means of two binomial distributions.

Closely related to these problems is the concept of estimating the confidence interval of the mean and variance of a population. The estimate is useful in conducting a random test of a program discussed in Chapter 11.

Since a binomial distribution can be approximated by a normal distribution, the discussion in this section is given by way of the normal distribution for convenience.

A. *Statistical Test*

A statistical test starts with forming two hypotheses H_1 and H_2 about the value of a population parameter (such as mean or variance). These hypotheses, one of which will be accepted, are judged according to statistical means using sample data. There are two kinds of errors associated with the test: the Type-I error rejecting H_1 while it is true, and the Type-II error rejecting H_2 while it is true. The risk is expressed in terms of probability.

A. **Testing the Mean of a Binomial Distribution Having Unknown Variance.** Since the population variance is unknown, the test is done by way of a distribution called the Student t distribution. A table of the distribution is given in Appendix 6. The following is a procedure for testing the mean:

a. State two hypotheses to be tested

$$H_1: \mu = \mu^*$$
$$H_2: \mu \neq \mu^*$$

where μ^* is an arbitrary value of the population mean to be tested.

b. Choose the desired probability α, called the significance level of the test, of Type-I error.

c. Find the value of $t_{n-1,\alpha/2}$ from Appendix 6.

d. Accept H_1 if the condition is satisfied

$$-t_{n-1,\alpha/2} \leq \frac{(\bar{x} - \mu^*)\sqrt{n}}{s} \leq t_{n-1,\alpha/2}$$

(H_1 is said accepted at the 100α% level of significance.)

e. Else accept H_2 at the 100α% level of significance.

Example 5.6

A sample of 210 units is taken from a binomial distribution. The sample mean and variance are 53.00 and 39.63 respectively. Test, at the 5% level of significance, the assumption that the population mean is 52.15.

The test is performed as follows:

a. Form two hypotheses

$$H_1: \mu = 52.15$$
$$H_2: \mu \neq 52.15$$

b. The level of significance is given as $\alpha = 0.05$.

c. The Student t values, $t_{210-1,\alpha/2}$, is found to be 1.96, from Appendix 6.

d. The condition

$$-1.96 \leq \frac{(\bar{x} - \mu^*)\sqrt{n}}{s} = \frac{(53 - 52.15)\sqrt{210}}{6.295} = 1.957 \leq 1.96$$

is satisfied. Thus H_1 is accepted. In other words, the population mean can be assumed at 52.15 at the 5% level of significance.

B. Testing the Variance of the Binomial Distribution. The variance of the binomial distribution can be easily computed after the population mean has been tested. Since $\mu = n\theta$, so $\theta = \mu/n$. Thus the variance σ^2 is $\sigma^2 = n\theta(1 - \theta) = \mu(1 - \mu/n)$. Let σ^* be the estimated population variance. Then $\sigma^* = \mu^*(1 - \mu^*/n)$, where μ^* is the estimated population mean at the 100α% level of significance. Because σ^* is computed from μ^*, σ^* is accepted as the population standard deviation also at the 100α% level of significance.

C. Testing the Difference between the Means of Two Binomial Distributions Having Unknown but Equal Variances. If two samples are taken independently from the same binomial distribution for testing the population mean and variance by two parties, the results should be statistically compatible if both parties follow basically the same random sampling procedure. The compatibility can be verified through statistical inference. The verification can be done by conceptually considering the binomial distribution as two populations. The population means are estimated using sample data. The difference between the means is then tested. If the difference is statistically acceptable, the results obtained by the parties are treated unbiased. It may be otherwise. Then a third sample may be taken for comparison. This concept is useful in software quality control particularly in resolving a dispute on software quality between a developer and a user. The verification can be done as follows:

Let $\bar{x}_1$ and s_1^2 be the mean and the variance of a sample of size n_1 taken from the binomial distribution with mean μ_1 and variance σ_1^2, and $\bar{x}_2$ and s_2^2 be the same from the binomial distribution with mean μ_2 and σ_2^2. As discussed in the preceding sections, μ_1 and σ_1^2 can be inferenced from $\bar{x}_1$ and μ_2 and σ_2^2 from $\bar{x}_2$. The difference $\mu_1 - \mu_2$ can be tested using $\bar{x}_1$, $\bar{x}_2$, s_1^2, and x_2^2 in a testing procedure similar to that of part A of this lettered list. The hypotheses to be tested are:

$$H_1\colon \mu_1 - \mu_2 = 0$$

$$H_2\colon \mu_1 - \mu_2 \neq 0$$

The condition to be satisfied is

$$-t_{n_1+n_2-2,\,\alpha/2} \leq \frac{\bar{x}_1 - \bar{x}_2}{g\sqrt{1/n_1 + 1/n_2}} \leq t_{n_1+n_2-2,\,\alpha/2}$$

where

$$g^2 = \frac{(n_1 - 1)s_1^2 + (n_2 - 1)s_2^2}{n_1 + n_2 - 2}.$$

If the condition holds, then H_1 is accepted at the $100\alpha\%$ level of significance. Otherwise H_2 is accepted.

Example 5.7

Two samples of sizes 51 and 71 are taken from a binomial distribution with mean μ and variance σ^2 by two inspectors. The first sample contains two defectives and the second contains three defectives. Are the inspectors biased in taking samples from the population (at the 5% level of significance)?

Since $n_1 = 51$, $n_2 = 71$, $\bar{x}_1 = 2$, $\bar{x}_2 = 3$, $\theta_1^\circ = 2/51$, and $\theta_1^\circ = 3/71$, hence

a. Form the hypotheses

$$H_1: \mu_1 - \mu_2 = 0$$
$$H_2: \mu_1 - \mu_2 \neq 0$$

b. The level of significance is given as $\alpha = 0.05$.

c. $t_{n_1+n_2-2,\,\alpha/2} = 1.98$, found from Appendix 6.

d. Since $s_1^2 = n_1\theta_1^\circ(1 - \theta_1^\circ) = 2(1 - 0.04) = 1.92$ and $s_2^2 = n_2\theta_2^\circ(1 - \theta_2^\circ) = 2.88$. Thus g is found to be 1.57. Hence the condition

$$-1.98 \leq \frac{\bar{x}_1 - \bar{x}_2}{g\sqrt{1/n_1 + 1/n_2}} = \frac{2 - 3}{1.57\sqrt{1/51 + 1/71}} = -3.5 \leq 1.98$$

is not satisfied. Thus H_2 is accepted. In other words, the population means estimated by thc inspectors are different at the 5% level of significance.

B. *Interval Estimators*

In many statistical applications, the interval estimators of population mean and variance can be of special interest since they give reliable information about the characteristics of the population. Two types of interval estimators are particularly important in software quality control: interval estimators of the mean and variance of a binomial distribution. The application of these estimators is illustrated in Chapter 11.

A. Interval Estimator of the Mean of a Binomial Population. Let $\bar{x}$ be the mean of a sample taken from the binomial distribution having mean μ and variance σ^2, then $\bar{x}$ has the normal distribution with mean μ and variance σ^2/n (see the central limit theorem in Section 5.1.2***B***). In practice, it is often necessary to estimate μ and σ of the binomial distribution from the sample mean $\bar{x}$ and sample variance s^2. The estimate of σ is discussed in the next section, while that of μ is treated here.

Replacing σ by $\sigma/\sqrt{n}$, the probability in the blank area under the curve of Figure 5.1 can be stated as

$$p\left[-z_{\alpha/2} \leq \frac{\sqrt{n}\,(\bar{x} - \mu)}{\sigma} \leq z_{\alpha/2}\right] = 1 - \alpha$$

which can be rewritten as

$$p\left[\bar{x} - z_{\alpha/2}\frac{\sigma}{\sqrt{n}} \le \mu \le \bar{x} + z_{\alpha/2}\frac{\sigma}{\sqrt{n}}\right] = 1 - \alpha \qquad (5.4)$$

Thus

$$\left[\bar{x} - z_{\alpha/2}\frac{\sigma}{\sqrt{n}}, \bar{x} + z_{\alpha/2}\frac{\sigma}{\sqrt{n}}\right]$$

is the $100(1 - \alpha)\%$ confidence interval of the population mean μ. The estimate involves σ, which is unknown in most practical applications. The sample variance s^2 can be used instead. This is done by replacing σ by s and $z_{\alpha/2}$ by $t_{n-1,\alpha/2}$ in Equation 5.4, where $t_{n-1,\alpha/2}$ is the value of a distribution called the Student t distribution at $n - 1$ degrees of freedom. (A Student t distribution table is given in Appendix 6.) Thus the interval is estimated by

$$\left[\bar{x} - t_{n-1,\alpha/2}\frac{s}{\sqrt{n}}, \bar{x} + t_{n-1,\alpha/2}\frac{s}{\sqrt{n}}\right] \qquad (5.4a)$$

Example 5.8

A set of 101 random numbers is sampled from Appendix 1 for estimating the number of 0's in the population. If the sample mean $\bar{x}$ is 10 and the sample variance s^2 is 9, what is the 95% confidence interval of the population mean μ?

Since $\bar{x} = 10$, $\alpha/2 = (1 - 0.95)/2 = 0.025$, $n = 101$, and $t_{100,\,0.025} = 1.99$ from Appendix 6, hence

$$\left[10 - 1.99\frac{3}{\sqrt{101}}, 10 + 1.99\frac{3}{\sqrt{101}}\right] = [9.403, 10.597]$$

is the 95% confidence interval of μ.

B. Interval Estimator of the Variance of the Binomial Distribution. Let s^2 be the variance of a sample taken from the normal distribution having mean μ and variance σ^2, then $(n - 1)s^2/\sigma^2$ has a distribution called the chi-square distribution, denoted by χ^2, with $n - 1$ degrees of freedom [2].

The interval of the variance σ^2 can be estimated by

$$p\left[\omega_1 \le \frac{(n-1)s^2}{\sigma^2} \le \omega_2\right] = 1 - \alpha \qquad (5.5)$$

where ω_1 is the value of $\chi^2_{n-1,1-\alpha/2}$ and ω_2 that of $\chi^2_{n-1,\alpha/2}$, which can be found from Appendix 7 given n and α. Equation 5.5 can be rewritten as

$$p\left[s\sqrt{\frac{(n-1)}{\omega_1}} \geq \sigma \geq s\sqrt{\frac{(n-1)}{\omega_2}}\right] = 1 - \alpha \qquad (5.6)$$

Thus the 100(1 − α)% confidence interval for σ is

$$\left[s\sqrt{\frac{(n-1)}{\omega_2}}, s\sqrt{\frac{(n-1)}{\omega_1}}\right]$$

Equation 5.6 is applicable to the binomial distribution having mean $\mu = n\theta$ and $\sigma^2 = n\theta(1-\theta)$.

Example 5.9

A set of 101 random numbers is sampled from Appendix 1 for estimating the number of 0's in the population. If the sample s^2 is found to be 9, estimate the 95% confidence interval of the population variance σ^2.

Since $1 - \alpha = 0.95$, thus $\alpha = 0.05$ or $\alpha/2 = 0.025$. From Appendix 7, $\omega_1 = \chi^2_{101-1, 0.975} = 74.2219$ and $\omega_2 = \chi^2_{101-1, 0.025} = 129.561$. Hence

$$\left[3\sqrt{\frac{101-1}{129.561}}, 3\sqrt{\frac{101-1}{74.2219}}\right] = [2.64, 3.48]$$

is the 95% confidence interval of σ of the population.

5.2 SEQUENTIAL SAMPLING

Sequential sampling was originated by Wald [10]. Under this method, sampling and inferencing are done after unit i is drawn from a population, $i = 1, 2 \ldots$. It may be considered as an alternative to the simple random sampling discussed in the preceding section. Explained in this section are the sampling procedure and sequential sampling from a binomial distribution. Its application to software quality control is discussed in Chapters 6, 11, and 12.

5.2.1 Sampling Procedure

The sample size determination method discussed in Section 5.1 is for simple random sampling involving a sample of fixed size. No inference is made after each unit is drawn from the population. The estimate of the parameters μ and σ^2 is done after the sample has been completely taken.

There is an alternative called sequential sampling, which may require a smaller sample to make the inference with the same degree of accuracy. The sample size is not predetermined and is treated as a random variable during the sampling procedure. The hypotheses to be tested are the following: H_1: The population has the continuous or discrete probability function $f_1(x)$. H_2: The population has the continuous or discrete probability function $f_2(x)$. The sample is taken by drawing a sequence of units $x_1, x_2, \ldots, x_r$, one at a time. After a unit is chosen a decision is made against three conditions. Let

$$F_r = \frac{f_2(x_1)f_2(x_2)\ldots f_2(x_r)}{f_1(x_1)f_1(x_2)\ldots f_1(x_r)}$$

The conditions are: (1) If $F_r \leq A$, then stop and accept H_1; (2) If $F_r \geq B$, then stop and accept H_2; (3) If $A < F_r < B$, then the next unit is drawn and sampling continues, where A and B are values chosen to make the probability of Type-I and Type-II errors equal to α_1 and α_2, respectively. In practice, the exact values of A and B are difficult to find and are approximated by

$$A = \frac{\alpha_2}{1 - \alpha_1}$$

and

$$B = \frac{1 - \alpha_2}{\alpha_1}$$

5.2.2 Sequential Sampling from the Binomial Distribution

The sequential sampling procedure given in the preceding section is applicable to any continuous or discrete probability function. Its application to the binomial distribution is of particular interest in software quality control.

The probability function of the binomial distribution is

$$f(x) = \binom{1}{x}\theta^x(1 - \theta)^{1-x}$$

where x is a random variable, $x = 1$ if the unit drawn is defective, and $x = 0$ otherwise. Let

$$f_1(x) = \binom{1}{x}\theta_1^x(1 - \theta_1)^{1-x}$$

$$f_2(x) = \binom{1}{x}\theta_2^x(1 - \theta_2)^{1-x}$$

The ratio F_r is given by

$$F_r = \frac{\binom{1}{x_1}\theta_2^{x_1}(1-\theta_2)^{1-x_1}\binom{1}{x_2}\theta_2^{x_2}(1-\theta_2)^{1-x_2}\cdots\binom{1}{x_r}\theta_2^{x_r}(1-\theta_2)^{1-x_r}}{\binom{1}{x_1}\theta_1^{x_1}(1-\theta_1)^{1-x_1}\binom{1}{x_2}\theta_1^{x_2}(1-\theta_1)^{1-x_2}\cdots\binom{1}{x_r}\theta_1^{x_r}(1-\theta_1)^{1-x_r}}$$

$$= \frac{\theta_2^{x_1+x_2+\cdots+x_r}(1-\theta_2)^{1-x_1+1-x_2+\cdots+1-x_r}}{\theta_1^{x_1+x_2+\cdots+x_r}(1-\theta_1)^{1-x_1+1-x_2+\cdots+1-x_r}}$$

which reduces to

$$F_r = \frac{\theta_2^{S_r}(1-\theta_2)^{r-S_r}}{\theta_1^{S_r}(1-\theta_1)^{r-S_r}} \tag{5.7}$$

where S_r is called the cumulative number of defectives in the sample of r units. Namely, $S_r = x_1 + x_2 + \cdots + x_r$, where $x_i = 0$ or 1.

The computation of the F_r value is tedious. However, it can be simplified graphically in practice. Since the sampling procedure continues when $A < F_r < B$, namely,

$$\frac{\alpha_2}{1-\alpha_1} < \frac{\theta_2^{S_r}(1-\theta_2)^{r-S_r}}{\theta_1^{S_r}(1-\theta_1)^{r-S_r}} < \frac{1-\alpha_2}{\alpha_1}$$

It follows, after taking natural logarithms, that

$$\ln\frac{\alpha_2}{1-\alpha_1} < S_r \ln\frac{\theta_2}{\theta_1} + (r - S_r)\ln\frac{1-\theta_2}{1-\theta_1} < \ln\frac{1-\alpha_2}{\alpha_1}$$

Then S_r may be defined by taking equality of the left two expressions, as follows:

$$S_r = \frac{\ln\dfrac{\alpha_2}{1-\alpha_1} - r\ln\dfrac{1-\theta_2}{1-\theta_1}}{\ln\dfrac{\theta_2}{\theta_1} - \ln\dfrac{1-\theta_2}{1-\theta_1}} \tag{5.8}$$

or, by taking equality of the right two expressions, as follows:

$$S_r = \frac{\ln\dfrac{1-\alpha_2}{\alpha_1} - r\ln\dfrac{1-\theta_2}{1-\theta_1}}{\ln\dfrac{\theta_2}{\theta_1} - \ln\dfrac{1-\theta_2}{1-\theta_1}} \tag{5.9}$$

A graph showing the three decision conditions defined by A, F_r, and B is given in Figure 5.3. The lines L_1 and L_2 represent Equations 5.8

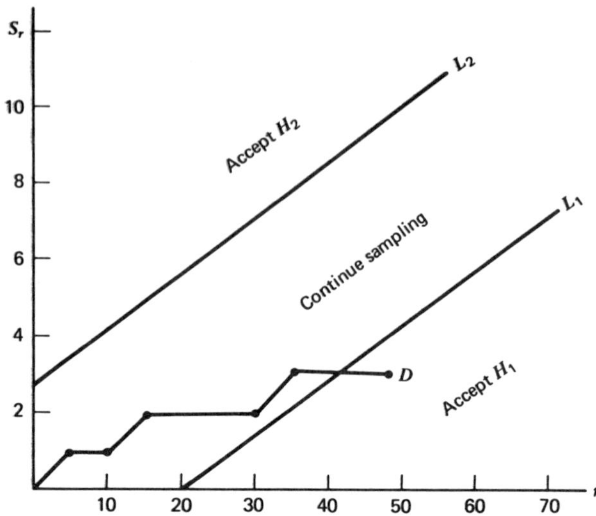

Figure 5.3 Three decision regions for the sequential test of the binomial distribution.

and 5.9, respectively. There are three regions in the figure. One for accepting hypothesis H_1, one for H_2, and the other for further sampling.

The point (S_r, r) is plotted in the figure after unit r is sampled and analyzed. If the point falls under L_1, then H_1 is accepted (rejecting H_2). Similarly, if the point falls above L_2,then H_2 is accepted (rejecting H_1). Otherwise, one more unit is drawn. This sampling process continues until an acceptance of H_1 or H_2 is made. The line leading to point D is an example of the sampling process that results in accepting H_1.

Example 5.10

Let x be a random variable having the probability function

$$F(x) = \binom{n}{x}\theta^x(1 - \theta)^{n-x}$$

where $x = 0$ or 1. Test the hypotheses, using the sequential sampling,

$$H_1: \theta = 0.05$$

$$H_2: \theta = 0.10$$

with $\alpha_1 = 0.10$ and $\alpha_2 = 0.10$.

The controlling lines L_1 and L_2 can be constructed by Equations 5.8 and 5.9 as follows:

a. Line L_1

$$S_r = \frac{\ln \frac{0.1}{0.9} - r \ln \frac{0.9}{0.95}}{\ln \frac{0.1}{0.05} - \ln \frac{0.9}{0.95}} = \frac{-2.197 - r(-0.054)}{0.693 - (-0.054)}$$
$$= 0.072r - 2.941$$

b. Line L_2

$$S_r = \frac{\ln \frac{0.9}{0.1} - r \ln \frac{0.9}{0.95}}{\ln \frac{0.1}{0.05} - \ln \frac{0.9}{0.95}} = \frac{2.197 + 0.054r}{0.693 - (-0.054)}$$
$$= 0.072r + 2.941$$

A graph similar to Figure 5.3 can be drawn using L_1 and L_2. The sequential sampling can be accomplished by drawing units from an object population, such as the random numbers given in Appendix 1.

REFERENCES

1. C. L. Brisley, "Work Sampling," in H. B. Maynard (Ed.), *Industrial Engineering Handbook*, McGraw-Hill, New York, 1956, pp. 3-62–3-76.
2. I. Guttman and S. S. Wilks, *Introductory Engineering Statistics*, Wiley, New York, 1965.
3. W. G. Cochran, *Sampling Techniques*, Wiley, New York, 1963.
4. H. F. Dodge and H. G. Romig, *Sampling Inspection Tables*, 2nd ed., Wiley, New York, 1959.
5. H. A. Freeman, M. Friedman, F. Mosteller, and W. A. Wellis, *Sampling Inspection*, McGraw-Hill, New York, 1948.
6. J. D. Braverman and W. C. Stewart, *Statistics for Business and Economics*, Ronald, New York, 1973.
7. J. E. Freund and F. J. Williams, *Elementary Business Statistics—The Modern Approach*, 3rd ed., Prentice-Hall, Englewood Cliffs, New Jersey, 1977.
8. G. W. Summers, W. S. Peters, and C. P. Armstrong, *Basic Statistics in Business and Economics*, 2nd ed., Wadsworth, Belmont, California, 1977.
9. A. E. Mace, *Sample-Size Determination*, Reinhold, New York, 1964.
10. A. Wald, *Sequential Analysis*, Wiley, New York, 1947.

EXERCISES

1. A sample of n units is randomly taken from a population of N units without replacement. Show that each of the $\binom{N}{n}$ units has an equal chance of being drawn. What is the chance?

2. Describe a procedure of drawing 10 light bulbs from a lot of 100 bulbs using the random number tables in Appendix 1.

3. If a sample of size n is taken from a binomial distribution containing 1% defective, what is the probability that the number of defectives in the sample differs from $0.01n$ by not more than $0.99\sqrt{n}$?

4. A sample of size 100 is taken from a population with an unknown popualtion mean μ and a known variance 32. What is the probability that the sample mean $\bar{x}$ differs from μ by more than three standard deviations?

5. A sample is drawn at random from a population having a known defective rate $\theta = 0.01$. Given the probability 0.95 that the sample mean $\bar{x}$ differs from the population mean μ by not more than 0.3σ, determine the sample size n.

6. Describe the procedure of drawing a sample of R random digits from the random number tables in Appendix 1.

7. The population of 12,000 random digits given in Appendix 1 contains approximately 10% of digit 0's. If the probability is 0.99 that the sample mean $\bar{x}$ and the population mean μ are different by not more than $0.1n\theta$, determine the sample size n.

8. A sample of 100 units is taken from a binomial distribution. The sample mean and variance are found to be 11 and 9 respectively. Is it reasonable to assume that the population mean is 9.5 at the 5% level of significance?

9. Take two samples of sizes 50 and 100 from the random number population in Appendix 1. Find the number of 0's in each sample and decide at the 5% level of significance if the samples are randomly taken.

10. If x is a random variable having the Poisson probability function

$$f(x, \mu) = \frac{\mu^x e^{-\mu}}{x!}, \qquad x = 0, 1, 2, \ldots$$

Discuss how to test the hypotheses

$$H_1: \mu = 1.0$$

$$H_2: \mu = 1.2$$

using the sequential sampling with $\alpha_1 = 0.1$ and $\alpha_2 = 0.05$. Draw a graph similar to Figure 5.3 showing the decision regions for the test.

CHAPTER 6

Acceptance Sampling

Acceptance sampling is an activity in the procurement of a product lot. The acceptance or rejection of the lot is based on the results of inspecting, or testing, a random sample from the lot. If the sample contains a tolerable number of defectives, then the lot is accepted. Otherwise it is rejected.

There are many different types of acceptance sampling such as single sampling, double sampling, multiple sampling, and sequential sampling. Each has advantages and disadvantages. The choice of method may depend on the agreement between the producer and the user of the product.

There are cases in sampling inspection in which rejecting a lot means scrapping the entire lot. For example, a light bulb is destroyed in testing its life span. Rejecting a lot of bulbs can mean scrapping the lot since testing all of the bulbs results in destroying all. If a product unit will not be destroyed during testing, the defective lot can be rectified by replacing the defective units. If the lot is of poor quality not worth the cost of rectification, the lot is either rejected or accepted with reduced payment.

The rectification of a product lot has a significant meaning in software development. Accepting a software system is equivalent to accepting all possible output units of the system. The rectification of the output lot is equivalent to removing from the system the errors that cause the defectiveness in the lot. Thus acceptance sampling is applicable to software development provided random test samples can be generated. Two sampling plans, single sampling and sequential sampling, are discussed in this chapter. The generation of random test cases and the application of acceptance sampling to software acceptance are discussed in later chapters.

6.1 SINGLE SAMPLING PLAN

A single sampling plan is one from which the acceptance or rejection of a product lot is dependent on one sample only. No second sample is to be inspected whether requested by the producer or the user of the product. The validity of the plan is based on either the hypergeometric, the binomial, or the Poisson distribution.

Since there are virtually an infinite number of such plans that can be used to accept a product lot, certain criteria are needed in formulating a plan acceptable to both the producer and the user. The criteria may be given in terms of the risks assumed by the parties. The characteristics of a plan so formulated can be represented by a curve called the operating characteristics curve. The probability of acceptance by the plan under any population defective rate θ can be easily obtained from the curve.

6.1.1 Foundation of Single Sampling

A single sampling plan works as follows: A sample of n units is drawn randomly from a lot of N units containing $N\theta$ defective units, where θ is the defective rate of the lot. If the sample contains less than d defectives, then the lot is accepted. Otherwise it is rejected.

The probability of getting x defectives in the sample is given by Equation (3.4) as follows:

$$h(x) = \frac{\binom{N\theta}{x}\binom{N - N\theta}{n - x}}{\binom{N}{n}}$$

Let the probability of accepting the lot be P_a. Then P_a is computed by adding the probabilities of obtaining 0, 1, 2, . . . , $d - 1$ defectives in the sample. Namely,

$$P_a = \sum_{x=0}^{d-1} h(x) \tag{6.1}$$

Since $h(x)$ can be approximated by the binomial distribution, when N is large,

$$b(x) = \binom{n}{x} \theta^x (1 - \theta)^{n-x}$$

the probability P_a may be calculated by

$$P_a = \sum_{x=0}^{d-1} b(x) \tag{6.2}$$

The probability P_a can be further approximated by the Poisson distribution, if n is large and θ is very small such that the value of $n\theta$ is moderate (e.g. $n\theta = 25$), as follows:

$$P_a = \sum_{x=0}^{d-1} \frac{(n\theta)^x e^{-n\theta}}{x!} \tag{6.3}$$

There are two types of risk in implementing a single sampling plan similar to the Type-I and Type-II errors associated with a statistical test given in Section 5.1.3. Namely,

A. A good lot can be rejected by the plan. The risk involved is called the producer's risks, denoted by α_1.

B. A bad lot can be accepted by the plan. The risk involved is called the user's risk, denoted by α_2.

Example 6.1

A large lot containing 1% defective units is to be accepted according to the single sampling plan: A sample of 79 units is randomly drawn from the lot. If it contains less than three defective units, then the lot is accepted. Otherwise, it is rejected. What is the probability of accepting the lot?

The probability of acceptance can be computed by Equation (6.3) as follows:

$$P_a = \frac{(79\theta)^0 e^{-79\theta}}{0!} + \frac{(79\theta)^1 e^{-79\theta}}{1!} + \frac{(79\theta)^2 e^{-79\theta}}{2!} = 0.954$$

6.1.2 Operating Characteristics Curve

The computation of the probability of accepting a product by a single sampling plan involves the population defective rate θ. Since the exact value of θ is difficult to find, it is desirable to have a simple means by which the probability under θ can be found without tedious computation. One possible way is through a curve called the operating characteristics (OC) curve of the sampling plan. The curve is constructed from a series of points $[\theta_i, P_a(\theta_i)]$, where θ_i is a value of θ, $\theta_i = i/N$, for $i = 0, 1, 2, \ldots, N$, and $P_a(\theta_i)$ is the probability of acceptance at θ_i. The value of $P_a(\theta_i)$ can be computed by Equations 6.1, 6.2, or 6.3. In other words, an OC curve is constructed with the points

$$\left[\frac{0}{N}, P_a\left(\frac{0}{N}\right)\right], \left[\frac{1}{N}, P_a\left(\frac{1}{N}\right)\right], \ldots, \left[\frac{N}{N}, P_a\left(\frac{N}{N}\right)\right]$$

An example is shown in Figure 6.1.

There are two types of OC curves of a single sampling plan: one is the ideal curve with no producer's and user's risk involved; the other is the realistic curve with both risks involved. In Figure 6.1(a) the probability of acceptance is 1 at $\theta = 0.01$ (or less) and 0 otherwise. However, the probability is about 0.95 at $\theta = 0.01$ and never equals 0 at other values, as shown in Figure 6.1(b). In the figure, α_1 is the producer's risk in having a good lot rejected by the sampling plan, and α_2 is the user's risk in accepting a bad lot by the same plan. Notice that the ideal curve rarely exists in practice.

Constructed from the probability of acceptance of Figure 6.2, the OC curve of the sampling plan of Example 6.1 is shown in Figure 6.3.

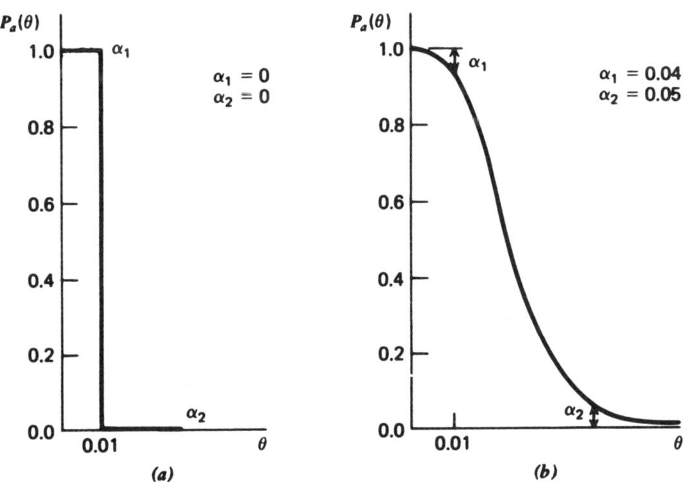

Figure 6.1 The ideal and realistic operating characteristics curves of a single sampling plan. (a) Ideal curve; (b) realistic curve.

Defective Rate θ	Probability of Acceptance, $P_a(\theta)$
0.00	1.000
0.01	0.954
0.02	0.789
0.03	0.578
0.04	0.388
0.05	0.246
0.06	0.148
0.07	0.087
0.08	0.050
0.09	0.028
0.10	0.015
0.11	0.008
0.12	0.004

Figure 6.2 The probabilities of acceptance of the sampling plan of Example 6.1.

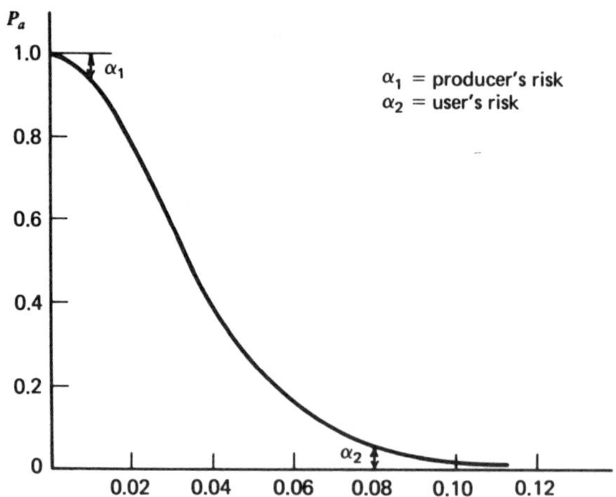

Figure 6.3 Operating characteristics curve of the single sampling plan $n = 79$ and $d = 3$.

With this curve, the value of $P_a(\theta)$ at any θ value is easily found. For example, $P_a(0.015) = 0.88$.

6.1.3 Formulation of a Single Sampling Plan

The formulation includes the determination of the sample size and that of the acceptable number of defectives in the sample. Since there can be many plans to choose from, the selection of the most appropriate one requires a careful study. As a plan is usually formulated toward accepting a good product lot, the risk of the producer and of the user must also be reduced to a minimum. If α_1 is the producer's risk at θ_1 and α_2 the user's at θ_2, then the values of θ_1, α_1, θ_2, and α_2 must be agreed on by both parties before a plan is generated.

A. *Family of Single Sampling Plans*

One important problem in acceptance sampling is the formulation of an economical plan that will satisfy the assurance of product quality while providing protection to both the producer and the user of the product. A sampling plan is usually established with the criteria called the acceptance criteria θ_1, α_1, θ_2, α_2, where α_1 is the producer's risk and α_2 the user's risk. It cannot be formulated by either θ_1 and α_1 or θ_2 and α_2 alone, since there is virtually an unlimited number of plans that can satisfy either of them. For example, if the criteria are given by $\theta_2 = 0.05$ and $\alpha_2 = 0.05$ only, then at least five single sampling plans

	$P_a(\theta)$				
Defective Rate θ	$n = 60$ $d = 1$ (1)	$n = 95$ $d = 2$ (2)	$n = 126$ $d = 3$ (3)	$n = 155$ $d = 4$ (4)	$n = 183$ $d = 5$ (5)
0.00	1.000	1.000	1.000	1.000	1.000
0.01	0.549	0.754	0.866	0.928	0.960
0.02	0.301	0.434	0.538	0.625	0.695
0.03	0.165	0.223	0.272	0.313	0.359
0.04	0.091	0.107	0.121	0.134	0.148
0.05	0.050	0.050	0.050	0.050	0.050
0.06	0.027	0.022	0.019	0.017	0.016
0.07	0.015	0.010	0.007	0.005	0.003

Figure 6.4 Probabilities of acceptance under various θ values by different single sampling plans.

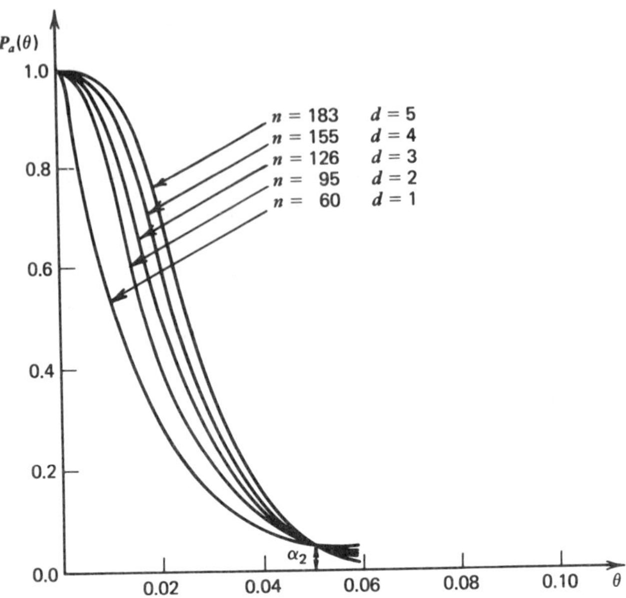

Figure 6.5 Operating characteristics curves of five single sampling plans satisfying $\theta_2 = 0.05$ and $\alpha_2 = 0.05$.

meet the requirements, as shown in Figure 6.4. The OC curves of the plans are given in Figure 6.5.

Although the plans satisfy the given criteria, the producer's risk α_1 at θ_1 is not taken into consideration. Clearly, plan 1 is the most economical one to use since it requires the smallest number of product units. But it provides the least protection to the producer. Conversely, plan 5 provides the greatest protection to the producer, but at the expense of the most sampling inspection. Therefore, it is essential to use all of the acceptance criteria in formulating a single sampling plan.

B. *Formulation of a Single Sampling Plan Satisfying Specific θ_1, α_1, θ_2, α_2*

A single sampling plan that satisfies the acceptance criteria exactly may be difficult, if not impossible, to formulate, since the sample size n and the number of defectives d in the sample must be integer. However, a plan that satisfies approximately may be found and is illustrated as follows:

The formulation is based on a working table such as the one shown in Figure 6.6. An entry in $n\theta_1(n\theta_2)$ is the value of $n\theta$ that makes the

Plan Number	Number of Defectives d	Values of $n\theta_1$ at $\alpha_1 = 0.05$ (1)	Value of $n\theta_2$ at $\alpha_2 = 0.05$ (2)	Ratio of $n\theta_2$ and $n\theta_1$ $R = (2)/(1)$
1	1	0.0513	2.9961	58.4381
2	2	0.3555	4.7422	13.3407
3	3	0.8184	6.2969	7.6945
4	4	1.3672	7.7539	5.6714
5	5	1.9707	9.1563	4.6462
6	6	2.6133	10.5156	4.0239
7	7	3.2852	11.8438	3.6052
8	8	3.9805	13.1250	3.2973
9	9	4.6953	14.4375	3.0749
10	10	5.4258	15.7500	2.9028
11	11	6.1680	16.8750	2.7359
12	12	6.9258	18.0000	2.5990

Figure 6.6 A combination of $n\theta_1$, $n\theta_2$, α_1, and α_2 for formulating a single sampling plan.

probability of acceptance equal to $1 - \alpha_1(\alpha_2)$ for the corresponding number d and is computed by Equation 6.3. For example, if $d = 3$, then

$$0.95 = e^{-n\theta_1}\left[\frac{(n\theta_1)^0}{0!} + \frac{(n\theta_1)^1}{1!} + \frac{(n\theta_1)^2}{2!}\right]$$

and

$$0.05 = e^{-n\theta_2}\left[\frac{(n\theta_2)^0}{0!} + \frac{(n\theta_2)^1}{1!} + \frac{(n\theta_2)^2}{2!}\right]$$

The values of $n\theta_1$ and $n\theta_2$ are found to be 0.8184 and 6.2969, respectively, as shown in the table.

Tables similar to that of Figure 6.6 for various combinations of the acceptance criteria can also be given. However, the computation of $n\theta_1$ and $n\theta_2$ values requires the solutions of nonlinear equations, which can be done easily by a binary search method. The details are left to the reader.

The following is a procedure for determining a single sampling from a working table:

A. Compute the ratio $T = \theta_2/\theta_1$.

B. Compare T with a value, for example, R_i of column R of the table, and find the value of d. There are two possibilities:

  a. If $T = R_i$, then take the value of d corresponding to R_i.

  b. If $R_{i+1} < T < R_i$, then arbitrarily select the value of d corresponding to R_i or R_{i+1}.

C. Compute n by $n = n\theta_1/\theta_1$ or $n = n\theta_2/\theta_2$.

If $T = R_i$, then there are two possible plans satisfying the acceptance criteria. Namely, one with sample size computed from $n\theta_1$ and the other from $n\theta_2$. If $R_{i+1} < T < R_i$, then four plans are satisfying the same criteria. The plan that satisfies the criteria the most is selected.

Example 6.2

Formulate a single sampling plan that satisfies approximately the acceptance criteria: $\theta_1 = 0.01$, $\alpha_1 = 0.05$, $\theta_2 = 0.08$, and $\alpha_2 = 0.05$.

The plan can be found as follows, using Figure 6.6:

A. $T = \theta_2/\theta_1 = 0.08/0.01 = 8$.

B. T is found to be $R_3 < T < R_2$. Namely, $7.6945 < 8 < 13.3407$. The value of d is 3 (or 2).

C. Compute n by $n = n\theta_1/\theta_1$ or $n = n\theta_2/\theta_2$. There are four possibilities:

  i. $n = 0.8184/0.01 = 82$

  ii. $n = 6.2969/0.08 = 79$

  iii. $n = 0.3555/0.01 = 36$

  iv. $n = 4.7422/0.08 = 60$

Thus there are four plans meeting the criteria: (1) $n = 82$, $d = 3$; (2) $n = 79$, $d = 3$; (3) $n = 36$, $d = 2$; and (4) $n = 60$, $d = 2$. The selection requires some analysis as shown in Figure 6.7.

Plan Number	n	d	θ_1	α_1	θ_2	α_2
1	82	3	0.01	0.0504	0.08	0.0416
2	79	3	0.01	0.0460	0.08	0.0489
3	36	2	0.01	0.0512	0.08	0.2178
4	60	2	0.01	0.1219	0.08	0.0477

Figure 6.7 A comparison of four single sampling plans.

Since the producer's risk and the user's risk associated with the second plan are 0.0460 and 0.0489, respectively, closest to those specified in the acceptance criteria, that plan is chosen.

A single sampling plan that meets approximately the acceptance criteria can also be found by a graphic method using a nomograph of the cumulative binomial distribution. Interested readers should consult Reference 9.

6.2 SEQUENTIAL SAMPLING PLAN

In single sampling, the sample size n is predetermined before implementing a plan. In another plan, called the sequential sampling plan, the size n is not prefixed but determined entirely by the sampling process.

A sequential sampling plan is formulated with the same acceptance criteria used in generating a single sampling plan. The characteristics of the plan can also be represented by an operating characteristics curve. The plan may require less sample inspection than does a single plan while providing almost identical results. It can be advantageous to consider this method carefully before adapting either one.

6.2.1 Foundation of Sequential Sampling

The foundation of sequential sampling plans has been discussed in Section 5.2. The probability of acceptance based on a sequential sampling plan with θ_1, α_1, θ_2, α_2 can be computed by [8]

$$P_a(\theta) = \frac{\left(\dfrac{1-\alpha_2}{\alpha_1}\right)^w - 1}{\left(\dfrac{1-\alpha_2}{\alpha_1}\right)^w - \left(\dfrac{\alpha_2}{1-\alpha_1}\right)^w} \tag{6.4}$$

where $w \neq 0$ and is determined by

$$\theta = \frac{1 - \left(\dfrac{1-\theta_2}{1-\theta_1}\right)^w}{\left(\dfrac{\theta_2}{\theta_1}\right)^w - \left(\dfrac{1-\theta_2}{1-\theta_1}\right)^w} \tag{6.5}$$

The value of w in Equations 6.4 and 6.5 ranges from $-\infty$ to ∞. If

$w = 0$, then θ and $P_a(\theta)$ are computed by

$$P_a(\theta) = \frac{\ln \dfrac{1 - \alpha_2}{\alpha_1}}{\ln \dfrac{1 - \alpha_2}{\alpha_1} + \ln \left| \dfrac{\alpha_2}{1 - \alpha_1} \right|} \tag{6.6}$$

and

$$\theta = \frac{\ln \dfrac{1 - \theta_1}{1 - \theta_2}}{\ln \dfrac{\theta_2}{\theta_1} - \ln \dfrac{1 - \theta_2}{1 - \theta_1}} \tag{6.7}$$

Example 6.3

A large lot is to be accepted by a sequential sampling plan with the criteria: $\theta_1 = 0.01$, $\alpha_1 = 0.05$, $\theta_2 = 0.08$, $\alpha_2 = 0.05$. Determine the decision lines L_1 and L_2 for the plan. What is the probability of acceptance of the product by the plan if the population defective rate is $\theta = 0.02$?

The decision lines L_1 and L_2 are determined by Equations 5.8 and 5.9 as follows:

$$S_r = \frac{\ln \dfrac{0.05}{1 - 0.05} - r \ln \dfrac{1 - 0.08}{1 - 0.01}}{\ln \dfrac{0.08}{0.01} - \ln \dfrac{1 - 0.08}{1 - 0.01}} = \frac{-2.94444 - r(-0.07365)}{2.07944 - (-0.07365)}$$

$$= 0.034r - 1.368$$

and

$$S_r = \frac{\ln \dfrac{1 - 0.05}{0.05} - r \ln \dfrac{1 - 0.08}{1 - 0.01}}{\ln \dfrac{0.08}{0.01} - \ln \dfrac{1 - 0.08}{1 - 0.01}} = \frac{2.94444 - r(-0.07365)}{2.07944 - (-0.07365)}$$

$$= 0.034r + 1.368$$

The decision regions defined by the sampling plan are given in Figure 6.8. The probability of acceptance is computed as follows: By Equation 6.5

$$0.02 = \frac{1 - \left(\dfrac{1 - 0.08}{1 - 0.01}\right)^w}{\left(\dfrac{0.08}{0.01}\right)^w - \left(\dfrac{1 - 0.08}{1 - 0.01}\right)^w}$$

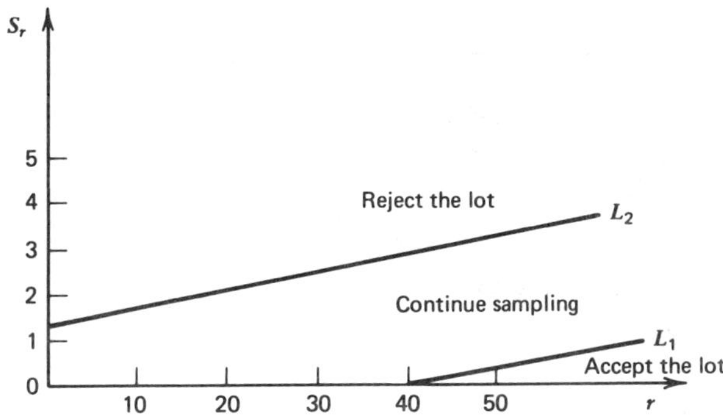

Figure 6.8 Decision regions defined by L_1 and L_2 of the sequential sampling plan of Example 6.3.

The value of w is found to be 0.44453. Thus $P_a(0.02)$ is given by Equation 6.4 as follows:

$$P_a(0.02) = \frac{\left(\frac{1-0.05}{0.05}\right)^{0.44453} - 1}{\left(\frac{1-0.05}{0.05}\right)^{0.44453} - \left(\frac{0.05}{1-0.05}\right)^{0.44453}} = 0.787$$

Notice that the value of w in Equation 6.5 can be easily found by a binary search method. The details are left to the reader. The computation of $P_a(\theta)$ requires natural logarithm arithmetics. A natural logarithm table is given in Appendix 8 for convenience.

6.2.2 Operating Characteristics Curves

The construction of the operating characteristics curve of a sequential sampling plan is similar to the construction of that of a single sampling plan. The probabilities of acceptance are computed by Equations 6.4 and 6.5, or by Equations 6.6 and 6.7. However, it is not necessary to solve Equation 6.5 for the value of w. The points $[\theta, P_a(\theta)]$ can be obtained by assigning a series of w values to Equations 6.4 and 6.5.

Constructed from the probabilities given in Figure 6.9, (obtained by solving Equation 6.5 for w at given θ values) the operating characteristics curve of the sampling plan of Example 6.3 is shown in Figure 6.10. The probabilities in Figure 6.9 are very close to those of Figure 6.2. Thus the OC curves of Figures 6.3 and 6.10 appear almost identical, which means either the single or the sequential sampling plan can be used with no difference under the same acceptance criteria.

θ	w	$P_a(\theta)$
0.00	∞	1.000
0.01	0.9969	0.950
0.02	0.4445	0.787
0.03	0.1289	0.594
0.04	−0.1473	0.393
0.05	−0.3840	0.244
0.06	−0.6207	0.139
0.07	−0.8180	0.083
0.08	−1.0152	0.048
0.09	−1.1731	0.031
0.10	−1.3703	0.017
0.11	−1.5281	0.011
0.12	−1.6860	0.007

Figure 6.9 The probabilities of acceptance under θ values for Example 6.3.

6.2.3 Formulation of a Sequential Sampling Plan

The formulation includes the determination of the decision regions defined by the decision lines L_1 and L_2 through Equations 5.8 and 5.9. The details are given in Section 5.2

Usually, the determination of the sample size n in advance is not necessary. However, it can be of interest to estimate n for budgeting or

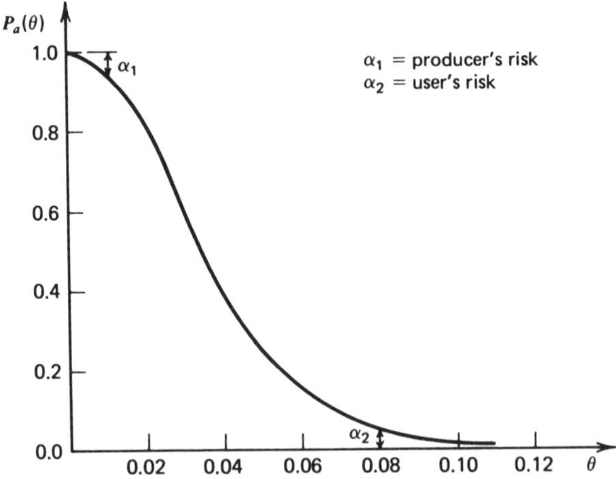

Figure 6.10 Operating characteristics curve of the sequential sampling plan of Example 6.3.

planning purposes. The value of n is dependent on the true but unknown population defective rate θ. It can be computed as follows [8]:

A. If $\theta = \theta_1$, then

$$n = \frac{(1-\alpha_1)\ln\dfrac{1-\alpha_1}{\alpha_2} - \alpha_1 \ln\dfrac{1-\alpha_2}{\alpha_1}}{(1-\theta_1)\ln\dfrac{1-\theta_1}{1-\theta_2} - \theta_1 \ln\dfrac{\theta_2}{\theta_1}} \tag{6.8}$$

B. If $\theta = \theta_2$, then

$$n = \frac{(1-\alpha_2)\ln\dfrac{1-\alpha_2}{\alpha_1} - \alpha_2 \ln\dfrac{1-\alpha_1}{\alpha_2}}{\theta_2\ln\dfrac{\theta_2}{\theta_1} - (1-\theta_2) \ln\dfrac{1-\theta_1}{1-\theta_2}} \tag{6.9}$$

Example 6.4

The producer and user of a product agree on the criteria $\theta_1 = 0.01$, $\alpha_1 = 0.05$, $\theta_2 = 0.08$, and $\alpha_2 = 0.05$ to accept the product, using a sequential sampling plan. Determine the sample size.

There are two cases:

a. If $\theta = \theta_1$, the sample size is determined by Equation 6.8. Namely,

$$n = \frac{(1-0.05)\ln\dfrac{1-0.05}{0.05} - 0.05\ln\dfrac{1-0.05}{0.05}}{(1-0.01)\ln\dfrac{1-0.01}{1-0.08} - 0.01\ln\dfrac{1-0.08}{0.01}}$$

$$= \frac{0.95(2.9444) - 0.05(2.9444)}{0.99(0.07324) - 0.01(2.07944)} \doteq 52$$

b. If $\theta = \theta_2$, the sample size is determined by Equation 6.9. Namely,

$$n = \frac{(1-0.05)\ln\dfrac{1-0.05}{0.05} - 0.05\ln\dfrac{1-0.05}{0.05}}{0.08\ln\dfrac{0.08}{0.01} - (1-0.08)\dfrac{1-0.01}{1-0.08}}$$

$$= \frac{0.95(2.9444) - 0.05(2.9444)}{0.08(2.07944) - 0.92(0.07324)} \doteq 28$$

REFERENCES

1. H. F. Dodge and H. G. Romig, *Sampling Inspection Tables—Single and Double Sampling*, 2nd ed., Wiley, New York, 1959.
2. A. J. Duncan, *Quality Control and Industrial Statistics*, 4th ed., Irwin, Homewood, Illinois, 1974.
3. E. I. Grant and R. S. Leavenworth, *Statistical Quality Control*, 4th ed., McGraw-Hill, New York, 1972.
4. I. Guttman and S. S. Wilks, *Introductory Engineering Statistics*, Wiley, New York, 1965.
5. J. M. Juran, L. A. Seder, and F. M. Gryan, Jr., *Quality Control Handbook*, 2nd ed., McGraw-Hill, New York, 1962.
6. A. E. Mace, *Sample-Size Determination*, Reinhold, New York, 1964.
7. Statistical Research Group, Columbia University, *Sequential Analysis of Statistical Data: Applications*, Columbia University Press, New York, 1945.
8. A. Wald, *Sequential Analysis*, Wiley, New York, 1947.
9. H. R. Larson, "A Nomograph of the Cumulative Binomial Distribution," *Industrial Quality Control*, Vol. 23, American Society for Quality Control, 1966, pp. 270–278.

EXERCISES

1. A box contains 100,000 nuts and is subject to acceptance. Formulate a single sampling plan with the criteria: $\theta_1 = 0.005$, $\alpha_1 = 0.06$, $\theta_2 = 0.05$, and $\alpha_2 = 0.05$. What is the probability of accepting the product if the box contains 4000 defective nuts? Construct the operating characteristics curve for the plan.

2. Formulate a sequential sampling plan for accepting the product of Exercise 1 with the same acceptance criteria. What is the probability of accepting the product plan? Determine the decision regions and construct the operating characteristics curve for the plan.

3. The lot of 12,000 random digits given in Appendix 1 is subject to acceptance based on the fraction of the digit 9's in the lot. Formulate a single and a sequential sampling for accepting the lot with the criteria $\theta_1 = 0.10$, $\alpha_1 = 0.05$, $\theta_2 = 0.102$, and $\alpha_2 = 0.05$. What is the probability of accepting the lot by either plan if $\theta = 0.097$?

4. Implement the sampling plans of Exercise 3 and make the decision of accepting or rejecting the lot. Compare the results of both plans.

CHAPTER 7

Modeling

Modeling is the activity of understanding the problems under consideration. A model is a representation of an existing or a conceptual object, an abstraction of a real world phenomenon that will be the basis for development of a piece of software. A model for software development is like a model for a tailor—essential if excellence is to be achieved.

Modeling is the activity of building a model, which may be considered as the goal of developing a piece of software. It covers almost every human activity imaginable, ranging from engineering, science, economics, business, and so on, to social science. There are many types of models: analytical, biological, computer performance, economic, engineering, operations research, parallel computation, regression analysis, simulation, mathematical, computer programming language. For example, in a triangle with angles x, y, z and sides opposite A, B, C, respectively, the equation $\sin^2 x + \cos^2 x = 1$ is a model abstracting a relationship between the angles and the sides. Similarly, the inequalities:

Maximize

$$c_1x_1 + c_2x_2 + \cdots + c_nx_n$$

subject to

$$\begin{aligned}
&a_{11}x_1 + a_{12}x_2 + \cdots + a_{1n}x_n \le b_1\\
&a_{21}x_1 + a_{22}x_2 + \cdots + a_{2n}x_n \le b_2\\
&\vdots\\
&a_{m1}x_1 + a_{m2}x_2 + \cdots + a_{mn}x_n \le b_m\\
&0 \le x_1, \quad 0 \le x_2, \ldots, \quad 0 \le x_n
\end{aligned} \tag{7.1}$$

form a linear programming model abstracting a phenomenon in the study of optimization in operations research, management science, economics, and so on.

Modeling often includes devising solution methods for the problem under consideration. In the foregoing linear programming model, the method of finding a set of values of $x_1, x_2, \ldots, x_n$ that maximizes the objective function may be considered as an integral study of the modeling activity. However, modeling is not just the selection of the appropriate equation or approximation. It is the study of all the factors necessary to solve a problem and generate a quality solution. In modeling, all aspects of input, processing, and output must be studied.

As will be shown in this chapter, the rigorous planning process enforced in the manufacturing industries for describing products and raw materials, specifying the manufacturing process and operations, and designing the manufacturing facilities provides important guidelines for software developers for how to approach thorough modeling of a piece of software.

7.1 MODELING IN THE MANUFACTURING INDUSTRIES

The manufacturing industries use many types of planning activities, descriptive documents, information resources, expertise, and strategies to model the manufacturing process for a desired product. First and foremost, a distinction is drawn between the product and the process used to manufacture the product. This is parallel to the distinction that must be drawn between the product of a piece of software, that is, the output, and the software itself, which is analogous to the factory. Following this practice, the modeling of products and raw materials will be described, and then the modeling of the manufacturing factory.

7.1.1 Modeling of Products and Raw Materials

The modeling of products and raw materials in the manufacturing industries, as it relates to software design, will be discussed under the following aspects:

Product description

Product prototype design, including product unit definition, product unit defectiveness definition, and tolerance

Raw materials description

Product strategies: simplification, diversification, standardization

Product quality planning

A. Product Description—Quality Characteristics. In the manufacturing industries, much effort goes into defining the desired characteristics of the product. A product description is developed which may include characteristics such as size, shape, weight, color, or chemical composition. Accuracies in dimensions of parts may be defined, or strength, wear, or corrosion resistance limitations identified. These characteristics are developed by product designers based on information from sales, product engineering, manufacturing engineering, and marketing. Niebel and Draper [1] identify some of the important factors that should be recognized in product design:

Utility value of the product
Need for the product
Product's sales appeal
Advantages and improvements over similar products on the market
Size of the potential market
Patentability of the product
Research and development costs
Setup and tool costs
Profit potential
Suitability of the company's engineering talent and production facilities
Suitability of the company's sales force and means of distribution
Strength of the company compared with the competition
Expected life of the product
Compatibility of the product with other company products

The product description, therefore, represents a design that is expected to minimize material, manufacturing, and storage costs, and make the most economical use of tools and factory facilities to produce a product of high utility value.

Once developed, the product description must be conveyed, formally and informally, to those engineers and operators responsible for producing the model or the actual product. Formal product descriptions can be nonpictorial descriptions such as the purchasing specification and, where common standardized parts are used, the standard parts index. Pictorial descriptions may be simple patterns or an engineering drawing such as a blueprint. In most manufacturing industries, the engineering drawing serves as the language in which designers, engineers, and operators communicate. A good drawing conveys the product description in a form that is presentable, that is, not confusing to those who must read it, economically producible, and standardizable to the degree desired. In best practice, each drawing describes only one part. This system simplifies numbering and indexing, allows changes to be made to one drawing without affecting other drawings unnecessarily, and makes distribution and reproduction of drawings more efficient.

B. Product Prototype Design. In the development of a new product, an important stage is that of product prototype design. Each component in the proposed product description is critically analyzed for functionality. The engineering drawings serve as a graphical model, and an experimental mechanical model, or prototype, is constructed to test and evaluate the functional design. The design is then optimized. That is, it is studied from a factory standpoint to adopt each component to the simplest method of manufacture, and thereby achieve the maximum economies in production.

Although the production design phase follows the functional design phase, good designers have their eyes on manufacturing quality and cost from the beginning. The designer's influence early in the product development process, as formalized in drawings and specifications, can set the limits on the manufacturing efficiencies achievable by later process enhancement, tooling, or purchasing efforts. By using his or her knowledge of alternative methods of manufacture, equipment, tooling, raw materials, and the suitability of available standardized parts and parts obtainable from other vendors, the designer can help ensure product quality and minimize costs. The total design effect on manufacturing costs has been estimated by Yankee [2] to average as much as 35 percent of the major overall costs.

From the manufacturing industries have emerged the following basic rules to ensure sound design and maximum production economy:

A. Design all functions and physical characteristics for the greatest simplicity.
B. Design for the most economical production method.
C. Design for a minimum number of machining operations.
D. Specify finish and accuracy no greater than what are actually needed.

Product prototype design includes definition of product unit, product unit defectiveness, and tolerance.

(i) PRODUCT UNIT DEFINITION. The capacity of a factory can be measured in many ways. In the manufacturing of "discrete" products such as screws, nuts, or automobiles, the capacity may be measured by the number of units produced per day. In the manufacturing of "continuous" products such as gasoline or flour, the capacity measure may be by volume or weight, that is, gallons or tons, per day. This type of measure—unit, gallon, ton—may be considered to define the product unit. Such a definition is necessary to perform product quality inspections using the quality control tool introduced in Chapters 2 through 6.

(ii) PRODUCT UNIT DEFECTIVENESS DEFINITION. As the product unit definition is the basis for applying quality control techniques, the product unit defectiveness definition is the basis on which to judge the quality conformance of a product unit. Product unit defectiveness for a particular product is generally difficult to define. For example, an automobile can be a product unit. To define the defectiveness of the unit first requires identification of the quality characteristics of an automobile, such as weight, physical properties, chemical components of each spare part, gas mileage, tire life, battery life, and so forth, and then definition of the defectiveness of each of the characteristics. For example, the defectiveness of gas mileage may be defined as 30 miles per gallon on the open highway; that of battery life may be defined as mean time to failure of 3 years. Failure to meet the criteria set forth in the definition would indicate defectiveness of the product unit. These definitions become the quality standards for manufacture of the product.

(iii) TOLERANCE. Tolerance is the total variation permitted for some characteristic of the product unit and, as such, can be part of the product unit defectiveness definition. For example, a weight, dimension, or performance characteristic may be specified to an accuracy of "± 5 percent." In manufacturing, tolerances are specified because it is unrealistic, given the nature of production facilities, to expect two product units to be exactly alike. The expected variation in product units is determined by the manufacturing process. The high and low limits within which the variation of a product unit is acceptable is specified by the designer.

C. Raw Materials Description. An exact and complete definition of raw materials is an integral part of the modeling activity. In the manufacturing industries, raw materials are described thoroughly in relation to the properties desired for the product. As part of planning a factory, the types and sources of the raw materials, and the means of transporting the materials to the factory, are well-defined before the factory is built.

The process of selecting raw materials from which to manufacture a desired product is a series of choices and compromises among a large number of materials, their useful characteristics, and cost. The following are some of the typical ways in which raw materials are described in the manufacturing industry:

(i) Types of Raw Materials. Materials are classified in general groupings, for example, metallic and nonmetallic, organic and inorganic. These classifications can be a guide to the general properties of the material. In planning for the manufacture of a product, the types of raw materials required must be exhaustively identified. The number of materials used in manufacturing even a relatively simple product may be large. Figure 7.1, for example, shows the diverse types of materials used in making an incandescent light bulb [3].

(ii) Characteristics of Each Type of Raw Material. Once the types of raw materials have been identified, the characteristics of each material must be analyzed. In the manufacturing industries, this is a sophisticated task. First, the salient characteristics are identified. These include numerous physical, chemical, thermal, electrical, and magnetic properties, as well as crucial mechanical properties such as tensile strength, hardness, fatigue, and impact endurance. Each characteristic is defined, usually by the results of engineering tests, which

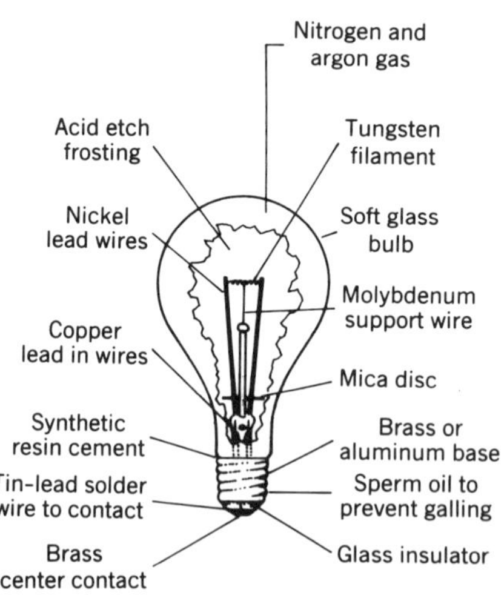

Figure 7.1 Materials used in an incandescent lamp. (M. L. Begeman and B. H. Amstead, Manufacturing Processes, 6th Ed., Wiley, Copyright © 1969 by John Wiley & Sons, Inc. Reprinted by permission of John Wiley & Sons, Inc.)

determine the average properties of each material, taking into account flaws, variations in composition, and variations caused by manufacturing fluctuations.

In analyzing the characteristics of the raw materials, the designer should ask such questions as: Are the characteristics of the material suitable to the manufacturing process? What side effects does each characteristic have on the operations of the factory? Are there any constraints on use of the materials? Is there any substitute for each of the materials?

The designer must know how to go about answering these types of questions. Reliable data on the properties of each specific material are recorded in handbooks or, for new materials, documented by the suppliers. Production engineering data, such as cost per unit volume or resistance to specific service environments, must usually be obtained from the supplier. It is essential to know which characteristics of the raw materials are crucial to manufacturing the product. In an example often cited, hardness and tensile strength would seem key characteristics in manufacturing a durable product, but turn out to be less predictive than yield strength or fatigue strength if the product must withstand impacts or sudden loads.

Analysis of the characteristics should go beyond the initial specification of a material as part of the functional design. It should include consideration of alternatives and factors that affect the manufacturing of the product as part of the production design.

Figure 7.2 shows an example of how the properties of raw materials are documented by the manufacturing industries [3].

(iii) RULES FOR USING RAW MATERIALS. The rules governing the use of raw materials in a manufacturing process are those that define the order and, in many cases, the timing with which the materials must be input into stages of the process. Such rules must be defined before a factory is built and strictly followed. It is well-known, for example, that many of the properties of metals depend on the material's crystalline lattice structure, which varies as a function of temperature. To achieve the desired properties, the material must be at the right temperature, which is accomplished by moving the material through the stations of the factory precisely at designated times. A variation of such rules may lead to poor quality products, waste, or even disaster.

(iv) SOURCES OF RAW MATERIALS. To obtain raw materials for a factory, it is necessary to know where to find the materials and to understand how the materials need to be processed before they can be

Metal	Tensile Strength, lb/in.^{2} [a]	Ductility (%)[a]	Metaling Point, °F[a]	Brinell Hardness[a]
		Ferrous Metals		
Grey Cast Iron	16,000–30,000	0–1	2500	100–150
Malleable Iron	40,000–50,000	1–20	2475	100–145
Steel	40,000–300,000	15–22	2600	110–500
White Cast Iron	45,000	0–1	2500	450
Wrought Iron	35,000–47,000	30–35	2800	90–100
		Nonferrous Metals		
Aluminum	12,000–45,000	10–35	1220	30–100
Copper	50,000–100,000	5–50	1977	50–100
Magnesium	12,000–50,000	9–15	1200	30–60
Nickel	60,000–160,000	15–40	2650	90–250
Lead	2,600–3,300	25–40	620	3.2–4.5
Titanium	80,000–150,000		3270	158–266
Zinc, cast	7,000–13,000	2–10	1445	80–100

[a] Depending upon the alloy.

Figure 7.2 Approximate properties of common metals (M. L. Begeman and B. H. Amstead, Manufacturing Processes, 6th Ed., Wiley, Copyright © 1969 by John Wiley & Sons, Inc. Reprinted by permission of John Wiley & Sons, Inc.).

used in the factory to manufacture the desired product. The sources of raw materials are described by origin, location, and required processing. Origin refers to whether the material comes from a naturally occurring source, such as an ore deposit, or as the by-product of another industrial process.

The materials used in the manufacturing industries seldom occur naturally in a usable form. Ore, for example, must first be extracted from extraneous materials, refined, sometimes alloyed with other materials, and then processed until the desired properties are obtained. The quality of the ore and the ease with which it can be processed determine the engineering effort and cost of converting the ore to a usable raw material. Geographic locations where quality ore is found in commercial quantities become the principal sources of the material.

Figure 7.3 illustrates how a number of raw materials required to manufacture a product originate in different forms and are obtained from different geographic sources [3].

D. Products Strategies—Simplification, Diversification, and Standardization. As part of developing the product design, three broad strategies of product planning need to be considered: simplification, diversification, and standardization. Studying how to apply these

Metal	Principal Ores or Raw Material	Principal Location
Aluminum	Bauxite (a mixture of gibbsite, $Al_2O_3 \cdot 3H_2O$, and diaspore, $Al_2O_3 \cdot H_2O$)	Guianas, Italy, Arkansas
	Cryolitre (Na_3AlF_5)[a]	Iceland, Greenland
Iron	Hematite (Fe_2O_3), red ore, 70% iron	Lake Superior District
	Magnetite (Fe_3O_4), black ore, 72.4% iron	New York, Alabama, Sweden
	Siderite ($FeCO_3$), brown ore, 48.3% iron	New York, Ohio, Germany, England
	Limonite [$Fe_2O_3X(H_2O)$], brown ore, 60–65% iron	Eastern United States, Texas, Missouri, Colorado, France
Tin	Cassiterite (SnO_2)	East Indies, Malaya, Bolivia
Magnesium	Magnesium chloride ($MgCl_2$)	Michigan
	Dolomite ($CaCO_3 \cdot MgCO_3$)	Unites States, Europe
	Sea water	
Zinc	Sphalerite (ZnS)	Missouri, Kansas, Oklahoma, British Columbia
Copper	Chalcocite (Cu_2S)	Arizona
	Bornite (Cu_3FeS_3)	Utah, New Mexico, Michigan, Nevada
Nickel	Miscellaneous sulfides	Canada
	Pentlandite [$(NiS(FeS)_2$]	
Lead	Galena (PbS)	Colorado, Missouri, Utah, Idaho, Montana, Oklahoma, Mexico
Silver	Argentite (Ag_2S)	Mexico, Utah, Nevada, Colorado, Peru, Bolivia

[a] Necessary to the process.

Figure 7.3 Metals, their ores, and sources (M. L. Begeman and B. H. Amstead, Manufacturing Processes, 6th Ed., Wiley, Copyright © 1969 by John Wiley & Sons, Inc. Reprinted by permission of John Wiley & sons, Inc.).

strategies to the product is a modeling activity that must be performed before the factory is built.

Simplification is the process of eliminating extraneous or marginal product lines. It is a move toward specialization in one product or a small number of products. Often, the motive for simplication is manufacturing economy. With simplified product liners, inventories can be reduced, materials can be purchased in large quantities, and the manufacturing can proceed in long runs that make installation of special production equipment economical and reduce setup costs.

Diversification is the process of expanding product lines. The need for diversification comes from the users of the products. Where the users' needs or desires are highly individualized and there is a demand for variety and differentiation among purchased goods, the factory must be planned to output diversified product lines in order to be competitive and satisfy the users.

Standardization is the process of applying dimensional, performance, and quality criteria to the components of the product. The benefits of using standardized interchangeable parts in assembly line manufacturing, and the necessity of standardization for such industries as electrical power supply and distribution are well-accepted. It should also be understood that standardization supports product diversification. This is certainly true, for example, in the electronics industry, where standardized components are used almost universally to develop a limitless number of applications.

In the manufacturing industries, selection of the standards to apply to the product is an important function. Management must establish internal standards and select industry-wide standards developed by appropriate trade and professional societies.

E. Product Quality Planning. Product design and manufacturing are not complete without a quality control plan that parallels all phases of development, manufacture, and delivery. Quality planning should include procedures to assure the quality of the design and also product conformance with the quality characteristics of the design.

The quality of the design is planned into the product unit defectiveness definition and tolerances established in the product description. Feedback on the quality of design should be obtained from users of the product, either through study of user complaints and specified requirements or, if appropriate, by conducting sample investigations of user satisfaction with the delivered product.

The product conformance to the design is controlled by quality assurance activities during the manufacturing phases. These activities include performing checks or inspections and monitoring the quality of product units. These activities should be supported by evaluations of supervisor and operator, personnel performance checks, maintenance and accuracy checks of tools and test equipment, and periodic review of files and other sources of manufacturing information.

7.1.2 Modeling of the Manufacturing Factory

Planing for the design of the manufacturing process and facilities, as it pertains to design of a piece of software, will be discussed under the following aspects:

Process description
Methods of manufacturing
Rules for processing raw materials
Material flows in the factory
Process control
Factory characteristics
Methods of building the factory

A. Process Description. Building or setting up a factory to manufacture a desired product must be based on process planning. The best materials and methods for manufacturing a quality product at a minimum cost must be determined. As discussed in Section 7.1.1***A***, this planning begins with interpretation of the product description, since product design has considerable influence on the formulation of manufacturing procedures. A complete and accurate product description is essential for process planning.

Determining the proper sequence of operations should be based on criteria for logic and economy. For example, the process should follow the layout of the equipment in the factory to minimize the distance traveled between steps. Operations that must be performed before others should come first. If there is a likelihood that the product may be abandoned during the process, then costly operations should be deferred to the last stages of manufacture. The sequence of operations can be indicated by a numbering system, as long as there is no confusion about simultaneous steps or work performed by different departments.

Often the determination of the proper sequence of operations is a top-down process. First, the primary areas of the factory are determined, based on geometrical or mechanical advantages, and the primary manufacturing operations set up. Then the secondary operations are arranged as seems best. Finally, allied operations necessary between stations, such as washing or heat-treating, are set up, until all operations have been included in the sequence.

The result of process planning is a process description, a written step-by-step set of instructions for how to manufacture the product. In many industries, this document is developed using a bottom-up approach. All operations required to complete each stage of manufacture at a given factory station are determined, grouped into logical blocks of operations, then placed into proper sequence in the total process. However, the process description is developed, it is crucial that all operations at the lowest level are completely identified. The number and type of operations at the lowest level give the basis for estimating costs and time required. Failure to identify even one operation could mean the difference between profit or loss.

In summary, the steps of process planning should be as follows:

A. Analyze the product description for an overall concept of what is required.
B. Consult with product engineering on product design changes to clarify all points and recommend enhancements in design and production.
C. Determine the most logical and economical method of manufacture.
D. Identify all operations required to manufacture the product.
E. Determine the best way to combine and sequence the operations.
F. Specify the gauging, that is, the tool and equipment accuracies, required to manufacture the product to meet the quality standards within the specified tolerances.

B. Methods of Manufacturing. As part of developing the process description, the best method of manufacturing the product must be selected. Usually there are various methods by which the product can be made, and one optimum cost method. The most thorough approach is to begin with a systematic evaluation of the advantages and disadvantages of all relevant manufacturing methods, eliminate the obviously inappropriate ones, and concentrate on a few promising methods that can be researched in detail.

To evaluate manufacturing methods, a processing checklist should be used. Such a checklist should include consideration of the following types of factors:

Suitability and properties of raw materials
Volume of production: maximum and minimum production quantities
Quality of product: tolerances, etc.
Advantages and limitations of types of equipment
Economies of general-purpose versus special-purpose machines
Lead time
Production rate of personnel
Factory production capability
Inventory
Cost factors associated with the preceding, including influence of special features desired by user

Identifying alternative methods should begin by classifying the available processes. In metal working, for example, the processes might be classified as follows:

Processes used to change the shape of material
Processes used for machining parts
Processes used for obtaining surface finish
Processes used for joining parts
Processes used to change physical properties

Each of the classifications can then be subdivided into processes. Under shape changing, for example, would be listed with such processes as casting, forging, piercing, and so on. The appropriateness of each process, and the types of equipment and operations required, can then be fully examined and a selection of the best method made.

As discussed in Section 7.1.1*A*, development of the process description should proceed simultaneously with development of the product description, and there should be open communication and feedback between the product and process engineers. All alternative methods of manufacture should be considered before the product design is finalized.

C. Rules for Processing Raw Materials. As part of planning a manufacturing process, the types and quantities of raw materials must be identified, the way the materials will be used must be described, and the time at which each material is needed must be specified. A system of raw material inspection must be established to assure that sufficient quantities of each material, with the necessary level of quality, are received and ready to enter the factory.

D. Material Flows in the Factory. The factory plan must consider material flows and temporary storage throughout the manufacturing process. The most efficient layout of equipment must be determined, and the process operations must be coordinated with material handling and storage facilities, analysis of operation movements, and availability of factory facilities.

E. Process Control. The flow of materials and intermediate products within a factory constitutes a complex network. The smooth movement of materials and semifinished parts through the factory, and the early detection of any problems affecting product quality, is essential to efficient manufacturing of the product. When and how to inspect the quality of the raw materials and intermediate products must be studied.

Planning for process control and inspections should begin at the same time that the manufacturing process is selected and described. In such planning, the following types of questions should be addressed:

A. What quality characteristics of the intermediate and final products can be measured to yield information for controlling the process?

B. Are these measurements properly organized with respect to the total process?

C. Are the means available to take these measurements?

D. What is the most effective and economical way to control the process: manual, numerical, or automatic; that is, are adjustments to be made by an operator, computer control system, or built-in feedback system?

Inspection planning should include selection of the sampling methods appropriate to the various types of operations in the factory, for example, repetitive manufacture, job lot production, and assembly. It should also include consideration of how the inspection data will be recorded, analyzed, and used to provide feedback for adjusting the process to assure that the product conforms to specifications within tolerance limits.

The goal of process control and inspection planning is to develop means of assuring product quality at early stages of the manufacturing process. Ideally, problems with equipment or operations are not allowed to continue or grow worse undetected until the final steps of the process. With an effective process control and inspection system, the process can be stopped or modified before many defective product units are manufactured.

F. Factory Characteristics. As part of modeling the manufacturing process, the characteristics of the factory itself should be planned before designing and building the factory. These characteristics include building type, production volume, production rate, construction materials, storage capacity for incoming materials, means of transportation within the factory, way of handling materials in the factory, and so on.

G. Methods of Building the Factory. The selection of the best method for building the factory can have an impact on factory design. Therefore, building methods need to be carefully investigated. The following types of questions should be addressed:

A. Should a model of the factory be built and studied before actual construction begins?

B. Should the factory be built and installed on-site, or fabricated at the most convenient or economical locations, then transported, and assembled on-site?

C. What types of impacts will each building method have on the factory design?

7.2 MODELING IN THE SOFTWARE INDUSTRY

When a piece of software is being developed, the designers should use a thorough modeling approach such as that used by product designers in the manufacturing industries. Modeling in the software industry should include the use of planning activities, descriptive documents, information resources, expertise, and strategies to study the software model and define the desired output. A good model should be capable of the following:

Mapping an input onto an output

Evaluating outcomes from a set of input data

Evaluating the impact of a change in the input data on the output

Identifying the input that yields a desired output

Searching the values of some input that yields the most desired results

Assessing the effect on the outcomes of systematic variation of the input

Comparing the results of two sets of input data with different assumptions (or comparing the actual versus estimated results)

Such a model will help avoid introducing errors into the software during the design and coding stages of development.

Modeling is the essential, and most difficult, task for developing reliable software. It requires a background in the problem area under consideration, mathematical reasoning capability, and proficiency in some programming language such as FORTRAN or COBOL. It is an activity that may involve the complete software life cycle. It is the first step on the journey of a thousand miles of software development. A job well-begun means a job half done.

7.2.1 Modeling of Inputs and Outputs

The modeling of inputs and outputs in software design can be discussed analogously to the modeling of products and raw materials in the manufacturing industries. The following aspects will be considered:

Output description

Output prototype design, including product unit definition, product unit defectiveness definition, and tolerance

Input description

Output strategies: simplification, diversification, standardization

Output quality planning

A. Output Description

It was demonstrated in Section 7.1.1*A* how much care and effort the manufacturing industries give to describing a product and its quality characteristics. This should be the same in the software industry, but it is not. As shown in Figure 1.8, three ingredients are missing from the software life cycle: product concept formulation, product quality characteristics specification, and product design. The life cycle is therefore an incomplete cycle. These missing ingredients have been cited as the root of the technical problems stated in Figure 1.3 [17] [18]. In order to solve these problems, it is essential that the three ingredients be analyzed.

In performing this analysis, it must be remembered that the overriding purpose of software development is to provide a tool to help the user's productivity in performing his or her daily work. Therefore, the ability to provide what the user needs from application of the software is the critical success criterion of software development.

(i) Product Concept Formulation. As discussed at the beginning of this chapter, one of the most crucial lessons that software developers can learn from the manufacturing industries is that the product of a software development process—the product desired by the software user—is the output of a piece of software, not the software itself. The user needs a piece of software to help him or her accomplish his or her work more efficiently. The user needs data generated or retrieved; numbers crunched; and information of all types printed out on a timely basis or displayed in numeric, tabular, or graphic form. He or she needs appropriate system responses in real-time or nonreal-time. The user has no need for a piece of software if it is not able to produce directly usable, quality output. This is just like buying an automobile. It is the automobile that helps a consumer do his or her job. It is not the automobile factory that a consumer is interested in buying. If the automobile is of poor quality, the consumer really does not care how good the factory is. Unfortunately, the software industry has conventionally treated the piece of software itself as the end product for the user. Anyone who doubts this can open up any software engineering and development book and search for treatment of product concept formulation. The emphasis is always on the piece of software itself as the product.

Product concept formulation, then, concerns output. This starts with the types of data being produced. For example, in developing a piece of software that prints employee paychecks, the types of data that can appear on a paycheck would include:

CHECK NO.	The check number can be preprinted on a blank check. The software can print the number if required.
PAYEE	The person who is entitled to cash the check
AMOUNT-N	The numeral dollar amount to be cashed, for example, $123.45
AMOUNT-L	The literal dollar amount, for example, One Hundred Twenty-Three Dollars and Forty-Five Cents
NAME OF PERSON	The person who is authorized to sign checks

Depending on requirements, a paycheck may be accompanied by a pay statement providing relevant information to the payee. For example:

DEPARTMENT	The department or department number to which the employee (payee) belongs
SOCIAL SECURITY NO.	This number given for employee reference
YEAR-TO-DATE GROSS	The total amount of gross pay received from beginning of fiscal year up to and including last paycheck
PERIOD ENDING	The work period, for example, two weeks, or dates which the paycheck covers

CURRENT GROSS	The amount of gross pay of the period from the last paycheck to the period ending date
NET PAY	The difference between the current gross and deductions. This is also the Amount-N on the paycheck.
TAXES AND DEDUCTIONS	This includes: Federal Tax FICA Tax State Tax Local Tax Life Insurance Medical Insurance Dental Insurance (Taxes and deductions are given for the current pay period and from year-to-date.)

The information required on a paycheck and a pay statement may vary from organization to organization. Therefore, a given organization's requirements must be formulated before any software design task begins. (A common, and costly, mixup in the software industry is that software personnel confuse the task of defining user requirements with the tasks of software design. This can result in a developer becoming committed to one design approach before the user's requirements are fully defined and understood. Then, when the software goes through acceptance, the developer finds that it does not do everything the user needs it to do, and costly revisions are necessary. It should be remembered that the product is the output: The user's requirements define the type of output desired, not the design of the software.) When users address software design in specifications or requests for proposals, it is only to require that the developer design the software in accordance with the principles of software engineering (see Chapter 8) as a means of trying to ensure quality.

(ii) PRODUCT QUALITY CHARACTERISTICS SPECIFICATION. Since the product of software development is the output, not the software itself, the product quality characteristics are the characteristics of the output that determine its usability for the user. Attention to detail in describing the desired output is essential. All data fields and formats must be described. Even a minor format discrepancy can make the output incompatible with the user's tasks, forms, regulations, reporting requirements, and so on and thus impair the user's efficiency. For example, the product quality characteristics of each type of data on a paycheck being produced by a piece of software would be ascertained by answering the following types of questions:

CHECK NO. If required to be printed by the software, should the number be numerical, nonnumerical, or alphanumerical? What is the maximum number of digits or characters to be printed?

PAYEE Should a title be printed? What are the titles: Mr., Mrs., Ms., Esq.? Should the surname be printed first? Should a period follow a first initial and a second initial? What is the maximum number of characters to be printed? What if a payee's name exceeds the maximum number of characters? Should it be truncated to fit on one line or should it be printed on two lines? If it is to be printed on two lines, how should the name be "broken"? For example, how should a payee's name such as COMPUTER AND INFORMATION SCIENCE LIBRARY be divided to fit on two lines, or abbreviated to fit on one line?

AMOUNT-N Should a $-sign be printed before the dollar amount? What is the maximum number of digits to be printed? Should commas be used to identify billions, millions, and thousands (e.g., $2,345,678,900.12) or not (e.g., $2345678900.12)? Should the cents columns be printed with an underline (e.g., $2,345,678,900.$\underline{12}$)? Should the number be rounded or truncated during computation?

AMOUNT-L What is the maximum number of characters to be printed? What if the literal dollar amount exceeds the maximum number of characters? Should it be "broken" into two lines, and if so, how? Does the limit on how many characters for the literal dollar amount can be printed affect how many digits in the numeral dollar amount to be printed (i.e., must the numeral amount be small enough to ensure the paycheck has enough space for the literal amount)?

NAME OF PERSON	Should the last name be printed first? Should a period follow a first and second initial? What is the maximum number of characters to be printed? And so on.

Similar questions can be asked pertaining to the printing of an accompanying pay statement. These are left to the interested reader.

(iii) PRODUCT DESIGN. After the tasks of product concept formulation and product quality characteristics specification have been completed, product design can be addressed. In the modeling phase, this begins with a rapid prototype method, as described in the following section.

B. Output Prototype Design. Like the output of a factory, the output of a piece of software must be defined by a product unit so that the output product population can be inspected using a quality control tool. A piece of software can be considered of good quality only when it is able to produce a good quality product population. The product unit definition is therefore a necessity. (Note: The product unit should not be confused with units to measure the productivity of the people developing the software. Productivity is sometimes measured by completion of milestones such as a routine, module, or program. The product unit always defines an output of the software that is desired by the user.)

The lack of product unit definition in the software industry is an obstacle to the development of high quality, cost-effective software [5] [17] [18]. Defining the product unit in the beginning stages of developing a piece of software is crucial to solving many of the problems in Figure 1.3 that arise in software development.

(i) PRODUCT UNIT DEFINITION. Conceptually, a piece of software maps an input onto an output. An input consists of a number of input data types. An output consists of a number of output data types. Formally,

$$O = F(I)$$

where F is a function implemented in the software that transforms an input I into an output O. Or,

$$(O_{i1}, O_{i2}, O_{i3}, \ldots, O_{ik}) = F(I_{i1}, I_{i2}, I_{i3}, \ldots, I_{im})$$

where $i = 1, 2, \ldots,$ represents an input and an output

k = total number of output data types

m = total number of input data types

$(O_{i1}, O_{i2}, O_{i3}, \ldots, O_{ik})$ is the ith output consisting of k pieces of output data $O_{i1}, O_{i2}, O_{i3}, \ldots, O_{ik}$, which is transformed from the ith input $(I_{i1}, I_{i2}, I_{i3}, \ldots, I_{im})$ consisting of m pieces of input data $I_{i1}, I_{i2}, I_{i3}, \ldots, I_{im}$. Thus the output $(O_{i1}, O_{i2}, O_{i3}, \ldots, O_{ik})$ is a product unit and the input $(I_{i1}, I_{i2}, \ldots, I_{im})$ is an input unit. In the paycheck example given in Section 7.2.1*A*, the product unit would be defined in terms of data types as follows:

O_{i1} = Check number
O_{i2} = Payee
O_{i3} = Amount-N
O_{i4} = Amount-L
O_{i5} = Name of person authorized to sign checks
O_{i6} = Department
O_{i7} = Social security no.
O_{i8} = Year-to-date gross
O_{i9} = Period ending
O_{i10} = Current gross
O_{i11} = Net pay
O_{i12} = Taxes and deductions

The product unit would be produced from the input unit (see Section 7.2.1*C*) in terms of input data types as follows:

I_{i1} = Employee identification
I_{i2} = Employee name
I_{i3} = Regular hours worked in pay period
I_{i4} = Vacation hours taken in pay period
I_{i5} = Regular pay rate
I_{i6} = Overtime hours worked in pay period
I_{i7} = Overtime pay rate
i_{i8} = Number of dependents
i_{i9} = Tax exemptions per dependent

I_{i10} = Federal tax withholding rate
I_{i11} = State tax withholding rate
i_{i12} = Local tax withholding rate
i_{i13} = Deductions
$I_{i13,1}$ = Life insurance
$I_{i13,2}$ = Medical insurance
$I_{i13,3}$ = Dental insurance
$I_{i13,4}$ = Retirement contributions

Each product unit is produced from a unique input unit. Therefore, the definition of the product unit can also be given in terms of the input unit.

(ii) PRODUCT UNIT DEFECTIVENESS DEFINITION. Once the product unit definition is given, it is essential to define the defectiveness of the product unit so that the quality of a product unit can be evaluated. The product unit defectiveness should be defined in terms of the product quality characteristics discussed in Section 7.2.1*A*(ii). In the paycheck example, a product unit would be defective if the net pay printed on the paycheck is computed incorrectly from the input. Clearly, the product unit defectiveness can be defined in terms of any combination of the quality characteristics.

(iii) TOLERANCE. Identifying tolerance limits is an important task in defining the defectiveness of a product unit. In the paycheck example, rounding and truncation errors in computing and printing the check might be considered tolerable. However, in other applications where rounding and truncation accumulate into a significant variation in the final results, such errors would not be considered tolerable.

C. Input Description. The input domain of a piece of software should be described as thoroughly as are the raw materials entering a factory. The description should include types of inputs, characteristics of each type, rules for using inputs, and sources of inputs. Each of these elements of the input description is discussed in the following sections:

(i) TYPES OF INPUTS. For a piece of software, the entities analogous to the raw materials entering a factory are the input variables. In the paycheck example, the types of input data would be as follows:

EMPLOYEE IDENTIFICATION	This can be a social security number or other number.
EMPLOYEE NAME	The name of the employee to whom the check is issued.
REGULAR HOURS WORKED IN PAY PERIOD	The total number of hours actually worked in the pay period. This is usually a maximum of 40; additional hours worked are considered overtime and treated as another data type.
VACATION HOURS TAKEN IN PAY PERIOD	Total number of vacation hours taken during the pay period
REGULAR PAY RATE	The rate to be used in computing compensation for the regular hours worked and vacation hours taken during the pay period.
OVERTIME HOURS WORKED IN PAY PERIOD	The number of hours that exceeds the limit, for example, 40, of the regular hours worked during the pay period.
OVERTIME PAY RATE	The pay rate for computing compensation for the overtime hours worked. The overtime pay rate can be the same as the regular pay rate or higher.
NO. OF DEPENDENTS	This is used to compute tax withholdings for federal, state, and local income tax.
TAX EXEMPTIONS PER DEPENDENT	The number of qualified dependents for computing tax withholdings.
FEDERAL TAX WITHHOLDING RATE	The rate used to compute federal income tax withholding.
STATE TAX WITHHOLDING RATE	The rate used to compute state income tax withholding.
LOCAL INCOME TAX	The rate used to compute county and city taxes in the state in which the employee is subject to state taxes.
DEDUCTIONS	The deductions include life, medical, and dental insurance, and retirement contributions.

Once the input types have been identified, the quality characteristics of each type must also be defined so that they can be used to inspect the inputs units coming into the software. The quality characteristics are defined by asking the same kind of detailed questions as discussed for output data types (see Section 7.2.1*A*(ii)).

The raw materials entering a factory can be classified in general groupings which indicate something of their properties. The equivalent process for the input to a piece of software is the decomposition of input data types into subtypes. For example, in the development of a mailing list data base management system, the input data type is an address. However, an address consists of a number of entities such as title, name, street number, street, city, state, zip code, and possibly a phone number. Each of the entities also contains a number of subentities. For example, the entity "title" can be Dr., Mrs., Ms., Esq., and so on. Similarly, a first name can be either a full name or an initial. It can be seen that the address can be decomposed into a tree structure with a number of levels. An example of such decomposition is given in Figure 7.4.

Each of the boxes in Figure 7.4 represents an input data type or subtype. For example, TITLE is a subtype of ADDRESS, and DR. is a subtype of TITLE, and so on. Each label in a box in the figure represents an input variable.

(ii) Characteristics of Each Type of Input. The characteristics of the input variables should also be analyzed before developing the software. In this analysis, the following types of questions should be addressed:

A. Is a variable assuming numerical or nonnumerical values?

B. What are the lower and upper bounds of the variable?

C. If a variable assumes nonnumerical values, what types of data are to be assigned to the variable?

D. What are the components of the variable? (e.g., if NAME is a variable assuming people's names, the components would be FIRST NAME, MIDDLE NAME, and LAST NAME.)

E. What are the characteristics of each component?

For example, some of the characteristics of the component FIRST NAME might be that FIRST NAME cannot use any of the special characters in the set {+ * / " & # @ ; :) (! ? =] [% ¢} or any of the numerical characters in the set {0 1 2 3 4 5 6 7 8 9}. All such characteristics of all of the input variables must be defined as a basis for the later phases of software development.

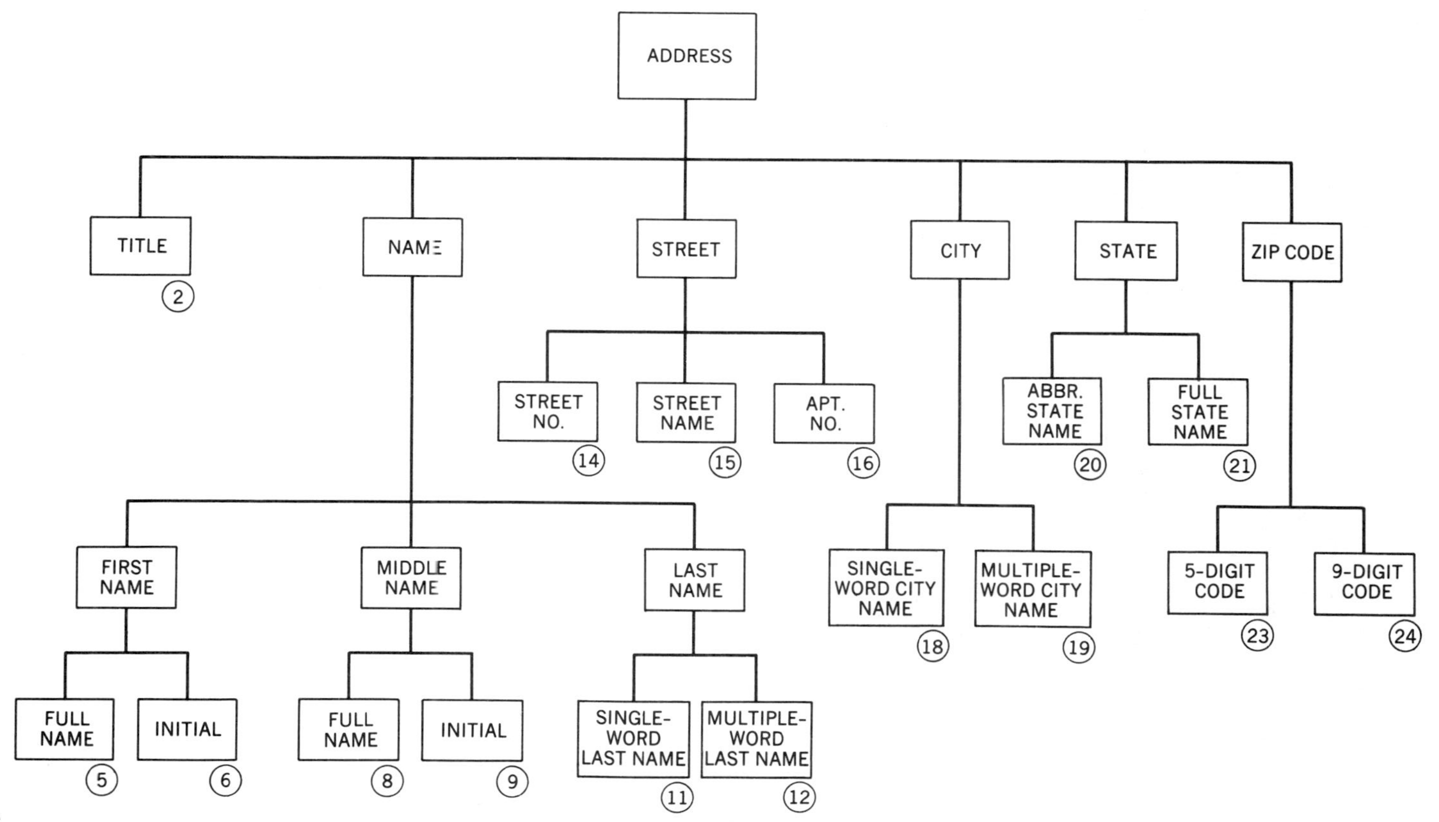

Figure 7.4 An address tree structure.

(iii) RULES FOR CONSTRUCTING INPUTS. As discussed in Section 7.1.1*C*(iii), the rules governing the use of raw materials entering a factory are closely allied with the properties of the raw material types to ensure proper use of the materials (e.g., a metal with desirable properties at a certain temperature must be at that temperature at the right time and place in the factory to ensure quality output). Following such rules can be the difference between success and disaster in the factory. Similarly, the rules for constructing inputs to a piece of software are the what, when, how and interrelationships among the input data types, and are closely allied with the characteristics of the input variables.

For example, considering again a mailing list data base management system, it was noted that the data type NAME might consist of subtypes FIRST NAME, MIDDLE NAME, and LAST NAME. One of the characteristics of LAST NAME might be that it consists of a minimum of 2 characters and a maximum of 20 characters. To ensure proper construction of inputs, the piece of software must be designed to handle these characteristics. Therefore, the rules governing the use of input data would include:

A. The number of characters (or field length) of NAME is the total number of characters of FIRST NAME, MIDDLE NAME, and LAST NAME.

B. The number of characters of LAST NAME is from 2 to 20.

Such rules can make the difference between success and failure in software development. It is all too common to find a piece of software that produces errors because the developer did not base the design on sufficiently comprehensive rules to cover all the possible characteristics of the input data.

(iv) SOURCES OF INPUTS. The sources of inputs to a piece of software can be a data base, a terminal, a real-time data acquisition system, a remote site, or a document. The sources of the data, the volume of data, and the means of transmitting the data to the software, such as tape or communication through telephone lines, must be completely studied and specified as thoroughly as the sources of raw materials are studied in the manufacturing industries. This is essential to successful, cost-effective software development. Just as a raw material, for example, an ore, may require refining before it can be used in a factory, it is very frequently the case with sources of input that the data must be processed, for example, reformatted, before it can be used by a piece of software. The feasibility and cost of such preprocessing of data from a given input source can have considerable effect on the software design.

D. Output Strategies. In software development, as in the manufacturing industries, the developer should consider how to apply the strategies of simplification, diversification, and standardization, as discussed in Section 7.1.1***D***. Throughout the software industry, developers are currently assessing the advantages and disadvantages of each of these strategies. Many business applications, for example, spread sheet programs, tax computation, and so on, are being addressed through the use of standardized packages. Other larger applications, for both commercial and military users, still demand custom software. However, in the interests of cost-reduction, it is now expected that the user will require the developer to evaluate the suitability of available "off-the-shelf" software before committing to development of a completely custom design. It has become common for a developer to adopt the strategy of simplification, producing a specialized package and periodically introducing updated revisions with additional capabilities, for example, new features, greater computational power, greater portability. In some fields, such as real-time simulation, one strategy has been to model a range of real-world systems or processes in a way that allows development of standardized software modules which the developer can customize to satisfy diverse users more cost effectively than by producing custom software for each user.

The developer should be aware of any applicable standards in use at his or her company or any adopted by the industry. Currently, the software industry is in a largely open-ended competitive mode, and it is not uncommon to encounter a lack of protocol for one piece of software or system to "talk" or "handshake" with another piece of software or system. In many applications, the developer must design his or her own interfacing software in order to support all required input/output operations and data communications.

There are many factors affecting the selection of an output strategy. Each developer must analyze his or her own situation. The time to perform that analysis is during the modeling phase.

E. Output Quality Planning. Quality planning is as essential in software development as it is in the manufacturing industries to ensure user satisfaction. It is a theme of this book that output quality, indicated by a developer's ability to offer the user a meaningful software warranty, results from following the principles of software engineering and applying the techniques of statistical quality control. To plan properly for output quality requires an understanding of the materials presented in Chapters 5 and 6.

Output quality planning is a software development activity that should begin during the modeling phase. The quality planning tasks include:

(i) DETERMINATION OF SAMPLING METHODS. There are many sampling methods that can be used for software testing and acceptance. The simple and sequential sampling methods discussed in Chapter 5 are for estimating the defective rate of a software product population. The single and sequential acceptance sampling methods discussed in Chapter 6 are for determining the acceptability of the product population of a piece of software. Which of these sampling methods should be used for the development of the software must be studied and identified.

(ii) REFINEMENT OF PRODUCT UNIT DEFINITION. The product unit definition is essential in order to apply the sampling methods selected in Section 7.2.1***E***(i). This definition is discussed in Section 7.2.1***B***(i) and is refined as a task of the quality planning activity.

(iii) REFINEMENT OF PRODUCT UNIT DEFECTIVENESS DEFINITION. The product unit defectiveness definition is essential in judging the goodness of a product unit produced by the software being developed. This definition, discussed in Section 7.2.1***B***(ii), is also refined as part of the quality planning activity.

(iv) DETERMINATION OF SAMPLING PARAMETERS. There are a number of parameters that must be determined in order to apply any of the sampling methods. These parameters are discussed in the following list for each sampling method:

A. **Simple Sampling Parameters.** This method requires determination of values for z and a in Equation (5.3a) so that the defective rate of the software product population can be estimated by the iterative sampling process.
B. **Sequential Sampling Parameters.** In this method for estimating the defective rate of the software product population, values must be determined for α_1, θ_1, α_2, and θ_2. The parameters θ_1 and θ_2 are the two defective rates of the software product population to be inferred, and α_1 and α_2 are the Type I and Type II errors, respec-

tively, that can occur in making the statistical inference, as explained in Sections 5.1.3 and 5.2.

C. **Single Acceptance Sampling Parameters.** The parameters required to formulate a single acceptance sampling plan are α_1, θ_1, α_2, and θ_2, where α_1 and θ_1 represent the producer's risk and α_2 and θ_2 represent the user's risk.

D. **Sequential Acceptance Sampling Parameters.** The parameters required to formulate a sequential acceptance sampling plan are the same as those required for a single acceptance sampling plan in item C.

(v) SELECTION OF SOFTWARE PRODUCT POPULATION ACCEPTANCE CRITERIA. Acceptance of the software product population can be based on one of two criteria: the defective rate of the product population, or the producer's risk and user's risk in accepting the population. Using the first criterion, the acceptable defective rate θ_a can be specified as:

$$\theta_a < \epsilon$$

where ϵ is a small number desired by the user. (The defectiveness criterion ϵ can also be given as $\epsilon_1 < \theta_a < \epsilon$, but $\epsilon_1 < \theta_a$ can be dropped since the value of θ should be as small as possible, ideally, close to 0.) With the given values of z, a, and ϵ, the sample size n required for simple sampling can be computed as follows for budgeting purposes:

$$n = \frac{z^2(1-\theta)}{a^2\theta} = \frac{z^2(1-\epsilon)}{a^2\epsilon}$$

For example, if $z = 1.96$ (at the 95 percent level of confidence), $a = 0.25$, and $\epsilon = 0.05$, then

$$n = \frac{1.96^2(1-0.05)}{0.25^2 \times 0.05} = 1168$$

It can be seen that the values selected for z, a, and ϵ have a significant impact on the cost of testing. In general, the smaller the values of a and ϵ, and the larger the value of z, then the larger the sample size n and the greater the cost of testing. If the user insists on assuring that θ_a is very close to 0, then the number of sample units required will approach infinity, which would be infeasible or too costly to test. Therefore, the user should choose the values of z, a, and ϵ carefully to fit his or her needs and resources.

Using the second criterion, an acceptance sampling plan (m, c) is formulated from the parameters α_1 and θ_1 (producer's risk) and α_2 and

θ_2 (user's risk). If a sample of m units is taken randomly from the software product population and the sample contains less than c defective units, then the population is acceptable. Otherwise, it should be rejected.

7.2.2 Modeling of Software

The modeling of a piece of software itself, as distinct from its output, can be discussed analogously to the modeling of a manufacturing process and facilities. The following aspects will be considered:

Process description
Rules of using inputs
Methods of producing outputs
Data flows in a process being automated
Process control
Software characteristics
Methods of developing the software system

A. Process Description. The purpose of developing a piece of software is (1) to automate an existing manual operational process to increase operational efficiency and the quality of operations, or (2) to automate a conceptual operational process for understanding that leads to attaining some intended purpose. Therefore, the process description task is to develop a document that defines the "problem" or system to be automated. This task includes the following activities:

A. Identify the types of input to the process and the types of output (see Section 7.2.1), just as in a factory the types of raw materials and products are identified.

B. Identify every stage of the process that transforms inputs into outputs. This is analogous to identifying the work stations in a factory where materials are transformed into intermediate products. (Defining the nature and structure of each stage of the process in an actual piece of software, for example, module, routine, task, package, etc., is a design task and is discussed in Chapter 9.)

C. Identify all functions performed at each stage of the process identified in activity B, just as in a factory all operations performed at each work station are identified.

D. Identify all of the inputs and outputs at each stage of the process.

E. Identify all of the process flows from input to output throughout the entire process.

F. Identify the requirements at each stage of the process for temporary storage of the data being input and output at each stage of the process.

G. Determine the volume and rates of data flows through stage of the process.

H. Determine constraints at each stage of the process.

These activities should be performed on a top-down basis. Then the top level description of the process should be reviewed for completeness. The description of each stage of the process is then decomposed into a second level of detailed descriptions, followed by a second review to ensure the properness and correctness of these descriptions.

For simplicity, the process descriptions generated by this method should be organized in a work flow diagram. Figure 7.5 shows a level-one work flow diagram, where $W_1, W_2, \ldots, W_6$ are stages of the process (analogous to factory work stations), each performing a number of functions, that is operations, that transform input into output; $S_1, S_2, \ldots, S_5$ are temporary data storage, if any, between two or more stages of the process; $A_1, A_2, \ldots, A_{16}$ are work flows from the input side to the output side; $M_1, M_2, \ldots, M_m$ are m types of input (analogous to raw materials); $P_{11}, P_{12}, \ldots, P_{1k_1}$ are the product population consisting

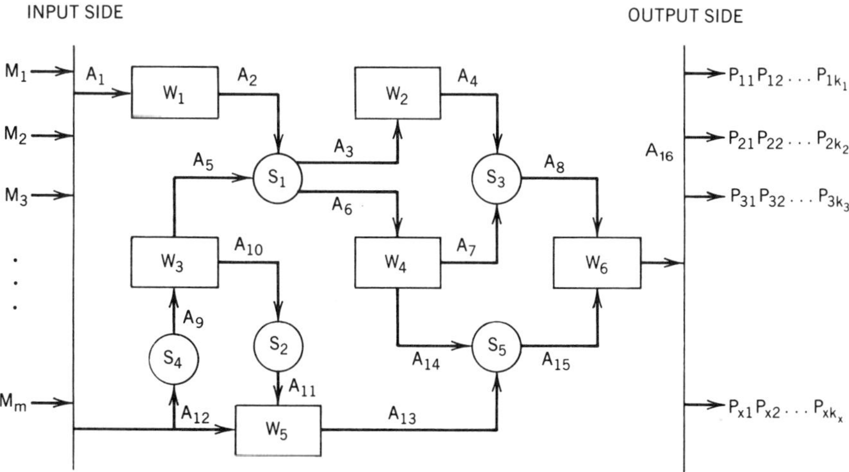

Figure 7.5 A level-one process work flow diagram.

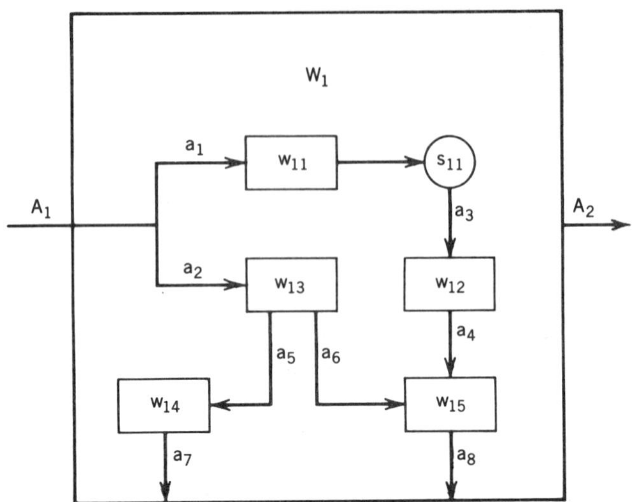

Figure 7.6 A level-two flow diagram of work station W_1.

of k_1 product units of type 1; $P_{21}, P_{22}, \ldots, P_{2k_2}$ are the product population of k_2 units of type 2; and so on.

In the same figure, the input and output at each stage of the process should be defined in terms of product unit and product unit defectiveness so that the quality of work at each stage can be assessed by the statistical quality control tool.

The level-one work flow diagram can be decomposed into a number of level-two diagrams for a more detailed analysis. Figure 7.6 shows a level-two work flow diagram for the stage of processing identified as W_1 in Figure 7.5. This decomposition can be continued to as deep a level of work flow diagrams as desired. The result is a thorough process description of even a very complex process.

B. Rules for Using Inputs. As discussed in Section 7.2.1*C*(iii), the developer must identify the rules that govern the construction of inputs to the piece of software. In modeling the existing or conceptual process being automated, the developer must identify the rules that govern input operations. These rules will define data organization for input, volume of input per unit of time, speed of input operations, inspection of incoming data, processing of missing data, constraints on processing incoming data, overflow handling and temporary storage of incoming data, how to proceed with processing where poor quality data are received, and so on. The user must identify and document all such rules for the entire process, that is, for the input side as shown in Figure 7.5, and for each stage of the process, as shown in Figure 7.6. These rules provide another important basis for the software design.

C. Methods of Producing Outputs. As part of the process description, the best method for generating the desired outputs should be selected. As in a factory, there are many available methods for solving a given problem. For example, to find the roots of equations of one variable, the software designer could select the bisection method, Newton's algorithm, the secant method, fixed-point iteration, the modified Regula-Falsi, the Steffensen iteration method, or others. The most thorough approach in software development, too, is to study as many methods as possible, then narrow the choices to a few promising ones to be studied in detail.

D. Data Flows in a Process Being Automated. Data flows in a process being automated are analogous to the flows of materials between work stations in a factory, and should not be confused with control flows (see Section 7.2.2***E***). Data flows refer to the relay of data output from one stage of the process to be input to another stage of the process, whereas control flows refer to the control of the operations that transform input into output within each stage of the process. For example, in Figure 7.5, the arcs $A_1, A_2, \ldots, A_{16}$ are data flow segments; the control flows are shown within each stage of the process.

The data flows in a work flow diagram may be defined in terms of who generates what; when to relay generated data from one stage to another; how the relay of the data is to take place, for example, real-time, near real-time, or nonreal-time; timing considerations; speed and volume of data transmission; and so on. The data flows defined here are an important part of the modeling that should precede the design tasks.

E. Process Control. In a factory, process control refers to the control of operations that transform materials at a work station. In a piece of software, process control refers to the control of operations that transform input into output at a stage of the process. Since the operations performed on the input must vary under different conditions (reflected in the design by IFTHENELSE and other similar types of statements), process control means defining when to do what. Process control is sometimes referred to as control flows, that is, the flow of control of input-output transformations within a stage of the process from one operation to another as conditions vary. For example, in Figure 7.6, the arcs $a_1, a_2, \ldots, a_8$ represent control flow segments.

The modeling of control flows must include identification of the following:

All operations performed at the stage of the process

All conditions under which the operations are performed

All logical sequences of operations and conditions, and timing of the operations

All constraints on the operations

F. Software Characteristics. The characteristics of a piece of software analogous to those necessary to design and build a factory can include the output data generation capacity, speed, memory size, data storage capacity, data flows, and the like. As in manufacturing, these characteristics impact on the design of the process and should be well-planned before the software is designed and implemented. The following are some of the major factors that must be considered in planning software characteristics:

(i) ACCURACY. As a general rule, a piece of software should be able to produce accurate output to fulfill its intended purpose. However, accuracy is probably the most difficult factor to control in terms of software characteristics, since the accuracy of the software product depends on the type of application. Accuracy can be fairly easy to achieve in business applications such as data base processing, but extremely difficult to control in scientific applications such as inversion of large matrices, especially ill-conditioned ones. Furthermore, accuracy may not be significant in some applications such as simulation and business trend forecasts, and is actually irrelevant in applications such as random number generation, where the randomness, not the accuracy, of the numbers determines the usability of the output. In addition, accuracy may be difficult or costly to achieve.

(ii) USABILITY. Usability refers to the software product, that is, the output. As discussed earlier in Section 1.4, this is the user's prime concern. If the output is not usable for the user's application, the software may be scrapped. Usability is difficult to address in terms of software characteristics. The developer should, however, be aware of this ultimate criterion of software acceptability from the start of the software development process and address it in the modeling, requirements specification, and software design phases. The more the developer understands that the software is no good if it does not meet the needs of its intended users, the more likely he or she will produce usable software.

The reader should note that there are many other quality factors, such as readability and complexity, being proposed in the literature. These factors are secondary in nature. If a piece of software is not useable, then all of the other factors would serve no purpose at all. Therefore these factors are not addressed in this book.

(iii) PORTABILITY. The software should be portable between people and between computers. Portability betwen people is associated with understandability and related factors such as conciseness, structuredness, self-descriptiveness, legibility, and consistency. Portability between computers is associated with factors such as computer independence and self-containedness.

(iv) RELIABILITY. A reliable piece of software performs its intended functions satisfactorily, that is, produces reliably usuable output (see Chapters 8 and 14). Some of the software modeling factors that contribute to reliability are usability, accuracy, completeness, robustness, consistency, and self-containedness.

(v) COMPUTER INDEPENDENCE. The software should be able to execute on different computers with minimum effort. This implies the use of standard languages such as ANSI COBOL, Ada®, or FORTRAN.

(vi) ROBUSTNESS. The software should be able to continue execution under certain imperfect conditions, such as when input data are out of order or in a different format. For example, a data set may be improperly prepared in an input stream. The software should not stop running when the error is encountered. Instead, it should generate an error message and continue to read and execute the next data set.

(vii) CONSISTENCY. Notation, terminology, or symbology used should be consistent. The sequence of code should correspond to its design, which in turn should correspond to its requirements. For exam-

®Ada is a registered trademark of the U.S. Government (Ada Joint Program Office).

ple, a uniform style of program indentation should be used throughout the code, and variable names should be given in an orderly manner.

(viii) MODIFIABILITY. Enhancement of the software functions should be easy to implement. Modifiability means accommodation of changes to existing functions, for example, alteration of convergent criteria for more accurate results in finding the roots of a polynomial. Modifiability should not be confused with augmentability, which is accommodation of expansion in size such as more data storage or additional functions.

(ix) MAINTAINABILITY. The software should be easy to maintain, and changes for improving operational efficiency should be easy to accommodate. Failed operations should be easy to restore to satisfactory conditions.

(x) LEGIBILITY. The functions of the software should be easy to understand by reading the code. For example, a complex expression should be properly split by parentheses; a lengthy instruction should be continued by breaking it at a proper point. Instructions such as:

```
SUM = (METHOD - SQUARE)/(E**M*TO
TAL + 2.0)
```

are confusing and should be coded more legibly:

```
SUM = (METHOD - SQUARE)/
(E**M*TOTAL + 2.0)
```

(xi) HUMAN ENGINEERING. The software should serve its intended purpose with minimum user effort. For example, instructions should be sequentially numbered; diagnostic messages should be self-explanatory; module interfaces should be simple and data flows easy to trace; documents should be easy to understand and contain no errors. Human engineering is associated with other factors such as understandability, accessibility, robustness, and communicativeness.

(xii) TESTABILITY. Software accuracy, usability, and performance should be easy to test and measure. Useful messages should be provided for testing and debugging purposes.

(xiii) COMPLETENESS. All components of the software should be fully designed, coded, and tested. All external references must be available.

(xiv) COMMUNICATIVENESS. Man-machine interfaces should be simple and easy to understand. Contents and formats of input and output data should be self-explanatory.

(xv) UNDERSTANDABILITY. The software should be easy to understand. Variable names should be meaningful; redundant data names and data removed from the code; comments brief and to the point; program control constructs simple; instructions easy to follow; module interfaces and data flow among modules easy to trace; references provided. To ensure software understandability requires the developer to prepare at least eight documents:

Modeling
Requirements specification
Software design
Test design
Software implementation (code)
Test implementation (test inputs)
Test and integration
Software acceptance

These documents must be prepared at each of the appropriate quality programming stages: modeling, requirements specification, concurrent software design and test design, concurrent implementation of software design and test design, test and integration, and acceptance (see Figure 1.10).

(xvi) EFFICIENCY. The software should be able to accomplish its functions with minimum resources. An efficient piece of software should possess the following characteristics:

A. **Accountability.** Its performance should be measurable so that statistical data can be gathered for analysis and improvement.
B. **Device Efficiency.** It should not use any hardware component or peripheral equipment unnecessarily. Input and output operations should be reduced to an absolute minimum.

C. **Computing Efficiency.** It should be developed so that redundant computation is not present. For example, if the instruction N = I * (2 * * 10 − 1) is executed many times, it should be coded as N = I * 1023.

D. **Accessibility.** The software should be easy to use and access. For example, a loop should not be controlled by a constant.

(xvii) AUGMENTABILITY. The software should be developed in such a manner that enhancement of computing functions and addition of data storage capacity is easy to accommodate. For example, the flying variable phenomenon, as described in Chapter 9, should be avoided.

(xviii) STRUCTUREDNESS. The software should possess an effective organization of code. The standard constructs of SEQUENCE, IFTHENELSE, DOWHILE, DOUNTIL, and CASE should be closely followed.

(xix) SELF-DESCRIPTIVENESS. The software should provide within itself sufficient information concerning its purpose, assumptions, constraints, input and output descriptions, revision status, and references for a reader to determine its usability for his or her applications.

(xx) SELF-CONTAINEDNESS. The software should be a complete entity, containing within itself all of its functions, whether implicit or explicit. It should be able to perform its functions without requiring foreign functions or modules. For example, input error detection and data intialization should be incorporated into the piece of software.

(xxi) CONCISENESS. The software should be brief and to the point. Excessive instructions, data, and comments should not appear in the code. Unnecessary modularization creates module interfacing complexity and should be avoided. Repetition of the same sequence of instructions results in unnecessarily lengthy code and obscures the readability of the code.

G. Methods of Developing the Software System. As there are many way of building a factory, there are many ways to approach software development. Questions such as the following should be considered:

A. Should the software be developed from scratch?
B. Are there software packages available that should be used?
C. Should a software model be developed first?

Answers to these types of questions early in the software development process will facilitate the later stages of software design.

7.3 CURRENT SITUATION IN THE SOFTWARE INDUSTRY

It is fitting to end this chapter with a discussion of the current situation in the software industry regarding software modeling. First, current practices, some of which have been mentioned throughout this chapter, will be briefly considered. Then, some of the resources that the software industry needs to develop will be examined.

7.3.1 Current Practices

In observing current software development practices, one cannot help but notice that the modeling tasks discussed in this chapter are often not sufficiently addressed by software developers, and rarely are they performed in a clearly organized modeling phase. Most conspicuously absent are the major tasks of input description, and definition of product unit and product unit defectiveness. Without these three tasks, statistical quality control techniques cannot be applied, and many of the problems regarding testing and acceptance of the software result. It is not uncommon to find developers conducting feasibility studies, preparing preliminary design documents, estimating project budgets and schedules, and sometimes even proceeding with design and coding—without fully knowing the nature or extent of the data the software must handle (input description), the user's detailed output requirements (product unit definition), or the level of performance the user will demand as a criterion of acceptability (product unit defectiveness definition).

As pointed out in this chapter, a major flaw in the current modeling approaches used in the industry is the confusion of the software product, that is, the output, with the software itself. This is one reason why crucial modeling tasks such as product unit definition are so often missing in all of the methodologies based on the so-called structured-software-development technology (e.g., structured programming, proof of program correctness, structured design) and on the emerging object-oriented design approaches. Granted that a piece of software must be correct. But ensuring the correctness of the software is at most solving only 50 percent of the problem. The other 50 percent is to ensure that the software is able to produce usable output for its intended users.

The inadequacy of much of the currently produced documentation to serve as effective communication tools between designer, developer, marketing personnel, and users is a common complaint in the software industry. Frequently, the available documentation does not perform the functions of a product description and process description, as in the manufacturing industries. Developers of standardized software packages sometimes attempt to supplement their documentation by offering telephone information services for users and other developers incorporating the software into new designs for new applications. Thus, many developers have a "hot-line" that others can call to ask questions about the features of the software, its capabilities, revision levels, and modifiability for interfacing with other software. With custom software, however, such an option is not generally available. On a large project, programmers move around, and the software becomes a patchwork with few of the desirable software characteristics described in Section 7.2.2***F***. A newly assigned programmer has to guess what his or her predecessors were trying to do, with regard not only to the design approach, but to the modeling tasks as well. In other words, the new programmer may not be sure, and may have no way to find out, precisely what functions the software is intended to perform or what the user's detailed performance requirements are. In current practice at its worst, such requirements may be documented but simply ignored during the stress of trying to design, implement, and test the software on a tight schedule.

Another feature of the current situation is a lack of attention to finding solutions to the 20 problems stated in Figure 1.3. In the six years since these problems were identified in the literature, the only published articles proposing solutions that offer a viable alternative to current practices have been those of the author Cho [5, 17, 18, 19]. One may ask why. Do developers not want users to know the existing problems? Do developers not want to offer software warranties? Do developers not have solutions to these problems, or do they have proprietary solutions they are not willing to publish? Whatever the reason, traditional software methodologies continue to be practiced despite their "inability" to solve any of the 20 problems.

The issue of software warranty remains to be addressed by developers and users. The drive for change may come from the users, once they realize that statistical quality control is an available technology for offering a meaningful software warranty. In current practice, users may try a number of unsatisfactory approaches to ensure quality, for example, specifying that the developer follow a certain design approach thought to guarantee quality output, conduct frequent design reviews with user personnel present, and submit the software in the so-called thorough inspection during acceptance testing. Much of the current confusion could be eliminated if the selection of a software methodology were based on one fundamental question: Can the methodology enable the developer to offer the user a meaningful software warranty?

7.3.2 What Is Missing from the Current Software Industry

In the manufacturing industries, building a factory and designing, manufacturing, and marketing a product require a combination of expertise in diverse areas of engineering, architecture, operations research, management science, human engineering, economics, and statistical quality control. The same is true of a piece of software, but software designers frequently do not have access to such resources during the modeling phase. Input descriptions, product unit definition, and product unit defectiveness definition are not programming tasks: They are modeling tasks that require knowledge of systems, applications, users' needs, constraints, and so forth beyond the programmer's expertise. Yet in current practice, modeling a piece of software is often the programmer's responsibility. To change the current situation, the broader expertise required for proper modeling and understanding of the user's requirements must be made available.

Another resource needed in the software industry is knowledge of statistical quality control. Expertise in applying statistical quality control techniques to produce quality, cost-effective products can be found in the manufacturing industries, where they have been in use for 50 years. However, few professionals in the software industry have manufacturing backgrounds, and few are familiar with statistical quality control. Without such a background, it is doubtful that one can offer a software warranty intelligently.

As indicated in Thayer, Pyster, and Wood [16], many software projects are plagued with poor quality, cost overruns, late delivery, and dissatisfied users. Inadequate attention to the modeling tasks discussed in this chapter has contributed a significant share to these problems.

Now is the time for users to decide whether to continue to be victims of software malpractices. Proper software modeling is a first step toward demanding meaningful software warranty.

REFERENCES

1. B. W. Niebel and A. B. Draper, *Product Design and Process Engineering*, McGraw-Hill, New York, 1974.
2. H. W. Yankee, *Manufacturing Processes*, Prentice-Hall, Englewood Cliffs, New Jersey, 1979.
3. M. L. Begeman and B. H. Amstead, *Manufacturing Processes*, 6th ed., Wiley, New York, 1969.
4. S. E. Elmaghraby, *The Design of Production Systems*, Reinhold, New York, 1966.
5. C. K. Cho, *An Introduction to Software Quality Control*, Wiley, New York, 1980.
6. M. L. Shooman, *Software Engineering*, McGraw-Hill, New York, 1983.
7. G. J. Myers, *Software Reliability Principles and Practices*, Wiley-Interscience, New York, 1976.
8. R. T. Yeh, *Current Trends in Programming Methodology, Vol. I: Software Specification and Design*, Prentice-Hall, Englewood Cliffs, New Jersey, 1977.
9. R. T. Yeh, *Current Trends in Programming Methodology, Vol. II: Program Validation*, Prentice-Hall, Englewood Cliffs, New Jersey, 1977.
10. R. W. Jensen and C. C. Tonies, *Software Engineering*, Prentice-Hall, Englewood Cliffs, New Jersey, 1979.
11. R. C. Tausworthe, *Standardized Development of Computer Software*, Prentice-Hall, Englewood Cliffs, New Jersey, 1977.
12. R. C. Tausworthe, *Standardized Development of Computer Software Part II Standards*, Prentice-Hall, Englewood Cliffs, New Jersey, 1977.
13. E. Yourdon, *Techniques of Program Structure and Design*, Prentice-Hall, Englewood Cliffs, New Jersey, 1975.
14. J. M. Buxton, P. Naur, and B. Randell, *Software Engineering Concepts and Techniques*, Petrocelli/Charter, New York, 1976.
15. O. J. Dahl, E. W. Dijkstra, and C. A. R. Hoare, *Structured Programming*, Academic, New York, 1972.
16. R. H. Thayer, A. Pyster, and R. C. Wood, "The Challenge of Software Engineering Project Management," *IEEE Computer*. Vol. 13, No. 8, pp. 51–59.
17. C. K. Cho, *Software Engineering and Quality Assurance—A Statistical Approach*, Continuing Engineering Education Course No. 705 Handouts, George Washington University, June 1986.
18. C. K. Cho, "Statistical Methods Applied to Software Quality Control," in G. Gordon Schulmeyer, and J. MacManus (Eds.), *Handbook of Software Quality Assurance*, Van Nostrand Reinhold, New York, 1987.

19. C. K. Cho, "Software Engineering with Statistical Quality Control," *Proceedings, METS '86*, Chinese Institute of Engineers-USA, Taipei, Taiwan, Nov. 17–29, 1986.

20. C. R. Vick and C. V. Ramamoorthy, *Handbook of Software Engineering*, Van Nostrand Reinhold, New York, 1984.

21. G. Booch, *Software Engineering with Ada*, Benjamin/Cummings, Menlo Park, California, 1983.

22. M. L. Begeman, B. H. Amstead, *Manufacturing Processes, 6th Ed.*, Wiley, New York, 1969.

CHAPTER 8

Requirements Specification

Requirements specification is the number one current problem in the software industry (see Figure 1.3). The reasons for this are examined in this chapter from the perspective of using statistical quality control in a manufacturing factory. It is pointed out that up to 50 percent of the requirements for software development never get addressed in a proper manner in the industry. Specifically, in current practice, test requirements are missing from the requirements specification.

The result of the requirements specification phase of software development must be a requirements specification document that can be used to communicate to the software developer, designer, test designer, user, and all other concerned parties. As a start, the structure of this chapter can serve as a framework for the requirements specification document. Each section in this chapter can be a section in the document. In the following discussions, each item that should be included in the requirements specification is identified, the type of information that should be addressed for each item is explained, and the source of this information is indicated. References are given to other chapters of this book where this information is discussed in greater depth. For example, product unit definition is discussed in Chapter 7; in this chapter, it is shown where to include this definition in a requirements specification.

Requirements specification should be a step-by-step procedure, documented in four parts to cover all necessary requirements:

Software engineering (development) requirements
Software requirements
Test requirements
Documentation requirements

8.1 SOFTWARE ENGINEERING (DEVELOPMENT) REQUIREMENTS

Software engineering, as discussed throughout this book, means applying the goals and principles of engineering and manufacturing disciplines to software development. In requirements specification, it is important to identify the general goals and principles to be followed. Some of the techniques available to the software designer to achieve these goals and follow these principles are discussed in Chapters 9 through 12.

The specification of software engineering requirements is discussed below under two broad headings: software engineering goals and software engineering principles.

8.1.1 Software Engineering Goals

The following are generally recognized in the industry as the goals of software engineering:

Modifiability
Understandability
Reliability
Efficiency

A. Modifiability

The requirements specification document should include a requirement that the proposed software be structured to support later expected modifications resulting from changes to the performance requirements, desired output, or correction of errors. Techniques or programming approaches that minimize the impact of modifications on the complexity of the system and on the engineering effort required to implement the modifications can be specified by the user or the software developer, as appropriate.

B. Understandability

To be understandable, a piece of software must have a design structure in which the way the software relates to the real-world problems it is intended to solve, and the way the software generates the desired output are clear. Understandability should be required at all levels of software development, from a readable coding style, to data structures and algorithms that are easy to isolate within the design. Understandability is essential to achieve the other software engineering goals.

The documents produced at each stage of software development (see Figure 1.10) and discussed in detail in Chapters 7 through 12 are essential to develop software with understandability.

C. Reliability

The requirements specification document should require reliability to be built into the design of the software from the start and to be a feature of every phase of the design. Reliability features such as failure prevention and recovery, failure modes, and graceful degradation should be considered early in the design effort, and it should be specified that the design must indicate how it will assure reliable performance of the software. Techniques to achieve reliability are discussed throughout this book.

D. Efficiency

Efficient use of time and memory should be required, with emphasis on those aspects of the output that are most crucial to the user's purposes. In real-time systems, for example, the time resources necessary for program execution to support the required system response rates will be a major concern. Where the selected hardware has size constraints or power limitations, space resources must be used with maximum efficiency, and trade-offs between time and space resources must be studied.

Methods for achieving efficiency in software design can be specified, based on hardware and algorithm selections that seem appropriate. However, it may be a good practice to allow the software developer some latitude to discover the best means to this end, based on a unified understanding of the problem and desired results. Using the most appropriate overall software design and program structure is the best approach to achieving system efficiency.

8.1.2 Software Engineering Principles

To achieve the software engineering goals of modifiability, understandability, reliability, and efficiency requires a disciplined development approach to software design. The requirements specification document, therefore, should require that the software be developed by applying the following software engineering principles:

Abstract data typing
Information hiding
Modularization
Localization
Uniformity
Completeness
Confirmability
Statistical quality control [Cho's proposal (14)]

A. *Abstract Data Typing*

Abstract data typing is a fundamental tool for managing the complexity of a piece of software. For each part of the software, there will be an appropriate level of abstraction to best implement the purposes of that program. For example, in a piece of software that must interact with a disk drive, the abstract data types for a data base management system may be those appropriate to manipulate a set of logical files, whereas the abstract data types for a device driver may be those appropriate to access an addressable block of words. Using the appropriate abstract data types for each function of parts of the software makes the system more understandable and helps ensure that it is structured efficiently.

The requirements specification document should include these kinds of requirements, such as the need for programs to interact with a disk drive, so that abstract data types can be identified and this tool used to its full advantage.

B. *Information Hiding*

The second principle of software engineering to be considered in the requirements specification is information hiding. Following this principle requires that design details not appropriate to a part of the software system be made inaccessible to the programmer or user interfacing with that program element. For example, within a program part for a data base management system, information relating to the physical details of the disk drive should be hidden and inaccessible.

Information hiding is an important tool for achieving modifiability, because it supports independent programming of higher-level and lower-level designs. In the preceding example, suppressing lower level details encourages the designer to make the interface of the data base management system with the disk drive independent of the physical organization of files on the disk. Changing disk drives to provide more storage capacity can then be accomplished without affecting the logical file structure.

The requirements specification document should address information hiding as it is to be used in identifying higher-level and lower-level design decisions, so that this tool can be used in developing the software.

C. *Modularization*

Modularization refers to a design strategy with the following characteristics:

- **A.** The software consists of hierarchical levels of modules, with each module composed of lower-level modules, developed either by a top-down decomposition or a bottom-up assembly of modules.
- **B.** Each module is a functionally and logically dependent unit of closely related internal elements.
- **C.** The modules at each level are relatively independent of each other, so that the module interfaces are kept as simple as possible.

The requirements specification document should require modularization in development of the software design to ensure the modifiability, reliability, understandability, and efficiency of the software. The specification should require that functions be programmed separately at each level of the modular design.

D. *Localization*

Localization refers to the placement of logically related computational resources in the same physical module. This results in well-structured modules relatively independent of each other. Like modularization, this approach can limit the effects of a modification to a small number of modules. As part of requirements specification, the designer should identify those resources to which the principle of localization should be applied.

E. *Uniformity*

Uniformity means applying a consistent notation, control structure, and calling sequence for operations in coding the modules. At any given level in the design, logically similar objects and operations are represented similarly. Uniformity is an important aid in achieving understandability and should be required in the requirements specification document. Any type of conventions or standards for coding the modules preferred by the user or software developer should be identified.

F. Completeness

Completeness of the software design means that all important functions and elements are included so that the modules developed are necessary and sufficient. To achieve completeness, programming language capabilities, however powerful, are not enough. Software management tools must be applied. Following the step-by-step procedure presented in this book for requirements specification can be an important aid in ensuring that the software design is complete.

G. Confirmability

The principle of confirmability refers to the ease with which the software design can be decomposed into elements that can be readily tested. As discussed in detail in Section 8.3, a major step toward achieving confirmability is the inclusion of test requirements—both system test requirements and module test requirements—as an essential part of requirements specification.

H. Statistical Quality Control

The user should require that the software be developed applying not only the software engineering goals and principles discussed previously, but also the principle of statistical quality control. Specifically, the user should require that the developer present statistical evidence that quality is built into the software. This should be in the form of a meaningful software warranty.

The materials presented in this book provide the minimum requirements for specifying the type of software warranty desired. As discussed in Chapter 7, in the manufacturing industries statistical quality control is integral to a total quality assurance approach. This means inclusion of the tasks of product design, raw materials identification, quality standards on raw materials and finished products, inspection of incoming raw materials, inspection of intermediate products at each step of the manufacturing process, and statistical testing of finished goods. It should be the same in the software industry. Quality should be built in by attention to the tasks of product design, input identification, quality standards for input and output data, inspection of incoming input data, inspection of module output, and statistical testing of output.

8.2 SOFTWARE REQUIREMENTS

After identifying the software engineering goals and principles which should guide development of the software, the next major requirements specification activity should be to specify the detailed input, output, and processing requirements for design of the software. As discussed in Chapter 7, this activity should be performed with the same thoroughness used in the manufacturing industries to develop requirements for raw materials, industrial processing, and product design, taking into account real-world constraints.

This phase of requirements specification should be an iterative refinement of definitions, constraints, resources, and formats until all requirements are identified and the requirements specification document is finalized. As in the manufacturing industries, the development of requirements is a process of optimization, resulting in the most efficient, cost-effective design of the products, that is, the output; and the best design and use of factory facilities, that is, the software.

8.2.1 Input Requirements

Quality–in–quality–out should be the ideal of software development. Therefore, the requirements for input data quality must be established. The detailed efforts of the manufacturing industries to ensure quality of raw materials should be emulated. During requirements specification, the types of input data and the rules for using input data should be specified and refined, taking into consideration organizational environment and the availability of technology and resources.

Once identified, the input requirements can be represented in a convenient form called the symbolic input attribute decomposition (SIAD) tree for software design and test design. The SIAD tree is a way to achieve clarity, conciseness, completeness, and measurability in the specification of input requirements. The types of SIAD trees—regular, weighted, ruled, and "network"—and their uses are described in Section 8.2.1*G*.

A. Types of Input Data

The types of inputs, as discussed in Section 7.2.1*C*(i), should be identified. The sources of each type of input data, as discussed in Section

7.2.1*C*(iv), should be identified and applied here. These requirements, addressed in the modeling document produced in the modeling phase of software development, should be refined during requirements specification.

B. Characteristic of Each Type of Input Data

An analysis of the characteristics of each type of input data should be performed, as described in Section 7.2.1*C*(ii), and refined here, taking into account real-world constraints and limitations. Constraints refer to consideration of the availability of appropriate technology; limitations refer to the availability of resources. For example, it may be too costly to require that the square root of a number used as input be accurate to the 100th decimal place. The cost would come from the need to develop a special piece of software. In addition, probably no hardware is available for this purpose. Even though the technology is available, it may take too long to compute the result. Therefore, realistic constraints on the quality characteristics of input data must be carefully studied and established during requirements specification.

C. Rules for Using Input Data

The rules governing the use of the input data should be defined as described in Section 7.2.1*C*(iii) and recorded in this section of the requirements specification document.

D. Critical and Noncritical Parameters

Key parameters in the software development effort, as determined by management and the user, should be prioritized. Then the types of inputs and their characteristics, rules, and sources should be analyzed with respect to these parameters. If low cost, for example, is given priority over other factors, then the designer must be aware that the decision between two otherwise equivalent input data sources should be determined by cost.

E. Data Base Requirements

As part of the analysis of inputs, at this stage, any special requirements of the user of the proposed software that affect the sources of input data or the characteristics of the data should be identified. For example, the user may require that the software interface with an existing system, restricting the designer in the definition of input data characteristics to already established formats. Communicating with the user to ensure that all special requirements are known and understood is a crucial part of requirements specification that can save a project from expected design changes in later phases of development.

F. Input Domain

The term "input" is defined by *Webster's New World Dictionary* as:

> What is put in, as electric current or other power put into a machine.

The term "domain" is defined as:

> (3) field of sphere of activity or influence: as, the domain of science.

In the context of this book, the term "input domain" is defined as:

> The field of knowledge from which inputs into software are generated.

Conventionally, software input domain has never been properly included in software requirements specification. This is a major area of the requirements problem (see Figure 1.3). As a result of this missing ingredient, a developed piece of software still requires frequent maintenance—a costly activity in the computer industry.

Based on the definition previously discussed, software input domain comprises four components: types of input, characteristics of each type of input, rules for using the input, and constraints on using the input. In specifying the input domain requirements, the first three of these components should be refined from the results of the modeling phase, as discussed in Sections 7.2.1*C*(i) to 7.2.1*C*(iii). The fourth component is generated by taking into consideration factors such as the availability of the first three components, current technology availability, the environment in which the software is to be used, and development cost and schedule.

G. SIAD Tree

One of the major problems in software development (see Figure 1.3) is ambiguity in requirements specification, particularly specification of input domain. One way of providing a clear definition of these requirements is to use an input domain vehicle called the SIAD tree. The term SIAD tree is defined in Cho [14] as:

> A tree element, representing the input domain of a software entity, arranged in a linear list with the structure preserved by a set of tree symbols for random sampling.

To handle the different types of software applications, it is useful to have a number of different types of SIAD trees. Four types of SIAD trees have been developed by this author so far: regular, weighted, ruled, and "network".

(i) REGULAR SIAD TREE. Figure 8.1 shows an example tree structure. The symbols $A, B, \ldots, U$ are called the tree elements. The symbols E, F, G, H, I, and J are called the basic elements. The tree is arranged in a SIAD tree as shown in Figure 8.2. A tree symbol in Figure 8.2 shows the relationship of an element to other elements. For example, the symbol X1, 2, 2 indicates that element H is subordinate to element C (whose symbol is X1, 2), which, in turn, is subordinate to element A (whose symbol is X1). A tree so arranged is a regular SIAD tree, as each element is indexed by a tree number in the index column.

a. Usage of an SIAD Tree. An SIAD tree can be used as a tool for describing the input domain of a piece of software and as a basis for construction of test input units using random sampling, which makes it possible to apply the principle of statistical quality control. The construction of test input units using an SIAD tree can be accomplished as follows.

Let N be the number of elements in the SIAD tree. Each element in the tree is indexed by a number ranging from 1 to N. A random number between 1 and N is produced using a generator such as the one shown in

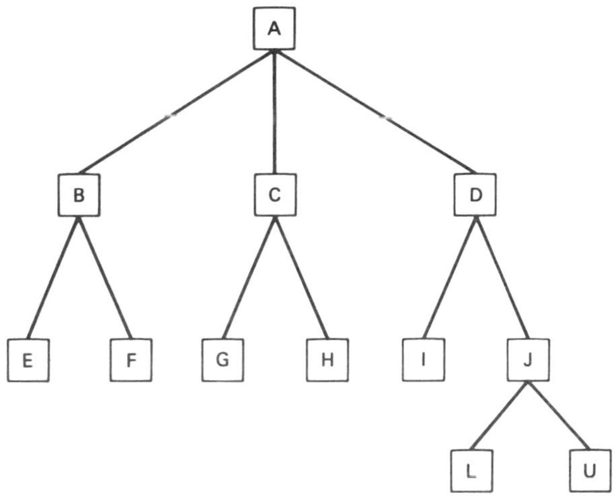

Figure 8.1 A tree structure.

Index	Tree Symbol	Tree Element
1	X1	A
2	X1, 1	*B*
3	X1, 1, 1	*E*
4	X1, 1, 2	*F*
5	X1, 2	*C*
6	X1, 2, 1	*G*
7	X1, 2, 2	*H*
8	X1, 3	*D*
9	X1, 3, 1	*I*
10	X1, 3, 2	*J* (numerical)
11	X1, 3, 2, 1	*L* (lower bound)
12	X1, 3, 2, 2	*U* (upper bound)

Figure 8.2 A regular SIAD tree of Figure 8.1.

Figure 4.1. The element with its index equal to the random number is selected. A total of K elements will be randomly sampled from the tree for designing a test input unit. For example, there are 12 elements in the SIAD tree in Figure 8.2. Three elements are to be taken from the tree using the random numbers 9, 5, and 12. The elements I, C, and U are drawn for constructing the test input unit. However, it is difficult to understand the meaning of the elements without referring to the original SIAD tree. This referencing can be tedious. Thus it is desirable to associate the meaning with the sampled element. This can be done by listing with an element all other relevant elements by way of tree symbols. In the preceding example, the relevant elements can be listed with each sampled element as follows:

Index	Tree Symbol	Tree Element	Remarks
1	X1	*A*	Descriptive element
5	X1, 2	*C*	Sampled element
1	X1	*A*	Descriptive element
8	X1, 3	*D*	Descriptive element
9	X1, 3, 1	*I*	Sampled element
1	X1	*A*	Descriptive element
8	X1, 3	*D*	Descriptive element
10	X1, 3, 2	*J*	Descriptive element
12	X1, 3, 2, 2	*U*	Sampled element

The relevant element of C is the element A, to which C is subordinate. The relationship between A and C can be seen by looking at the tree symbols $X1$ and X1, 2. It is clear that C is the second subordinated element of A, as shown in Figure 8.1. The element A is listed with C as a descriptive element. Similarly, the sampled element I is listed with two descriptive elements, A and D. The sampled element U is listed with three descriptive elements, A, D, and J.

This listing gives a meaningful description of each sampled element for guiding test input unit design. The following sections present FORTRAN and COBOL examples illustrating test input unit design using an SIAD tree:

b. FORTRAN SIAD Tree. A FORTRAN SIAD tree is shown in appendix 2 of Cho [12]. It is constructed using the ANSI FORTRAN [1] and the IBM 360/370 FORTRAN [2]. Although the tree covers most of the FORTRAN features, it is given as a working example for this book and should not be considered as complete. A detailed discussion of the tree is given in chapter 13 of Cho [12]. The construction and usage of the tree for test input design is introduced with the input attribute of READ statements in this section.

Every programming language must have an input and output mechanism, called the INPUT/OUTPUT attribute. The INPUT attribute is implemented in FORTRAN by a READ statement with the following syntax:

READ(INPUT LOGICAL NUMBER, FORMAT SPECIFICATION) INPUT LIST

For example, READ (5, 1) A is valid in FORTRAN. The READ statement can be decomposed into the elements: READ, INPUT LOGICAL NUMBER, FORMAT SPECIFICATION, and INPUT LIST. The last three elements may be considered as subordinate to the READ element. Assigning tree symbols to the elements gives the following:

Tree Symbol	Tree Element
X1	INPUT/OUTPUT
X1, 1	READ
X1, 1, 1	INPUT LOGICAL NUMBER
X1, 1, 2	FORMAT SPECIFICATION
X1, 1, 3	INPUT LIST

The element INPUT LOGICAL NUMBER can be decomposed into the elements POSITIVE INTEGER NUMBER and INTEGER VARIABLE. For example, READ (5,1) INPUT LIST and READ (IN,1) INPUT LIST are valid.

The element FORMAT SPECIFICATION can be decomposed into the elements: for FORMATTED READ and for UNFORMATTED READ. For example, READ (5,1) INPUT LIST and READ (5) INPUT LIST are valid. The element FORMATTED READ can be decomposed into the elements STATEMENT NUMBER OF A FORMAT and INTEGER 1-DIMENSIONAL ARRAY STORING FORMAT SPECIFICATION. For example, READ (5,1) INPUT LIST and READ (5, FMT) INPUT LIST are valid, where FMT stores a FORMAT specification being read in during the execution of the program. The decomposition of the element UNFORMATTED READ is not needed since it requires no FORMAT specification.

The element INPUT LIST can be decomposed into the elements SINGLE VARIABLE and ARRAY. For example, READ (5,1) and READ (5,1) (A(I), I = 1,5) are valid. The element SINGLE VARIABLE can be decomposed into the elements REAL SINGLE VARIABLE and INTEGER SINGLE VARIABLE (some elements such as DOUBLE PRECISION VARIABLE are omitted in this discussion for simplicity). The element ARRAY can be decomposed into the elements ARRAY ELEMENT and WHOLE ARRAY. For example READ (5,1) B(5) and READ (5,1) (INP(I), I = 1, N)—or more simply, READ (5,1) INP—are valid.

The element ARRAY ELEMENT can be decomposed into the elements 1-DIMENSIONAL, 2-DIMENSIONAL, and 3-DIMENSIONAL ARRAY ELEMENTS. For example, READ (5,1) B(5), READ (5,1) P(1,2), and READ (5,1) W(1,2,3) are valid. Under each ARRAY ELEMENT are two elements: POSITIVE NUMBER SUBSCRIPT and INTEGER SINGLE VARIABLE SUBSCRIPT. For example, READ (5,1) B(5) and READ (5,1) P(I, J) are valid. The element WHOLE ARRAY can be decomposed in a similar manner.

The results of these decompositions are then assigned proper indices and tree symbols, and listed as a SIAD tree in Figure 8.3. The use of this tree is demonstrated with the following example:

Let K, the total number of elements to be sampled for constructing a test input unit, equal 3. Three random numbers—45, 14, and 26—are generated for sampling. The descriptive and sampled elements are listed as follows:

Index	Tree Symbol	Tree Element
1	X1	INPUT/OUTPUT
2	X1, 1	READ
3	X1, 1, 1	INPUT LOGICAL NUMBER
4	X1, 1, 1, 1	POSITIVE INTEGER NUMBER
5	X1, 1, 1, 2	INTEGER VARIABLE
6	X1, 1, 2	FORMAT SPECIFICATION
7	X1, 1, 2, 1	FORMATTED READ
8	X1, 1, 2, 1, 1	STATEMENT NUMBER OF A FORMAT
9	X1, 1, 2, 1, 2	INTEGER 1-DIMENSIONAL ARRAY STORING A FORMAT SPECIFICATION
10	X1, 1 2, 2	UNFORMATTED READ
11	X1, 1, 3	INPUT LIST
12	X1, 1, 3, 1	SINGLE VARIABLE
13	X1, 1, 3, 1, 1	REAL SINGLE VARIABLE
14	X1, 1, 3, 1, 2	INTEGER SINGLE VARIABLE
15	X1, 1, 3, 2	ARRAY
16	X1, 1, 3, 2, 1	ARRAY ELEMENT
17	X1, 1, 3, 2, 1, 1	1-DIMENSIONAL ARRAY ELEMENT
18	X1, 1, 3, 2, 1, 1, 1	1-DIMENSIONAL REAL ARRAY ELEMENT
19	X1, 1, 3, 2, 1, 1, 1, 1	POSITIVE NUMBER SUBSCRIPT
20	X1, 1, 3, 2, 1, 1, 1, 2	INTEGER SINGLE VARIABLE SUBSCRIPT
21	X1, 1, 3, 2, 1, 1, 2	1-DIMENSIONAL INTEGER ARRAY ELEMENT
22	X1, 1, 3, 2, 1, 1, 2, 1	POSITIVE NUMBER SUBSCRIPT
23	X1, 1, 3, 2, 1, 1, 2, 2	INTEGER SINGLE VARIABLE SUBSCRIPT
24	X1, 1, 3, 2, 1, 2	2-DIMENSIONAL ARRAY ELEMENT
25	X1, 1, 3, 2, 1, 2, 1	2-DIMENSIONAL REAL ARRAY ELEMENT
26	X1, 1, 3, 2, 1, 2, 1, 1	POSITIVE NUMBER SUBSCRIPT
27	X1, 1, 3, 2, 1, 2, 1, 2	INTEGER SINGLE VARIABLE SUBSCRIPT
28	X1, 1, 3, 2, 1, 2, 2	2-DIMENSIONAL INTEGER ARRAY ELEMENT
29	X1, 1, 3, 2, 1, 2, 1, 1	POSITIVE NUMBER SUBSCRIPT
30	X1, 1, 3, 2, 1, 2, 2, 2	INTEGER SINGLE VARIABLE SUBSCRIPT
31	X1, 1, 3, 2, 1, 3	3-DIMENSIONAL ARRAY ELEMENT
32	X1, 1, 3, 2, 1, 3, 1	3-DIMENSIONAL REAL ARRAY ELEMENT
33	X1, 1, 3, 2, 1, 3, 1, 1	POSITIVE NUMBER SUBSCRIPT
34	X1, 1, 3, 2, 1, 3, 1, 2	INTEGER SINGLE VARIABLE SUBSCRIPT
35	X1, 1, 3, 2, 1, 3, 2	3-DIMENSIONAL INTEGER ARRAY ELEMENT
36	X1, 1, 3, 2, 1, 3, 2, 1	POSITIVE NUMBER SUBSCRIPT
37	X1, 1, 3, 2, 1, 3, 2, 2	INTEGER SINGLE VARIABLE SUBSCRIPT
38	X1, 1, 3, 2, 2	WHOLE ARRAY
39	X1, 1, 3, 2, 2, 1	1-DIMENSIONAL WHOLE ARRAY
40	X1, 1, 3, 2, 2, 1, 1	1-DIMENSIONAL REAL WHOLE ARRAY
41	X1, 1, 3, 2, 2, 1, 2	1-DIMENSIONAL INTEGER WHOLE ARRAY
42	X1, 1, 3, 2, 2, 2	2-DIMENSIONAL WHOLE ARRAY
43	X1, 1, 3, 2, 2, 2, 1	2-DIMENSIONAL REAL WHOLE ARRAY
44	X1, 1, 3, 2, 2, 2, 2	2-DIMENSIONAL INTEGER WHOLE ARRAY
45	X1, 1, 3, 2, 2, 3	3-DIMENSIONAL WHOLE ARRAY
46	X1, 1, 3, 2, 2, 3, 1	3-DIMENSIONAL REAL WHOLE ARRAY
47	X1, 1, 3, 2, 2, 3, 2	3-DIMENSIONAL INTEGER WHOLE ARRAY

Figure 8.3 A SIAD tree of the FORTRAN input attribute-READ statement.

1. Index Equals 45

Index	Tree Symbol	Tree Element	Remark
1	X1	INPUT/OUTPUT	Descriptive element
2	X1, 1	READ	Descriptive element
11	X1, 1, 3	INPUT LIST	Descriptive element
15	X1, 1, 3, 2	ARRAY	Descriptive element
38	X1, 1, 3, 2, 2	WHOLE ARRAY	Descriptive element
45	X1, 1, 3, 2, 2, 3	3-DIMENSIONAL WHOLE ARRAY	Sampled element

2. Index Equals 14

Index	Tree Symbol	Tree Element	Remark
1	X1	INPUT/OUTPUT	Descriptive element
2	X1, 1	READ	Descriptive element
11	X1, 1, 3	INPUT LIST	Descriptive element
12	X1, 1, 3, 1	SINGLE VARIABLE	Descriptive element
14	X1, 1, 3, 1, 2	INTEGER SINGLE VARIABLE	Sampled element

3. Index Equals 26

Index	Tree Symbol	Tree Element	Remark
1	X1	INPUT/OUTPUT	Descriptive element
2	X1, 1	READ	Descriptive element
11	X1, 1, 3	INPUT LIST	Descriptive element
15	X1, 1, 3, 2	ARRAY	Descriptive element
16	X1, 1, 3, 2, 1	ARRAY ELEMENT	Descriptive element
24	X1, 1, 3, 2, 1, 2	2-DIMENSIONAL ARRAY ELEMENT	Descriptive element
25	X1, 1, 3, 2, 1, 2, 1	2-DIMENSIONAL REAL ARRAY ELEMENT	Descriptive element
26	X1, 1, 3, 2, 1, 2, 1, 1	POSITIVE NUMBER SUBSCRIPT	Sampled element

A test input unit may be constructed using the three sampled elements as follows:

	A FORTRAN Compiler Test Program	SIAD Tree Index
	DIMENSION A(6, 5, 2), M(10, 10)	
	READ(5, 1) A	45
1	FORMAT (1X, 7F10.2)	
	READ (5, 2) N	14
2	FORMAT (1X, I10)	
	READ (5, 2) M (5, 5)	26
	WRITE (6, 1) A	
	WRITE (6, 2) N	
	WRITE (6, 2) M (5, 5)	
	STOP	
	END	

The three sampled elements—3-DIMENSIONAL WHOLE ARRAY, INTEGER SINGLE VARIABLE, and POSITIVE NUMBER SUBSCRIPT—are implemented in the three FORTRAN statements corresponding to the indexes 45, 14, and 26, respectively.

In order to conduct the test, the test program must be constructed in a form acceptable to the compiler. Thus some auxiliary statements such as DIMENSION, FORMAT, WRITE, STOP, and END are required. Otherwise, the compiler may not produce a compiled program such as in an assembly list. Some of the statements, such as all of the WRITE statements in the preceding test program, are supplied for convenience in producing output for examination. Strictly speaking, the correctness of the compiler in handling the test input unit should be examined by verifying the correctness of the assembly code it produces. However, such examination can be time-consuming and error-prone. It is better to compile and execute the program to generate output. In this latter approach, the assembler and loader are assumed to be correct.

A more detailed discussion of constructing test input units using this FORTRAN SIAD tree can be found in chapter 13 of Cho [12].

c. COBOL SIAD Tree. The input domain of a COBOL compiler can also be specified in an SIAD tree format. An input to the compiler is a COBOL program, which can be considered as constructed from a number of elements randomly sampled from the SIAD tree, following the syntax rules of the programming language.

A COBOL SIAD tree is shown in appendix 3 of Cho [12]. It is constructed using the ANSI COBOL [3] and the IBM 360/370 COBOL

[4]. Although the tree covers most of the COBOL features, it is given as a working example in this book and should not be considered complete. A detailed discussion of the tree is given in chapter 14 of Cho [12]. The construction and usage of the tree for test input unit design is introduced with the external program attribute of subroutine statements in this section.

The subroutine feature in COBOL is implemented by a subroutine definition and a calling statement. The syntax structure is:

```
CALL 'SUB' USING arguments.
```

and

```
IDENTIFICATION DIVISION.
PROGRAM-ID.SUB.
:
PROCEDURE DIVISION USING arguments.
:
EXIT PROGRAM.
```

The external subroutine statements can be decomposed into the elements SUBROUTINE DEFINITION and CALLING SUBROUTINE. Assigning arbitrary tree symbols to the elements gives:

Tree Symbol	Tree Element
X6, 3	EXTERNAL SUBROUTINE
X6, 3, 1	SUBROUTINE DEFINITION
X6, 3, 2	CALLING SUBROUTINE

The element SUBROUTINE DEFINITION can be decomposed into the elements SUBROUTINE NAME, USING, and DUMMY ARGUMENTS. The element DUMMY ARGUMENTS can be decomposed into the elements SINGLE ELEMENT and TABLE. The element SINGLE ELEMENT can be further decomposed into SINGLE VARIABLE (and others, such as GROUP OF VARIABLES, not listed for simplicity), which, in turn, can be decomposed into the elements SINGLE LITERAL VARIABLE, SINGLE NUMERIC VARIABLE, and SINGLE ALPHANUMERIC VARIABLE. The element TABLE can be decomposed into 1-DIMENSIONAL, 2-DIMENSIONAL, and 3-DIMENSIONAL TABLES. Each of these can be alphabetic, numeric, or alphanumeric.

The element CALLING SUBROUTINE can be decomposed into the elements CALLING SUBROUTINE, USING, and CALLING ARGUMENTS. The element CALLING ARGUMENTS can be decomposed into lower level elements in the same manner as DUMMY ARGUMENTS. The results of these decompositions with proper indexes and tree symbols are listed in the SIAD Tree in Figure 8.4. The use of this tree is illustrated by the following example.

Index	Tree Symbol	Tree Element
606	X6, 3	EXTERNAL SUBROUTINE
607	X6, 3, 1	SUBROUTINE DEFINITION
608	X6, 3, 1, 1	SUBROUTINE NAME
609	X6, 3, 1, 2	USING
610	X6, 3, 1, 3	DUMMY ARGUMENTS
611	X6, 3, 1, 3, 1	SINGLE ELEMENT
612	X6, 3, 1, 3, 1, 1	SINGLE VARIABLE
613	X6, 3, 1, 3, 1, 1, 1	SINGLE LITERAL VARIABLE
614	X6, 3, 1, 3, 1, 1, 2	SINGLE NUMERIC VARIABLE
615	X6, 3, 1, 3, 1, 1, 3	SINGLE ALPHANUMERIC VARIABLE
616	X6, 3, 1, 3, 2	TABLE
617	X6, 3, 1, 3, 2, 1	1-DIMENSIONAL TABLE
618	X6, 3, 1, 3, 2, 1, 1	1-DIMENSIONAL LITERAL TABLE
619	X6, 3, 1, 3, 2, 1, 2	1-DIMENSIONAL NUMERIC TABLE
620	X6, 3, 1, 3, 2, 1, 3	1-DIMENSIONAL ALPHANUMERIC TABLE
621	X6, 3, 1, 3, 2, 2	2-DIMENSIONAL TABLE
622	X6, 3, 1, 3, 2, 2, 1	2-DIMENSIONAL LITERAL TABLE
623	X6, 3, 1, 3, 2, 2, 2	2-DIMENSIONAL NUMERIC TABLE
624	X6, 3, 1, 3, 2, 2, 3	2-DIMENSIONAL ALPHANUMERIC TABLE
625	X6, 3, 1, 3, 2, 3	3-DIMENSIONAL TABLE
626	X6, 3, 1, 3, 2, 3, 1	3-DIMENSIONAL LITERAL TABLE
627	X6, 3, 1, 3, 2, 3, 2	3-DIMENSIONAL NUMERIC TABLE
628	X6, 3, 1, 3, 2, 3, 3	3-DIMENSIONAL ALPHANUMERIC TABLE
629	X6, 3, 2	CALLING SUBROUTINE
630	X6, 3, 2, 1	CALL
631	X6, 3, 2, 2	SUBROUTINE NAME
632	X6, 3, 2, 3	USING
633	X6, 3, 2, 4	CALLING ARGUMENTS
634	X6, 3, 2, 4, 1	SINGLE ELEMENT
635	X6, 3, 2, 4, 1, 1	SINGLE VARIABLE

Figure 8.4 A SIAD tree of the COBOL external subroutine attribute-SUBROUTINE statements.

Index	Tree Symbol	Tree Element
636	X6, 3, 2, 4, 1, 1, 1	SINGLE LITERAL VARIABLE
637	X6, 3, 2, 4, 1, 1, 2	SINGLE NUMERIC VARIABLE
638	X6, 3, 2, 4, 1, 1, 3	SINGLE ALPHANUMERIC VARIABLE
639	X6, 3, 2, 4, 2	TABLE
640	X6, 3, 2, 4, 2, 1	1-DIMENSIONAL TABLE
641	X6, 3, 2, 4, 2, 1, 1	1-DIMENSIONAL LITERAL TABLE
642	X6, 3, 2, 4, 2, 1, 2	1-DIMENSIONAL NUMERIC TABLE
643	X6, 3, 2, 4, 2, 1, 3	1-DIMENSIONAL ALPHANUMERIC TABLE
644	X6, 3, 2, 4, 2, 2	2-DIMENSIONAL TABLE
645	X6, 3, 2, 4, 2, 2, 1	2-DIMENSIONAL LITERAL TABLE
646	X6, 3, 2, 4, 2, 2, 2	2-DIMENSIONAL NUMERIC TABLE
647	X6, 3, 2, 4, 2, 2, 3	2-DIMENSIONAL ALPHANUMERIC TABLE
648	X6, 3, 2, 4, 2, 3	3-DIMENSIONAL TABLE
649	X6, 3, 2, 4, 2, 3, 1	3-DIMENSIONAL LITERAL TABLE
650	X6, 3, 2, 4, 2, 3, 2	3-DIMENSIONAL NUMERIC TABLE
651	X6, 3, 2, 4, 2, 3, 3	3-DIMENSIONAL ALPHANUMERIC TABLE
652	X6, 3, 3	EXIT PROGRAM

Figure 8.4 continued

Let K, the number of elements to be sampled for constructing a test input unit, equal 2. Two random numbers, 631 and 615, are generated for sampling. The descriptive and sampled elements for each number are as follows:

1. **Index Equals 631**

Index	Tree Symbol	Tree Element	Remark
606	X6, 3	EXTERNAL SUBROUTINE	Descriptive element
629	X6, 3, 2	CALLING SUBROUTINE	Descriptive element
631	X6, 3, 2, 2	SUBROUTINE NAME	Sampled element

2. **Index Equals 615**

Index	Tree Symbol	Tree Element	Remark
606	X6, 3	EXTERNAL SUBROUTINE	Descriptive element
607	X6, 3, 1	SUBROUTINE DEFINITION	Descriptive element
610	X6, 3, 1, 3	DUMMY ARGUMENTS	Descriptive element
611	X6, 3, 1, 3, 1	SINGLE ELEMENT	Descriptive element
612	X6, 3, 1, 3, 1, 1	SINGLE VARIABLE	Descriptive element
615	X6, 3, 1, 3, 1, 1, 3	SINGLE ALPHANUMERIC VARIABLE	Sampled element

A test input unit may be constructed using the two sampled elements as follows:

A COBOL Compiler Test Program	SIAD Tree Index
IDENTIFICATION DIVISION.	
PROGRAM-ID. MAIN.	
ENVIRONMENT DIVISION.	
SOURCE-COMPUTER.	
OBJECT-COMPUTER.	
INPUT-OUTPUT SECTION.	
FILE-CONTROL.	
SELECT OUTPUT-FILE ASSIGN TO UT-S-PRINT.	
DATA DIVISION.	
⋮	
LINKAGE SECTION.	
77 VAR PICTURE X(14) USAGE DISPLAY.	
PROCEDURE DIVISION.	
CALL 'SUB' USING VAR.	631, 615
DISPLAY VAR.	
STOP RUN.	
IDENTIFICATION DIVISION.	
PROGRAM-ID. SUB.	631
ENVIRONMENT DIVISION.	
SOURCE-COMPUTER.	
OBJECT-COMPUTER.	
DATA DIVISION.	
⋮	
LINKAGE SECTION.	
77 AN PICTURE X(14) USAGE DISPLAY.	
PROCEDURE DIVISION USING AN.	615
MOVE 'THIS IS A TEST' TO AN.	
EXIT PROGRAM.	

The two sampled elements, SUBROUTINE NAME and SINGLE ALPHANUMERIC VARIABLE, are implemented in the COBOL statements corresponding to indices 631 and 615 in the program.

In order to conduct this test, the test program must include auxiliary statements such as the IDENTIFICATION DIVISION and LINKAGE SECTION statements to be acceptable to the compiler. Statements such as MOVE and DISPLAY are included for convenience in producing output for inspection. Strictly speaking, the correctness of a COBOL compiler in handling the test input unit should be examined by verifying the correctness of the object code. However, such examination can be time-consuming and error-prone. It is better to compile and execute the program to generate output, on the assumption that the assembler and loader are correct.

A more detailed discussion of construction of test input units using the COBOL SIAD tree can be found in chapter 14 of Cho [12].

(ii) WEIGHTED SIAD TREE. A weighted SIAD tree is identical to a regular SIAD tree, except that each tree element in the weighted SIAD tree is indexed with selected weights or multiple indices. Figure 8.5 shows an example of a weighted SIAD tree modified from the regular SIAD tree shown in Figure 8.2.

In a sampling process, a uniform random number between 1 and 84, where 84 is the total number of indexes in Figure 8.5, is generated. An element whose index range covers the random number is taken. For example, if a uniform random number 43 is generated, then the tree element H is taken, since 43 falls into the range of H's index, that is, 41–45. With the control of the weights, different tree elements can have different probabilities of being sampled for test input unit construction.

Weight	Index	Tree Symbol	Tree Element
3	1–3	X1	*A*
7	4–10	X1, 1	*B*
10	11–20	X1, 1, 1	*E*
4	21–25	X1, 1, 2	*F*
10	26–35	X1, 2	*C*
5	36–40	X1, 2, 1	*G*
5	41–45	X1, 2, 2	*H*
20	46–65	X1, 3	*D*
5	66–70	X1, 3, 1	*I*
10	71–80	X1, 3, 2	*J* (numerical)
2	81–82	X1, 3, 2, 1	*L* (lower bound)
2	83–84	X1, 3, 2, 2	*U* (upper bound)

Figure 8.5 A weighted SIAD tree.

This is what makes the weighted SIAD tree of Figure 8.5 differ from the regular SIAD tree of Figure 8.2. Each element in the regular SIAD tree has an equal probability of being taken to be used to construct a test input unit, whereas each element in the weighted SIAD tree has a specified probability of being taken. For example, in Figure 8.5, the tree element *A* has three chances of being taken, while the tree element *B* has seven chances. These chances are shown in the Weight column of the tree.

(iii) Ruled SIAD Tree. A ruled SIAD tree is similar to a regular SIAD tree, except that rules for using the inputs are incorporated into the tree. Figure 8.6 gives an example of a ruled SIAD tree representing the input domain of the mailing list data base management system discussed in Sections 7.2.1*C*(i) to 7.2.1*C*(iii). In the figure, the Rule Index column is added to a regular SIAD tree. A number of the column points to a rule defined as shown in Figure 8.7. In order to use a rule in Figure 8.7, a number of subrules must be applied. These subrules are listed in Figure 8.8. For example, in order to use the tree element ADDRESS, rules 1 and 15 must be followed. Rule 1, taken from Figure 8.7, means that the data length in number of characters (or bytes) of ADDRESS, K1, equals the data length of TITLE, FIRST NAME, MIDDLE NAME, LAST NAME, STREET NO., STREET NAME, APARTMENT NO., CITY NAME, STATE NAME, and ZIP CODE; that is, K1 = K2 + K4 + K5 + K6 + K8 + K9 + K10 + K11 + K12 + K13. Similarly, rules 2, 14, 15, 16, and 18 apply if TITLE is to be used. For example, rule 14 means excluding any of the numeric characters $0, 1, 2, 3, \ldots, 10$ in a title in an address. Thus a title such as Mr., Mrs., Dr., or Esq. cannot have any of these characters embedded in the string to be input to the piece of software.

In using a rule from Figure 8.7, there may be subrules that must be followed. For example, subrules 2, 3, and 4, taken from Figure 8.8, are required in order to use rule 3, K3 = K4 + K5 + K6. Subrule 2 defines the length of FIRST NAME in an ADDRESS to be from 1 to 20 characters long, inclusive. Similarly, subrule 3 defines the length of MIDDLE NAME to be from 1 to 20 characters long, inclusive, and so on.

(iv) "Network" SIAD Tree. The "network" SIAD tree can be used for applications in which the regular, weighted, and ruled SIAD trees cannot conveniently represent the software input domain. Such applications include operating systems, communication networks, and compilers. For example, Figure 8.9 shows a syntax chart for the entity

Index	Tree Symbol	Tree Element	Rule Index
1	Y1	ADDRESS, K1 bytes	1 15
2	Y1, 1	TITLE, K2 bytes	2 14 15 16 18
3	Y1, 2	NAME, K3 bytes	3 14 15 16 17 19
4	Y1, 2, 1	FIRST NAME, K4 bytes	4 14 15 16 17 20
5	Y1, 2, 1, 1	FIRST INITIAL, K4 bytes	4 14 15 16 17 20
6	Y1, 2, 1, 2	FULL FIRST NAME, K4 bytes	4 14 15 16 17 20
7	Y1, 2, 2	MIDDLE NAME, K5 bytes	5 14 15 16 17 20
8	Y1, 2, 2, 1	MIDDLE INITIAL, K5 bytes	5 14 15 16 17 20
9	Y1, 2, 2, 2	FULL MIDDLE NAME, K5 bytes	5 14 15 16 17 20
10	Y1, 2, 3	LAST NAME, K6 bytes	6 14 15 16 17 19
11	Y1, 2, 3, 1	SINGLE-WORD LAST NAME, K6 bytes	6 14 15 16 18
12	Y1, 2, 3, 2	MULTI-WORD LAST NAME, K6 bytes	6 14 15 16 17 19
13	Y1, 3	STREET, K7 bytes	7 15 16 17
14	Y1, 3, 1	STREET NO., K8 bytes	8 15 17
15	Y1, 3, 2	STREET NAME, K9 bytes	9 14 15
16	Y1, 3, 3	APARTMENT NO., K10 bytes	10 15 16 17 20 21
17	Y1, 4	CITY NAME, K11 bytes	11 14 15 16 18 20
18	Y1, 4, 1	SINGLE-WORD CITY NAME, K11 bytes	11 14 15 18 20
19	Y1, 4, 2	MULTI-WORD CITY NAME, K11 bytes	11 14 15 16 18 20
20	Y1, 5	STATE NAME, K12 bytes	12 14 15 16 18 20
21	Y1, 5, 1	ABBREVIATED STATE NAME, K12 bytes	12 14 15 16 18 20
22	Y1, 5, 2	FULL STATE NAME, K12 bytes	12 14 15 18 20
23	Y1, 6	ZIP CODE, K13 bytes	13 15 17 21
24	Y1, 6, 1	5-DIGIT ZIP CODE, K13 bytes	13 15 17 21
25	Y1, 6, 2	9-DIGIT ZIP CODE, K13 bytes	13 15 17 21

Figure 8.6 Example of a ruled SIAD tree.

EXPRESSION in the Ada language. The chart can be transformed into a "network" SIAD tree as shown in Figure 8.10. The transformation is accomplished as follows.

Each entry in the Tree Element column in Figure 8.10 is an element, such as RELATION, in Figure 8.9. An entry in the Index column in Figure 8.10 identifies an element in Figure 8.9, and so on. If an element in Figure 8.9 branches to another element, then an index for the element

Rule Index	Rule Description	Subrule Index
1	K1 = K2 + K4 + K5 + K6 + K8 + K9 + K10 + K11 + K12 + K13	1 2 3 4 5 6 7 8 9 10
2	K2	1
3	K3 = K4 + K5 + K6	2 3 4
4	K4	2
5	K5	3
6	K6	4
7	K7 = K8 + K9 + K10	5 6 7
8	K8	5
9	K9	6
10	K10	7
11	K11	8
12	K12	9
13	K13	10
14	Excluding characters 0 1 2 3 4 5 6 7 8 9	
15	Excluding characters + * / ' " ⟨ ⟩ $ & # @ ≠ ; :) (! ? =] [% ¢	
16	Can include one character . or space	
17	Can include character -	
18	Excluding character -	
19	Including character ,	
20	Excluding character ,	
21	Including spaces	

Figure 8.7 Example of rules of the ruled SIAD tree in Figure 8.6.

is given in the Rule Index column in Figure 8.10 with an assumed probability of 1.0 for branching to that element. If the element branches to more than one other element, then multiple indexes, each with a predetermined probability of branching, are given. The 1 in the Index column denotes that the corresponding element is an entry into the tree. A 0 in the Rule Index column denotes that the corresponding element is an exit from the tree. For example, in Figure 8.9, the element RELATION indexed by 1 branches to the elements AND, OR, XOR, AND, OR and exit. Therefore, the indexes, 2, 3, 4, 5, 7, and 10 are given for these elements, respectively, in Figure 8.10, with corresponding probabilities of branching of 0.1, 0.1, 0.1, 0.3, 0.3, and 0.1.

Using the "network" SIAD tree, test input units can be constructed systematically for testing the syntax entity by generating a random

Subrule Index	Subrule Description	Remark[a]
1	$1 \leq K2 \leq 7$	Length of TITLE
2	$1 \leq K4 \leq 20$	Length of FIRST NAME
3	$1 \leq K5 \leq 20$	Length of MIDDLE NAME
4	$2 \leq K6 < 30$	Length of LAST NAME
5	$1 \leq K8 \leq 10$	Length of STREET NO.
6	$1 \leq K9 \leq 20$	Length of STREET NAME
7	$1 \leq K10 \leq 10$	Length of APARTMENT NO.
8	$1 \leq K11 \leq 20$	Length of CITY NAME
9	$2 \leq K12 \leq 20$	Length of STATE NAME
10	$5 \leq K13 \leq 10$	Length of ZIP CODE

[a] Each length in number of bytes (characters).

Figure 8.8 Example of subrules of the rules of the ruled SIAD tree in Figure 8.7.

number of elements. For example, on entering the entity, a random number R between 0 and 1, exclusive, is generated. An index in the Rule Index column is selected according to the predetermined probability of branching, and the element that corresponds to the selected index is taken for sampling. Thus, if $R = 0.376125$, then the element indexed by

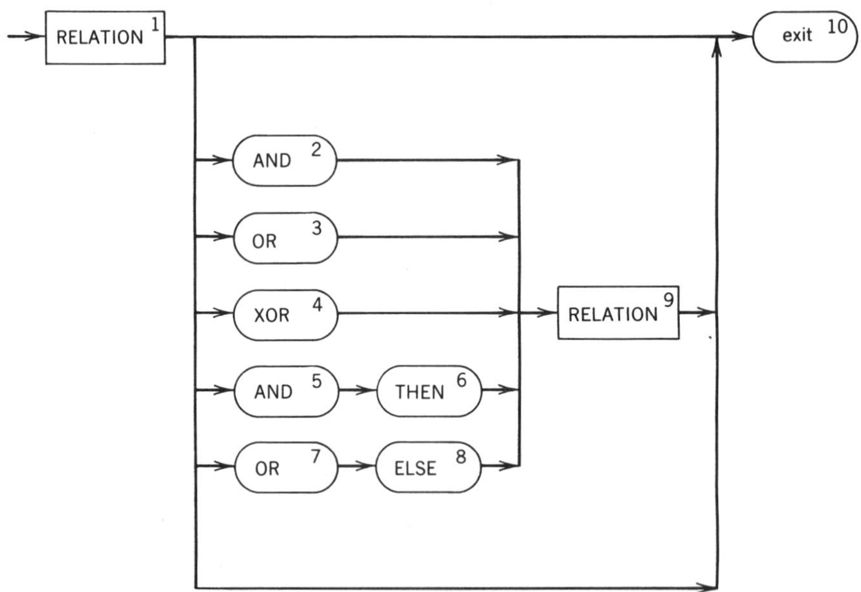

Figure 8.9 A syntax chart of Ada EXPRESSION.

Index	Tree Symbol	Tree Element	Rule Index (Probability)[a]
1	X1	RELATION	2 3 4 5 7 10 (0.1 0.1 0.1 0.3 0.3 0.1)
2	X2	AND	9 (1.0)
3	X3	OR	9 (1.0)
4	X4	XOR	9 (1.0)
5	X5	AND	6 (1.0)
6	X6	THEN	9 (1.0)
7	X7	OR	8 (1.0)
8	X8	ELSE	9 (1.0)
9	X9	RELATION	2 3 4 5 7 10 (0.1 0.1 0.1 0.3 0.3 0.1)
10	X10	exit	0 (1.0)

[a]Arbitrarily assigned probability.

Figure 8.10 A network SIAD tree transformed from the syntax chart of Ada Expression in Figure 8.9.

5, that is, AND, is being branched to, according to the probability. A random number of elements will be so branched to or chosen randomly. An element sampling process is shown in Figure 8.11. A total of eight elements, excluding the exit element, are selected by the random sampling process. These elements are then used to construct a test input unit of the syntax entity. For example, an Ada expression can be so constructed as follows:

```
NEXT_CAR.OWNER/= null AND THEN
NEXT_CAR.OWNER.AGE < 30 OR ELSE
N = 0 AND M/= N
```

where NEXT_CAR.OWNER/= null, NEXT_CAR.OWNER.AGE < 30, N = 0, and M/= N are instances of the element RELATION. This expression can then be used to test the Ada compiler's handling of that type of expression.

Random Number	Selected Rule Index	Selected Tree Element
—	1	RELATION
0.376125	5	AND
0.801962	6	THEN
0.112984	9	RELATION
0.650449	7	OR
0.049632	8	ELSE
0.771025	9	RELATION
0.091625	2	AND
0.491209	9	RELATION
0.961083	10	exit

Figure 8.11 A sampling process with the network SIAD tree in Figure 8.10.

The sampling process can be accomplished for each of the Ada language entities. The result of the entire sampling process would be considered a product unit for testing an Ada compiler. The same entire process can be repeated many times, generating many test input units.

H. Input Data Error Processing Requirements

It is important at this stage of requirements specification to identify processing requirements for correcting or rejecting input data that are unacceptable because of coding errors, incompleteness, or other problems. This is equivalent to the inspection of raw materials coming into a factory in order to remove defective materials or reject unacceptably defective shipments.

Incoming data must conform to the processing requirements of the software. Where the data are collected and transmitted by sources other than the software developer, such as a user-designated subcontractor or agency with statistical and data collection responsibilities, the checking of the input data for conformity with content, format, and processing guidelines established by the developer and user is a necessity. Incomplete or inappropriate input data can have a devastating impact on the cost and schedule of software usage. The requirements specification phase is the right time to address this potential problem.

I. User Friendliness Requirements

An analysis of the proposed software should be performed to identify the features that will contribute to the user friendliness of the system. User friendliness should be considered a necessity of the software design to be built in from the start, following established principles of human engineering. Procedures for data entry, system initialization, and so on should be studied for simplicity and forgivingness. Implementing such features cost effectively depends in part on the designer's thoroughness in the specification of input requirements. Careful attention to input data characteristics, such as the permissible range of each variable, and to the rules for using the inputs, can show the designer how to make the system easy to use and difficult to misuse—a gain in efficiency and productivity for all.

J. *Other Input Requirements*

Finally, any other special conditions or requirements that may affect data input should be identified. Such requirements may include telecommunication from remote locations or the use of dedicated communication lines, and the like.

8.2.2 Processing Requirements

Processing requirements are an essential part of requirements specification. These requirements cover functions, function interfaces, data bases, software sizing, software performance, hardware, data communication, software security, module input domain, language, and so on. The requirements specification document should identify these requirements as completely and with as much detail as practical.

A. *Functional Requirements*

As discussed in Chapter 7, the modeling of a piece of software should address processing requirements as thoroughly as a factory process is described in the manufacturing industries. All of the functions that the software must perform should be specified, including manipulation of data, methods of producing outputs, data flows, process control features, and so on. All of the aspects of the modeling of a piece of software, analogous to the modeling of a factory, as described in Section 7.2.2, should be included in the requirements specification document. Whether the designer follows a function-oriented or object-oriented design approach (see Chapter 9), all functional requirements should be identified at this stage of software development.

B. *Functional Interface Requirements*

The interfaces between the functions must also be defined so that the proposed software design is complete and each interface conforms to all other processing requirements. Some of the factors that affect the definition of interface requirements are discussed in Section 8.2.2***D***.

C. Data Base Processing Requirements

All requirements for processing the data base should be identified. At this stage, the user must decide whether to develop software for this function or use existing software. With either approach, the user must define how to ensure that the developed or selected software performs acceptably. A method to obtain statistical evidence that the software functions as desired must be identified.

D. Software Sizing

At this stage of requirements specification, the user must consider the size constraints of the proposed software as determined by the modeling activity discussed in Chapter 7.

E. Software Performance Requirements

The user must identify performance requirements, such as throughput and response times, and develop a method to ensure that the software will work, and work right. Software performance test requirements are discussed further in Section 8.3.

F. Hardware Requirements

Identification of hardware requirements and the definition of the proposed system components and devices to be used is a crucial part of requirements specification. It is a frequent practice that if the system is to be designed from scratch, the selection of the hardware is the responsibility of the software developer, who will propose to the user a system that most efficiently and economically meets the other software requirements and best suits the user's needs. In many cases, however, the user will have a preference for equipment from a specific manufacturer, frequently because the user has already installed or has extensive experience with a certain system.

As part of selecting hardware, the user must identify what bench mark tests or other hardware performance data will be used to ensure that the selected system will provide the necessary performance, power, and memory capacity. It can be seen that a clear understanding and complete definition of all software processing requirements, as part of requirements specification, is essential in evaluating hardware suitability.

G. *Data Communication Requirements*

The user should identify all data communication requirements, such as use of local area networks, wide area networks, and dedicated communication lines. The choice of appropriate local area network features such as ring, star, or bus topology; point-to-point or broadcast modes; cable medium, and data transmission rates should be considered in the light of performance and processing requirements. Any additional software that must be developed, and the attending technical risks, to accommodate the data communication requirements must be identified.

The user must also identify pertinent data communication standards and protocols and, if such standards have not been implemented by the software industry, seriously review the feasibility of the proposed design. Where such standards are in practice throughout the industry, the designer must ensure that the proposed design conforms to all applicable standards and protocols.

H. *Software Security Requirements*

The requirements specification document should include identification of provisions for ensuring system protection, data integrity, error recovery, and a convenient means of system backup. The necessary extent of software security requirements should be determined based on a clear understanding of the user's needs and the critical parameters of the design.

I. *Module Input Domain Requirements*

In comparing a piece of software to a factory, each module is like a station in the factory where partially processed materials come in and intermediate products are generated. In the requirements specification document, the input domain of each module should be demanded, following the same procedures described in Chapter 7 for the entire piece of software. The modeling of each module input domain should include the development of module SIAD trees.

J. *Language Requirements*

The appropriate language in which to program the proposed software may be selected as part of requirements specification. Generally, the user should allow the software developer to make this decision. Sometimes, however, the user has special considerations. For example, the user might specify programming in a high-level language to maximize the software's portability. For software contracted out by the Department of

Defense, a certain language may be specified for mission-critical and embedded software, or the user may require that the software be written in the Ada programming language.

K. *Other Processing Requirements*

Any other processing requirements that the user can identify should be included in the requirements specification document. The importance of identifying requirements as completely as possible during the early stages of software development cannot be overemphasized.

8.2.3 Output Requirements

The output requirements that should be included in the requirements specification document are those discussed in Chapter 7 as being analogous to product design, prototype design, and product strategies. These requirements are addressed at two levels:

System output requirements
Module output requirements

A. *System Output Requirements*

The system output requirements should be specified as follows:

(i) OUTPUT PRODUCT UNIT DEFINITION. The product unit definition developed as part of the software output modeling activity should be included here as part of the requirements specification document.

(ii) OUTPUT PRODUCT UNIT DEFECTIVENESS DEFINITION. The product unit defectiveness definition should also be included here. As discussed in Chapter 7, this definition is complex. It must address all essential quality characteristics of the output, and identify the defectiveness criteria for each characteristic.

(iii) OUTPUT FORMATTING REQUIREMENTS. All requirements for the format of the output should be identified, such as whether the output is text or numerical, tabular or graphic plot, what notation is used, what engineering units and labels are used, and so on.

(iv) OUTPUT MEDIA REQUIREMENTS. The media, for example, disk, tape, terminal, that will be used for the output of the software should be identified, and any special formatting or data communication requirements associated with the media should be addressed.

(v) Output Security Requirements. All requirements for controlling access and ensuring adequate backup, and so on should be identified.

(vi) Other Output Requirements

As a final step, any other special requirements pertaining to the output of the proposed software should be identified and included as part of the requirements specification document.

B. Module Output Requirements

The same process of requirements specification should be applied to the output of each module in the proposed software design as to the entire system. Treating each module as a crucial entity with its own requirements is an important step in ensuring quality in the software design. As will be discussed in Section 8.3, this careful approach to development of a modular design is essential for testing the software during its stages of development, and identifying problems before they lead to costly modifications.

(i) Module Output Product Unit Definition. As part of the modeling activity, a product unit definition should be developed for each module output. These definitions should be included here in the requirements specification document.

(ii) Module Output Product Unit Defectiveness Definition. Product unit defectiveness definitions for the module outputs should be included here to the level of complexity required for applying statistical quality control techniques (see Section 8.3.2.***D***).

(iii) Module Output Media Requirements. The media to which module output is transmitted for temporary storage should be identified, and any requirements or problems associated with use of the media, as related to processing requirements, system response rates, and so on, should be addressed.

(iv) Module Output Security Requirements. Requirements for data integrity and backup at the module level should be identified.

(v) OTHER MODULE OUTPUT REQUIREMENTS. As a final step, any other special requirements pertaining to the output of the modules should be identified.

8.3 TEST REQUIREMENTS

As stressed repeatedly in this book, with reference to the 20 problems stated in Figure 1.3, the lack of attention to effective ways of testing the quality of a piece of software is one of the most serious problems in the software industry—but a problems whose solution is at hand: testing by using statistical quality control.

As part of requirements specification, the user should include two types of requirements pertaining to the use of statistical quality control. First, the user should demand statistical evidence that quality is built into the software, to provide the basis for a meaningful software warranty. This is addressed in Section 8.1.2***H***. Second, the user should ensure that all necessary requirements for conducting statistical tests, including requirements for test methods, sampling plans, and so on, are specified. This is addressed in the following sections for both system test requirements and module test requirements.

8.3.1 System Test Requirements

System test requirements should be identified in the modeling document produced during the modeling activity, and refined as necessary during requirements specification.

A. Test Methods

There are five software test methods currently applicable for software testing: regular, weighted, boundary, invalid, and special tests. It may not be necessary to conduct all these tests in testing a piece of software. However, a combination of the methods is required to properly conduct the tests. Each method is explained as follows:

A. Regular Test. In software testing, if a test input unit is constructed using a regular SIAD tree, as discussed in Section 8.2.1***G***(i), then this is called the regular test method.

B. Weighted Test. If a weighted SIAD tree is used in constructing test input units for testing a piece of software, as discussed in Section 8.2.1***G***(ii), then this is called the weighted test method.

C. **Boundary Test.** If a test input unit is constructed using only one of the lower or upper bounds of an input data type, then this is called the boundary test method. For example, if a piece of software finds the root of the polynomial:

$$A_{100}X^{100} + A_{99}X^{99} + \cdots + A_0X^0 = 0$$

then, supposing that each of the coefficients assumes either of its lower or upper bound values, there are 2^{101} possible cases that can be processed by the piece of software.

D. **Invalid Test Method.** If a test input unit is constructed from the "invalid input domain" (i.e., from data beyond the types, rules, and subrules of the input domain) of a piece of software, then this is called the invalid test method. For example, in testing a piece of software that maintains a mailing list data base, test input units constructed from data that does not conform to the rules and subrules defined in a ruled SIAD tree, as discussed in Section 8.2.1***G***(iii) would be used to conduct the invalid test.

E. **Special Test Method.** If there are cases in which the software must be specially tested, then the test input unit is so specified, this is called the special test method. For example, in the polynomial discussed in Section 8.3.1***A***, Item C, the special case might be:

$$A_5X^5 + A_4X^4 + A_3X^3 + A_2X^2 + A_1X^1 + A_0X^0 = 0$$

This case is then tested separately from the regular, weighted, boundary, and invalid tests.

The user should specify the requirements for using these methods in conducting software testing or module testing.

B. Statistical Sampling Methods with Product Unit Definitions

The user should specify the most appropriate statistical sampling methods consistent with the product unit definitions developed as part of the modeling activity. Chapters 5 and 6 of this book provide a detailed discussion of single and sequential sampling techniques applicable to software testing.

To properly conduct each of the test methods defined in Section 8.3.1***A***, at least two sampling processes should be used: the sampling process for estimating the defective rate of the product unit population of the software, as discussed in Chapter 5; and the acceptance sampling process for accepting the software product unit population, as discussed in Chapter 6. This is the best approach to obtain statistical evidence that quality is built into the software.

C. *Statistical Inference Requirements*

Statistical tests are based on various concepts which determine the type of inferences which can be made from the results of the tests. In Chapters 5 and 6 of this book, the concepts of statistical testing are discussed in detail. These concepts include: the confidence level of the population mean, the accuracy factor, the level of significance, and Type I and Type II errors.

The designer should understand these concepts and the types of inferences appropriate to testing the proposed software. As part of requirements specification, the user should require that proper data be collected in order to perform the necessary statistical tests.

D. *System Acceptance Criteria*

Statistical inferences yield probabilistic assessments of the goodness of the product unit population. The requirements specification document, however, should also specify system acceptance criteria, that is, how good the product unit population must be and how thorough the system testing must be to satisfy the developer and the user that the software is acceptable and has been sufficiently tested. Several aspects of system acceptance criteria are discussed in the following sections.

(i) PRODUCER'S RISK AND USER'S RISK. Chapter 6 discusses the two types of risk associated with a statistical test and level of significance. The probability that a good population will be rejected is called the producer's risk. The probability that a defective population will be accepted is called the user's risk.

As part of requirements specification, the system acceptance criteria should include a statement of the level of risk considered acceptable by developer and user.

(ii) OUTPUT PRODUCT UNIT POPULATION DEFECTIVE RATE. The user and developer must establish acceptable software product unit population rates, that is, the values of $\epsilon_R, \epsilon_W, \epsilon_B, \epsilon_I, \epsilon_S$ such that $\theta_R < \epsilon_R, \theta_W < \epsilon_W, \theta_B < \epsilon_B, \theta_I < \epsilon_I, \theta_S < \epsilon_S$ under the regular, weighted, boundary, invalid, and special test methods, respectively. In addition, the software acceptance criteria $\alpha_1, \theta_1, \alpha_2, \theta_2$ that represent the producer's risk and user's risk are to be specified. The details of these are given in Chapter 6.

(iii) ACCEPTANCE SAMPLING METHODS. With the four criteria $\alpha_1, \theta_1, \alpha_2, \theta_2$ specified as discussed in Section 8.3.1***D***(ii) a statistical sampling plan that most economically, that is, with an optimal sample size, meets the specified producer's risk and user's risk levels can be selected, as described in detail in Chapter 6.

(iv) Acceptance Dispute Resolution Method. As a final aspect of system acceptance criteria, the requirements specification document should identify the method of acceptance dispute resolution to be used in the event of disagreement betwen the user and the developer. Both parties should agree to the preferred method before the software is developed and tested. Dispute resolution methods are discussed further in Chapter 12 of this book.

E. Other Test Requirements

The user and developer should, as a final step in developing system test requirements, identify any special cases that should be included in the tests. For example, there may be absolutely necessary cases, as when human lives are at stake, which might not get tested when using a random sampling technique.

8.3.2 Module Test Requirements

The developer should employ a similar approach to defining the test requirements for each module in the software system.

A. Module Test Methods

The test methods to be used in module testing and the requirements for using the methods should be specified. As with the software system, this means a combination of regular, weighted, boundary, invalid, and special tests.

B. Statistical Sampling Methods with Product Unit Definitions

The most appropriate statistical sampling methods consistent with the module product unit definitions during the modeling activity should be identified.

C. Statistical Inference Requirements

The user should understand the types of inference appropriate to testing each module, and identify the data that must be collected in order to perform the necessary statistical tests.

D. *Module Output Product Unit Population Defective Rate*

The user should establish the product unit population defective rate for each module output.

E. *Other Module Test Requirements*

As a final step in the statement of test requirements, any other requirements or special cases for module testing should be identified and included in the requirements specification document.

8.4 DOCUMENTATION REQUIREMENTS

Sections 8.1 to 8.3 have presented a step-by-step procedure for developing a requirements specification document that can help ensure that all requirements for the proposed software development are identified. As discussed in Chapter 7, documentation of requirements is a crucial part of modeling in the manufacturing industries. Documents such as the product description, in textual or blueprint form, and written instructions called the process description are fundamental tools for communication among designers, engineers, and customers. In the software industry, too, the modeling process should produce key documents that are used to ensure conformance to specifications throughout the development and testing of the software.

Documentation in the software industry is often considered a burden on the developer. This burden can be reduced or eliminated if the documentation is made a key part of each step of software development and testing, and is used as instructions to be followed rigorously, the way that the process description is used in the manufacturing industries. The type of documents to be produced should be identified as part of requirements specification. The eight documents: modeling, requirements specification, software design, software test design, software implementation, software test implementation, test and integration, and software delivery should be produced during the six stages of software development as shown in Figure 1.10.

REFERENCES

1. American National Standard Institute, Inc. (*ANSI*), *ANSI FORTRAN*, *X*3.9-1966, ANSI, New York, 1966.
2. International Business Machines Corporation, *IBM Systems*/360 *and System*/370 *FORTRAN IV Language*, IBM, White Plains, New York, 1971.

3. American National Standard Institute, Inc. (*ANSI*), *ANSI COBOL*, *X*3.23-1974, ANSI, New York, 1974.

4. International Business Machines Corporation, *IBM OS Full American National Standard COBOL*, IBM, White Plains, New York, 1972.

5. G. D. Brown *Advanced ANS COBOL with Structured Programming*, Wiley-Interscience, New York, 1977.

6. A. Ralston and C. L. Meek (Eds.), *Encyclopedia of Computer Science*, Petrocelli/Charter, New York, 1976.

7. A. Ralston, *A First Course in Numerical Analysis*, McGraw-Hill, New York, 1965.

8. B. Carnahan, H. A. Luther, and J. O. Wilkes, *Applied Numerical Methods*, Wiley, New York, 1969.

9. R. W. Llewellyn, *Linear Programming*, Holt, Rinehart & Winston, New York, 1966.

10. G. B. Dantzig, *Linear Programming and Extensions*, Princeton University Press, Princeton, New Jersey, 1966.

11. A. Charnes and W. W. Cooper, *Management Models and Industrial Applications of Linear Programming*, Vols. 1 and 2, Wiley, New York, 1961.

12. C. K. Cho, *An Introduction to Software Quality Control*, Wiley-Interscience, New York, 1980.

13. C. K. Cho, "Statistical Methods Applied to Software Quality Control," in *Handbook of Software Quality Assurance*, Edited by G. Gordon Schulmeyer and J. McManus, Van Nostrand Reinhold, New York, 1987.

14. C. K. Cho, *Software Engineering and Quality Assurance*, International Seminar Handouts (CE705LE), George Washington University, Washington, D.C., July 1986.

15. R. H. Thayer, A. Pyster, and R. C. Wood, "The Challenge of Software Engineering Project Management," *IEEE Computer*, Vol. 13, No. 8, August 1980, pp. 51–59.

EXERCISES

1. Perform a random sampling of four tree elements from the FORTRAN SIAD tree of Figure 8.3. Construct a test case using the sampled elements.

2. Perform a random sampling of three tree elements from the COBOL SIAD tree of Figure 8.4. Construct a test case using the sampled elements.

3. Using the techniques discussed in Sections 8.2 and 8.3 specify the requirements of each of the following programs:

   (a) One that will perform the matrix operation $AB = C$, where A is a matrix of size $N \times M$; B that of size $M \times K$; C that of size $N \times K$.

(b) One that will find the inverse of the matrix A such that $AA^{-1} = I$, where I is the identity matrix A, B of size $N \times N$.

(c) One that will find the values of $x_1, x_2, \ldots, x_n$ that maximizes the objective function $c_1x_1 + c_2x_2 + \cdots + c_nx_n$ in the linear programming problem (7.1).

4. A company has decided to develop a payroll program. The phenomenon is given as follows: The information about each employee contains:

   (a) Employee identification
   (b) Employee name
   (c) Hours worked in the week (vacation and sick leave hours taken are considered hours worked)
   (d) Base pay rate
   (e) Overtime pay rate ($/hour worked over 40)
   (f) Number of dependents
   (g) Tax exemptions per dependent
   (h) Tax withholding rate on taxable income (taxable income = gross pay—exemptions)
      i Federal withholding rate
      ii State withholding rate
   (i) Vacation hours
      i Hours entitled
      ii Hours taken
   (j) Sick leave hours
      i Hours entitled
      ii Hours taken
   (k) Deductions
      i Health insurance
      ii Life insurance
      iii Retirement

   Build a model and specify the requirements for developing the payroll program.

CHAPTER 9

Concurrent Software Design and Test Design

Software designers have many techniques for enhancing the reliability of a piece of software: error avoidance, error detection, error correction, error tolerance, and so on. However, starting with a good design to avoid introducing error into the software is recognized as the best technique. By performing the modeling and requirements specification tasks described in Chapters 7 and 8, the software developer can take the first two essential steps toward producing quality software. The modeling and requirements specification documents produced during these phases of software development state the goals which the designer is trying to attain.

To produce a quality software design, the designer must have strong technical ability. He or she must be able to understand the modeling and requirements specification documents; identify constraints, potential problems, and possible solutions; and conduct tradeoff studies and decide among alternatives. The designer must be also able to draw on a strong background in technology, and understand the 20 problems of the software industry stated in Figure 1.3. A multidisciplinary background in computer science, management science, engineering, statistics, operations research, optimization, simulation, and so on, will serve a good designer well.

The designer must keep in mind the software engineering goals of modifiability, understandability, reliability, and efficiency as he or she proceeds with the software design. The software engineering principles of abstract data typing, information hiding, modularization, localization, uniformity, completeness, confirmability, and statistical quality control must be observed carefully in developing the design.

Well-prepared modeling and requirements specification documents will allow the software design and test design tasks to proceed concurrently. If the software design and test design cannot be developed concurrently, then it means that the modeling and requirements specification documents are not sufficiently prepared. Refinement of those documents is essential before design tasks are continued.

In selecting a design methodology, the designer must decide between a function-oriented design and an object-oriented design approach. Function-oriented design is associated with use of the "conventional" programming languages such as FORTRAN and COBOL. Object-oriented design is appropriate for software written in the newly developed Ada®* language, and is of emerging importance in the software industry. In this chapter, both of these overall design approaches are described, and how to use either approach to produce a quality design is considered. It will be seen that both approaches have limitations when viewed from the perspective of software engineering using statistical quality control.

Software testing is a major problem area in software development. Even though testing receives frequent attention in the literature, there are two major questions that have not been satisfactorily answered: How much software testing is sufficient, and how good is the piece of software after testing? Until these two issues are resolved, software testing will remain a major problem area. In this chapter, an effective method for resolving these issues is proposed: a test design based on the use of statistical quality control to produce quality software.

9.1 SOFTWARE DESIGN

In a well-organized software development project, the design tasks should follow the modeling and requirements specification phases, and precede the implementation phase. This is not always an easy matter for the designer to arrange. The design methods in use in the software

*®Ada is a registered trademark of the U.S government (Ada Joint Program Office).

industry do not always carefully distinguish between development phases or between the tools appropriate to each phase. As will be seen in this section, the literature sometimes promotes general design methods—function-oriented or object-oriented design as modeling tools, that is, ways to understand the problem; and sometimes encourages use of implementation tools, that is, programming languages, which are aids to design of the software structure. This confusion of tasks, methods, and tools can have serious consequences for the software design. General principles for evaluating design methods, tools, and strategies are examined in the following sections from the perspective of software engineering.

9.1.1 Design Methods

A design method is a general guideline for proceeding with the conceptual design tasks, for example, top-down, bottom-up, structured analysis and design technique (SADT). With the emerging importance of the Ada programming language, the designer is now faced with an initial choice between function-oriented design and object-oriented design. These overall design approaches are examined separately in the following sections. To be considered are how well each approach organizes the design tasks, how well each addresses modeling and requirements specification, and how well each supports effective software testing and the use of statistical quality control.

A. Function-Oriented Design

Most software is developed using function-oriented design. This is the approach supported by the first three generations of programming languages. These languages are oriented toward abstracting real-world operations more than real-world objects, and provide a powerful set of constructs for implementing operation to produce the desired output. The stages of function-oriented design are:

Review of requirements specification
Design of data process
Design of algorithms

(i) Review of Requirements Specification. The literature of function-oriented design recognizes that software development begins with modeling and requirements specification, but does not always emphasize a clear modeling effort or sufficient modeling tasks, as described in Chapter 7, or generate a complete requirements specification, as described in Chapter 8. If these phases are conducted properly, the designer should have available a modeling document and a requirements specification document. The first design task is, therefore, to review these documents and to understand the problem thoroughly, the desired output, and the user's requirements. The designer should pay particular attention to the following as he or she reviews the requirements:

Completeness and uniformity of what is being stated in the documents. Any discrepancies or missing information must be identified

Identification of hardware constraints in the requirements

Identification of programming language constraints in the requirements

Identification of software constraints in the requirements

Identification of peculiar requirements that may affect the design of the software

(ii) DESIGN OF THE DATA PROCESS. Design of the data process includes three stages:

Define data flows

Define control flows

Define data structures

a. Define Data Flows. Data flows refer to the relay of data output from one stage of the process to be input to another stage of the process, as described in Section 7.2.2***D***, and are analogous to the flows of material between work stations in a factory. If the developer follows the principles of software engineering, the designer will have the data flows defined in the modeling document for his or her review and use in the software design.

b. Define Control Flows. Control flows refer to the control of the operations that transform input into output within each stage of the process, as described in Section 7.2.2***E***, and are analogous to the control of operations that transform materials at a work station in a factory. The control flows should also be defined in the modeling document for the designer to review and use in the software design.

c. Define Data Structures. Data structures are analogous to the space, tools, and apparatus with which materials are shipped and stored in a factory. In a software process, there are many different types of data structures, including variables, arrays, lists, stacks, and queues, which can be used.

1. Variable. A variable is a single element that processes a unique data type such as integer. A variable is created by declaring its data type, such as INTEGER in FORTRAN. The deletion of a variable is accomplished by removing the declaration of, and not using, the variable. A variable is selected by simply using the variable. For example, $I := 1$; in Ada means selecting I to be assigned the value of 1.

2. Array. An array is a linear assembly of data elements of the same or different data types. An array is created by declaring its data types. For example, the declaration

```
01  COUNTRY-NAME
    05  STATE-NAME PICTURE A(20) OCCURS 50 TIMES
      10  COUNTY-NAME PICTURE A(20) OCCURS 100 TIMES
        15  CITY-NAME PICTURE A(20) OCCURS 100 TIMES
```

in COBOL creates the three-dimensional array COUNTRY-NAME. The removal of the declaration, and nonusage of the array, deletes the array.

An element may be selected from the array by a selector called the index, such as I. For example, COUNTRY-NAME(I, J, K) selects the Kth city in the Jth county of the Ith state.

3. List. A list is an assembly of blocks of data elements. The blocks are arranged in a linear or nonlinear relationship called a link. If the linkage between blocks can be deduced simply from the order in which the blocks are specified, then the list is called a linear list. Otherwise, it is a nonlinear list. The following are types of linear lists:

One-Way List. Each block in the list contains one pointer to the next block. For example:

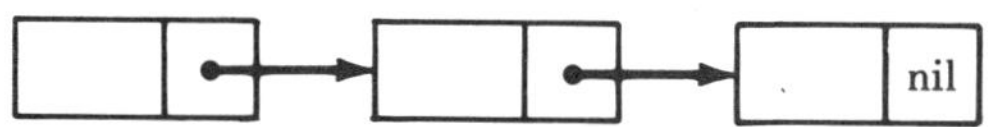

is a one-way list. The last block contains no pointer, usually denoted by "nil."

Two-Way List. Each block in the list contains two pointers. One points to the next block and the other to the previous block. For example:

is a two-way list. The terminal blocks contain "nil" pointers.

The following are types of nonlinear lists:

Circular List. If the pointer at the end block of a one-way list points to the starting block of the list, then the list is a circular list. For example:

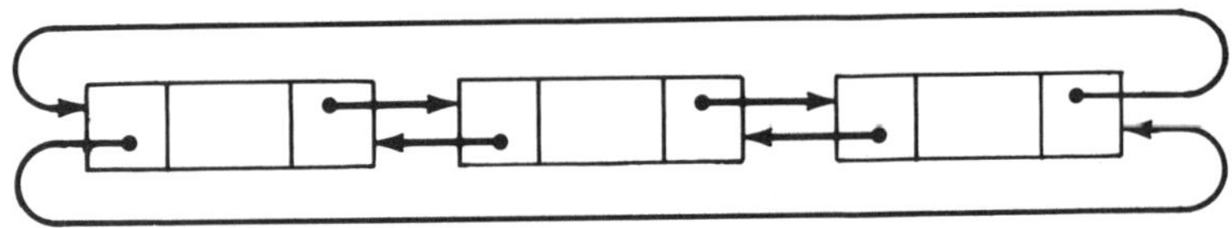

Tree List. If a list is arranged in a hierarchical relationship, then it is a tree list. For example:

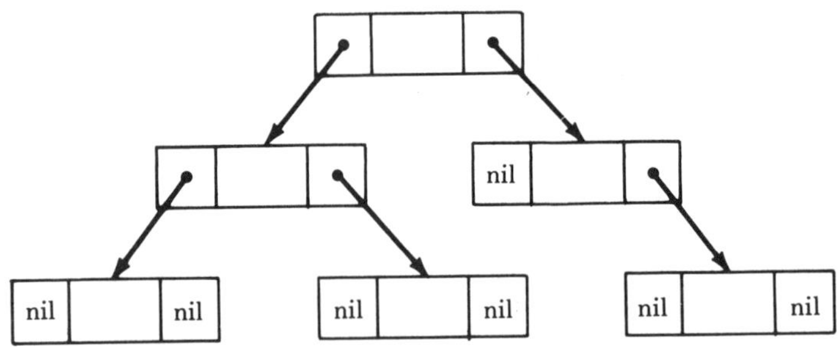

is a tree list. The block at the top level has at least one branch; a block at the lowest level has only one parent, and no branches. Every other block in the structure has a parent and at least one branch.

Network List. A network list is similar to a tree list except that a block can have more than one parent in the list. For example:

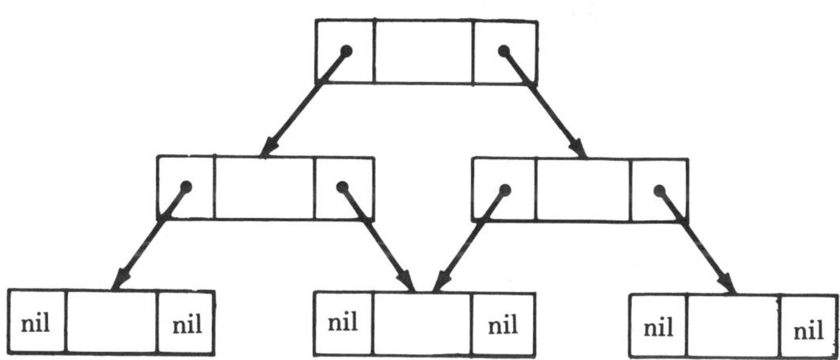

is a network list.

An element in a list can be selected by traversing the pointer chain, starting at the beginning block of the structure. An element in a list is created by inserting a new block into the list and then updating the pointers to reflect the insertion. For example, if block A is inserted into the list

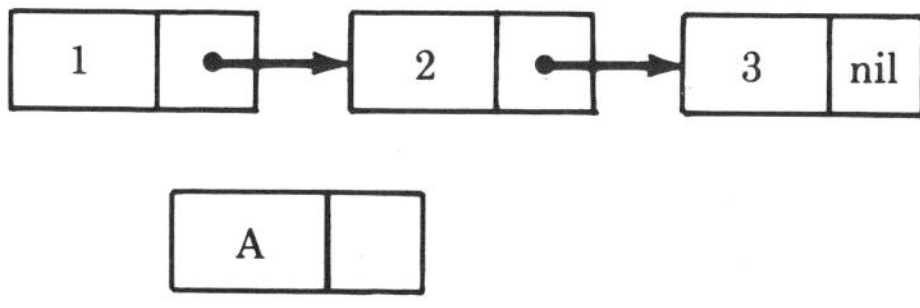

the result would appear as

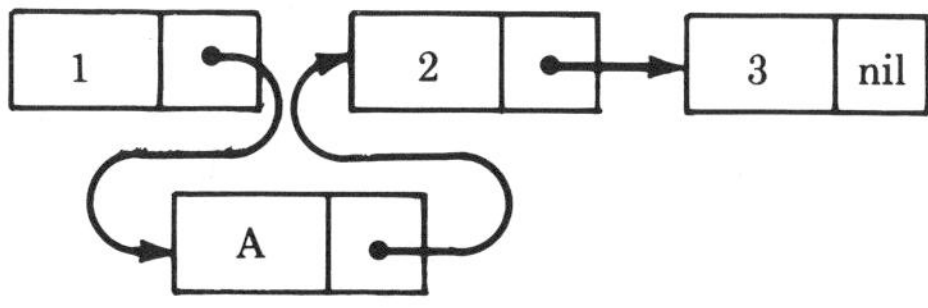

Deletion of a block from a list is accomplished by erasing the block from the list and then updating the pointers to reflect the change. For example, if block 2 is deleted from the list

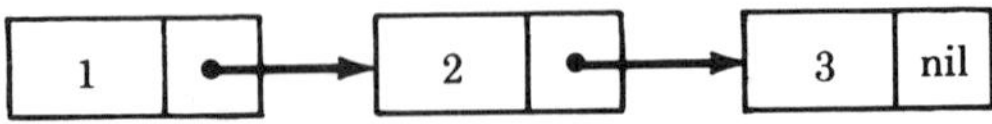

the result would appear as:

4. *Stack.* A stack is a linear list whose data elements are selected, created, or deleted in a last-in, first-out (LIFO) manner. Only the top element in the list can be accessed. To select another element in the list requires removal of all of the elements on top of the selected element. All elements in the list are "pushed" down when a new element is added on top of the list. All elements in the list are "popped" up when the top element is removed. Thus, pushing and popping are the two operations required to access and maintain the data structure.

5. *Queue.* Similar to a stack, a queue is a linear list whose elements are selected, created, or deleted in a first-in, first-out (FIFO) manner. Only the bottom element in the list can be accessed. To select another element in the list requires removal of all of the elements below the selected element. Addition of a new element on top of the list does not push down the elements, and the top element cannot be removed from the list. Thus, in a queue, pushing and popping operations are not required to access and maintain the data structure.

(iii) DESIGN OF ALGORITHMS. Once the data flows, control flows, the data structures have been defined, design of the algorithms used to process the data can begin. This stage of software design should include the following major design tasks:

Derivation of software functions from the software model
Design of the software functional structure

Design of the user interface
Review of module SIAD tree
Review of product unit definition
Review of product unit defectiveness definition
Design of module interfaces
Design of modules

These tasks should be performed in the preceding order shown and should be refined along with the test design on completion.

a. Derivation of Software Functions from the Software Model. In function-oriented design, the emphasis is on identifying functions, that is, the operations that transform input into output at each stage of the process. As discussed in Section 7.2.2, this is a modeling task. The designer must study the model developed during the modeling phase and decompose it into unique functions. This is a top-down, step-by-step process. The first step is to identify the major functions of the model. Then each function is decomposed into the next lower level of detailed functions. Each of the lower-level functions is then further decomposed into still another lower level of functions, and so on, until further decomposition is impossible. This process is similar to construction of a SIAD tree, as discussed in Section 8.2.1.

b. Design of the Software Functional Structure. After all of the functions have been identified, the interrelationships among them must be defined. The functions can then be organized into a tree structure based on the defined interrelationships. Such a structure allows understanding of a complicated problem on a level-by-level basis. A function at any given level of the tree is an abstraction of the subfunction(s) at a lower level, and hides some detailed information from the subfunction(s). The resulting structure becomes the structure of the software being developed.

As the designer develops the software structure, he or she will probably find that there are cases in which the same lower-level function is part of the decomposition of more than one higher-level function, for example, when a procedure is called by a number of procedures. When there are nodes in the tree structure that belong to more than one branch, the software is really a network (or plex) structure, as shown in Figure 9.1. For example, in the figure, the node $F_{1,3,1,1}$ ($F_{1,3,2,1}$) represents a function that belongs under both $F_{1,3,1}$ and $F_{1,3,2}$. Clearly, having many functions call the same procedure is efficient design, but to

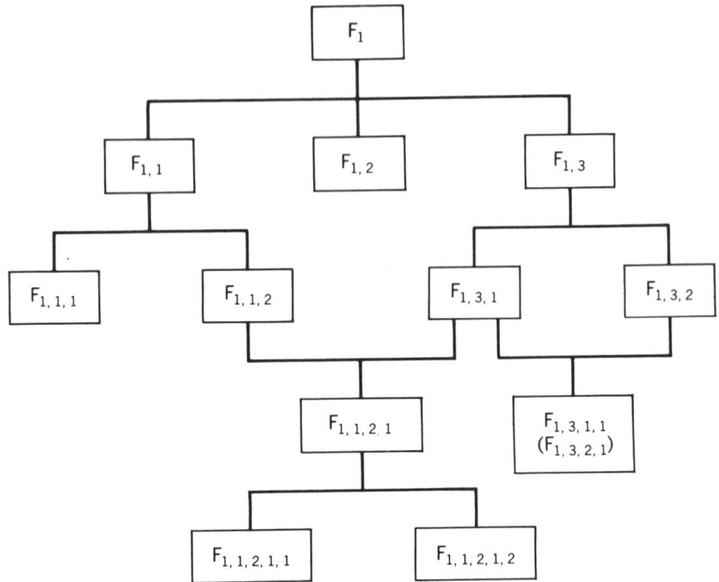

Figure 9.1 A software network structure design.

document the design as a network can make tracing the control flows a complex task that is difficult to understand.

To solve this problem, the designer can conceptualize the network as a "broken" tree structure, as shown in Figure 9.2. Here, each function is repeated where necessary so that each branch of the tree is shown with all of its nodes, and thus the complete decomposition of each higher-level function can be traced with ease. For example, $F_{1,1,2,1}$ belongs under $F_{1,1,2}$ and $F_{1,3,1}$. Therefore, it is shown under both higher-level functions. Under $F_{1,3,1}$, it is $F_{1,3,1,2}$. The designer must be sure to use a system of notation that indicates these nodes representing the same function, that is, the function, although repeated in the broken tree structure, appears only once in the actual software implementation.

This broken tree structure reduces the complexity of the network structure and increases the top-down understandability of the software design. To understand the design in a network structure, as shown in Figure 9.1, requires intrusions into other branches of the structure. In large-scale applications, the complexity of such network intrusions can be astronomical.

c. Design of User Interface. The preparation of the input and interpretation of the output of a piece of software form a man–machine

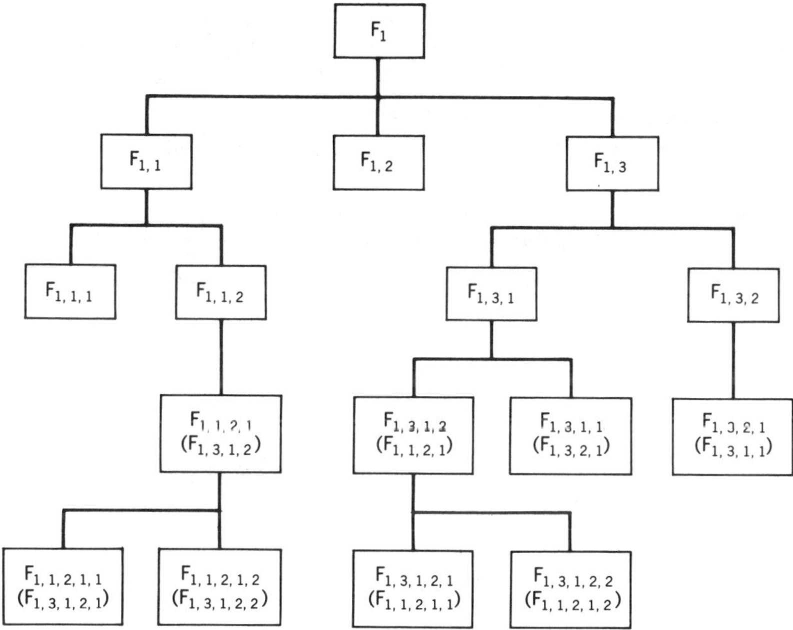

Figure 9.2 A software tree structure design "broken" from the software network structure design of Figure 9.1.

interface through which the user interacts with the system. Such an interface must incorporate human factors in its design and implementation. The following are basic guidelines for designing a quality man–machine interface:

A. Input data should be echo printed, where necessary, so that the user knows exactly what he or she is working with.

B. The order in which input data are prepared should not be restrained. It is very easy for a user to mix up the ordering.

C. The preparation of data should be straightforward. For example, it is a mistake to ask a business-oriented user to prepare numbers in an exponential format, for example, 0.1234E-05.

D. Do not provide the user with too many options. The more options, the more chance for errors. Always provide a default option for the inexperienced user.

E. Provide meaningful diagnostic messages to the user when an error occurs during execution.

d. Review of Module SIAD Tree. Similar to a complete software system, each module of a piece of software produces an output from an input designed to interface with the module. Therefore, the input domain of a module can also be represented by a SIAD tree, as described in Section 8.2.1*G*. A module SIAD tree is required because:

A. It ensures testability of a module, as inputs to the module can be constructed systematically from the tree to facilitate test design.

B. It forms a convenient basis for designing module interfaces.

C. It enables concurrent development of module design and module test design.

Since data generated by a module can be used by many other modules, it is desirable to associate a tree element with its originating module for cross-reference purposes. This can be accomplished by associating the name of the generating module with the tree symbol of the element. For example, if a module is named $X1$, then the data produced by the module can be represented in the tree with a symbol that begins with $X1$. Such an association is meaningful only under the condition that the element is not changed by any but its originating module. An example of generating module SIAD trees for the development of the automatic random number generator test program is given in Section 8.2 of Cho [12].

The design of a module SIAD tree is the test designer's task, as discussed in Section 9.2.2***A***. In the design of algorithms phase, the software designer should review the input domain of the software.

e. Review of Product Unit Definition. As discussed throughout this book, the product unit definition is essential to software development and the use of statistical quality control. The product unit is defined during the modeling phase and recorded in the requirements specification document (see Chapter 8). The product unit for each module in the software design is defined by the test designer, working concurrently with the software designer (see Section 9.2.2***B***). These definitions must be reviewed and understood by the software designer as he or she proceeds with the design tasks. Clearly, in the literature of function-oriented design, it is not uncommon to find this task overlooked.

f. Review of Product Unit Defectiveness Definition. The definition of product unit defectiveness is needed for quality inspection of product units. The product unit defectiveness at the system level is defined during the modeling phase, based on the user's requirements, and recorded in the requirements specification document (see Section 8.2.3*A*(ii). The definitions of module product unit defectiveness are given by the test designer (see Section 9.2.2*C*). The software designer must review and understand these definitions in designing the software and software modules. This review is crucial in obtaining proper software design. For example, in a piece of software that finds the roots of the quadratic equation:

$$AX^2 + BX + C = 0$$

product unit defectiveness would be defined as:

$$|AX_1^2 + BX_1 + C| > \epsilon$$

$$|AX_2^2 + BX_2 + C| > \epsilon$$

where X_1 and X_2 are the roots and ϵ is the defectiveness criterion whose value is specified by the user. If the user specifies a value of $\epsilon = 10^{-2}$, then the defectiveness criterion is fairly easy to meet. A 16-bit-word computation would be sufficient. However, if ϵ is specified as 10^{-8}, then special care should probably be taken. For example, the data types of DOUBLE PRECISION in FORTRAN or LONG FLOAT in Ada may have to be used on a 32-bit-word computer. If the value of ϵ is specified as 10^{-12}, then a 32-bit-word computer may not be sufficient, even with the FORTRAN DOUBLE PRECISION or Ada LONG FLOAT. A 36- or 64-bit-word machine may be required. If a software designer is not aware of the product unit defectiveness definitions, he or she may end up developing unusable software for the user. Again, this task is generally not addressed in the literature of function-oriented design.

g. Design of Module Interfaces. A module interface is the calling and passing of data between two modules. For example, the following FORTRAN CALL and SUBROUTINE statements form such an interface:

```
CALL SUB(A,B,OUT)
:
.
END
SUBROUTINE SUB(A,B,OUT)
:
.
OUT = A + B**2
RETURN
END
```

The variables A and B are passed to SUB, and the output of SUB is returned to the calling routine by way of OUT.

The design of an interface begins with studying the SIAD tree of a module and selecting proper tree elements to go into the interface. If a tree element is numerical, then only the element is chosen. The lower and upper bounds of the element can be designed in the module for range-checking purposes. If the input is well-defined or is user-independent, then the range checking may not be necessary and can be omitted for the sake of simplicity.

The following are basic guidelines for designing a quality module interface:

1. Avoidance of Content Coupling. A module calling another module should not reference data in the called module by using an absolute displacement, such as extracting the content at an absolute address from the called module. Any modification to the called module may alter the address and result in an error. Fortunately, this mistake is difficult to make in most high-level languages.

2. Avoidance of Bad Common Coupling. In some programming languages, data can be passed from one module to another through a construct known as common data storage. For example, the blank COMMON in FORTRAN and EXTERNAL in PL/I are such constructs. The literature has reported problems in using such features [3]. For example, variable names in common data storage bind modules together when the names are initially coded, making it difficult to reuse the modules for other applications; it is difficult to change the variables since modification and recompilation of many modules are required each time a variable is altered; it reduces program readability; and so on. However, most of the problems in using common data storage are caused by bad programming practice, namely, lack of discipline. A solution to this problem, based on a radio broadcasting concept, is given in Section 9.1.3***A***.

As a rule, then, two modules should not be "glued" together by the interface. Once developed, a module should be reusable. For example, a variable in an interface should be given a significant name within the module, instead of tying the name to the function of a calling module.

3. Avoidance of Control Coupling. The logic of a module should not depend on the logic of a calling module, or vice versa. For example, in the segments of FORTRAN code:

```
    :
    I = 1
    CALL SUBA(I,A,B)
    :
    I = 2
    CALL SUBA(I,A,B)
    :
    END
    SUBROUTINE SUBA(I,A,B)
    IF(I .EQ. 1) THEN A = B*2 END IF
    IF(I .EQ. 2) THEN A = B**2 END IF
    :
    END
```

The logic of SUBA is controlled by the value of I defined in the calling routine. This type of design should be avoided for reusability and logic simplicity.

4. Avoidance of Excessive Data Coupling. Excessive data should not be passed from a calling module to a called module. For example, module *A* calls module *B* with a student record. Module *B* is receiving excessive data if some data in the record, such as birthdate, are not needed by module *B*. Unnecessary data obscure module readability and tend to increase the chances of the data being modified by the called module. A technique for reducing excessive data in module interfacing is discussed in Section 9.1.3.

h. Design of Modules. A module consists of data structures and algorithms. Since there are many types of data structures and algorithms that can be developed to perform the intended function of the module, design alternatives and simplicity should be considered in designing the module.

The design of a module starts with studying the model on which the software is based and the module SIAD tree. It is essential in this design phase to provide input data verification and error message generation for the user interface. Of particular importance is range checking of array indexes. If an index exceeds its range, severe errors that are extremely difficult to find can occur. For example, if the size of the array *A* is 10 and the value of the index I is 11, then the instruction $A(I) = 12$ can write over the contents of a location outside of the array. The result is unpredictable. Some computer architecture and programming languages provide protection against such errors. Even so, errors may remain undetected. Therefore, error detection facilities must always be considered. If the input is well-defined or user-independent, then such checking may not be necessary and the software can have greater simplicity.

Some guidelines follow for designing quality modules,

1. One Function-One Module. The purpose of decomposing a piece of software into a set of smaller entities is to simplify its logic and increase its understandability. In software design, each of the smaller entities is called a module. Each module may be implemented in a PROCEDURE, SUBROUTINE, or FUNCTION, depending on the programming language used. Each module can be compiled independently and can be called by any other modules constructed to call.

Program modularization is widely used in the software industry. However, despite its power as a design strategy, its use has not resulted in a high level of software simplicity and understandability. There are several reasons for such slow progress in applying modularization to full effect [20]:

A. Since software requirements are not generally well-defined before the software design phase, modularization usually begins with an incomplete understanding of the software functions. Many functions are identified late in the design phase and are embedded into the software design in a nonmodular fashion.

B. Designers tend to design modules too broadly, making each module do too many related but different functions, thus obscuring the module's logic. This is caused partially by insufficient requirements specification and partially by insufficient design.

C. A common function is not identified early enough and is designed into the software by distributing parts of it among different modules, thereby increasing the functional complexity of the software.

D. Modules can interact on common data in an unexpected way, resulting in module interface complexity.

To achieve the potential of modularization, it is necessary to design a module to perform only one function. To do this, the designer must have well-prepared software modeling and requirements specification documents.

2. *Module Sizing.* It makes sense that a small module is simpler and easier to understand than a large one. As a result, practitioners tend to follow arbitrary rules to limit the size of a module. For example:

A. A module should contain 10 to 100 executable high-level language statements [8].

B. A module is anything that fits into 4,096 bytes of memory [8].

C. A module is whatever can be written and debugged in one man-month, or is equivalent to 200 to 300 programming language statements [8].

Approaches like these are not only primitive in nature, they do not guarantee the understandability of the module and have adverse effects on the complexity of the module interfaces. Limiting module size arbitrarily tends to increase the number of modules. The complexity of the module interfaces increases exponentially as the number of modules increases. For example, a piece of software containing M modules sharing N pieces of data in common storage, such as the blank COMMON in FORTRAN, has $NM(M-1)$ data paths along which data traces, changes, and errors can propagate [3]. Adding a module to the software means an increase of $NM(M+1) - NM(M-1) = 2NM$ data paths. The same phenomenon can be observed in using other features such as calling sequences. There is a trade-off between module size and module interface complexity that must be carefully studied. The principle of one module-one function is a good guideline for the designer to follow. A more detailed discussion of module interface complexity and techniques for reducing such complexity are given in Section 9.1.3*A*.

3. *Logic Simplicity.* Generally, the fewer parts in a mechanical product, the more reliable the product. This maxim also holds true in software development. Simplicity means understandability of the software. Therefore, the logic of an algorithm in a module should be kept simple. Module simplicity can be achieved by the following steps:

A. Design at least two algorithms as design alternatives.

B. Compare the algorithms in terms of number of statements, variable names, arithmetic operations, IF statements, array indixes, and so on.

C. Select the best algorithm as a result of this comparison.

D. Divide the selected algorithm into segments and repeat steps A through C for each of the segments.

Time spent on this aspect of the design will be repaid many times over in later developmental stages, and will help to produce a more reliable module.

4. Data Structure Simplicity. Understandability and efficiency of an algorithm depend heavily on the structure of the data that the algorithm manipulates. Most data are organized in a linear list, one-, two- or three-dimensional array, tree, network, queue, stack, and so on, as discussed in Section 9.1.1***A***(ii)c. Each of these structures has its own special properties suitable for some applications and not for others. For example, in a linear list, the list elements can be arranged in an ascending or descending order for rapid search of an element, whereas in a stack such an arrangement may not be desirable and can be difficult. The proper data structure for an algorithm, or vice versa, must be selected carefully. The following are basic guidelines for designing simple data structures:

A. Study the model on which the software is being based.

B. Understand the properties of the data structures that correspond closely to the physical or conceptual process being automated.

C. Select the data structures closest to the physical or conceptual process being automated for the module. Modifications to a module design may be necessary so that the best design of both data structures and algorithms can be realized.

It can be seen that simplicity in data structures and in algorithms is complementary. A detailed discussion of data structures can also be found in chapter 9 of Cho [12].

5. Separation of Module Input and Output. A common mistake in software modularization is the intermixture of module input and output. This practice increases module interface complexity and makes it difficult to trace the source and destination of a particular piece of data among the modules. Reading of the entire program may be necessary to trace a single data path.

A new approach based on the concept of radio broadcasting has been developed to solve this problem (see Cho [12] and Section 9.1.3***A***). In brief, a module serves as a broadcasting station transmitting data to other modules. Those modules serve as radios receiving and using data. No module serving as a radio can modify the data received. Each receiving module can, in turn, be considered as a broadcasting station, transmitting data to other modules, and so on.

The newly developed Ada language has a feature available for implementing the separation of module input and output, as discussed in

Section 9.1.1.*B*(iv). However, such implementation does not greatly help with tracing data paths or reducing module interface complexity. This subject is discussed further in Section 9.1.3*A*.

6. Use of Program Design Language. Module design can be expressed in a Program design language (PDL), a design tool discussed in general in Section 9.1.2. The PDL can be used to provide a description of a module in six major parts:

A. **Module Name.** This is for module identification.
B. **Level Number.** This is the level of detailed design of the module (not to be confused with the level of functions in a tree structure).
C. **Description.** This is the description of the function or subfunction(s) of the module, the constraints on the module, and other information related to the module.
D. **Input.** This is the description of the input domain of the module in terms of input variables with which the data are to be passed to the module. The description includes the types and the structures of the variables and the rules for constructing input data, and so on.
E. **Output.** This is the description of the output of the module and is given in similar detail to that of the input variables.
F. **Process.** This is the body of the module design. It uses simple English to describe the constructs of the module logic.

The input and output parts of the design are the interfaces of the module with other modules. The constructs used in the body of the module include SEQUENCE, IF-THEN-ELSE, DO-WHILE, and DO-UNTIL, which are written in simple English. These basic constructs are described as follows:

1. SEQUENCE. The basic SEQUENCE structure is:

where each box is anything except a GOTO statement. The statements in a box can be instructions, a control structure, or a combination of both. Each sequence should contain only one entry and one exit for better understandability. The following are FORTRAN, COBOL, and

Ada examples:

A. FORTRAN SEQUENCE

```
A = B + C
D = (A*B)**2
```

B. COBOL SEQUENCE

```
COMPUTE A = B + C
COMPUTE D = (A*B)**2
```

C. Ada SEQUENCE

```
A := B + C;
D := (A*B)**2;
```

2. *IF-THEN-ELSE (ENUMERATION).* The basic IF-THEN-ELSE structure is:

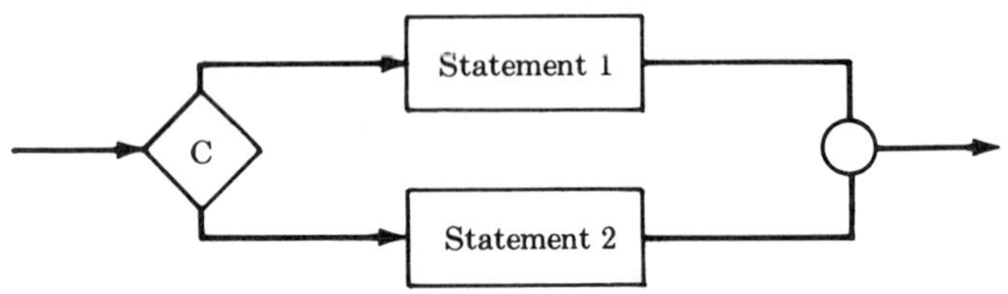

which is IF C THEN Statement 1 ELSE Statement 2. Either, but not both, of the statements can be null. Each statement can be an instruction, a control structure, or a combination of both. The following are examples:

A. FORTRAN IF-THEN-ELSE

```
IF (A .LT. 5.0) THEN
   B = C + D*E
ELSE
   B = C + D*E + 1
ENDIF
```

B. COBOL IF-THEN-ELSE

```
IF A IS LESS THAN 5.0 THEN COMPUTE B = C + D*E
                      ELSE COMPUTE B = C + D*E +1
```

C. Ada IF-THEN-ELSE

```
IF A < 5.0 THEN
   B := C + D*E;
ELSE
     B := C + D*E + 1;
ENDIF;
```

3. DO-WHILE, DO-UNTIL (REPETITION). There are two forms of repetition. The DO WHILE places control of the repetition at the beginning of the loop, and the DO UNTIL places control at the end of the loop. The basic structure is:

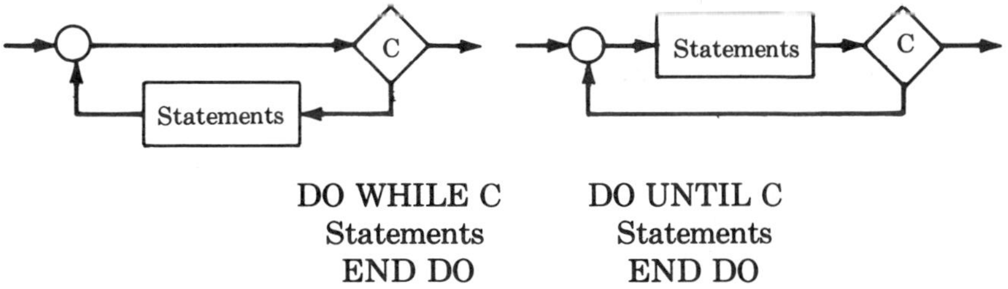


```
DO WHILE C          DO UNTIL C
 Statements          Statements
  END DO              END DO
```

The following are DO-WHILE AND DO-UNTIL examples:

A. FORTRAN REPETITION

```
  DO WHILE*
  DO 1 I = 1, N
      A = A + B
1 CONTINUE
```

*When N = 0, the loop
is not executed

B. COBOL REPETITION
The DO WHILE structure in COBOL can be implemented by the PERFORM UNTIL statement:

```
PERFORM A–1 UNTIL B > 0
    A–1.
        COMPUTE A = A + B
    A–1-EXIT.
        EXIT.
```

Any form of the PERFORM is valid, such as:

```
PERFORM A-1 VARYING I FROM 1 BY 1 UNTIL I > 100.
```

Strangely, the PERFORM UNTIL DOES NOT IMPLEMENT THE DO UNTIL in COBOL, since the statements are not executed by the PERFORM when the condition is met. The DO UNTIL is implemented by executing the statements once and then performing the DO WHILE as follows:

```
PERFORM A-1.
          PERFORM A-1 UNTIL A > 0.
          A-1.
                COMPUTE A = A + B.
          A-1- EXIT.
                EXIT.
```

C. Ada REPETITION

DO WHILE	DO UNTIL
WHILE CONDITION LOOP	LOOP
A := A + B;	:
END LOOP;	A := A + B;
	EXIT WHEN DONE;
	END LOOP;

The SEQUENCE, ENUMERATION, and REPETITION constructs are basic design elements which can be embedded within each other in any combination to expand the design. Each of the embedded constructs can be expanded by further embedding, and so on. For example, in the sequence of statements:

```
A = B + C
IF C = D THEN
   A = B**2
ELSE
   A = B**3
END IF
D = E + F
```

the IF-THEN-ELSE is embedded among other statements. With this expansion by embedding, the three basic constructs are sufficient for software design for any application.

If a module is complicated, then the PDL description can be developed in three levels. Level-one PDL is an abstraction of the level-two PDL, hiding some detailed information from the level-two PDL. Similarly, level-two PDL is an abstraction of the level-three PDL, hiding some information from the level-three PDL, and so on. The lowest level PDL is very close to the language to be used. The criteria used in developing these levels of abstraction are:

	Level		
PDL	1	2	3
Input Variable	Basic description and how it is used	Adding the structure of the variable	Adding data type, lower and upper bounds, rules for using the variable
Output Variable	Basic description and how it is used by other modules	Adding the structure of the variable	Adding data type, lower and upper bounds, rules for using the variable
Process	Basic functions and the logic order in which the functions are to be performed in simple English	Adding constraints, decomposing each basic function into subfunctions, with description of necessary initialization; using SEQUENCE, IF-THEN-ELSE, LOOP, and CASE constructs in simple English to design the algorithm	Decomposing each subfunction into smaller pieces with detailed description of initialization, conditions conditions, constraints, etc.

The advantages of using the three-level approach are:

A. After each level of the PDL has been completed, a design review or walk-through can be conducted by the software designer and user to ensure that nothing is missing from the PDL before going on to the next level of the PDL.

B. After the review, the design can be refined, and the PDL can be used as a design document for that level.

C. The level of abstraction in the PDL creates a top-down understandability of the design, enhancing tremendously the readability of the software being developed.

The level-one PDL for the software modules can be reviewed by all parties concerned who may not have a programming language background, such as user and developer high-level officials. The level-two PDL for the modules can be reviewed by all parties who have some programming language background, such as the user's technical persons, the developer's project manager, and the software engineers. The level-three PDL can be reviewed by the software engineers and programmers who are to implement the design. This three-level PDL description encourages more people to get involved in design activities.

An example of a three-level PDL description of a matric multiplication module is given in Figure 9.3.

(iv) LIMITATIONS OF CONVENTIONAL FUNCTION-ORIENTED DESIGN METHODS. From the perspective of this book, conventional function-oriented design methods are limited in their ability to ensure development of quality software. The methods currently being practiced do not include sufficient review of definitions of input domain and product unit, and do not seem able to solve any of the 20 problems stated in Figure 1.3. In the preceding sections, especially Sections 9.1.1***A***(iii)e and 9.1.1***A***(iii)f, the author has proposed approaches to make software developed by using function-oriented design more understandable and reliable.

Some software designers have argued that the problem with function-oriented design methods is that the physical or conceptual process being automated consists of objects as well as operations, and that conventional programming languages, by emphasizing functional aspects, that is, operations, lack features for abstracting and symbolically manipulating objects in the software design. It is argued that software developed with a function-oriented design approach is, therefore, not a balanced model of the process being automated. As a result, the problems the software must solve (and thus, the user's needs) cannot be fully described and are therefore difficult to understand. This, in turn, affects the quality of the software design.

The solution proposed by such designers is object-oriented design using the Ada programming language. In the following sections, object-oriented design methods will be described. It will be considered whether object-oriented design and the Ada language truly offer a way to ensure software quality.

```
MODULE NAME:          MODULA
LEVEL:                1
DESCRIPTION:          This module performs multiplication of
                      two matrices.
INPUT:            A = This is a multiplicant matrix.
                  B = This is a multiplier matrix.
OUTPUT:           C = This is a matrix storing the result of the
                      multiplication.
PROCESS:
    DO .;
         Multiply matrix A by matrix B and store the result in
         matrix C;
    END ;
END ;

MODULE NAME:          MODULA
LEVEL:                2
DESCRIPTION:          This module performs multiplication of
                      two matrices.
INPUT:            A = This is a 2-dimensional multiplicant ma-
                      trix.
                  B = This is a 2-dimensional multiplier matrix.
OUTPUT:           C = This is a 2-dimensional matrix storing the
                      result of the multiplication.
PROCESS:
     DO ;
         Multiply each row of matrix A by each column of
         matrix B ;
         Store the result in matrix C ;
     END ;
END ;

MODULE NAME:          MODULA
LEVEL:                3
DESCRIPTION:          This module performs multiplication of
                      two matrices.
INPUT:        A = This is a 2-dimensional, double precision,
                  of size 3 × 3, multiplicant matrix.
              B = This is a 2-dimensional, double precision,
                  of size 3 × 3, multiplier matrix.
OUTPUT:       C = This is a 2-dimensional, double precision,
                  of size 3 × 3, matrix storing the result of the
                  multiplication.
PROCESS:
   DO ;
      DO I FROM 1 TO 3 ;
         DO K FROM 1 TO 3 ;
            C(I,K) = 0 ;
            DO J FROM 1 TO 3 ;
               C(I,K) = C(I,K) + A(I,J)*B(J,K) ;
            END ;
         END ;
      END ;
   END ;
END ;
```

Figure 9.3 Example of a three-level Program Design Language.

B. *Object-Oriented Design*

Object-oriented design attempts to move beyond purely functional design techniques to create a balanced treatment between abstracted objects and abstracted operations. Software objects are treated as entities, each with its own defined set of applicable operations. The rationale for using the Ada language for software development is that Ada has a rich set of features to facilitate object-oriented design, in which the software is intended to resemble the physical or conceptual process being automated more closely than would software developed using other languages. Since the Ada language is ideal for the implementation of an object-oriented design, it would be beneficial to express object-oriented design in terms of the features of the language, that is, using Ada itself as a program design language. (The appropriateness of this use of Ada is discussed in Section 9.1.1***B***.) There are four major features in the Ada

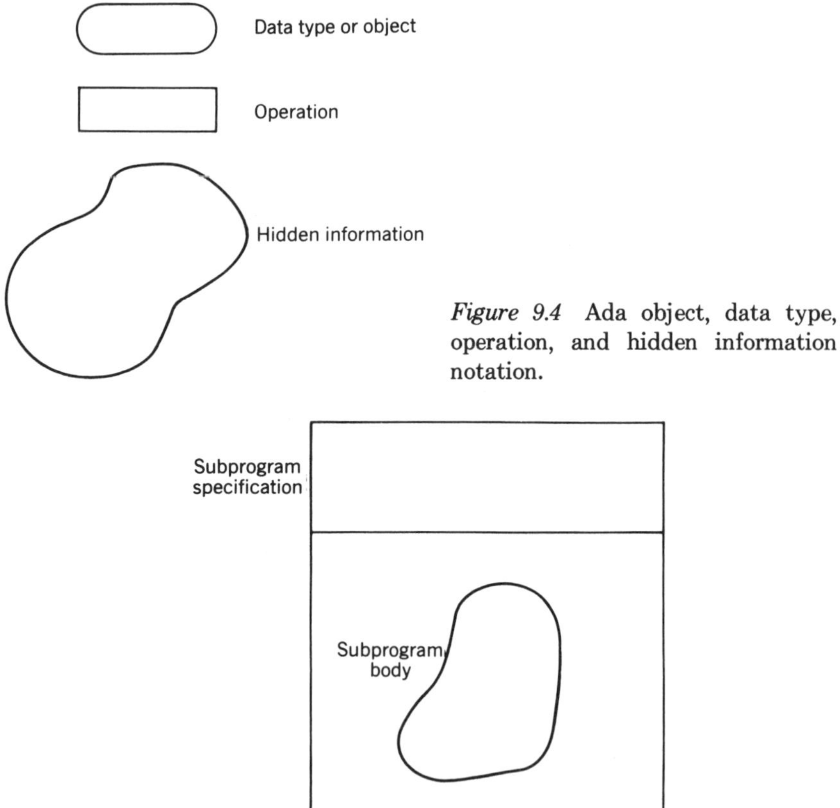

Figure 9.4 Ada object, data type, operation, and hidden information notation.

Figure 9.5 Ada subprogram notation.

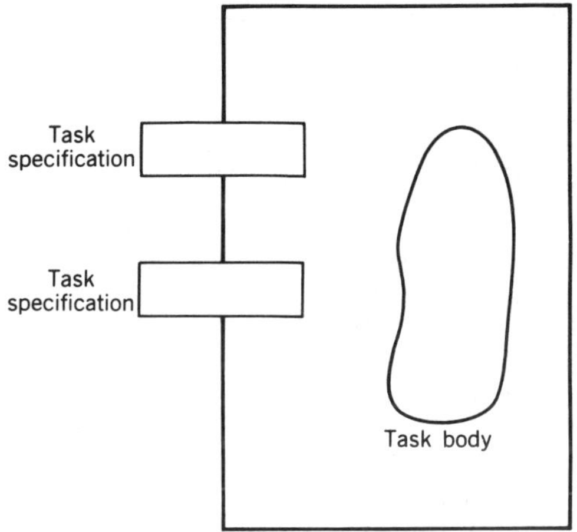

Figure 9.6 Ada task notation.

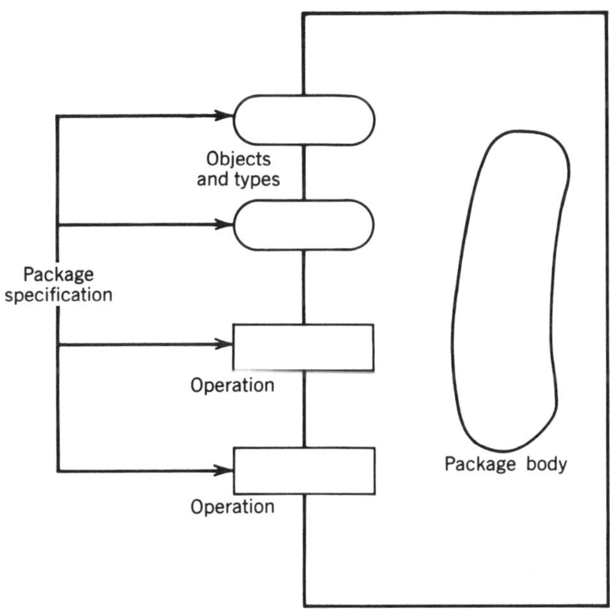

Figure 9.7 Ada package and generic notation.

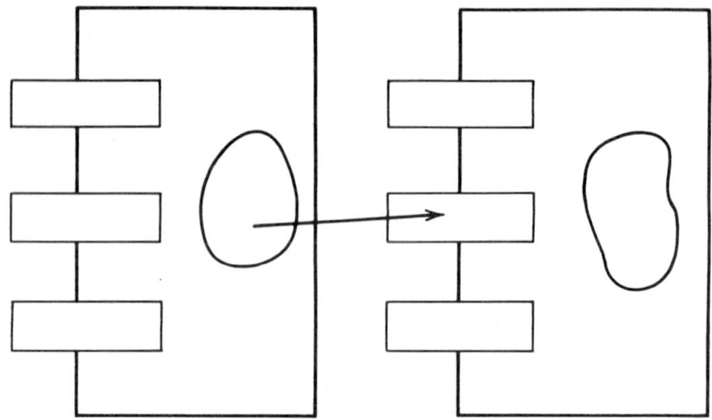

Figure 9.8 Ada inter-task communication notation.

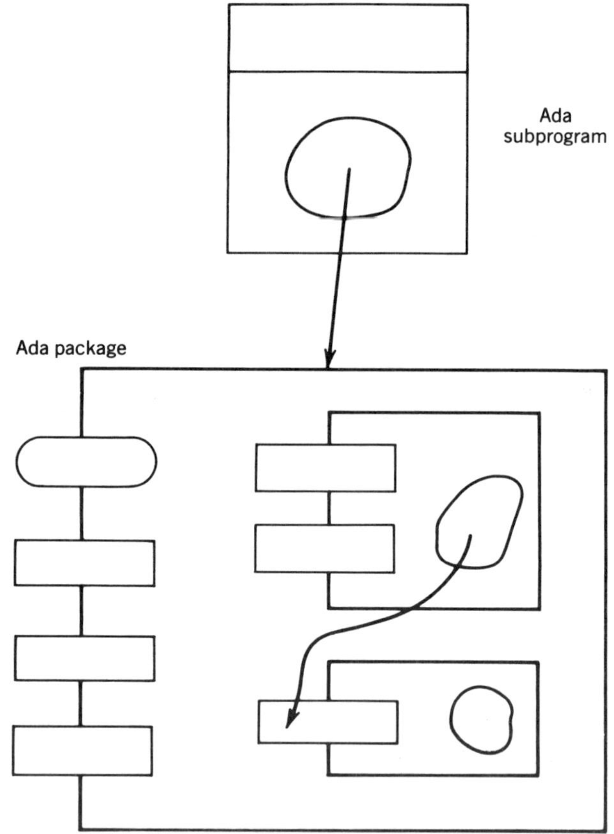

Figure 9.9 Ada unit nesting notation.

language: subprogram, package, generic, and tasking. The notation system for these Ada features would also be a convenient notation system for object-oriented design. These notations are shown in Figures 9.4 through 9.9.

The stages of object-oriented design are:

Define the problem
Develop an informal strategy
Formalize the strategy

(i) DEFINE THE PROBLEM. The problem is defined using whatever tools, such as data flow diagrams, are appropriate. In object-oriented design, defining the problem means understanding it as a number of interrelated entities which will be represented by modules in the software design. This process is iterative, and later stages of the design can be expected to contribute further insights into the nature of the problem. With modularization, increased insight into the problem can, in turn, enhance the design without requiring major changes beyond the module level.

(ii) DEVELOP AN INFORMAL STRATEGY. Once the problem is generally defined, an informal strategy should be developed, using natural English descriptions and concepts drawn from the real world. At this point, there is no need to think in terms of the structure of the design, or restrict descriptions to the formal expressions of a programming language. In object-oriented design, the formal implementation of the strategy will develop naturally as part of the approach. First, it is important to develop an informal understanding of the strategy that will later be formalized.

(iii) FORMALIZE THE STRATEGY. Formalizing the strategy requires the following design tasks:

Identifying objects and their attributes
Identifying operations on the objects
Establishing the interfaces
Implementing the operations

a. Identify Objects and Their Attributes. The objects and attributes of a programming language correspond to the nouns and qualifying adjectives occurring in the natural English descriptions of the informal strategy. By extracting the noun phrases from the informal strategy, several categories of nouns can be identified:

A. Common Nouns. These name a class of entities, for example, table, terminal, sensor, switch.

B. **Mass Nouns and Units of measure.** These name a quality, activity, or substance, or a quantity of the same, for example, water, matter, fuel.

C. **Proper Nouns and Nouns of Direct Reference.** These name a specific being or entity, for example, nozzle-pressure sensor, my table, abort switch.

In identifying objects in the software design, the common and mass nouns, along with units of measure, will represent abstract data types. The proper nouns and nouns of direct reference identify specific objects that refer to real-world objects of the problem.

The nouns' qualifying adjectives identify the attributes, or qualities, of each object. Attributes can indicate constraints, such as a range of possible values, or define timing relationships, such as asynchronous, concurrent, or independent. The selection of attributes can therefore begin to reveal some of the structures of the developing software design.

b. Identify Operations on the Objects. In the same way that nouns can be used to identify objects, the verb phrases that occur in the natural English descriptions of the informal strategy can be used to identify operations. In this process, each operation must be associated with an object. In addition, the adverbial phrases associated with each verb can be used to identify attributes of the operations, such as timing relationships, sequence of control, and number of iterations. As with attributes of objects, this process can reveal structures of the developing design such as tasks that will execute concurrently with other tasks.

c. Establish the Interface. The next step is to establish the relationships among the objects by defining the scope, that is, number and type of interfaces, and the visibility of the interfaces to each object. Ada provides a means to make a contract between the user of each object and the object itself, and enforces the contract by not permitting operations other than those specifically defined for each object. Again, the informal strategy provides a source for this information.

d. Implement the Operations. Once the objects and operations have been identified, and the interfaces among them established, the operations associated with each object can be implemented in the programming language. The informal strategy provides direction in designing the proper sequence of control, parallel tasking, and so on. The final result of this step of design is an executable program.

During implementation of the operations, lower levels of objects and operations will be identified. These are treated as in any hierarchical decomposition of a problem; namely, the process of defining the problem

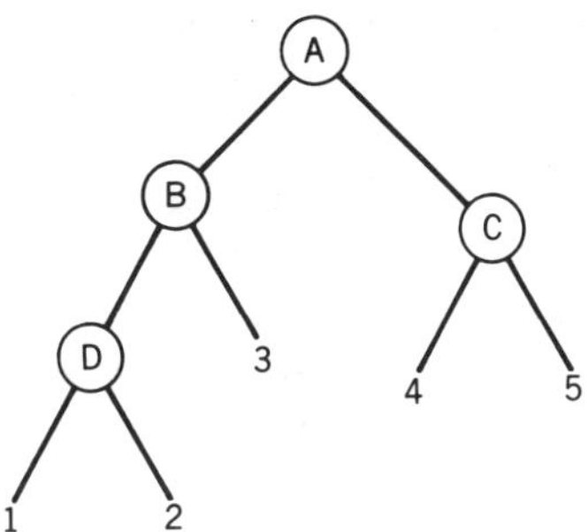

Figure 9.10 A binary tree.

and developing first an informal, then a formal strategy is reiterated as often as necessary to reach the lowest level of detail and produce a complete implementation of the software design.

(iv) DESIGN INTO ADA—AN EXAMPLE*. The following example of designing a program to count the leaves on a binary tree demonstrates the stages of object-oriented design discussed above and the implementation of this methodology in Ada.

a. Define the Problem. A binary tree is a simple data structure often found in compilers, gaming programs, and data base systems. As Figure 9.10 indicates, a binary tree consists of nodes (nonterminals A ··· D) and leaves (terminals 1 ··· 5). In a complete binary tree, each node has two branches. Thus, a given node consists of either a leaf or two subtrees. If a tree is just a leaf, then,

NUMBER_OF_LEAVES(TREE) = 1

If it consists of two subtrees:

NUMBER_OF_LEAVES(TREE) = NUMBER_OF
_LEAVES(RIGHT_SUBTREE) + NUMBER_OF
_LEAVES(LEFT_SUBTREE)

This recursive definition still applies if one of the subtrees is empty (a null tree). The goal is to develop a system that counts the leaves of a given tree.

b. Develop an Informal Strategy. There are many ways to count the leaves of a binary tree, for example, starting at one node and traversing the tree until all the leaves have been visited. However, this is an imperative method that requires high-level knowledge of how the ele-

*Source: G. Booch, *Software Engineering with Ada*, The Benjamin/Cummings Publishing Company, Menlo Park, California, 1983. Reproduced with permission of the publisher.

ments of the tree are physically connected (an implementation detail). Instead, an algorithm that appeals to an intuitive approach will be used. In this manner, if the representation of the tree changes physically, perhaps for efficiency reasons, the logic structure of the system should remain invariant.

It is assumed that the language used to express the algorithm has the three basic control structures (SEQUENCE, ENUMERATION, and REPETITION), and that it has no predefined objects or operations. It is also assumed that the designer has a facility for defining objects and their attributes for the abstract world (extensibility). Given these constraints, the informal strategy is as follows:

> Keep a pile of the parts of the tree that have not yet been counted. Initially, get a tree and put it on the empty pile; the count of the leaves is initially set to zero. As long as the pile is not empty, repeatedly take a tree off the pile and examine it. If the tree consists of a single leaf, then increment the leaf counter and throw away that tree. If the tree is not a single leaf but instead consists of two subtrees, split the tree into its left and right subtrees and put them back on the pile. Once the pile is empty, display the count of the leaves.

Figure 9.11 gives an example of the use of this informal strategy.

c. Formalize the Strategy. The next step in the design is to take this informal strategy and express it formally using Ada.

1. Identify the Objects and Their Attributes. As noted above, this is a simple task. Repeat the informal strategy, this time underlining the nouns and adjectives:

> Keep a <u>pile</u> of the <u>parts of the tree</u> that have not yet been counted. Initially, get a <u>tree</u> and put <u>it</u> on the <u>empty pile</u>; the <u>count</u> of the <u>leaves</u> is initially set to zero. As long as the <u>pile</u> is not empty, repeatedly take a <u>tree</u> off the <u>pile</u> and examine <u>it</u>. If the <u>tree</u> consists of a <u>single leaf</u>, then increment the <u>leaf counter</u> and throw away that <u>tree</u>. If the <u>tree</u> is not a <u>single leaf</u> but instead consists of <u>two subtrees</u>, split the <u>tree</u> into its <u>left and right subtrees</u> and put <u>them</u> back on the <u>pile</u>. Once the <u>pile</u> is empty, display the <u>count of the leaves</u>.

From this evaluation, the basic objects are:

LEFT_COUNT
PILE
LEFT_SUBTREE, RIGHT_SUBTREE; TREE

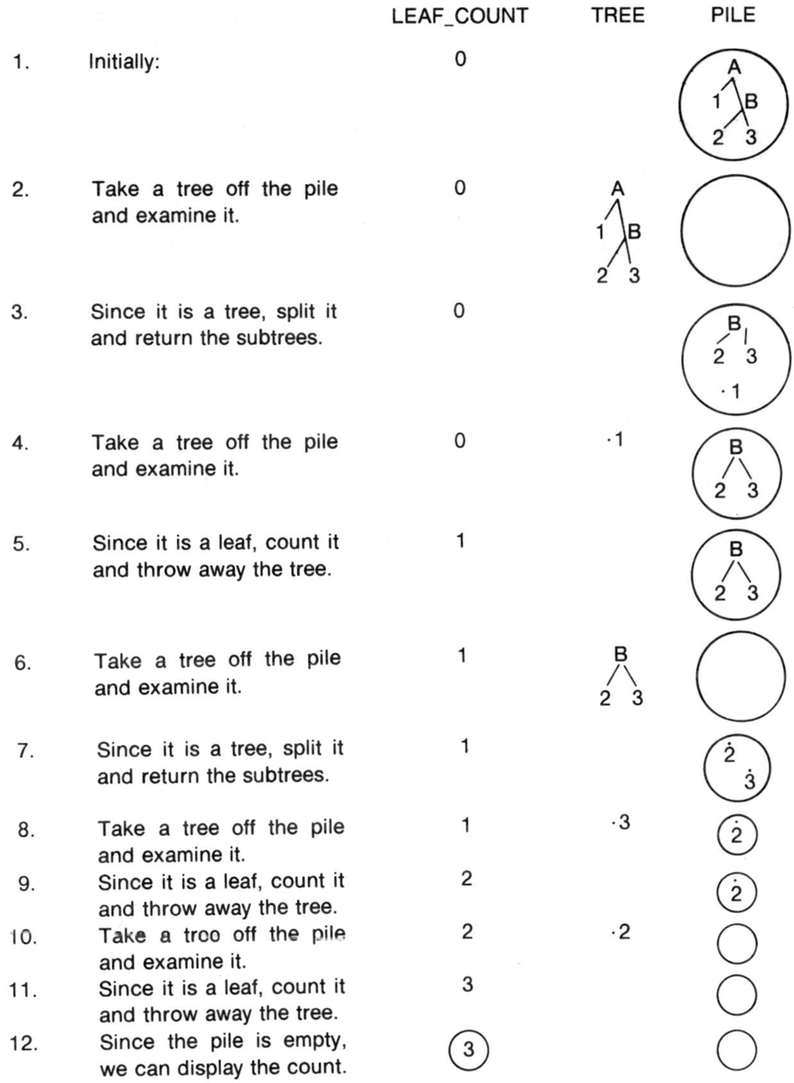

		LEAF_COUNT	TREE	PILE
1.	Initially:	0		A 1 B 2 3
2.	Take a tree off the pile and examine it.	0	A 1 B 2 3	
3.	Since it is a tree, split it and return the subtrees.	0		B 2 3 ·1
4.	Take a tree off the pile and examine it.	0	·1	B 2 3
5.	Since it is a leaf, count it and throw away the tree.	1		B 2 3
6.	Take a tree off the pile and examine it.	1	B 2 3	
7.	Since it is a tree, split it and return the subtrees.	1		2 3
8.	Take a tree off the pile and examine it.	1	·3	2
9.	Since it is a leaf, count it and throw away the tree.	2		2
10.	Take a tree off the pile and examine it.	2	·2	
11.	Since it is a leaf, count it and throw away the tree.	3		
12.	Since the pile is empty, we can display the count.	3		

Figure 9.11 Example of counting the leaves.

These are all abstract objects; they are a logical part of this problem space. Note that LEFT_SUBTREE, RIGHT_SUBTREE, and the TREE are all just instances of the same type of object, which can be called TREE_TYPE. Similarly, it will be assumed that LEAF_COUNT and PILE are both objects of the type COUNTER_TYPE and PILE _TYPE, respectively.

2. Identify Operations on the Objects. This, too, is a simple task. Repeat the informal strategy, this time underlining the verbs and adverbs:

> Keep a pile of the parts of the tree that have not yet been counted. Initially, get a tree and put it on the empty pile; the count of the leaves is initially set to zero. As long as the pile is not empty, repeatedly take a tree off the pile and examine it. If the tree consists of a single leaf, then increment the leaf counter and throw away that tree. If the tree is not a single leaf but instead consists of two subtrees, split the tree into its left and right subtrees and put them back on the pile. Once the pile is empty, display the count of the leaves.

Note that verbs implying existence (e.g., keep) are not underlined. This is because declaration of an object (PILE, in this example) already implies its existence.

Stepping through the informal strategy this second time, each operation is associated with its object. Furthermore, any adverbs encountered act as modifiers to the basic operations, indicating the time of an event (INITIAL) or the conditions under which an event occurs (while the pile IS_NOT_EMPTY). From this evaluation, the operations applicable to the objects are:

```
LEAF_COUNT
    DISPLAY
    INCREMENT
    ZERO
PILE
    IS_NOT_EMPTY
    PUT
    PUT_INITIAL
    TAKE
LEFT_SUBTREE, RIGHT_SUBTREE, TREE
    GET_INITIAL
    IS_SINGLE_LEAF
    SPLIT
    THROW_AWAY
```

As noted earlier, since LEFT_SUBTREE, RIGHT_SUBTREE, and TREE are all instances of the same abstract type, the applicable operations can be grouped together.

3. Establish the Interfaces. Given the objects in the abstract world, plus the operations that can be performed on them, the relationships among them can now be described. Using the notation introduced in

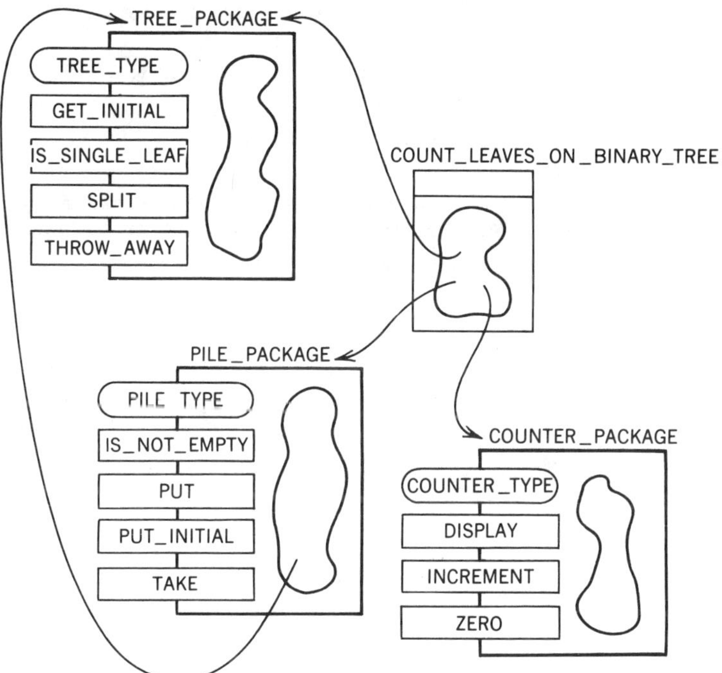

Figure 9.12 Design of COUNT_LEAVES_ON_BINARY_TREE.

Section 9.1.1***B***, the design of the solution is visualized as shown in Figure 9.12. In particular, note that the main action of the solution is indicated by a subprogram and that the objects are represented by three packages. The packages encapsulate the definition of the underlying types of each object; the name of each type is exported, along with the specification for each of the applicable operations. (Export means making something available outside of the package definition.) The arrows indicate which program units can see other program units. Thus, the main subprogram can see all three packages, but not the reverse. The PILE_PACKAGE must see the TREE_PACKAGE, however since the PILE must understand the structure of what is being PUT or TAKEN.

Given this design, the interface of each package can next be described. This interface will establish a contract between the package and its user; the details of each entity are hidden, and only the interfaces are visible. Furthermore, this logical abstraction of the objects is enforced in the solution by revealing the specification of only the applicable operations. It is not important for the package user to understand how these operations are implemented; it is only important that a user be able to apply these operations.

Using Ada as the design language, the interfaces of the entities in the solution are formally declared. A package specification provides the visible part of the interfaces, while the package body, which is separately compilable, provides the implementation of the operations. These package specifications provide the definition of the abstract data types.

For the LEAF_COUNT, which is an instance of a COUNTER _TYPE, the interface is implemented as:

```
package COUNTER_PACKAGE is
   type COUNTER_TYPE is limited private;
   procedure DISPLAY     (COUNTER : in      COUNTER
                                            _TYPE);
   procedure INCREMENT   (COUNTER : in out  COUNTER
                                            _TYPE);
   procedure ZERO        (COUNTER : out     COUNTER
                                            _TYPE);
private
   ...
end COUNTER_PACKAGE;
```

In this package specification, the operations are named with procedures. The **in**, **in out**, and **out** reserved words are known as modes and indicate the direction of data flow relative to the subprogram. The COUNTER_TYPE is declared as limited private, which indicates that the structure of the type is not visible (and thus not usable) outside the package. (The implementation of each private part is not included in this example.)

For the PILE, which is an instance of a PILE_TYPE, the interface is implemented as:

```
with TREE_PACKAGE;
package PILE_PACKAGE is
   type PILE_TYPE is limited private;
   function    IS_NOT_ EMPTY (PILE   : in
                         PILE_TYPE) return BOOLEAN;
   procedure  PUT               (TREE  : in out  TREE
                                 _PACKAGE. TREE_TYPE;
                                 ON    : in out  PILE
                                 _TYPE);
```

```
    procedure PUT_INITIAL   (TREE : in out TREE
                             _PACKAGE. TREE_TYPE;
                            ON    : in out PILE
                             _TYPE);
    procedure TAKE          (TREE : out    TREE
                             _PACKAGE. TREE_TYPE;
                             OFF  : in out PILE
                             _TYPE);
private
    ...
end PILE_PACKAGE;
```

In this package specification, a limited private type (not included in this example) is again used. Note that, with a limited private type, the only operations available outside the package are those listed in the package specification; operations of assignment or the test for equality or inequality are not even available to users of the package. The style of using procedures has been applied to name the abstract actions, while a function names a predicate (that is, an expression that evaluates TRUE or FALSE).

Within this PILE_PACKAGE, the form of the things that can be kept on the PILE must be known. To indicate a dependency among program units, a **with** clause is applied. In this case, the TREE _PACKAGE is made visible, and thus usable, throughout the PILE _PACKAGE. Once visible, the services of the TREE_PACKAGE can be named using dot notation, as TREE_PACKAGE.TREE_TYPE.

To complete the definition of the interfaces, the TREE_TYPE is described as:

```
package TREE_PACKAGE is
   type TREE_TYPE is private;
   procedure GET_INITIAL     (TREE        : out
                               TREE_TYPE);
   function  IS_SINGLE_LEAF  (TREE        : in
                               TREE_TYPE)
                              return BOOLEAN;
   procedure SPLIT           (TREE        : in out
                               TREE_TYPE;
                               LEFT_INTO   : out
                               TREE_TYPE;
                               RIGHT_INTO  : out
                               TREE_TYPE);
```

```
    procedure THROW_AWAY    (TREE          : in out
                              TREE_TYPE);
  private
    ...
  end TREE_PACKAGE;
```

In this declaration, the implementation of the private part is again not included. In several of the procedure declarations, note that the **in out** mode has been used, and for good reason. For example, in SPLIT, it is desired to take one TREE and break it into its composite parts, returning only those parts and a null value for the original TREE. If the original TREE were not exported, the tree would have been CLONED, not SPLIT.

4. Implement the Operations. Now that the specifications for the COUNTER_TYPE, PILE_TYPE, and TREE_TYPE have been declared, a set of tools is available to employ in the solutions to the problem. The final step in the solution process is to implement the informal strategy, along with the operations defined earlier. Working from the top down, starting with the informal strategy, the Ada solution that results is highly readable, since it matches the problem space very closely:

```
with COUNTER_PACKAGE, PILE_PACKAGE, TREE
     _PACKAGE;
use COUNTER_PACKAGE, PILE_PACKAGE, TREE
     _PACKAGE;
procedure COUNT_LEAVES_ON_BINARY_TREE is
  LEAF_COUNT      : COUNTER_TYPE;
  LEFT_SUBTREE    : TREE_TYPE;
  PILE            : PILE_TYPE;
  RIGHT_SUBTREE   : TREE_TYPE;
  TREE            : TREE_TYPE;
begin
  GET_INITIAL(TREE);
  PUT_INITIAL(TREE, ON => PILE);
  ZERO(LEAF_COUNT);
  while IS_NOT_EMPTY(PILE)
    loop
      TAKE(TREE, OFF => PILE);
      if IS_SINGLE_LEAF(TREE) then
        INCREMENT(LEAF_COUNT);
        THROW_AWAY(TREE);
```

```
        else
          SPLIT(TREE,
                LEFT_INTO ⇒ LEFT_SUBTREE,
                RIGHT_INTO ⇒ RIGHT_SUBTREE);
          PUT(LEFT_SUBTREE, ON ⇒ PILE);
          PUT(RIGHT_SUBTREE, ON ⇒ PILE);
        end if;
      end loop;
    DISPLAY(LEAF_COUNT);
  end COUNT_LEAVES_ON_BINARY_TREE;
```

The first part of this procedure uses the **with** clause to name the package it needs to see; the **use** clause has a subtle purpose (not included here). Together, these two clauses formally implement the relationships indicated in Figure 9.12. Following the name of the main procedure itself are the declarations for the objects as named. Finally, the implementation of the algorithm follows the **begin** of a block. Notice how the Ada code reads just like the informal strategy.

The final part of the implementation would include completion of the package bodies, along with the private parts. Further Ada tools would be required to do this. In particular, several high-level abstract data types must be implemented at a lower level.

(v) PROBLEMS WITH OBJECT-ORIENTED DESIGN. Object-oriented design is intended to provide advantages over function-oriented design in supporting the principles of software engineering. Features of the Ada language, such as abstraction, information hiding, and parallel tasking, can enforce the design steps of decomposing a problem into hierarchical levels and representing portions of the problem in a strictly modular fashion. Therefore, an object-oriented design should help ensure completeness and confirmability.

However, from the perspective of software engineering, there are a number of problems in using object-oriented design. The following sections discuss these major problems:

No review of requirements specification
No input domain definition
No means for using statistical quality control
Equivalence with function-oriented design

a. No Review of Requirements Specification. As seen in Sections 9.1.1***B***(i) through 9.1.1***B***(iv) (reproduced from Booch [11] and other Ada and object-oriented design publications), preparation and review of a software requirements specification document is not considered part of the design method. At least, there is little mention in the literature of requirements specification or of what should be the requirements to facilitate test and development of the software. Thus, object-oriented design is not different from conventional software development methods in this regard. Without a requirements specification effort, object-oriented design has no intrinsic advantage over function-oriented design in facilitating an understanding of the user's requirements. Therefore, even using object-oriented design, the developer's understanding of the problem may differ from the user's, and this difference may lead increasingly to serious misunderstandings as the software development proceeds.

b. No Input Domain Definition. Object-oriented design (at least as discussed in the literature) does not specifically designate an effort to define the input domain of the software. In defining the problem and developing an informal strategy, input data types and input operations may be identified, but there are no intrinsic methods for ensuring that the designer has a full understanding of the input domain. As discussed in Chapter 7, this would include types of input, characteristics of each type, rules for constructing inputs, and sources of inputs, plus—to understand the process—rules for using the inputs. Without such full definition, object-oriented design offers no more guarantees than function-oriented design that the problem has been fully understood by the designer.

c. No Means of Using Statistical Quality Control. Like the other software development methods, object-oriented design does not address definitions of product unit and product unit defectiveness. Therefore, testing a piece of software developed in Ada is still a problem. Without such definitions, there is no basis on which to apply statistical quality control, no way for a developer to show statistical evidence that quality is built into a piece of software, and, therefore, no effective way to offer a software warranty.

d. Equivalence with Function-Oriented Design. Although object-oriented design may appear different from conventional function-oriented design, the approach described in Sections 9.1.1***B***(i) through 9.1.1***B***(iv) is, really, another way of decomposing a piece of software into a "functional" structure. To see this, the design of COUNT_LEAVES_ON_BINARY_TREE in Figure 9.12 can be organized into a tree structure, as shown in Figure 9.13. The only difference between the two

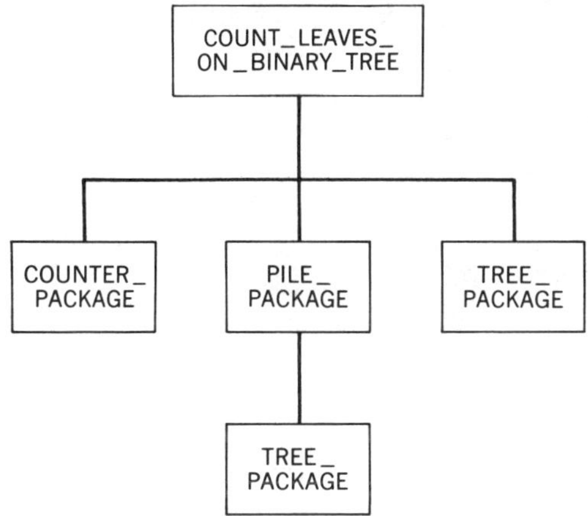

Figure 9.13 A "broken" tree structure of the design in Figure 9.12.

structures is that in Figure 9.13, the TREE_PACKAGE (which needs only a copy in implementation) is shown under the "driver" COUNT _LEAVES_ON_BINARY_TREE and under the PILE_PACKAGE in the design. Thus, the object-oriented design is equivalent to the function-oriented design "broken" tree structure shown in Figure 9.2 (see Section 9.1.1***A***(iii)). In general, there is no evidence that a piece of software developed in Ada using object-oriented design is more reliable than that developed by other methods. This can be seen in the example discussed in Chapter 13. The real advantage of object-oriented design would seem to be better software understandability.

(vi) USE OF ADA AS A PROGRAM DESIGN LANGUAGE. Ada has been proposed as a program design language. However, since a piece of software is analogous to a factory, Ada, as a programming language, is analogous to the building material of the factory, just like brick, plaster, aluminum siding, and concrete. In manufacturing, building materials cannot be used as a factory design tool, or as a means of communication among users, developers, and designers—that is the function of the engineering blueprints. The building materials are selected on the basis of their characteristics to implement the design. Similarly, the function of the Ada language is to implement a software design, not to develop or communicate that design. Despite its advantages in greater understandability, Ada is not an aid to modeling a design; it has no features for requirements specification, input domain definition, or product unit and product unit defectiveness definition.

In addition, the use of Ada as a program design language tends to reduce the degree of user involvement in software design, as the user would need some Ada background to communicate with the software designer. This can be a major stumbling block between the user and developer. It is suggested that the three-level program design language discussed in Section 9.1.1*A*(iii)h be used for designing each of the procedures or functions in a package, such as the GET_INITIAL, IS_SINGLE_LEAF modules in the TREE_PACKAGE in Figure 9.12.

Even though it is claimed that the Ada language has the necessary features to incorporate the software engineering principles of abstract data typing, information hiding, modularization, localization, uniformity, completeness, and confirmability to attain the goals of modifiability, understandability, reliability, and efficiency, evidence to support this is not yet available. In addition, solutions to some of the technical problems stated in Figure 1.3, such as Success, Warranty, Reliability, and Goodness, cannot come from Ada, as none of those problems are programming-language related! The solutions must come from another source. The approach discussed in this book serves this purpose.

9.1.2 Design Tools

Design is a set of mental activities that finds a solution to a problem. The realization of such activities in physical representation requires some conveying media, for example, languages, symbols, notations such as mathematical and logical expressions, and so on. Some of the tools available for software design include the Software Design Language, flowcharts, and Hierarchy plus Input-Process-Output.

A. The Software Design Language

As implied by its name, the Software Design Language (SDL) is used in designing and describing software systems. This language is also referred to as program design language (PDL), semicode, pseudocode, structured English, system design language, and system development language. The major characteristics of the language include:

Description of software design in a sequence of simple English sentences

The use of symbols, notations, and characters with the sentences

The use of IF_THEN_ELSE to describe conditional expressions

The use of DO WHILE and DO UNTIL to describe repetitions

No use for the GOTO statement

The use of END to denote the end of a repetitive operation or the end of a module

The description of a module divided into six parts: module name, level number, description, input, output, and process

The SDL is easy to learn to use. It can be used to express a design in any level of detail. The designer can start with a high-level concept and progress to a lower level of design. The coding of the program should closely resemble the design, resulting in a structured program. A design expressed in the SDL can be stored as a data base for retrieval and update purposes. An excellent description of the language can be found in Chapin [22]. An example illustrating the use of the SDL in the design of matrix multiplication module is given in Section 9.1.1***A***(iii)h. The reader should note that the SDL is less advantageous in satisfying the software engineering principle of information hiding than the 3-level PDL discussed in Section 9.1.1***A***(iii)h.

B. Flowchart

This widely used tool shows the logic flow of data manipulation in the software. Recently, use of flowcharts has been criticized for the following reasons:

A. Program design is an iterative process that requires many changes before it is completed. It is cumbersome to modify or redraw a flowchart to reflect the changes.

B. A flowchart is difficult to read. It can spread over many pages, requiring cross-page references.

C. A flowchart cannot be stored as a data base for automatic retrieval and update.

D. A flowchart is not compatible with the emerging technique of structured programming.

Despite these objections, a flowchart remains a powerful tool for software design. Almost all engineering disciplines employ drawing to express design. Designing an airplane without drawings is an impossible task. Software engineering is probably no exception. The old saying is certainly worth considering:

A picture is worth 1,000 words.

A sample is worth 1,000 pictures.

The usefulness of this tool, however, is situation-dependent. The designer should not assume its applicability without study.

C. Hierarchy Plus Input-Process-Output (HIPO)

This tool shows the organization of software modules, the input and output data, and the description of the processing of the input into the output. A HIPO chart is shown in Figure 9.14. The hierarchy of the software is shown in Figure 9.14(*a*). The content of each module is stated in Figure 9.14(*b*). Module input, output, and processing is described in Figure 9.14(*c*). The symbols P1, P1, 1 . . . , are called the program symbols and show module relationships in Figure 9.14(*b*).

Similar to the objections to the use of flowcharts, there are arguments against HIPO charts. Again, the usefulness of this tool is situation-dependent and should not be assumed to be universally applicable.

9.1.3 Design Strategies

Having looked at design methods and tools, some consideration will be given to two other aspects of design. The first is part of the art of software design: the techniques available for avoidance of module interface complexity. The second is a design strategy called proof of design correctness, which attempts to ensure the quality of the design. This strategy is one of the few proposed alternatives to software testing, and thus it is fitting to consider its merits and limitations before proceeding to a discussion of test design.

A. Module Interface Complexity Avoidance

Although structured programming has received considerable attention, discussions have focused on language and data manipulations, and little has been done in the area of structuring module interface schemes for transferring data from one module to another within a software system. The transfer of such data is performed through a combination of module calling statements (such as CALL in FORTRAN) and common storage statements (such as COMMON in FORTRAN). In conventional practice, there are virtually no rules for constructing such an interface

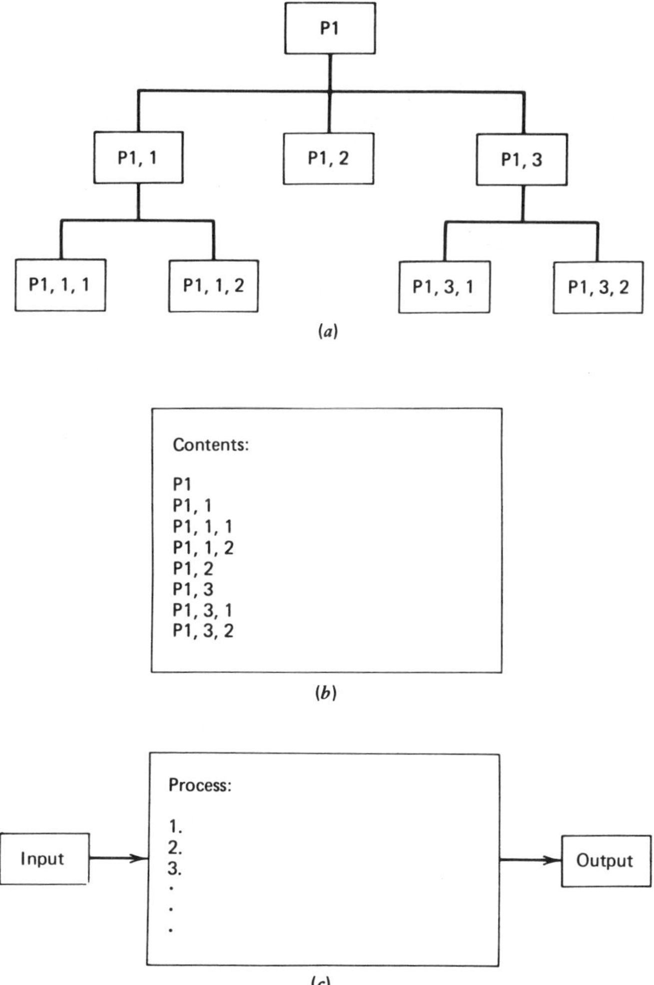

Figure 9.14 A HIPO chart.

scheme, and, as a result, modularization is plagued with problems such as data type definition, structural misalignment, and data flow tracing complexity, particularly in large, complex systems consisting of hundreds of modules.

In this section, a structured module interface technique is discussed. The technique includes: (1) the selection of external module constructs, (2) the selection of module interface constructs, (3) "read-only" file allocations, (4) data naming techniques, and (5) interface scheme construction for easing the problems. With this technique, the sources, destinations, and types of the data used in a module interface are explicitly indicated. The complexity of data flow tracing in the entire system is greatly reduced.

The technique can be applied to any high-level language program, provided that the language has proper module interface constructs. There are languages lacking such valuable constructs. For example, the COMMON STORAGE constructs required by the technique is not available in the ANSI Ada or COBOL, except in some versions such as that in Sperry Rand Corporation [6]. FORTRAN and PL/I are among the languages having the required constructs. An application of the technique using FORTRAN and an example are given. This emerging technique will not only help solve module interface problems and produce more reliable software, it will also increase human productivity in program development and maintenance.

(i) SOFTWARE MODULARIZATION PROBLEMS. Modularization in software development means the organization of a piece of software into functional units. One major advantage in doing so is better manageability of both software complexity and understandability. However, this is true only to a certain extent, which can be observed as follows:

In theory, if a project requires one man-year to complete, then only 0.5 years are needed if two people are working on it. Similarly, only 0.25 years are required if four people are assigned to it. Thus, it takes only one second if 31,536,000 people are put to work. In reality, of course, this is simply not true, even if unlimited resources are available. If nothing else, communication and coordination required for a team of this magnitude would make effective functioning impossible.

The productivity of a single person decreases as the number of people, denoted by M, increases. The productivity of the team increases with M, but only to a certain point beyond which the productivity decreases as the team expands in size. The project completion time tends to decrease as M increases, but not always. A relationship between the completion time and productivity versus the number of people is shown in Figure 9.15. The productivity and completion time reach the optimum points when the number of people reaches M. Beyond M, the completion time starts to deteriorate and the productivity begins to drop. This phenomenon follows the law of diminishing returns in economics.

Similar observations apply to software modularization. A relationship between software understanding time and understandability versus the number of modules is shown in Figure 9.16. The time is 0 when no

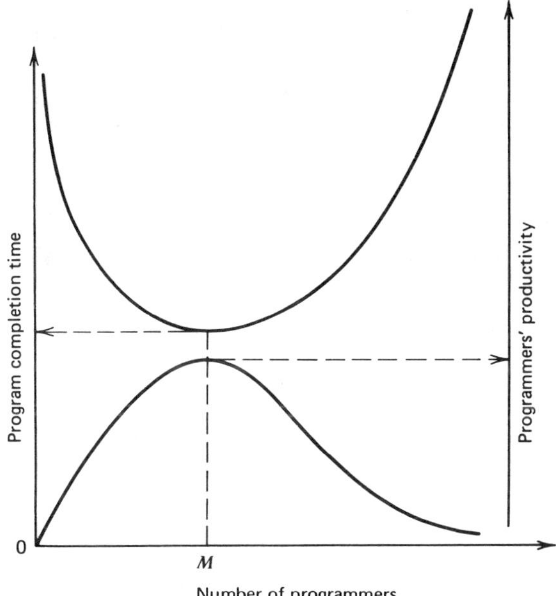

Figure 9.15 A relationship between program completion time and programmers' productivity versus number of programmers.

module is developed, and is t if the software is organized in only one module. It reaches a minimum at the point M.

Software understandability is defined as the number of instructions understood per unit of time. It is also 0 when no module is developed, and is u if the number of module is 1. It reaches a maximum at point M. Understandability decreases as the number of modules grows beyond M. The deterioration is primarily caused by the complexity of the module interface, that is, the passing of data from module to module. This phenomenon also follows the law of diminishing returns.

(ii) MODULE INTERFACE PROBLEMS. Module interfacing is an extremely complex phenomenon in software development and maintenance. The problems of module interfacing have not been well-understood in the software industry, as evidenced by such practices as arbitrarily limiting module size [8]. This arbitrariness inevitably leads to creation of an unnecessarily large number of modules. Since software understandability is governed by the law of diminishing returns, as discussed in Section 9.1.3*A*(i), no module can be added freely to the

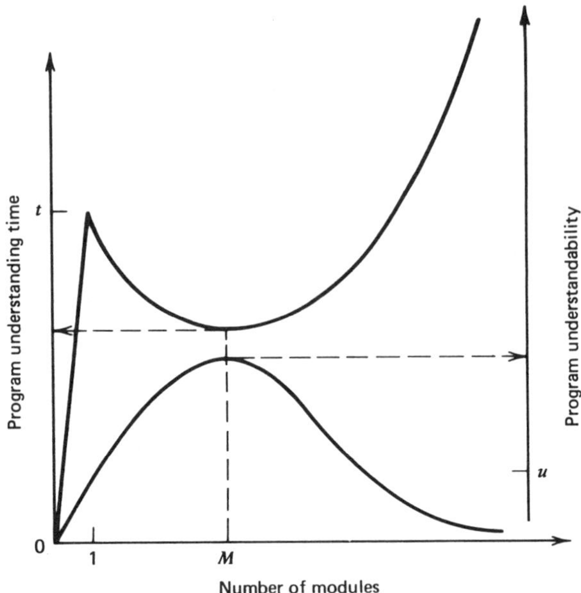

Figure 9.16 A relationship between program understanding time and program understandability versus number of modules.

software without limitation. As the number of modules increases, the complexity in tracing data flows among modules also increases—exponentially.

The following sections describe some of the severe problems in module interfaces constructed from commonly available features of high-level programming languages:

a. Problems in Using Common Storage for Module Interface. Common storage is defined as a portion of memory space shared by software modules. The allocation of the space and the sharing of the data in the space is accomplished by using a language construct in a module, such as the COMMON feature in FORTRAN or the EXTERNAL feature in PL/I. Some of the severe problems with using common storage are discussed in the following section. An approach to help solve these problems is discussed in Section 9.1.3***A***(iii).

1. Data Misalignment. Module interfacing through COMMON storage requires a one-to-one correspondence of variables among modules. This correspondence can easily lead to misalignment of data type, such as integer to real, and of data structure, such as array size. A variable missing from a COMMON statement in a module can mix up the interface for the entire program. For example:

```
SUBROUTINE SUBA
COMMON/A/B, C, D, I, J, K
:
RETURN
END
SUBROUTINE SUBB
COMMON/A/B, C, I, J, K
:
RETURN
END
```

In the subroutines, variable *D* is missing from the COMMON statement in SUBB. The data type of I in SUBB is mixed up with that of D in SUBA. In addition, variables I, J, and K in SUBB are sharing wrong data with SUBA. An error of this kind can be difficult to identify, particularly in a large and complex program.

2. *Difficult Data Source Identification.* A data source is defined as the module that is the "last" one generating the data being examined in another module. The source can be anywhere in the software. For example, it can be module 99 while the data is being examined in module 5. It can be module 20 while the data is being inspected in module 80. Thus, it is difficult and time-consuming to isolate the source while reading the program.

The data source within a module is the last statement generating the data. It is easier to isolate the source with a variable cross reference list produced by a compiler such as the IBM 360 FORTRAN H compiler. However, such a list only describes variables within the module. A cross-module variable cross-reference list would be of great value to ease the data source identification problem.

3. *Difficult Data Destination Identification.* The data destination is defined as the module that actually uses the data. A datum specified in a nonexecutable statement only (such as COMMON or INTEGER) or in a calling sequence—but that never appears in an executable statement in a module—is not considered as being used by the module. Since the use of a COMMON statement requires a one-to-one correspondence of variables among modules, redundant variables are also required for proper

data alignment in the statement. Such variables obstruct the readability of the module.

4. Complex Data Flow Tracing. There are two types of COMMON statements in FORTRAN: blank COMMON and labeled COMMON. The use of the blank COMMON requires not only a one-to-one correspondence of variables among modules, but also on COMMON statements among the modules, resulting in extreme complexity in tracing data flows. The complexity can be quantified as follows [3]:

$$P = NM(M - 1) \tag{9.1}$$

where P = total number of data tracing paths
N = total number of variables specified in a blank COMMON statement
M = total number of modules.

For example, a program consisting of 100 modules with 100 variables in a blank COMMON statement can result in up to $100 \times 100(100 - 1) = 990{,}000$ paths.

The complexity can be reduced by using the labeled COMMON so that the one-to-one correspondence of the blank COMMON statements among modules can be controlled. If the total set of variables can be divided into groups, and each group is needed by a subset of modules, then the situation can be greatly improved. However, the problem of the one-to-one correspondence of variables still remains.

5. Difficult Modification. A change to variables specified in a COMMON statement requires modification to many modules. It is a time-consuming and error-prone procedure. In addition, recompilation of the modules affected by the change is required. Frequent modification of software specifications worsens the situation.

b. Problems in Using a Calling Sequence for Module Interface. A subroutine code starts with an identification construct, such as SUBROUTINE SUBA in FORTRAN or PROGRAM ID.SUBA with PROCEDURE DIVISION in COBOL. The subroutine can be invoked by a call statement, such as CALL SUBA in FORTRAN or CALL 'SUBA' in COBOL.

A calling sequence is defined as the sequence of the call statement and the subroutine identification construct. Associated with a calling sequence can be a list of variables for passing data to, and for returning data from, the subroutine. For example:

```
CALL SUBA(A, B, C)
SUBROUTINE SUBA(A, B, C)
```

is a valid sequence in FORTRAN. Similarly:

```
CALL 'SUBA' USING A, B, C.
IDENTIFICATION DIVISION.
PROGRAM ID. SUBA
:
PROCEDURE DIVISION USING A, B, C.
:
```

is a valid sequence in COBOL.

There are variations in specifying variables in a calling sequence in different languages. For example, in FORTRAN, the variables need not appear in a sequence if they appear in a COMMON statement. However, in ANSI COBOL, variables are required to appear in the sequence since the COMMON feature is not available in that language, with the exception of the version described in Sperry Rand Corporation [6].

The use of a calling sequence for module interface also has a number of severe problems, for which it seems that no technique can be developed to solve. The problems may be eased somewhat with a program document, but this is not an efficient approach.

1. Data Type Misalignment. Module interfacing through a calling sequence also requires a one-to-one correspondence of variables among modules. This correspondence can lead to a misalignment of data type, such as integer to real, and of data structure. A variable missing from either the CALL statement or the subroutine statement can mix up the module interface for the entire program. For example:

```
SUBROUTINE SUBA(A, B, A)
:
CALL SUBB(B, C, I, J, K)
:
RETURN
END
SUBROUTINE SUBB(B, C, D, I, J, K)
:
RETURN
END
```

In the subroutines, variable D is missing from the CALL statement. The data type of D in SUBB is mixed up with that of I in SUBA. Variables D, I, J, and K in SUBB are sharing wrong data with SUBA. Fortunately, some FORTRAN compilers can detect errors of this kind.

2. *Difficult Data Source Identification.* Data source identification is also a difficult problem in using calling sequences for module interface, probably as difficult a problem as in using COMMON statements. This problem has been discussed previously.

3. *Difficult Data Destination Identification.* Data destination identification is also a problem in using calling sequences for module interface, as discussed previously for COMMON statements.

4. *Complex Data Flow Tracing.* Tracing data flows among modules using calling sequences is probably easier than tracing data flows through blank COMMON statements, but no better than through labeled COMMON statements. The magnitude of the complexity of tracing data flows among modules using COMMON statements has been discussed previously.

5. *Flying Variables.* A variable is called a flying variable if it has to be specified in many calling sequences before it is used in a module or subroutine. For example, Figure 9.17 shows four FORTRAN subroutines A, B, C, and D. Subroutine A calls B, and B calls C, which in turn calls D. The variable V is being passed to A from a calling subroutine. If V is not used in A, B, or C, but only in *D*, it still must be specified in all of the calling sequences from A through D. Thus, V is a flying variable since it "flies" over A, B, and C before it is used in D.

Since flying variables must be specified through many modules, they add complexity to the module interfaces. In many situations, the number of variables that can be specified in a calling sequence is limited. This limitation may force the use of some other interface feature, further complicating the problem. For example, the maximum number of continuation statements for a FORTRAN statement is 19. If the flying variables require a specification beyond the limit, then the COMMON feature must be used, adding a new dimension of complexity.

(iii) STRUCTURED MODULE INTERFACE TECHNIQUE. The problem associated with module interfaces constructed from a common storage can be solved by using the structured module interface technique [1]. A detailed discussion of this technique follows. The application of the technique to FORTRAN programs is illustrated in Section 9.1.3*A*(iv).

```
SUBROUTINE A(N, V)
:
CALL B(M, V)
:
RETURN
END
SUBROUTINE B(M, V)
:
CALL C(K, V)
:
RETURN
END
SUBROUTINE C(K, V)
:
CALL D(MN, V)
:
RETURN
END
SUBROUTINE D(MN, V)
:
W = (V*MN)**2
:
RETURN
END
```

Figure 9.17 A flying variable phenomenon.

a. Reduce the Number of Module Constructs to a Minimum. There are two types of external routine constructs in some programming languages that can be used for module development. One is the subroutine, and the other is the function. The invocation of a subroutine is performed by way of an explicit call instruction; that of a function is performed by way of an implicit call instruction. For example, the SUBROUTINE and FUNCTION are such constructs in FORTRAN. In other languages, there is only one such construct, for example, the SUBROUTINE in COBOL.

Such constructs are aids to coding convenience, but they add complexity to module readability. For example, the expression B(N, M) is ambiguous; it can be an array element or an implicit call statement invoking the function B with arguments M and N. Thus, the number of such constructs should be reduced to a minimum for simplicity. In almost all high-level languages, the subroutine feature is sufficient to construct all modules. The function construct should not be used because of this confusion.

b. Reduce the Number of Module Interface Constructs to a Minimum. The number of common storage and calling sequence constructs used should be reduced to a minimum in structuring the module interfaces. Selection of which construct to use may depend on the application. For example, a calling sequence may be more appropriate in some multiprogramming situations [3]. On other occasions, the common storage construct may be better. In general, the common storage construct is preferred, since techniques can be developed to structure an interfacing scheme that can solve most of the problems described in Section 9.1.3***A***(ii)a, as shown in Section 9.1.3***A***(iv). However, it is almost impossible to use such techniques with a calling sequence.

c. Use Read-Only File When Possible. As discussed in Item 5 Section 9.1.1***A***(iii)h, one practice which can ease data source and destination identification problems is the separation of module input and output. When module input and output are intermixed—that is, a module receives a datum, modifies it through computation or other manipulation, then returns it to common storage—problems result.

Separation of module input and output can be based on the concept of radio broadcasting. The source of a particular datum serves as a radio station broadcasting the datum to receiving stations. A receiving station can, in turn, serve as a broadcasting station, sending the data it generates to other receiving stations. However, a receiving station cannot change the data it receives from the original station. Only the data source is allowed to do so.

Thus, a module can be considered as a broadcasting station and a receiving station. Each module interface serves either as a radio, receiving data (which it is not allowed to modify) from its sources, or as an antenna, sending data to other stations for the module, depending on the function of the module. The interface scheme may be considered as a read-only file, since other modules using the data cannot change the contents of the file.

A ready-only file can be constructed using common storage. Each module receives data from other modules or sends data to other modules through a combination of (1) specifying the file name in the module, (2) moving the contents of the file to other storage within the module, and (3) using an intramodule reference to read the data for the module. The intramodule reference can be achieved by aligning some storage in the module with the file, using a construct such as the EQUIVALENCE feature in FORTRAN or the DEFINED feature in PL/I. The EQUIVALENCE construct is discussed in Section 9.1.3*A*(iv).

d. Use Standardized Names for Modules, Files, and Variables. Standardization of the names of the modules, files, and variables used in the interfacc, if done properly, can make the sources, destinations, and types of data self-evident, reducing the need for constant referencing of documents while also maintaining operational efficiency.

e. Construct the Module Interface Scheme. Following the principles discussed in a through d, the designer can construct a module interface scheme that avoids most of the problems of module interface complexity. The designer may find that it is difficult to develop a general approach, and that for each application it is better to begin by carefully studying the interface constructs available in the programming language being used and to design the interfaces accordingly.

(iv) APPLICATION OF STRUCTURED MODULE INTERFACE TECHNIQUE TO FORTRAN PROGRAMS. In this section, the structured module interface technique is applied to the FORTRAN program shown in Figure 9.19. An example of a module interface scheme is shown in Figure 10.2.

a. Reduce the Number of Module Constructs to a Minimum. As discussed above, FORTRAN has SUBROUTINE and FUNCTION features for module development, but the FUNCTION feature causes ambiguity and confusion (see Section 9.1.3*A*(iii)a). Therefore, the first step in designing the module interfaces is to decide to use only the SUBROUTINE feature for module development.

b. Reduce the Number of Module Interface Constructs to a Minimum. The designer should next consider whether to use the blank COMMON storage, labeled COMMON storage, or CALL sequence constructs. This selection may depend on the application, but, as discussed previously, in general the labeled COMMON storage construct is preferred.

c. Use Read-Only File When Possible. The designer should next decide the extent to which the radio broadcasting concept for separating input and output can be applied to constructing the module interfaces. In some applications, implementation of this concept may be tedious, in which case other techniques, such as grouping data according to the data's function using a labeled COMMON statement, may be applied. Development of such techniques is left to the interested reader.

d. Use Standardized Names for Modules, Files, and Variables. Standardization of module names, read-only files, and variables is illustrated for the interface scheme for a FORTRAN subroutine in Figure 9.18. The symbol X is an alphabetical character signifying a module name. The symbol NNNN is part of the module name. The symbol T is a character signifying the type of the data stored in the array TNNNN. For example, R means real data and I means integer data. The array TNNNN stores all data of type T generated by module XNNNN. The character K is a positive integer representing the size of array TNNNN.

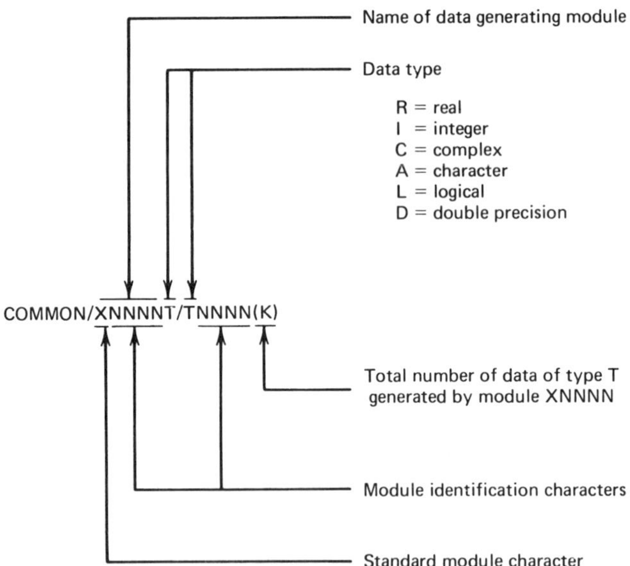

Figure 9.18 Standardization of a labeled COMMON for a FORTRAN module interface.

e. Construct the Module Interface Scheme. Figure 9.19 shows a structured FORTRAN module interface scheme using a standardized labeled COMMON statement for intermodule reference, and an EQUIVALENCE statement in the module for intramodule reference. The EQUIVALENCE statement is used both for specifying data generated by the module which will pass through the interface to other modules, and for extracting data from the interface for use within the module.

In the scheme, the data stored in array $T_{11}NNNN_1$ are generated by module $XNNNN_1$. All or part of the data are used by the module $XNNNN_m$ through the EQUIVALENCE statement. If no data of

---

SUBROUTINE $XNNNN_m$

COMMON/$XNNNN_1T_{11}$/$T_{11}NNNN_1(K_{11})$

COMMON/$XNNNN_1T_{12}$/$T_{12}NNNN_1(K_{12})$

⋮

COMMON/$XNNNN_1T_{1t_1}$/$T_{1t_1}NNNN_1(K_{1t_1})$

COMMON/$XNNNN_2T_{21}$/$T_{21}NNNN_2(K_{21})$

COMMON/$XNNNN_2T_{22}$/$T_{22}NNNN_2(K_{22})$

⋮

COMMON/$XNNNN_2T_{2t_2}$/$T_{2t_2}NNNN_2(K_{2t_2})$

⋮

COMMON/$XNNNN_mT_{ml}$/$T_{ml}NNNN_m(K_{ml})$

COMMON/$XNNNN_mT_{m2}$/$T_{m2}NNNN_m(K_{m2})$

⋮

COMMON/$XNNNN_mT_{mt_m}$/$T_{mt_m}NNNN_m(K_{mt_m})$

EQUIVALENCE

1 $(V_1,\ T_{i_1j_1}NNNN_{i_1}(I_{i_1j_1}))$,

1 $(V_2,\ T_{i_2j_2}NNNN_{i_2}(I_{i_2j_2}))$,

⋮

1 $(V_v,\ T_{i_vj_v}NNNN_{i_v}(I_{i_vj_v}))$

⋮

RETURN
END

Figure 9.19 FORTRAN module interfacing scheme.

$T_{11}NNNN_1$ are used by $XNNNN_m$, then, for simplicity, the COMMON statement must not appear in the scheme. Similarly, if some data of $T_{11}NNNN_1$ are used by $XNNNN_m$, then only those data names should be specified in the EQUIVALENCE statement. Each of the variables specified in the EQUIVALENCE statement $V_1, V_2, \ldots, V_v$ can be a single variable or an array of different dimensions. The specification of the scheme should also follow the rules of FORTRAN. An example of the scheme is discussed in chapter 10 of Cho [12] and in Figure 10.2.

B Proof of Design Correctness

Proof of design correctness (also called design correctness proof) is a way of promoting software quality that has received only minimal research attention, much less than design verification and walk-through. The idea is to prove that the piece of software has quality built in during development and is checked for errors early in the development process, since there is a better probability of uncovering and correcting an error at an early stage of development than at a later stage. Correcting an error costs much less the earlier the error is found and fixed.

The proof may consist of the following parts:

A. Prove that requirements are translated into software design correctly.

B. Prove that requirements are translated into software design completely.

C. Prove that the methods of processing inputs into outputs given in the requirements specification are correct.

D. Prove that the software design is correct in terms of the user's requirements.

This is an ambitious undertaking, and one that still has many flaws, as indicated in the literature Cho [12] and Myers [13]. From the perspective of this book, proof of program correctness is one step too far from the user's requirements to achieve maximum effectiveness of cost savings in error detection and correction. As currently practiced, proof of program correctness fits into software development as follows:

Requirements Specificationon	Modules' Internal Specifications	Implemented Modules
	Design verification	Proof of program correctness

A module (subroutine) is proved correct with respect to its internal specifications. Here, the modules' internal specifications are the result of software design. As shown, the proof of program correctness is two steps away from requirements specification. It would be more advantageous if proof of design correctness were integrated with software development as follows:

Requirements Specification	Modules' Internal Specifications	Implemented Modules
	Proof of design correctness	Test of software usability

This moves the proof of design correctness one step closer to the user's requirements. Also, as discussed in Cho [12] and supported with counterexamples in Chapter 11 of this book, just because a piece of software is correct does not mean that it will be usable by the user. Therefore, a test of the software's usability must be included as part of software development.

9.2 TEST DESIGN

Although proof of design correctness would be a meaningful way to help ensure software reliability, its development into a pragmatic methodology is many years away at best. Thus, testing remains the only pragmatic way to evaluate software quality and usability. However, all one has to do is to ask when to stop testing a piece of software and how good the software is after testing to realize that no confidence of any sort can be placed in the reliability of a piece of software tested by conventional methods and verified by program correctness proof, regardless of the extent of the testing and proof efforts.

The test design described in this chapter is based on the application of statistical quality control. This powerful and widely used tool in the manufacturing industries has not been used in the software industry because it is new to most software professionals. Yet, in the manufacturing industries it is the essential element that helps consumers demand and manufacturers deliver warranties on their products. Statistical quality control can also help software users demand and software developers deliver warranties on their software.

Statistically, testing a piece of software is equivalent to finding the defective rate of the product unit population that can be generated by the software. The defective rate is defined as the ratio of the number of product units that are defective to the total number of product units that the software can generate. The total number of product units, denoted by N, of any nontrivial piece of software ranges from extremely large to infinite, but still can be treated as an object of statistical interest. Although impossible in practice, it can be conceptually assumed that all N units have been produced and analyzed. Each of them can be classified as defective and nondefective. If there are D units that are defective, then the product unit population defective rate, denoted by θ, is $\theta = D/N$. Since it is impossible to obtain all N units, the best approach is to estimate θ by means of statistical sampling. If the population is conceptually shuffled, it provides a basis for applying the principle of binomial distribution sampling. A sample of n units is taken randomly from the population. If it contains d defective units, then the sample defective rate, denoted by $\theta°$, is $\theta° = d/n$. If n is large enough, then the rate $\theta°$ can be used to estimate the product unit population defective rate θ. Addressing the two major testing issues—when to stop testing, and how good the software is after testing—Equations (5.3a) and (5.4a), respectively, provide a starting point. Equation (5.3a) is an iterative sampling process that determines the sample size n; Equation (5.4a) can be used to estimate the mean, denoted by μ, of the product unit population. Once the value of μ is estimated, the product unit population defective rate θ can be computed by $\mu = n\theta$. If the value of θ is acceptable, then the product unit population is acceptable. The piece of software is acceptable only when the product unit population is acceptable. Therefore, the estimated product unit population defective rate θ can be viewed as the software quality index.

As discussed in Chapters 5 and 6, the principles of statistical quality control apply to establishing the product unit population defective rate and to software acceptance. The difference between testing for the defective rate and testing for software acceptance is in the sampling plan formulation. Acceptance testing is discussed separately in Chapter 12.

The major advantages of using the statistical method for testing are as follows:

A. Testing can be performed based on the user's actual utilization of the software. In this approach, each time that a user operates the software is considered equivalent to "sampling" a product unit from the product unit population.

B. Numerical confidence levels, such as 95 percent, can be imposed on the test results, consistent with the availability of resources for testing. The more resources available, the more sampling can be conducted, and the higher the confidence level that can be specified, as shown in Equation (5.3a).

C. Statistical quality control is applicable to software developed for diverse applications, scientific or business, batch or real-time, large or small, as long as valid SIAD trees are defined during software development.

D. In many applications, testing can be completely automated, from generation of test cases to analysis of test results.

Test design using statistical quality control is discussed in the following section first for the software system, then for testing of modules.

9.2.1 Software System Test Design

The task of estimating the product unit population defective rate for a piece of software is based on statistical quality control principles, using a step-by-step procedure:

Review of the software modeling and requirements specification documents prepared as discussed in Chapters 7 and 8
Review of product unit definition
Review of product unit defectiveness definition
Selection of test methods
Design of sampling plans
Design of input units using SIAD trees
Generation of expected test results

This procedure is applicable both to the entire software system and the modules of the system.

A. Review of Requirements Specification

Like the software designer, the test designer must begin by reviewing the software modeling and requirements specification documents. Communication among the user, developer, software designer, and test designer should be encouraged to ensure that all necessary and sufficient requirements are identified. The concept of "necessary" means that no significant requirements are missing and that no extraneous or redundant requirements are included. The concept of "sufficient" means that each necessary requirement is defined in appropriate detail. For example, if an application requires a cosine function, it may not be necessary to design one if a sine function is available, as the cosine value of an angle can be computed by:

$$\sin^2 x + \cos^2 x = 1$$

To define the requirement sufficiently would be to specify whether an angle should be expressed in radian or angle, which range of the angle value is desired, and so on. The test designer should apply the "necessary and sufficient" criteria in his or her review of requirements for:

Software input domain
Software processing requirements
Software product unit definition
Software product unit defectiveness definition
Test methods
Sampling plans
Software acceptance criteria

B. *Review of Product Unit Definition*

The product unit to be generated by the software system being developed is defined in the modeling and requirements specification documents, based on the developer's understanding of the user's requirements. It is the test designer's task to review this definition based on his or her understanding of the materials in Chapters 5 and 6. The test designer must take the user's point of view in designing a test that will give statistical evidence that the software is producing the output desired by the user.

The product unit for each module of the software is not defined in the requirements specification document. This definition is the test designer's task, as discussed in Section 9.1.1***A***(iii)e. In reviewing the software system product unit definition, the test designer must check for consistency between the module product unit definitions and the complete system's input and output processing.

C. *Review of Product Unit Defectiveness Definition*

The test designer must review the quality characteristic of each product unit and the defectiveness criteria which determine the goodness or defectiveness of the unit. The requirements specification document must be reviewed to determine which characteristic is the most crucial in determining the goodness of a unit. For example, for a piece of software that finds the root of:

$$AX^2 + BX + C = 0$$

The most crucial quality characteristic would be the accuracy of the product unit, that is, the roots found by the software. In other words:

$$|AX_i^2 + BX_i + C| < \epsilon$$

is considered good, where ϵ is a given small positive number, X_i is a root found by the software, and $i = 1, 2$. When this condition is met, then the unit is said to be usable; otherwise, the unit is not usable to the user. Other characteristics, such as modifiability, understandability, and efficiency, may also need to be considered in reviewing the product unit defectiveness definition.

Depending on the application, product unit defectiveness may be classified into four categories of defective units:

A. Severely Defective Unit: Contains wrong, improper, or unusable results. In the previous example, if:

$$|AX_1^2 + BX_1 + C| > \epsilon$$

$$|AX_2^2 + BX_2 + C| > \epsilon$$

then the unit could be considered to be severely defective.

B. Seriously Defective Unit: Contains correct but unusable results, or is difficult to use for user's daily operations. If:

$$|AX_1^2 + BX_1 + C| < \epsilon$$

$$|AX_2^2 + BX_2 + C| > \epsilon$$

then the unit could be considered to be seriously defective.

C. Minor Defective Unit: Contains an error that will not affect its usability. If:

$$|AX_1^2 + BX_1 + C| < \epsilon$$

$$|AX_2^2 + BX_2 + C| = \epsilon$$

then this could be considered a minor defective unit.

D. Irregularly Defective Unit: Contains results that are beyond expected limits of good workmanship but will not affect its usability. If:

$$|AX_1^2 + BX_1 + C| = \epsilon$$

$$|AX_2^2 + BX_2 + C| = \epsilon$$

then the unit could be considered to be irregularly defective.

D. Review of Selected Test Methods

The test designer must review the combination of regular, weighted, boundary, invalid, and special tests identified in the requirements specification document as appropriate for testing the piece of software to be developed.

E. Review of Sampling Plans

Understanding of the materials in Chapters 5 and 6 is essential in reviewing the sampling plans identified in the requirements specification document. The test designer must determine the consistency of the parameters and the sampling plans. For example, in determining the sample size required to estimate the defective rate of the product unit population, two parameter values must be specified in Equation (5.3a):

$$n_{i+1} = \frac{z^2(1 - \theta_i^\circ)}{a^2\theta_i^\circ}$$

namely, the confidence level z and the accuracy factor a. If the requirements specification states that $\theta < \theta^1$, then given the values of z and a, the minimum sample size n could be computed by:

$$n = \frac{z^2(1 - \theta^1)}{a^2\theta^1}$$

If the value of n so computed does not conform to the value of n in the requirements specification, then some action must be taken to correct it.

The test designer should pay particular attention to the acceptance requirements of the product unit population so that a predelivery acceptance test can be conducted to maximize the probability of acceptance upon software delivery. In reviewing an acceptance sampling plan, the consistency of the user's risk and producer's risk and the plan must be checked. Corrective action may be necessary before test design begins.

F. Design of Input Units Using SIAD Tree

Test design involves selection of a random number generator and design of inputs units using a software SIAD tree. Understanding the materials in Chapter 4 is crucial in selecting a random number generator. This task involves testing the generator to ensure the randomness of the numbers generated. A detailed discussion of the automated testing of a random number generator is given in Cho [12].

The construction of input units must be undertaken for each of the five test methods: regular, weighted, boundary, invalid, and special. In this section, it will be seen how the software SIAD tree is used in this task. Since there are three types of tree elements that can be specified in an SIAD tree—numerical, nonnumerical, and data value—the construction of a random input unit can be based on any one of these types:

A. Numerical Elements. If LA and UA are two tree elements representing the lower and upper bounds of a variable A in a SIAD tree, then the value of A may be generated randomly by:

$$A = LA + (UA - LA)r$$

where r is a random number, $0 < r < 1$. For example, if $LA = -0.5$, $UA = 10$, and $r = 0.2314$, then $A = -0.5 + (10 + 0.5) \times 0.2314 = 1.9297$.

B. Non-Numerical Elements. If a tree element randomly sampled from a SIAD tree represents non-numerical data, the actual data are to be selected by the designer, as will be illustrated in the next section.

C. Data Value Elements. If a piece of data is specified directly in the SIAD tree, then it is entered into an input unit directly, if sampled. For example, if a SIAD tree is specified as:

Index	Tree Symbol	Tree Element
1	Y1	X
2	Y2	MM
3	Y3	PPP
4	Y4	AAAA
5	Y5	FFFFF
6	Y6	HHHHHH

then AAAAXMM is an input unit if elements 4, 1, and 2 are randomly sampled in that order.

Construction of input units for the regular, weighted, boundary, invalid, and special tests is described in the following section.

(i) Regular Test. The construction of a sampling input unit starts with random sampling of elements from the SIAD tree of the piece of software. The sampled elements are used to construct the test input unit. Then the software processes the unit and generates a product unit. This process is equivalent to sampling a product unit from the product unit population of the software. In random sampling of the elements from the SIAD tree, if every element has an equal probability of being sampled, then the test is called a regular test, as discussed in

Section 8.3*A*(i). The following is an example of designing a regular test for testing a mailing list data base management system using the SIAD tree given in Figure 8.6.

The data base management system is being developed to perform the following functions:

Function C. Creation of a new address
Function A. Addition of field data to an address
Function D. Deletion of an address
Function M. Modification of field data in an address
Function R. Retrieval of addresses for mailing use

There are other functions that may be performed by the data base management system, such as copying of addresses from one storage medium to another, merging two lists of mailing addresses, and so on. But for the purpose of illustrating test design, these functions are not included. With the five functions listed previously, a regular test can be constructed as follows:

First the test designer must consider the product unit definition. In this example, the product unit is likely to be defined in one of two ways. In Definition 1, the product unit is defined as correct execution of one of the five functions C, A, D, M, or R, with proper data to be used for testing the function. In Definition 2, the product unit is defined as correct execution of a sequence of functions with proper data for testing these functions. These two possible definitions are illustrated in Figure 9.20.

In Definition 1, each unit consists of only one function. The function is selected as follows: A uniform random number between 1 and 5 is generated. The function that corresponds to the random number is selected for constructing a test input unit. For example, if the first

Unit	Definition 1	Definition 2
1	R	ADCCM
2	A	MMCARRDARD
3	D	CCA
4	A	RRRADAACCCDRMCC
⋮	⋮	⋮
n	M	CCDMRACCDDMRRCCAARAA

Figure 9.20 Example of functional product unit definitions.

random number generated is 5, then the fifth function, that is, R (retrieval of addresses for mailing use) is used for unit 1; if the second random number generated is 2, then the second function, that is, A (addition of field data to an address) is used for unit 2; and so on.

In Definition 2, each unit consists of a sequence of F functions. Each of the functions is selected randomly in the same manner as described in the preceding paragraph. The number F is also a random number which simulates a user performing a different number of functions each time he or she uses the system. The number F is selected as follows: Let K be the maximum number of functions a user can perform at any one time. Then:

$$F = [Kr] + 1$$

where $[Kr]$ means the truncation of the contents of Kr to an integer, and r is a uniform random number, $0 < r < 1$. Once the value of F is determined, each of the functions are then selected as described in the preceding paragraph.

Proper data for testing each function must then be generated.

a. Data for Testing Function C: Creation of New Address. Let m be the maximum number of tree elements in the SIAD tree. (The value of m should be less than or equal to the total number of the bottom-most tree elements of all of the branches of the tree. For example, the total number of such elements in the tree shown in Figure 7.4 is 16, as indicated by the circled numbers. These elements are also shown in the SIAD tree in Figure 8.6 indexed by the indixes 2, 5, 6, 8, 9, 11, 12, 14, 15, 16, 18, 19, 20 21, 23, and 24). For each function in the product unit, for example, C, a random number K such that $1 \leq K \leq m$ is generated. Then K random indixes, $i_1, i_2, \ldots, i_K$ are generated, where $1 \leq i_j \leq 25$, and 25 is the number of tree elements in the SIAD tree, as shown in Figure 8.6. The K tree elements corresponding to the K indexes are then selected to construct data for a function in the product unit. For example, let m be 16, K be a random number 5, and the five random indexes be 3, 13, 20, 23, and 24. The tree elements NAME, STREET, ABBREVIATED STATE NAME, 5-DIGIT ZIP CODE, and 9-DIGIT ZIP CODE would be selected for constructing data.

The construction of data for each sampled tree element must follow the rules for using that element. For example, the sampled third element in Figure 8.6., NAME, must follow rules 3, 14, 15, 16, 17, and 19 in Figure 8.7, and subrules 2, 3, and 4 in Figure 8.8. A name can then be constructed as follows: Using subrules 2, 3, and 4 in Figure 8.8, three numbers, $K4$, $K5$, and $K6$, are generated, where $1 \leq K4 \leq 20$, $1 \leq$

$K5 \leq 20$, and $2 \leq K6 \leq 30$. Let 5, 2, and 8 be the random numbers generated for $K4$, $K5$, and $K6$, respectively, that is, $K4 = 5$, $K5 = 2$, and $K6 = 8$. Thus, the first name has five characters, the middle name has two characters, and the last name has eight characters. Now the data for the name can be generated following rules 14, 15, 16, 17, and 19 in Figure 8.7. For example, the five characters ABCDE can be used for the first name, since they satisfy rules 14, 15, 16, 17, and 19. Similarly, the two characters XY can be used for the middle name, and the eight characters SMITH JR can be used for the last name. Hence, the data for testing function C would be:

ABCDE XY SMITH JR

The data for each occurrence of the C function in the product unit can be similarly constructed.

b. Data for Testing Function A: Addition of Field Data to an Address. In the mailing list data base management system, it is possible that some fields, such as APARTMENT NO., in an address do not have data at the time of initial data entry, but are filled in from time to time. Therefore, to design test data for this function, let H be the maximum number of addresses into which the user can add field data each time he or she uses the system. A random number G such that $1 \leq G \leq H$ is generated, where G is the number of addresses a user works with in a certain work session. Now the user retrieves G addresses randomly from the data base. (In a sequential or random access device such as a tape or disk, the addresses can be retrieved by G random record numbers. The retrieval can also be accomplished by specifying G values of a search key such as LAST NAME, if such values are known.) Random field data are then generated for those randomly selected empty fields of the retrieved addresses. Data for each field are generated similarly to those for testing Function C.

c. Data for Testing Function D: Deletion of an Address. Data for testing the deletion of addresses from the mailing list data base can be generated the same way as for the addition of field data into addresses, except that instead of adding field data to the retrieved address and then storing it back into the data base, the retrieved address is deleted.

d. Data for Testing Function M: Modification of Field Data in an Address. Data generation for Function M is similar to that for Function A, as explained previously, except that random field data are generated to modify randomly selected fields of the retrieved addresses.

e. Data for Testing Function R: Retrieval of Addresses for Mailing Use. The purpose of maintaining a mailing list data base is to expedite repetitive mailings. Therefore, retrieval of addresses is an essential function of the data base management system. The user may desire retrieval of the entire data base, or he or she may want to select addresses for various purposes. The need for testing retrieval of the entire data base is less crucial than the need for testing retrieval based on selected criteria, which would require some consideration. For example, the retrieval might be based on the selection of some criteria such as zip code, for example, $10000 \leq$ ZIP CODE ≤ 10500. Then, only those addresses satisfying the criterion are to be retrieved. The retrieval criteria might be simple or complex, such as:

LAST NAME = SMITH

or:

(LAST NAME = SMITH) AND (ZIP CODE = 10000)

or:

((TITLE = ESQ) OR (TITLE = ESQUIRE)) AND
(10000 ≤ ZIP CODE ≤ 12000)

Notice that the value of each field name in the criteria must exist in the data base. Otherwise empty retrieval may result.

Retrieval selection criteria can be constructed as follows: Let S be the maximum number of field names (or keys) that can be used in a retrieval selection. Let T be a random number, $1 \leq T \leq S$. Then T field names are selected to be the keys for constructing a retrieval criterion. Proper data are generated randomly for each of the keys, where proper data means data available in the data base.

(ii) WEIGHTED TESTS. Input data units for a weighted test design can be constructed in the same way as the input for a regular test design, except that the test samples elements from a weighted SIAD tree, as shown in Figure 8.5. The process of weighting, explained in Section 8.2.1***G***(ii), gives each tree element a greater or lesser probability of being sampled than other tree elements, and is a way for the test designer to simulate the frequencies with which the user is likely to use the system functions.

(iii) BOUNDARY TEST. In applications where many boundary conditions exist, another type of test design is required. For example, in a piece of software that finds the roots of:

$$A_{100}X^{100} + A_{99}X^{99} + \cdots + A_0X^0 = 0$$

the bounds of each of the coefficients $A_{100}, A_{99}, \ldots A_0$ are defined, that is:

$$L_{A_{100}} \leq A_{100} \leq U_{A_{100}}$$
$$L_{A_{99}} \leq A_{99} \leq U_{A_{99}}$$
$$\vdots$$
$$L_{A_0} \leq A_0 \leq U_{A_0}$$

Thus, in cases where each coefficient assumes either its lower or upper bound value, there are 2^{101} boundary conditions that need to be tested. Since testing of 2^{101} conditions is impossible, statistical sampling must be used, and a boundary test must be designed in which randomly sampled boundary conditions are the input data units.

In the mailing list data base management system example, the boundary conditions are the cases shown in Figure 8.8, where the length of each field name assumes either of its upper or lower bound value. There are $2^{10} = 1024$ boundary conditions in Figure 8.8. In addition, there are other boundary conditions such as the maximum number of addresses that can be stored by the data base management system, the maximum number of users who can access the systems at the same time, the maximum number of field names in a retrieval selection criterion, and so on. It is the test designer's job to identify those conditions to be tested if they are not specified in the requirements specification document.

(iv) INVALID TEST. The invalid test is for testing a piece of software's capability to handle invalid data. The design of the test is identical to the design of the regular, weighted, and boundary tests, except that the input units are constructed by generating data that go against the rules, subrules, and boundary conditions defined in the SIAD tree. For example, with reference to Figures 8.6 and 8.7, invalid input data for the tree element LAST NAME can be constructed by including numerical characters, for example, SM1TH. For numerical applications, an invalid input can be generated as a number outside of the defined boundary conditions. For example, in a piece of software that finds the roots of the polynomial:

$$A_{100}X^{100} + A_{99}X^{99} + \cdots + A_0X^0 = 0$$

the boundary values for coefficient A_{100} would be:

$$L_{A_{100}} \leq A_{100} \leq U_{A_{100}}$$

If a number A^*_{100} is generated outside the boundary conditions of A_{100}, for example, $A^*_{100} < L_{A_{100}}$, then that value for coefficient A_{100} would be an input unit for the invalid test.

(v) SPECIAL TEST. In applications where special tests must be conducted but the number of special cases prohibits full testing, then statistical sampling of special cases is necessary. Input units for the special test can be constructed as for the other types of tests, except that the units are sampled from the special cases specified in the requirements specification document or identified by the test designer.

G. Generation of Expected Test Results

After reviewing the combination of regular, weighted, boundary, invalid, and special tests necessary to adequately test the software, and designing sampling plans to generate input units for each test, the test designer must identify and document the expected test results. This task requires identification of the values of the product units to be produced by the software. The values will be sampled and tested against the defectiveness criteria to determine the goodness or defectiveness of each product unit. However, in many applications, such as those involving complex calculations, it may be difficult to find the values of the product units before the software is implemented and performs the actual calculations. For example, consider a piece of software that will find the inverse A^{-1} of a matrix A. As long as the size of the matrix is small, the test designer can generate the expected test results fairly easily. In a 2×2 matrix, the values of x and y in the linear equations:

$$2x + y = 5$$
$$5x + 3.5y = 6$$

can be found as follows. The equations are expressed in matrix form:

$$\begin{pmatrix} 2 & 1 \\ 5 & 3.5 \end{pmatrix} \begin{pmatrix} x \\ y \end{pmatrix} = \begin{pmatrix} 5 \\ 6 \end{pmatrix}$$

Thus:

$$A = \begin{pmatrix} 2 & 1 \\ 5 & 3.5 \end{pmatrix}$$

The inverse of A is found to be:

$$A^{-1} = \begin{pmatrix} 1.75 & -0.5 \\ -2.5 & 1 \end{pmatrix}$$

Therefore,

$$\begin{pmatrix} x \\ y \end{pmatrix} = \begin{pmatrix} 1.75 & -0.5 \\ -2.5 & 1 \end{pmatrix} \begin{pmatrix} 5 \\ 6 \end{pmatrix} = \begin{pmatrix} 5.75 \\ -6.5 \end{pmatrix}$$

However, if the matrix size is 1,000 × 1,000, this task becomes infeasible before the software is implemented.

To generate expected test results during the test design phase, then, may require the test designer to use his or her ingenuity in finding alternatives. In the matrix inversion software, for example, the test designer can express test results in terms of the identify matrix I:

$$A^{-1}A = I$$

Now, the test designer can apply the defectiveness criteria to the values of the identity matrix indexes:

$$A^{-1}A = \begin{pmatrix} 1.75 & -0.5 \\ -2.5 & 1 \end{pmatrix}\begin{pmatrix} 2 & 1 \\ 5 & 3.5 \end{pmatrix} = \begin{pmatrix} 1 & 0 \\ 0 & 1 \end{pmatrix} = \mathrm{I}$$

Taking into account potential rounding and truncation errors, he or she can identify conditions such as $|I_{ij}| < \epsilon$ for $i \neq j$, and $|1 - I_{ii}| < \epsilon$ for all i and j, where i and j are row and column numbers of the indices. With this definition of expected results, the test operator will be able to determine whether a product unit A^{-1} is acceptable or defective. Given that $\epsilon = 0.00001$, for example, the test operator can see that:

$$I = \begin{pmatrix} 1.000001 & 0.000001 \\ 0.000002 & 1.000003 \end{pmatrix}$$

conforms to the expected result and indicates that the input units to the test resulted in output of an acceptable product unit A^{-1}. Likewise, the test operator can see that:

$$I = \begin{pmatrix} 1.01 & 0.000001 \\ 0.000002 & 1.000003 \end{pmatrix}$$

does not conform to the expected result (i.e., $I_{11} = 1.01$, and $1.01 - 1 = 0.01$, and $0.01 > 0.00001$) and indicates that the product unit A^{-1} is defective. This method would allow the test designer to generate expected results for a 1,000 × 1,000 matrix without needing to calculate the values of actual product units.

In other applications, the expected test results can often be obtained in a straightforward manner. For example, in testing the mailing list data base management system, each product unit must be correctly reflected in the data base; otherwise, a unit can be considered defective.

9.2.2 Module Test Design

Virtually all software is implemented in a test and integration phase of development in which small portions of the piece of software, that is, modules, are tested separately and then integrated until the software system is complete. Designing tests for each module is the responsibility of the test designer, and the time to design module tests is during the test design phase of development.

Looking at current practices in the software industry, one observes the same problems in module testing as in software system testing. There are many methods being used, such as the so-called top-down, bottom-up, big-bang, and sandwich testing [13]. These approaches tend to confuse testing the module with testing the module output, just as software design in general tends to confuse the software product, that is, output, with the software itself. For example, some module test methods propose the following tests:

A. Every statement in a module must be executed at least once during testing.

B. Every control path in a module must be traversed at least once during testing.

Such methods do not address how to determine the usefulness of the module output.

Clearly, the best way to approach module test design is to treat each module as if it were a piece of software whose input domain can be specified and whose output can be defined in product units which can be tested for goodness or defectiveness by statistical sampling. As discussed previously, the definitions of product units for a software system are based on the user's requirements. If the output of a module is directly usable by the user, then the test designer can base the product unit definition for that module on the requirements specification document. Otherwise, where the module output is used solely by other modules of the system, it is the test designer's task to define the product unit for each module to be tested.

A. *Design of Module SIAD Tree*

Just as the function of a software system is to map a system input onto a system product unit, the function of a module is to process a module input unit into a module output unit. Therefore, module input units are constructed from a module input domain. The specification of the module input domain is also essential to the success of software development. Unfortunately, this task is missing from many of the software development methodologies being practiced today.

The specification of the input domain of a module is the test designer's job. The test designer must work closely with the software designer in designing the module and the input domain. Once the module and its input domain are finalized, a SIAD tree can be constructed for the module and used in designing and constructing the module test. The process of construction of a module SIAD tree is identical to that of a system SIAD tree, as discussed in Section 8.2.1***G***.

The design of a module SIAD tree is essential to designing a reusable module. A module designed for one application is reusable for another application only when the input domains required for each application are identical. Otherwise, the module must be modified before it can be reused.

As seen in Section 9.1.1***B***, the design of input domains is missing from object-oriented design (the term input domain is not even mentioned in Booch's *Software Engineering with Ada* [11]). Therefore, it is necessary to include a SIAD tree for each of the functions in a designed Ada package for the object-oriented design to be complete. For example, in the TREE_PACKAGE in the example in Section 9.1.1***B***(iv), the test designer would need to define:

Input data types, that is, variables that are to be used in inputting data into the procedure GET_INITIAL.

Characteristics of each of the input data types, for example, number of levels of the tree to be input, number of nodes subordinated to a parent node (in the binary tree application, the number is either 0 or 2), the maximum number of tree nodes to be input, data to be input for each tree node, and so on.

Rules for using the data types, such as: in what way the tree is to be input into the GET_INITIAL, how the maximum number of tree nodes is to be input, in which format, what is considered valid and invalid input, the order in which the data are to be input, and so on.

B. Module Product Unit Definition

Each module of a software system transforms input units into product units. The product unit for each module can therefore be defined by using the same procedure as for the software system product unit. Definition of the module product unit will allow application of the statistical quality control tool to the module's product unit population.

C. Module Product Unit Defectiveness Definition

Module product unit defectiveness can be defined in the same manner as software system product unit defectiveness, as shown in Chapters 7 and 8.

D. Selection of Module Test Methods

The five software system test methods—regular, weighted, boundary, invalid, and special tests—are also applicable to module testing, provided that the module SIAD tree, module product unit, and module product unit defectiveness are defined. Detailed discussions of these methods are given in Chapters 7, 8, and 9.

E. Design of Module Sampling Plans

The same sampling plans used for software system testing can be used to test each module of the system. These sampling plans are given in the modeling and requirements specification documents, as discussed in Chapters 7 and 8.

It may be advantageous to use additional or alternative sampling plans for module testing. For example, if the requirements specification document specifies that the simple sampling method is to be used to estimate the defective rate of a software product unit population, then the sequential sampling method can be used in addition, or as an alternative, to the simple sampling plan. An understanding of the materials in Chapters 5 and 6 is essential to designing module sampling plans.

F. Design of Input Units Using Module SIAD Tree

This task is identical to the task of designing input units using the software system SIAD tree, except that a module SIAD tree is used instead (see Section 9.2.1***F***).

G. Generation of Expected Module Test Results

This task is identical to the task of generating expected test results for the software system, as discussed in Section 9.2.1*G*.

H. Design of Module Driver for Testing

A module driver for testing is a simple program that reads in or generates the data required to test a module, prints or displays the test data, calls and passes the data to the module being tested, and prints out results produced by the module for analysis. It also prints out the test data after calling the module, to check whether the data have been changed by the module. This step is of vital importance, as the input data should not be changed, as discussed in the radio broadcasting concept in Section 9.1.3***A***.

Because a piece of software is organized in a hierarchical structure, the module being called by the driver may call its subordinated modules (which, in turn, may call still other modules). The design of the driver should not be concerned with what other modules are being called by the module being tested. The construction of the driver should be guided by the SIAD tree of the module being tested only.

9.3 VERIFICATION OF SOFTWARE DESIGN AND TEST DESIGN

The first principle in developing reliable software should be the avoidance of errors. The cost of removing an error after coding is substantially higher—in a magnitude of, perhaps, hundreds of times that of removing errors during the design stage. The verification of software design and test design is to ensure that error avoidance is rigorously practiced. The following sections described the tasks required to verify the software design and test design.

9.3.1 Review of Software Modeling and Requirements Specification Documents

Any discrepancies among the software design, test design, modeling document, and requirements specification document must be resolved before implementation of the software design and test design begins.

9.3.2 Verification of Software Design

The software design must be verified as complete and correct.

1. Verification of Software Design Completeness. Use of SIAD tree for the software being developed as a checklist to examine the completeness of the design. Every tree element, rule, and subrule should be reflected in the software design. Make sure that every function is also reflected in the software design.

2. Verification of Software Design Correctness. Correctness is verified in two steps:

a. Trace module interfaces to ensure that all necessary and sufficient chainings among the modules are included in the design. Trace the transforming of the defined software input into output units.

b. Check the correctness of each module design in processing its input units into output units. Make sure that all necessary and sufficient processing is included in the design.

9.3.3 Verification of Test Design

The test design must be verified as complete and correct.

1. Verification of Test Design Completeness. Completeness is verified in two steps:

A. Make sure a proper random number generator is selected. (The generator should have been tested using the methods discussed in Chapter 4.)

B. Use the SIAD trees of the software and modules of the software as a checklist to examine the completeness of the test design. Every tree element, rule, and subrule should be reflected in the test design. Make sure that every function is also reflected in the test design.

2. Verification of Test Design Correctness. Check that the test design can be used to provide statistical evidence that the user's requirements stated in the requirements specification document have or have not been met. Make sure that all necessary and sufficient processing for performing the tests is included in the test design.

9.3.4 Cross-Verification of Software Design and Test Design

After the software design and test design have been separately verified, a cross-verification should be performed. Use the test design to walk through the software design, making sure that the two designs are complete, correct, and compatible. Modifications to either or both of the designs may be required if they are found to be incompatible.

REFERENCES

1. C. K. Cho, "Structured Data Interfacing for Software System," *Proceedings of the* 1977 *ACM Annual Conference*, ACM, New York, 1977, pp. 145–152.

2. ANSI, *American National Standard Programming Language COBOL*, ANSI X3.23-1974, American National Standards Institute, Inc., New York, 1974.

3. W. P. Stevens, G. J. Myers, and L. L. Constantíne, "Structured Design," *IBM Systems Journal*, Vol. 13, No. 2, 1974, pp. 115–139.

4. International Business Machines Corporation, *IBM System/360 and System/370 FORTRAN IV Language*, 10th ed., IBM, White Plains, New York, 1972.

5. G. D. Brown, *Advanced ANS COBOL with Structured Programming*, Wiley-Interscience, New York, 1977.

6. Sperry Rand Corporation, *Sperry Univac* 1100 *Series American National Standard COBOL (ASCII) Programmer Reference*, UP-7923 Rev. 2, Sperry Rand Corporation St. Paul, Minnesota, 1975.

7. J. K. Hughes, *PL/I Structured Programming*, Wiley, New York, 1979.

8. E. Yourdon, *Techniques of Program Structure and Design*, Prentice-Hall, Englewood Cliffs, New Jersey, 1975.

9. International Business Machines Corporation, *OS PL/I Checkout and Optimizing Compilers: Language Reference Manual*, 5th ed., IBM, White Plains, New York, 1976.

10. G. J. Myers, "A Controlled Experiment in Program Testing and Code Walkthrough/Inspection," *Communications of the ACM*, Vol. 21, No. 9, September, 1978, pp. 760–768.

11. G. Booch, *Software Engineering with Ada*, Benjamin/Cummings, Menlo Park, California, 1983.

12. C. K. Cho, *An Introduction to Software Quality Control*, Wiley-Interscience, New York, 1980.

13. G. J. Myers, *Software Reliability Principles and Practices*, Wiley-Interscience, New York, 1976.

14. R. W. Jensen and C. C. Tonies, *Software Engineering*, Prentice-Hall, Englewood Cliffs, New Jersey, 1979.

15. M. L. Shooman, *Software Engineering*, McGraw-Hill, New York, 1983.

16. R. C. Tausworthe, *Standardized Development of Computer Software*, Prentice-Hall, Englewood Cliffs, New Jersey, 1977.

17. R. C. Tausworthe, *Standardized Development of Computer Software, Part II Standards*, Prentice-Hall, Englewood Cliffs, New Jersey, 1979.

18. R. T. Yeh (Ed.), *Current Trends in Programming Methodology Vol. I Software Specification and Design*, Prentice-Hall, Englewood Cliffs, New Jersey, 1977.

19. R. T. Yeh (Ed.), *Current Trends in Programming Methodology Vol. II Program Validation*, Prentice-Hall, Englewood Cliffs, New Jersey, 1979.

20. B. H. Liskov, "A Design Methodology for Reliable Software," *Proceedings of the 1972 Fall Joint Computer Conference*, AFIP Press, Montvale, New Jersey, 1972, pp. 191–199.

21. C. K. Cho, "Statistical Methods Applied to Software Quality Control," in G. Gordon Schulmeyer and J. I. McManus (Eds.) *Handbook of Software Quality Assurance*, Van Nostrand Reinhold, New York, 1987.

22. N. Chapin, "Semi-code in Design and Maintenance," *Computers and People*, Vol. 27, No. 6, June 1978, pp. 2–12.

EXERCISES

1. Generate a program design and a test design for the development of the payroll program of Exercise 4 of Chapter 8, using the requirement specifications of Exercise 4 of Chapter 8.
2. Generate a program design and a test design for the development of the program that will perform the matrix operation $AB = C$, using the requirement specifications of Exercise 3(a) of Chapter 8.
3. Generate a program design and a test design for the development of the program that will find the inverse of the matrix A, using the requirement specifications of Exercise 3(b) of Chapter 8.

CHAPTER 10

Concurrent Implementation of Software Design and Test Design

One of the essential purposes of Chapters 7 through 9 is to emphasize to the developer and user how much planning should go on before the actual coding of a piece of software. Conducting thorough modeling, requirements specification, and design phases can help the developer avoid many of the costly problems that can occur during software development, and ensure that the software will meet the user's needs.

When it becomes time to implement the software design, the implementer should have a number of resources to draw on. First, there are the modeling, requirements specification, and design documents. Second, there are the implementer's knowledge of programming languages and environments, and his or her experience in using good programming practices. These topics are discussed in this chapter under human factors and selection of programming languages. It will be demonstrated which kinds of considerations are important in implementing the software design.

A theme of this book is that design and testing tasks should proceed concurrently so all necessary software and test programs are ready for the test and integration phase of development. Software design and test design are complementary activities that, together, allow the use of statistical quality control techniques. Chapter 7 shows how the modeling activity addresses both design and test requirements. Chapter 8 provides guidance in how to ensure that during requirements specification all design and test requirements are identified and documented. In Chapter 9, software design and test design are discussed in detail as activities that proceed concurrently. In this chapter, it will be seen that implementation of the test design should proceed concurrently with implementation of the software design. Important considerations in the implementation of the test design are addressed.

10.1 IMPLEMENTATION OF SOFTWARE DESIGN

The major factors important in implementation of software design are discussed as follows:

Human factors
Selection of programming language
Implementation strategies
Code documentation

10.1.1 Human Factors

Human factors have their place in software engineering as they do in all technologies. When software is being developed, the designer must include features that will make the software easy to use and difficult to misuse, and that will facilitate use and maintenance of the software. Human factors in software engineering are discussed below under the following major headings:

Man-machine interfaces
Software portability
Programming support environments

A. Man-Machine Interfaces

Man-machine interfaces are the points of contact between the user and the software system. These interfaces must be designed to be user-friendly, that is, to support the understandability and efficiency of the system at each step of the user's involvement with the software. The areas of concern in the design and development of man-machine interfaces include, but are not limited to:

Training in use of the software system
Input/output preparation and usage
User error handling
System response time

(i) Training in Use of the Software System. Instructive help should be provided to guide the user in preparing input and interfacing with the software system. The most common means of first introducing the user to a system are a user's manual and a tutorial program. The tutorial program is usually a combination of instructions and practice exercises designed to explain the features of the system and provide the user with hands-on experience in using the system. At the present time, users' manuals and tutorials are often difficult to understand and use effectively. A better approach to the design of manuals and tutorials, perhaps involving greater collaboration between designers, users, and technical writers, is an area of man-machine interface design that needs increased attention.

(ii) Input/Output Preparation and Usage. Providing features that aid the user in entering data and interpreting output is one of the most important aspects of man-machine interface design. This calls for a thorough analysis by the designer of the input/output operations; and an anticipation of how the user is likely to proceed, what common mistakes are likely to be made, and what guidance and information will be helpful to the user at each step of the operations.

a. Input Operations. The software design should enable the user to prepare data for input to the system in a straightforward manner, logically related to the application and consistent with the user's orientation, without arbitrary or rigid rules for order or format of the data. The user should not have to convert data from a format meaningful to the application to a different format acceptable to the system. For example, a business-oriented user should not have to prepare numbers in an exponential format such as 0.12345E-0.5.

The use of "free format" data preparation should be maximized. At the same time, each input operation should be clearly defined by the system. It is not good practice to provide the user with a confusing or overwhelming number of options for structuring input operations. The more options, the more possibilities for errors.

Input data should be echo-printed with self-explanatory messages. There should be no confusion for the user as to whether or not the system has accepted a data entry, or what data has already been entered. Messages that clarify the procedure, identify the engineering units being used, and prompt for missing data without making the user refer back to paper or call up a listing are effective aids in data preparation and entry.

In many applications, the data to be input is not merely numbers or character strings, but more complex graphic or pictorial information. Therefore, the man-machine interface for input operations should be designed with consideration of state-of-the-art technologies such as optical input devices, for example, digitizers and optical scanners. Each of these types of devices presents its own challenges to software and man-machine interface design.

No matter what device is used for data entry, a terminal should be provided for interactive use of the system. If appropriate, voice recognition and touch-sensitive screen devices should be considered. At the least, the terminal should use a menu-driven system to reduce keyboard typing by the user. State-of-the-art user-friendly design of the terminal interface includes such features as:

A. Indexing and help message displays on each screen, identifying which key to press to page forward or page backward through the screens, what options are available from the screen being displayed, and so on.
B. Use of cursor and command displays to control interactions, for example, enabling the user to enter a lengthy command by moving the cursor to a display field and pressing the return key, rather than by typing in a long character string.
C. Making keyboards "monkey-proof" so that pressing inappropriate keys does not enter an error or cause the system to go down. This feature is especially important when off-the-shelf hardware is used and the terminal is being reconfigured by the software designer for new functions.

b. Output Operations. Output data should be produced with self-explanatory messages in a format meaningful to the user. Output can include numerical, textual, tabular, graphic, or pictorial information. The software should therefore be capable of generating the type of output required. Headings, scale labels, engineering units, and other information necessary for direct, immediate interpretation of the data should be included. In real-time applications, the output may include status messages on the process or system being controlled by the software, and automatic updates of changing parameters. The man-machine interface for output operations must be designed to present such information in a clear, accessible manner.

The software designer must fully understand the user's output interface requirements and, if necessary, include consultation with the user on the acceptability of the proposed man-machine interface design during the development of the software.

(iii) User Error Handling. No matter how much training or how many instructive prompts are provided, the user is likely to make mistakes in operating the system. The designer should anticipate the types of mistakes that will be made and design the software to handle errors with minimal interruption of system operations for the user. Anticipation means the designer should think through every possible action that the user might take, right or wrong, at the keyboard, and build in means for the system to respond to and handle each user action. For example, the system should not go down or misinterpret data entries if the user presses an unexpected combination or sequence of keys.

Helpful features for error handling include:

A. Meaningful error messages. The use of error codes should be avoided. Instead, the system should generate a self-explanatory message, clarifying the type of error and indicating to the user what actions should be taken to recover from the error.
B. A simple means to clear an unintentional mistake, escape from a sequence of commands the user realizes is wrong, and so on.
C. Use of edit buffers. This common feature provides a copy of the data base for the user to modify, so that the user can make mistakes without losing a previously stored file.

(iv) System Response Time. Human factors psychologists have studied response time to establish the most effective response rates for machines interacting with human beings. Software design should ensure that the system responds to commands without inordinately long or irritating delays. Most users will require "on-line" operations, that is, immediate system response to command entries with no perceptible delay. System response time in generating output will depend on the user's requirements. However, the trend is toward interactive systems which provide immediate feedback to the user. Real-time applications impose their own special timing requirements on system response rates.

B. *Software Portability*

Software portability is becoming an increasingly important factor in software design, especially for ensuring the maintainability of software. Enhancing, correcting, and modifying software functions frequently requires porting a piece of software from one computer system to another, or assigning new personnel to maintain the software. As discussed in Myers [3], software maintenance accounts for approximately 50 percent of the cost of software systems.

To achieve software portability requires understandability, one of the goals of software engineering. The software must be understandable, both to machines and to people. Each of these types of portability is discussed in the following sections.

(i) Portability Among Machines. To port a piece of software from one computer system to another requires compatibility between various aspects of the systems:

A. The computers must be compatible in such characteristics as word size, for example, 32-bit words.

B. Peripheral equipment and file management facilities must be compatible.

C. The new system must have available a set of tools compatible with the tools used to develop the software.

D. The user interfaces must be compatible, or the cost of conversion may be prohibitive.

The most common principle in developing portable software is to use a high-level language, such as FORTRAN or COBOL. Use of a low-level language such as Assembly language makes software portability extremely difficult.

The use of a high-level language does not in itself guarantee that the porting of an implemented code will be easy, even when an industry standard language is used. For example, FORTRAN 77 is an American National Standards Institute (ANSI) standard language, but, nonetheless, variations of the language exist among different vendors. IBM FORTRAN, to cite one case, contains extensions to the standard. Extensive modifications would be required to port a piece of software from machine to machine if such a language is used.

Recognizing this problem, the Department of Defense, which has sponsored development of the Ada language, has ruled that no superset or subset of the ANSI-standard Ada language (ANSI-1815A) may be called Ada. This is a major step toward software portability among machines.

Recently, as the UNIX operating system is coming into widespread use on many machines, a piece of software written on a computer system under UNIX can be easily ported to other systems, whether or not the language used is a standard language. For example, the C language, although not an ANSI standard, can be moved with minimum modification to many systems under the UNIX operating system. Similarly, if an Ada program is developed under UNIX, it can then be ported to another system under the same operating system with ease. (The reader should realize that a majority of UNIX operating systems were not developed for real-time applications or porting under such an environment.)

(ii) Portability Among People. Understandability is the key to ensuring software portability among the various personnel who work with the system. All too frequently, new project personnel find that they cannot make use of already existing software, despite its applicability, because they cannot understand what their predecessors have programmed. Similarly, new software maintenance personnel frequently find that, until they have an unacceptably long time to become familiar with the system, they cannot perform their tasks effectively.

To reduce the extent of these problems, the following approaches should be taken:

A. A standard language should be used to minimize the time and effort required to train people. New personnel should not have to learn another language on the job in order to be able to work with the software being developed.

B. A methodology should be applied to ensure that all personnel working on the software project have a top-down understanding of software development, from modeling and requirements specification to software design and coding, as detailed in Chapters 7 through 9 of this book.

C. Programmers should be made familiar with the principles of statistical quality control, so that they can communicate with the software test designers and implementers during the implementation of the software design.

D. Good documentation should be provided for understanding of the coding. The modeling, requirements specification, and design (whether function-oriented or object-oriented) must be documented, as discussed in Chapters 7 to 9, to communicate effectively what the user expects from the software and to identify the input, processing, and output requirements of each part of the software design. For full understandability, new personnel require both a guide to the structure of the program and coding so that programmers can modify the software, and a user's manual that explains how to use the software at the man-machine interface level. This type of documentation, together with the coding document, provides a sound basis to ensure software portability among people.

C. *Programming Support Environments*

All software is developed in a programming support environment which consists of software tools, development methodologies, languages, compilers, linkers, loaders, text editors, management tools, and so forth. Some of these tools, such as a development methodology, support the life cycle of the software, whereas others, such as compilers, linkers, and loaders used in a language, support only the implementation phase of software development.

A major problem in the software industry is the lack of a complete, coordinated set of tools that not only facilitates software development, but also supports software engineering by helping project management in planning, scheduling, and controlling software development. To increase software quality and productivity, this problem must be considered in software development.

As part of software development, the implementer must identify the tools available and understand their coordination. For example, the Ada Programming Support Environment (APSE) is conceptualized as a three-level hierarchy of tools which addresses both generic tools and methology-specific tools, as shown in Figure 10.1. Generic tools are those which apply to all programming tasks; these tools include linkers, loaders, and so on. Methodology-specific tools define or support a particular programming or management discipline; these tools include preprocessors and configuration managers. The three levels of the APSE are:

A. Kernel Ada Programming Support Environment (KAPSE). This is the host operating system, which provides elementary run-time support for the rest of the environment, the logical-physical mapping needed for program portability, access control for the program library, and the logical interface to peripheral devices, including terminals.

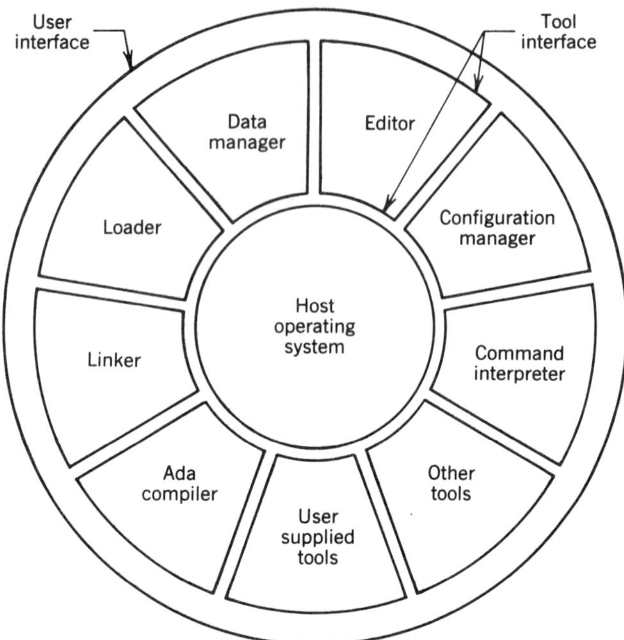

Figure 10.1 The Ada programming support environment.

B. Minimal Ada Programming Support Environment (MAPSE). This contains the basic tools for program development, such as text editor, pretty printer, compiler, linker, set-use static analyzer, control-flow static analyzer, dynamic analysis tools, terminal interface routines, file administrator, command interpreter, and configuration manager.

C. Ada Programming Support Environment (APSE). This includes tools for creation of data base objects, modification, analysis, transformation, display, execution, and maintenance. Such tools may include syntax-directed editors, real-time debuggers, and so on. This level is the MAPSE plus user-supplied tools for software development.

The implementer should realize that the programming support environment is a crucial factor in how the developer and user will be able to interact with the software.

10.1.2 Selection of a Programming Language

Programming languages are analogous to the materials used to build a factory. The selection of the right materials has a major impact on the success or failure of the factory. For example, plastic cannot be used for metal-cutting tools, and glass cannot be used for high-temperature oven walls. Similarly, selection of the right programming language for development of a particular piece of software must be carefully considered. In Chapters 7 through 9, it has been seen how the user's requirements pertaining to selection of a programming language are addressed in the modeling, requirements specification, and design phases. Here, the discussion of programming languages is continued into the implementation phase.

The factors in choosing a programming language may include:

The type of software being developed, for example, scientific or commercial, real-time or non-real-time, graphic or textual, and so on.

Algorithm complexity, for example, numerical computation, logic manipulation, or input/output operations.

Data structure complexity, for example, one- or two-dimensional arrays, linked list or queue, and so on.

Performance requirements, for example, response time or processing throughput.

Programming support environment, for example, availability of development tools and knowledgeable personnel.

Software portability, for example, portability among computers or among programming staff.

Support of software engineering principles to attain the software engineering goals.

These factors may be prioritized for different applications.

Currently, there are many languages being used in the software industry. In scientific and engineering applications, FORTRAN, PL/I, and PASCAL are the commonly used languages. In commercial and data base development applications, COBOL, RPG, and PL/I are the widely used languages. In artificial intelligence applications, LISP (LISt Processing) is the most widely used language. For embedded and mission-critical software mandated by the United States Department of Defense, the newly developed Ada language is required.

Selection of a programming language is considered further in the following sections. The aspects of language selection discussed include:

Characteristics of existing languages
Characteristics of software applications
Modern program constructs and data abstraction
Module interface schemes
Language selection criteria

A. *Characteristics of Existing Languages*

The characteristics of the most widely used languages—FORTRAN, COBOL, PL/I, PASCAL, Ada, and LISP—vary because of the different purposes for which the languages were designed. FORTRAN is primarily for number crunching, COBOL for input/output operations. PL/I is a "combined" language of FORTRAN and COBOL. PASCAL and Ada are close relatives, while LISP differs markedly in syntax and structure from all of the other languages. Because of their differences, each language facilitates some applications and is of limited use in others.

The features of the languages selected may also affect the design concepts of the software being developed. Two common examples of this effect concern recursion and abstract data typing:

A. Recursion. Recursive functions have great utility in many types of programs for such operations as binary sorting of numbers, and early in the design effort, the designer may decide on the type of recursive concept that will be most effective for the application. However, if FORTRAN, which has no direct recursion construct, is selected as the programming language, the implementer may have to change the planned recursion concept during the coding phase because of the inherent limitatons of the language.

B. Abstract Data Typing. The importance of abstract data typing lies in its utility in reducing the possibilities of programming errors. FORTRAN 77 allows the designer to define only six data types: real, integer, logic, character, double precision, and complex. This can hinder implementation of a design requiring more sophisticated data typing. It might have been more appropriate to select Ada as the programming language, since Ada provides many data types and enables the implementer to define his or her own data types.

B. Characteristics of Software Applications

A piece of software can be developed for scientific, commercial, real-time, non-real-time, graphic, textual, or artificial intelligence applications. Each application has characteristics that make special demands on the programming language. For example, in scientific applications, it is essential that rounding and truncation errors be limited to as small a magnitude as possible (since these kinds of errors cannot be removed). This requirement means that the language used must have a long storage word capacity, such as the DOUBLE PRECISION in FORTRAN or the LONG_FLOAT in Ada. In commercial applications, the language must handle extensive input and output operations; COBOL was specifically designed for this purpose. Real-time applications require a language with strong features for inter-task communication and service calls to the operating system in order to provide fast system response. In graphic applications, the interface between a program and a graphic device must be compatible. Artificial intelligence applications require a language with convenient features for symbolic manipulation of data; the LISP language was developed for this purpose. Thus, the implementer needs to study the characteristics of the intended application carefully before using a particular language.

C. Modern Programming Constructs and Data Structures

As pointed out in discussions of the Program Design Language (PDL), a software design is built using a few basic design constructs: SEQUENCE, IF_THEN_ELSE, and REPETITION. To implement the design, the programming language selected must have convenient features to allow coding of these constructs. The implementer should note that languages such as PASCAL, Ada, and FORTRAN 77 have these features. However, others, for example, FORTRAN IV and LISP, may only have some of these features, but not all.

Similarly, the programming language selected should facilitate implementation of all of the data structures discussed in Section 9.1.1***A***(ii)c, for example, stack, queue, list, network. Again, some languages cannot conveniently implement these structures. For example, it is not easy to implement stack or network structures in FORTRAN or COBOL.

D. Module Interface Schemes

Selecting a language that has the necessary features to implement a structured module interface (see Section 9.1.3***A***(iii)) is essential to achieve clear module logic and interfaces, traceability from code to design and vice versa, and, thus, understandability of the code. As explained in Section 9.1.3, the worst case for module interface complexity is given by the equation:

$$P = NM(M - 1)$$

where P is the number of data paths along which flows of data among all of the modules of the software can be traced; N is the total number of pieces of data in the module interface; M is the number of modules, assuming that the blank COMMON in FORTRAN is used. Although it has been argued that calling sequences should be used for module interfacing [1], use of this construct results in almost the same degree of complexity as using the COMMON construct. Unless the number P can be reduced to NM, the understandability of the implemented code that can be achieved is, at best, 50 percent.

The following is an example implementation of the module interface design described in Section 9.1.3*A*(iii). Figure 10.2 is taken from Cho [2]. To trace the source of a piece of data in a module, one need only read a variable name given in a module as it appears in an EQUIVALENCE statement. The array that corresponds to the variable name indicates immediately where the piece of data comes from. For example, in the main routine X0001 in Figure 10.2, the data in FF comes from R0012, as shown in the EQUIVALENCE statement:

```
      EQUIVALENCE     (NP, I0001(1)),
     1                (FF, R0012(1)),
     1                (FS, R0013(1)),
     1                (FP, R0014(1)),
     1                (FG, R0015(1))
```

Similarly, the data in FG is from R0015. Therefore, one needs only to find out what happens in the two routines SUBROUTINE X0012 and SUBROUTINE X0015, as shown in Figure 10.2, to find out information about the variables FF and FG. There is no need to trace what happens in any other routines. In the same EQUIVALENCE statement, it is immediately clear that the main routine X0001 generates a piece of integer data NP to be used by the other routines through the array I0001.

The advantages of the structured interfacing are as follows:

A. Since all data of one type generated by a module are stored in one array, there is virtually no chance of data type misalignment.

```
C      MAIN X0001.
       COMMON/X0001I/I0001(1)
       COMMON/X0012R/R0012(1)
       COMMON/X0013R/R0013(1)
       COMMON/X0014R/R0014(1)
       COMMON/X0015R/R0015(1)
       EQUIVALENCE (NP,        I0001(1)),
      1            (FF,        R0012(1)),
      1            (FS,        R0013(1)),
      1            (FP,        R0014(1)),
      1            (FG,        R0015(1))
          .
          .
          .
       STOP
       END
       SUBROUTINE X0002
C
C      THIS SUBROUTINE GENERATES A SEQUENCE OF 1000 RANDOM DIGITS
C      EACH TIME IT IS CALLED.
C
       COMMON/X0002I/I0002(1001)
       COMMON/X0008R/R0008(1)
       EQUIVALENCE (S(1),      I0002(1)),
      1            (K,         I0002(1001)),
      1            (RN,        R0008(1))
          .
          .
          .
       RETURN
       END
       SUBROUTINE X0003
C
C      THIS SUBROUTINE GENERATES A MATRIX FROM A SEQUENCE OF
C      1000 RANDOM DIGITS.  IT CALLS X0009, X0010, AND X0011 TO COMPUTE
C      THE ROW SUMS, COLUMN SUMS, AND GRAND TOTAL OF THE MATRIX M.
C
       COMMON/X0003I/I0003(101)
       COMMON/X0002I/I0002(1001)
       COMMON/X0009R/R0009(10)
       COMMON/X0010R/R0010(10)
       COMMON/X0011R/R0011(1)
       EQUIVALENCE (M(1,1),    I0003(1)),
      1            (N,         I0003(101)),
      1            (S(1),      I0002(1)),
      1            (K,         I0002(1001)),
      1            (R(1),      R0009(1)),
      1            (C(1),      R0010(1)),
      1            (G,         R0011(1))
          .
          .
          .
       RETURN
       END


       SUBROUTINE X0009
C
C      THIS SUBROUTINE FINDS THE ROW SUMS OF THE MATRIX M.
C
       COMMON/X0003I/I0003(101)
       COMMON/X0009R/R0009(10)
       EQUIVALENCE (M(1,1),    I0003(1)),
      1            (N,         I0003(101)),
      1            (R(1),      R0009(1))
          .
          .
          .
       RETURN
       END
       SUBROUTINE X0010
C
C      THIS SUBROUTINE FINDS COLUMN SUMS OF THE MATRIX M.
C
       COMMON/X0010R/R0010(10)
       COMMON/X0003I/I0003(101)
       EQUIVALENCE (C(1),      R0010(1)),
      1            (M(1,1),    I0003(1)),
      1            (N,         I0003(101))
          .
          .
          .
```

Figure 10.2 A structured FORTRAN module interface example.

```
      RETURN
      END
      SUBROUTINE X0011
C
C     THIS SUBROUTINE FINDS THE GRAND TOTAL OF THE MATRIX M.
C
      COMMON/X0011R/R0011(1)
      COMMON/X0003I/I0003(101)
      EQUIVALENCE (G,          R0011(1)),
     1            (M(1,1),     I0003(1)),
     1            (N,          I0003(101))
          .
          .
          .
      RETURN
      END


      SUBROUTINE X0004
C
C     THIS SUBROUTINE PREPARES DATA FOR THE FREQUENCY CHI-SQUARE TEST.
C
      COMMON/X0004R/R0004(11)
      COMMON/X0003I/I0003(101)
      EQUIVALENCE (T(1),       R0004(1)),
     1            (EF,         R0004(11)),
     1            (N,          I0003(101))
          .
          .
          .
      RETURN
      END
      SUBROUTINE X0012
C
C     THIS SUBROUTINE PERFORMS THE FREQUENCY CHI-SQUARE TEST.
C
      COMMON/X0012R/R0012(1)
      COMMON/X0004R/R0004(11)
      COMMON/X0009R/R0009(10)
      COMMON/X0003I/I0003(101)
      EQUIVALENCE (FF,         R0012(1)),
     1            (T(1),       R0004(1)),
     1            (EF,         R0004(11)),
     1            (R(1),       R0009(1)),
     1            (N,          I0003(101))
          .
          .
          .
      RETURN
      END
      SUBROUTINE X0005
C
C     THIS SUBROUTINE PREPARES DATA FOR THE SERIAL CHI-SQUARE TEST.
C
      COMMON/X0005R/R0005(101)
      COMMON/X0003I/I0003(101)
      EQUIVALENCE (T(1,1),     R0005(1)),
     1            (ES,         R0005(101)),
     1            (N,          I0003(101))
          .
          .
          .
      RETURN
      END


      SUBROUTINE X0013
C
C     THIS SUBROUTINE PERFORMS THE SERIAL CHI-SQUARE TEST.
C
      COMMON/X0013R/R0013(1)
      COMMON/X0005R/R0005(101)
      COMMON/X0003I/I0003(101)
      EQUIVALENCE (FS,         R0013(1)),
     1            (T(1,1),     R0005(1)),
     1            (ES,         R0005(101)),
     1            (M(1,1),     I0003(1)),
     1            (N,          I0003(101))
          .
          .
          .
```

Figure 10.2 continued

```
      RETURN
      END
      SUBROUTINE X0006
C
C     THIS SUBROUTINE PREPARES DATA FOR THE POKER CHI-SQUARE TEST.
C
      COMMON/X0006I/I0006(1)
      COMMON/X0006R/R0006(11)
      COMMON/X0002I/I0002(1001)
      EQUIVALENCE (N,          I0006(1)),
     1            (P(1),       R0006(1)),
     1            (T(1),       R0006(6)),
     1            (EP,         R0006(11)),
     1            (S(1),       I0002(1)),
     1            (K,          I0002(1001))
          .
          .
          .
      RETURN
      END
      SUBROUTINE X0014
C
C     THIS SUBROUTINE PERFORMS THE POKER CHI-SQUARE TEST.
C
      COMMON/X0014R/R0014(1)
      COMMON/X0006I/I0006(1)
      COMMON/X0006R/R0006(11)
      EQUIVALENCE (FP,         R0014(1)),
     1            (N,          I0006(1)),
     1            (P(1),       R0006(1)),
     1            (T(1),       R0006(6)),
     1            (EP,         R0006(11))
          .
          .
          .
      RETURN
      END

      SUBROUTINE X0007
C
C     THIS SUBROUTINE PREPARES DATA FOR THE GAP CHI-SQUARE TEST.
C
      COMMON/X0007R/R0007(19)
      COMMON/X0007I/I0007(1)
      COMMON/X0002I/I0002(1001)
      EQUIVALENCE (W(1),       R0007(1)),
     1            (T(1),       R0007(14)),
     1            (EG,         R0007(19)),
     1            (N,          I0007(1)),
     1            (S(1),       I0002(1)),
     1            (K,          I0002(1001))
          .
          .
          .
7     RETURN
      END
      SUBROUTINE X0015
C
C     THIS SUBROUTINE PERFORMS THE GAP CHI-SQUARE TEST.
C
      COMMON/X0015R/R0015(1)
      COMMON/X0007R/R0007(19)
      COMMON/X0007I/I0007(1)
      EQUIVALENCE (FG,         R0015(1)),
     1            (W(1),       R0007(1)),
     1            (T(1),       R0007(14)),
     1            (EG,         R0007(19)),
     1            (N,          I0007(1))
          .
          .
          .
      RETURN
      END
      SUBROUTINE X0008
C
C     THIS SUBROUTINE GENERATES A UNIFORM RANDOM NUMBER BETWEEN 0 AND 1,
C     EXCLUSIVE, AND AN INTEGER RANDOM NUMBER BETWEEN 0 AND 2**31, EXCLUSIVE.
C
      COMMON/X0001I/I0001(1)
      COMMON/X0008R/R0008(1)
      EQUIVALENCE (N,          I0001(1)),
     1            (RN,         R0008(1))
          .
          .
          .
      RETURN
      END
```

Figure 10.2 continued

B. Data sources are clear from the interface scheme. Searching of intermediate modules to locate a data source is not necessary. For example, the type of source of the data of G used in module X0003 is available from the EQUIVALENCE statement; namely, G is of type real coming from module X0011.

C. Data destinations can be easily identified by scanning all of the EQUIVALENCE statements in the entire program. For example, the destinations of N, specified in I0003(101), are found to be modules X0009, X0010, X0011, X0004, X0012, X0005, and X0013.

D. Data flow tracing complexity is greatly reduced. Since there are 64 variables specified in the interface of the entire program, it requires only 64 paths along which to trace data. However, it requires up to $P = NM(M - 1) = 22 \times 15 \times (15 - 1) = 4{,}620$ such paths if the blank COMMON feature is used without the structured technique. Thus, the complexity is reduced by $4{,}620/64 = 72$ times. (A similar comparison can be made using the CALL sequence. This is left to the interested reader.)

E. Since no variables are passed to a module through CALL sequences, it requires less time to execute the module. This savings can be significant if the module is called a number of times.

Only FORTRAN, PL/I, and some versions of COBOL have the features needed to structure a module interface in this way. Unfortunately, the Ada language does not have these features. Therefore, avoidance of module interface complexity with Ada code may be difficult to achieve.

E. Language Selection Criteria

In addition to the language selection criteria discussed in Sections 10.1.2***A*** through 10.1.2***D***, other factors should be considered, namely, the software engineering principles of abstract data typing, information hiding, modularization, localization, uniformity, completeness, confirmability, and statistical quality control. In selection of a language, the implementer should consider each of these principles as follows:

Abstract data typing	Support of user-defined data types
Information hiding	Support of hiding of object or operation implementations at desired levels in the design

Modularization	Support of the implementation of a system of modules (such as SUBROUTINE and FUNCTION in FORTRAN, and PROCEDURE and FUNCTION in Ada) and support of "one-way traffic" module interface implementations; that is, input variables to and output variables from a module are not mixed
Localization	Support of the collection of logically related procedures and/or functions in a physical module
Uniformity	Support of coding styles, for example, indentation, consistent data declaration, and so on
Completeness	Support of the complete implementation of software design with minimum alteration of design concepts
Confirmability	Support of the implementation of modules so that each module, as well as the software system, is independently testable
Statistical quality control	Support of the application of statistical quality control to testing the usability of each module and the software system (This depends more on the development methodology than on the programming language)

Figure 10.3 gives a comparison of several existing languages in terms of their support of software engineering principles and types of applications. For each criterion, the languages are rated on a scale of 0 (least supportive) to 4 (most supportive). It can be seen that, based on total score, Ada appears to be the best among the languages, as evaluated by these criteria.

10.1.3 Implementation Strategies

The following basic strategies should be kept in mind during software implementation. The result will be better software with greater understandability.

Language	Abstract Data Typing	Information Hiding	Modularization	Localization	Uniformity	Completeness	Confirmability	Statistical Quality Control	Scientific	Commercial	Data Base Management	Artificial Intelligence	Total
FORTRAN	0	2	4	4	3	2	3	1	4	2	2	1	28
COBOL	0	2	3	3	2	3	1	1	1	4	3	0	23
PL / I	0	2	4	4	3	2	3	1	4	3	3	1	30
PASCAL	0	2	4	4	3	2	3	1	4	3	3	1	30
Ada	4	4	4	4	4	4	3	1	4	3	3	1	39
LISP	0	0	1	1	3	2	1	1	1	1	1	4	16

Figure 10.3 Selection criteria of some languages.

A. *Use Meaningful Variable Names*

This is the most important strategy that every software engineer and programmer should follow. This practice not only helps the original author remember what each variable means, but makes understanding the code much easier for new personnel. Unfortunately, not every programming language allows the use of meaningful variable names all the time. For example, with some FORTRAN compilers, each name must be eight or fewer characters. When a name cannot be used in full, it should be abbreviated meaningfully, and a comment to explain it should be immediately inserted into the code. Other languages such as Ada allow a concatenated name which fully expresses its meaning. For examples, THIS_IS_TEMPERATURE_INPUT is a valid variable name in Ada.

B. *Limit the Use of GOTO Statements*

The use of GOTO statements has been blamed for obscuring the understandability of software modules [4]. Although some have recommended prohibiting the use of GOTO statements entirely, the reader should not be too fanatical on this point. As discussed in section 9.3.1 of Cho [2], the removal of GOTO statements sometimes can result in an exponential increase in module interface complexity. As a rule, GOTO statements should be used only to forward the logic. It may not be advantageous to use GOTO statements to go back to a sequence within a module.

C. *Use Libraries of Existing Functions*

Usually a programming language makes available a library of functions. Rather than reinventing the wheel, the implementer should use these functions. There is no point in recoding an existing function, unless the function is not usable due to errors or limitations.

D. *Observe Software Engineering Principles*

The software engineering principles of abstract data typing, information hiding, modularization, localization, uniformity, completeness, confirmability, and statistical quality control should be closely observed in implementing a piece of software. These principles are crucial during the design phase, and there is no reason to be lax during implementation of the design.

10.1.4 Code Documentation

Code documentation is a necessity to ensure that the code is readable and that the structure of the software design is clear to all personnel working with the code. These goals can be achieved in a straightforward manner if the design follows the principles of software engineering and the code has been developed in a step-by-step modular process. The code documentation for each module of the design can be generated during the coding phase by following the guidelines given below, referring to Section 9.1.1*A*(iii):

A. Coding of each module should begin with the level-three PDL description of the module.

B. Coding should proceed by implementing each statement of the PDL in the selected programming language. The implemented code can be inserted after each PDL statement.

C. After the code has been developed, the PDL statements can be used directly as comments on the code.

D. Detailed comments can be inserted appropriately if desired.

With this procedure, the code is automatically linked to the level-three PDL and provides easy traceability from the requirement design to the code.

The comments on the code should be checked to ensure that all necessary aspects of the design are included. The following list gives some of the information that should be included in the code documentation:

A. Description of module calling relationships, for example, the names of the other modules which call the documented module, and the names of the other modules which the documented module calls
B. Version or revision numbers, and dates of modification
C. Implementation details, including:
    a. Memory map
    b. Timing mechanisms
    c. Interrupt handling procedures
    d. Example inputs and outputs
    e. Lists of error conditions and messages, and cross-references to design documents
    f. Hardware and software constraints
    g. Procedures and other information such as file names necessary for compilation, linking, and loading, and so on, of the module
    h. Guide to modifying the module

The implementation lines of the code should be indented for easier understandability.

10.2 IMPLEMENTATION OF TEST DESIGN

As discussed in Chapter 9, the tasks of test design can proceed simultaneously with those of software design. Similarly, the implementation of the test design can proceed simultaneously with implementation of the software design. This means that, in accordance with the test design, test input units can be constructed efficiently as software modules and systems are ready to be tested. The testing and debugging of the software should be an iterative process, requiring well-planned scheduling and prioritization of tasks to achieve efficiency.

For each module or system to be tested, the basic strategy for implementation of the test design is as follows:

A. Review the test design documents. The test design should be developed following a step-by-step procedure based on the statistical quality control techniques used in the manufacturing industries.

After review of these documents, the software testing personnel should:

a. Understand the product unit definitions used for testing each module and the entire software system.

b. Understand the product unit defectiveness definitions used for testing each module and the entire software system.

c. Understand the sampling plans used for estimating the software product unit population defective rate and for the software acceptance sampling plan. (The sampling plans for the entire software system are defined in the requirements specification document; the plans for testing each module are defined in the test design documents.)

B. Select a random number generator for implementing the test design.

C. Test the usability of the random number generator.

D. Implement the test design:

a. Construct test input units.

b. Construct supporting devices or software, for example, simulation software for some applications, if necessary.

E. Generate test results.

F. Document generated test results, identifying the expected results if obtained.

After these steps have been followed, the test results can be analyzed and statistical inferences can be made as to the acceptability of the module or software system. The appropriate actions in the implementation of the software design can then be taken.

Implementation of the test design is discussed further under the following headings:

Types of software errors
Test strategies
Selection of random number generators
Test design implementation considerations
Test documentation

10.2.1 Types of Software Errors

A program error can originate from many sources within the software and from outside of it. In a modern computer system, particularly in a multiprogramming environment, an error foreign to a program (such as a hardware error) can manifest itself as a software error and vice versa. An understanding of the sources of errors is particularly important to effective program testing, debugging, and developing quality software.

A. *Environment Errors*

An environment error is one that is foreign to the piece of software. It can come from hardware malfunctioning, a software system that supports hardware operations, compilers, human errors in data acquisition, and so on.

(i) Hardware Errors. A computer is a complex assembly of millions of circuit elements. The failure of a single element can cause failure of the entire system. Despite this vulnerability, most modern computers operate for thousands of hours with very high reliability. However, such reliability does not mean that a computer is perfect. It can fail. The cause of failure can be difficult to isolate, and the effect of the failure can propagate into the end results of a program. The following are some sources of hardware failures;

A. **Peripheral Devices.** Card readers, printers, tape drives, and disk drives provide input and output to the central processing unit. They contain many sophisticated parts that perform functions with mechanical movement and can wear out.
B. **Data Storage Media.** Cards, tapes, disks, and drums are fragile and subject to being scratched. Temperature and humidity also affect the quality of the media. A defect in the media can cause incorrect data transition among components of a computer.
C. **Central Processing Unit, Logical and Arithmetic Units.** These units are composed of electronic elements without moving parts and may fail because of temperature variations, humidity changes, electrical surges, and so on. The sources of failure can be extremely difficult to identify, since the failure can be transient, and the nature of the failure can be complex.

Most computers are designed with the concept of self-detecting hardware errors. A detected error can cause the system to issue an interrupt for identifying the location of the error, shutting down the entire system, and other operations necessary for diagnostic purposes.

(ii) Hardware Constraints. Many data manipulations are constrained by hardware limitations. The amount of data that can be handled at any one time is restricted by available resources. Overflow and underflow conditions can occur if the magnitude of data exceeds the upper and lower bounds of the word capacity. The accuracy of data representation is subject to limited word size. Mathematical manipulations of data, such as addition and multiplication, must be rounded to fit the representation, resulting in an error called the round-off error. Conversions of data from real to integer to fit the data representation scheme are subject to truncation, such as truncating the real number 3.1416 to the integer 3, resulting in an error called the truncation error.

(iii) Language Errors. Errors of this kind stem mostly from the ambiguity of the semantics of the language. A language statement may not mean what one assumes it means. An error can be easily created by misinterpreting the semantics of a language feature. A second source of language error comes from language deficiencies. A user has to fight to solve his or her problems using limited language capabilities, increasing the chances of making errors.

(iv) System Software Errors. A computer cannot operate without supporting software such as operating systems, compilers, and utility packages. Computer architecture is complex enough. System software is more so. It consists of millions of low-level instructions, such as assembly statements. It is not perfect, containing an unknown number of errors. An error in a system program can also propagate into a user's program. It is extremely difficult to detect an error of this nature since the software was developed by many people in different organizations.

(v) Data Entry Errors. Program input data are acquired by manual or automatic means. Errors can be easily introduced into the data by a manual procedure, since human activities are error-prone. Any defect in data acquisition instruments or equipment in an automatic environment is likely to produce errors in the input. Errors of this kind can be difficult to detect since the source may be beyond the user's control.

B. Software Errors

A software error is one that exists in a piece of software. It can originate in a defective model, bad program design, bad programming practice, and so on.

(i) Modeling Errors. An error in a model will be transplanted into a piece of software through requirements specification, design, implementation, and documentation. Every effort must be made to ensure the technical feasibility and correctness of the model. Sources of modeling errors include:

A. Technology Deficiencies. A real-world problem cannot be tackled by currently available technology.

B. Limited Resources. Modeling can be constrained by budget and personnel availability, as well as by lack of technical background of available personnel.

C. Wrong Attitude. Modeling is considered unsubstantial or unimportant by many people in the software industry. It is not even included in many software projects as an important action item.

(ii) Requirement Errors. Requirements are rules governing the development of a software system. Any defects in the rules will certainly cause a tremendous reliability problem in the final product. Sources of requirement errors include:

A. Modeling Errors. Errors in the model are transplanted into the requirements specification.

B. Representation Deficiencies. Most requirements are defined with a natural language, symbols, or notations. The semantics of the language can be ambiguous and misinterpreted.

C. Inaccurate Translation. The model is translated incorrectly into the requirements specification.

(iii) Design Errors. Traditionally, the design phase of software development has been one of the major steps at which errors are introduced into a piece of software. For example, an analysis of 200 types of errors found during a large software development project revealed that as many as 64 percent of the errors were design errors [5]. Worst of all, most of the design errors were not detected until the later phases of testing and maintenance. The cost of removing such errors increases exponentially with time. If it costs one dollar to remove an error at the design phase, it can cost hundreds of dollars to do so at the testing phase. Therefore, every effort must be made to ensure the correctness of the software design. Sources of design errors include:

A. Improper Translation. Requirements are wrongly translated into the software design.

B. Wrong Logic. The logic of data manipulation is defective.

C. Improper Use of an Algorithm. Generally, a real-world problem can be solved by more than one method. For example, a polynomial can be solved by (1) half-interval search, (2) the method of false position, (3) the Newton-Raphson method, and (4) the Bairstow method. Each method is suitable for a particular type of polynomial and unsuitable for another. The selection of the right method can mean the difference between success and failure of the project.

D. Truncation. The representation of a real-world problem may involve an infinite process. For example, the series:

$$e^x = 1 + x + \frac{x^2}{2!} + \frac{x^3}{3!} + \cdots$$

has an infinite number of terms in computing the value of e^x. The series must be cut short to be accommodated on a computer. The cutting of the series creates a sure error in the problem. An error of this type is called a truncation error.

E. Improper Data Structure. The data structure selected for an algorithm has a significant impact on the performance of the algorithm. The selection of a data structure should be complementary to selection of an algorithm.

(iv) Coding Errors. Coding is another step at which errors are easily introduced into the software. For example, an analysis of 200 types of errors found during a large software development project revealed that as many as 36 percent of the errors were coding errors [5]. Fortunately, most coding errors can be detected by manual means or by a compiler. However, a small number of errors may remain undetected. Sources of coding errors include:

A. Design Errors. Errors in the design are unknowingly translated into the program code.

B. Data Entry Errors. The character I can the entered as a 1 and vice versa, as can be characters 0 and O, "," and "·", and so on. Most of these data entry errors can be detected by the compiler. However, there are cases where such errors will remain undetected. For example, the variables A0 and AO will be treated as two entities by the compiler.

C. Syntax Rules. Violation of the syntax rules of the programming language can remain undetected. For example, a data type misalignment in passing variables to a subroutine with a CALL statement or a COMMON statement can be a difficult problem.

D. Initialization. A variable may be used with improper initialization.

E. Commingling of Data Flows. Data coming to a subroutine can be modified by the subroutine and then returned to the calling routine in the same data area. In a large system consisting of hundreds of subroutines, such modification complicates data flow tracing among the routines as well as increases the chances for errors.

(v) Document Errors. A program is a document "read" by a computer. A document is a "program" read by a human being. Errors in modeling, requirements specification, software design, and software coding are also document errors. Thus, a program and a document share the same sources of errors, except that the language used in the document is a natural language, such as English, rather than a programming language.

10.2.2 Test Implementation Strategies

The design of random test input units using a SIAD tree has been discussed in Chapter 9. The implementation of the test design and analysis of the test results require a set of carefully formulated strategies in order to secure maximum returns. The following sections give some of these strategies:

A. Assign the Best Personnel to the Task

Testing has been considered a less prestigious activity in the software industry than design. It is looked on as a tedious, uninteresting task. Too often, inexperienced and junior people are assigned to this important activity, resulting in the unreliability of many software products.

Testing demands great creativity. Test personnel are responsible for preventing unreliable software from reaching the user. They can help save users millions of dollars and even prevent loss of human lives. The best personnel must be assigned to design, implement, and analyze test data and test results.

B. Testing Must Be Done by an Independent Party

Testing a piece of software should not be the responsibility of those who develop it, since it is natural to defend the correctness of one's own efforts. With a well-developed model and requirements specification, an independent party can do a far better job of testing, and finding errors in the software can be a challenging assignment.

C. *Provide Expected Test Results If Possible*

It has been observed that one of the most common mistakes made in software testing is the failure to provide expected results for the test [2]. As discussed in Chapter 9, providing such results when large computations are involved can be a challenge to the test designer. Sometimes it is not feasible. For example, testing the random number generator shown in Figure 4.1 requires only one piece of input data. The randomness of the generated numbers cannot be supplied in advance. In general, however, expected test results should be provided if possible.

D. *Execute a Test Case Under Valid and Invalid Conditions*

Each software operation should be tested under conditions of both valid and invalid input data. The software should be expected to generate correct results when the input data are valid, and to generate correct diagnostic messages when the input data are invalid. Invalid testing is discussed in Chapters 8 and 9.

E. *Keep the Software Static During Testing*

The software must not be modified during implementation of the set of designed test input units. Such modification can cause three problems:

A. Errors can be easily introduced. Any program statement modified for ease of testing must be restored to its original form. A forgotten statement is a sure error left in the software.
B. It is difficult to identify the source of an error detected during testing if the error might be a result of the modification.
C. The correctness of the modified version does not guarantee the correctness of the original. For example, a DO loop working properly for 50 iterations does not necessarily mean that it will work for 200 iterations.

F. *Document Test Cases and Test Results*

Bookkeeping is one of the most important ingredients in the success of a business. Software testing is no exception. Every test case and test result must be documented for later reference.

G. *Keep in Mind the Difference between Correctness and Usability*

There are many cases in which the correctness of the software does not assure its value to the user. For example, the usability of the random number generator shown in Figure 4.1 is based on the randomness of the numbers it generates, not the accuracy of the numbers. Similarly, a business simulation program is useless if it cannot predict the right trend of business conditions even though the software is correctly producing accurate results. This important point must be considered in conducting software testing.

10.2.3 Selection of a Random Number Generator

As discussed in Chapter 9, selection of a random number generator is an important part of test design. The following sections discuss aspects of the availability and testing of a random number generator in the context of test design implementation.

A. Availability of Random Number Generators

Random number generators are available in many publications, and every computer system should have one. Also, a user can easily develop one. The FORTRAN and COBOL generators given in Section 4.3 are but two examples. These generators, which are based on Equation 4.3, are designed for 32-bit-word computers, but can be easily modified to run on 36-bit, 48-bit, or 64-bit machines. The modification can be accomplished by replacing the two numbers 65,539 and 2,147,483,647 with two new numbers appropriate to a non-32-bit computer.

For example, the FORTRAN generator:

```
SUBROUTINE RANDU (N, R)
N = N*(2**(K/2) + 3)
IF (N.LT.0) N = N + ((2**(K - 2) - 1)*2 + 1) + 1
R = N
R = R/((2**(K - 2) - 1)*2 + 1)
RETURN
END
```

can be modified to run on a computer of any word size by varying K, where K is an even-numbered word size. Replacing K by 64, for example, implements the generator on a 64-bit computer. Similarly, replacing K by 48 implements the generator on a 48-bit computer.

As part of the modification, to increase execution speed, the numbers (2**(K/2) + 3) and (2**(K − 2) − 1)*2 + 1 should be spelled out for the selected word size. For a 64-bit machine, the numbers should be (2**(64/2) + 3) and (2**(64 − 2) − 1)*2 + 1, or 4294967299 and

9223372036854775807, respectively. Similarly, for a 36-bit computer, the numbers should be (2**(36/2) + 3) and (2**(36 − 2) − 1)*2 + 1, or 262144 and 34359738367, respectively.

The generators based on Equation 4.3 can be implemented in other languages, such as PL/I and Ada, on a computer of any word size. The details of these implementations are left to the user.

Selection and modification of a random number generator for a software development computer are necessary but insufficient tasks for using the generators in the implementation of sampling plans. The generator must also be tested to ensure its usability for the intended purpose, as is discussed next.

B. Testing of Random Number Generators

As discussed in Chapter 4, the usability of a random number generator for a particular software application is determined by four major characteristics: efficiency, reproducibility, long period, and statistical acceptability. How these characteristics can be realized by a computerized random number generator is discussed as follows:

A. Efficiency. A uniform random number generator, such as the one discussed in Section 10.2.3*A*, can be used to produce a sequence of millions of numbers in a very short time. The precise length of time required depends on the make and word size of the computer used. If the application requires great computational efficiency, then the speed with which the generator produces a sufficient sequence of random numbers should be accurately measured.

B. Reproducibility. All computerized random number generators possess the characteristic of reproducibility. To reproduce a sequence of numbers, a positive and odd integer is selected as a starting "seed" for calling the generator m times. Whenever the seed is used and the generator called m times, the sequence of m numbers is reproduced.

C. Long Period. The period of a random number generator depends on the word size of the computer on which the generator is implemented. The longer the word size, the longer the period. For example, on a 16-bit computer the period is $2^{(16-2)}$ or 16,384; on a 32-bit computer, the period is $2^{(32-2)}$ or 1,073,741,824; on a 64-bit computer, the period is $2^{(64-2)}$ or 4,611,686,018,627,387,094. Software testing personnel must bear in mind that the length of the period has a tremendous effect on the test results to be achieved. For any nontrivial software development application, a generator implemented on a 16-bit machine should never be used, because the period, that is, 16,384, is too short.

D. Statistical Acceptability. This is the most important characteristic that a random number generator must possess. Statistical acceptability means that the sequence of random numbers produced by the generator is statistically random. If a generator cannot produce numbers whose randomness is statistically acceptable, the other three characteristics are meaningless in determining the usability of the generator.

The only way to determine the statistical acceptability of a random number generator, that is, to determine if the numbers it produces are random, is to test the generator. The following is an example of a procedure for testing the uniform random number generator:

```
SUBROUTINE RANDU (N, R)
N = N * 65539
IF (N.LT.0) N = N + 2147483647 + 1
R = N
R = R/2147483647
RETURN
END
```

The testing of this generator is accomplished by the following step-by-step procedure:

(i) Define Product Unit. The product unit of the generator is defined for an application as follows: A sequence of 1,000 digits is produced by the generator by using an initial seed and calling the generator 1,000 times. Each digit is obtained by multiplying 10 by a number returned via the variable R in the generator, $0 < R < 1$, and by truncating the result to an integer digit. Figure 10.4 is an example product unit generated by the seed 751003.

(ii) Define Product Unit Defectiveness. The product unit, a sequence of 1,000 digits, is defined as defective if the digits are not random, as determined by failure to pass at least one of the frequency tests, serial tests, poker tests, and gap tests, as discussed in Chapter 4. It is nondefective if it passes all four tests. (Note: There are many other tests that could be used to determine the randomness of the digits. The four tests cited here are given for discussion purposes only.)

95821 83466 63187 92943 09251 98094 55391 83576 36309 42365
10164 33176 26597 56242 67059 01728 90123 01497 24567 48907
28972 41977 90837 96315 20371 90670 10099 35849 89726 46631
00885 42047 43021 19347 63824 34010 53734 29501 09249 87629
74801 85448 12921 30716 25115 40649 57460 13498 13489 64531
84201 48778 99494 44289 65100 83685 68638 85573 70897 70222
77660 09285 73945 88492 83412 53037 95742 96749 42558 75039
17247 69728 73179 35299 88208 85461 33087 45019 66944 85828
97634 34579 11156 54996 09943 07378 87863 22220 16489 50273
96174 49490 04979 67720 04690 03767 99918 17353 10934 55072
83190 66399 62523 18749 17401 63843 16937 35172 33610 96399
38811 83468 17131 40639 41533 53247 83570 38857 63459 95473
71604 03629 55708 70586 64513 58415 22295 41770 68855 35332
13918 78832 14453 22099 38834 87984 74237 60621 11890 78129
07449 14861 32842 43201 62727 42951 05072 72314 64355 92834
46531 03692 41294 50743 97567 10921 43406 21536 45435 10350
01349 92539 71328 44909 68070 38877 25770 48164 66139 90677
98103 43110 36954 98012 20548 23424 55238 59382 51045 61640
05984 77972 92943 89846 22381 50091 15782 69458 32770 08189
70138 28250 12987 34880 18573 11153 01933 95878 44081 93418

Figure 10.4 A sequence of 1,000 random digits.

(iii) Understand Sampling Plan. An appropriate sampling plan for testing the generator would be the simple sampling plan for estimating the defective rate of the product unit population produced by the generator, as described in Section 5.1.

(iv) Implement the Test Design. Once the product unit and product unit defectiveness have been defined and a sampling plan selected, the test design can be implemented as follows: First, 300 random "seed" numbers, shown in Figure 10.5, are generated independently of the generator to be tested. Each of these seeds will be used by the generator to produce a sequence of 1,000 digits. There will be, therefore, 300 product units to be tested for randomness. Implementation of the test design requires development of a Chi-square test program to automate the frequency, serial, poker, and gap tests. The complete implementation of the test program and the random number generator is shown in Figure 10.6.

(v) Generate Test Results. The generator is used to produce 300 sequences of 1,000 digits, that is, 300 product units. It is impossible at this point to determine whether the results are those expected, that is,

1920180917	1793661063	1058745351	497958259	180580185	471878913
1367993651	279522951	244350599	1660810721	2037765155	1940376187
1299828947	1941715183	830341861	1766318479	1967445175	1370006357
325884427	305560821	1354612019	215957881	141358185	455684353
1422558441	818063305	78188651	1153072021	1727529905	337237097
1003808933	996564053	483266879	170226483	303966599	796732433
211734279	1496047501	1321556271	627218307	1865602795	482930865
139116285	17958209	297872663	1065209647	1649997759	1552189753
1952070413	396340481	907473585	129839667	327785113	874096733
2094640827	941263709	2033131853	234307623	1747303933	238583943
1202144259	771678901	70293821	786282085	1226077141	1080671951
1657160733	717625241	368891163	1619117451	232039123	485760733
1740224697	1352753841	1625608747	976234035	1592557921	220906151
1268319399	1957337789	700888811	191383793	1476540725	1497903627
2091645905	1097664241	1580033629	135143097	928467321	545791363
1502317375	583618003	532852547	1164482375	923702513	1616316009
529587131	665126123	180240743	222664013	1313882381	981218645
1635114557	1609865509	803261315	520578005	1233088611	447626249
1949731635	1669520085	816955283	1082677113	780896633	154227045
790720863	516611647	1172142181	1694732669	695360417	1389987677
486978733	826223625	477861841	619634415	2102778077	1924550837
526838573	236620693	505928519	2016161339	908214417	1388271389
1613469495	769363769	689643027	887413081	577992279	56157029
99814551	198308843	324625851	1737739273	2043802939	219734921
2062167	563478875	712972289	587580701	102413191	1734713423
2091517991	1093337039	1237884969	1197775969	646103717	464400743
1145267699	1607517691	2081064689	28747689	745854081	1153726355
2072889485	529162833	1030035343	1974537057	1472660543	874816825
458401863	453484181	901006503	51292225	1947548181	795934343
1918257665	2140596471	831064225	992964945	620338569	843538293
1070784759	1874388925	423527727	1111880823	1311319243	850568105
1515347259	587344327	761969501	557141453	326951257	655133325
998490031	1340956343	91634203	1992091675	1898708169	324027901
1458443305	217006129	265665295	420414181	1296336469	1000601155
1901602363	720924531	440896647	833444625	751414897	1188807689
1454552491	430363131	1286156353	1218427693	302927579	1303923251
2029374391	187842701	61345103	1093095703	1358411971	610718667
1442204665	1928573725	873683261	2129611625	609412081	2095748909
930273119	1770761105	803719715	1045744435	741944375	1326764053
156024709	1799411443	1019326347	602631129	1170505599	1788674327
35674777	1264454449	1426456177	1495161835	1558699143	1192514151
754823619	1307840973	1142149311	2134801313	467033675	230543607
995575721	1250609583	390674015	887610647	355888951	1073259485
1718139019	498633893	1344482965	223862305	1446212787	1153637515
1082356341	344388205	1208523529	164979585	1197623203	629230353
255491459	1213105467	578607253	838829273	1688319121	623803865
1370774423	1162780183	121081309	1491499081	454643077	463006963
1292398153	1136077117	293597931	1777477149	1944457003	1752659849
102963649	627854661	1631620029	214525589	588721009	1776381295
1730175031	1690504499	814172495	582101525	1172893459	663308089

Figure 10.5 Three hundred random seeds for testing the uniform random number generator.

sequences of random numbers. Thus, the results must be analyzed further to determine whether the product units are defective or nondefective.

(vi) Estimate the Defective Rate of the Product Unit Population of the Generator. The estimation of the product unit population defective rate requires two steps: analyzing the test results and performing statistical inference.

a. Analyzing Test Results. Figure 10.7 shows a step-by-step result of sampling and determination of the sample size required. Initially, 20 product units (i.e., 20 sequences of 1,000 digits) are sampled, using the

```
C       MAIN X0001.
        INTEGER K,N,NSEED,NP,NSEQ,NFF,NFS,NFP,NFG
        INTEGER M(10,10),S(1000)
        REAL G,FF,FS,FP,FG,R(10),C(10)
        DIMENSION NN(10)
        READ(5,1) NSEED
1       FORMAT(I10)
        NSEQ=0
        NPASS=0
        N=10
        DO 4 I=1,NSEED
          READ(5,1) NP
          WRITE(6,5) I
          WRITE(6,15) NP
          NSEQ=NSEQ+1
          CALL X0002(NP,K,S)
          WRITE(6,6) S
          CALL X0003(K,S,N,M,R,C,G)
          DO 2 II=1,N
            NN(II)=II-1
2         CONTINUE
          WRITE(6,7) NN
          DO 3 II=1,N
            NN(II)=C(II)
            IR=R(II)
            IJ=II-1
            WRITE(6,8) IJ,(M(II,J),J=1,N),IR
3         CONTINUE
          NG=G

          WRITE(6,9) NN,NG
          CALL X0004(N,R,EF,FF,CHISQF)
          CALL X0005(N,M,K,ES,FS,CHISQS)
          CALL X0006(K,S,EP,FP,CHISQP)
          CALL X0007(K,S,EG,FG,CHISQG)
          WRITE(6,10)
          WRITE(6,11) CHISQF,CHISQS,CHISQP,CHISQG
          WRITE(6,12) EF,ES,EP,EG
          IF(FF+FS+FP+FG.EQ.4.0) NPASS=NPASS+1
          WRITE(6,13) NPASS
          WRITE(6,14) NSEQ
4       CONTINUE
5       FORMAT(1H1,15HTEST CASE NO.     ,I5/)
6       FORMAT(1H1,31HSEQUENCE OF 1,000 RANDOM DIGITS//(7X,10(5I1,1X)))
7       FORMAT(//1X,10HMATRIX M   //14X,10I5,8H   TOTAL///)
8       FORMAT(7X,I2,5X,10I5,3X,I5)
9       FORMAT(///1X,8H   TOTAL,5X,10I5,3X,I5///)
10      FORMAT(//28X,50HFREQUENCY TEST  SERIAL TEST  POKER TEST   GAP TEST
       1///)
11      FORMAT(1X,27HCOMPUTED CHI-SQUARE VALUE  ,2X,F10.5,5X,F10.5,2X,
       1F10.5,1X,F10.5/)
12      FORMAT(1X,27HEXPECTED CHI-SQUARE VALUE  ,2X,F10.5,5X,F10.5,2X,
       1F10.5,1X,F10.5////)
13      FORMAT(/1X,52HCUMULATIVE NO. OF SEQUENCES PASSING ALL FOUR TESTS =
       1,I5/)
14      FORMAT(/1X,52HCUMULATIVE TOTAL NO. OF SEQUENCES TESTED           =
       1,I5/)
15      FORMAT(/1X,22HSTARTING ODD NUMBER =   ,I10/)
        STOP
        END


        SUBROUTINE X0002(NP,K,S)
C
C       THIS SUBROUTINE GENERATES A SEQUENCE OF 1000 RANDOM DIGITS
C       EACH TIME IT IS CALLED.
C
        INTEGER NP,K,S(1000)
        K=1000
        DO 1 I=1,K
          CALL X0008(NP,RN)
          S(I)=RN*10.0
1       CONTINUE
        RETURN
        END
```

Figure 10.6 An automatic random number generator test program.

```
      SUBROUTINE X0003(K,S,N,M,R,C,G)
C
C     THIS SUBROUTINE GENERATES A MATRIX FROM A SEQUENCE OF
C     1000 RANDOM DIGITS.  IT CALLS X0009, X0010, AND X0011 TO COMPUTE
C     THE ROW SUMS, COLUMN SUMS, AND GRAND TOTAL OF THE MATRIX M.
C
      INTEGER K,S(1000),N,M(10,10)
      REAL R(10),C(10),G
      N=10
      DO 2 I=1,N
        DO 1 J=1,N
          M(I,J)=0
1       CONTINUE
2     CONTINUE
      I=S(1)
      I=I+1
      ITEMPT=I
      DO 3 L=2,K

        J=S(L)
        J=J+1
        M(I,J)=M(I,J)+1
        I=J
3     CONTINUE
      J=ITEMPT
      M(I,J)=M(I,J)+1
      CALL X0009(N,M,R)
      CALL X0010(N,M,C)
      CALL X0011(N,M,G)
      RETURN
      END


      SUBROUTINE X0009(N,M,R)
C
C     THIS SUBROUTINE FINDS THE ROW SUMS OF THE MATRIX M.
C
      INTEGER N,M(10,10)
      REAL R(10)
      DO 2 I=1,N
        ROWSUM=0.0
        DO 1 J=1,N
          ROWSUM=ROWSUM+M(I,J)
1       CONTINUE
        R(I)=ROWSUM
2     CONTINUE
      RETURN
      END


      SUBROUTINE X0010(N,M,C)
C
C     THIS SUBROUTINE FINDS COLUMN SUMS OF THE MATRIX M.
C


      INTEGER N,M(10,10)
      REAL C(10)
      DO 2 J=1,N
        COLSUM=0.0
        DO 1 I=1,N
          COLSUM=COLSUM+M(I,J)
1       CONTINUE
        C(J)=COLSUM
2     CONTINUE
      RETURN
      END


      SUBROUTINE X0011(N,M,G)
C
C     THIS SUBROUTINE FINDS THE GRAND TOTAL OF THE MATRIX M.
C
      INTEGER N,M(10,10)
      REAL G
      G=0.0
      DO 2 I=1,N
        DO 1 J=1,N
          G=G+M(I,J)
1       CONTINUE
2     CONTINUE
      RETURN
      END
```

Figure 10.6 continued

```
      SUBROUTINE X0004(N,R,EF,FF,CHISQ)
C
C     THIS SUBROUTINE PREPARES DATA FOR THE FREQUENCY CHI-SQUARE TEST.
C
      INTEGER N
      REAL R(10),FF,T(10)
      KK=100
      DO 2 I=1,N
        T(I)=KK
2     CONTINUE
      EF=16.919
       CALL X0012(N,R,T,EF,FF,CHISQ)
      RETURN
      END


      SUBROUTINE X0012(N,R,T,EF,FF,CHISQ)
C
C     THIS SUBROUTINE PERFORMS THE FREQUENCY CHI-SQUARE TEST.
C
      INTEGER N
      REAL R(10),T(10),EF,FF
      CHISQ=0.0
      DO 1 I=1,N
        CHISQ=CHISQ+(R(I)-T(I))**2/T(I)
1     CONTINUE
      FF=0.0
      IF(CHISQ.LT.EF) FF=1.0
      RETURN
      END


      SUBROUTINE X0005(N,M,K,ES,FS,CHISQ)
C
C     THIS SUBROUTINE PREPARES DATA FOR THE SERIAL CHI-SQUARE TEST.
C
      INTEGER N,M(10,10),K
      REAL FS

      REAL T(10,10)
      KK=10
      DO 2 I=1,N
        DO 1 J=1,N
          T(I,J)=KK
1       CONTINUE
2     CONTINUE
      ES=113.145
      CALL X0013(N,M,T,ES,FS,CHISQ)
      RETURN
      END


      SUBROUTINE X0013(N,M,T,ES,FS,CHISQ)
C
C     THIS SUBROUTINE PERFORMS THE SERIAL CHI-SQUARE TEST.
C
      INTEGER N,M(10,10)
      REAL T(10,10),ES,FS
      CHISQ=0.0
      DO 2 I=1,N
        DO 1 J=1,N
          AM=M(I,J)
          CHISQ=CHISQ+(AM-T(I,J))**2/T(I,J)
1       CONTINUE
2     CONTINUE
      FS=0.0
      IF(CHISQ.LT.ES) FS=1.0
      RETURN
      END
```

Figure 10.6 continued

```
      SUBROUTINE X0006(K,S,EP,FP,CHISQ)
C
C     THIS SUBROUTINE PREPARES DATA FOR THE POKER CHI-SQUARE TEST.
C
      INTEGER K,S(1000)
      REAL FP
      INTEGER Y,U(10)
      REAL P(5),T(5),EP
      KK=250
      DO 1 I=1,5
        P(I)=0.0
1     CONTINUE
      I=0
      DO 7 INDEX1=1,KK
        DO 2 J=1,10
          U(J)=0
2       CONTINUE
        DO 3 INDEX2=1,4
          I=I+1
          J=S(I)
          J=J+1
          U(J)=U(J)+1
3       CONTINUE
        Y=1
        DO 4 J=1,10
          IF(U(J).NE.0) Y=Y*U(J)
4       CONTINUE
        IF(Y.NE.4) GO TO 6
        DO 5 J=1,10
          IF(U(J).EQ.2) Y=5
5       CONTINUE
6       P(Y)=P(Y)+1
7     CONTINUE

      U(5)=P(1)
      U(4)=P(2)
      U(2)=P(3)
      U(1)=P(4)
      U(3)=P(5)
      U(2)=U(2)+U(1)
      DO 8 I=1,4
        P(I)=U(I+1)
8     CONTINUE
      AK=KK
      T(1)=0.037*AK
      T(2)=0.027*AK
      T(3)=0.432*AK
      T(4)=0.504*AK
      EP=7.81473
      N=4
      CALL X0014(N,P,T,EP,FP,CHISQ)
      RETURN
      END


      SUBROUTINE X0014(N,P,T,EP,FP,CHISQ)
C
C     THIS SUBROUTINE PERFORMS THE POKER CHI-SQUARE TEST.
C
      INTEGER N
      REAL P(4),T(4),EP,FP
      CHISQ=0.0
      DO 2 I=1,N
        CHISQ=CHISQ+(P(I)-T(I))**2/T(I)
2     CONTINUE

      FP=0.0
      IF(CHISQ.LT.EP) FP=1.0
      RETURN
      END
```

Figure 10.6 continued

first 20 seeds given in Figure 10.5. The product units are analyzed by the Chi-square test program. The sample defective rate is $1 - 14/20 = 0.30$. The sample size is found to be 57 (from Appendix 2) with $\theta = 0.30$, $a = 0.40$, and $z = 1.96$. Since 20 is less than 57, 37 additional product units must be sampled.

After 30 additional product units are generated, the sample defective rate remains 0.30. To reach the required sample size of 57, another 7

```
      SUBROUTINE X0007(K,S,EG,FG,CHISQ)
C
C     THIS SUBROUTINE PREPARES DATA FOR THE GAP CHI-SQUARE TEST.
C
      INTEGER K,S(1000)
      REAL W(13),T(5)
      DO 1 I=1,K
        IF(S(I).EQ.0) GO TO 3
1     CONTINUE
      FG=0.0
      GO TO 7
3     J=I+1
      JJ=I
      DO 4 I=1,13
        W(I)=0.0
4     CONTINUE
      TZERO=0.0
      DO 5 I=J,K
        IF(S(I).NE.0) GO TO 5
        L=I-JJ
        TZERO=TZERO+1
        JJ=I
        IF(L.GT.13) L=13
        W(L)=W(L)+1
5     CONTINUE
      J=0
      DO 6 I=1,12,3
        J=J+1

        W(J)=W(I)+W(I+1)+W(I+2)
6     CONTINUE
      W(5)=W(13)
      T(1)=TZERO*0.271
      T(2)=TZERO*0.198
      T(3)=TZERO*0.144
      T(4)=TZERO*0.105
      T(5)=TZERO*0.282
      N=5
      EG=9.48773
      CALL X0015(N,W,T,EG,FG,CHISQ)
7     RETURN
      END


      SUBROUTINE X0015(N,W,T,EG,FG,CHISQ)
C
C     THIS SUBROUTINE PERFORMS THE GAP CHI-SQUARE TEST.
C
      INTEGER N
      REAL W(5),T(5),EG,FG
      CHISQ=0.0
      DO 2 I=1,N
        CHISQ=CHISQ+(W(I)-T(I))**2/T(I)
2     CONTINUE
      FG=0.0
      IF(CHISQ.LT.EG) FG=1.0
      RETURN
      END


      SUBROUTINE X0008(N,RN)

C
C     THIS SUBROUTINE GENERATES A UNIFORM RANDOM NUMBER BETWEEN 0 AND 1,
C     EXCLUSIVE, AND AN INTEGER RANDOM NUMBER BETWEEN 0 AND 2**31, EXCLUSIVE.
C
      INTEGER N
      REAL RN
      N=N*65539
      IF(N.LT.0) N=N+2147483647+1
      RN=N
      RN=RN/2147483647
      RETURN
      END
```

Figure 10.6 continued

product units must be generated. After another 30 additional product units are sampled, the defective rate is found to 0.25 with a total of 80 sequences. (Theoretically, 57 sequences would have been sufficient. Because more sampling results in greater accuracy, 80 sequences are sampled.) The sample size is found to be 73, which is less than 80; therefore, the sampling process is completed.

Cumulative Number of Test Cases	Cumulative Number of Test Cases Passing All Four Tests	Sample Defective Rate	Estimated Number of Test Cases Required
20	14	0.30	57
50	35	0.30	57
80	60	0.25	73

Figure 10.7 Determination of sample size in estimating the defective rate of the random number generator of Figure 4.1.

b. Performing Statistical Inference. The sampling process discussed above represents taking outputs at random from a binomial distribution. The sample defective rate is found to be $\theta^0 = 0.25$. The next step is to estimate the mean μ and the variance σ of the product unit population. This can be done by testing hypotheses as follows:

Let the hypotheses be formulated as:

$$H_1\colon \mu = \mu_1 = 19.2$$
$$H_2\colon \mu = \mu_2 \neq 19.2$$

on the basis of the mean $\bar{x}$ and variance s^2 of the sample of 80 sequences at the five percent level of significance.

The sample mean $\bar{x}$ and variance s^2 can be computed by:

$$\bar{x} = n\theta^0 = 80 \times 0.25 = 20$$
$$s^2 = n\theta^0(1 - \theta^0) = 80 \times 0.25 \times 0.75 = 15$$

The procedure for testing the mean of a binomial distribution having an unknown variance is given in Section 5.1.3*A*. This procedure can be used for testing the hypotheses. From Appendix 4, the student t value of $t_{n-1,\alpha/2} = t_{80-1,0.05/2} = 1.96$. The value of $(\bar{x} - \mu_1)\sqrt{n}/s$ is

$$\frac{(20 - 19.2)\sqrt{80}}{3.87} = 1.85$$

Since $-1.96 < 1.85 < 1.96$, the hypotheses H_1 is accepted. In other words, the sample mean 20 is not different from 19.2 at the five-percent level of significance.

This conclusion can be verified by the confidence interval of the population mean μ as follows. Using Equation 5.4a, the $(1 - 0.05)$-percent confidence interval of μ is:

$$\left[20 \pm 1.96\frac{3.87}{\sqrt{80}}\right]$$

which is:

$$[19.152, 20.848]$$

(vii) Determine Whether or Not To Use the Generator. The 95-percent confidence interval of the mean of the product unit population produced by the generator is found to be [19.152, 20.848]. The defective rate of the population is found to be from 18.152/80 to 20.848/80, or from 0.2394 to 0.2606. If an application requires that the rate must be less than 0.05, this generator is not usable.

It is important to note that generalizations about the usability of the generator, as determined previously, should be avoided. The determination that the generator is usable or not usable is valid only for a given test design. If a different test design is used, then the defective rate of the product unit population may also be different, even though the generator is the same. Thus, although a piece of software may not be usable under one set of conditions, it may be 100 percent usable under another set.

It is also important to note that the usability of the generator is determined by the four characteristics: efficiency, reproducibility, long period, and statistical acceptability. None of these characteristics is related to the number of errors in the generator. In fact, there is no error in the generator, as is proved in Section 11.5.2*A*. This generator serves as a counterexample to almost all of the software reliability models currently existent in literature and, therefore, invalidates the applicability of these models as software reliability measures. This subject is discussed further in Chapter 14.

10.2.4 Test Design Implementation Considerations

A number of factors must be considered in implementing the test design for the software system and for each module. The purpose of identifying these factors is to ensure that the implementation carries out the test design and fulfills its intended function: to provide a means of offering statistical evidence of the quality of the software as a basis for a meaningful warranty.

A. System Test Design Implementation

The major considerations in implementing the software system test design are:

A. The number of test cases necessary to test the system should be determined either by a sample size determination equation such as

Equations 5.3 or 5.3a if specified in the test requirements in the requirements specification document. Test cases should be generated for each of the regular, weighted, boundary, invalid, and special test designs as applicable.

B. Use a uniform random number generator only if the generator has been tested, as discussed in Section 10.2.3***B***.

C. If inputs to the software system are from multiple sources, such as number of terminals, then the time at which the test cases are fed into the system at a terminal should be randomized. If it is necessary to measure the throughput of the system, that is, the number of product units per unit of time, then do the following:

a. Generate n random time instances at which the n test cases are to be input into the system from the various sources. Measure the time t required to process the n cases.

b. Repeat this procedure (Step A) n times, obtaining n timed input results, that is, $t_1, t_2, \ldots, t_n$.

c. Compute the average of $t_1, t_2, \ldots, t_n$ by:

$$\bar{t} = \sum_{i=1}^{n} t_i/n$$

d. Find the variance of $t_1, t_2, \ldots, t_n$ to determine the spreadness of these results by:

$$\sigma^2 = \sum_{i=1}^{n} (t_i - \bar{t})^2/(n-1)$$

B. Module Test Design Implementation

The major considerations in implementing module test designs are:

A. The implementation of the test design for each module should be prioritized to correspond to the implementation schedule for the software modules. Just as the most critical module should be implemented first, then the next most critical module, and so on; in complementary order the test design for the most critical module should be implemented first, then the test design for the next most critical module, and so on. This approach to prioritizing the implementation of module test designs will facilitate the testing of the software modules.

B. Develop a module driver for testing each module being implemented.

C. Implement a test design by a manual means or by coding a test case generation program based on the test design.

D. The number of test cases necessary to test each module should be determined either by a sample size determination equation, such as Equation 5.3, if specified in the test design, or by the iterative Equation 5.3a. Test cases should be generated for each of the regular, weighted, boundary, invalid, and special tests, as applicable.

E. Use a uniform random number generator only if the generator has been tested, as discussed in Section 10.2.3***B***.

F. If a module processes inputs from multiple sources concurrently, such as from a number of terminals, then the time at which the test cases are fed into the module at a device should be randomized. If it is necessary to measure the throughput of the module, that is, the number of inputs processed per unit of time, then the procedure described in Section 10.2.4***A***.**C** for the software system should be used at the module level.

10.2.5 Test Documentation

After test designs have been implemented, a test document should be prepared to record test results for later analysis and reference. The test document should contain the following information:

Name of the module being tested
Document revision level number
Cross-reference to test design documents
Name of person conducting the test
Date of test
List of implemented test cases
List of computer programs used to generate the test cases
Results for each test case
Listing of module driver
Instructions for using the test cases to test the module or system

The testing of each module and of the entire software system should be documented separately. The test cases and test results can be used to test later versions of the same piece of software, whether it is a module or the entire system, allowing a comparison of test results from different versions.

10.3 VERIFICATION OF SOFTWARE IMPLEMENTATION AND TEST IMPLEMENTATION

A code walk-through or reading to examine the software code which implements the software design is required to ensure that the implemented code realizes the software design. The engineer or programmer who implements each module must explain the module to a group of people doing the code walkthrough. This practice usually uncovers errors here and there.

A test implementation walk-through should also be conducted to ensure that the implementation represents the test design and satisfies the user's needs. Then, after the code reading and test walk-through have been conducted separately, a cross-reading of the implementation should be performed to further uncover possible errors.

REFERENCES

1. W. P. Stevens, G. J. Myers, and L. L. Constantine, "Structured Design," *IBM System Journal*, Vol. 13, No. 2, 1974, pp. 115–139.
2. C. K. Cho, *An Introduction to Software Quality Control*, Wiley-Interscience, New York, 1980.
3. G. J. Myers, *Software Reliability—Principles and Practices*, Wiley-Interscience, New York, 1976.
4. E. W. Dijkstra, "The Humble Programmer," *Communications of the ACM*, Vol. 15, No. 10, October 1972, pp. 859–866.
5. E. Horowitz (Ed.), *Practical Strategies for Developing Large Software Systems*, Addison-Wesley, Reading, Massachusetts, 1975.

EXERCISES

1. Implement the software design and test design of the payroll program, using the designs of Exercise 1 of Chapter 9.
2. Implement the software design and test design of the matrix operation $AB = C$, using the designs of Exercise 2 of Chapter 9.
3. Implement the software design and test design of the matrix inversion program, using the designs of Exercise 3 of Chapter 9.

CHAPTER 11

Software Testing, Integration, Verification, Validation, and Debugging

11.1 SOFTWARE SUCCESS CRITERIA —SOFTWARE ENGINEERING GOALS

Lack of criteria, or inappropriate criteria, for determining the successfulness of a piece of software is one of the 20 major problems in software engineering project management. It is certainly one reason why many software projects have been plagued with poor quality or unusable software, that is, not maintainable, unreliable, difficult to use, and insufficiently documented, as indicated in Figure 1.3.

The current literature abounds with discussions of software modifiability, understandability, reliability, and efficiency as the goals of software engineering. These goals may also be considered the success criteria for software development. Unfortunately, the need for meaningful measurements of these goals has still not received proper attention.

11.1.1 Problems with Currently Used Measures for Success Criteria

The difficulties in developing and applying meaningful measures of modifiability, understandability, reliability, and efficiency are discussed as follows:

A. *Modifiability (Maintainability)*

Software modifiability is difficult to measure directly. Therefore, indirect measures have been proposed, such as those in Gilb [35]:

Problem recognition time
Administrative delay time
Modification tools collection time
Problem analysis time
Modification specification time
Active modification time
Local testing time
Global testing time
Modification review time
Total recovery time

The biggest problem with this type of quantification is that the time required to modify a piece of software is not a statistically developed measure like the time required to replace a hardware component, for example, Mean Time To Failure (MTTF). There is no way to control personnel or the nature of the modification. Thus, the author of the software, a new person assigned to the task, and persons of varying proficiency in software development and application areas may all require different lengths of time to perform similar modifications. Likewise, whether the modification is being undertaken to enhance software functions, improve software efficiency, or remove errors will affect interpretation of any value found for the modification time. For these reasons, the time required to modify a piece of software may not be a meaningful measure of that software's modifiability.

B. *Understandability*

Software understandability is defined as the number of instructions that can be understood per unit of time in Cho [20]. Understanding the instructions means understanding what these instructions do in the code. Many factors contribute to software understandability: sufficiency of software documentation, simplicity in the code and data structure, software modularization, module interface, and so on. However, the quantification of understandability cannot be objective. Like modifiability, understandability also depends on many factors such as one's background, programming proficiency, familiarity with the software application area, and so on.

C. *Reliability*

Conventional software reliability has been discussed in terms of models in the three categories:

Models based on hardware reliability theory

Models using program internal characteristics

Models derived from "inserting" known errors into software and finding the number of inserted errors detected versus actual number of errors detected

A major flaw in all of these models is that they are based on errors existing in the software. In practical applications, there are many cases in which program errors are irrelevant to program usability. An error-free program can be useless to its user under certain conditions, and can be 100 percent useful under other conditions. Ample counterexamples that invalidate all of these models exist. Software reliability and some of these counterexamples are given in Chapter 14.

D. *Efficiency*

Software efficiency is the ability of a piece of software to perform its intended functions with a minimum of effort. It is a performance requirement established during the modeling and requirements specification stages of software development. Many factors contribute to software efficiency: design, coding, memory usage, input/output processing, and so on. Conventionally, software efficiency is quantified by using two measures: execution time (i.e., response time per transaction) and throughput (i.e., the amount of input data being processed into output, or the amount of work performed per unit of time).

One important measure of software efficiency that has not received proper attention is capacity. It is not addressed in many software engineering books, for example, Shooman [36], Yeh [10], Jensen and Tonies [31], and Vick [37], and receives only minimal mention in others, such as Pressman [32], Tausworthe [33, 34]. Capacity measures have many important characteristics: storage, memory, software input, expandability of storage, and so on. In many applications, capacity is a much more important measure of efficiency than execution time and throughput. A software system is inefficient if it lacks sufficient capacity, even if its execution time and throughput are superb in meeting performance requirements. (Consider the time and effort that would be spent on a piece of software if its capacity could not be expanded to meet operational needs.)

Although the importance of efficiency cannot be overemphasized, software developers should always keep in mind that efficiency is important only to the extent that the software works and is usable to its user. If a piece of software is efficient but does not work right all the time, then it would damage its user—efficiently. This is an important factor to be considered in applying efficiency as a success criterion.

11.1.2 Proposed Measures of Reliability and Efficiency

As discussed, the software engineering goals of modifiability, understandability, reliability, and efficiency may be considered software success criteria. However, meaningful quantification of modifiability and understandability is difficult because of the subjective factors involved, and proper measures of reliability and efficiency are still lacking until now. In the context of this book, the following are proposed as measures of software reliability and efficiency:

Reliability: The software product population defective rate θ as defined in Chapter 7. The smaller the value of θ, the more reliable the software. The determination of the value of θ is based on statistical principles and is independent of time and of the number of errors remaining in the software.

Efficiency: Execution speed, throughput, and capacity as obtained by statistical procedures.

These measures of reliability and efficiency are discussed further later in this chapter.

11.2 SOFTWARE SAMPLING PROCESS

The simple sampling and sequential sampling processes discussed in Chapter 5 can be used to sample product units from a software product population. The following is a simple sampling process that can be applied to software testing (the reader should apply a sequential sampling process to software testing):

A. Take an initial sample of small size n_0 units (e.g., $n_0 = 100$) from a software product population by executing n_0 input units.

B. Let θ_0^0 be the defective rate of the sample of size n_0.

C. Compute the sample size n_{i+1} by Equation (5.3a) as follows:

$$n_{i+1} = \frac{z^2(1 - \theta_i^0)}{a^2\theta_i^0}$$

where θ_i^0 is the cumulative defective rate of the cumulative sample units n_i already taken after the ith iteration, for $i = 0, 1, 2, \ldots$

D. If $n_{i+1} > n_i$, then take $(n_{i+1} - n_i)$ additional units and repeat Steps C and D.

E. Else stop. The total number of sample units taken is sufficient.

The process is illustrated by the following example. It is assumed that a software system is designed to produce a product unit population of exactly 104,000 units. It is also assumed that the software product population has been produced and analyzed. Each of the units in the population is either defective or nondefective. A digit of 0 is marked on a unit that is defective in the population after analysis, while a non-zero digit is marked on a unit that is nondefective in the population. The population so marked is given in Appendix 1 of this book. The reader is to estimate the population defective rate by the sampling procedure stated previously.

The iterative sample process is shown in Fig. 11.1. The probability that $|\theta - \theta^0| = 0.1\theta$ is 95 percent. The value of z is found to be 1.96 from Appendix 3 of this book. Therefore,

$$n_{i+1} = \frac{1.96^2(1 - \theta_i^0)}{0.1^2\theta_i^0}$$

There are several ways to take product units from the population. One is to take the sample randomly on a unit-by-unit basis. Another is to take the sample randomly on a block by block basis, for example, a block of 100 units. For simplicity, a block of 100 units will be sampled randomly from the population. The sampling of a block is done by first generating a random number for a page (between 414 and 434, inclusive) from which a block is to be taken. Next a random number is obtained for a row block from which the block is to be taken (between 1 and 5, inclusive). Finally, a random number (between 1 and 10, inclusive) is produced for a column

Iteration i	Page No.	Row Block No.	Column Block No.	Sample Units Taken	Cumulative Sample Size n_i	No. of Defectives in Sample	Cumulative Sample Defective Rate θ_i^0	Next Iteration Sample Size n_{i+1}
0	425	2	8	100	100	18	0.1800	1,751
1	433	2	1	100		16		
	420	1	1	100		7		
	421	3	8	100		16		
	418	4	4	100		15		
	417	4	5	100		7		
	431	1	9	100		13		
	425	3	3	100		19		
	430	3	6	100		9		
	427	4	7	100		10		
	433	1	3	100		17		
	416	3	1	100		17		
	420	1	7	100		13		
	431	2	2	100		8		
	426	2	1	100		9		
	430	3	5	100		8		
	414	3	7	100		17		
	428	4	5	51	1,751	15	0.1336	2,492
2	429	1	9	100		13		
	417	5	7	100		11		
	432	1	6	100		12		
	429	5	2	100		20		
	426	3	1	100		14		
	428	4	3	100		15		
	423	2	1	100		10		
	425	5	1	41	2,492	9	0.1356	2,449
3	(Stop, since the total no. of sample units taken is 2,492, which is greater than 2,449)							

Figure 11.1 An iterative sampling example.

block from which the block is to be taken. For example, in the initial iteration, the three random numbers generated are 425, 2, and 8, which indicate that a block of 100 units is to be taken from row block 2 and column block 8 on page 425. The step-by-step sampling procedure is explained as follows:

A. An initial sample of 100 units from the population on pages 414 to 434 is taken. The actual sample taken is the 100 units of block (12, 2, 8), which is on page 425, row block 2, and column block 8. This is given in iteration 0 in Figure 11.1.

B. There are 18 0s in the block, so $\theta_0^0 = 18/100 = 0.18$, as shown in iteration 0 of Figure 11.1.

C. Compute the sample n_1 by:

$$n_1 = \frac{1.96^2(1 - \theta_0^0)}{0.1^2\theta_0^0} = \frac{1.96^2(1 - 0.18)}{0.1 \times 0.1 \times 0.18} = 1{,}751$$

as given in iteration 0 of Figure 11.1.

D. As $n_1 > n_0$, therefore, $(n_1 - n_0) = (1{,}751 - 100) = 1{,}651$ additional units are needed.

E. The additional 1,651 units taken are indicated in iteration 1 of Figure 11.1. There are 216 0s in the 1,651 units. Therefore,

$$\theta_1^0 = \frac{18 + 216}{100 + 1{,}651} = 0.1336$$

and:

$$n_2 = \frac{1.96^2(1 - \theta_1^0)}{0.1^2\theta_1^0} = \frac{1.96^2(1 - 0.1336)}{0.1^2 \times 0.1336} = 2{,}492$$

F. $n_2 > n_1$. Therefore, $(n_2 - n_1) = (2{,}492 - 1{,}751) = 741$ additional units are required.

G. The additional 741 units taken are indicated in iteration 2 of Figure 11.1. There are 104 0s in the 741 units. Therefore,

$$\theta_2^0 = \frac{18 + 216 + 104}{100 + 1{,}651 + 741} = \frac{338}{2492} = 0.1356$$

and:

$$n_3 = \frac{1.96^2(1 - 0.1356)}{0.1^2 \times 0.1356} = 2{,}449$$

H. $n_3 < n_2$. Therefore, stop. The total number of 2,492 sample units taken is sufficient.

The details of the sampling procedure are shown in Figure 11.1. The statistical inference of the population defective rate θ is discussed in Section 11.3.

11.3 STATISTICAL INFERENCE BASED ON SOFTWARE PRODUCT UNIT POPULATION DEFECTIVE RATE

As discussed in Chapter 5, there are many statistical inference principles that can be applied to software quality assessment. An example of finding the mean and the defective rate of a software product population is given here:

The range of the mean of a binomial population is (see Equation 5.4a):

$$\left[\bar{x} - t_{n-1,\alpha/2}\frac{s}{\sqrt{n}}, \bar{x} + t_{n-1,\alpha/2}\frac{s}{\sqrt{n}}\right]$$

From Section 11.2, the sample defective rate θ^0 of a sample of 2,492 units taken from the population in Appendix 1 of this book is

$$\theta^0 = 0.1356$$

$$\bar{x} = n\theta^0 = 2{,}492 \times 0.1356 = 338$$

$$s = \sqrt{n\theta^0(1 - \theta^0)} = \sqrt{2{,}492 \times 0.1356 \times (1 - 0.1356)} = 17.09$$

$$t_{n-1,\alpha/2} = t_{2{,}492-1,0.01/2}$$

$$= 2.576 \text{ (from Appendix 4 of this book)}$$

$$\sqrt{n} = \sqrt{2492} = 49.92$$

Thus, the range of the population mean μ is found to be:

$$[337.118, 338.882]$$

Therefore, the range of the defective rate of the population θ at the 99-percent level of confidence is:

$$\left[\frac{337.118}{2{,}492}, \frac{338.882}{2{,}492}\right]$$

or:

$$[0.1350, 0.1360]$$

The true defective rate θ is:

$$\theta = \frac{\text{total number of 0's}}{\text{total number of digits in the population}}$$

$$= \frac{14{,}143}{104{,}000} = 0.13599$$

which falls within the computed range.

This example shows sampling can be very effective in estimating the defective rate of a population. The cost in this sampling is 2,492 units, while that of finding the true defective rate is 104,000 units. The cost saving is $1 - 2{,}492/104{,}000 = 0.9760$ or 97.60 percent of exhaustive inspection.

The cost of sampling is almost negligible compared with that of a 100-percent inspection. In fact, if a population contains millions and millions of units, sampling is the only practical way to determine the defective rate of the population.

11.4 SOFTWARE TESTING AND INTEGRATION PROCEDURE

Test and integration are the activities that assemble modules into a complete software system. Following the software engineering approach described in this book, test and integration are also the phases of software development in which software implementation and test implementation come together.

There are many test and integration methods being practiced in the industry. Myers [2] describes several of them based on bottom-up, top-down, modified top-down, "big-bang," "sandwich," and modified "sandwich" approaches. However, as currently practiced, all of these methods are based on the assumption that a software module will be correct if:

A. Every statement can be executed at least once during testing.
B. Every logic path can be executed at least once during testing.
C. The module is error-free.

This assumption may seem to make sense from the developer's point of view—but not from the user's point of view. For the user, the purpose of testing should be to determine directly whether the software produces good results. The only way to do this is by using software product population sampling.

Software developers should consider, as pointed out in this book, that a piece of software is analogous to a factory. Testing and integration of a piece of software is analogous to building a factory. As practiced in the manufacturing industries, the planning and design of the factory must use a top-down approach. Blueprints of the factory facilities, the machinery layout, and sources of construction materials and machinery must be ready before starting construction. But there is only one approach for building the factory, and that is from the ground up. This is not only due to physical necessity, but also because the components of the factory are assembled on a "secure quality part" basis.

Thus, there is only one suitable approach for testing a piece of software: bottom-up that assembles quality modules into the system. There are many examples which invalidate many of the other approaches, as will be shown in later chapters. If bottom-up testing and integration cannot be carried through, then there might be something seriously wrong with the software design.

The following sections present some step-by-step "bottom-up" procedures using software product population sampling for module testing, module integration, and system testing.

11.4.1 Module Test Procedure

Each module will be tested using the module product population sampling. If the defective rate meets module requirements, then it is to be integrated. The procedure is:

A. Review the software modeling document to understand the role and rationale of the module being tested.

B. Review the software requirements document to understand the requirements of the module and the software system.

C. Review the software design document to understand why and how the module is designed, and the interrelationships between the module being tested and other modules in the software system.

D. Review the test design of the module to verify that the software design and test design are complete and correct.

E. Review the implementation of software design and test design to determine whether the module is ready for testing.

F. Review the module driver for testing the module.

G. Review the product unit definition for testing the module.

H. Review the product unit goodness definition for test-result analysis.

I. Review the sampling plan(s) for testing the module. As discussed in Chapter 8, there are five types of sampling:

Regular sampling
Weighted sampling
Boundary sampling
Invalid sampling
Special sampling

Select the most appropriate sampling plan(s) to be applied to testing the module.

J. Make sure that Steps **A** through **I** are performed so that the software engineering principles of uniformity, completeness, confirmability, and statistical quality control are practiced throughout the module testing.

K. Test each module using the test procedure discussed in Section 11.2 for each sampling plan in Step **I** above, using the test input units implemented as discussed in Section 10.2.

L. Perform statistical inference on the population defective rate θ from each sample defective rate θ^0 found in Step **K**, using the methods discussed in Chapter 5 and Section 11.3.

M. If the test results satisfy the requirements of the module, release the module for further development (integration).

N. Or else return the module to the designer and implementer for debugging (further details on debugging are given in Section 11.6).

O. Repeat Steps **A** through **N** for all software modules that are required to be integrated and tested, until the entire software system is integrated.

11.4.2 System Test Procedure

After all of the modules have been tested and integrated according to the procedure discussed in Section 11.4.1, the entire system is ready for system testing. The test procedure is:

A. Review the software modeling document to understand the "goal" of the software system.

B. Review the software requirements document to understand the requirements of the software system.

C. Review the product unit definition of the software system.

D. Review the product unit defectiveness definition of the software system.

E. Review the sampling plan(s) for testing the software system. As discussed in Chapter 8, there are five types of sampling:

Regular sampling
Weighted sampling
Boundary sampling
Invalid sampling
Special sampling

that can be used for testing a software system.

F. Make sure Steps **A** through **E** are performed so that the software engineering principles of uniformity, completeness, confirmability, and statistical quality control are practiced throughout.

G. Use the set of test input units implemented in Section 10.2 to test the software system, using the process discussed in Section 11.2, for each of the sampling methods stated in Step **E**.

H. Perform statistical inference on the defective rate θ of the software product population from each sample defective rate θ^0 found in Step **G**.

I. If the test results satisfy the test requirements, as discussed in Section 8.2, then release the software system for preacceptance test.

J. Or else return the software system to the designers and implementers for debugging (further details on debugging are given in Section 11.6).

11.5 INDEPENDENT VERIFICATION, VALIDATION, AND CERTIFICATION

Verification and validation are two major tasks of software development. Their purpose is to determine that the software performs its intended functions with reliability. However, the actual activities that should constitute verification and validation are not clear in the literature. For example, in Myers [2], verification is "an attempt to find errors by executing a program in a test or simulated environment," and validation is "an attempt to find errors by executing a program in a given real environment." According to Jensen and Tonies [31], verification "assures that each level of requirements or specification correctly echoes the intentions of the immediately superior level of requirements," and validation "assures that each end item product functions and contains the feature as prescribed by its requirements and specifications at the corresponding level." None of these definitions are sufficient for verification and validation. To end possible confusion, the following section provides standard definitions of the terms verification and validation in the context of this book and identifies the specific activities that should constitute each of these phases of software development.

Section 11.5.2 gives an example of the proof of program correctness method in helping ensure the correctness of a program in complementing program testing. As indicated in the literature [9], verification and validation should be conducted by a third party to maintain an independent perspective of the software being developed.

11.5.1 Verification and Validation Activities

In the context of this book, the definitions of verification and validation will be according to the *Webster's New World Dictionary*, respectively:

> To test or check the accuracy or correctness of, as by investigation, comparison with a standard, or reference to the facts

and:

> To prove to be valid.

Thus, the activities that constitute software verification and validation are identified as follows:

A. Verification Activities. Verification activities consist of the following:

- **a.** Ensure the accuracy or correctness of the contents of the documents produced during the modeling, requirements specification, concurrent software design and test design, concurrent software implementation and test implementation, and testing and integration stages of the software development process.
- **b.** Ensure that the developed software performs its intended functions by checking the analysis of the test results.
- **c.** Ensure that the defective rates of the software product populations of the sampling plans, where applicable:

  Regular sampling
  Weighted sampling
  Boundary sampling
  Invalid sampling
  Special sampling

  satisfy the test requirements stated in the requirements specification document.

B. Validation Activities. Validation activities consist of the following:

- **a.** Ensure that the software modeling document is complete and approved. This document contains the first set of "facts for software development," as discussed in Chapter 7.
- **b.** Ensure that (1) the software requirements specification document is complete and logically correct, and consistent with the

software modeling document; (2) the software test requirements are based on statistical quality control principles; and (3) both the software requirements specification document and the test requirements document are approved. These documents also contain the "facts" for software development, as discussed in Chapter 8.

c. Ensure that (1) the software requirements and test requirements are correctly translated into software design and test design, respectively; and (2) the software design and test design documents are complete and approved, as discussed in Chapter 9.

d. Ensure that (1) the software design and test design are implemented correctly; and (2) the software design implementation and test design implementation documents are complete and approved, as discussed in Chapter 10.

e. Ensure that (1) testing and integration are conducted based on statistical quality control principles; and (2) the test document is complete and approved, as discussed in Chapter 11.

f. Ensure that (1) if any error is found at any stage of the development process, the activities in Items **a** through **e** are performed in a logical order to ensure that the error is properly corrected; and (2) the detection and correction of this error is documented.

11.5.2 Proof of Program Correctness

A common approach to program proving is that of the informal method of Floyd [13] and Naur [14]. The method starts with generation of input and output assertions for a program. Program loops and paths are then identified. Verification conditions are generated for each of the loops and paths that are to be proved correct. Finally, the program is examined for normal termination.

The input and output assertions and the verification conditions are stated in some formal logic system such as the first-order predicate calculus. A logical variable or an expression is assigned the value of true or false. There are many notations associated with the calculus, some of which are shown in Figure 11.2. The discussion of the calculus is beyond the scope of this book and can be found in any mathematical logic or artificial intelligence references. A proof procedure is:

A. Draw a flowchart for the program

B. Generate the input and output assertions

C. Specify an inductive assertion for each loop, if any.

D. Identify all paths within the program (each path starts with an assertion and ends with another).

E. Write the verification conditions for each path from the semantics of the program statements.

F. Prove every verification condition. There are two possible outcomes if the proof cannot be completed:

   a. The program contains errors.

   b. The verification conditions are incomplete or wrong.

G. Prove that the program will stop normally.

Connective	Symbol	Example	Meaning
Conjunction	$\vee$	$a \vee b$	a or b
Disjunction	$\wedge$	$a \wedge b$	a and b (same as if a then b else false)
Negation	$^{-}$	$\bar{a}$	not a
Implication	$\supset$	$a \supset b$	a implies b (same as $\bar{a} \vee b$)
Equivalence	$\equiv$	$a \equiv b$	a is equivalent to b [same as $(a \supset b) \wedge (b \supset a)$]
Universal quantifier	$\forall$	$\forall a(f(a))$	For all values of a, $f(a)$ is true
Existential quantifier	$\exists$	$\exists a(f(a))$	There exists some value of a such that $f(a)$ is true

Figure 11.2 Predicate calculus connectives.

A. *A Case Study of Program Proof*

The following is an example of proving the correctness of the uniform random number generator of Figure 4.1.

A. A flowchart of the program is drawn in Figure 11.3.

B. The input and output assertions are generated as follows:

$$A1: \quad (0 < N < 2^{31}) \wedge (N \text{ is an integer})$$
$$A2: \quad (0 < N < 2^{31}) \wedge (0 < RN < 1) \wedge (N \text{ is an integer}) \wedge (N \text{ is altered})$$

C. Since there is no loop in the program, no inductive assertion is needed for a loop.

D. There are two paths in the flowchart. One is 2-4-5-6 and the other 2-3-4-5-6. (The path from 1 to 2 is trivial and is not included.)

E. The verification conditions for each path are generated as follows:

   a. The assertion at point 6 is the same as the output assertion. Namely,

$$(0 < N < 2^{31}) \wedge (0 < RN < 1) \wedge (N \text{ is an integer}) \wedge (N \text{ is altered})$$

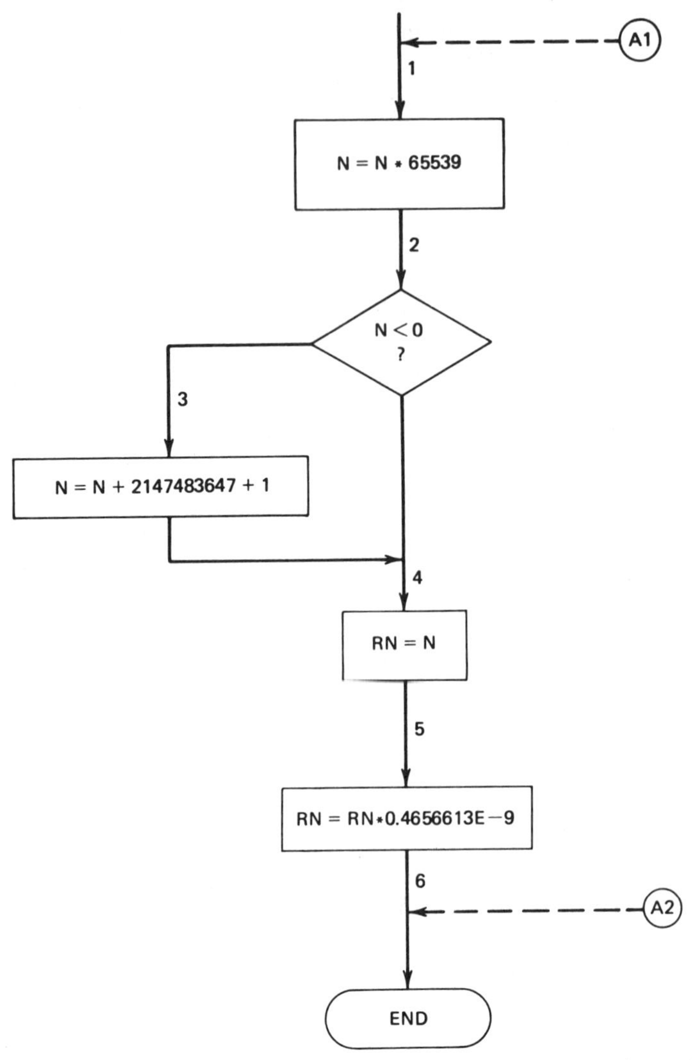

Figure 11.3 A flowchart of the random number generator of Figure 4.1.

b. The assertion at point 5 is:

$$(0 < N < 2^{31}) \land (0 < RN * 0.4656613E\text{-}9 < 1) \land (N \text{ is an integer}) \land (N \text{ is altered})$$

c. The assertion at point 4 is:

$$(0 < N < 2^{31}) \land (0 < RN * 0.4656613E\text{-}9 < 1) \land (N \text{ is an integer}) \land (N \text{ is altered})$$

d. The assertion at point 3 is:

$$(0 < N + 2^{31} < 2^{31}) \wedge \left[0 < (N + 2^{31}) * 0.4656613E\text{-}9 < 1\right]$$
$$\wedge (N \text{ is an integer}) \wedge (N \text{ is altered})$$

e. There are two assertions at point 2, using the assertions at **c** and **d** above:

$$(0 < N < 2^{31}) \supset \left[(0 < N < 2^{31}) \wedge (0 < N * 0.4656613E\text{-}9 < 1) \wedge (N \text{ is an integer}) \wedge (N \text{ is altered})\right]$$

$$(-2^{31} < N < 0) \supset \left[0 < N + 2^{31} < 2^{31}) \wedge (0 < (N + 2^{31}) * 0.4656613E\text{-}9 < 1) \wedge (N \text{ is an integer}) \wedge (N \text{ is altered})\right]$$

Since there are two paths in the program and two verification conditions have been generated for the paths, the program is ready to be proved.

F. The verification conditions are proved as follows:

a. To prove the condition

$$(0 < N < 2^{31}) \supset \left[(0 < N < 2^{31}) \wedge (0 < N * 0.4656613E\text{-}9 < 1)\right]$$
$$\wedge (N \text{ is an integer}) \wedge (N \text{ is altered})$$

requires the verification of:

i. $0 < N < 2^{31}$. Since the random number generator was developed to run on a 32-bit word computer such as an IBM 370 system. The maximum number a word can store is $2^{31} - 1$. In addition, $0 < N$ is an input condition. Thus the relationship holds.

ii. $0 < N * 0.4656613\text{E-}9 < 1$. Let every number in the relationship $0 < N < 2^{31}$ be divided by 2^{31}. Then

$$0 < \frac{N}{2^{31}} < 1$$

which is $0 < N * 0.4656613\text{E-}9 < 1$.

The other conditions of N are clear.

b. To prove the condition:

$$(-2^{31} < N < 0) \supset \left[(0 < N + 2^{31} < 2^{31}) \wedge (0 < (N + 2^{31})\right.$$
$$\left. * 0.4656613E\text{-}9 < 1\right) \wedge (N \text{ is an integer}) \wedge (N \text{ is altered})$$

requires the verification of:

i. $-2^{31} < N < 0$. The minimum odd number a 32-bit word can store is $-2^{31} + 1$. Thus, when N becomes negative, it is always greater than -2^{31}. To many readers the value of N becoming negative is a strange phenomenon, since the input of N is always positive. This is because of the instruction $N = N * 65539$ in the program. It is possible that the product of N and 65539 exceeds $2^{31} - 1$. When this occurs, the sign bit of the word may be set to negative. Thus $N < 0$ does occur. Hence $-2^{31} < N < 0$ holds.

ii. $0 < N + 2^{31} < 2^{31}$. Let every number in the relationship $-2^{31} < N < 0$ be increased by 2^{31}. Then $0 < N + 2^{31} < 2^{31}$ holds.

The other conditions of N are clear.

G. To prove that the program will stop normally requires that it will not loop infinitely. This is true since there is no loop in the program.

The correctness of the random number generator of Figure 4.1 has been established.

The proof procedure is sometimes accused of being a fancy disguise for the common code reading or walk-through process with formality [2]. The degree of formality is a question of individual preference. The following section is a discussion of some problems of proof of program correctness:

B. Problems of Correctness Proof

The following are some serious problems associated with proof of program correctness:

A. The validity of a program proof is based on the assertions generated from the program. There is no guarantee that the assertions will be correct.

B. Errors in module interfaces, such as data type misalignment in a calling sequence, cannot be detected by a proof.

C. It is extremely complicated to account for program constraints such as rounding, truncating, overflow, and underflow conditions. Such constraints are usually omitted from the proof. Consequently, serious errors may not be detected by a proof.

D. The semantics of some languages can be easily misinterpreted. A program may not perform in the way defined by an instruction. The following is a FORTRAN example:

```
    ⋮
CALL SUB (A, B, 5)
I = 5
WRITE (6, 1) I
END
SUBROUTINE SUB (A, B, N)
N = N + 1
RETURN
END
```

To many readers the written result of I is 5. Surprisingly, some version of the language will produce 6 instead of 5. Errors of this kind can never be detected by proofs.

E. Most serious of all, a proof itself can contain errors. For example, an ALGOL program written by Naur [3], using techniques of program correctness proof, was found to contain at least seven errors [4]. The proof is equivalent to a "program" subject to another proof, which in turn requires still another proof, and so on.

F. Understanding of a proof requires extensive background in mathematics, the first-order predicate calculus, and the application field in which the program is being used. It can be extremely difficult to understand or detect errors in a proof. The following three "theorems" and "corollaries" are given for the reader's enjoyment. The reader is asked to "debug" each of the "programs." An interesting treatment of these and other mathematical fallacies can be found in Maxwell [1].

"*Theorem*" 1: $16 = 0$.

"*Proof*": Since in trigonometry,

$$1 = \sin^2\theta + \cos^2\theta$$

so:

$$1 - \sin^2\theta = \cos^2\theta$$

Taking the square root of both sides,

$$\sqrt{1 - \sin^2\theta} = \cos\theta$$

Adding 1 to both sides,

$$1 + \sqrt{1 - \sin^2\theta} = 1 + \cos\theta$$

Raising both sides to the power of 4,

$$(1 + \sqrt{1 - \sin^2\theta}\,)^4 = (1 + \cos\theta)^4$$

Letting $\theta = \pi = 3.14159\ldots$,

$$(1 + \sqrt{1}\,)^4 = (1 - 1)^4$$

Thus,

$$16 = 0$$

"*Corollary*": $2^n = 0$, for $n = 1, 2, \ldots$.

"*Theorem*" 2: $16 = 1$.

"*Proof* ": In the binomial expansion,

$$\{[x + (1 - x)]^n\}^4$$
$$= \left\{x^n + \frac{nx^{n-1}(1 - x)}{1!} + \frac{n(n-1)x^{n-2}(1 - x)^2}{2!} + \cdots + nx(1 - x)^{n-1} + (1 - x)^n\right\}^4$$

Letting $n = 0$,

$$1^4 = \{1 + 0 + 0 + \cdots + 0 + 1\}^4 = 2^4$$

Thus,

$$1 = 16$$

"*Corollary*": $2^n = 1$, for $n = 1, 2, \ldots$.

"*Theorem*" 3: $16 \leq -1$

"*Proof* ": Let $T = 1 + 2 + 4 + 8 + 16 + \cdots$. Multiplying both sides by 2,

$$2T = 2 + 4 + 8 + 16 + 32 + \cdots$$

Adding -1 and 1 to the right-hand side,

$$2T = -1 + 1 + 2 + 4 + 8 + 16 + 32 + \cdots$$

So,

$$2T = -1 + T$$

Thus,

$$T = -1$$

Hence,

$$-1 = 1 + 2 + 4 + 8 + 16 + 32 + \cdots$$

Finally,

$$-1 \geq 16$$

"*Corollary*": $2^n \leq -1$, for $n = 1, 2, \ldots$.

The purpose of stating these problems is neither to discredit nor to discourage the use of proof of program correctness and structured programming. On the contrary, the reader is encouraged to use it—but with the greatest caution. A software system even proven correct could do more harm than good to the user because of the psychological consideration that the user may place absolute confidence on the software without realizing potential errors in the proof. To help place structured programming in perspective, Maurits C. Escher's "Waterfall" is given in Figure 1.4 as an example.

11.6 SOFTWARE DEBUGGING

Debugging is an activity of finding and removing errors from a program. It is a difficult task in software development. The majority of commercial programmers use as much as 50 percent of project time on debugging [12]. Millions of dollars are spent worldwide on this activity. Yet debugging has received far less attention in the industry than it deserves.

Debugging itself is a minisoftware life circle equivalent to the regular one, differing only in the scope of activity. It is directed toward developing a program "part" to replace a wrong "part" in the program. Requirements definition, design, and coding for the "part" are very much like those for software development. The debugged program is subject to retesting using the same set of random test cases.

11.6.1 Software Debugging Procedure

Software debugging activities should follow the quality programming process in Figure 1.10 as follows:

A. Debugging Requirements Definition

The requirements for debugging a software "part" should be defined after all the random test cases are executed by the program and the results analyzed, to avoid piecemeal debugging. All errors found in the test are to be used to devise a "repair" plan, which is essential to the success of this vital activity. Owing to the nature of the program "part," the definition may include modification of the original model, SIAD tree, and even the original requirements.

B. Design

The design of a program "part" includes modification of the existing wrong one or a completely new one. For example, the random number generator of Figure 4.1 has been found defective in satisfying the user's requirements, as concluded in Section 10.2.3***B***. Modification of the generator is meaningless since it contains no error. The design of a new algorithm is required since the current one is not suitable for the user. (This does not mean that the generator cannot be used in other applications requiring different randomness.)

Unless an error comes from the original model or requirements, new test cases for testing the debugged program are not necessary. The same set of test cases can be used for this purpose.

C. Coding

Coding is the implementation of a debugging plan to replace wrong program "parts." It must be done with extreme care. As with regular software development, there are many sources from which new errors can be introduced into the entire program. A backup copy of the program must be made available.

D. Testing

Testing the debugged program is similar to testing the original program. The same set of random test cases can be used for both purposes so that adverse effects or errors can be detected.

E. Analysis of Test Results

The test results of the original and the debugged programs can be compared to detect any discrepancies. Such discrepancies should show the correctness of the debugging activity. Otherwise, new errors may have been introduced.

11.6.2 Debugging Techniques Using Software Product Unit Population Defective Rate

The effectiveness of the debugging activity can be measured by reducing the software product population defective rate θ. If the rate is increased, it is a clear indication that new errors have been made. The debugging activity will be repeated until the rate θ is improved to the user's requirements.

11.7 SOFTWARE EFFICIENCY TESTING

Every practitioner knows that efficiency is an important criterion in judging the success or failure of a piece of software, and especially, of a

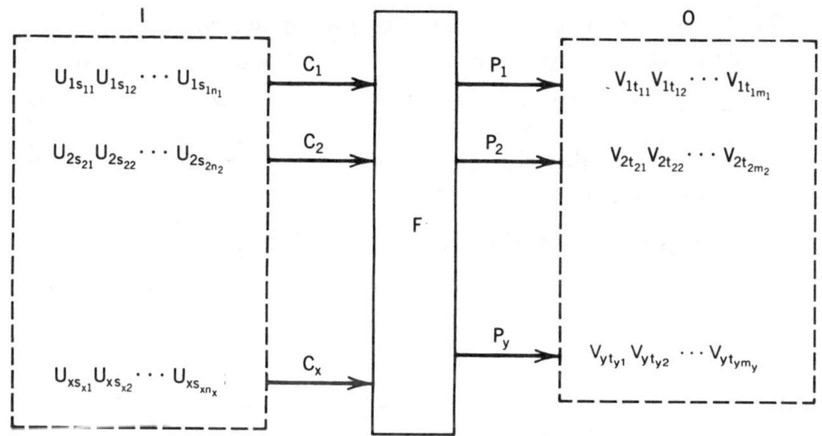

Figure 11.4 Software efficiency test configuration.

real-time system. As proposed in Section 11.1.2, the proper measures of efficiency are execution speed, throughput, and capacity as obtained by statistical procedures. The following sections present step-by-step procedures, based on statistical sampling, for testing execution speed, including concurrent characteristics and capacity.

11.7.1 Execution Speed Testing

The same set, I, of test input units implemented as discussed in Section 10.2, and used in system testing as discussed in Section 11.4.2, can be used to assess the execution speed of the software system. With reference to Figure 11.4, the step-by-step procedure is:

A. Build proper timing mechanisms into the software system F.

B. From set I, randomly select n_1 input units to be read into F via channel C_1.

C. Generate a time, for example, s_{11}, at which to feed an input unit, for example, $U_{1s_{11}}$, into channel C_1.

D. Repeat Step **C** n_1 times to get n_1 time instances, each at a random interval, at which to read in the n_1 input units.

E. Repeat Steps **B** through **D** for channels $C_2, C_3, \ldots, C_x$.

F. Execute the system F to generate the product units from the input units, reading in each input unit precisely at the time instance assigned to the unit.

G. Find the time required to produce each unit from input to output.

H. Find the total time required to produce the units.

I. Find the average execution time of each product unit.

J. Find the variance of the execution time.

The details are discussed as follows: Figure 11.4 shows a software efficiency test configuration where:

F = the integrated software system.

C_1 = input channel 1 to F. The channel can be a terminal input line, real-time input line, disk input line, telephone line, and so on.

$C_2, C_3, \ldots, C_x$ = input channels $2, 3, \ldots, x$, where x is the total number of input channels with which F is designed to process.

P_1 = output channel 1 from F. The channel can be a terminal output line, a disk output line, a printer line, a telephone line, and so on.

$P_2, P_3, \ldots, P_y$ = output channels $2, 3, \ldots, y$, where y is the total number of output channels with which F is designed to work with.

s_{11} = a random time instance on C_1, $L \leq s_{11} \leq U$, where L is the beginning time of a software execution period and U is the ending time of the period.

n_1 = a random number, the number of units to be read into F through channel C_1, $0 \leq n_1 \leq n$, where n is the sample size in testing F.

$n_2, n_2, \ldots, n_x$ = similar to n_1 for each of the $C_2, C_3, \ldots, C_x$ channels.

$U_{1s_{11}}$ = an input unit, from the input unit set W in testing F, to be read through channel C_1 at time instance s_{11}.

$U_{1s_{12}} \cdots U_{1s_{1n_1}}$ = same as $U_{1s_{11}}$, each is to be read into F through channel C_1 at time instances $s_{12}, s_{13}, \ldots, s_{1n_1}$.

$U_{2s_{21}}, U_{2s_{22}}, \ldots, U_{2s_{2n2}}$ = same as $U_{1s_{11}}, U_{1s_{12}}, \ldots, U_{1s_{1n_1}}$, the input units to be read into channel C_2, and so on.

t_{11} = the time instance at which a product unit is finished through channel P_1.

$V_{1t_{11}}$ = the product unit finished through channel P_1 at time instance t_{11}.

$V_{1t_{12}}, \ldots, V_{1t_{1m_1}}$ = the product units finished through product channel P_1 at time instances $t_{12}, \ldots, t_{1m_1}$.

m_1 = a random number, the number of product units being output through channel P_1.

$m_2, m_3, \ldots, m_y$ = similar to m_1 for each of the $P_2, P_3, \ldots, P_y$ channels.

$V_{2t_{21}} V_{2t_{22}} \cdots V_{2t_{2m_2}}$ = similar to $V_{1t_{11}} V_{1t_{12}} \cdots V_{1t_{1m_1}}$ through product channel P_2, and so on.

I = the input set containing all of the input units $U_{1s_{11}} U_{1s_{12}} \cdots U_{xs_{xn_x}}$ in the dotted square on the left-hand side of Figure 11.4.

O = the product set containing all of the product units $V_{1t_{11}} V_{1t_{12}} \cdots V_{yt_{ym_y}}$ in the dotted square on the right-hand side of Figure 11.4.

$$n(I) = \text{number of input units in the set } I,\ n(I) = \sum_{i=1}^{x} n_i.$$

$$n(O) = \text{number of product units in the set } O,\ n(O) = \sum_{i=1}^{y} m_i.$$

$$(\text{Note } n(I) = N(O))$$

$$T_{ij} = t_{ij} - s_{pq}$$

where: $1 \le i \le y, \quad 1 \le j \le m_i$
$1 \le p \le x, \quad 1 \le q \le n_p$
$V_{ij} = F(U_{pq})$

$$T = \sum_{i=1}^{y} \sum_{j=1}^{m_i} T_{ij}$$

$$\mathrm{T} = T/n(O) \quad \text{or } \mathrm{T} = T/n(I)$$

$$\sigma^2 = \left(\sum_{i=1}^{y} \sum_{j=1}^{m_i} (t_{ij} - \mathrm{T})^2 \right) \Bigg/ (n(O) - 1)$$

The efficiency of the software system can be represented by the average response time T and the standard deviation σ of the execution times.

This execution speed test can be modified to obtain other useful efficiency measures. For example, the test can be repeated M times, with

M different pairs of input sets, Is, and product sets, Os, obtaining M sets of T and σ^2 values. The average of the M values of T will be the real software execution speed. A major consideration in this approach is cost. In many non-real time applications, one value of T is close enough to the real system speed.

The execution speed test can also be used to assess the software system's ability to handle concurrency characteristics. This assessment is of particular importance in real-time applications where events may occur at the same time instance. The concurrency test can be performed easily by modifying the input time instances $s_{11}, s_{12}, \ldots, s_{xn_x}$ so that input units can be fed into F on the x channels at precisely the same instance. To demonstrate, let $s_{11}, s_{21}, \ldots, s_{x1}$ be the same time; for example, h_1, so that $U_{1s_{11}}, U_{2s_{21}}, \ldots, U_{xs_{x1}}$ are read into F at the same time instance h_1. Similarly, let $s_{12}, s_{22}, \ldots, s_{x2}$ be the same time h_2, where $h_1 > h_2$, so that $U_{1s_{12}}, U_{2s_{22}}, \ldots, U_{xs_{x2}}$ are sent into F at h_2, and so on. The timing results will be the concurrency characteristics of the software system.

11.7.2 Capacity Test

Software input capacity is defined as the number of input units that can be processed concurrently within given constraints. Figure 11.5 shows a software capacity characteristic. In the figure, the X axis represents capacity in terms of the number of input units that a software system is designed to process; the Y axis is the average response time; the curve C represents the average response time as a function of the capacity. The

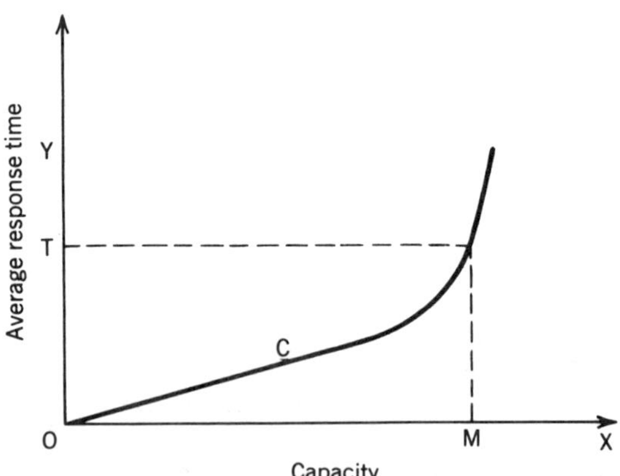

Figure 11.5 Software capacity characteristic.

line T represents the maximum software response time requirement. The response time is 0 when there is no input unit to be processed. It increases with increases in the number of input units to be processed. The increase is due to the contention of system resources for processing the units. The point M on the X axis is the maximum capacity at which the software can meet the required response time T. Beyond M, the response time increases rapidly and exponentially, and should be considered carefully. If the system cannot meet the requirements of M and T, even though the software product population satisfies the requirement of $\theta < \epsilon$, it still is not acceptable. The developer must do everything possible to ensure all of the requirements are met before delivery of the system for acceptance.

A step-by-step procedure for capacity testing is as follows:

A. Use the execution speed test procedure in Section 11.7.1 to find the time T and σ^2.

B. If T is less than T, then repeat Step **A**, using a binary search method to increase the number of units to be read into the system F in the given interval P.

C. Else, repeat Step **A**, using a binary search method to decrease the number of units to be read into the system F in the given interval P.

D. If T = T, then stop. The maximum number of input units, M, that can be processed by F to meet the response time requirement T has been found. Else, repeat Step B or Step C.

11.8 COMPARISON OF SOFTWARE SYSTEMS USING SOFTWARE PRODUCT UNIT POPULATION DEFECTIVE RATE

Comparisons of software systems are required under two circumstances: selection of software for an application, and modification of software for an application. In the first case, the comparison is necessary when there is more than one system available for an application and the developer or user must choose among the packages of systems on the market or between two systems developed by competing developers. In the second case, when a system is modified to remove errors, increase execution speed, or enhance the system functions, it is necessary to compare different versions of the same system. In either case, the comparisons should be based on software product population defective rate and execution speed.

Comparisons of available systems for an application can be performed by following the modeling and requirements specification tasks of the software development process discussed in Chapters 7 and 8 before making a selection. The only way in which selecting among available systems differs from developing a system is that the systems are already developed. Therefore, the software design and implementation channel, as indicated in Figure 1.10, is not necessary. The software test design, implementation, and system test channel, also indicated in Figure 1.10, is essential for making the selection. A system should be selected only when it satisfies the test requirements for the application. This can be easily determined by comparing the software population defective rates of the available systems, for example, comparing the range of a defective rate, as discussed in Section 11.3.

Comparisons of different versions of the same system are discussed in Section 11.6.

11.9 PREACCEPTANCE TESTING

Once the test requirements of the software system are satisfied according to the testing and integration procedure discussed in this chapter, the system is ready to be delivered to the user for acceptance testing. In order to increase the probability of passing the test, the developer may conduct the test before delivery, simulating the user's test. Procedures for pre-acceptance testing are the same as the software acceptance test discussed in Chapter 12.

11.10 SOFTWARE WARRANTY

It is a widely accepted belief in the software industry that current technology limits developers from offering a meaningful warranty. In fact, most off-the-shelf software packages offer no warranty at all except disclaimers. But now, with the deployment of statistical quality control to software development as introduced in Cho [20] and in this book, this limitation is no longer valid.

Since the software product population defective rate, θ, obtained by statistical sampling, measures the goodness (or defectiveness) of the software, it provides a vehicle with which software warranty can be delivered. The defective rate θ means that each time a unit is taken randomly from the population, the probability of the unit being defective is θ. Therefore, the probability of the unit being good is $1 - \theta$. This probability is, of course, associated with a confidence factor, for example, 95 percent confidence that the probability of the unit being defective is θ. Therefore, a software warranty can be written in terms of the requirements:

Software input domain, as explained in Section 8.2

Software product unit definition, as explained in Section 8.2

Software product unit defectiveness definition, as explained in Section 8.2

Sampling plans, as explained in Section 8.3

Sampling methods, as explained in Section 8.3

Level of confidence for sampling, as explained in Section 8.3

The defective rate being less than ϵ, as explained in Section 8.3

The warranty is invalid if any of the requirements is undefined or changed. No user (developer) can demand (deliver) a warranty unless he or she understands all of these requirements. Costly consequences may result otherwise.

An example warranty is given in Chapter 13.

11.11 CASE STUDIES

The application of the test principles discussed in this chapter are illustrated by three example: a nonnumerical application program, a scientific application program, and a data processing program. The details of these examples are given in Sections 11.5.2 through 11.6.2 in Cho [20].

REFERENCES

1. E. A. Maxwell, *Fallacies in Mathematics*, The Cambridge University Press, Cambridge, Great Britain, 1963.
2. G. J. Myers, *Software Reliability—Principles and Practices*, Wiley, New York, 1976.
3. P. Naur, "Programming by Action Clusters," *BIT*, Vol. 9, No. 3, 1969, pp. 250–258.
4. J. B. Goodenough and S. L. Gerhart, "Toward a Theory of Test Data Selection," *IEEE Transactions on Software Engineering*, Vol. SE-1, No. 2, 1975, pp. 156–173.
5. S. L. Hantler, and J. C. King, "An Introduction to Proving the Correctness of Programs," *Computing Surveys*, *ACM*, Vol. 8, No. 3, 1976, pp. 331–353.

6. J. C. Huang, "An Approach to Program Testing," *Computing Surveys, ACM*, Vol. 7, No. 3, 1975, pp. 113–128.

7. E. Horowitz (Ed.), *Practical Strategies for Developing Large Software Systems*, Addison-Wesley, Reading, Massachusetts, 1975.

8. E. Miller (Ed.), *Program Testing Techniques*, IEEE Computer Society, New York, 1977.

9. W. C. Hetzel (Ed.), *Program Test Methods*, Prentice-Hall, Englewood Cliffs, New Jersey, 1973.

10. R. T. Yeh (Ed.), *Current Trends in Programming Methodology*, Vols. 1 and 2, Prentice-Hall, Englewood Cliffs, New Jersey, 1977.

11. J. C. King, "Symbolic Execution and Program Testing," *Communications of the ACM*, Vol. 9, No. 7, 1976.

12. A. R. Brown and W. A. Sampson, *Program Debugging*, American Elsevier, New York, 1973.

13. R. W. Floyd, "Assigning Meanings to Programs," in J. T. Schwartz (Ed.), *Mathematical Aspects of Computer Science*, American Mathematical Society, Providence, Rhode Island, 1967, pp. 19–32.

14. P. Naur, "Proof of Algorithms by General Snapshots," *BIT*, Vol. 6, No. 4, 1966, pp. 310–316.

15. O. J. Dahl, E. W. Dijkstra, and C. A. R. Hoare, *Structured Programming*, Academic Press, New York, 1972.

16. T. A. Linden, "A Summary of Progress toward Proving Program Correctness," *Proceedings, 1972 Fall Joint Computer Conference*, AFIPS, Montvale, New Jersey, 1972, pp. 201–211.

17. G. J. Myers, "A Controlled Experiment in Program Testing and Code Walkthroughs/Inspection," *Communications of the ACM*, Vol. 21, No. 9, September 1978, pp. 760–768.

18. S. S. Kuo, *Numerical Methods and Computers*, Addison-Wesley, Reading, Massachusetts, 1965, pp. 168–169.

19. J. L. Mize and W. W. Cotterman, *Essentials of Structured Cobol Programming*, Wadsworth, Belmont, California, 1978, pp. 71–82.

20. C. K. Cho, *An Introduction to Software Quality Control*, Wiley, New York, 1980.

21. C. K. Cho, *High Quality Software—An Introduction* (in Japanese), Translated and published by Kindai Kagaku Sha, Tokyo, Japan, November 1982.

22. C. K. Cho, *AERA (Automated En Route Air Traffic Control System) Package 1 Test Bed Software Quality Assurance Tests of the Aircraft Data Manager*, Working Paper NO. WP-81W00285, MITRE Corporation, Bedford, Massachusetts, June 1981.

23. C. K. Cho, *AERA (Automated En Route Air Traffic Control System) Horizontal Route Analysis Test Results*, Memo No. W41-M4782, MITRE Corporation, Bedford, Massachusetts, April 1980.

24. C. K. Cho, *AERA (Automated En Route Air Traffic Control System) Horizontal Route Analysis (HRA) and Horizontal Route Generation (HRG) Program Retest Results*, Memo No. W41-M4922, MITRE Corporation, Bedford, Massachusetts, May 1980.

25. C. K. Cho, "Statistical Methods Applied to Software Quality Control," in G. Gordon Schulmeyer and J. MacManus (Eds.), *Handbook of Software Quality Assurance*, Van Nostrand, New York, 1987.

26. C. K. Cho, *Software Engineering and Quality Assurance*, Continuing Engineering Education Course No. 705 Handouts, George Washington University, Washington, D.C., December 1985.

27. Robert V. Fultyn, *Computer Assisted Software Testing*, Digital Equipment Corporation, Maynard, Massachusetts, 1982.

28. Harvey Wohlwend, "An Application of Statistical Sampling to Software Quality Measurement," in *Proceedings, National Conference on Software Quality and Productivity*, National Security Industries Association, Williamsburg, Virginia, March 6–8, 1985.

29. Lance B. Jump, *Software Quality Control: A Case Study*, Applied Data Systems, Laurel, Maryland, 1983.

30. C. K. Cho, *Performance Evaluation of the Aircraft Data Manager and Display Data Manager of the AERA (Automated En Route Air Traffic Control System) Build 1 System*, Memo No. W41-M5578, MITRE Corporation, Bedford, Massachusetts, August 1981.

31. Randall W. Jensen and Charles C. Tonies, *Software Engineering*, Prentice-Hall, Englewood Cliffs, New Jersey, 1979.

32. Roger S. Pressman, *Software Engineering: A Practitioner's Approach*, McGraw-Hill, New York, 1982.

33. Robert C. Tausworthe, *Standardized Development of Computer Software*, Prentice-Hall, Englewood Cliffs, New Jersey, 1977.

34. Robert C. Tausworthe, *Standardized Development of Computer Software Part II Standards*, Prentice-Hall, Englewood Cliffs, New Jersey, 1979.

35. T. Gilb, *A Comment on the Definition of Reliability*, ACM Software Engineering Notes, Vol. 4, No. 3, July 1979.

36. M. L. Shooman, *Software Engineering*, McGraw-Hill, New York, 1983.

37. C. R. Vick and C. V. Ramamoorthy (Ed.), Handbook of Software Engineering, Van Nostrand Reinhold, New York, 1984.

EXERCISES

1. Devise a sampling plan for estimating the defective rate of the payroll program of Exercise 1 of Chapter 10, using $z = 1.96$ and $a = 0.01$.

2. Estimate the defective rate of the payroll program, using the sampling plan of Exercise 1, and the test design of Exercise 1 of Chapter 9.

3. Devise a debugging plan for correcting the program being tested in Exercise 2 if it contains errors and implement the plan.

4. Estimate the defective rate of the matrix multiplication program of Exercise 2 of Chapter 10, using the test design of Exercise 2 of Chapter 9.

5. Estimate the defective rate of the matrix inversion program of Exercise 3 of Chapter 10, using the test design of Exercise 3 of Chapter 9.

CHAPTER **12**

Software Acceptance

Stix [10] makes the following observation on the possible consequences of poor software quality:

> At least once during a career, a manager will hit that major lemon: a system that takes in raw data and spews out raw sewage. ...a former IBM systems analyst and a member of the team that developed COBOL had to sell his family's 200-year-old farm to pay debts incurred when a faltering Honeywell minicomputer drove his fledgling service bureau out of business.

Poor quality software that results in damage to the user and possible lawsuits is too costly for any business to accept and must be avoided by all means. The user should remember the old saying that it is better to prevent than to mend, and before acquiring a software system, the user should do his or her homework. The following are the homework tasks that can help a user avoid costly consequences:

A. Ensure that software modeling and requirements specification activities have been conducted, as discussed in Chapters 7 and 8.

B. Ensure that all software requirements have been specified, as discussed in Chapter 8.

C. Survey the market to see if any existing software system meets the requirements.

D. If there is an existing software system that meets the requirements, then conduct test design, implementation, and testing of the system to estimate the defective rate of the product unit population of the system, as discussed in Chapters 9, 10, and 11. If the defective rate is acceptable, then conduct acceptance procedures on the population, as discussed in this chapter. Demand a warranty from the vendor of the software, if possible.

E. If there is no existing software system that meets the requirements, then contract out for development to a contractor or, possibly, to more than one contractor, following the methods discussed in Chapters 9 through 12. Be sure to demand a warranty on the software developed.

F. If there are systems, either existing or developed, to select from, then use the same set of test input units constructed for the acceptance procedure to determine the acceptability of each system. Ignore a developer who cannot deliver warranty on the software system he or she develops.

A software acceptance procedure is the user's means to determine whether the software being developed will help or damage him once it is delivered. Therefore, there are many factors that must be considered in software acceptance: meeting software engineering goals in software development, acceptance test methods, acceptance sampling plans, the step-by-step acceptance procedure, methods for acceptance of software efficiency, acceptance dispute resolution, and selecting a system from among available systems. These factors are discussed in the following sections. Two examples illustrating software acceptance sampling and testing are given.

12.1 MEETING SOFTWARE ENGINEERING GOALS

As discussed throughout this book, the goals of software engineering are modifiability, understandability, reliability, and efficiency. After a piece of software has been developed and delivered to the user, it is the user's responsibility to decide whether or not to accept the software. Software acceptance is the crucial step before the software is put into operation.

Therefore, in evaluating whether or not the piece of software meets the goals of software engineering, it is necessary to prioritize these goals according to what is most important to the user. Generally, reliability has top priority. The user's primary concern is to ensure that the software works, and works right, to a measurable degree. The measurement for software reliability is $1-\theta$, where θ is the defective rate of the software product unit population. (This measurement is different from conventional software reliability measures, as discussed in Chapter 14.) If the defective rate θ meets the test requirements given in the requirements specification document, that is, $\theta < \epsilon$ as discussed in Section 8.3, then the goal of reliability has been met. If the goal is not met, it is not necessary to consider whether or not the goals of modifiability, understandability, or efficiency are met. The software will be considered unacceptable.

If the software does meet the goal of reliability, then the goal of efficiency should be considered next. A measure of efficiency in terms of response time or throughput can be obtained by using the method discussed in Section 11.7. The response time may be measured in units of time per number of simultaneous users, for example, 1 second when 10 users are using the same piece of software. Throughput can be measured in terms of the number of product units produced by the software per unit of time, for example, 100 units per second. Again, the goal of efficiency must be met before deciding whether or not to accept the software. If the efficiency of the system is too low, it may not be acceptable, even if it has met the goal of reliability.

Software understandability should rank third in evaluating the software's acceptability. Since this goal cannot be properly quantified, it is up to the user to decide. One approach would be to determine that all of the software documentation is complete and acceptable. The documents for modeling, requirements specification, software and test design, software code and test generation, test and integration results, and analysis are but the minimum requirements in judging software understandability.

The goal of modifiability should rank fourth. Like understandability, modifiability cannot be properly quantified. Each type of modifiability —error correction, requirement changes, and function enhancement— needs to be measured in an appropriate way. The measure for error correction is the defective rate of the software product unit population. The smaller the number θ, the less the need to correct the software. For software modifications arising from changes to the requirements, the defective rate θ is not appropriate. For example, if the length of the data field LAST NAME needs to be changed from 30 (see Figure 8.8) to 35, then the piece of software should not require a modification. The change should be made to the input domain (shown in Figure 8.8) only; that is, these field lengths should be read in, instead of coded, to the piece of software. This dimension of modifiability may be measured by $M = m_r/m_s$, where M is the modifiability, m_r is the number of requirement changes, and m_s is the number of modifications to the software. The larger the number M, the better the software modifiability. Note that $m_r = m_d + m_s$, where m_d is the number of times the input domain is changed to meet the m_r requirement changes. In other words, a requirement change can be accomplished by either change to the software input domain or change to the software itself. For example, if 10 requirements are to be changed, the changes may be accomplished by making 6 changes to the input domain and 4 to the software. Therefore, $m_r = m_d + m_s = 6 + 4 = 10$. Hence $M_1 = \frac{10}{4} = 2.5$. If, however, the changes are accommodated by only one change to the software and nine changes to the input domain, then $M_2 = \frac{10}{1} = 10$. In this case, the software with a modifiability of M_2 would be considered four times more modifiable than the software with a modifiability of M_1. Thus, the larger the number M, the better the modifiability of the software. The rationale for this measure is that modification of the software is a time-consuming, error-prone process, whereas modification of the input domain is easy and precise. For the last dimension of modifiability, function enhancement, no proper measure is available, since upgrading software functions may require major modifications to the software.

12.2 SOFTWARE ACCEPTANCE TEST METHODS

As discussed in Chapters 8 through 11, there are five test methods with which a piece of software can be tested: the regular, weighted, boundary, invalid, and special tests. Each test samples a product unit population and estimates the defective rate of that population. These methods are also to be used to test the software for acceptance. The same single and sequential sampling plans described in Chapter 6 can be applied to each of the test methods. The test design, implementation, and actual conduct of acceptance testing is similar to the software testing conducted by the developer.

12.3 ACCEPTANCE OF THE SOFTWARE PRODUCT UNIT POPULATION

As pointed out in Section 12.1, software acceptance is equivalent to acceptance of the software product unit population. Figure 12.1 shows the rationale for this equivalence.

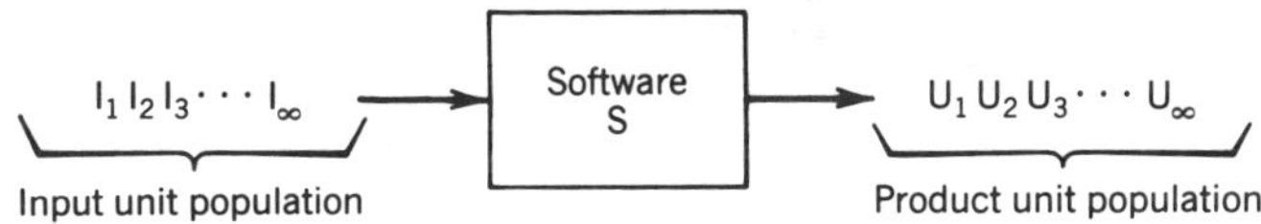

Figure 12.1 The operation of software.

With the definition of the product unit produced by the software, there is a one-to-one correspondence between each input unit and the output unit produced when the input data is processed by the software. For any nontrivial piece of software, the number of product units that can be generated is extremely large or infinite. The units $U_1, U_2, U_3, \ldots, U_\infty$ are all of the possible product units and constitute an infinite population. The number of input units is also infinite and form a population of infinite input units.

As the piece of software S is put into operation, daily use of S is equivalent to randomly selecting product units, for example, $U_8, U_{2978}, \ldots, U_{12345}$ from the infinite product unit population. This is the same as randomly selecting input units $I_8, I_{2978}, \ldots, I_{12345}$ to generate the product units $U_8, U_{2978}, \ldots, U_{12345}$. If the product unit population is acceptable, then S is acceptable. Otherwise, S is unacceptable. Therefore, software acceptance is equivalent to product unit population acceptance. The acceptability of the product unit population, and thus the software, is now a matter of statistical acceptance sampling.

12.4 ACCEPTANCE SAMPLING METHODS

The acceptance sampling methods discussed in Chapter 6 can be used to accept a piece of software. An example of an acceptance sampling method is given below.

It is assumed that a piece of software has been developed to produce a population of exactly 104,000 product units. It is also assumed that each of the units in the population has been analyzed and classified as

Sampled Unit	Page Number	Page Row	Page Column	Defectiveness Digit
1	426	20	39	2
2	414	18	15	0
3	417	40	58	7
4	425	6	81	1
5	427	17	47	8
6	421	38	68	2
7	433	48	52	9
8	427	19	44	0
9	423	36	22	0
10	414	5	78	9
11	424	49	3	9
12	431	47	22	5
13	428	34	69	3
14	426	36	63	7
15	416	42	41	0
16	427	18	23	9
17	429	41	53	2
18	414	31	26	1
19	422	34	81	7
20	423	42	35	3
21	425	37	46	0
22	428	26	54	6
23	431	8	45	4
24	416	29	28	0
25	420	20	93	2
26	416	35	70	2
27	423	9	51	0
28	429	41	11	7
29	417	34	64	0
30	425	42	8	5
31	418	6	38	3
32	428	16	72	0
33	421	10	34	2
34	419	5	53	2
35	428	24	15	9
36	419	42	86	9
37	427	26	10	0
38	423	5	22	8
39	432	47	72	6
40	431	23	85	9

Figure 12.2 A random sample of 79 units from the population in Appendix 1.

Sampled Unit	Page No.	Page Row	Page Column	Defectiveness Digit
41	426	28	100	1
42	432	22	26	4
43	424	47	59	3
44	423	39	14	8
45	421	31	73	9
46	427	38	34	9
47	417	48	72	6
48	430	36	31	2
49	426	42	60	4
50	423	11	50	3
51	415	48	58	4
52	430	18	98	5
53	414	9	23	8
54	416	43	8	7
55	420	19	55	9
56	417	21	42	7
57	422	32	30	4
58	429	48	25	3
59	418	20	84	7
60	418	29	34	0
61	432	49	83	6
62	430	40	72	8
63	425	29	58	0
64	416	19	96	5
65	418	1	59	2
66	429	47	51	1
67	426	26	35	1
68	422	14	16	6
69	420	11	73	0
70	423	31	51	9
71	415	17	60	8
72	428	25	9	9
73	417	32	14	7
74	419	22	45	4
75	431	48	22	0
76	418	6	73	7
77	430	17	75	6
78	417	12	1	2
79	425	3	7	1

Figure 12.2 continued

defective or nondefective. Each defective product unit is identified by a digit of 0; each nondefective product unit is identified by a digit of $1, 2, \ldots,$ or 9. This population of defective and nondefective product units is given in Appendix 1. A single sampling plan, described in Section 6.1.3, will be used to determine the acceptability of the population.

Given the acceptance criteria of $\alpha_1, \theta_1, \alpha_2, \theta_2$, a single sampling plan is formulated in terms of n and d, where n is the sample size of the plan and d is the acceptable number of defects in the sample. The acceptance sampling plan with $n = 79$ and $d = 3$, formulated with the criteria $\alpha_1 = 0.05$, $\theta_1 = 0.01$, $\alpha_2 = 0.05$, and $\theta_2 = 0.08$ (explained in Section 6.1.3), will be used to accept or reject the product unit population.

A sample of 79 product units is randomly selected from the population. The page, row, and column from which each unit is taken, and the unit's defectiveness-indicating digit, that is, 0 or $1, 2, \ldots, 9$, are given in Figure 12.2. Since the sample contains 14 0's, that is, 14 defective units, which is greater than $d = 3$, the population is rejected. (This rejection is valid only for the criteria values of $\alpha_1 = 0.05$, $\theta_1 = 0.01$, $\alpha_2 = 0.05$, and $\theta_2 = 0.08$.) This conclusion can be verified by estimating the population defective rate, which is found to range from 0.1350 to 0.1360 (see Section 11.3). The criterion $\theta_2 = 0.08$ is much smaller than the product unit defective rate. Thus, there is virtually no chance for the product unit population to pass the test.

In an actual software acceptance procedure, it is not necessary (and sometimes impossible) to generate all of the product units in the output population. But, as can be seen by this example, only 79 units need to be generated randomly and analyzed to reach a valid conclusion as to the acceptability of the population under the defined acceptance criteria.

The sampling method illustrated is the single acceptance sampling method. There are other methods available, such as the sequential sampling method described in Chapter 6. An example of using the sequential sampling method in acceptance of a PL/I program is given in Section 12.3 of Cho [9].

12.5 ACCEPTANCE PROCEDURE

A software acceptance procedure based on the principles of statistical quality control consists of the following steps:

A. Decide the software quality characteristics and their priorities in acceptance testing

B. Review the product unit for sampling

C. Review product unit defectiveness
D. Review an acceptance sampling plan
E. Select acceptance criteria for formulating a sampling plan
F. Formulate an acceptance sampling plan
G. Construct the operating characteristic (OC) curve of the sampling plan
H. Construct random test input units using a SIAD tree
I. Analyze test results
J. Accept or reject the software

Some steps of this procedure are identical to the steps of the software defective rate estimating procedure. Namely, the definition of product unit and product unit defectiveness, the construction of random test input units using the SIAD tree of the program, and the analysis of test results are identical in both procedures.

12.5.1 Decide Software Quality Characteristics and Their Priorities in Acceptance Testing

There are many quality characteristics affecting software performance. Some of them, such as readability, maintainability, and human engineering, are qualitative and cannot be measured in numerical terms. Others, such as accountability, accuracy, efficiency, and reliability, can be quantified.

It is important to determine which characteristics should be evaluated in acceptance testing and how they should be prioritized. It is natural to examine the quantifiable characteristics first. It can be a waste of resources to examine the qualitative characteristics before determining whether the software meets its measurable requirements.

12.5.2 Review Product Unit for Sampling

The definition of product unit for acceptance sampling is the same as that for estimating the software product unit population defective rate (see Chapters 8 and 9).

12.5.3 Product Unit Defectiveness

The definition of product unit defectiveness for acceptance sampling is the same as that for estimating the software product unit population defective rate (see Chapters 8 and 9).

12.5.4 Determine an Acceptance Sampling Plan

As discussed in Chapter 6, there are many types of sampling plans that can be used for acceptance testing. The single, double, multiple, and sequential sampling plans are used in the manufacturing industries today. The adoption of a plan for software acceptance may depend on an agreement between the developer and the user of the software system under consideration.

12.5.5 Select Acceptance Criteria for Formulating a Sampling Plan

As discussed in Chapter 6, the formulation of an acceptance sampling plan is dependent on the criteria α_1, θ_1, α_2, and θ_2, where α_1 is the producer's risk if the population defective rate is θ_1, and α_2 is the user's risk if the population defective rate is θ_2. The values of these criteria are to be agreed upon by all parties so that an economical sampling plan can be generated to provide protection to the developer and the user.

12.5.6 Formulate an Acceptance Sampling Plan

A good acceptance sampling plan should possess the following characteristics:

A. The software producer's risk should be reduced to a minimum.

B. The software user's risk should be reduced to a minimum.

C. The software producer should be motivated by the plan to employ statistical quality control to develop better software.

D. The damage potential in using the software system should be reduced to a minimum.

E. The cost of management, inspection, and implementation of the plan should be reduced to a minimum.

A sampling plan satisfying these characteristics can be formulated using the criteria $\alpha_1, \theta_1, \alpha_2, \theta_2$.

12.5.7 Construct the Operating Characteristic Curve of the Sampling Plan

The operating characteristic (OC) curve of a sampling plan states the producer's risk and the user's risk in numerical terms. In practice, it is important to know the OC curve before implementing a plan in order to be aware of the sampling risk. The details of constructing an OC curve are given in Chapter 6.

12.5.8 Construction of Random Test Input Units

The construction of random test input units can be accomplished by sampling elements from the SIAD tree of the program (see Chapters 8 and 9).

12.5.9 Analyze the Test Results

The analysis of test results for conformance to the software requirements is very time-consuming and must be done with extreme care. The outcome of the analysis is a classification of the software output into defective and nondefective product units which, in turn, leads to acceptance or rejection of the software. Any unfair bias can increase the producer's risk of having a good program rejected or the user's risk of accepting a poor-quality program.

Test results can be analyzed by manual, semimanual, or automatic means. There are cases in which the results are better verified manually, particularly in nonnumerical applications such as updating a data base. A combination of manual and automatic means may be best in applications such as data transmission in a computer network. Completely automatic means may be the most advantageous in numerical applications, particularly complex ones such as finding the inverse of large matrices (see Section 9.2.1*G* for a discussion of how to simplify such calculations by using the identity matrix).

12.5.10 Accept or Reject the Software

Following this procedure, software acceptance can be a routine task. If the number of defective units in the sample is less than the acceptable number of defective units determined in the selected sampling plan, then the software is accepted. Otherwise, it is rejected.

The major advantage of using statistical quality control principles in software development is that of confidence. If the acceptance procedure is followed and the sample is random, one can be reasonably sure of making the right decision—whether accepting a good program, or rejecting a poor-quality program.

12.6 ACCEPTANCE PROCEDURE FOR SOFTWARE EFFICIENCY

The two measures of software efficiency that should be used in the software acceptance procedure are: average execution speed for generating a product unit from an input unit, and capacity expansion.

12.6.1 Average Execution Speed

This measure can be determined by using the same set of sampled input units that were used for testing the piece of software. The average and the standard deviation of the execution speed can be obtained, as discussed in Section 11.7. The number of defective units d in the sample can be obtained, where a defective unit is defined as one whose execution time exceeds the specified execution time requirement. If the number of defective units satisfies the requirements of the acceptance sampling plan, that is, $d < c$, then the efficiency of the software is acceptable. Otherwise, improvements are needed before acceptance.

12.6.2 Capacity

The acceptance procedure for software capacity may be based on the results of capacity testing, as discussed in Section 11.7.2. Otherwise, similar tests can be conducted to determine the acceptability of the software capacity.

12.7 SOFTWARE ACCEPTANCE DISPUTE RESOLUTION

The success of developing a reliable software system depends on many factors. Software acceptance sampling is the final activity before the user starts using the system. Every precaution must be taken by both the developer and the user to ensure that the system is performing its functions properly. Before delivering the system, the developer should estimate the software product unit population defective rate and perform a simulated acceptance procedure to reduce the risk of having his or her good system rejected. The user should conduct the acceptance procedure in an unbiased manner to reduce the risk of accepting a poor-quality system. However, there is always a chance of bias, resulting in a possible dispute between the parties.

12.7.1 Some Factors Affecting Software Acceptance Accuracy

The following are some of the factors that might contribute to inaccurate sampling results:

A. Intermediate Errors

As discussed in Chapter 10, there are many sources from which errors can propagate. There is one type of error which adds a new dimension to software acceptance complexity. Since a key to the success of software acceptance is the ability to generate random samples of the product unit population, and the most convenient form of sampling is by using random numbers to select test input units, the randomness of the numbers used can become an important issue. For example, the random number generator shown in Figure 4.1 has a defective rate of about 0.25. If this generator is used in acceptance sampling, there is a strong possibility that it will introduce a bias into the test results.

B. Falsification

In analyzing the test results, it can be too inconvenient for the inspector to perform a detailed examination of each product unit generated, and taking shortcuts is tempting. For example, in the FORTRAN example given in section 11.3.2D of Cho [9], the value of *I* can be easily interpreted to be five by merely reading the code without actually executing the program. Mistakes of this kind can lead to inaccurate results and affect acceptance or rejection of the software. A possible approach for solving this problem would be reexamination of the same output by different inspectors.

C. Involuntary Errors

Human activities are error-prone. There is no way to avoid errors of this kind. This example from Juran, Seder, and Gryna, Jr. [5] illustrates the point:

> The following sentence has been used thousands of times:
>
> FEDERAL FUSES ARE THE RESULT OF YEARS
> OF SCIENTIFIC STUDY COMBINED WITH
> THE EXPERIENCE OF YEARS

The sentence is flashed before the audience for 30 seconds or for a full minute. Each member is asked to count the number of times the letter

"F" appears. When the record slips are collected and tallied, it is usual to find that only about 80 to 90 percent of the Fs to be found are actually found.

The situation in software defectiveness analysis is much worse than in this simple illustration. Human factors including visual errors, blunders, and fatigue may interact with the actual software errors, complicating the activity in an unpredictable manner. A possible safeguard against such errors would be to offer a recheck of the analysis after the inspector has finished his examination of the test results.

12.7.2 Dispute Resolution

The method of dispute resolution must be predetermined by both the developer and the user of the system. There are two approaches that may be used for resolving a dispute between these parties:

A. Following the same acceptance sampling plan originally used, another sample is taken by an independent third party. The results of the acceptance procedure, using the new sample, is used to accept or reject the software.

B. Following the procedure for estimating the software product unit population defective rate described in Chapter 11, another sample is taken by an independent third party. If the defective rates estimated by the developer and the third party are not different statistically, then the burden of justifying rejection of the software may be assumed to be on the user. If the defective rate estimated by the third party does differ statistically from that originally estimated, the burden of justifying acceptance of the software may be assumed to be on the developer.

Sampling plans for estimating the product unit population defective rate and for acceptance testing are described in Chapters 5 and 6, as well as in this chapter. The details of dispute resolution are left to the reader.

12.8 SELECTION OF A SOFTWARE SYSTEM FROM AMONG SEVERAL SYSTEMS

Selecting a software system in a competitive market poses an interesting challenge to the user. Often, there is more than one system commercially available that appears suitable for the user's application. For example,

	Input Domain 1		Input Domain 2	
Test Method	System 1	System 2	System 1	System 2
Regular Test	$\theta_{R_{11}}$	$\theta_{R_{12}}$	$\theta_{R_{21}}$	$\theta_{R_{22}}$
Weighted Test	$\theta_{W_{11}}$	$\theta_{W_{12}}$	$\theta_{W_{21}}$	$\theta_{W_{22}}$
Boundary Test	$\theta_{B_{11}}$	$\theta_{B_{12}}$	$\theta_{B_{21}}$	$\theta_{B_{22}}$
Invalid Test	$\theta_{I_{11}}$	$\theta_{I_{12}}$	$\theta_{I_{21}}$	$\theta_{I_{22}}$
Special Test	$\theta_{S_{11}}$	$\theta_{S_{12}}$	$\theta_{S_{21}}$	$\theta_{S_{22}}$

Figure 12.3 A framework for software system selection.

many word processing systems with similar capabilities are available on the market. Also, the user may contract out to two developers to develop software performing the same functions. Making the selection usually involves considerable time and effort in studying each available system to identify its capabilities and to compare its performance with that of other systems. Generally, each system has its advantages and disadvantages, and it is difficult to choose among them.

The test methodology presented in this book offers an effective way to make such decisions. The user can apply the same set of test input units for each of the regular, weighted, boundary, invalid, and special test methods to obtain the defective rates θ_r, θ_w, θ_b, θ_i, and θ_s of the product unit populations generated for each test method, respectively. Use of the same test input units is the most efficient way to determine the compatibility of the software with the user's application. Weighted tests can be used to evaluate how well each system performs those functions called most frequently by the user; minor features can be given low weights. Special tests can be used for essential features without which the software is unacceptable.

A framework for comparing the defective rates of these product unit populations under different conditions for a number of software systems is shown in Figure 12.3. The system with the best set of θ values is the system to be chosen.

12.9 CASE STUDIES

Software acceptance procedures for two programs, a random number generator and a PL/I line edit program are illustrated in Sections 12.2 and 12.3 in Cho [9].

REFERENCES

1. B. W. Boehm, J. R. Brown, and M. Lipow, "Qualitative Evaluation of Software Quality," *Proceedings of Second International Conference on Software Engineering*, ACM, IEEE, and National Bureau of Standards, 1976, pp. 592–605.
2. International Business Machines Corporation, *System/360 Scientific Subroutine Package* (360*A*-*CM*-03*X*), *Version III*, *Programmer's Manual*, 4th ed., IBM, White Plains, New York, 1968.
3. International Business Machines Corporation, *Random Number Generation and Testing*, Reference Manual GC20-8011-0, IBM, White Plains, New York, 1959.
4. I. Guttman and S. S. Wilks, *Introductory Engineering Statistics*, Wiley, New York, 1965.
5. J. M. Juran, L. A. Seder, and F. M. Gryna, Jr., (Eds.), *Quality Control Handbook*, 2nd ed., McGraw-Hill, New York, 1962.
6. A. Wald, *Sequential Analysis*, Wiley, New York, 1947.
7. Rand Corporation, *A Million Random Digits with* 100,000 *Normal Deviates*, The Free Press, Glencoe, Illinois, 1955.
8. C. K. Cho, "Statistical Methods Applied to Software Quality Control," in G. Gordon Schulmeyer and J. McManus (Eds.), *Handbook of Software Quality Assurance*, Van Nostrand Reinhold, New York, 1987.
9. C. K. Cho, *An Introduction to Software Quality Control*, Wiley-Interscience, New York, 1980.
10. G. Stix, "User vs. Vendor: To Sue or to Settle," *Computer Decisions*, Vol. 17, No. 21, Hayden Publishing Co., October 1985, pp. 66–75.

EXERCISES

1. Formulate a single and a sequential sampling plan using the acceptance criteria $\theta_1 = 0.01$, $\alpha_1 = 0.05$, $\theta_2 = 0.30$, and $\alpha_2 = 0.05$.
2. Accept the random number of Figure 4.1 using the sampling plans formulated in Exercise 1.
3. Use the single and sequential sampling plans of this chapter to accept the payroll program debugged in Exercise 3 of Chapter 11.
4. Formulate a sequential sampling plan using the acceptance criteria $\theta_1 = 0.005$, $\alpha_1 = 0.025$, $\theta_2 = 0.01$, and $\alpha_2 = 0.025$.
5. Use the sequential sampling of Exercise 4 to accept the payroll program debugged in Exercise 3 of Chapter 11.
6. The following is a single sampling plan satisfying the acceptance criteria $\theta_1 = 0.01$, $\alpha_1 = 0.05$, $\theta_2 = 0.08$, and $\alpha_2 = 0.05$: A sample of

79 units is randomly generated. If the sample contains less than three defective units, then the program is accepted. Otherwise it is rejected. Use the single sampling plan to conduct an acceptance test of the matrix multiplication program of Exercise 2 of Chapter 10.

7. The following is a single sampling plan satisfying the acceptance criteria $\theta_1 = 0.01$, $\alpha_1 = 0.05$, $\theta_2 = 0.08$, and $\alpha_2 = 0.05$: A sample of 79 units is randomly generated. If the sample contains less than three defective units, then the program is accepted. Otherwise it is rejected. Use the single sampling plan to conduct an acceptance test of the matrix inversion program of Exercise 3 of Chapter 10.

CHAPTER 13

Quality Programming: A Case Study

The quality programming methodology described in Chapters 7 through 12 to develope quality programs can now be illustrated by an example that follows each step in the process and shows how the methodology incorporates the principles of software engineering and statistical quality control. The example programming problem is the development of a routine to find the roots of the quadratic equation:

$$AX^2 + BX + C = 0$$

Based on the software engineering principles discussed in this book, this software should be developed in the following stages:

Modeling
Requirements specification
Concurrent software design and test design
Concurrent implementation of software design and test design
Testing and integration
Software acceptance

13.1 MODELING

The modeling tasks are to develop a product description and process description, based on the concept that a piece of software is analogous to a factory. The results of performing these tasks are recorded in a modeling document.

13.1.1 Problem Description

In this example, the problem is to develop a routine to find the roots of the quadratic equation:

$$AX^2 + BX + C = 0$$

13.1.2 Types of Raw Materials

The raw materials are the inputs to the routine. In this case, there are three raw materials: the coefficients A, B, and C.

13.1.3 Characteristics of Raw Materials

The characteristics of each raw material are then identified:

A. Each coefficient will be a whole (integer) number
B. Each coefficient will be represented in floating point
C. Each coefficient will be single precision

At this stage, it should be noted that, given these characteristics, the routine must be able to handle cases in which $A = 0$ or both A and B are 0. The design for handling these cases is considered as part of modeling the manufacturing process.

13.1.4 Rules for Using Raw Materials

The following rules for using the raw materials are identified:

A. The coefficients will be input in decimal numbers
B. The coefficients will remain unchanged during computation

13.1.5 Definition of Product Unit

The product unit definition identifies the desired output of the software. In this example, the product unit is defined to be the root(s) of the equation, which may be real or complex, and a status flag to indicate error status during computation.

13.1.6 Definition of Product Unit Defectiveness

Based on the product unit definition, a product unit will be considered defective if one or both of the roots are not usable, or if the status flag fails to indicate an error during computation. A root, X_1, will be considered not usable if:

$$|AX_i^2 + BX_i + C| > \epsilon$$

where $i = 1$ if $A = 0$, or $i = 1$ and 2 if $A \neq 0$, and ϵ is a given criterion to be decided on during requirements specification (see Section 13.2.2).

13.1.7 Methods of Manufacturing

At this stage, the availability of methods for finding the roots of the quadratic equation should be considered. A survey shows that many methods are available, including the Newton-Raphson, regula-falsi methods, and the formula

$$X = \frac{-B \pm \sqrt{B^2 - 4AC}}{2A}$$

Each of these methods has advantages and disadvantages that will be analyzed during software design (see Section 13.3.1).

13.1.8 Characteristics of Factory

The next step in modeling is to identify the characteristics of the software necessary to produce the desired output. In this case, the routine should be easily understandable and maintainable. To keep the example simple, the processing time and memory requirements will not be considered critical, although an efficient routine is still desirable.

13.1.9 Manufacturing Process

The stages of software processing, analogous to stations in a factory, are next identified. In the example, the processing stages are as follows: The input coefficients are examined to decide if they meet the required input characteristics. If both A and B are 0, then the input is considered defective. If at least one of the coefficients assumes a value beyond its defined input domain, then an error message is generated. If $A = 0$ and $B \neq 0$, then the equation is linear, and the root is found by solving the linear equation. If both $A \neq 0$ and $B \neq 0$, then the root(s) will be found by using one of the methods identified in the preceding Section 13.1.7.

13.1.10 Methods of Building Factory

The routine will be built by using a top-down design methodology and a "critical-module-first" schedule, with bottom-up implementation and testing. This implementation strategy ensures that the "factory" is built on a "secure quality part" basis. To aid development of the piece of software with maintainability and understandability, a high-level language such as FORTRAN, PL/I, or Ada should be used.

13.2 REQUIREMENTS SPECIFICATION

Following the steps of requirements specification, the software design and test requirements for the development of the quadratic equation root finding routine are identified below. All requirements specified at this stage of the software development process are recorded in a requirements specification document.

13.2.1 Software Design Requirements

The software design requirements include input domain, processing, output, performance, and software quality characteristics.

A. Input Domain

The input domain of the software is defined using a SIAD tree and input domain rules, as shown in Figures 13.1 and 13.2

B. Processing

As modeled in Section 13.1.9, the routine will check whether one or both of the coefficients *A* and *B* are 0, then find the root(s) of the equation in real or complex real (and imaginary) components. Proper error messages will be generated.

Index	Tree Symbol	Tree Element	Rule Index
1	Y1	A, the coefficient	1
2	Y1, 1	LA, lower bound of A	1 2
3	Y1, 2	UA, upper bound of A	1 3
4	Y2	B, the coefficient	1
5	Y2, 1	LB, lower bound of B	1 4
6	Y2, 2	UB, upper bound of B	1 5
7	Y3	C, the coefficient	1
8	Y3, 1	LC, lower bound of C	1 6
9	Y3, 2	UC, upper bound of C	1 7

Figure 13.1 A SIAD tree of the input domain of a quadratic root finding routine.

Rule Index	Rule Description	Subrule Index
1	An integer number in input. (converted into a floating point number for computation)	0
2	LA = −7	0
3	UA = 7	0
4	LB = −7	0
5	UB = 7	0
6	LC = −7	0
7	UC = 7	0

Figure 13.2 Input domain rules for the SIAD tree in Figure 13.1.

C. *Output*

The routine will output up to two roots. Each root will consist of two parts: real and imaginary. If the imaginary part is 0, then the root is a real root. Otherwise, it is a complex root. If the equation has only one root, then the root will be repeated in the output. A status flag will be provided to indicate whether the roots have been computed successfully. Otherwise, the flag will indicate the nature of the error (error types and codes are to be determined).

Since this routine communicates with other software modules within an application, there is no direct user interface, and no output formatting specifications are required.

D. *Performance*

As modeled in Section 13.1.8, the routine is not to be operated in a real-time environment, nor in a system where space or other such resources are constrained. No time or space performance requirements are imposed on the routine. However, it should be developed with maximum efficiency.

E. *Software Quality Characteristics*

The requirements specification is not complete unless it includes the software quality requirements discussed throughout this book. Thus, the routine will be developed in accordance with the software engineering goals of modifiability, understandability, reliability, and efficiency, and will incorporate the software principles of abstract data typing, information hiding, modularization, localization, uniformity, completeness, confirmability, and statistical quality control as much as possible. The developer will deliver the routine with a warranty that it will work according to the specified requirements.

13.2.2 Test Requirements

The test requirements include the definitions of product unit and product unit defectiveness, software acceptance criteria, and sampling methods for determining acceptability of the routine being developed.

A. Definition of Product Unit

The product unit definition developed in the modeling stage in Section 13.1.5 can be transferred to the test requirements document.

B. Definition of Product Unit Defectiveness

The product unit defectiveness definition developed in the modeling stage in Section 13.1.6 can be transferred to the test requirements document. At this point, a value for the defectiveness criterion ϵ should be decided. In this example, $\epsilon = 0.00001$.

C. Software Acceptance Criteria

There are two sampling methods employed in accepting a piece of software: one for estimating the defective rate of the software product population, and one for software product population acceptance by the user. For this example, only the first sampling methods will be given. The reader can do software acceptance sampling as an exercise following the acceptance methods discussed in Chapters 6 and 12.

The acceptance criteria for the first sampling method are: a sample of n units is to be taken randomly from the product unit population such that the sample defective rate θ° and the population defective rate θ differ with an accuracy factor of 0.25, that is $|\theta^\circ - \theta| = 0.25\ \theta$, and $\theta < 0.01$.

D. Sampling Method

The regular test method, discussed in Section 9.2, using the input domain and rules given in Figures 13.1 and 13.2, will be required to test the routine. (Application of other test methods, including weighted, boundary, invalid, and special tests, is left to interested readers.)

13.3 CONCURRENT SOFTWARE DESIGN AND TEST DESIGN

The modeling document and the requirements specification document prepared during the modeling stage (see Section 13.1) and the requirements specification stage (see Section 13.2) enable the developer to proceed concurrently with the software design and test design phases of the project. At this stage, the developer decides whether to use a function-oriented or object-oriented software design. In this example, a function-oriented design will be used. (Application of the other design methods to this example is left to the interested reader.)

13.3.1 Software Design

The function-oriented design approach includes: identification of methods for finding the roots of the quadratic equation, selection of a method to use, identification of the function required for solving the equation, organization of the identified functions into a tree structure, development of a design for implementation of each of the functions including module interface and algorithm design, and consideration of man–machine interface design.

A. Identification of Methods

The availability of methods for finding the roots of the quadratic equation was considered in the modeling stage of development (see Section 13.1.7). Now, all appropriate methods are identified and analyzed. As many methods as possible should be considered at this stage. These will include the Newton-Raphson, regula-falsi, and analytic methods. Each of these methods is now analyzed based on such factors as execution speed, memory requirements, constraints, development schedule, and so on.

B. Selection of Method

Based on the analysis performed in Section 13.3.1*A*, a method is selected. In this example, the analytical, that is, the formula, method will be used.

C. Function Identification

The routine will accept as input three pieces of data for the values of the coefficients A, B, and C, find the root(s), and return the results with a status flag indicating the occurrence and nature of any errors. If $A \neq 0$, then the roots will be found by the formula:

$$X = \frac{-B \pm \sqrt{B^2 - 4AC}}{2A}$$

If $A = 0$ and $B \neq 0$, then the root will be computed using the linear equation:

$$X = -\frac{C}{B}$$

If both A and B are 0, then the routine will return an error message.

To perform these operations, the routine will consist of the following four functions:

A. Check input data for the value of A and B. (It is assumed that the value of each of the coefficients is within its defined range. The routine will not check the ranges.)

B. Compute the root(s) by the quadratic formula with status flag, or compute the root(s) by the linear equation with status flag.

C. Compute the value of $B^2 - 4AC$.

D. Organization of Functions into Tree Structure

The four functions identified in Section 13.3.1*C* may be organized into a tree structure as follows:

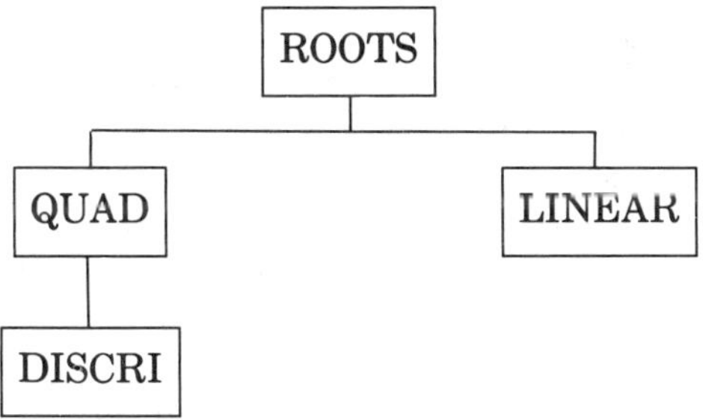

Each function is now identified as one module in the software design.

E. Module Design

The design of each of the four modules is approached in a top-down manner. The module is designed in a program design language (PDL) in a three-level description, as discussed in Sections 9.1.1 and 9.1.2. After

MODULE NAME: ROOTS LEVEL OF DESIGN: 1

DESCRIPTION: This module is the "driver" of the routine that finds the root(s) of a quadratic equation.

INPUT: A, the coefficient of the equation, a whole number.
B, the coefficient of the equation, a whole number.
C, the coefficient of the equation, a whole number.

OUTPUT: REAL1, the real part of the first root, if any.
IMAG1, the imaginary part of the first root, if any.
REAL2, the real part of the second root, if any.
IMAG2, the imaginary part of the second root, if any.

STATUS: An error flag.

PROCESS:

```
BEGIN
    Initialization;
    Find two roots of the equation by QUAD;
    Find one root of the equation by LINEAR;
    Generate STATUS, if any;
END;
```

Figure 13.3 ROOTS module design in level-one PDL.

the first-level PDL is completed for all of the four modules, a design review is conducted to make sure that the design is complete in terms of the identified functions. The second-level PDL description is then developed for each module based on the first-level PDL description. After the second-level PDL is completed, another design review is conducted. This design process is repeated to produce the third-level PDL description for each module. At this level, the PDL is close to the code and is ready to be implemented.

First-level PDL descriptions for each module are given in Figures 13.3 through 13.6.

13.3.2 Test Design

Software test design includes four tasks: review of the product unit definition, review of the product unit defectiveness definition, design of a sampling plan, and design of random input units for producing sample

MODULE NAME: QUAD LEVEL: 1

DESCRIPTION: This module finds the roots of a quadratic equation of the form $AX^2 + BX + C = 0$, where $A \neq 0$.

INPUT: A, the coefficient of the equation, a whole number.
B, the coefficient of the equation, a whole number.
C, the coefficient of the equation, a whole number.

OUTPUT: REAL1, the real part of the first root, if any.
IMAG1, the imaginary part of the first root, if any.
REAL2, the real part of the second root, if any.
IMAG2, the imaginary part of the second root, if any.

PROCESS:

```
BEGIN
     Find two roots of the equation;
END
```

Figure 13.4 QUAD module design in level-one PDL.

MODULE NAME: LINEAR LEVEL: 1

DESCRIPTION: This module finds the root of a quadratic equation of the form $AX^2 + BX + C = 0$, where $A = 0$ and $B \neq 0$.

INPUT: B, the coefficient of the equation, a whole number.
C, the coefficient of the equation, a whole number.

OUTPUT: REAL1, the real part of the root.
REAL2, (not used).

PROCESS:

```
BEGIN
     Find the root of the equation;
END;
```

Figure 13.5 LINEAR module design in level-one PDL.

MODULE NAME: DISCRI LEVEL: 1

DESCRIPTION: This module computes the value of $B^2 - 4AC$ for finding the roots of a quadratic equation of the form $AX^2 + BX + C = 0$, where $A \neq 0$.

INPUT: A, the coefficient of the equation, a whole number.
B, the coefficient of the equation, a whole number.
C, the coefficient of the equation, a whole number.

OUTPUT: DISCRI, the value of $B^2 - 4AC$.

PROCESS:

```
BEGIN
  Compute the value of B² – 4AC;
END;
```

Figure 13.6 DISCRI module design in level-one PDL.

product units. These tasks are performed concurrently with software design to shorten the design, implementation, test, and integration time. Test design should be the responsibility of a party other than the software designer.

A. *Review of Product Unit Definition*

In accordance with the requirements specification document, a product unit of the quadratic root finding routine is defined to be the root(s) of the equation and a status flag. For the purpose of testing, a product unit can also be considered to be an input unit to the testing routine and is identified in terms of the randomly generated coefficients A, B, and C.

B. *Review of Product Unit Defectiveness Definition*

In accordance with the requirements specification document, a product unit produced by the root finding routine is defined to be defective if:

$$|AX_i^2 + BX_i + C| > 0.00001$$

where X_i is a root found by the routine and $i = 1$ if $A = 0$, or $i = 1$ and 2 if $A \neq 0$.

C. *Design of a Sampling Plan*

Several sampling methods can be formulated to satisfy the software acceptance criteria given in Section 13.2.2*C*, for example, the simple sampling and sequential sampling methods described in Chapter 5. The iterative sampling process discussed in Section 5.1.2.***D*** will be used as an example for testing the quadratic root finding routine. This sampling method uses the following equation (Equation 5.3a):

$$n_{i+1} = \frac{z^2(1 - \theta_i^0)}{a^2\theta_i^0}$$

where $z = 1.96$ and $a = 0.25$, as specified in the test requirements (see Section 13.2.2***C***).

D. Construction of Random Input Units Using SIAD Tree

The input domain of the routine is represented by the SIAD tree given in Figures 13.1 and 13.2. There are five test methods that must be considered in software testing; regular, weighted, boundary, invalid, and special (discussed in Section 8.3), but, in this example, only the regular test method will be used.

The construction of random input units for the regular test method can be accomplished as follows:

$$A_j = \lfloor LA + (UA - LA + 1)R_{A_j} \rfloor$$

$$B_j = \lfloor LB + (UB - LB + 1)R_{B_j} \rfloor$$

$$C_j = \lfloor LC + (UC - LC + 1)R_{C_j} \rfloor$$

where $[e]$ means the truncation of e; R_{A_j}, R_{B_j}, and R_{C_j} are random numbers, $0 < R_{A_j} < 1$, $0 < R_{B_j} < 1$, and $0 < R_{C_j} < 1$, for $j = 1, 2, \ldots, n$. For example, if $R_{A_1} = 0.31563$, $R_{B_1} = 0.69387$, and $R_{C_1} = 0.95869$, then from Figures 13.1 and 13.2:

$$A_1 = [-7 + (7 - (-7) + 1) \times 0.31563] = [-7 + 4.73445] = -2$$

$$B_1 = [-7 + (7 - (-7) + 1) \times 0.69387] = [-7 + 10.4081] = 3$$

$$C_1 = [-7 + (7 - (-7) + 1) \times 0.95869] = [-7 + 14.3804] = 7$$

Thus, the numbers -2, 3, and 7 are to be used for the coefficients A, B, and C, respectively, and this set of values is taken as input unit 1. This sampling process can be automated along with the sampling process discussed in Section 13.3.2***C***.

In order to generate the random input units for the sampling process, a random number generator is required. Before beginning the sampling, the randomness of the numbers generated by the generator must be tested.

For example, the test designer may use the random number generator RANDU shown in Figure 4.1. The testing of this generator is described in Section 10.2.3, using the χ^2 test program in Figure 10.6. Notice that the results of the testing showed that the generator is defective about 25% of the time under the defined conditions of the test. To make use of the generator, the test designer should modify it so that the defective rate of the product unit population of the generator is reduced to an acceptable number. The modification can be accomplished using the quality control concept of ratification. In this approach, the test designer should modify the program shown in Figure 10.6 so that the entire χ^2 test program becomes a random number generator. This generator will return a sequence of 1,000 random digits to the calling routine only if the sequence is "ratified" by passing the χ^2 test. If a sequence does not pass the test, it is not returned to the calling routine. Another sequence is then generated and tested. With this modification, the defective rate of the product unit population of the generator can be reduced from 25 percent to less than a given number, for example, 5 percent.

In addition, a test driver that will call the modified random number generator to construct the input units, call the quadratic root finding routine to output the input units, and verify that the defectiveness of each product unit can be automated. The design of such a driver is left to the interested reader. A driver developed in Fortran with the routine for testing is given in Figure 13.7.

13.4 CONCURRENT IMPLEMENTATION OF SOFTWARE DESIGN AND TEST DESIGN

The software design and test design discussed in Section 13.3 are implemented on an IBM 4381 32-bit computer system in both the FORTRAN and Ada languages. The FORTRAN versions of the software design and test design are given in Figures 13.7 and 13.8, respectively. (The Ada implementation of the software design is given in Figure 13.9.)

13.5 TESTING AND INTEGRATION

Once the software design and the test design have been implemented (Figures 13.7 and 13.8), the software developer can proceed to the testing of the quadratic root finding routine using statistical quality control. As

```
      REAL LA, UA, LB, UB, LC, UC
      INTEGER AUNITS, AN
      WRITE(5,10)
10    FORMAT(1H1)
      LA = -7.0
      UA = 7.0
      LB = -7.0
      UB = 7.0
      LC = -7.0
      UC = 7.0
      AN = 0.0
      NN = 12359
      N = 0
      EPSLON = 0.00001
      Z = 1.96
      ACCURA = 0.5
      AUNITS = 50
      DO 100 IX = 1, 10000
         AN = 0
         DEFECT = 0.0
         DO 50 IZ = 1, AUNITS
         CALL RANDU(NN, R)
         NA = LA + (UA - LA + 1.0) * R
         A = NA
         CALL RANDU(NN, R)
         NB = LB + (UB - LB + 1.0) * R
         B = NB
         CALL RANDU(NN ,R)
         NC = LC + (UC - LC + 1.0) * R
         C = NC
         CALL ROOTS(A,B,C,REAL1,AMAG1,REAL2,AMAG2,STATUS)
         IF (STATUS .EQ. 0) THEN
            AN = AN + 1
            XC1 = A * (REAL1 ** 2 - AMAG1 ** 2) + B * REAL1 + C
            XC2 = A * (REAL2 ** 2 - AMAG2 ** 2) + B * REAL2 + C
            IF (ABS(XC1) .GT. EPSLON .OR. ABS(XC2) .GT. EPSLON) THEN
     1         DEFECT = DEFECT + 1
            END IF
         END IF
50       CONTINUE
         DEFTOT = DEFTOT + DEFECT
         N = N + AN
         THETAI = DEFTOT / N
         NNEXT = (Z * Z * (1.0 - THETAI)) /
     1             (ACCURA * ACCURA * THETAI)
         ASIZE = NNEXT - N
         IF ( AUNITS .LE. 0 ) GO TO 110
         WRITE(6,90) IX, NNEXT, N, AUNITS, THETAI
90       FORMAT(1X,5I10,5X,F10.6)
100   CONTINUE
      STOP
110   WRITE(6, 120) N, THETAI
120   FORMAT(///,15H SAMPLE SIZE = ,I5,5X,18H DEFECTIVE RATE = ,F10.6)
      STOP
      END

      SUBROUTINE RANDU(N,R)
      N = N * 65539
      IF(N .LT. 0) N = N + 2147483647 + 1
      R = N
      R = R / 2147483647
      RETURN
      END
```

Figure 13.7 A test driver for testing the routine in Figure 13.8.

```
SUBROUTINE ROOTS(A,B,C,REAL1,AMAG1,REAL2,AMAG2,STATUS)
STATUS = 0
REAL1  = 0
REAL2  = 0
AMAG1  = 0
AMAG2  = 0
IF(A .NE. 0) CALL QUAD(A,B,C,REAL1,AMAG1,REAL2,AMAG2)
IF(A .EQ. 0 .AND. B .NE. 0) CALL LINEAR(B,C,REAL1,REAL2)
IF(A .EQ. 0 .AND. B .EQ. 0) STATUS = 1
RETURN
END
SUBROUTINE QUAD(A,B,C,REAL1,AMAG1,REAL2,AMAG2)
DISC = DISCRI(A,B,C)
IF(DISC .GE. 0) THEN
   REAL1 = -B / (2 * A) + SQRT(DISC) / (2 * A)
   REAL2 = -B / (2 * A) - SQRT(DISC) / (2 * A)
ELSE
   REAL1 = -B / (2 * A)
   REAL2 = REAL1
   AMAG1 = SQRT(-DISC) / (2 * A)
   AMAG2 = - AMAG1
END IF
RETURN
END
SUBROUTINE LINEAR(B,C,REAL1,REAL2)
REAL1 = - C / B
REAL2 = REAL1
RETURN
END
FUNCTION DISCRI(A,B,C)
DISCRI = B * B - 4 * A * C
RETURN
END
```

Figure 13.8 A FORTRAN quadratic root finding routine implemented from the designs in Figures 13.3 through 13.6.

discussed, in this example the sampling plan implements Equation 5.3a with $z = 1.96$ and $a = 0.25$.

The results of sampling are shown in Figure 13.10. The sampling process stops at iteration 2 with a sample size of 706 units and a sample defective rate of 0.087819. In other words, at iteration 1 the sample size is determined by

$$n_1 = \frac{1.96^2(1 - 0.08)}{0.25^2 \times 0.08} = 706$$

and at iteration 2:

$$n_2 = \frac{1.96^2(1 - 0.087819)}{0.25^2 \times 0.087819} = 638$$

```
WITH REALFUNC ;
PACKAGE QUAD_ROOTS IS
   USE REALFUNC ;
   PROCEDURE ROOTS(A : IN FLOAT ; B : IN FLOAT ; C : IN FLOAT ;
                    REAL1 : OUT FLOAT ; AMAG1 : OUT FLOAT ;
                    REAL2 : OUT FLOAT ; AMAG2 : OUT FLOAT ;
                    STATUS : OUT FLOAT) ;
   PROCEDURE QUAD(A : IN FLOAT ; B : IN FLOAT ; C : IN FLOAT ;
                   REAL1 : OUT FLOAT ; AMAG1 : OUT FLOAT ;
                   REAL2 : OUT FLOAT ; AMAG2 : OUT FLOAT)
   PROCEDURE LINEAR(B : IN FLOAT ; C : IN FLOAT;
                    REAL1 : OUT FLOAT ; REAL2 : OUT FLOAT) ;
   FUNCTION DISCRI(A : IN FLOAT ; B : IN FLOAT ; C : IN FLOAT) RETURN
      FLOAT ;
END QUAD_ROOTS ;
PACKAGE BODY QUAD_ROOTS IS
   PROCEDURE ROOTS(A : IN FLOAT ; B : IN FLOAT ; C : IN FLOAT ;
                    REAL1 : OUT FLOAT ; AMAG1 : OUT FLOAT ;
                    REAL2 : OUT FLOAT ; AMAG2 : OUT FLOAT ;
                    STATUS : OUT FLOAT) IS
   BEGIN
      STATUS := 0.0 ;
      REAL1 := 0.0 ;
      REAL2 := 0.0 ;
      AMAG1 := 0.0 ;
      AMAG2 := 0.0 ;
      IF A /= 0.0 THEN
         QUAD(A, B, C, REAL1, AMAG1, REAL2, AMAG2) ;
      ENSIF B /= 0.0 THEN
         LINEAR(B, C, REAL1, REAL2) ;
      ELSE
         STATUS := 1.0 ;
      END IF ;
   END ROOTS ;
   PROCEDURE QUAD(A : IN FLOAT ; B : IN FLOAT; C : IN FLOAT ;
                   REAL1 : OUT FLOAT ; AMAG1 : OUT FLOAT ;
                   REAL2 : OUT FLOAT ; AMAG2 : OUT FLOAT) IS
      DISC : FLOAT ;
   BEGIN
      DISC := DISCRI(A, B, C) ;
      IF DISC >= 0.0 THEN
         REAL1 := -B / (2.0 * A) + SQRT(DISC) / (2.0 * A) ;
         REAL2 := -B / (2.0 * A) - SQRT(DISC) / (2.0 * A) ;
      ELSE
         REAL1 := -B / (2.0 * A) ;
         REAL2 := REAL1 ;
         AMAG1 := SQRT(-DISC) / (2.0 * A) ;
         AMAG2 := - AMAG1 ;
      END IF ;
   END QUAD ;
   PROCEDURE LINEAR(B: IN FLOAT ; C: IN FLOAT ;
                     REAL1 : OUT FLOAT ; REAL2 : OUT FLOAT) IS
   BEGIN
      REAL1 := -C / B ;
      REAL2 := REAL1 ;
   END LINEAR ;
   FUNCTION DISCRI(A : IN FLOAT ; B : IN FLOAT ;
                    C : IN FLOAT) RETURN FLOAT IS
      DISCRIM : FLOAT ;
   BEGIN
      DISCRIM := B * B - 4.0 * A * C ;
      RETURN DISCRIM ;
   END DISCRI ;
END QUAD_ROOTS ;
```

Figure 13.9 An Ada quadratic root finding routine implemented from the designs in Figures 13.3 to 13.6.

ITERATION	N(I+1)	N(I)	N(I+1)-N(I)	DEF. RATE
1	706	50	656	0.080000
2	638	706	-68	0.087819

SAMPLE SIZE = 706 DEFECTIVE RATE = 0.087819

Figure 13.10 An iterative sampling test results in testing the routine in Figure 13.8 using the driver in Figure 13.7.

Since $n_2 = 638$ is less than $n_1 = 706$, the total number of units sampled at iteration 1, the sampling process stops.

The 95-percent confidence interval of the mean of the population (for $z = 1.96$) can be estimated by Equation 5.4a as follows:

$$\left[\bar{x} - t_{n-1,\alpha/2}\frac{s}{\sqrt{n}}, \bar{x} + t_{n-1,\alpha/2}\frac{s}{\sqrt{n}}\right]$$

where $\bar{x} = n\theta^0 = 706 \times 0.087819 = 62$, and $s = \sqrt{n\theta^0(1 - \theta^0)} = 7.52$, and $\alpha = 0.05$.

Therefore,

$$\left[62 - 1.96\frac{7.52}{26.6}, 62 + 1.96\frac{7.52}{26.6}\right]$$

namely,

$$[61.4453, 62.5547]$$

The defective rate of the output population of the routine is estimated from the mean. Thus, the 95-percent confidence interval of the defective rate may be computed by:

$$[61.4453/706, 62.5547/706]$$

or:

$$[0.087, 0.089]$$

This estimate will be used to determine whether or not the software is acceptable (see Section 13.6). To give the reader an idea of the accuracy of this estimate, the true defective rate of the population can be found by 100-percent inspection, since the output population consists of only 3,375 product units, excluding 15 units in which both coefficients A and B are 0. It can be seen that the true defective rate of the output population is 0.0571, which is close enough to the 95-percent confidence level of θ from 0.087 to 0.089 for purposes of testing the routine. (The small variation is due to the fact that the random number generator RANDU of Figure 4.1 used for the test is not quite random, as discussed in Section 10.2.3.

Before taking the results of testing into the software acceptance phase, the developer should make sure all parties concerned understand how to interpret the results. It is crucial to understand that the results are valid only for the specified conditions of the test and cannot be generalized to performance of the software under other conditions. In this example, the 95-percent confidence interval of the defective rate from 0.087 to 0.089 is valid only under the defined conditions of $\epsilon =$ 0.00001 and the input domain of coefficients A, B, and C, where $-7 \leq A \leq 7$, $-7 \leq B \leq 7$, and $-7 \leq C \leq 7$, and A, B, and C are all whole numbers. Under different conditions, the defective rate will be different.

For example, Figure 13.11 shows how testing the quadratic root finding routine (Figure 13.7), using the same random number generator (Figure 4.1) but different values of ϵ and different input domains for coefficients A, B, and C, will generate varying estimates of the defective rate. In the figure, domain 1 is:

$$-7 \leq A \leq 7, \text{ and } A \text{ is a whole number in input}$$

$$-7 \leq B \leq 7, \text{ and } B \text{ is a whole number in input}$$

$$-7 \leq C \leq 7, \text{ and } C \text{ is a whole number in input}$$

	Population Defective Rates			
ϵ	Domain 1		Domain 2	
Value	True	Sampled*	True	Sampled*
10^{-1}	0.0000	0.0000	—	0.0000
10^{-2}	0.0000	0.0000	—	0.0000
10^{-3}	0.0000	0.0000	—	0.0100
10^{-4}	0.0000	0.0000	—	0.4100
10^{-5}	0.0571	0.0829	—	0.9300
10^{-6}	0.5810	0.4922	—	0.9600
10^{-7}	0.8095	0.7565	—	0.9700

*Note: The sample size = 193 for each of the sampled entries.

Figure 13.11 Comparison of software product population defective rates under different conditions of the routine of Figure 13.8.

and domain 2 is:

$$-100 \le A \le 100, \text{ and } A \text{ is a whole number in input}$$

$$-100 \le B \le 100, \text{ and } B \text{ is a whole number in input}$$

$$-100 \le C \le 100, \text{ and } C \text{ is a whole number in input}$$

As should be expected, varying the value of ϵ has a marked effect on the estimated defective rate of the population. But notice that the differences between estimates for domain 1 and domain 2 for the same value of ϵ are equally striking. For example, the defective rates at $\epsilon = 10^{-5}$ are 0.0829 and 0.93 under domain 1 and domain 2, respectively —and these are the results of tests of the exact same routine.

Figure 13.11 also shows the true defective rate of the population of domain 1 for each value of ϵ. It can be seen that the sampling test method is effective in estimating the true defective rate of the population. For example, at $\epsilon = 10^{-6}$, the true defective rate is 0.5810, and that of the sample is 0.4922. (The true defective rates under domain 2 are not shown, as the population is fairly large, that is, $201^3 = 8{,}120{,}601$. These calculations are left to the interested reader.)

The variation in the defective rates shown in Figure 13.11 also illustrates how the software developer can assess risks in offering a software warranty. The routine can be guaranteed to work 100 percent under domain 1 and for ϵ values of 10^{-4} or larger. This warranty cannot be given under domain 2 or ϵ values smaller than 10^{-4}. In general, there are risks involved in offering a warranty for applications where the

Population Defective Rates

Value	Domain 1		Domain 2	
	True	Sampled*	True	Sampled*
10^{-1}	0.0000	0.0000	—	0.0000
10^{-2}	0.0000	0.0000	—	0.0000
10^{-3}	0.0000	0.0000	—	0.0000
10^{-4}	0.0000	0.0000	—	0.0103
10^{-5}	0.0000	0.0000	—	0.2167
10^{-6}	0.0429	0.0673	—	0.6788
10^{-7}	0.5500	0.5440	—	0.7047
10^{-8}	0.5690	0.5751	—	0.7098
10^{-9}	0.5690	0.5699	—	0.7202

*Note: The sample size is 193 for each of the entries.

Figure 13.12 Comparison of software product population defective rates under different conditions of the Ada routine of Figure 13.9.

software product unit population is very large or consists of an infinite number of units. These risks are assessed by the value of z in Equation 5.3a. (Analyses for the Ada routine of Figure 13.9 are given in Figure 13.12.)

13.6 SOFTWARE ACCEPTANCE

When testing and integration are complete, the software developer can proceed to determine the acceptability of the piece of software. Since the developer has followed the principles of software engineering, documented all requirements, and defined the desired performance of the software in a way that allows application of statistical quality control techniques, this determination is straightforward.

The software acceptance and test requirements documented in the requirements specification state that to be accepted, the software must

The subroutine in Figure 13.8 is sold with the following warranty under the conditions:

1. The subroutine will find the root or roots of the quadratic equation on a 32-bit computer:

$$AX^2 + BX + C = 0$$

2. The product unit is defined as one or two roots of the quadratic equation returned by the subroutine under the input domain:

$-7 \leq A \leq 7$ and A is a whole number in input

$-7 \leq B \leq 7$ and B is a whole number in input

$-7 \leq C \leq 7$ and C is a whole number in input

3. A product unit is defined if either of the roots results in

$$|AX_i^2 + BX_i + C| > \epsilon$$

where $\epsilon \geq 0.0001$, $i = 1$ or 2. If both $A = 0$ and $B = 0$ in an input, then an error status will be returned by the subroutine.

With the conditions defined above, the entire risk as to the usability and performance of the subroutine is with us. If the subroutine is found to be defective under the defined conditions, we assume the entire cost of all necessary servicing, repair, or correction. This warranty gives you specific rights and you may have other rights which vary from state to state.

This warranty does not cover the loss resulted from the use of the subroutine under the defined conditions. The developer does not warrant that the subroutine will work outside the conditions defined above.

Figure 13.13 An example software warranty.

have a product unit population defective rate of $\theta < 0.01$ at the defectiveness criterion of $\epsilon = 0.00001$ (see Sections 13.2.2***B*** and 13.2.2***C***).

The test results documented in the testing document show that the estimated product unit defective rate at $\epsilon = 0.00001$ is from 0.087 to 0.089 (at the 95-percent confidence level).

Clearly, 0.087 > 0.01, and therefore, the software product population does not meet the acceptance criteria. The software developer should conclude that the software is not ready for delivery to the user. Further development is required to reduce the defective rate and improve the quality of the software.

The user can verify the defective rate reported by the developer by conducting a test of his or her own, following the sample procedure given in the preceding sections. Now the user has a tool to help him or her decide whether to accept or reject a piece of software.

13.7 EXAMPLE SOFTWARE WARRANTY

As a result of the software development discussed in this chapter, a software warranty may be written for marketing the subroutine in Figure 13.8. An example warranty is shown in Figure 13.13. The reader should compare this warranty with that in Figure 1.1.

REFERENCES

1. C. K. Cho, *An Introduction to Software Quality Control*, Wiley, New York, 1980.
2. C. K. Cho, "Statistical Methods Applied to Software Quality Control," in G. Gordon Schulmeyer and James McManus (Eds.), *Handbook of Software Quality Assurance* Van Nostrand Reinhold, New York, 1987.
3. C. K. Cho, *Software Engineering and Quality Assurance*, Course Handouts of CE705, George Washington University, Washington, D.C., June 1986.
4. C. K. Cho, *Software Engineering with Statistical Quality Control*, *Proceedings*, METS '86, Taipei, Taiwan, November 17–21, 1986.

CHAPTER 14

Software Reliability

Quality and productivity are the two essential weapons used by all companies in the competition for market shares in the modern age. Quality refers to a product's performance of its intended functions to satisfy its customers' needs reliably. Productivity means outputting the products abundantly so that the cost is bearable to the consumers. In the preceding chapters, quality and productivity have been discussed in relation to software development. In this chapter, software reliability—essential for quality—is examined.

Most discussions in the literature of software reliability are based on hardware reliability theory: a well-developed set of mathematics that allows prediction of the reliability of hardware products subject to wear, tear, burn, and so on. This mathematics has provided many familiar parameters, for example, mean time to failure (MTTF), residual errors, and so on, that since the 1970s have been proposed as measures of software reliability. Some of these models are discussed in this chapter: the mean time to failure, Jelinski–Moranda, Schick–Wolverton, Musa, and Nelson models. These models estimate software reliability based on a piece of software's error history, using hardware reliability theory.

Despite the attractiveness of the mathematics, this basis for software reliability models has often been viewed skeptically [1], [9], [10]. It will be seen that gathering the data for the error history of a piece of software requires a long period of time, and even then, the reliability measure is often difficult to quantify. The applicability of hardware theory to software is in general questionable, because a piece of software is not subject to deterioration such as wear, tear, or burn, that is, the reliability of a piece of software is independent of time, but dependent on the frequency and nature of software usage.

Three counterexamples are given in this chapter to show that in many cases these hardware-theory-based models are not applicable to software reliability. The deficiencies of these models are pointed out from the perspective of statistical quality control, and a reliability measure based on the defective rate of a software product population is proposed. A comparison of the above-mentioned models and this model is given. Finally, a criterion for selecting a model to use for a given application is proposed: the software warranty.

14.1 DEFINITIONS OF SOFTWARE RELIABILITY

Current definitions of software reliability bear a marked similarity. The following definition is given in Shooman [3]:

> Software reliability is the probability that the program performs successfully, according to specifications for a given time period.

Similarly, in Ramamoorthy and Bastani [1]:

> Software reliability is defined as the probability that a software fault which causes deviation from required output by more than specified tolerance, in a specified environment, does not occur during a specified exposure period.

A third definition is given in Myers [2]:

> Software reliability is the probability that the software will execute for a particular period of time without a failure, weighted by the cost to the user of each failure encountered.

The common element in all of these definitions is that software reliability is treated as a function of time.

In contrast, this author defines software reliability as follows:

> Software reliability is 1–θ, the probability that the software performs successfully, according to software requirements, independent of time.

where θ is the defective rate of the software product population. This definition is a natural consequence of following the principles of software engineering with statistical quality control.

In estimating software reliability, many factors affecting software failure, including errors in the programming language, compiler, operating system, assembly, and hardware must be considered. These factors are ignored in estimating the reliability of a particular piece of software, but are included in the overall system reliability.

Mathematically, software reliability R is defined as follows [1]. Let:

$$R(i) = P\{\text{no failure over } i \text{ runs}\}$$

or:

$$R(t) = P\{\text{no failure in time interval } [0, t]\}$$

assuming that inputs are taken independently according to some probability distribution function:

$$R = 1 - \lim_{n \to \infty} \frac{n_f}{n} \tag{14.1}$$

where n is the number of software runs and n_f is the number of failed runs in n runs.

14.2 CONVENTIONAL SOFTWARE RELIABILITY MODELS

Conventionally, software reliability is expressed in a reliability function as follows [3]:

$$\begin{aligned} R(t) &= P\{\text{no failure in time interval } [0, t]\} \\ &= e^{-[\kappa E_r(m)]t} \\ &= e^{-\kappa[(E_T/I_T) - E_c(m)]t} \end{aligned} \tag{14.2}$$

where: κ = an arbitrary constant
m = software debugging time in months
$E_r(m)$ = number of errors remaining in software after n months of debugging
E_T = total number of known errors in software
I_T = total number of machine instructions in software
$E_c(m)$ = total number of errors corrected in m months
t = software operating time in hours

This function means that the probability of successful software operation without errors is an exponential function of software operating time.

The following models of software reliability are all based on this approach.

14.2.1 Mean Time To Failure (MTTF) Model [3]

The MTTF model is given as: Let $z(t)$ be a function called the hazard function in t as follows:

$$z(t) = K\left[E_T/I_T - E_c(m)\right]$$

The MTTF is then defined as:

$$\text{MTTF} = \frac{1}{z(t)} = \frac{1}{K\left[E_T/I_T - E_c(m)\right]} \tag{14.3}$$

where K, E_T, I_T, $E_c(m)$, and m are the same as given in Equation 14.2. Equation 14.3 can be rewritten as:

$$\text{MTTF} = \frac{1}{b(1 - am)} \tag{14.4}$$

where $b = KE_T/I_T$

$a = g_o I_T/E_T$ (g_o is a constant rate of error correction)

Equation 14.4 can be plotted as shown in Figure 14.1.

It can be seen that the greatest improvement in mean time to failure occurs in the last quarter of debugging time [3]. It is claimed in [3] that this is an "extremely important point." If there is no model to guide debugging activities, the developer may waste resources, patience, and credibility during the debugging process without achieving the goal of debugging.

14.2.2 Jelinski–Moranda Model

The Jelinski–Moranda model is the hazard function of the form:

$$z(t) = M\left[N - (k - 1)\right] \tag{14.5}$$

where M = an arbitrary constant

N = total number of errors present in the software

k = number of errors found by debugging time m_k

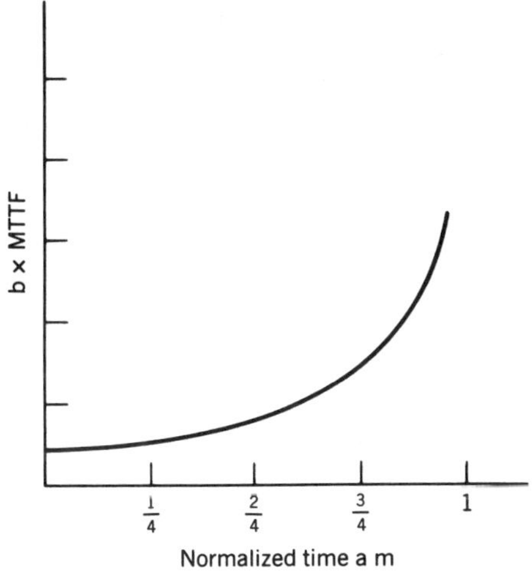

Figure 14.1 Mean time to failure vs. debugging time.

14.2.3 Schick–Wolverton Model

The Schick–Wolverton model is a modification of the Jelinski–Moranda model. Equation 14.5 becomes:

$$z(t) = M[N - (k - 1)]t \tag{14.6}$$

where t is the operating time of the software.

This model assumes that the failure rate is proportional to the number of remaining errors and increases with operating time t.

14.2.4 Musa Model

The Musa model is of the form:

$$R(t) = e^{-(t/T)} \tag{14.7}$$

where t = execution time of the software after release

T = mean time to failure,

$$= T_o e^{[t'C/(M_o T_o)]} \tag{14.8}$$

where T_o = mean time to failure at the beginning of test ($t' = 0$)

C = ratio of equivalent operating time to test time

M_o = number of errors which must occur to reveal all errors ($M_o = E_T$)

$t = t'C$, where t' is the execution time or central processor time used in software testing (rather than months of calendar time)

14.2.5 Nelson Model

The Nelson model is based on Equation 14.1 in selecting test cases according to the operational distribution. The software reliability is estimated by:

$$\tilde{R}(1) = 1 - \frac{n_f}{n} \tag{14.9}$$

where n = total number of runs

n_f = number of failed runs out of these n runs

The size of the errors, or the probability of inputs in uncovering these errors, remaining in the software, $S(E_r)$, is defined to be;

$$S(E_r) = 1 - \tilde{R}(1)$$

The estimate of $S(E_r)$ is given by:

$$\tilde{S}(E_r) = \frac{n_f}{n}$$

14.3 COUNTEREXAMPLES TO CONVENTIONAL SOFTWARE RELIABILITY MODELS

Existing software reliability models are often viewed skeptically [9], [10], as mentioned earlier, because of, among others, the number of cases in which they are not applicable. Three such cases are discussed below: a random number generator, a quadratic root finding routine, and a matrix inversion routine. In each case, the conventional software reliability models described in Section 14.2 are shown to fail to provide a meaningful reliability prediction.

14.3.1 Counterexample 1: A Random Number Generator

The random number generator shown in Figure 14.2 is an implementation of the congruence method of Equation 4.3 in FORTRAN on an IBM 4381 32-bit system. It has been proven correct, that is, error free, in Cho [4]. The reliability of the generator as measured first by the defective rate of the product unit population of the generator, and then by the conventional models discussed in Section 14.3, is estimated in the following sections.

```
SUBROUTINE RANDU(N,R)
N = N * 65539
IF(N .LT. 0) N = N + 2147483647 + 1
R = N
R = R / 2147483647
RETURN
END
```

Figure 14.2 A uniform random number generator on a 32-bit computer.

A. *Prediction Based on Product Unit Population Defective Rate*

The generator can be tested using the method discussed in Sections 4.4 and 4.5. The product unit is defined to be a sequence of 1,000 digits, as shown in Figure 4.4. A product unit is defined to be defective if it fails to pass at least one of the frequency, serial, poker, and gap tests using the χ^2 goodness-of-fit test discussed in Section 4.5. A sampling test using the χ^2 test program shown in pages 200 to 204 of Cho [4], and the iterative Equation (5.3a) has been conducted. The test results are given in Figure 14.3. The sampling process stops at iteration 3 with a sample defective rate of 0.25, using $z = 1.96$ and $a = 0.4$ for Equation 5.3a. The total sample size is 80 units. The 95-percent confidence interval of the mean, μ, of the population is, using Equation 5.4a:

$$\left[20 \pm 1.96\frac{3.87}{80}\right]$$

or:

$$[19.152, 20.848]$$

The estimated product unit population defective $\theta = \mu/n$ is:

$$[19.152/80, 20.848/80]$$

or:

$$[0.2394, 0.2606]$$

i	n_{i+1}	n_i	$n_{i+1} - n_i$	θ_i^0
1	57	20	37	0.30
2	57	50	7	0.30
3	73	80	−7	0.25

Figure 14.3 Estimating the defective rate of the random number generator of Figure 14.2 using sampling Equation (5.3a).

In other words, the product unit population defective rate is about 25 percent, that is, the probability of getting a defective product unit from the population is 0.25. Thus, the "mean time to failure" is one in every four units and is independent of time. Notice that this conclusion is valid only under the defined conditions. If different definitions of product unit and product unit defectiveness are used, then the defective rate may not be 0.25. For example, a product unit could be defined to be a sequence of 1,000,000 digits for the sampling inspection.

B. Predictions of Conventional Software Reliability Models

The models described in Section 14.2 would measure the reliability of the random number generator as follows:

(i) MTTF MODEL. Since the generator contains no error on the IBM 4381 32-bit computer system, $E_T = 0$ and $E_c(m) = 0$. The MTTF is found by Equation 14.3:

$$\text{MTTF} = \frac{1}{K(0/I_T - 0)} \rightarrow \infty$$

Therefore, the MTTF is infinite, that is, the generator will never fail. However, as shown in the test results obtained in Section 14.3.1*A*, the generator will fail 25% of the time.

(ii) JELINSKI–MORANDA MODEL. In this case, $N = 0$ and $k = 0$. The hazard function of Equation 14.5 is:

$$Z(t) = M(0 - (0 - 1)) = M$$

Plugging the value of $Z(T)$ into Equation 14.3, the MTTF is:

$$\text{MTTF} = \frac{1}{M}$$

Thus, the mean time to failure of the generator can be arbitrarily selected from 0 to infinity, as the value of M is an arbitrary constant in Equation 14.5. This prediction also fails to measure the reliability of the random number generator correctly, as evidenced by the test results obtained in Section 14.3.1*A*.

(iii) SCHICK–WOLVERTON MODEL. The values of N and k in Equation 14.6 are both 0. Thus,

$$Z(t) = M[0 - (0 - 1)]t = Mt$$

The mean time to failure is computed by:

$$\text{MTTF} = \frac{1}{Mt}$$

Again, the mean time to failure would range from 0 to infinity, depending on the operation time t. Since the random number generator contains no error, there is no need to use operation time for error correction. Therefore, t would be equal to 0, and the mean time to failure would be infinite. Again, this is not true.

(iv) MUSA MODEL. Using Equation 14.8, the value of M_0 is 0. Therefore,

$$T - T_0 e^{[t'C/0]} \to \infty$$

Again, the mean time to failure is predicted to be infinite.

(v) NELSON MODEL. As there are no errors remaining in the software, the size of the error $S(E_r)$ is 0 in Equation 14.9. Therefore, $n_f = 0$. But this is not the case, as shown in Section 14.3.1*A*.

14.3.2 Counterexample 2: A Quadratic Equation Root Finding Routine

The routine shown in Figure 14.4 is an implementation in FORTRAN of the design given in Section 13.3.1 on an IBM 4381 32-bit computer system. A test conducted on this routine is given in the following section.

A. Prediction Based on Product Unit Population Defective Rate

As shown in Chapter 13, the true defective rates of the routine's product unit population varies under different ϵ values. For convenience, these results are repeated in Figure 14.5. It can be seen that for values of ϵ from 10^{-1} to 10^{-4}, the product unit population is defect free, that is, the probability of getting a defective unit from the population is 0. For example, if each of the coefficients A, B, and C is a whole number within the range of -7 to 7, then the roots returned by the routine are 100 percent good. However, the defective rate θ is 0.0571 when $\epsilon = 10^{-5}$, $\theta = 0.5810$ when $\epsilon = 10^{-6}$, and so on. The defective rate varies, not because of any changes to the software, but because of different values for the defectiveness criterion.

Thus, the routine contains no errors for ϵ values of 10^{-1} through 10^{-4}, but is not error-free for ϵ values from 10^{-5} through 10^{-7}. The

```
SUBROUTINE ROOTS(A,B,C,REAL1,AMAG1,REAL2,AMAG2,STATUS)
STATUS = 0
REAL1  = 0
REAL2  = 0
AMAG1  = 0
AMAG2  = 0
IF(A .NE. 0) CALL QUAD(A,B,C,REAL1,AMAG1,REAL2,AMAG2)
IF(A .EQ. 0 .AND. B .NE. 0) CALL LINEAR(B,C,REAL1,REAL2)
IF(A .EQ. 0 .AND. B .EQ. 0) STATUS = 1
RETURN
END
SUBROUTINE QUAD(A,B,C,REAL1,AMAG1,REAL2,AMAG2)
DISC = DISCRI(A,B,C)
IF(DISC .GE. 0) THEN
   REAL1 = -B / (2 * A) + SQRT(DISC) / (2 * A)
   REAL2 = -B / (2 * A) - SQRT(DISC) / (2 * A)
ELSE
   REAL1 = -B / (2 * A)
   REAL2 = REAL1
   AMAG1 = SQRT(-DISC) / (2 * A)
   AMAG2 = - AMAG1
END IF
RETURN
END
SUBROUTINE LINEAR(B,C,REAL1,REAL2)
REAL1 = - C / B
REAL2 = REAL1
RETURN
END
FUNCTION DISCRI(A,B,C)
DISCRI = B * B - 4 * A * C
RETURN
END
SUBROUTINE RANDU(N,R)
N = N * 65539
IF(N .LT. 0) N = N + 2147483647 + 1
R = N
R = R / 2147483647
RETURN
END
```

Figure 14.4 A FORTRAN quadratic root finding routine.

"errors" come from rounding during computation. The rounding errors are cumulative in nature, cannot be numbered one by one, and cannot be removed by debugging. (The exception is where single precision may be changed to double precision. However, this only moves the problem from one area to another; i.e., the problem reappears under stringent requirement; for example, $\epsilon = 10^{-15}$.)

The results of the sampling procedure used in Chapter 13 are shown in Figure 14.6.

ϵ Value	True Defective Rate*
10^{-1}	0.0000
10^{-2}	0.0000
10^{-3}	0.0000
10^{-4}	0.0000
10^{-5}	0.0571
10^{-6}	0.5810
10^{-7}	0.8095

*100-percent inspection of all $15 \times 15 \times 15 = 3375$ units in the product population.

Figure 14.5 True product population defective rates under different ϵ values of routine in Figure 14.4.

i	n_{i+1}	n_i	$n_{i+1} - n_i$	θ_i^0
1	706	50	656	0.0800
2	638	706	−68	0.0878

Figure 14.6 Estimating the defective rate of the quadratic root finding routine of Figure 14.4 using sampling Equation 5.3a.

The magnitude of rounding errors during computation depends on the magnitude of the input data to the routine: the larger the magnitude of the input data, the larger the rounding error. This is due to the storage word size limitation on a computer system. As shown in Chapter 13, the defective rates found for different ϵ values are markedly different under input domain 1, where each of the coefficients A, B, and C is a whole number ranging from -7 to 7, than under input domain 2, where each coefficient is a whole number ranging from -100 to 100. For convenience, this data is repeated in Figure 14.7. The true defective rates under domain 1 are shown in Figure 14.5; those under input domain 2 are unknown. It can be seen that no single defective rate can measure the reliability of the routine properly.

B. *Predictions of Conventional Software Reliability Models*

As seen in Section 14.3.1***B***, the mean time to failure, Jelinski–Moranda, Schick–Wolverton, Musa, and Nelson models predict an infinite or arbitrary mean time to failure when the software is error free. Thus, when ϵ values range from 10^{-1} through 10^{-4}, these models may or may not measure the reliability of the quadratic root finding routine properly. Furthermore, none of these models can predict the effect of changing the input domain on the reliability of the routine (see Figure 14.7).

ϵ Value	Input Domain* 1	2
10^{-1}	0.0000	0.0000
10^{-2}	0.0000	0.0000
10^{-3}	0.0000	0.0100
10^{-4}	0.0000	0.4100
10^{-5}	0.0829	0.9300
10^{-6}	0.4922	0.9600
10^{-7}	0.7565	0.9700

*Sample size = 193.

Figure 14.7 Sampled population defective rates under different defectiveness criteria and input domains.

In the cases in which the values of ϵ range from 10^{-5} through 10^{-7}, all of the models reveal their inability to measure reliability meaningfully when "errors" are due to rounding during computation. Since rounding errors cannot be removed one by one, the terms in the equations for debugging time and remaining errors become meaningless. (Even if double precision is used in the routine, these models still fail to measure reliability properly under different defectiveness criteria, e.g., $\epsilon = 10^{-15}$.)

14.3.3 Counterexample 3: A Matrix Inversion Routine

The matrix inversion routine shown in Figure 14.8 implements the Gauss-Jordan elimination method in [11] on an IBM 4381 32-bit computer system. The routine finds the inverse A^{-1} of a matrix A such that $A^{-1}A = I$, where I is an identity matrix and the matrices A^{-1}, A, and I are of size $N \times N$. A test conducted on this routine is discussed in the following section.

A. Prediction Based on Product Unit Population Defective Rate

A test of the routine shown in Figure 14.8 is conducted according to the test method discussed in this book. Let a_{ij} be an element of A. The input domain of A is $-100 \leq a_{ij} \leq 100$ for each element a_{ij}. The rule of using a_{ij} is that it is a whole number in the range for all a_{ij}'s and A is nonsingular. A product unit is defined to be a matrix of size 2×2, or $3 \times 3, \ldots,$ or 8×8. The definition of product unit defectiveness is $|I_{ij}| \geq \epsilon = 0.000001$ for $i \neq j$ and $|I_{ij} - 1| \geq \epsilon = 0.000001$ for $i = j$. Using the iteration equation (5.3a), the test results are shown in Figure 14.9, given $z = 1.96$, or probability being 0.95, $a = 0.05$, and the matrix size being 2×2. The sampling process stops at iteration 5. The total number

```
      SUBROUTINE MATINV(A, N, DET)
      DIMENSION PIVOT(8), IPVOT(8), INDEX(8, 2)
      DIMENSION A(8, 8)
      INTEGER ONE, TWO
      ONE = 1
      TWO = 2
      DET = 1.0
      DO 10 I = 1, N
         IPVOT(I) = 0
10    CONTINUE
      DO 60 I = 1, N
         T = 0.0
         DO 30 J = 1, N
            IF(IPVOT(J) .NE. 1) THEN
               DO 20 K = 1, N
                  IF(IPVOT(K) .NE. 1) THEN
                     IF(IPVOT(K) .GT. 1) THEN
                        RETURN
                     END IF
                     IF(ABS(T) .LT. ABS(A(J, K))) THEN
                        IROW = J
                        ICOL = K
                        T = A(J, K)
                     END IF
                  END IF
20             CONTINUE
            END IF
30       CONTINUE
         IPVOT(ICOL) = IPVOT(ICOL) + 1
         IF(IROW .NE. ICOL) THEN
            DET = -DET
            DO 35 L = 1, N
               T = A(IROW, L)
               A(IROW, L) = A(ICOL, L)
               A(ICOL, L) = T
35          CONTINUE
         END IF
         INDEX(I, ONE) = IROW
         INDEX(I, TWO) = ICOL
         PIVOT(I) = A(ICOL, ICOL)
         DET = DET * PIVOT(I)
         IF(DET .EQ. 0.0) THEN
            RETURN
         END IF
         A(ICOL, ICOL) = 1.0
         DO 40 L = 1, N
            A(ICOL, L) = A(ICOL, L) / PIVOT(I)
40       CONTINUE
         DO 50 LI = 1, N
            IF(LI .NE. ICOL) THEN
               T = A(LI, ICOL)
               A(LI, ICOL) = 0.0
               DO 45 L = 1, N
                  A(LI, L) = A(LI, L) - A(ICOL, L) * T
45             CONTINUE
            END IF
50       CONTINUE
60    CONTINUE
      DO 80 I = 1, N
         L = N - I + 1
         IF(INDEX(L, ONE) .NE. INDEX(L, TWO)) THEN
            JROW = INDEX(L, ONE)
            JCOL = INDEX(L, TWO)
            DO 70 K = 1, N
               T = A(K, JROW)
               A(K, JROW) = A(K, JCOL)
               A(K, JCOL) = T
70          CONTINUE
         END IF
80    CONTINUE
      RETURN
      END
```

Figure 14.8 A FORTRAN matrix inversion routine.

i	n_{i+1}	n_i	$n_{i+1} - n_i$	θ_i^0
1	5,780	100	5,680	0.2100
2	6,664	5,780	884	0.1874
3	6,809	6,664	145	0.1841
4	6,840	6,809	31	0.1834
5	6,825	6,840	−15	0.1834

Figure 14.9 Estimating the defective rate of the matrix inversion routine of Figure 14.8 using Equation 5.3a.

of matrices taken randomly from the input domain is 6,840. The sample defective rate is 0.1834. Therefore, one can conclude that the defective rate of the population of the inverted matrixes of size 2×2 is from 0.1818 to 0.1854, computed from Equation 5.4a. The defective rate can be verified by a 100-percent inspection of the population of 201^4 or 1,632,240,801 matrices of size 2×2, which is left to interested readers.

Again, it is crucial to the developer to realize that the conclusion given above is valid only under the defined input domain, product unit, and product unit defectiveness definitions, and cannot be generalized. The conclusions valid under different definitions will be different. To illustrate this point, the same routine is tested under the definitions shown in Figure 14.10. The input domains are:

$$-100 \le a_{ij} \le 100 \text{ and } a_{ij} \text{ a whole number}$$

$$-1000 \le a_{ij} \le 1000 \text{ and } a_{ij} \text{ a whole number}$$

$$-10000 \le a_{ij} \le 10000 \text{ and } a_{ij} \text{ a whole number}$$

$$-100000 \le a_{ij} \le 100000 \text{ and } a_{ij} \text{ a whole number}$$

From Figure 14.10, it can be seen that the smaller the value of ϵ, the larger the defective rate. However, the larger the matrix size N, the larger the defective rate. This variation of defective rate is due to the cumulation of rounding errors during computation.

To more properly assess the reliability of the matrix inversion routine, a combination of the remaining test methods: weighted, boundary, invalid, and special would also be required. Therefore, additional tables like the one shown in Figure 14.10 can be obtained by the sampling of product units. The generation of these tables is left to the interested readers.

Input Domain	ϵ Value	Matrix Size N* 2	3	4	5	6	7	8
1	10^{-1}	0.00	0.00	0.00	0.00	0.00	0.00	0.00
	10^{-2}	0.00	0.00	0.00	0.00	0.00	0.00	0.00
	10^{-3}	0.00	0.00	0.00	0.00	0.00	0.00	0.00
	10^{-4}	0.00	0.01	0.00	0.02	0.01	0.01	0.04
	10^{-5}	0.02	0.02	0.13	0.14	0.14	0.14	0.16
	10^{-6}	0.21	0.54	0.83	0.98	1.00	1.00	1.00
	10^{-7}	0.96	1.00	1.00	1.00	1.00	1.00	1.00
2	10^{-1}	0.00	0.00	0.00	0.00	0.00	0.00	0.00
	10^{-2}	0.00	0.00	0.00	0.00	0.00	0.00	0.00
	10^{-3}	0.00	0.00	0.01	0.00	0.00	0.00	0.01
	10^{-4}	0.00	0.01	0.03	0.00	0.02	0.00	0.02
	10^{-5}	0.01	0.04	0.14	0.12	0.09	0.09	0.17
	10^{-6}	0.13	0.51	0.74	0.89	0.97	1.00	1.00
	10^{-7}	0.90	1.00	1.00	1.00	1.00	1.00	1.00
3	10^{-1}	0.00	0.00	0.00	0.00	0.00	0.00	0.00
	10^{-2}	0.00	0.00	0.00	0.00	0.00	0.00	0.00
	10^{-3}	0.00	0.00	0.00	0.00	0.00	0.00	0.00
	10^{-4}	0.00	0.00	0.00	0.01	0.00	0.01	0.00
	10^{-5}	0.02	0.02	0.06	0.09	0.07	0.16	0.18
	10^{-6}	0.15	0.47	0.69	0.87	0.90	0.99	1.00
	10^{-7}	0.93	1.00	1.00	1.00	1.00	1.00	1.00
4	10^{-1}	0.00	0.00	0.00	0.00	0.00	0.00	0.00
	10^{-2}	0.00	0.00	0.00	0.00	0.00	0.00	0.00
	10^{-3}	0.00	0.00	0.00	0.00	0.00	0.00	0.00
	10^{-4}	0.00	0.00	0.02	0.02	0.02	0.00	0.02
	10^{-5}	0.02	0.02	0.11	0.10	0.13	0.21	0.16
	10^{-6}	0.30	0.61	0.81	0.86	0.92	0.96	0.99
	10^{-7}	0.94	1.00	1.00	1.00	1.00	1.00	1.00
5	10^{-1}	0.00	0.00	0.00	0.00	0.00	0.00	0.00
	10^{-2}	0.00	0.00	0.00	0.00	0.00	0.00	0.00
	10^{-3}	0.00	0.00	0.00	0.00	0.00	0.01	0.00
	10^{-4}	0.00	0.00	0.02	0.01	0.01	0.03	0.00
	10^{-5}	0.05	0.00	0.11	0.10	0.11	0.17	0.15
	10^{-6}	0.40	0.79	0.92	0.97	0.97	1.00	1.00
	10^{-7}	0.99	1.00	1.00	1.00	1.00	1.00	1.00

*Sample size = 100 (matrices) for each entry.

Figure 14.10 Test results under regular test method under different conditions in testing the matrix inversion routine of Figure 14.8.

B. Predictions of Conventional Software Reliability Models

The same comments given in Section 14.3.2*B* can be made about the conventional reliability models in measuring the reliability of the matrix inversion subroutine in Figure 14.8. The mean time to failure, Jelinski–Moranda, Schick–Wolverton, Musa, and Nelson models would not measure the reliability of the routine properly, as the errors in the routine are rounding errors during computation. Since rounding errors cannot be removed one by one, the terms in the equations for debugging time and remaining errors cannot be reduced. Again, even if double precision is used in the routine, these models still would fail to measure the reliability of the routine properly under some other stringent defectiveness criteria, for example, $\epsilon = 10^{-15}$. In addition, no single reliability measure can predict the performance of a piece of software properly. The defective rates shown in Figure 14.10 illustrate the point.

14.4 DEFICENCIES OF CONVENTIONAL SOFTWARE RELIABILITY MODELS

This chapter has shown that the mean time to failure, Jelinski–Moranda, Schick–Wolverton, Musa, and Nelson models for predicting software reliability all appear deficient in providing a meaningful measure of the probability of failure of a piece of software. The prime cause of this deficiency is that all of these models assume that:

A. The errors in a piece of software can be counted.
B. The number of errors remaining in the software decreases as debugging progresses.
C. Errors can be removed one by one.
D. No new errors are introduced into the software as debugging progresses.

The reason these assumptions were made would be the lack of appropriate definitions of product unit and product unit defectiveness. As has been shown throughout this book, a piece of software is analogous to a factory, and the output analogous to the manufactured product. As long as the developer thinks of the piece of software as his or her product, he or she will think of product defectiveness in terms of programming and coding errors. This in turn leads to thinking of software reliability in terms of debugging to remove such errors. However, once the developer defines product defectiveness in terms of the output of the software, then it can be seen that there are causes of defective output other than programming and coding errors.

Specifically, conventional reliability models do not take into account:

Rounding and truncation "errors"
Necessary storage overflow
Changes in the conditions of software usage

With these types of "errors," there is no relationship between the number of remaining errors and debugging time; there are always "new" errors in some software, and in some applications the errors can never be removed.

For example, suppose a piece of software is designed to find the value of e^x by:

$$e^x = 1 + x + \frac{x^2}{2!} + \frac{x^3}{3!} + \cdots + \frac{x^k}{k!} + \cdots + \frac{x^m}{m!}$$

for all real values of x. Even if there is no programming or coding error in the software, the truncation of the series at some term; for example, k, required for computation using a fixed word size digital computer, is a sure source of defectiveness in the software output. This "error" can be detected and corrected by adding more terms, for example, up to the mth term, to the series for computation. However, the error of truncation remains no matter what. In this case, a known error is removed and just as certainly a new error is added.

In scientific computation, due to the limitation of computer word size, rounding and truncation errors cannot be avoided. In fact, these types of errors are the general rule, rather than the exception. In many applications, they cannot be easily counted, and they are cumulative in effect. They cannot be removed one by one.

In most numerical applications, storage overflow is considered an error. However, storage overflow is required in many applications such as in a random number generator. This is yet another case which demonstrates the necessity of defining errors in terms of product unit defectiveness, that is, in terms of the output, not of the program error.

Finally, as discussed throughout this book, the output of a piece of software can be unusable to the user, regardless of whether the software itself is error-free. Let the user change the conditions, for example, input domain or defectiveness criterion, and an error-free program will generate defective output. As shown in this chapter, software reliability models based on the mathematics of hardware reliability theory cannot provide a meaningful measure of reliability in many applications.

For these reasons, some conventional models cannot measure software reliability properly. The appropriate measure of software reliability is the estimated defective rate of the product unit population, as determined by application of the principles of statistical quality control.

REFERENCES

1. C. V. Ramamoorthy and F. B. Bastani, "Software Reliability—Status and Perspective," *IEEE Transactions on Software Engineering*, Vol. SE-8, No. 4, July 1982, pp. 354–371.
2. G. J. Myers, *Software Reliability Principles and Practices*, Wiley-Interscience, New York, 1976.
3. M. L. Shooman, *Software Engineering*, McGraw-Hill, New York, 1983.
4. C. K. Cho, *An Introduction to Software Quality Control*, Wiley-Interscience, New York, 1980.
5. C. K. Cho, "Statistical Methods Applied to Software Quality Control," in G. G. Schulmeyer and J. I. McManus (Eds.), *Handbook of Software Quality Assurance*, Van Nostrand Reinhold, New York, 1987.
6. J. D. Musa, "A Theory of Software Reliability and Its Application," *IEEE Transactions on Software Engineering*, Vol. SE-1, No. 3, September 1975, pp. 312–327.
7. Z. Jelinski and P. Moranda, "Software Reliability Research," in W. Freiberger (Ed.), *Statistical Computer Performance Evaluation*, Academic, New York, 1972, pp. 465–484.
8. G. J. Schick and R. W. Wolverton, *Assessment of Software Reliability*, 11th Annual Meeting, German Operations Research Society, Hamburg, Federal Republic of Germany, September 1972.
9. B. Littlewood, "How to Measure Software Reliability and How Not to...," *IEEE Transaction on Reliability*, Vol. R-28, June 1979, pp. 103–110.
10. M. V. Zelkowitz, "Perspectives on Software Engineering," *Computing Survey*, Vol. 10, June 1978, pp. 197–216.
11. S. S. Kuo, *Numerical Methods and Computers*, Addison-Wesley, Reading, Massachusetts, 1965.

CHAPTER 15

Software Quality and Productivity: What Top Management Must Do

Show Software Credibility. Show Software Warranty.

The only way the U.S. software industry can remain competitive is to produce the best quality software through statistical quality control. And top management must lead.

Chin-Kuei Cho

The author of reference [1] in this chapter is Dr. W. Edwards Deming, the internationally renowned consultant. Deming's work in statistical quality control introduced new principles of management into Japanese industry and revolutionized Japanese product quality and productivity. As a result, Japanese industry now dominates the worldwide market of consumer goods. In recognition of his contribution to the economy of Japan, the Union of Japanese Science and Engineering established the Annual Deming Prize to be awarded for advancements in precision and dependability of products. In

1960, the Emperor of Japan awarded Deming the Second Order Medal of the Sacred Treasure. Deming is considered the father of the third wave of the industrial revolution [3]. The first wave was the machinery-based factory initiated by Eli Whitney. The second wave was mass production as developed by Henry Ford. The third wave is the use of statistical quality control to improve quality, and is due to the insight and efforts of Deming.

Quality is everyone's job, but responsibility for quality must begin with top management. Deming has identified 14 obligations that the top management of any organization in the service or manufacturing industries must fulfill in order to be responsible to stockholders and consumers [1]. Ten of these obligations can be applicable in the software industry and are discussed below.

15.1 TEN OBLIGATIONS FOR TOP MANAGEMENT OF ANY SOFTWARE DEVELOPER OR USER ORGANIZATION

Based on the material presented in this book, Deming's 14 obligations for top management can be adapted for the software industry. The following 10 obligations apply to the top management of any software developer or user organization.

A. **Create constancy of purpose to increase software quality and productivity.** With a plan to become competitive and to stay in business. Top management is responsible to the general public, especially the software users whose satisfaction is the supreme justification for the existence of a software business.

B. **Adopt the new philosophy of quality and cost-effective software**—with the understanding that we can no longer live with delays, mistakes, poor quality and costly software.

C. **Cease dependence on conventional software methods**—requiring, instead, statistical evidence that software quality is built in to eliminate need for inspection and correction on the job where the software is used. Top management of every computer and software developer and user company has a new job and must learn it. Every user company can now demand meaningful software warranty using statistical quality control. Every developer company must now show credibility by delivering software warranty.

D. **End the practice of awarding software business on a lowest cost basis**—demanding, instead, meaningful measures of quality along with price. Software developers who cannot qualify with statistical evidence of quality must be eliminated.

E. **Find problems**—Management must work continually on improving software practices: training, supervision, retraining, and improvement of software development methodologies using statistical methods.

F. **Institute modern methods and rigorous programs of training in software engineering and quality assurance with statistical quality control.**

G. **Institute modern methods of supervision of software personnel**—The responsibility of software personnel must change from sheer numbers to both numbers and quality. Achievement of quality will automatically increase productivity.

H. **Drive out fear**—so that everyone in a software company will work effectively.

I. **Break down barriers among departments**—Personnel in research, design, development, sales, and production must work as a team to foresee problems of software development.

J. **Create a structure in top management that will direct and control every day on the above nine points.**

These 10 obligations are elaborated in the following sections:

15.1.1 Create Constancy of Purpose to Increase Software Quality and Productivity

Today's problems in the computer and software industry, summarized in the 20 problems stated in Figure 1.3, have been a theme of this book. A company will not stay competitive for long if it does not learn how to solve these problems. In the future, the industry can expect that creation of and commitment to constancy of purpose and dedication to improvement of competitive position will be imperative to keep companies alive and to provide jobs for their employees.

Top management of software companies must think long term to be responsible to software users, stockholders and general public. Quick profits benefit no one. Long-term existence—10, 20, 30 years—of a company does. Should a software company be considered committing a crime in providing poor quality software to its users in making a quick profit?

Top management must accept the following responsibilities in creating a constancy of purpose:

A. **Innovation.** Resources must be allocated to long-term planning. The factors that need to be considered in planning include:
   a. Commitment to attaining the software engineering goals of:
      Modifiability
      Understandability
      Reliability
      Efficiency
   using the software principles of:
      Abstract data typing
      Information hiding
      Modularization
      Localization
      Uniformity
      Completeness
      Confirmability
      Statistical quality control
   b. Training of supervisors
   c. Training and retaining of software personnel
   d. Software quality and productivity
   e. Software cost
   f. Software user satisfaction

B. **Resource allocation.** Put resources into software research, development, and into education.

C. **Constantly improve software practices.** New technologies in software modeling, requirements specification, design, implementation, testing, and maintenance need be considered and incorporated into software development.

15.1.2 Adopt the New Philosophy of Quality and Cost-Effective Software

We live in a new information age which offers a new challenge for developing good quality and cost-effectiveness. Everyone in the software industry must adopt the new philosophy. Poor quality and costly software are no longer tolerable. Is a warranty such as the one shown in Figure 1.1 tolerable? Should a user be treated with that kind of nonsense? Software users have every right to demand a real software warranty from the developer. Should top management make a commitment to eliminate the conventional software methodologies which have not been able to solve any of the 20 problems stated in Figure 1.3, and to use new methods that would help solve these problems. Otherwise, the company may not be able to survive and stay in business. The materials presented in this book provide ample evidence that software engineering with statistical quality control offers solutions to some of the technical problems of the 20 problems, as illustrated in Chapters 8 through 14.

15.1.3 Cease Dependence on Conventional Software Methods

Since the dawn of the new information age, many software development methodologies and standards have been devised and practiced with the intent of developing quality and cost-effective software. Among these methodologies are structured programming, structured analysis, structured design, structured testing, and the like. Among these standards is perhaps IEEE 730. However, the contributions of these methodologies and standards to the industry have been meager, as evidenced by the 20 problems stated in Figure 1.3. Isn't it time for the software industry to reevaluate the practices of conventional software methodologies? Shouldn't we ask the question of whether or not continuing the practices of conventional methodologies will solve any of these 20 problems?

The materials discussed in this book present ample evidence that software users can and should demand statistical evidence that quality is built into the software they purchase. Using software engineering with statistical quality control can minimize the need for inspection and maintenance after the software is put into operation, a costly practice from which tremendous damage can result.

15.1.4 End the Practice of Awarding Software Business on a Lowest-Cost Basis

Price has no meaning without a measure of the quality being purchased.* According to Deming [1]:

> Without adequate measures of quality, business drifts to the lowest bidder, low quality and high cost being the inevitable result. American industry

*Walter A. Shewhart, *The Economic Control of Quality of Manufactured Products*, Van Nostrand, 1931. Reprinted in 1981 by the American Society for Quality Control).

and the U.S. government, civil and military, are being rooked by rules that award business to the lowest bidder. ...

Awarding software business on a lowest-bid basis without demanding meaningful quality measurement should be considered malpractice by software users. Conventionally, because of the lack of tools that could help users disqualify developers offering lowest bids without quality, many software developers have been enjoying a lucrative business in the software industry. Software users could end up being the victim. Worry no more. The tools that are necessary and sufficient for a user to screen out those developers who shouldn't be in the business are available in this book. Software developers who cannot qualify with statistical evidence of quality need be eliminated from the software industry.

15.1.5 Find Problems

Everyone in a software company must be provided with appropriate statistical methods with which to identify the software quality problems that can be corrected "locally," and those that belong to the system and require the attention of management. It is top management's job to work continually on every phase of the software life cycle: modeling, requirements specification, concurrent software design and test design, concurrent implementation of software design and test design, testing and integration, acceptance, and maintenance.

15.1.6 Institute Modern Methods of Rigorous Programs of Training in Software Engineering with Statistical Quality Control

There are virtually hundreds of long and short training courses and seminars on software engineering or software quality assurance being held in the software industry in the United States and abroad each year. Are those training courses and seminars good and helpful? To get a clear answer, one should refer to the 20 problems stated in Figure 1.3 and to the materials in this book, and ask the instructors and organizations giving the courses the following questions:

A. Do you know how many problems in the software industry that prevent users from getting good-quality and cost-effective software?

B. Do you know what each of these problems means?

C. Do you know how to solve any of these problems?

D. Do you teach how to measure software quality in meaningful numerical terms?

E. Do you have a statistical quality control background?

F. Do you have practical software engineering experience?

If the answer to any of these questions is no or not clear, then one should think twice. Top management must be able to recognize training programs that are good for the organization, and to eliminate those that are poor.

15.1.7 Institute Modern Methods of Supervision of Software Personnel

The goal of supervision of software development personnel is to develop good quality and cost-effective software, while that of supervision of software user personnel is to ensure product quality and cost-effectiveness of the software being produced by the developer. Modern methods of software supervision are based on understanding of the 20 problems stated in Figure 1.3 and providing solutions to these problems. The conventional supervision of software development by number of lines developed or number of production runs is no longer an acceptable method. Top management has a new job to do and must learn how to do it.

15.1.8 Drive Out Fear So That Everyone in a Software Organization Will Work Effectively

Fear in an organization can cost millions of dollars. The following article appeared in *The Washington Star*, April 15, 1981 (p. A-5):

U.S. WORKERS FEEL THAT REPORTING WASTE DOESN'T DO ANY GOOD, SURVEY FINDS

by Phillip Schandler

The board mailed a questionnaire to 13,000 randomly chosen employees of 15 agencies. About 8,600 responded. Of these, nearly 45 percent, about 4,000 said they had "personally observed or obtained direct evidence of a wasteful or illegal activity within the past year," the report says.

And one in 10 of those who claimed knowledge of an improper activity said it involved more than $100,000.

However, only 30 percent of the workers who claimed knowledge of improper activity reported it to anyone else.

Fifty-three percent of those who failed to report an impropriety said it was because they "did not think anything would be done to correct the activity." Another 20 percent said they didn't think anything could be done.

Twenty percent said they didn't say anything because to do so would be "too great a risk to me." This shows

> that fear of reprisal is "an important, although secondary, consideration" in failure to disclose wrongdoing, the report says.

It is a common phenomenon in a software industry that a software developer is very much afraid of having his software found to be defective by a third party. A software user is also too afraid of it being known that he or she has accepted a piece of poor-quality software to admit it. This kind of fear has resulted in many problems, for example, on-the-job inspection of what goes wrong and corrections of what might have been wrong with the software, delaying daily production and idling many personnel. It is the responsibility of top management to drive out fear and to ensure that statistical evidence of software quality be demonstrated before putting the software into operation.

15.1.9 Break Down Barriers Among Departments

The software developer and user must work as a team in developing good-quality and cost-effective software. In the developer's organization, software designers and implementers must also work in concert with software quality assurance personnel. Everyone in the organization must understand the goals and objectives of the organization and know what one's role is in the environment. Barriers that block cooperation and working relationships must be eliminated by top management.

15.1.10 Create a Structure in Top Management That Will Direct and Control Every Day on the Previous 9 Obligations

In order to fulfill the nine obligations discussed previously, the top management of a software company needs to create a structure to guide itself. This requires not an organizational structure, but a structure for performing statistical work. The aim of the structure is to utilize statistical knowledge and ability to serve the best interests of the company. An example structure is given in Figure 15.1. The structure is headed by a theoretical statistician competent to provide statistical leadership. The functions of the structure are:

A. Coordinating the teaching and dissemination of information on the nine obligations for top management

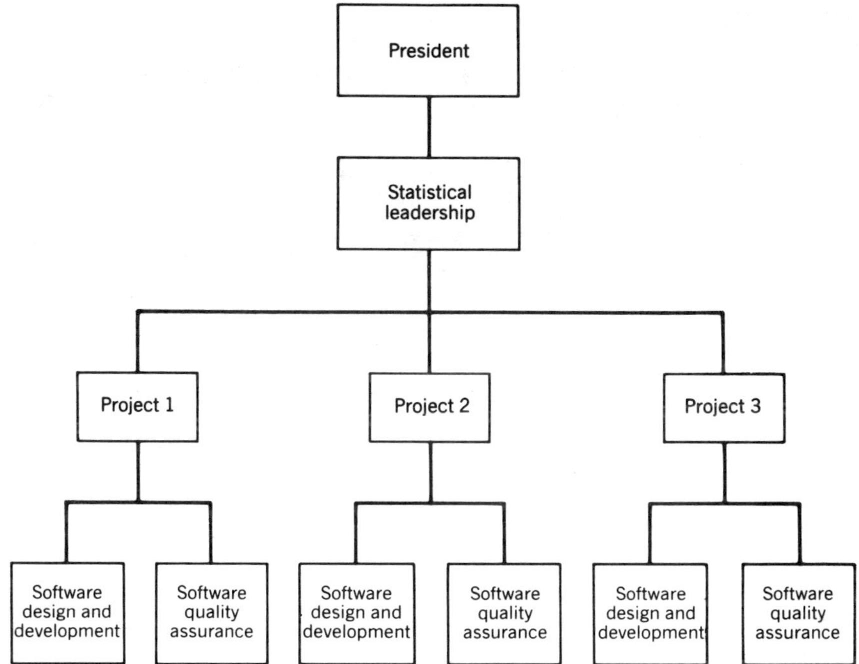

Figure 15.1 Example of top management structure to fulfill its nine obligations.

B. Teaching techniques for top management and for everyone else in the company

C. Identifying problems in the organization and in the software projects that other people could not be expected to perceive

A software company, whether developer or user, must employ people with a statistical quality control background to guide the company toward increasing software quality and productivity to stay in business.

15.2 WHERE TO START

To fullfill the 10 obligations of top management in the software industry, this book serves as a starting step of a journey of a thousand miles.

REFERENCES

1. W. E. Deming, *Quality, Productivity and Competitive Position*, Massachusetts Institute of Technology, Center for Advanced Engineering Study, Cambridge, Massachusetts, 1982.
2. W. E. Deming, *Methods for Management of Productivity and Quality*, George Washington University, Washington, D.C., 1982.
3. D. Halberstam, "W. Edwards Deming, the Man Who Taught Japan about Quality, Believes: Yes We Can!" *Parade, Parade Publications, Inc., New York*, July 8, 1984, pp. 4–7.

APPENDIX **1**

104,000 "Random" Digits (No. of 0's = 14143)

7110867876 4499593960 7730006367 4818014250 0248060786 0069785991 2200278539 7681573137 8900096123 7608213249
0261073411 3607017202 8194079038 3308942007 7234774838 5040784712 7922501786 2472560122 7002768409 6300681339
0700813793 4730082640 5008010088 1670302350 8380822084 0022033730 2101108115 1597014229 8066000368 1309294138
9389491498 6269247464 2435513257 0622656407 5199589168 7138920526 3887458337 0450417273 8811535656 6007995088
8683242934 3267113733 6836677095 2545964403 2322778484 3987861563 3991403340 9237017963 8721277667 9587675883
2852987204 1512957937 6363563033 5355069568 7635353268 3057840751 5190100132 3623291305 2711242507 0588341365
2816718171 4036439300 1149731356 2419407806 0570642501 0780576433 6727883792 2510996713 1130028570 1139395821
4234047721 0394010883 7820030307 7662380999 4107677897 2524992675 1797329203 1420004242 8316107045 0519459945
6917057711 8008368927 4780112941 5094935440 9313690131 1291071076 2367803254 0478833876 5259566817 4552842688
8031678307 3991832877 9833542110 6269078879 8304006950 5911108155 7463297259 6567955535 3618878630 3689766257

9578586483 1755124796 6023769685 6353113787 6989524336 4665802565 1658282064 9258346842 8836993690 5913883889
3499127036 0956235683 5932404025 3728394540 1883607132 6339112837 4959008084 7418231724 5757706898 0472223810
8820313614 5653645427 8259084922 5416583666 8151596267 5612077432 2975480742 6813044286 2023516706 8670401965
5144010408 4428201194 9825094187 6292915102 1158862099 5395088956 5020172114 0870442086 9434174860 2363475766
0204551619 7360790669 5437606024 0229912489 9845446144 6309234965 0599089658 4432924752 7232836079 5935423247
1077909912 8704171509 0663559192 6402959860 4634908370 8802767018 8743818801 0234955445 6840920038 0823711607
4298026373 4130912302 0844987028 6221703290 1946728487 0825029416 4995563740 2515812107 5983243709 9140542602
4884169640 1255009007 8111762201 0266256769 8486637057 5970001000 9041452349 0811721002 5599005063 1120440640
1959401455 4821259827 8861058275 6797072170 4741705572 8219879891 3597384026 9826701851 0949692626 1297125936
3767140742 0662218360 9003907828 4957112150 4050973301 0900187071 1052473730 0488942054 6009249585 9889207538

0695949276 9774089712 8017869135 3366475460 3635532268 0094968045 6549434602 5824199081 1470377878 7142003847
2377926611 1150157351 8169819420 0520925618 4022474072 5684234440 5823563965 1864880508 6431970670 1457795661
8504668966 2484407055 9197458463 2923091706 3450575124 9669591624 7321398703 7689314740 1878696804 5863927321
9094790087 1780739536 3368199176 2114332992 4513548154 9126659693 3902520973 1365445635 1693922306 8243619685
9705678892 1196957317 5250034479 7369504916 6183752992 0452169934 5694937943 2576447978 7730046304 7765084368
2060386001 8900041565 0479090999 0195059908 4140100120 1000260050 0260455398 0062659543 1502822971 0500180590
0115900246 2524531908 3050215904 3984760266 0601975101 1120801966 4052539030 1450093773 2008038305 0307333292
0516635400 8223510530 5279494858 3688761101 8024078314 9862291111 1896689326 1000818649 9448247617 5678482971
3011190296 4630955522 3817509081 0100322629 2461719033 5823326084 5890032603 0127380377 0439544900 9449567512
3560314907 0049102036 0054966331 2220592485 2837980036 4098905427 6000004525 5565090070 3010494727 0948641123

8255541475 1251752379 1567212120 4736811525 5139553702 5375753929 5114952001 2889688443 8253102152 1934601654
4504266917 2955023810 1376136835 5453154271 8887504332 6358976837 4919265394 6903316414 7083183560 7577906954
8467500032 0730605790 3099601519 3962000860 0008560400 7608270139 5207040008 9085900009 0080761703 3286300007
0303194380 2552440297 8156317792 7562512361 0244494562 1169072534 6052254538 0272754084 6403861525 6891329195
6568734689 1078522542 5408260115 9212811826 5013083497 9511781439 6511844745 5204245090 4154549439 4797015179
5505348858 7081213329 1969256121 1227216869 1870235459 0271916505 9557637240 6035222221 2365979078 1943059705
5281809046 0136055103 7005268444 7122143732 2720053852 1632805346 9721923279 1274943189 2851778480 6973264975
7386692235 0108992392 2759159687 8023524908 8315891675 3749850322 1854043091 2949785074 3566024009 1060762541
9809219403 9253011006 5516338911 4730197647 8304545205 8226093444 7010656607 1719804607 3684484088 6860460892
2208183022 7410928076 6604050925 9783200443 8232854583 0002801607 6236426730 2881264082 6087000770 3428303742

9704019033 1290099007 5100284970 6743004840 0327549038 0460010313 3108000300 9449080005 0552103104 8552781505
3807050997 0238000000 7502654011 6700606068 0640006459 0070061830 2160044180 0700102700 0502062300 0699307600
4410112552 4085213076 5421530542 4030797158 1732606304 6580174042 4221571940 0185801090 6645479703 4907185704
2231664639 0289200414 5940215892 0277601345 5865651144 1498594065 3381290487 1317011667 7787739729 3681053612
2428720757 5966284518 3800098024 8063713212 3551567839 9565287955 8193158053 6742216380 1690878256 2976399222
6274813678 5840691056 0091074021 8128257649 9288811412 9095250073 8592901356 2418076243 0065763614 1191149100
6336361668 5806719434 8153788763 9363064574 0120202995 5395733748 2627642613 7817563598 7203655329 2255767013
0575504337 1834452797 8919949266 1015700770 3545517653 2019115687 0993629611 1878643183 3636290790 5961591213
2958077377 2251950147 1115872197 6638327797 1358773596 1430422739 9162730828 5066989253 2452813179 0820451368
8036552900 1435438387 9874855325 5308929574 3360990039 1487402248 3088959607 4610314002 0433080975 3423579592

0230987843	9055731441	8069388429	6951269128	0093215364	6795191424	1715428254	0554918801	7717637120	4542255299
8522523406	1310813788	6429214173	2400898196	1054631884	2600130894	0346896660	7824033958	9081352879	0053721896
3121980216	0645466477	3506974214	5079092482	6501198368	1582496662	8886066719	0113199221	9998478895	6252024570
7000505140	9940422007	6610919608	6317010360	6995406609	6003006948	0145050007	7094101616	0041977036	3986206860
8493956798	9895641342	2436928495	4684177982	0732705166	3850661775	4437123305	0092506131	5574767950	2269145013
4869255723	4628991318	0047055740	5056529942	0350305760	8639782586	8100601037	4123608865	3714084195	8202289297
4254258466	7603348758	4443100601	8483832197	5604789825	1323543996	4217211528	1898285014	7976249111	1833510096
3883426985	1465694437	1989526894	0487270777	4791967704	5906938050	4230284278	8244443659	7577607228	0928762341
8108349505	8680100004	4003078140	9707757639	6736872692	0518952530	2950010260	0590805200	8302684583	9000366503
0050607704	3087069000	5875806931	1508103801	1507913309	3500746900	6703100369	3477658275	8366848008	0031390208
2715211070	7265076863	2247478539	5620786444	4540791426	5385257838	9046075152	0328552225	1727641599	2585483149
8087085000	9900080398	4718509016	0622151733	3008192715	1680444753	1503192272	0061070006	5509069603	3804564906
9673174619	7908745378	2010330100	5045361040	0000870323	9071771500	7381403410	8378171400	7840576783	0017130302
7374483182	8161633270	9275640348	4171860109	8845057900	0282047586	6052065055	0239674520	7963743075	3485565709
0569432346	7778696561	7279430216	9881338232	8333383853	8932610525	6378696394	1562615238	5399696543	4948302635
8765364054	9692087923	6551709432	9085485279	6018975281	6908405369	4879898761	2130290692	3140084409	6829142685
4589344792	5975173740	8911631822	0236295745	6271801141	8953592498	6862149828	8986511685	8832204006	5393311502
2526050284	3687844953	2051589241	2819972161	7003449814	1396703840	7040174818	5141605961	7527522963	2163865045
0270048834	4578610116	3703506497	5820368503	8661976030	5551278123	3375403052	1088588258	5128340158	6351967780
3308078178	5773983754	3670650391	5158274220	0741875514	6260607539	4809062006	6460681277	0950102700	9440046072
6944837538	4273661218	4690997370	6134760835	5214402456	1638052559	7622002927	8047936566	3126670775	5415840330
7260722503	7567310187	8294360882	0211303402	7402886476	5536160544	2100935458	3456598744	9350960073	6869475332
3712068962	2386743318	8744391259	2426262083	8164429118	1777836100	8843018331	5132621147	1106962589	1386716302
4400654945	2026245562	5337829483	7213053275	2982654792	0227510595	4110229888	0529423284	5453001307	7313869609
3202773834	1986392518	2569019347	1593441983	9639802001	4789857068	7862956302	6806327732	5359504866	2672715406
2277950663	1689996240	0076466565	3591607061	6916421364	2469338581	0028518245	0309374502	8547600952	9524180316
7883372362	6252456798	9462599472	5178716295	1155594767	5033491524	1592539550	2560228496	1556177476	5012121396
0236926384	9763788920	9482179376	1016821336	6813236683	2936601243	6345457882	4364850986	4912069953	9155872777
4175211115	5968637003	3800007373	3000805128	0125689070	2329829602	9708006422	6000170609	4645140173	0153390304
6790956119	4845757380	7766462236	3366850202	1769992041	5747313510	2016464305	3765872712	3492125987	0953734040
7043964657	0167733083	9943959673	1606112319	6309800473	6545074607	2551656559	7281913493	9062541166	7365570637
3837021847	6787534443	4517084281	8922771966	3422272685	1529361145	9917315544	0348604907	6140751548	2421085886
5952448256	4596356137	0978883383	9253418489	0351594406	0942801521	8272123090	4493967275	7470217956	9921359780
7872728998	9298236403	4944794596	9266660102	0154642597	1870821285	6849322149	2905447894	8039159196	5240868389
4589352814	2756093591	0366489375	6891656377	5085675317	4337818585	7335907735	0290049487	5710008243	6834149648
4425248982	5202933451	8707000502	2600006596	8810776006	3410014731	7920306118	3980577166	2172850200	0155805311
0726514239	7980640775	7502980914	5871982851	5008861881	2420111301	2282202413	4656859749	1259672199	1840615304
7474938015	2906219751	9648468854	6266031368	4279605828	3843975669	5151511928	9685166769	4942268047	5392954968
9213526070	1700843086	6070105349	0184008730	1372004543	7506042890	8160336616	0210756043	8248174950	7700542342
8160372724	7704513964	1444321692	6464919379	4536797208	7014464739	3970789346	8317491389	6256090324	5301638480
4057130081	4183929048	1605194315	3288737687	1826293020	3993119192	4945213315	3079638348	1292431396	5405824048
4948802408	4188197380	7429174788	5285000340	7552003281	0576102770	8090132960	2320099147	0606707007	2106180000
8420055786	5255993328	0658380445	0050006005	9204186105	0008825228	0332005899	0522113010	4054800129	1169008061
1061904035	2313381888	5186648267	0183709566	6533265051	5712411060	6721739558	3940199651	3382944913	3178526163
2274392835	9685357753	0187527983	8102890631	2461622240	0693389954	4832954155	8006306814	1031636686	0050540335
0099931940	8352293874	4466568123	5092850812	6285930089	4585825326	0820008360	2155690080	0901373111	1032097516
3290368803	2889362282	4218562602	5667040283	2606061048	1016518542	3228852645	1415313311	1217222388	8961127341
7268396654	8152430032	2765725513	6518724043	3870713317	9829970419	4019420759	2007608685	8988408705	7471507234
3538019105	4292050865	8955974646	9349710830	5960471090	5320001693	4609088751	6017128397	0354580742	3641559772
5807719119	6260166070	0284108040	2442008880	4832328783	1509743747	5683004202	6031997146	5900860230	8391026078

4885251711 6172260528 7103197897 0651281000 4668043538 6420488782 2333804852 2008746013 5063095807 0782302944
2388881663 2184120476 5565253090 6523986560 0156270873 9404956592 2595884076 6395136714 1974452721 9170857930
4892900421 5040691461 6900195234 3650752090 0437242641 6916117645 6103557762 1120269629 8265265049 4351405011
3865092822 5142575698 0731189547 9537816482 6823279999 5642611764 0177774957 3324914310 7539589514 0070121549
2604308927 5785538607 0706626107 2381666433 5192118757 9649407337 9367523479 7956643466 6528050300 9243274837
9784292008 2174161179 5468865789 2263652519 2502229795 3984043725 1735788155 3157584104 0236661065 2714963781
9907037120 6873048074 8061004677 0742391303 0106908096 7302564484 0037227644 4786063022 7363820028 4216117466
6846497683 4754028134 7413228040 9101300670 8852571491 9626745743 0183142787 7103544202 1861546408 5073700571
6025101189 2980740893 3772731159 4965237331 3148164133 1847620854 3974065386 3946169784 7853113800 8880087435
8892954265 2901623977 8516767589 9994019149 5823774328 4652221985 0966919445 7929269055 4563888974 2633392843

4515582300 8811027507 1008097223 5482649204 1577409131 3697366279 0010715442 4592041171 9020422880 8800946935
4407244159 3304244538 3311373485 4051615554 2444759608 8593461779 0694932093 3795863101 5142561104 4767192450
6596736441 0652050257 8685843548 3413607130 4956180619 8979181505 4370891729 5924173427 8542556399 4895391189
3379470069 3837571038 1350363073 5204988047 9267064145 4818987812 7092346440 4197006728 7842938068 0288632615
9660771333 5724930922 1143169545 7301918589 2075066237 1926390843 0083338665 3302062372 4877612166 3402852106
9635144637 4036709717 1946788304 0239077880 0150466406 8060260970 8448010107 7939908389 9770194213 0532006288
2067276152 9255924724 8016671565 2139594859 7182711346 4774578649 0995099665 0703628507 9024897834 0368788242
4164163097 5085143230 3876742889 3094752763 2606360956 4187782318 9472303327 6570286267 4309399046 5385129518
3918022075 6076410317 0303042410 0350536090 8245384800 2163650222 4200474092 0747862380 7718640923 3004257871
8003385050 0957882428 1660000513 3350091192 5872007683 9167460280 8804332150 0580596170 0279990009 0169642432

0786038805 2200750002 0543109080 3509230445 6947002128 1001215237 0340805741 0006630010 0015802904 5800710031
7385224424 0144984611 8546295262 3975666286 7750507239 2552430649 6869070564 0070208064 1566562663 1442972094
9566118167 9635410943 7110782948 5580544937 9244064189 2057318598 7921760392 1335612793 2687490211 0062833336
5000910808 0060780081 0510367800 4252361710 5089410409 2067025070 7558390509 0001261030 7264037705 0401034005
8093588573 0732642674 1212612816 6049304383 9468476747 8263562174 8095282897 0392282883 0371992486 7268950352
4440573244 1807399465 9357718853 7460139327 9085777615 7916403658 8903664534 6867704480 4284736514 5649523775
0545206027 0566257027 4096492870 8977418002 7368335708 0017201362 0077102504 7992560178 0209202056 9872230090
9427970381 4717512702 9845224524 0500672987 1682444566 8265850055 7188494125 6357425930 5091535694 3037051083
0025381790 2251802395 9013984000 8747020302 1130402104 6450406030 7985683234 0003917034 9718994389 6774673103
4139436188 6663464336 7509416119 6629487909 3225889455 1241857965 5717290902 0344150871 8543358531 7198219084

9001005210 9801574085 1040050033 0105090050 0339064754 3560790451 5508909008 0661864701 2351026770 7507307250
3975983758 4156368587 8616727168 2318940320 1683095767 7915944659 5564252103 6171121232 2690025522 2151811233
9610236467 3195563434 2044989621 5449285361 3463031288 7295969265 3262168039 2278757039 8376693502 7871969675
5544692027 1340080050 2315955355 6064894255 5436224552 4551741298 3543463793 2392290174 2818580587 6481044484
1193750279 9746717351 6742275671 1887610319 1557277232 8959614669 5526265142 5715450736 5854507747 7857874178
2608357477 3573655653 5555989637 6089090482 0344380097 9308087453 0056582308 1212280025 9093963455 8058639970
3722128270 7608816047 5859829652 7476116798 9454743144 7266703527 4572337716 5915357422 2467563984 7682271721
6891737404 3284840463 9015115347 2866404016 0413539438 5127820894 8770292191 1402133039 6829138611 9067164265
0015005152 6571356288 3077664280 1600697954 5020057731 6070445039 6484307365 1578658513 6542004160 6981310603
7016116370 0700907546 9051488056 8080567261 1804008446 5892602090 3809007206 4104080635 0070944994 0040506080

4660336493 2530757204 3794096208 0099498963 5799990999 7708469061 7198771614 3904344512 7883961054 7602311915
1080309094 1990718047 3002001902 5455391730 0402275529 6009240155 8099015045 0523605586 0881494260 0054002056
8744105706 0318980989 9500414208 2483044587 9149300517 8006791958 3602401096 6270982733 6385526280 5867019611
5037220680 4360176231 2337048430 1045232603 8701709572 3377622944 6519822878 6964039263 2515223191 8513611739
5748031573 6706208845 1777187112 5468890096 7670166058 2304015687 8847297561 1301813358 4542557646 1884064071
0859751805 7469884100 9026348101 5400869488 5074602944 4088441489 8215729225 0098771578 4951962925 4091064004
6420868031 9023003092 0778508039 3628045463 8903020001 9006977217 0708098055 0084038080 9000420080 1079079502
1590794880 3484173339 1933658182 5585937208 5628344460 2887227206 8819447495 4804130291 0473022355 8829928254
9504004268 0980162805 6946580563 0877279505 9423462682 8800960721 6618388581 2982586323 8640376272 1504932122
3608337607 82[illegible]2131917 2946137869 7895047925 0305736638 0209663307 5402048604 3540220653 4035503406 6108620942

3401059542 5316886837 6989131128 9371756464 5497764424 6756265156 3828885429 8764468559 2812495880 4799754833
9615680667 1586675019 3160530439 1127768757 5516632358 2076454393 7506592623 6240397886 6007768303 5247655684
2948692528 6201945913 6935317227 4251034149 1803320800 2809181796 0801066785 3287912182 8851269399 0006935814
9665063316 6459903053 7993183792 8010921495 7781656819 5868263784 6912334215 4767897856 0117004388 1289363952
2852621537 0588598442 7047558774 334290727 0 97735365 2340890161 5343156533 5777148937 9698758652 0666975664
7141703579 0051550261 3899873793 8429165066 5993297775 4691921354 3809855681 1031216919 7882625530 7879605804
2007102106 3906892091 6780473375 006627119 8460060413 5508855247 1568078000 6470007191 0608706002 0032801856
79 8492995 1311772668 6615776606 4865103138 4239655862 2161213631 5582367384 3201056877 9069667071 2850972158
2994691189 2495251057 0556658354 0554028157 6358472536 6973847455 8069557184 4792136724 0882141821 9196171637
4151317353 9530290731 8517271525 8287397086 9197073917 3954983101 4205921026 2356726588 4533215698 5709891852

1003413770 5655789148 1890409211 8564055483 7657969067 8529797564 1128369025 4143071931 6855359429 3933542286
2003491081 4845450503 0343603040 0155907902 0090376007 6478857076 8039405085 6130642400 0907904354 0610687987
3879801636 3547134631 8576391532 5427227953 3868366740 7807153736 9215145605 1220916064 3733523322 2515902317
3661279725 6117733315 8949919478 9977747127 2173258790 8219748579 8827993035 9085893613 9540401469 5469047170
2099527888 8591417312 1238361050 9283223010 1157180106 4832872293 6391122660 1199361605 8226838762 9687701629
1528615719 0244812514 5278743114 8666002909 3658542194 9407596927 1172361334 2624422614 1243838524 6513603997
2370628838 2181927627 4330678127 8641156801 0933995349 4650495272 9876043316 2654388423 6991011455 4180705984
5660579029 6331420910 1789527797 4174496378 4008886094 5435153780 5284388192 1336479422 0895840847 0861385809
0777500059 4507877388 0140489521 2557735047 5154729942 4817644288 1214441731 0967624837 8798535802 6574178829
2101308309 7116860248 8660705805 8903905441 6148040493 4230401006 4938271902 4539419122 1907733840 8505286270

0929246797 0943655324 1737200373 6703115252 3799477327 4845960053 9581842922 6305744082 7446315038 6847969913
6472033800 7202317270 6929876882 3353459601 7075582170 2951356843 9150717813 6517429221 0690192783 1000507138
0384090097 5394808381 8830223103 1356700000 0980124524 1178204870 3167602551 3092079441 4094886375 3126808777
2691343837 7706141652 9340266636 5650897736 1359497133 5888556251 1001785685 7241428972 1634561591 1697735047
7640145759 6893708522 6436313224 2604812302 8323587898 9839964517 3261886755 4764142241 4192421812 1306776888
5609447526 9706719858 3266326647 8535010163 7037465106 9479768774 5884557718 2745544345 7063157448 2534978329
1785690596 5465439336 4787589268 6156159063 6225981927 4005004089 8516773950 2894447510 8291530759 9238743489
2611783865 1664746981 9730492990 3768300879 4419469666 6030798561 3475691745 1592719814 7640401995 9197846393
3281340806 3915750828 0964805347 9206588678 6484387285 6652480233 7959838932 8348237459 8226364660 8755074447
5079866148 5747883492 8044893564 3660084424 8688936772 2458178930 2724100233 9363698674 7426345428 5762470015

9881704404 3067836008 3574461981 0543474849 0937541291 5243291518 7842988796 0291556115 2096536804 8539828565
8581621273 5807479282 6854034976 9878175480 6943637921 9463920268 6234587469 3919090094 3552418049 5158007657
8693616879 7493299150 5483205902 5875459403 9147118188 2146286016 0134056005 7006257423 2049509139 7422966862
3968958766 6198801362 9395706276 5425269644 9857306583 1619645510 8180362370 2808671689 4811832546 7013972658
9092163447 9289890432 6402479247 0309876467 3799684185 5649899864 4625716135 6070778807 9944981465 0391518129
3122878684 8246131871 5076025239 8465380264 7897063529 0235996980 8178494975 5789358351 0925826781 1343841783
3068471316 4070559186 9080570078 2277714501 7629159248 5677021824 7394437165 4698734480 2291087173 3522212981
3952314351 2052417920 7859844699 0952367663 2864979172 6262804506 0125297681 5350248075 3620375304 0759367928
0242070160 8002185947 1672019588 9516998076 1964229830 9959091056 3894906870 2943131700 9490256437 2008752138
5570899659 6380442525 5111067576 8044992642 1920963100 7242474771 5345566885 0695059175 5936418313 3190371068

1657927219 3893545472 3958751089 5271265809 3197227986 3277151895 4900865399 8913961516 0100072055 3059194366
3012605893 2107119330 0250004038 1269802223 5504151530 7231285008 3688232792 4079036233 9839742789 1098363708
3513584244 4935939848 3555975874 8997092006 1396988838 1835781027 3852888023 7526262847 2740391481 7843093554
3769929246 7540690404 6191150330 3163003078 6964970393 9654830048 3827062423 1023702529 1191689738 2731272847
0227243301 4186552957 8987481810 6703151802 3528806535 9777678943 5814344204 4214659691 1258973938 7080121126
9301656589 1890204185 7224103827 1329483460 7050349124 6001704361 9997667476 8705100230 2927686508 6218238110
7795017342 6846693851 6308293955 6535014639 0932520838 0209282266 4623270402 7209524944 9378086413 1074484006
1892114084 3304443444 1330704199 6194214142 1292805326 9964160791 1015511533 8650991150 7311866007 6072590323
5333461925 3107334280 3736025412 2648108094 2851238374 4512412168 6379738060 7132077384 9080916710 2727148381
9610420752 1545812436 8345755491 6927464038 7096748374 9717685307 8762853207 7022656649 8797613460 1483217022

9465433988	8691596685	7840659076	7711851210	1245032962	8272763029	4224633670	3929630545	1529011249	1321781980
4686022357	8203374448	4494797672	8567987768	8238419141	7303931851	0111326228	5349707924	8827561118	9159187859
5049005010	0270232996	8303630805	8010501000	2021586915	7077782154	4036790163	7537798603	9307354142	3634909519
4584572705	4719247739	1425387683	3567719778	4573243854	4194510651	8382963556	6441634835	4615032750	3612588408
0293680608	7693195887	4073191639	2553671516	8825927413	2918088251	8998767438	3443966366	0376895584	5698003222
1197013202	0918320080	1199488000	7407850318	2747787504	4354175813	1109765032	9571412750	1768400130	3971849781
0404886210	9906022803	2003021906	9288563339	0016023640	9063694157	7054917790	0006612248	0000526112	9915044370
8145055511	4182700068	2919527273	2474250969	1263448820	0381597959	1748779628	5633860041	8882183896	1348162400
2960544245	2226657365	2183786419	0723499424	1969149445	2724521795	4575497708	5542108609	6792736639	7021920526
6456556943	2916228978	6321535944	8640832682	6685516263	5518269307	4932658814	4287937718	9389093770	9766150854
8015097256	2537741972	7144972929	8224300464	8077088150	3068808020	0136966088	7605060946	6924006665	6247532577
0751061350	1161037258	9739804889	4503379535	0472205519	9931651264	5378147349	7707954310	5204523795	6819119654
2030186535	8082759791	7200590091	1864254380	8760906855	6074340099	9501970144	7740206089	9003842257	2480677890
2026471237	9152831350	4623294860	6051422990	1018960976	2320203245	9793484391	9154873238	1956173452	1182497233
1308203530	0010101891	0004709525	2007551930	0905300019	4059007782	1210878166	9940380078	4761745280	0564000072
3519508224	5730134297	7940382576	9067355026	5735850276	2005771014	2975573336	8464038112	1983881569	8136626181
8331156336	5888641921	9005974217	0725570656	2095399630	5168993813	0189249124	3164435243	0607770467	6848949513
8013571793	6346166854	1449406463	9520572161	7317550262	2241837318	7142818818	3063838263	9557004467	7770874501
8937673175	5322642142	4812389015	4160814237	8303675264	8970109312	5719540738	1028066747	8538336731	0542445808
8220873106	7957608347	5729165992	3400198144	3670090584	9003082076	4598638549	0600621408	3157445471	2605216024
6149644937	0026786701	7876043585	5472863900	5354987008	0808156703	6090206093	0004406907	3853028735	9990026372
0049783047	2028092700	5203527042	5004725997	2708240929	2027495570	6026565575	0005004884	8593835301	0000084393
1885930150	6013952172	0519466658	3076489272	9921522767	4286933173	4566442924	7928120201	9997088179	4348115696
5234972616	1385252748	0348066156	2353820798	1422300354	3838174519	5794868878	0684914829	8543183949	3526233938
9436211423	0759110646	0600031204	0957036226	5312731408	9086917580	8599166080	8088860422	4014093004	9628366403
7100488013	4305219004	0260044105	2169170150	7079801666	5280004579	6068702004	4421900020	9479395709	0425663475
9532128156	4458645141	1542107529	8525290888	4644637325	6835388279	4976062431	4786342045	6274460272	0442042534
9435873109	7999277909	3653747331	3532037394	9327069142	6524038615	8316560019	4238277023	3387969672	5067375446
2345322334	1278755019	3366842251	0620413328	5433704663	8012394696	8839633565	0896624103	0730403473	6779525754
3181069073	5959027244	8386616940	2897093160	5369225586	3651715636	1647615758	7878072140	5466781246	7188298905
0860937248	9029158003	0625021683	0140786099	1630800780	5596098959	3403250934	2071960715	5420553267	8571716448
4292123625	6545794909	4797548729	5742751085	7088451622	8318554510	8182924880	8102291090	4755566927	8138909332
6075398136	3832589084	7273577737	0472265683	2135225250	5092837723	0192165984	1755270283	8161224261	0614842246
2016702546	1022458695	0173514215	3443040813	7476051147	2455046577	1164451578	3200116561	3778047162	9570029318
3735406965	1307973776	8562147920	2573864362	7964187184	5126759796	9179741572	2198103274	4122719417	1030687481
2332476865	0938577533	4851311151	1179854219	6079339563	5167405308	3467103545	4521546787	8014485597	7213396824
3033313993	8358491113	7114771504	4181986348	6642437580	9174199258	2599996418	6599681626	4505338163	4145106656
5060031000	2201988085	6104037004	7038330002	1840990328	8600905701	0104040550	0080180416	2405576457	9056663008
0318562082	2409405546	9398748673	9023223805	3823593774	4664856982	4968394690	5983970970	4081992991	4509221684
0203968041	1807150128	7679069323	9235490108	1505412912	3415308802	5745431006	4406010777	0074602002	2120657857
2435699901	9520639328	6166307201	3849281290	9547732190	0317995660	9402997596	7737755478	2249203098	1906660126
0586417926	5129639539	8107922204	8118763470	9952899882	0495646051	6317341730	9947102853	3522667507	6287313579
0840861397	5976697807	5965492467	7304201600	5039204920	3212780465	0978704025	5056560412	9728004079	7067208369
2045641121	1650615593	8194321941	1574563758	4959648438	7843606727	9393937855	7819164263	3112188921	4107224154
5418066055	1996237459	2417542839	0621027373	1021231641	4150064264	0976259588	0001167059	9713222396	2054761091
9395475907	5167579006	5253497642	0612913417	6697890309	1007405673	6662031340	3295506379	5808292303	3850419737
6399159032	0469750810	3283628803	6451301600	8428144094	7820907755	7029840578	3656822247	7046190086	3626042716
7442635199	8383721779	1326026673	2388348380	2753099554	2697212315	5516454677	0047020618	4113792972	8666340252
3369193138	2905562353	2360129151	5522965120	2764906994	7453478774	2359448911	5289042437	1294704126	7180608277
7386565337	1173620664	5572020494	0693746475	8349129242	1748769474	8788812274	1759138014	4053283592	2715206964

7387303080	7520492907	7667220707	0702444156	0109102076	9689037354	8214040266	4390565076	0102626036	3108791306
6026870139	5865664540	5558514025	7898706436	1457663549	7157208288	5090662815	8262268319	6561511457	2896949545
7890898508	0777606800	6401578514	4090061416	1321380177	5164874024	4709202954	0020240976	6480518629	5004035350
0867291581	2014937656	9504864456	3826690802	4199053682	8278047209	0364000130	4888429542	3377512733	3023156070
4200861399	5998508860	6230870869	8226604200	4880805718	1029333971	5107012926	6920300803	1135562370	8650076594
0820325468	2516862525	8920453152	1512868607	1228969590	2848361849	5193630993	8556988095	2150059450	9495363698
7612067224	7896614761	8741699733	9650048584	9117293510	4402317681	1157737645	1118859442	6436409596	8417134340
8570202078	0769311099	9019404115	5409570180	2853802000	3258162782	3987586766	0625356107	3600871314	0096464061
3267999356	0474415848	8220994515	2138876441	9633461820	5496843021	5443231780	7506144739	3677285100	8902396215
0683466348	9601294489	8600590717	7970293907	8783500515	8517027256	8989289594	0518598490	1820700201	6084999065

4730967272	7572462216	3131437171	2433663917	3950467430	5184527131	2295023384	1870496501	3305354888	2734069462
0092610649	2469034420	3564920640	4351102059	7808736999	4012753506	6356813707	8807309033	7033700932	9160620938
0206600201	4042179045	6588851174	6733001070	2050062005	3370203510	4400000752	8672417896	5014312280	0278331503
7089917260	4495917411	2127660626	0138723678	5926590435	8251533840	1837790756	3535310087	1112440018	0244593551
0928707483	8950505371	6512008113	6032682011	4232718562	6861690722	1152823486	3154859408	4130374812	3480139969
6900202724	4707713819	1046338204	2154409716	7287216089	3445409475	9288386323	1056004520	0864902108	6290708383
6884100066	7313467778	3478530200	6275673011	0704119054	7032052503	5923388639	6827744681	4347880944	8416911633
0030082979	7535931987	3000458029	5328667871	4420130436	0258409136	3121050305	5546055362	9291346402	4078913782
6759470009	2895178940	5375094992	5874637930	3112448730	0136175370	2509951008	7453084721	8995417523	5439586343
8211901701	6066829765	6334003641	3848001004	0033970606	7068991019	0298375772	0526730012	4983314009	5357595074

5695682795	4612691110	2494611168	0129126215	9615915183	5264678015	5801312584	2563102831	8993059660	9192467584
9510079611	3119417114	0934749743	1680924192	5893429316	5070967363	8903362917	8323541112	0172043786	5669176537
4016595110	7147306239	6400412937	7110302575	8163767094	9751122933	1213655144	5667201986	7412365209	0689167743
9590173785	1069330766	1180289131	8422901689	7078706739	9931086338	6907320111	7192631531	9601537865	4095508417
5449522923	3711513847	0610664666	3576732077	0208681124	6740063635	6560043928	8362732407	9640981890	6005854230
2980600117	4800382461	0484110648	0284040208	4045261603	6575921647	5207003302	8750199054	3730749165	9028601155
9729772743	7284524135	8155618803	2843734880	2802699247	1939494140	3659303266	9856315430	9929510892	4417443381
7069107300	2701767599	0102328140	3966007155	3301710020	0008546041	5660961507	7110237093	0588301420	6805010410
0170607662	2693626886	2112131948	6023808467	9310513550	8853129232	5981568191	6812880325	1898635865	9553967460
6147743561	7841460513	3033700981	2668279984	3027417683	6269890353	1306695483	5272397666	0743348177	3113426332

5617216674	1110637869	4040279693	5820933518	5920269224	3500823321	9339167378	3583275821	6985757195	4808252062
4476187023	7133995751	4320414653	0495863238	5135083356	3914688278	7995421441	8157410159	3858102974	5441922441
2132066927	3746532091	8797404368	2270631452	4364411005	5564900305	5748997705	7083706011	3932157073	0774841381
7806713071	0126458870	2748474130	1557618889	3501724004	3643251434	2805863905	2923364003	9022423000	6007527905
2520081710	0011026006	0084981346	0217534213	5602909981	9522527096	5185125509	7323155921	0623202711	0105201003
1212837497	9435879833	8510438627	6149007095	6946095624	3204579433	9871167043	7983993371	5918017623	6309449465
7278194891	7647669660	2650866003	5183778923	6302144106	3391930520	7078046086	0772734184	9224898379	0246435061
8674917067	4068541301	0776078532	2382589721	7147905278	7488046301	9647997064	3217982024	0812307283	7815839250
5975648657	0102199455	0987079198	9409020902	9669892929	4970529091	4184008249	1718525370	9168342967	3194206015
3991328418	4145421460	2736685315	6171935267	6075355319	3355865512	2580762686	3653829875	0674500400	7841782820

3497260602	1803687260	4062428818	1325902911	5853601442	6656792397	2792536833	7555272791	5088848959	2081776458
9817242193	7619603738	0259712901	8126031162	8011317202	3137691597	8051848359	6472557558	9972191823	0685509329
5930313460	3951270103	3286808765	2448368373	8029351520	7200497600	2904473058	6005340404	8533189131	9640726069
9203845021	0338634067	6470040070	3160070722	1141402999	0801009010	2863022907	2900350700	6045500025	5002592500
1828947044	9201556144	0047037746	4514218099	3713556600	1747867783	3695860186	8185439089	0143017624	8869375425
8795974022	6207900406	8224989200	7581546416	2479911915	2212602174	4490569059	9288019132	0687023194	2906826469
2209045719	5678250936	9205002690	8440782305	9703906442	8716248390	5032053782	1160360227	3222820554	6280016049
5780521073	4502532001	0535021960	0436023411	7546308201	6006303784	0940530560	9030069846	8500594227	8813020275
3137623380	6332027899	6343265347	8811589099	8567610045	6267078051	0893068196	6049001168	3099344027	8225598690
0754629789	4421546254	1249486835	5842068383	1890924661	5904334825	8268259583	4231610694	2460361015	6109332333

5363968113	6165195797	5310458976	6141210939	7307472428	8077955823	5556084476	1853659766	9461733541	3261532022
4812646599	2348410038	2166793377	6493880624	0389323615	9066285592	6209523002	5480873930	8204666129	5639408865
0608220382	6692656236	1580670589	8681892711	8144292806	6639886191	1889608031	2576615299	3063384878	8362897049
1351422827	5170824596	0733505049	3801693332	3216118210	6213246947	6578132921	5217852257	7528168289	3337210451
6079517694	2236019952	3133339506	3107978298	3575323797	7608876495	6787938184	2904205769	1138343431	1357532752
6729747875	8633682187	8380843666	1168767160	3663104707	2119672386	0757083280	5879661491	5021114252	8628477266
7540336196	4913547411	8889944207	9255905703	9933212275	2300263356	2053108716	5517849006	5121591519	9148249757
9997029397	3558810112	9299519678	4104147037	1839133987	3244088540	7986545025	6102119344	8015809503	9677436768
1642371640	0698135750	6612229715	4635323445	6100121899	2894548544	1410978852	6283217723	0194933908	8336611340
9979985222	3807030548	7885564074	7169549285	3370291124	6579498159	4466593573	7248017429	5599912189	3479019807

7888187563	4547242067	1682433182	2289537882	4047259376	5284838225	4272272006	4509171002	7705271831	7839525257
0100377737	3377150239	0980667293	1407143607	0070768856	0230022308	1627192219	1516247579	1429509890	9840127011
2709823551	6818021711	3601939884	4075901260	5305570310	7007177810	8567490947	4805043582	1004004472	9966466947
1365243494	3917208349	6675426227	2891755099	5022158785	3365823699	2253160571	7113783056	9938463089	2837026273
9163611191	5526833034	7188434196	1069598240	4762755370	7367510232	6412571644	2925137460	3436204028	4037383705
6223038604	4270079258	6059988540	5351076303	0539031292	7258812701	3936257762	6281237319	8270357726	8002905053
7655249462	1962845725	1513897053	4936244447	0039476927	1410910399	2507295888	1746727098	7912005106	0628179882
2152968880	3127714007	8511288319	4626040197	7674632176	1038058320	1655211492	7663845721	4743456562	6419785353
5904729280	7150195377	3901503591	8300504296	0055569005	1431900508	0020010178	1902522535	0404204984	0578253217
8532288362	8001324124	9934626643	5945115028	7096747235	5524158250	5170465288	2128516084	1343230462	5626792902

1158605398	1713782180	4796859963	0688423983	6150506009	1116571447	3522160698	2105195667	5926953126	4888916103
7443374865	4922279491	7920506116	0720638318	7562771886	3146712796	2479639238	9258335945	7305321554	8388135344
5254089743	3430800644	5100688096	0700605519	2860895071	1920863586	3399381086	8025727606	3193960761	5566751998
4451343565	4241463373	4421007600	7527184055	7445043558	0882226768	1839128074	2269385383	4752322827	4084779556
9525968142	0973676008	6100259703	0061084119	7217015068	7803500083	6863000740	8231005320	8331794195	6049207599
4686256440	9704075263	5979074224	4623744941	2445640200	5343554434	4322972133	4304899420	1390228723	8613404267
4082146680	4976058904	0706292246	2430326641	1325421975	5302792939	7064815358	0259590894	5051583984	1966078968
7856039082	7934087116	9104103387	8376491388	4602303982	0421989663	7530436324	4531042604	3952524257	8831717930
3586034847	6828770945	0696739761	0532801317	5639510134	3645815860	5217375906	8160162554	7716000979	9736870888
3888382762	2497716359	3936980753	7207814827	1633263214	9158054520	5245636780	2342914228	7583957192	3920232506

1903372293	4424212994	7279733619	0522041211	7845093041	3004756663	3468597103	0697959742	2127887331	5640452320
6142693696	2085605059	5451967534	8833089279	2733211757	3027254364	1980844330	3952921564	2866230666	4247502844
0912354296	7855069108	8084985359	4341512618	5903135931	0282333146	4432935824	1817833384	5251931462	7497156211
1787145781	0284821021	8782273816	0503867079	8533149090	2686336024	4033496878	0283000245	3244937088	6547590658
4400687055	3282798827	2283861022	3435421458	4534167948	8638799199	3015735215	9286351381	8605593311	9075317469
8025142804	6617200200	0694184901	5507344150	7172398536	4131593305	3440652007	6704056253	1362500611	2900302224
5740148495	8750932084	1350020030	4007452251	1285100082	3235070250	3625320869	4007200134	7380302053	6905036325
9907349173	4199441905	5683592305	0699175317	7292462199	3028686618	7548977999	1691789237	4419264257	0941039132
8623507580	4205460741	1026557606	7259525938	9636331691	2558170885	9290013799	0154187045	9950842750	0276176795
5228044752	4617729448	7566303794	6045922914	9250444700	7587498896	1588559235	2163189888	8927628664	8699911963

0300908703	0807899945	9582033031	3159490411	8194262533	6312169895	2864018805	5050628339	5560397304	4879767026
9491081267	7408930007	4089008833	6303430723	5711270513	8301383927	7023014304	7290840818	6280972566	1418409590
5825899132	1126974300	9782246921	6717141212	4538162763	7395222563	7003585559	7116070071	2708891259	3408194015
6637072321	6165436100	7433406033	1328838517	9253088918	0585827686	4397470224	9216112426	7690356397	6092987881
4191631739	4832259848	4969847488	1563002246	0443113874	2597457668	7921694865	4279413142	7860645613	2777207067
6847499053	6074124385	5423666590	9138997216	2747923506	1215086909	4443503918	6070124459	2082519950	5551319703
0563399685	9964443254	6285743728	5047960818	7359750233	2963828380	1692159255	0321958342	2885928120	4092668951
3440795348	8108069682	4990203396	6547230522	6634968008	9054010827	3486500848	2852907782	3064716854	0837704992
6743014605	2804795690	9836375212	4850066855	9700839085	3462374204	2120505944	3771713934	1457602186	5834681936
1750000576	3818470406	1397144515	9920793701	9075582635	0471582872	4630565505	0525429050	6950155901	2469073040

4837400505 7466194517 1442300055 9516035454 2640068881 9299060496 4436771451 5499939643 2398930657 7720820185
3401749062 7051465082 2547274408 5268385783 1875763909 5002839400 3182591492 5775122325 5599345707 9876395138
8810300065 0935026091 3612212780 7839020527 1960529745 9705713040 6055502345 0001007060 5207190378 6447202660
3652573312 0892347254 8507276308 2037990486 6494092360 1150060829 6009592025 0850208970 3050030566 8020629683
0433220011 0691508411 0003100820 8493218420 5700481074 0980609640 8738920289 2010260060 5078151636 5626085078
3139585075 4111548068 9215080215 7268488025 7970615870 3506670607 2965880207 0258142429 5215309523 3020830173
0757115000 0714506320 1102815111 0711114072 8175779041 7203000236 3703765969 1857617264 4029810991 9057091851
4432606325 3377284695 9635229904 0066834435 2163750548 2213844851 1816906001 3633861401 1402707399 3217706005
8078678204 1288079366 0592994724 3315536578 3578909298 4701558099 4724851679 7103043782 5180681275 1853499371
0450902729 5068177377 6722562900 8532670000 0144169408 7228572773 4089730808 5412285606 4166650397 4895856028

4380665028 8548010506 3140144821 8773744605 2678423638 6128730795 6964234744 0530270064 6380065000 0770453237
6021201100 4044855238 3350041454 2008800170 1601944211 2425658091 1530306530 8454253586 6668400974 5690522688
1534157725 0795025781 2333808380 3303710186 5220096935 9570100334 0920808832 6052535747 0271326532 2775747012
0008873026 8078300100 1353305076 0322024050 2500606508 9059710930 5297102882 8534800003 8204121575 2093600065
7429464404 9669648247 9772121603 9297455184 2868498733 1732070406 3219376626 5349943968 2419510159 0937568392
0156118022 0000680703 0000825727 8920078125 9064461053 0030528503 6302107492 6809997621 2097290704 3039914355
1625470470 4101501470 9570891104 4658176987 8078782126 7708428714 9926995623 8253056573 6537195404 4684155609
6416043735 7426361554 3220155419 0562684874 7597710419 3156363694 2897308139 9781097491 1877776028 0925288717
5317128884 1660850728 3989911140 9954012827 6450394892 0663430434 9245729651 9042876690 8663993110 4229001702
7442760700 1089922667 0700024672 4989203970 9990068000 9086296136 0997069924 1580022992 6680070966 3050453341

3313150984 8333496634 4071948890 5848994207 1422177282 4402587356 8357464713 5312239659 5448619794 1067469627
4223076870 7627924183 1400521150 8731480602 9935126487 3017611965 7459128109 6126922461 7800840895 1081924917
2391167429 1942055040 2213566074 5018402735 6002769725 4228352947 1661092924 8222096201 1943649469 0006651690
1559119315 0526525070 8596835471 3814019013 2744003250 1329915278 0763808327 0343056056 5432734621 3730793514
0854673004 0705090753 1708000894 1500040652 1084504039 6609906319 3097707825 5772086670 6670906500 0771033530
3428858678 1482220281 1760138715 6057770063 9249461286 1983734043 9182228676 0127443690 6351951326 7175271878
7129808039 3300002020 2385055713 7600721002 3008063822 4972057198 5471101060 0940645000 3670560048 0202000007
7024502450 7458324807 3023495140 9667997553 2161505269 1202341755 5895296084 2346317652 4710942888 1783037476
4990512110 4806046290 0046690102 6805100986 0685996502 2506060428 0588300630 7323495800 0140158547 5009354955
0020270241 5260691058 0004462025 1159139048 2707874030 7365381090 2069970624 3462757952 1858002607 5388183755

6909952006 6797388003 4352645080 1736168864 0606085347 1721812064 1142553573 6990259289 1202765237 5013728240
4306489126 4312613016 4973791160 4879777763 3632586350 8643423856 6760759210 4760022457 9188562642 2888540073
9485010129 2526748206 7501843600 3792248558 9592763841 6963290638 6350984170 0043902765 8620518091 2538988549
5470311428 8226500237 2000082390 8807359410 0178746806 3941302017 0030662711 2029692360 1032780080 5254585520
5471324420 7240013520 9743734620 6484545813 3296564367 1898723367 8128700136 8611888645 7991863697 0925058508
9016203561 1925238376 6666852749 4738044926 1175796747 0049259713 6866421572 4732670308 0206958972 5404443684
0994370709 7546989482 3570911462 9846480724 3797731210 6086810605 1755225606 4290842244 5846423921 3880984852
3323546439 3076495234 0100931812 1277062689 2061670142 2008198297 4422459298 0774300217 9891614934 7564624622
5906489415 2824922687 6194638763 8955731673 9704915799 4024256006 5349626691 2297813327 2901510873 1028373674
1591600918 6046138301 9937607760 2592718500 0603803641 0069047539 7071631293 0980805882 9103505618 8613750505

3026260675 0421448330 0737625594 1737593799 5248664766 7984582796 0987161214 6236169620 8279179190 3522227192
1836441541 9015896089 0217265532 2871986387 7919200633 6907659897 8680510260 4410240089 6252616296 9275386835
0000778103 8100002360 6509060183 6813601986 3065966680 7077715662 6635586308 3021859586 8230601920 8403522880
8340182749 8640713656 5756953265 3106133806 3594634860 4995059153 6113018487 4526119979 4414443318 4639345058
0317026168 1803751195 7152617257 4672908231 9342169043 3665322645 9057995726 8212120661 0798194073 1358087715
5817486247 8814353610 0308316354 3211216469 5090661277 0950239663 9388145762 0104113757 0339974544 8718112305
4337200595 8656744023 8420875041 7692719968 1940856213 7672508728 3230506330 4080550000 7360129938 3089750833
1222989912 1489728328 5510718468 3041272411 2307341774 6133182638 7806100052 6202364004 3434854026 2200804498
3698884096 4608896465 0807560161 3879039073 2029121472 9164960186 7859512914 9486783806 2889443692 1221220794
2899333071 4938939611 9233986655 9413015829 9009213124 9586005224 3809122487 9999881162 2925033654 2210743615

4390979398	7150430185	4987118325	0075603015	5612129847	6154622270	9206192817	2438220516	0709260882	2255613664
2292058119	7906461179	9806157071	0394804288	4546289735	0641620386	5666257292	3612317138	0536671224	8579307291
2171820768	9794296685	3369724290	8817484360	6459748870	0232317231	1805513153	1882031661	8009496563	9983429502
9290140806	5859880369	7542657074	4397495556	8524808060	7728283439	3348445423	7117661221	1503997870	9349567184
7193572769	3755245148	3809708087	4942501257	2793374407	7242251821	5267618489	9845531009	3850984247	6790322685
9924347350	6170003651	5312931661	0201164015	9703771700	7227336112	6310943662	8115681290	5327752711	0540147939
4174850560	0415757402	1770749115	9800900608	4132504009	2703534106	6790490046	5353910146	7400470260	4851799868
6629930170	7710646783	7027269352	1102544600	0640040347	9578181960	9450022174	4004250428	1990912358	3190141762
9242615453	2853336750	1930521688	5730438902	9842643308	3989167518	2843202661	4747680667	3564577349	2946797484
9770590739	9323343040	4380053098	7310283095	9029544470	1993800112	0659210812	7011755644	6445391485	0268607482

8698721475	4961380328	9973524369	7684166419	8166248583	2886446523	9559652924	2839510378	0789119611	6921698495
6098105585	0716912030	6912377059	0018005701	9084487812	0309977605	6173909017	4044440085	0005853410	7777680555
4804848326	4529539182	8781580380	6121471807	3806820203	6529895508	0361014320	0890107133	3190776654	0656470025
2235826279	8962568864	7261658945	3722984039	7062493245	5559314302	2436924829	5933982536	6971692626	8480835016
0003509716	4010532602	0430050954	1858619122	4860606292	3347409638	0646700688	0543212993	3718250083	5700603767
0616619152	0847871427	1784846115	3857597498	7294404181	3937265283	9789733616	3372824781	6544720817	4336880210
0816817446	9346594736	8954083970	1139568544	3138458427	7426595272	2400659966	5642675940	4711950271	2842683950
7251672038	3757111734	1155164229	7687140515	9070741990	2386253671	7484367633	4732782438	1186693208	1855806224
6636611355	9612564540	0093005177	9426770824	1310345300	7610525463	8923103576	3789481202	7125442101	8863132638
3341488015	4991238930	6572903328	5084355217	1247949555	2918916796	8105371068	5356790691	2539919452	8089264481

3146692577	1623462210	0648347258	6208749748	5621753931	4123190259	9276685416	0734263714	7435814932	5120173831
0275769718	2218467572	2081115846	5485265932	7456966875	5266924500	9038104991	2715730467	3887155932	0496827224
1129973353	2063122552	7164389855	7210744330	2772998587	9726681514	1030742707	8877808518	3678224112	5590201288
5091567539	2619572845	1473103764	3459493819	9819684585	7482888732	8909337114	7965812495	1409845424	8507491056
5437724533	1441040780	6995152965	9784404043	2128967043	7516063576	1893834449	0942672051	9448427156	7841258979
7119041696	1250251842	2453244486	8443330320	7086160680	8473740528	8747061389	9561247393	9070509987	5308068882
1368219967	0458178445	1532086568	1095781138	8980832016	1714200080	6939970510	5001076050	3026369007	6646062872
7057301195	84[illegible]9881187	3049606963	9128002375	8981368090	0862419292	4430260866	7584826661	6548468751	8176230332
2898838134	4739570907	7428037928	3662600862	6994800832	1347244454	0209449484	6398947384	4573346254	0702239420
4652580678	5172260726	7485360505	4461753371	0364905672	3082938174	9008644590	0311160159	7908691751	7553549930

7608231778	7051181066	4656594982	4961377461	4616540054	5005191892	2706190958	0573896806	8446532101	1258593166
3305322763	8333179165	3641612994	4042070226	2502257547	7341860637	0002904981	9863624676	4056206025	8976547057
8577622719	8815606214	9188544983	2643507053	6156363221	0218376873	7791294149	1775463723	6427731312	5050448321
8825738744	4578628133	3078652776	5240511735	5413855754	0530445964	2152763332	2917376005	7257172424	5906696383
4376635566	9765056548	9282093014	2690883570	3361030756	6133730704	4453694040	3618843189	7123221548	4892140205
0045132464	4828299841	5226568159	9579088556	4742743795	2631573074	6110212050	8372725380	6758374434	7808076542
2693275341	0201039964	8755057117	0518837737	0059374277	0068556694	3093122915	0516947441	4016017462	5060981895
2122821196	1693604283	0555019387	4875118176	1522698303	2098885026	2308954136	2289328667	1057499719	7109819367
7011465505	6859683688	1212028928	1545371566	4301178016	5654211063	7558016642	4114360614	6208117348	1252874294
6579609904	5377797086	3509625355	8988644604	1062557868	3812050978	3112232099	2813712887	3222632452	2875266341

9990981105	4031854201	6455842924	2548992257	8788006016	8202734861	9571860158	1121836943	2806226064	1159799429
3241130470	0455479271	1613025169	1919983853	7103670095	5663307853	6057515557	0959852239	5928535593	7020590522
0752876773	0125292626	8624958435	0096957894	5147441474	5363358616	1140546053	9398299926	0533404965	1761623542
6228897456	6604698124	5969863110	4690175359	9219866194	8580944340	7214128147	4729405732	1672920783	5749951278
9352925559	0978069370	7080097753	2719072384	7739800365	4795483137	9520189610	7454754957	7585501049	9901717440
6419081157	6290688815	8454951933	1153964342	0700443626	5592844665	6722621763	0716163060	9532417646	5065157913
1684635403	3438999508	4453228770	7477424951	9139982282	6439591417	7678763069	3066398063	9421551861	4515840135
9700061472	2260396239	3801088355	4418152418	5030757612	8793208898	0163864997	5770597756	9537241252	2743504903
7619758888	6633887240	7605356889	4825869598	8567665588	2696019079	2750278949	9558196538	2687324643	1464538563
5074152782	1346775266	1380373121	8059282713	4017359832	6627551984	6447969146	0966815959	9895316457	9893670167

1689329514 7601059484 7108200929 4852976076 0144857298 0699221849 1751410968 8030548789 3327079550 6867432581
8275453225 7690773830 7313853007 0046669835 7972330054 3487461250 0530305161 4747245540 0007724049 0020361035
8414511222 7847231434 4244546837 2987208943 5876947782 8982532906 6428652083 7119908365 4691235465 6490890715
5611299138 4217270324 3132029948 2075703727 9134558625 8085227307 3627360980 5549700068 2837597955 6801897496
0434479935 3166415795 1875186852 5122270538 0926524463 7587951321 1787350653 9246907796 1308150845 5285600669
0227349308 9501409866 6727456648 7345448101 8275456864 4642402460 4086205103 7507829549 7213976931 4088727298
7433746280 4238393001 0030069061 0455606440 0023279791 0963730217 4140306233 1792666349 8909399561 9632002350
5935630251 0200252702 7630299822 2714508811 5743852010 3783137430 6106911558 0649509375 0420553667 6521978122
0908446184 4497168610 5178205127 1466006002 1227277851 0152022358 5911938130 6224517774 1607288522 4555116559
5221442588 1108569512 0840513634 6593778339 0674358179 5462164242 6705310184 2537720146 0223836565 3981443765

7186848959 7864003525 9855608871 3879553500 4732555843 6342626791 6910923895 8571826267 0290412959 2940625761
0102570800 9331701334 5879831144 5026220626 5973055178 9176667249 0716200530 2701020099 0888061336 2972934557
8615844881 2708705073 5889469175 8989565582 3253021461 2416879612 7451273578 4100069300 8080000759 6766959761
1409098603 4250054740 5569375633 3873043305 7178287737 6626989254 8800673285 8610633017 6646814398 2702726891
3955935885 7835263171 1955986437 3028235756 6758922023 1420622067 3705026412 1248307128 4019754014 9632291604
0823820665 2956093397 5825361576 7037944987 9860694341 6059430846 2757417118 5250372507 5621085288 5253392855
6226591318 6420144451 1839071409 8309337737 2336225340 7430563065 3423136904 1525759374 4434157595 4306060214
2584532324 5123759654 5567681626 8928382123 0604777274 0636546497 5280510037 8120796184 7897844785 6926991068
8239363532 3426904451 0433710065 6645606200 7037552053 0091700004 6279798032 5169759560 9068580242 5641082048
9527789815 0577062957 5078330407 3328856228 5533154434 9449973114 3105942267 5435796722 1929173475 1838471402

0037865896 9675925213 2439875754 8092472266 6675057780 8185923270 6476051699 7847960790 2106615814 6673325976
7206252973 6151452612 7842972640 0210396890 2046015321 3077780165 6184424194 4213807893 4711508274 0357430733
4677923021 0051518744 3380391314 0180807643 2734316061 4215680316 8882656732 9738127315 2816320056 0898352877
2000287469 6238325237 5253582994 5218477934 9886534372 4807288970 6750387535 9553820462 4747664378 9823931373
4273775565 2773709045 4203594402 0965871585 6316860577 3904675535 6305435518 2722231146 4217767286 1511082610
5423854343 7710135023 3514743577 2148796691 8893128387 0169242967 1001049891 5444948839 2789000782 7757253728
8174643873 8281126352 3231261957 9164988728 8572430007 3225845006 4151863272 3850860446 3750679716 7736919777
0740090040 4087110040 7627903917 7834980830 1864258014 9673181685 5533772962 1104686456 0269006647 2106301650
5485462789 3646764913 5371389252 1615223200 2749653068 7713371200 6921183163 3784017796 0391345641 9906619654
4683603965 7791336178 4615766894 9853407749 4985433824 7684417882 3926089028 8700547300 0065846625 4132513789

7840001077 4266715308 9376976586 4074389628 3012007816 9262510561 7856047473 4043927657 7668058477 1387725860
6895400490 4799944505 4300807635 0160680179 0823909223 9891059730 7689741622 6801478390 9015601947 5192521593
2464628942 0482736188 7012755095 0950222889 5606005110 0416246500 5024942565 7394832143 4615879376 9600272117
2838309335 8078447577 3209835997 4232609883 4090379370 8318284581 7141029756 3875332495 8564819359 9256650923
9592623621 8678238038 2818816084 6725210249 0014986777 8033751253 4813555555 9352120010 3176310207 6615416707
7087165730 1197840963 9024348530 1880768941 4194441398 6167477120 3894801881 6672826741 8171029211 2629772594
4513377198 7705848034 7189051874 6115726503 0441097614 9390002083 4015647478 1791534006 4314212554 2992505804
1704522822 8556537580 3556284358 4276501506 6412726736 2474009754 7129633424 2218622174 4038366872 9652717265
8025535112 7848630978 0100304600 4002693550 1480029405 9008022601 4400067903 5077551425 8006963900 3054058049
4249810039 4143788636 8934673714 9512049099 0154037177 3633950229 2513465738 4776784773 4306713230 8543462208

8496068092 0513433314 7208920005 0100103400 4614078089 4004054025 0374620308 0488403667 6100004077 9283127366
0107141669 2895020787 3180200133 9882372009 1678058224 3700918751 9285558914 5136853848 3912791281 7091654726
5164532783 3770003127 1823259657 4983653584 8743810470 0851374983 4449782464 5970319926 6276320172 0540413165
0539503697 2758462808 6065105037 8432976194 7885215808 9444737826 2615400712 8542386356 0751514945 9035330195
3800492165 7072887934 8258832321 4237646631 9959401926 6120005879 4800881433 2563332604 4015557711 7434666768
1733629852 9582271239 5315919924 7605991424 4168339042 1389642263 3498273037 1887374824 6557788135 0759564572
0471835897 1948058926 8903913765 3699933979 5108551399 0357744951 2977678186 5436350561 8881326625 7145394361
1102505893 0790199929 9473615246 0529336680 8303418495 1405652334 4961066283 2034833172 0623262888 0458890088
2862479628 9481782692 5572828814 1623601271 9622270074 6126216472 9731163111 7385139090 9895178066 3316208793
3144542614 8565229373 6896770857 0[illegible]36427577 63[illegible]75[illegible]7848 8484576926 5514785685 9967460239 8158727903 4762837325

8800349365 3153015743 8550961632 4156362436 6 43802961 7147776830 8907040561 8049329410 1885597073 4395980137
2277930852 6803904126 9464270085 6406710401 6244898446 3718166825 1088139282 4646912494 7875049009 3241719595
5420526716 6857554249 8557732967 7013693145 0608872074 3905528754 5356695014 1929429773 8579338370 6932394164
0757438881 4551358307 8654516013 9250654301 8431306145 5787469330 8143965816 7932886953 4496361876 1896168899
8692041773 8043214568 7754470306 7533462509 1692570620 2092630869 6713321675 4444383059 3667681909 8785011567
2379167679 6380908470 5433249066 6677818189 5903602824 2310996793 9683004095 3183342759 8784816432 4189976422
6872761645 3112821770 6705665120 3957453134 7473779944 7996817744 1204717053 4048415029 7010785963 1908730173
1007216001 5730757492 5569700481 2085500442 3303250080 3200074740 9107689120 0399769919 7490563050 4790633923
9347151093 3401416690 7102034595 3419177407 3249602913 4276019874 1419565081 3396447959 9654574783 5709429877
2685061834 7061877496 9594684793 3414872151 5434222965 5507685981 4382040176 8712682054 6256753926 4979885123

8123280723 4521266540 5827800999 0100705470 8629370086 9674935510 6501109181 4775204700 2748300549 7470000826
6754845743 4669774443 8247465130 4076011391 0122652969 5842203072 2521324425 7958598198 2602509219 1236886095
1025493001 1087577522 9951760888 7059909205 7035043472 1813622368 4914806070 3416265850 7292185547 5481148367
7025881455 4679038452 0154653480 0708760733 9074257175 5613834585 9180640384 1257188390 6117606644 3501195613
7533099976 4544005432 1619886079 6397573948 9764417167 2534194127 3749552861 8982114086 0479854833 1214748028
3706488434 7613994654 9331176163 1388878250 4999155751 2503302008 7696421145 5245352126 4099111717 3096540324
4512561776 6654365346 1858314330 4040994490 0624805032 3200425782 7010344588 6383401689 5987017836 6671075936
1926031958 0204615628 1474914732 1231387168 1012221710 3675531179 9396404678 3311838995 9772819228 1844683259
2919269206 5496689239 2301000497 6166264453 0819057666 4499640637 1662623335 7326593770 6844408464 9918470064
8358055157 6246047079 1081153846 7224254876 2747370413 4926817739 4943441000 5868774475 2993688517 3396747979

0566768293 1326162180 7645442425 1562327243 9287204992 7581212726 5470968154 8723768313 9571724157 5827164313
8912502154 0760498925 4533361632 4622137696 7668467564 1400447262 1159646568 8975053713 0525107686 0725929665
1077329854 5297879935 6873001085 4849759529 6583043313 8558326524 0139390166 1270491628 3811024332 8974389615
5592646574 7360860964 9912030101 2899040420 9601605426 0302636969 9730248221 7841148032 2078065270 9682387894
1128324704 1336397757 4328215068 0997323843 8227609784 6861714854 0079386397 9365088375 4930485590 6726266465
6214830181 4817898553 7320546920 6003847336 9452263320 0310854473 8443401513 8171889437 9948450359 7577541439
0749292306 0650402999 8646900506 2103621430 5187407338 4400570907 2772306051 4740452908 6092111891 6068952030
8263551993 0549557905 8286758311 2498450967 9234390996 7321264646 2401628085 7902051000 8700200066 1059175237
3785195141 3014626503 7744487739 6030080906 6171478901 7102870189 0379200007 6002043335 5021884472 3250907668
1200519852 4564730236 7404363725 9634599491 1473132669 4484811808 1713682674 0460703179 2584489205 6500783465

3060564379 3660729078 7622927369 1610130402 8309890483 4863329748 0560255189 9792714659 8574649428 9075494892
4911803694 0896505867 3327881832 7113475465 2338972461 3392016164 1633602888 7546855555 7918144043 1292586017
2538325632 5252136606 2042532802 4422206475 6196321202 1396260028 5805615606 3642918992 0506920290 0559464720
4022109119 6020902432 8488272289 0905127732 5353543703 7763030782 7211121832 9703090013 8353010574 9380612254
0771014025 9248814547 2189495425 7798854025 8941149508 8806825928 1639538073 6719916747 7272674049 2223930056
4271262042 8602062006 5520478727 4289146605 5499208966 4956080024 9049200811 4964135458 2421017898 8119534740
8227570662 9722990456 4179847617 7612452804 4063705640 2265070280 0542464894 4833984051 2298511044 2758720580
3741235738 5864051365 7167833072 2431562088 3569475755 5416781747 7214580403 3654607443 0880673284 6260752269
5951784291 8326149867 1326610495 6508341998 9429988559 6008304218 1950763645 1112248557 3716209125 9476504450
0798083344 4307052770 4963132899 3554622990 1641281690 2402262151 8454991074 7117454087 5416249904 8618429326

7277431642 9471445958 2659180417 0852205831 2264306378 2946730867 6055668657 4800226385 0126545412 1947588036
9660884690 2316042952 4027694959 1776112961 2761756656 4848582268 7892797443 8155044548 7612895279 6093867925
0875745834 1027346586 7068514977 5568666013 0859293805 2325444221 5008250391 4696615609 1194272794 3059248227
1736846033 8508160631 3695800146 4350948290 5222713169 2800874167 6311738586 2214721753 3128296296 3627908812
7517744426 1382844934 1955091727 3015441307 5823878841 3984945762 8765246887 6010880544 7881069589 8957138002
3522770037 3513200965 9077070525 0748004505 6257306690 0008701943 0000471930 5786152586 7300927633 6005930069
8902372896 9172623482 0910609653 7888842191 9493423630 8023176936 7963330480 7961006144 5304972247 1697739152
4707650169 1699749025 1110657730 1114557320 0660083896 5130018744 0721555504 6520574616 1213072452 6162039711
9494377923 8855037083 5761813871 9425944681 2159109830 3477094367 9174023683 0090295462 2074424348 2784296877
3212374822 7364232831 9612186278 6963717123 9702097015 3632637765 8891324995 3885277985 1225413252 6328113623

0087340004 0189018204 0012917016 7025705061 5809009020 3016538208 0390608900 6023804006 0600850100 6007708010
0343348864 5904691134 8295817162 3045454990 0197530078 5284705787 9838175589 8607933957 9010891584 6196059203
0040051501 2062012547 9705000192 5227402294 0080663401 7820046823 3566655000 0907009180 4949020440 0616606090
2697141495 5208625035 3565093875 0834493927 7530196298 7983862923 0248792005 3656279056 7527572260 8843672962
4060379069 1543616234 4312806904 2787474531 2712921069 6559709894 1286740730 5018566220 9164019126 4040120960
9486762711 6489969999 7204427543 4365737254 9000610978 6383998176 1378074125 0776279979 1532615781 4935955983
3997933392 6554130441 9642440018 9838796613 7079107409 8384157289 3626321550 4952079148 0829948715 6393405551
5986936581 5498074857 1601049116 8770767809 1365800306 1757063440 8200256803 4525672966 4580409920 7901933438
0764707794 2838093473 3266512697 7678920977 5357640964 1350929484 7210574967 0472694252 1793430836 7948622201
8453479806 2000950905 0989245091 6489212011 6867545418 9744015702 6343974215 1740003553 0828183597 8040496002

2284830299 1249191699 5149994993 1647631374 2334079293 4215467638 2310628193 2540130356 5569257042 4119960375
3286324731 0438725900 0048076787 4640882800 2260033043 6378083544 1801019733 0070009908 0001741560 0318003703
8605526091 4249601739 7565514041 8484955770 7140178852 1225276048 2786933730 1949349121 7529311158 4730399249
4247302507 9847500407 7081850404 6436024972 7139000501 9134022100 4251204982 1403090174 0133855922 1020793487
8567120935 0544296884 9989638800 3913597215 7892001432 6384380056 5320452941 1864879121 8970893603 0575071733
1246768810 3981586839 3450208108 3463997317 5913827922 4115076036 9040230358 3227071654 6957901989 2598659311
0710595052 0995710911 0260031395 9055081261 3963252367 7418275443 7587305738 2302203528 7053336751 8207034310
2280487100 0104269396 7468007001 4189344451 9031543570 9925644139 1285090725 6437725531 1349974308 9477362190
0200579500 5237500631 0006293169 1861352247 6220273176 7329019394 0385105500 7310311062 8245015910 6031918548
0010082124 7078714602 3116203500 0060702977 6300137402 7319006430 3200830690 6607034642 6608009650 0097450500

0339812055 1599436087 0054965313 6371794927 5492654777 0240502289 3746616054 5460602252 0561458184 1364799422
3558495069 4868750432 9704043343 1841065019 2770587959 2452496092 7751258331 0703532029 2815766096 5379505100
8811930707 9834912383 1706495019 2048504452 6802486283 1314679530 6549034667 9004542900 5064859360 4415231261
0248046980 2400079166 7000460600 0220500040 0010944609 5062200470 0735823023 9105000009 5700140502 0330701003
5715395507 0061472245 9044204886 4842573773 2958746247 3816419379 7345900635 2577702138 7393023774 4287916227
4131805681 4355420186 6009593348 0700921269 0757079200 9066184979 1322289793 8323163025 4491806441 0937844197
0605881483 7385318378 2795214909 6630083831 5261892575 1088490031 1443790383 4140910736 8224747638 5684500603
7629446905 5882390300 7796488377 2866382472 7500708680 3861023834 7557046422 5593451216 2999612577 5263849163
5282408072 8670067263 9072180385 1340665005 6314600200 1609054023 0071408560 0076432062 0038310007 9109203232
2607404826 0065580750 9373661445 3026582400 8886680006 7737012406 2844890117 5390803055 0672321816 8386160670

6409598272 2668723783 2247639293 7154666880 1377920304 7923010038 4372539813 3203453815 8416059623 9851621319
5303396557 2452650207 9512881821 0963029820 4303520532 8732406522 7639004075 2070635982 0037906509 6790107025
0510870651 7805902301 9041241615 6443037392 3052657053 0540994786 3160041951 3427410083 9708522155 4080038336
5746950807 0896138716 4031450055 0618533117 4042928030 8752870784 6008000247 3720005007 8536066550 0015881760
2661994254 8237991744 6746949836 5124911133 1916030187 5325494192 1767246469 2928836411 8686404804 3047952785
0200010200 3668550364 3007200209 7059540920 5036809824 2603627909 0105000637 7000050730 5307000030 8107090002
9736321902 4717630680 7358185303 4471155986 0009803361 1006489837 5424528802 4219173405 3350064503 0550651441
8833328203 6984902509 7962830289 3199416495 3250106760 0050262038 7846994005 5002901022 5510210188 6800094601
0030943000 0008201662 5001496061 2300910766 3390367007 5069729172 5893070013 4048704073 5090000509 5845368003
5083000906 9441576016 9955251364 3124026929 0335964920 5876228874 4580890743 0054985365 6433505018 0034005505

5502370403 6477273163 2827043292 1316498280 4673717845 5181863621 7655060530 1000002215 7836298396 2692063280
0985012507 7979182037 6360009405 0002069909 4140382220 7226540216 6684620722 7568200993 0717306057 3072803282
4868109521 1771061209 7215115454 7848271278 9027127414 8979435390 3908206400 0116507777 9949121205 0002375224
0693071265 0511223710 7009744370 0888046269 7837601986 3752808993 5870003948 0345415239 0589577336 7599782006
7182655063 6085958277 6584687685 6008010689 0015009528 3229191980 0923039984 6115976270 4580023072 7114235675
7875519395 2187372425 8572566617 7961467090 6234433505 8362722531 0010281326 6826173942 6638960133 5521886724
3870028800 0280008004 1880024760 4020741050 3400541003 1572400806 0307006200 3604889008 3270062960 0308402005
0361701916 0373679603 0800700006 5633040840 7826070030 0066902025 9050000500 0030008737 9303160004 8655477268
5200000748 0273000090 8300000605 8404550206 8540242058 7167306714 5900074640 2090605100 2830614549 6105700064
9934349223 6083751413 0383303523 3089430606 8037261829 5352198756 7339102184 2550438998 3344987861 6712723260

4865106030	5695319017	2372245343	6230711001	4744649119	2559449066	9455899935	7086006105	3491480058	3655924872
7320523919	2994541440	1703009868	1764032202	2274043876	1233688810	1301360313	6927451977	6555600452	9081252771
2212317184	4019978997	9764116128	3359509477	4449698940	9527274684	4339324093	2562186338	8523310270	7764135174
2830063502	0480080054	6409834410	5429709705	5536964390	0083304165	4840076005	0355009507	9270462896	0117594151
9081988986	1655695716	3582165070	6389545408	6787207431	6597036229	2000977510	6846525609	3468607246	1154236800
7932237016	2950056001	5852911449	0593096017	1043908040	4501763815	0478549100	5848528027	7400885483	1318602232
5985369780	2462919413	2513840124	9502083349	4985045345	3144965022	0092955725	8597029748	4759724951	9586380824
2353640494	4360258762	7004284008	9594440693	2590821248	6878980977	4404711214	6536173973	6552260287	6387222954
6634562443	8712655209	3910259528	1219121982	4387393064	7041226423	1858090850	3150867229	7435021302	4919169208
6136517323	5466672680	8787905755	0166289027	3666619990	6283152855	4043756582	5670600802	6606656936	2967669115
8789167679	6776704082	1723579453	7317254684	9717386315	2758734243	9490863331	4619393405	5025956872	5633699859
9191677760	5002815884	8053059002	1700309076	0903847004	3235494606	9489093040	2040676105	5898098833	5019360727
1993532877	9960335242	0069335945	4429251309	3203426186	2338610372	6788204603	6372471995	2008176401	8429899742
9263343886	4261512404	0947781853	7081320683	5680540073	8774349202	5560426478	7001590321	5622155611	6377800442
5954102493	0318113195	8462407521	9974719878	2403962476	2443234613	2992459940	2912864511	8240117747	6274185644
1432881300	7535110819	5022336939	4331550851	0953717186	6002722881	5183678317	7942014891	5581810027	1628514382
3053188699	6243844946	1401826400	3210736351	6001904589	5965994955	0535340804	5159917979	3364842139	5667329805
3267421223	4227498803	4156331000	0643107000	6175377088	3695354038	1364850586	3465042133	1232751415	5035953058
3633108408	4271782645	8444382966	7491360300	8952253928	8036245794	3926386629	9557384113	4252639426	5938168369
8501747480	8697427524	8478006395	0912741820	3135888712	3206266698	3288963962	0953845972	2813931491	8462109574
3909880313	9695499700	5974502828	5881143042	5101710090	2075103054	3320808229	4002774763	7859734723	0126304023
9286508205	6948658802	9871655184	9148042545	5561240270	0969154306	8989339202	5463261459	9586694043	9495818317
9841557280	7610141731	8495783188	5481869419	1816356445	1009932130	8239125776	1145237227	5632335441	3677482412
7572528402	4158447297	0131670276	6402755023	0780606733	0371332731	0001607408	0830542681	4984422097	6206414013
7056246790	9890356027	7506005506	9274007680	5209514027	9156504025	5515433657	6809937160	0044512208	9032730783
1450250128	7708998345	2848604065	1409100680	4168462585	8178965530	1354092177	7730708882	6943994050	8422099286
8971445993	8862086385	6462451332	1334626416	7600003360	2571165242	8587523733	6898425568	9131998981	6054089044
7901590685	0459562358	2132842602	2190819887	5776921409	6640145756	2628308203	5252613565	6801343275	7294361281
8574679226	2002716783	5801023306	0066069803	0484305053	8941782339	7800026050	2904060218	6877107980	4053079549
1103110416	6012617233	3819638992	4948825126	4005189045	3735173477	0979323062	0157101766	8346774985	5938845584
8076280931	0462435832	9733431418	7415894607	8949366909	0117712300	0363000081	7810057645	6604329145	5744759229
8409336411	8262458975	2356410026	3987488910	2961606730	8894912451	6581262944	5443914384	9887690142	5551839163
7090100305	7224518916	3512974328	5349013534	6688113602	7107403346	4949505840	4944195334	5973734323	0824823597
9063268901	4968867923	3346208445	1725322051	4357413552	4487702867	8190621101	2467544354	2975335776	1347443162
9256050168	1253403018	6308939746	3561814184	9512013944	7267682891	5288403029	8168771309	4283688794	1529602283
2575675434	2092904089	8394641516	3510713635	6877136382	9118351173	1272683693	8022361671	8523511553	9109150116
3234860390	7563877469	6570230012	0614916882	3319456025	5631014517	6990843730	3595109156	1991448643	5579911726
9762236343	4830346162	2570216066	3070911651	5461820840	9062344865	1437396573	9823483491	5744714044	8146554299
0591600931	8685764309	1683799922	8435110694	3704623462	1826650493	1753198764	2771345089	0313481469	4915724104
4406014503	3427193208	5195419252	7543958993	8595630217	8634949261	2480172616	2472792456	6192239630	1617561017
0752184146	0880961094	3109751445	4945845257	8719806004	4115874287	1102178979	0233992638	1662093562	4162236525
2841730529	0087541780	9382706147	3990056394	2547028307	7917077564	6254316014	3986714643	0191595336	7231645646
1084687618	4214322218	0886951068	0260535008	9698554756	6289877841	7988389795	8877213317	7025088160	1643972612
4614911778	5115293534	7708532935	2230631089	9796295538	3852859818	7670742909	9415838985	2442833132	1196287834
6918844674	3157374615	7691136637	0203939248	7838039338	4390347707	7406290841	9780587031	7781148738	6631981349
6649462314	0391063559	9818103922	6339456943	1037774281	2323100786	7014565089	6341140395	7728868004	8787157654
6633138688	0543495595	6306350229	4752532614	0863918168	3815033939	8551021741	9335800984	2455699143	8805004831
4002834490	0930740810	3725494006	2830158815	4710022161	7148003850	8183405217	2807792860	7267776156	0561519378
2958870759	4370559667	6601544189	2937476760	7354269000	1193661367	6595850750	3634565390	7169627768	2964926047
8732373601	5018486992	3785920949	2680007939	7849322352	3823739414	3885147321	5378634101	3463221164	0691443974

9750457721 9492104135 0072931733 3983662069 5907470385 9668569741 8427300901 6687985529 0268562238 4954561881
5780813319 4351953957 3694636966 3958298873 6679035391 6341803246 0582077874 1026183529 5200494930 3684875236
8450616764 2219174081 2201860657 6034616846 1967479555 0093418585 5425231063 2883139310 7924247995 6373353575
3607770299 8097049955 8694029151 7513075700 5728979882 7251930342 6786471523 3780807108 9193244126 9240223359
0517071732 8903440533 7977485195 1890135076 9525681407 9094393948 0172461490 0174568944 7831364877 2915904614
7504300159 4272946446 7716877782 6371374364 1660853470 5075482832 0647406316 1218382643 1616434748 6448307324
9446954287 8464081663 1601233579 0574510516 1527087625 2109827293 5996576556 6540133943 5704559570 5189352775
4735642117 2884951547 5973596646 9438398316 0765244803 0288272166 1294544137 8616676405 5823283921 7741781432
1804522710 9412785908 7695496533 6587377601 2071418000 0421367650 5128047363 8190527197 2208057028 4738058257
1292275391 4020128578 5921314875 7273444169 1087457968 1086102792 5882753598 8716304522 7666641052 9311646231

6776793297 0839000346 4360403532 5457743608 3658566568 4310667121 2267920799 2094101524 4952771635 1060959055
4738387940 7317988036 7726195268 6287230091 7157155227 2972464748 8569939583 6302613080 4228560055 0255944558
0380220992 6087675789 0687210073 9517011700 4312131699 0211816179 8886946056 4601532390 7453227671 4932365193
0564107892 5025415866 6219910836 8300816093 4237733136 9973082934 9388972375 7507591604 2629826069 5586713299
0333594073 2043817253 4831657786 3371784986 2902515687 4609786316 4065929780 8439168204 9721642880 4681399600
4660832575 9294733614 8771084889 5819086766 6076976181 6673204902 3904756706 9658564883 9423439345 3212983998
5308903633 8983910401 7540213630 6847396525 8884708484 3695424151 4526890794 8252789972 6805282869 8573300679
6187888763 8088077629 9397192910 0680458975 4616800982 9233111917 9035723464 4277018946 9695275873 3016292507
9322350007 5937668836 7460214014 5155451177 8430692338 8486167197 8129126938 1548068206 5611225292 4966437607
6392715079 5227036784 3803632720 8261543479 6855917709 4077175045 2097371211 2078121216 6765315292 6135411157

6129364150 4863533925 2981867741 6274397207 7232062255 3512950301 6122723488 7054028093 2632493943 4518490173
1667176399 7463124299 0710312161 9032944361 9790267495 2796820155 7553018681 8962522172 6525842371 2079809510
4885740660 9418826641 5059057955 0615598951 5769677264 0524051001 5099880637 6257623552 9172947603 3130648061
8148714051 7702839239 5613522990 6626934542 8141416689 2704194574 6647415124 3248291690 8553207253 3698473949
4524417970 7767725155 9479338664 5972574209 5602698065 9357909222 2701709891 1315682780 8677371313 3057878748
8885959640 9297248944 2595233884 0578511717 3049385308 7635874120 3836580373 7170810820 6908737857 9884509662
0650580235 3432214286 9592676137 9666746579 2355784550 5054525686 0328784572 2261146294 1481391901 6054276519
1064511591 5624283734 1578305193 5805612087 5792359508 9150298988 8568470311 9429790957 9701325712 2220805450
7313352250 8983986796 5017774123 9335148616 5070172335 8611483497 7633284081 3507472640 8724083045 7490231481
7159704902 3394766523 8852257171 2244625452 4462615756 1409875293 0539137779 5360676407 3169730528 0954960031

2621381248 3794598347 0398422120 1049088568 2548446670 6939011302 5134628423 0742287987 2141347972 4445765825
8164810200 3325601726 2046992503 7577527818 4169890616 2189456479 8061923963 0876037815 0795532142 6966129690
0040776963 6602870597 5735262785 1388571610 4352077133 6511249640 4079332379 0973712664 9510999196 3739963551
5953713501 1487433813 0443139954 8305071141 1660812421 3730717744 3458694643 6378832300 3613964753 9181279568
8828336676 6006234161 2409247863 1674537034 1378687198 1628540342 9750046313 7285547735 7547330145 2917724424
8161665110 8857562190 0291483413 4318246966 2323481892 9555597751 2129460258 6045988246 9067517216 2617049244
2498536615 2946808793 7848217109 8946347356 4477977833 7437661765 8008076769 1587149441 9167678913 9435718870
9258670088 0612741390 8694643381 7389288254 4247648791 7739242691 2150713813 8448648508 9607636711 8684706622
3072366947 2782462127 3603922427 8805905306 6514419450 9356859660 7380645814 9013362235 4791079808 2659700155
8054220616 8299559186 7964692185 1336575527 0487035647 8432956566 7955811329 0361789117 7747662705 7865836192

7191754739 0680107739 3299071332 2017322800 3566035791 4475814704 1300382005 2559869986 6946327607 1771264700
7527994846 3263877622 6605759644 8926760502 3011325050 0180477245 9830209399 4479910857 3759149741 8390390033
0928305250 4893294258 6687851537 3437538277 8200683923 4771197888 4071676348 1773542715 7159290958 9785594564
0879879495 8588810078 5822983217 6203422573 2897615012 4567336187 8232626317 2727677487 4635221857 5255476746
8496802132 9887726852 3417757564 6501700191 8724615704 1959436219 2244098677 6550543104 1863353086 2695650561
4023845705 0848383460 8396002106 0143201564 5696113608 2534917163 8182922398 5374066330 9323474950 1233076241
9710243008 5342759292 3772546981 6437065552 7796340584 8129678054 3033441841 9245559314 1089847415 5257062577
0253184720 1551219017 2682871370 5220900500 6390047344 6727659300 9529303007 6403202260 2264964905 7800086202
1062760095 1051217422 5927474727 0314897056 3489881876 6973518764 5854140798 2464241118 7450046030 2130924664
3005225856 4221761503 8948608786 5796411194 9499359195 9218209867 1362597153 1604358335 4629266648 6979311039

1497882701 2092373521 8824865451 2642489700 0412908453 1013332206 8656058942 0948589981 5838263874 7399294352
7332003760 2070537018 7023681206 2171100604 1459508047 0180983408 8223830877 7905072483 0700443200 3903350282
4785374554 0071663159 4721171462 7473860507 6095507574 0596709295 7660407548 3732704361 1747782711 9684832912
0030005208 9590620439 5607013650 9895534759 8920945561 8602508720 6640961884 9044990600 7010773786 6805980040
3987333475 2152784522 7082462255 0765473418 2569667897 8868740055 7983593916 1549469840 9185330934 5949845335
4873018062 3589420507 6321376161 5042805370 0208045468 1080648900 1705490017 4000039384 9550480001 2609236005
4530976231 1361957994 2813265120 3513608634 7319475482 3123000185 7740827112 1522370296 4063494888 6600960315
6009940036 9885727097 2067460039 0492198024 0660995502 4050984506 6605883120 0807785050 9340045600 0601005092
7003459000 3280049400 4058030230 6462500740 9003693306 5707096972 0078505890 0004007293 6685007126 0400159880
7014718421 4474648697 3497819393 9474830805 7348476832 8994205066 9732644367 6697507982 3830939513 8533702398

7994020298 1184680432 1126814002 7860450058 1010273701 4080254633 2647506804 3016475560 8809506177 9060200706
1844826686 8959801567 8328311070 3006370969 0473560495 2153879940 8747923762 4651374800 8879183168 9405064124
6530342822 0957109347 0722093099 4088871007 7911210903 3253600803 9375050127 0823316794 1252358272 5007050024
1795098483 0650335310 9298780951 7322074841 2815863919 4619838917 7713426929 7762982060 0460362291 9747598028
2205484657 1015029606 1529441293 4003197794 5000880008 4178695578 2689169241 4761516702 3580504090 6272987457
2494251924 0222019936 9019707935 1897890746 0841202604 0433029846 2043776851 3047097640 5081140972 0588015266
5120809709 8400378390 5747338860 9603290565 8071201352 7137324582 3050759587 4122287450 3809412723 0109701505
1552900394 1330225974 5072434200 0030031709 3028652736 6802380500 9471070205 5060865374 3173940730 0219999051
8053885016 3583558563 7345035487 4244971747 4855887312 5474131024 5990744504 0071857377 9581169820 7634997414
1978800600 1200502596 0092890100 6342524063 8662374559 2400810900 7740634078 1860702178 1180970235 5543850632

4888045276 6776595748 8050861847 1252500972 0832450066 8418662530 8823330978 7413726794 8817697887 9123247831
0200147515 0039408375 0520207759 0806700077 0400000411 0492500100 1201100601 5085771175 2804488483 7195030570
5568830809 7050807003 8000356193 0956400910 8250203380 8000554078 3537089873 9000648534 0100868641 8406981708
3300323309 2115943213 8204737832 3001215643 3573389914 9383240719 7975923944 7995265316 8595473298 6794917252
2752222698 2578978762 5853202393 9690010236 0237201094 8589943804 2650234805 9807288817 4707008138 8775241401
5971916335 3430488710 7185039906 7741025709 8300545709 9266236480 5339013551 0118396747 2033451999 5951306419
3159415729 7926585812 4813059069 4462217020 9441559852 6728048916 9932270805 8377828090 7968162894 7659574139
6193428227 0000302901 6111957309 7211053717 4312892285 2117614751 4988402210 8722681891 2192694311 5353268689
4913753512 7390654088 9807286559 5300060100 2168680059 8800514084 9601047722 6916809258 5238560390 0354060896
0319297010 9974738409 7209414370 8043514164 8234005491 8153082460 6113851709 1186412105 0335061919 4414387800

3482226001 3724220827 1796874243 6051125353 6341483228 9425038088 0992662325 0610491629 4289803607 0999022665
8602096303 0375644008 4104390020 9503988053 0026006889 9060737952 5264220900 0083703515 0609488402 4604686821
3321650787 8896102373 9256306070 0252710106 0225039277 8783133090 1624390587 0682110946 7749340643 1320319585
8776011003 7044502752 0120024208 1058312645 2052279803 9080577002 9900907831 4407920034 1710725479 4020017403
9095772872 2796202045 7910544547 1825483384 7699894090 5586465636 5417624555 0517307845 6571619021 7194885956
4737406819 4397277108 7579954189 7638866078 4493195161 4845771467 7528367616 5210614042 6216917169 5770390627
3765305855 0650470936 3698406100 5104103669 7717335500 7083053571 6250579403 8400800269 0680929006 0189044043
2200995142 5687773288 9539145769 0746194733 6729463440 2786194960 4304428017 6719194679 7581703803 3026542575
4100501103 3762922862 6735623363 2281374644 1090271648 9973346738 1556344212 0366251655 8882786852 8432375925
7972861699 5224789631 1332653646 7509740517 5298862965 4163912395 5985452742 6475273852 7319193441 2816841877

2370629161 5235010483 0560983944 6029249032 1194481528 8459643129 2052531404 9142844298 7745099077 9420516723
6669043287 7020529249 1412817574 3592494658 2790662089 9024957108 0526107557 0271636270 7512406470 5039408952
6291302210 2870173404 0601507016 0061844382 6508207714 8205818663 0200032754 2791050005 8173460148 8060705102
0623700655 0989083785 2158432007 4520255728 8137001700 4090701086 9494376402 9906227000 3860371035 2081910000
1278718840 2492636774 5386719460 4366652105 2086792506 3977129327 9217657633 8769780230 4074249067 8065236366
6716507857 8728221860 1431806660 7377566121 8066835584 1636214971 8302112767 4901597915 5480573643 7317776459
0304539725 5446234327 5752995265 4075900781 1335991295 4235966627 9847108218 1973453384 3042106458 3575421374
8985964082 2174038608 1837202051 8925960104 3251307983 2505230435 0912630407 3200602080 0067040064 5670269092
8533950911 2098107113 3922859634 9816725053 0880911245 6972058502 4325148319 9221019702 0705304154 3810078445
7821809010 4646623042 3348063900 9900286449 8524010500 6302000080 8450822333 7159220720 6550970270 8723435207

9599821865 1807537426 9381836817 4494610713 2737543247 4324757660 4703711492 8416265782 4861198023 1071567015
8192597193 9009900070 9723371732 9494689715 5264902055 1185439938 6043647887 6711373865 6327431690 9203848841
3190140608 0879826047 1005050555 4349980930 0036712060 5077703684 8600092904 0201930126 8082658202 2054304100
0125376284 2940560239 5964609779 8988752216 1704003012 2330918244 2518471095 4425304032 1062096996 0584040600
7602749512 2929215394 8661282618 2610971614 1962472856 2116419165 9445230091 0541769156 9513995342 7983358142
2085237140 1108960902 0494925989 8989056609 3070951371 1673042625 2165898969 0543393014 4868590466 9771501589
1947605118 2107313125 0261690893 5394480372 2276796228 4102158954 7781742404 6574033435 3090351245 0777074425
8870784882 3162595992 3308161464 8509730996 1419745585 5956257707 7688849044 1259534675 7583869364 2972706890
3677154075 8804503452 1520856249 1904000470 0074023786 8151008782 1650308927 0115961002 2050572760 6056905156
7248444360 2122921006 0264727265 1560676442 2464439870 5203171716 0210893004 1978319573 8995639101 4159804099

8767882063 6287408495 5610946204 6952487156 0369121046 3674068564 1554037218 9392123657 7661807507 0937568952
9028553551 9372102293 1543436246 5314639231 9460607697 5245384227 0094659767 8307964461 8457393730 2980448171
4310560598 6421419717 1642400040 9591416755 5019500506 7913278283 7063213299 0910375524 2562055287 2292795769
0006358001 3720706010 1373203783 0003514373 7999753152 5920091110 4030018445 0604914903 3990228319 5059800569
4963426223 1737300310 8790957014 2374233306 0673588181 0768040388 7080035904 2341304210 3027972686 7690102809
6735008950 7522710709 0199793124 7275698646 5164413143 6043057098 5549034409 4256759707 3147419407 6160388141
4735007080 8288709341 2872052441 2059285591 9413982798 5785711067 0126106215 0041181221 5092971063 3190609169
8978902265 9344610780 4737055223 2306419667 4538705883 1368471144 8642556906 1800944488 3055632793 1468826876
3088016068 0152020651 0942060010 6024455746 6877409750 0600000064 0730000644 5836380090 2630105292 7638014190
3949969572 2819775785 3700400955 0681396609 0433676515 4023447397 7235429280 0148596896 9957928649 8803298310

0447687210 2077155448 6182125715 9768269026 6829876635 5379666517 4202492585 1633337545 6782171435 4503526998
3557287798 0380849608 9907913834 9733449665 1215550945 7217651083 7385729052 4076216928 5519334601 8093152669
0539980742 9010340810 2550745517 6056408043 9616412503 8447140424 4057203510 6760588507 4903550700 1094741890
1089691051 2949092293 5566881156 2473669868 3889763788 2499614335 5678967689 3336942130 2653107154 9131055094
3642960616 0580737190 0396496758 2415043781 1461500587 1279368875 5065735842 6163728862 2220933086 0788548652
0454474831 0630105431 6380190861 1901636734 4760208500 8629542890 5026567739 6589010222 8403082740 5525000363
9373575596 7875362860 3222795218 2322499716 3663858555 6680110038 1581033173 6947102133 0585893248 2229472287
7920577496 3065505360 1292023704 0108149613 0454602688 5709008270 4107767750 3710194451 7002153206 0449958603
3459000096 2499407484 1661254888 2252838293 0870036789 8580424184 5749079310 1017605484 9613133009 6151247714
8942803617 8099407525 0643760020 7048487507 9018275291 5789806289 5408750832 6255418460 0658484873 1271925797

9875586273 5079806777 3876632508 8505540488 2569127275 3341995578 5926568267 6614831954 7906277605 7127288931
5429441300 8606907814 6367645030 0973897609 6999350590 1327155481 8357049480 0170394506 6830204425 5906166070
0509097621 5770008627 0804493180 6980234180 8900181103 5963140717 4444270245 6209836924 5092080807 3812500092
8742103807 0507560670 0010040660 3238832094 0050001845 0460980031 9470987006 0224405130 1203269032 2878004313
5984093452 7318216001 8859031004 6383897210 0800390619 7091060507 7756203300 6224686484 0399709668 9050840042
2857087927 0113200724 9070689433 8340007001 8909280382 0530353163 9030880483 3883007605 3496445617 0396019896
0363230297 7318744899 1243327881 8102861977 7405556438 4998256015 1274005410 7493924923 2725254598 8532395286
9110878131 9520111349 2575028460 0759609269 9713059834 7190713053 3773938724 4258619901 7200222358 1369843087
0903249179 8308177868 7136892869 8475406238 0484332943 5890515092 5580870573 0505682327 4859914251 2992757018
8188883060 2290095975 2232115763 7235193338 4050608607 4501532694 9772456318 3454553082 5945609139 3798695090

5691062160 7667091830 9083085964 5061495912 1291253628 1424654202 9812677071 0162366605 6889987680 5243376547
6080008094 4404370886 1692604897 6772067264 0802160944 7600014090 2614750698 5508826437 5622700107 0407497246
5331379107 9170360607 9716609401 5900535878 0976850435 8175715300 6884030844 0000445518 6653074876 3081400639
0221128407 6038000707 0341506401 8304294200 4080875085 4211250268 9350276004 3101521939 8679853700 3064854923
2615858195 6708415350 9910980431 7078069403 7296088762 8314593479 8237333620 5289565099 4061340812 3948876782
9781626706 0397760960 7054206039 3350300441 3127780875 2440230703 6027040608 0904038029 0642272002 1900731237
0477373933 4358436420 2687511533 5404529718 9677734286 1752529234 1219038146 8115458799 2494209066 1129790201
8039697092 1454035343 5322364114 0302414960 6895649139 8250911710 0569591486 1182416049 8890745015 7373467119
0840567569 4009124920 9318750454 2212551676 2950534165 4014506994 0085416448 0023501572 2796930410 4048031376
7598197744 4293026285 0450417132 7539505672 5043283091 6798703082 0693898182 2961139969 0018950030 8200600705

1468307372 1949457531 0243107665 8653138615 6748053141 8992751630 1302494322 4402409838 2030816605 6165885040
2849646865 0917655419 7661192851 4813874145 3746884821 5785392449 8653435426 0587023265 1915819516 0324071888
0551739800 9610386292 8717358423 6243692635 4355837754 1738580504 0845168165 3100790200 9284315006 1472802058
7805775605 9255664483 4626610991 2647376833 3510419575 3714248121 9306017217 1936177794 7456536696 0691229870
2056838506 1278500799 0505006520 0205183133 9608680976 3815000373 8577421168 6029301909 5741105246 2900100809
4539819072 1224810411 4685310105 6067622659 9192108807 6437557397 2556948977 4729618790 4243840993 5996344631
0030848675 9094860901 3390611437 9289431498 9378040671 6324424542 5650722904 1830671684 7105094033 8750650069
6215219026 2007428903 3655714350 7305599836 0124317884 0183965617 5013542804 9580861756 8281872864 1842854782
4351747333 4109755197 8340872446 7449517323 2006543932 7824847468 0048625628 2007154416 1126338019 1420283733
8460283034 8747330411 8787509676 4528423337 7878530876 2705689545 3950062992 8794400462 6032670614 0050034043

9383041676 8730373075 2010475869 0610640457 6001000442 4900900203 0266582039 5580978529 3989245240 4964000206
0863877041 8743915238 6724599980 9081630535 7080506108 0917092226 8499392532 6429611827 1194802021 1595909219
0127210029 0177159063 0997318130 8667369507 8654549235 8569616303 1761991197 1465591174 5150075601 3402287582
2256632919 3606376878 0111521064 6963184624 1755512844 4850158468 0020316670 3952933791 8679027533 0159506085
0565091811 5759392059 0050387853 9552589592 9698270600 0506021493 9381836037 7692043909 2225074034 0305769404
3557757254 1003404246 2648689852 7554343683 1388958354 1567722988 8175825395 0230801024 8483158389 9393640113
1952250917 9422444603 9722485391 7671156994 4692668061 1031448508 4462759058 8461622690 5964072118 9877273162
8014458494 0107320412 1623868156 6794313255 4207482373 9212176640 5307123591 6458825514 5473016434 2560849580
1398964127 2571567424 1220172954 4662982515 6627085408 3278624910 5879504861 1075635542 9924039427 4703384841
9213066691 2913224064 5181395336 5849585009 6003468550 3338276904 8115245156 3672123134 1243914468 8557671894

4675251454 0820470632 3702095769 1397101076 3717054558 0900766484 0203412079 0109296992 5250319056 1316673281
7470006850 0937695781 7386734246 1598801204 7154238663 5419795161 5882799117 7182259632 1592299013 9642880077
7165688286 8630930847 7406939599 5262564472 4244330393 3362663357 5181624718 8599637088 9596638009 5446040345
5819039066 5108181938 7345660785 5657905105 2467842648 7460725236 5665192074 0763575181 7850620681 6970245614
3931118883 5326890102 5138932808 3148072977 5260735328 6374126701 1086744063 4965379127 3131145120 7961041773
9285186470 0820887276 3747318232 4402289216 1011984728 6836648211 6450755466 1563244631 4818478588 8021539581
6406981836 8096031332 7011600877 6642745237 6623272792 3679750610 8145285435 5740791726 3008823127 6118884005
1736980042 6634005303 0264258593 8001730518 5041362597 3524539608 4689071200 6726641756 0844000173 0746238087
5981705062 9467253457 0289932827 5242467552 8336940109 8783317365 1680522591 7400044835 7488101301 6926330195
4783973414 8586640854 7428190925 1124389867 5719279530 9590221134 2108603768 6399283872 8276777596 5401515218

2165120188 5632923137 7154449993 6451839926 5242143486 3232796709 4764599013 2864378542 1257764317 1524818704
7792077881 9741892924 7267812846 0380003737 6295109206 8333330558 7208849987 9484586584 0504569034 6759279785
0227156198 1541567629 2265092489 5793268054 2828692760 5180596934 7094404818 1404264547 2176443763 8041823271
7483250265 2218659583 0071046162 9496848062 8019768526 8210269050 2830212211 2552640771 7154213287 5822324636
1649590803 5438790135 9881667826 6474374585 7571608066 0342614072 6362296323 9819551248 9322071559 2426118776
2409515094 7322114088 8235913379 2755625356 1977888360 1267536481 6842753919 7342713069 1556538891 6824101276
0328667927 6945382051 2910113797 7660955796 1281721844 0041512810 0794869133 3409255209 4596184641 8229535289
9728728802 2265180895 8421329991 2273671954 3882639075 0894502222 5065171246 8557874944 8206074300 1221832806
8835902720 8072464944 4718829414 8228743753 5608498453 7710327943 8084323544 8082636699 9895466580 7965409810
9014713823 6949364878 1194430043 0389436546 6492818360 8007765722 7454396763 4886665285 8488605625 1049768645

7536702522 0995884944 3221175930 5928214170 7830530561 6699788059 0558528044 7654723055 0968765605 6346988191
8516872997 2673614006 4009710131 6484418703 3637193555 1437299248 1944050022 7859700172 0594938240 8900894914
7928147560 1664429984 5920515805 5099597072 5808736817 5356286149 1124363001 2854971260 7218826486 4197228309
7360566500 2703822800 9908609521 0267003589 6704863820 6890477861 1494213039 9930226934 3000980902 9707860490
8729019872 5522221313 0387655891 9546794874 2070385973 0921335728 3666153760 4487575030 0544294183 5160185233
1695023581 5216980690 4476217067 7873537185 4987492678 7267260431 7898325288 7939880004 3794223246 0955023536
0832691683 9658841817 4941865474 3926433623 3655489242 9945409639 2925386795 5699501631 6282682783 2554605345
5695664768 6049527410 3147549420 9064352253 2992000842 6595420674 6489580743 4137410257 0956865189 1747379862
2765784228 0432423357 3603413546 3879257804 5654918747 4427373950 3801592162 1943578320 6627241833 4564237827
0776718056 1099529152 9478989427 4150147262 1084146937 6348981342 4322956047 3433802940 1950227884 1257718607

0645206109 4755881112 0581738266 9756677009 0532857204 0972458325 6689518379 6051318597 7616747274 6771394300
2331736035 7755000002 9511084640 0013504110 1087060588 3521220192 8105401002 4548035000 4140047117 2498603934
9394715432 9225025882 8125602767 8976742252 3803688117 0507958645 0290605060 0687109760 8050607143 8384684359
0912356554 6038800049 9366128879 0892180922 4914032898 5570315383 1041022213 9873694572 5087652312 1920437803
4928800878 7095030417 3609474243 8706459322 8566831265 4488351071 3183047453 5091648440 2827834222 3325542928
8159415304 2903957938 5541004470 7645054819 5267524826 4461123821 4004290059 8617326070 8588951589 6727544687
2562541798 2151762000 1071498027 4522688444 1327804983 5695450313 4962798983 3157251821 8825541145 1363187476
0609967789 9668034096 2777303477 0033274045 8569420318 5406663477 3196217161 0618281432 6060276250 3281659142
8849975178 8804788440 3300865265 5729130019 2060008516 4182004234 1474028373 3384128310 5902766174 9469910016
2730373216 2081480936 6216932229 0954995441 4570174200 9703614153 0453705029 1285126328 4500464088 4887835998

0615123014 2742978829 7579244267 1912295348 9280552497 2956165027 9688276018 2114870807 5925463371 0559138333
6965007900 3022261398 6141254208 7118300014 7086646361 3060737086 3774340781 8790887587 6683285377 2838171059
3964295545 5117518421 9572239770 4806005254 1895299050 7733014307 5445852246 9534684061 4377610499 0963624199
4578909845 2768286611 6944928935 6204971633 5869864024 6220125855 5970011694 2929150978 3345505299 8927562941
9076105852 0510539206 0820073309 9202814505 9233714702 0121050655 7070502760 2380107657 0808012683 4110476203
5903557234 4175608269 9237294806 0103666750 4366114986 0083495007 6005198213 0089269298 1739136727 0879858045
1079545983 4800566287 3985239151 4200603467 7491309377 0365809836 5916626105 7589090962 9053080477 6688160603
2031683467 4715298688 5712720118 3563316883 6748287904 2515181586 0884434902 0232434324 3651845712 6929544862
8898004421 1988181258 4426453269 9685580192 4459351466 5901088914 8601866305 4263703628 1018093893 6665503984
3441323411 0352639763 5057127178 4993518286 1500032407 9695907983 3840939757 2474472880 3884566902 9776202992

2338844540 3390918513 3314597166 8242238088 2924639567 4714183695 6705650358 7713313805 8275690224 2419572252
1720647147 1111587281 2517430951 4081755526 5498895137 4381473497 0392748372 3187473384 3889016090 0100417462
2981942756 8684359787 6070581692 4613997876 1152279244 1430644605 9662530444 1526673721 0645935640 8545473354
7345025930 0678546683 5402830291 7856143248 6423301118 4040953488 3403092630 9885361397 1697208601 3927363819
0681860999 5386432876 9708140403 0000643394 8910837729 3350158683 0440917623 0061054356 6730567504 5463003297
0713458061 6661802676 6649554606 6481844436 2584580098 4204927653 7200129553 8788214866 9249394376 0553090764
4585365709 8973378173 7963725010 2959714721 3778125667 8396584338 7919439578 9823683203 4198072890 3069960016
3431008755 9378955680 4807366195 5031875445 3015538557 0930386138 5832355789 1316279056 6703063202 7907926480
0356628979 3648776404 0270006439 8660682200 3013169053 6087703425 5100275585 8501608858 2634007066 7869290741
0173713704 3666672070 5085944196 5693502326 3350189680 0964810007 7780823693 5490955042 9326059196 2929071752

1864642895 4502253007 9727014501 7068102629 3075270312 2826608742 3232578060 5200672731 4484841852 0851802552
3731065907 0085810835 5275155115 3177123733 6986547060 3114052858 1084244028 4146228532 2630544675 9409914683
5100297307 9144954984 5403013022 4057520145 2474035781 7949318184 7284933372 9866646075 7574564562 6321773549
5242977380 5196451097 2310557869 1576706917 1535639467 5404437835 8921440398 1534029664 6711413505 0086859884
2961604845 9118647223 6920342529 6883581308 8094113546 3149476156 7199027226 5197936138 3147977011 3265646932
0049689871 5222981747 3688643315 3224860714 7583750944 1667834348 2622140756 1491939016 5911223669 2644253951
3966668758 3707487603 3899562345 0577070255 9243213764 2821053781 3252345789 7672456053 8731267657 8060368828
4226339640 4828724130 3941607114 6956639011 6057068696 0159612913 9848092901 4747050672 2845025816 7187082457
7586193106 0729556754 0543836226 8533463965 5524657036 8632515070 5056975129 2268508874 5833090094 2720509670
6053897474 2347310276 6752480213 8009348334 3329434886 9902856182 1605796797 0372610264 1843550793 8813304144

1552703688 4365381804 2164009784 1359152437 2027407675 9457741100 6973683565 8881089422 4145477361 8348567375
3245140840 6040376160 5393044669 4160654829 2617323560 6902110702 1294138367 0860631234 8260666519 1406954354
0003100409 2303505801 3030002700 8001007630 0887820170 4560578406 7650759490 0321202620 7490890793 5620820003
1571739850 5703703431 7655259020 9049224000 2028220702 8626361897 8975125088 3850447722 9284820901 4774501545
0740579320 0539049062 0537908841 5009450806 2993569464 6905345367 0895374667 2761480567 1475980577 0169574544
9210423980 2289936214 2033785837 7147073120 8055107814 7859875262 8002700525 6301273093 1409636019 9235726580
4698750798 6587064346 4548023372 4231281352 1169068858 8703911569 7662778173 6368699271 0439063019 6329198996
0754769727 2203697868 9027267678 5096309187 7469360867 6004096395 3740788793 9604005195 6812358133 1161914708
8989618906 8741639913 2284155469 5296596044 0475219887 4208958090 7532643139 2590870468 0321541587 6553179257
9660730154 3300847135 8309201568 4300184160 0509641737 6781588423 8330087119 9781971977 8831911323 8152145547

1609169838 0052307204 5017072196 1772424744 0043386942 8416986754 0301209016 0822305679 7366981558 7133193104
1960939224 0591916763 8847155749 6194089761 5299267387 8906102921 3711474134 8372133580 4634631263 4491305570
6077560484 0902923615 7633680468 4385280624 0524017768 9161051635 0021253277 8202562224 1800012646 0634252155
0489541524 5119103184 5743095911 7675698454 4807896753 7050282454 8955193083 9869651333 3954464003 5815414333
2912901078 2399960211 3339915627 8809714305 4214989144 9795346616 1238777484 1406557112 5730187606 6387693493
7750017362 9504063183 6481834454 3406557302 4853078964 5061266300 2570407416 7161310248 8189419536 1496520060
1536464155 6184197119 6591720910 1917824443 7448114287 5728426381 6027457749 6774096281 6405428632 1812343086
2477255350 5081525621 4923699361 8167730031 8814898603 9508464440 0660650653 6381793507 6866203714 4473188971
0445082003 5025099997 9004566391 3403760006 0009590059 0353454093 6827180024 8200112906 5300001700 8493407069
6895763439 5492781331 0565450008 7564225635 6164437693 8119427865 2755077489 2607064188 1623151106 0699261442

0840658016 6191809951 3280786186 9664324964 0719469909 7209047173 1630138245 7829841049 0773147041 3524691177
2977002395 5824844502 9444259303 3755933366 5134945812 2775982630 1906420412 8118543214 7588800920 3040309447
2204929481 9222394505 3316948013 2666598378 5863994191 6707139536 2943706970 7639558840 0317518006 6976035056
4459105380 3113361510 8858579762 8174464769 6941209324 1752454549 9050202642 1667130698 7000501052 1639719921
0101015590 7487243301 8810178543 0465905369 8675133533 4951952185 5171145729 2549648688 7525150570 8505752588
1897280771 6437777814 3731031727 8957357541 5263526719 0838593741 7827549445 3217840876 1428817009 7867975658
3230028035 9450449511 3541894324 2458630992 0267357805 9682928492 8581465385 5329778237 6797085542 5032360055
3841194269 6775170384 2543483706 0039738741 7785206086 8131833002 1910362587 0128137259 0419521982 6570095145
6543589481 2421345961 1149671918 2304994550 8604154636 3132982540 8636118852 6810923127 1776094462 2436830429
8231941622 7881382606 3785529936 5269606987 3064012338 9802585210 9940812892 3749560735 3204272888 9707521821

1401431055 1982902466 9300231217 1207436764 6690856200 9097507083 3885637300 3661742864 8560308033 2628806736
2325006934 0682050853 5493045003 4500098300 6407211580 1932480479 6796876268 0068600083 1773062452 1948004016
5445604888 6079592027 0941367907 9042993024 8111786668 9991697276 7180677512 2909301887 1096749922 3408921701
9580137223 3395107135 2902583180 9441264556 6046492087 6688910451 5247977696 6731602745 1237310882 0400022869
9874056978 5061064205 7960368949 4710123269 0934916823 8600048400 3695933006 5720181434 5598809957 0559536496
1213468519 0920277027 6420203196 0353931582 0162444686 2544309525 2702574325 7686554528 5737812403 5138382305
4817906579 3506820692 0000203007 8456967064 1607259199 1503028085 1750626392 4809495407 8879008051 0658908079
5026535483 2688980875 7353249531 6186571907 2202662670 5855694903 3062069301 7750001516 3854984402 9425656936
1290800777 7097178040 0613186067 2089284466 5897605775 0328598840 0778387765 6874153992 4844149711 0082221618
5458301790 1814302579 7718039026 7230373215 9432690374 4340676383 9870638293 1963361994 7855060872 0576989592

9284334147 6472699260 1490327915 9070926293 1431885488 4327770375 8200062063 5522692930 1030226925 6906491211
4006502503 0755560906 6006700480 1498665630 7208730300 5053153100 8805917695 3550630006 1956830957 1702603063
6793994584 6367147283 9363236305 4854399602 7857689138 1250818135 6129833523 6205838359 5873697726 2399782462
8998592100 7569422191 0927481801 9926158321 0001247005 0090127377 0590111373 0000306420 5279281222 0533333003
8933471551 3806276306 1842773180 4582188718 0499053986 4510016178 0917382716 8063591937 9172638543 1215526933
3860286256 8491227517 3630033252 8661138451 6437926259 6181585564 0284259710 2713102671 0989765951 4632145551
8547190586 5922334344 5271790861 5623263140 4264940751 8732223740 9092896662 2610688455 8669409457 6288252547
5816711428 8939152081 8914094988 9780634971 6088210234 4030005530 4103599273 7148537745 3795058769 5001690557
7373075428 9894352856 2367561305 4165842373 0409190066 9150618760 1049062079 1929901599 6266380978 2630014165
3642705941 3895186352 2039586553 2238248586 5162544732 9698120200 7341990994 6508206631 6858930677 8075515072

6722122591 2213713086 7634734489 5672032327 8703112446 4449949967 7170356329 6680046052 2364508740 0681972714
3286972983 6799868902 9819999978 1889605477 3596823439 2679320433 5280789002 5981664547 7017355549 2750306265
3236831360 5235498614 3227884494 7733519108 1078851984 5792471415 0178582472 3563363935 6605967636 0505436133
2241043600 5788196841 5030300400 0363549803 0041603021 0109803340 4203043501 6042284049 2524725972 3478066010
1001007264 0200516803 2607718170 9006082848 0185303271 7080996700 8213907080 8605490079 0005006062 2006928080
3173627044 4607104311 3610073956 7718459653 5183017203 7071116110 8023061206 2141738294 5052057241 4989810305
1377736521 2098700281 6007505639 7257201305 0112170395 7438065050 5960134614 1686325020 1058099309 3050818623
1161933248 8884341064 0822696225 3783789456 4092709209 9503037391 3159301799 7131753580 2305788585 4550709940
3327238703 2202215604 1578402962 3915909069 4309907008 1767390481 8240322939 9149246566 3860374672 0869372738
4181124114 5276914987 0071004040 0320058903 3293070046 6951308815 1678438480 1517759569 7082344798 0067703174

1185347538 0680715475 0156364866 2701383751 4142536739 5005558265 0466279530 8398928570 6771385221 4071877974
3853400105 8821450956 3668034866 3157003000 5803087304 7020707617 0817075828 3245183151 8037006519 1986491186
5374652791 1285702632 6032312900 1921061965 4716103160 5109965655 9023447880 1675320462 2566511962 5259873727
7851504012 3794205887 0148087044 4954029762 7967285505 1914257467 3604668477 9272351290 4418478119 9754397016
7543565062 1000086910 0584580020 0774801605 0807099800 0950080295 6647604980 7653103340 6602000005 0410486200
6493124401 0954550405 4662807210 0343161412 8047189411 9308493713 9215149734 5966455016 5055407582 7993980166
3062948283 0168044776 3577911562 6603204273 2129363332 3752733363 9484803214 5078772828 1383952898 1484540856
6635721427 4726472178 1210782286 8448849506 6042648531 1441282495 1693549606 5511159313 6779769128 6809569326
9008566369 3864079989 3327239282 8232820535 5825369344 3504863103 0799537790 9840282847 1636698183 9703398484
2600743317 0390618676 0069954182 7533764775 3331871244 5138635034 0876003559 8037091445 4457400462 6486906480

6136700663 6003036339 2010072690 5892574611 6501764828 9074342480 8216797057 6601228793 4326655715 5057245102
3935929563 0248631103 1290818321 9317859950 9945010487 8949828415 4832354929 2759610743 9241427187 6997415895
8212494054 4859591629 4992746188 7344326763 3793908750 5946965703 0884489772 2499693889 3306402229 7246173328
4934358781 5603451026 0090028705 5131301490 8873190258 0953255955 4098663096 1642511421 0187910146 5242792626
5883840585 1138580368 6784455515 1855872194 5383014945 2640178408 4318722996 9714394185 2894643831 1996509698
0051970480 3508948126 6263272928 5980313991 6504706195 0822848711 8724466453 2152148755 1010046862 9099258571
1802456080 8003261014 4341491981 7831871029 2200626603 6362004450 4431010211 9249548805 0125703296 6485728028
7803849101 2031697093 7704248487 9551854749 2681938442 7891369902 4799065479 1860935246 2291658596 0153043170
2144033023 0270586324 6012156994 9428921553 9040552646 7767943289 8690200855 6821211254 4357212854 3201691975
5890381285 5442286031 0562514105 5245629334 5944522807 9047317765 5557612246 8297511002 0630326585 9007402623

7590759163 1570043000 7020910909 1570560584 0780360678 6050570706 7000457085 5020227807 8160399600 5461423600
0578784764 0769587187 6212724386 7425942906 5817478923 9366804278 0224691328 8608256697 9826605545 9489077929
2404335076 8988261587 1346583742 2092077341 0117535451 4812881411 2246169848 1298206455 7572719667 6795526780
0756663964 0772120717 4349721527 9221542844 3567850653 1283211425 5458016864 2051729727 1634002837 6860848376
0305000911 0060400407 0904360601 0033323405 1044022010 2475084403 0232934689 9593177003 0064354200 8094058843
5904189432 7710511716 6676255928 7326841665 3088374979 0736002335 0749748611 4472828598 7296077302 7799758727
1746298057 1435269054 2700739959 9470806457 3091700919 9649780580 7490575871 3036058388 7040724221 3036795058
1352512252 7187163189 5626512374 4825242107 7891853528 4774749483 2473976424 3071014911 4231274257 2011341723
5746863908 8261227518 8637270625 2176787560 0523893939 3922858338 8364753316 4221045846 8408211202 4947862919
9183306510 1927646753 6523905444 3817311050 0566372319 8573796365 7534728795 7977257201 3174616232 3495288305

0065693692 2992354352 1402469180 4855394099 0948315766 5072998711 8379979053 6648916645 8948125618 7242060784
5641785641 2327162557 8230632672 4465867791 5989620226 1133578674 8258014351 8973587989 4723961576 7887200568
3738674339 4029609030 3792288903 2692344806 5523763100 5395796849 0152365593 3998546665 8077992309 5758506590
8538422161 4904627304 0160685688 5231170915 3204812403 4378149163 2888525256 2769241975 0388634951 3226520269
3687404818 5199105590 0484315353 8714682934 1836727445 7174698684 1960713950 8265948182 5543680832 0285414135
5976300032 6273680510 2364301419 0838764565 0834528421 2921766607 2720725234 0708482170 1298709012 0057843715
0183234661 3545774010 1470427481 9419867493 2602606596 5075005401 0926910000 9190736657 2940001039 4202460083
9680050701 2281836955 2399803659 5931728392 1223921594 6410825286 7028585664 1171334383 7657384614 3648465460
0964394643 3094298100 6878294067 9109390665 0564845539 0660013343 1017076800 9183403500 2003674030 0719735009
3220481777 6608441794 8780987491 3197127684 6580107526 8991694015 0763757528 5929489514 7754899152 8823947853

2946277906 5422143455 4727375303 8207599485 4089776756 7651722260 4728387691 1761774835 0200985299 4024012049
1272320864 4940529678 2133193955 9170057763 4393759555 5698242029 4881658183 0665165891 8951269109 2839003703
1543734578 5721192382 3023641363 7577567542 5788569189 5927085181 4509412777 4067231645 8886870823 7647435405
4001490364 0002128024 5204070872 4810070300 0246302136 1210506963 5007877037 0703000310 3001000720 9201000238
3929707453 1852969926 7500437923 7671281021 9054142789 6288815061 4965218047 5508617504 2210120022 8540732227
9074107102 7838898740 6274294802 4612958689 8374877473 0408763893 4106887504 1094754299 0653605984 5626438432
5076110342 9950572240 8493755296 0546152972 6218631093 0730120098 7973752381 9785440463 6520980426 9169929769
4929630963 1168562519 4370378173 9913571668 4814630146 7910656472 8599887800 3457753044 3868135553 3341324016
9953209932 1888213062 2075253648 9064513059 0396881265 5060443189 6938503242 7157108251 2540278647 0230661960
6334854231 7433350632 2610636077 9973434300 3518161437 5295867303 4216762346 1657642144 3259144169 3330039054

0288043156	1706719303	3258597910	1644122084	8949568631	7178795910	4728058229	6906106724	4007777059	8095086295
3200032955	9065142505	5321657310	5805960347	6035983370	8387473945	8091590831	4334678183	6552123855	9319545801
7610114201	6845704562	7706396731	9226478966	2786507346	8620555487	6547352146	6622865341	7751950095	4367759999
8155479882	9391307633	5794535981	6974056215	5189033124	8148950921	3816372472	6043236955	6276540610	4391105204
8030660576	0643243290	8617001935	2799346530	6872664618	7592662304	8219082230	4101795308	7163856451	5682009515
6735323606	7616098606	1907295657	9188749947	9957900520	6098502522	2025885485	7465216739	6180275658	2939475161
2110369149	1485088177	2299213863	4124190117	0273653250	3731103562	0388912768	0134000263	3457081236	9053937918
5984395484	8795234531	4880241565	7236901819	9831536829	1030518062	8417243825	8914896617	4915153516	4036953622
7629282035	1419528324	0552257692	7850211079	4445030978	4846429136	8945559725	6610066086	7982278986	5835092502
4416651922	7120780063	9492140797	0801725505	3080512293	6611009681	1693445074	2319885656	4358485931	6425897037

9421126531	3389878130	2894400369	6037916736	9297190721	3263320993	6602560535	0556277140	5197787251	6828291559
7119705702	3006077552	9672401482	7939941383	3211414434	0107498283	5675906128	4288237068	3753337204	1677038876
0602415598	9389111607	0810537269	5735925310	0545455449	4838355908	0205708845	0352013061	9068919984	1895129779
8638929239	6473732268	2354778324	5722955600	5548341853	7851749338	2410076668	9121849476	6630503713	1797653152
2884459038	0255684055	6439086456	9916755368	2281096533	9862167179	1456547273	3777694700	4249922067	4475753854
8004476684	6356801521	9559104818	1828681265	5543740231	3933653898	8220776795	3009218748	0299467418	6532868370
7569695346	1827682175	7590253188	5163075260	8880327951	8586462022	6212950198	9369460641	4061206169	7443537804
2618015557	9155786441	2206311220	6506702292	2380986228	2049808670	7007841934	9697415566	0175402940	1068811868
8021873137	4018041370	9004131777	0785028498	7378195719	0375711430	9504512517	4543285921	2293863502	1731274685
4898896379	0271582484	1144712935	8751526644	5381745108	7540659865	1161665511	9594902819	3706206957	8540582255

5515507842	1882391318	7942711910	8469748022	0479270222	6874016489	1983617956	8559563071	8359941681	6943261486
9351730666	9823581810	0547743871	6264117857	3608185902	2116855564	4982277691	7585869862	0386997080	4199058509
9962125633	9681101953	6398231201	7237685457	8295479878	9322490583	1924028059	6906007749	0394996050	8329870834
6012451305	6293688343	3427296369	3085976071	1078271012	4793250295	3665331886	2171357144	1196213382	0833345538
7445281486	5218061614	6715306519	0337779218	6254551998	1564584314	0486602179	7078679106	9361791415	8572863207
7678303406	6116262714	2500090955	6756009100	0138429325	3554923618	2543185793	9776285580	0099485578	7111749692
1090064652	9166789111	0386743854	3463053602	5983449121	0967005545	5978760291	6175558766	8107685924	0820834652
1972850789	9324176495	4224047323	1044953073	8215591019	8965647831	2654299646	3850867769	6775042805	8418022576
6684140475	9684644171	3913039654	2278440044	4627635094	4409656155	5933027741	6106849384	5751768993	7903659948
5619309117	3830368872	0264410929	1488076956	6915976532	5035470671	5030069686	4618032559	2720013654	3630957330

3547293799	2508217610	3353307764	9368588492	1780033346	0449810697	5158785206	2266569011	4640182942	6514881542
3385608191	7832956412	4470308049	1423622565	0041599894	0961970130	5283422678	9722464207	0291551176	6144218240
7175620646	2618736544	1754675557	4269388093	4803577045	4510874508	8356562189	3369723407	1043248234	5854097624
4631001602	5581604434	5579719386	5360239059	0334987635	2061483932	3501606625	4860899392	9787298491	7911149047
8361786307	0682322953	9476178260	2685773784	0276579521	8903648393	5217127773	4307148772	6441588453	1126844887
4569347533	8488001649	8862748785	8913750092	0508689967	2707906103	0081283069	3200630417	3889958688	6797717250
3092086619	2115858662	9418080204	1466817893	1168056270	7615666646	5010210009	8792510156	0595519993	1646200381
2580974988	8747719954	1757503236	9503828937	4260735024	7460967335	0643606511	0312102653	0267200600	9983118227
0975374491	7026576085	7615967474	6193410508	9855604222	4708358190	2253335172	2013204790	3666696056	9729246708
9990000643	7563335263	2276989799	2958088089	6796765216	5974367432	4229658046	3154751560	1749021833	0834941442

APPENDIX 2

A Table of Sample Sizes*

*Standard deviation factor $z = 1.96$
Risk = 5%

Defective Rate θ	Accuracy Factor a							
	1%	5%	10%	15%	20%	25%	30%	40%
0.01	3803184	152128	38032	16904	9508	6086	4226	2377
0.02	1882382	75296	18824	8367	4706	3012	2092	1141
0.03	1242118	49685	12422	5521	3106	1988	1381	777
0.04	921984	36880	9220	4098	2305	1476	1025	577
0.05	729904	29197	7300	3245	1825	1168	812	457
0.06	601851	24075	6019	2675	1505	963	669	377
0.07	510384	20416	5104	2269	1276	817	568	290
0.08	441784	17672	4418	1964	1105	707	491	277
0.09	388429	15538	3885	1727	972	622	432	243
0.10	345744	13830	3458	1537	865	554	385	217
0.11	310821	12433	3109	1382	778	498	346	195
0.12	281718	11269	2818	1253	705	451	314	177
0.13	257092	10284	2571	1143	643	412	286	161
0.14	235984	9440	2360	1049	590	378	263	148
0.15	217691	8708	2177	968	545	349	242	137
0.16	201684	8068	2017	897	505	323	225	127
0.17	187561	7503	1876	834	469	301	209	118
0.18	175007	7001	1751	778	438	281	195	110
0.19	163774	6551	1638	728	410	263	182	103
0.20	153664	6147	1537	683	385	246	171	97
0.25	115248	4610	1153	513	289	185	129	73
0.30	89638	3586	897	399	225	144	100	57
0.35	71344	2854	714	318	179	115	80	45
0.40	57625	2305	577	257	145	93	65	37
0.45	46953	1879	470	209	118	76	53	30

* Standard deviation factor (z) = 1.96
Risk = 5%

APPENDIX **3**

Standardized Normal Distribution Function Values

Values of the Standardized Normal Distribution Function $\Phi(z)$

z	0.00	0.01	0.02	0.03	0.04	0.05	0.06	0.07	0.08	0.09
-3.4	0.00034	0.00032	0.00031	0.00030	0.00029	0.00028	0.00027	0.00026	0.00025	0.00024
-3.3	0.00048	0.00047	0.00045	0.00043	0.00042	0.00040	0.00039	0.00038	0.00036	0.00035
-3.2	0.00069	0.00066	0.00064	0.00062	0.00060	0.00058	0.00056	0.00054	0.00052	0.00050
-3.1	0.00097	0.00094	0.00090	0.00087	0.00084	0.00082	0.00079	0.00076	0.00074	0.00071
-3.0	0.00135	0.00131	0.00126	0.00122	0.00118	0.00114	0.00111	0.00107	0.00104	0.00100
-2.9	0.00187	0.00181	0.00175	0.00169	0.00164	0.00159	0.00154	0.00149	0.00144	0.00140
-2.8	0.00256	0.00248	0.00240	0.00233	0.00226	0.00219	0.00212	0.00205	0.00199	0.00193
-2.7	0.00347	0.00336	0.00326	0.00317	0.00307	0.00298	0.00289	0.00280	0.00272	0.00264
-2.6	0.00466	0.00453	0.00440	0.00427	0.00415	0.00403	0.00391	0.00379	0.00368	0.00357
-2.5	0.00621	0.00604	0.00587	0.00570	0.00554	0.00539	0.00523	0.00509	0.00494	0.00480
-2.4	0.00820	0.00798	0.00776	0.00755	0.00734	0.00714	0.00695	0.00676	0.00657	0.00639
-2.3	0.01073	0.01045	0.01017	0.00990	0.00964	0.00939	0.00914	0.00889	0.00866	0.00843
-2.2	0.01390	0.01355	0.01321	0.01288	0.01255	0.01223	0.01191	0.01161	0.01131	0.01101
-2.1	0.01787	0.01743	0.01700	0.01659	0.01618	0.01578	0.01539	0.01500	0.01463	0.01426
-2.0	0.02275	0.02222	0.02169	0.02118	0.02068	0.02018	0.01970	0.01923	0.01876	0.01831

-1.9	0.02872	0.02807	0.02743	0.02681	0.02619	0.02559	0.02500	0.02442	0.02385	0.02330
-1.8	0.03593	0.03515	0.03438	0.03363	0.03289	0.03216	0.03145	0.03075	0.03006	0.02938
-1.7	0.04457	0.04364	0.04272	0.04182	0.04093	0.04006	0.03921	0.03837	0.03754	0.03673
-1.6	0.05480	0.05370	0.05262	0.05156	0.05051	0.04948	0.04846	0.04746	0.04648	0.04552
-1.5	0.06681	0.06553	0.06426	0.06301	0.06179	0.06058	0.05939	0.05821	0.05706	0.05592
-1.4	0.08076	0.07928	0.07781	0.07637	0.07494	0.07354	0.07215	0.07079	0.06944	0.06812
-1.3	0.09681	0.09511	0.09343	0.09177	0.09013	0.08852	0.08692	0.08535	0.08380	0.08227
-1.2	0.11508	0.11315	0.11124	0.10936	0.10750	0.10566	0.10384	0.10205	0.10028	0.09853
-1.1	0.13568	0.13351	0.13137	0.12925	0.12715	0.12508	0.12303	0.12101	0.11901	0.11703
-1.0	0.15867	0.15626	0.15388	0.15152	0.14918	0.14687	0.14458	0.14232	0.14008	0.13787
-0.9	0.18407	0.18142	0.17880	0.17620	0.17362	0.17107	0.16854	0.16604	0.16355	0.16110
-0.8	0.21187	0.20898	0.20612	0.20328	0.20047	0.19768	0.19491	0.19216	0.18944	0.18675
-0.7	0.24198	0.23887	0.23578	0.23271	0.22966	0.22664	0.22364	0.22066	0.21771	0.21478
-0.6	0.27427	0.27095	0.26764	0.26436	0.26110	0.25786	0.25464	0.25144	0.24827	0.24511
-0.5	0.30855	0.30504	0.30155	0.29807	0.29461	0.29118	0.28776	0.28435	0.28097	0.27761
-0.4	0.34460	0.34092	0.33726	0.33361	0.32999	0.32637	0.32277	0.31919	0.31563	0.31208
-0.3	0.38211	0.37830	0.37450	0.37072	0.36695	0.36319	0.35944	0.35571	0.35199	0.34829
-0.2	0.42076	0.41685	0.41295	0.40906	0.40518	0.40131	0.39745	0.39360	0.38976	0.38593
-0.1	0.46019	0.45622	0.45226	0.44830	0.44435	0.44040	0.43646	0.43252	0.42859	0.42467
-0.0	0.50002	0.49603	0.49204	0.48805	0.48406	0.48008	0.47609	0.47211	0.46814	0.46416

Values of the Standardized Normal Distribution Function $\Phi(z)$

z	0.00	0.01	0.02	0.03	0.04	0.05	0.06	0.07	0.08	0.09
0.0	0.50002	0.50401	0.50799	0.51198	0.51597	0.51995	0.52394	0.52792	0.53190	0.53587
0.1	0.53984	0.54381	0.54777	0.55173	0.55569	0.55963	0.56357	0.56751	0.57144	0.57536
0.2	0.57927	0.58318	0.58708	0.59097	0.59485	0.59872	0.60258	0.60643	0.61027	0.61411
0.3	0.61792	0.62173	0.62553	0.62931	0.63308	0.63684	0.64059	0.64432	0.64804	0.65174
0.4	0.65543	0.65911	0.66277	0.66641	0.67004	0.67366	0.67725	0.68083	0.68440	0.68794
0.5	0.69147	0.69498	0.69848	0.70195	0.70541	0.70885	0.71227	0.71567	0.71905	0.72241
0.6	0.72576	0.72908	0.73238	0.73566	0.73892	0.74216	0.74538	0.74858	0.75175	0.75491
0.7	0.75804	0.76115	0.76424	0.76731	0.77036	0.77338	0.77638	0.77936	0.78231	0.78524
0.8	0.78815	0.79103	0.79390	0.79673	0.79955	0.80234	0.80511	0.80785	0.81057	0.81327
0.9	0.81594	0.81859	0.82122	0.82382	0.82639	0.82895	0.83147	0.83398	0.83646	0.83891
1.0	0.84135	0.84375	0.84614	0.84850	0.85083	0.85314	0.85543	0.85769	0.85993	0.86214
1.1	0.86433	0.86650	0.86864	0.87076	0.87286	0.87493	0.87697	0.87900	0.88100	0.88297
1.2	0.88493	0.88686	0.88876	0.89065	0.89251	0.89435	0.89616	0.89795	0.89972	0.90147
1.3	0.90320	0.90490	0.90658	0.90824	0.90987	0.91149	0.91308	0.91465	0.91620	0.91773
1.4	0.91924	0.92073	0.92219	0.92364	0.92506	0.92647	0.92785	0.92921	0.93056	0.93188

1.5	0.93319	0.93447	0.93574	0.93699	0.93821	0.93942	0.94061	0.94179	0.94294	0.94408
1.6	0.94519	0.94629	0.94738	0.94844	0.94949	0.95052	0.95154	0.95253	0.95351	0.95448
1.7	0.95543	0.95636	0.95728	0.95818	0.95906	0.95993	0.96079	0.96163	0.96245	0.96327
1.8	0.96406	0.96484	0.96561	0.96637	0.96711	0.96784	0.96855	0.96925	0.96994	0.97061
1.9	0.97128	0.97193	0.97256	0.97319	0.97380	0.97440	0.97499	0.97557	0.97614	0.97670
2.0	0.97724	0.97778	0.97830	0.97881	0.97932	0.97981	0.98029	0.98077	0.98123	0.98168
2.1	0.98213	0.98256	0.98299	0.98341	0.98382	0.98421	0.98461	0.98499	0.98536	0.98573
2.2	0.98609	0.98644	0.98678	0.98712	0.98745	0.98777	0.98808	0.98839	0.98869	0.98898
2.3	0.98927	0.98955	0.98982	0.99009	0.99035	0.99061	0.99085	0.99110	0.99134	0.99157
2.4	0.99179	0.99202	0.99223	0.99244	0.99265	0.99285	0.99305	0.99324	0.99342	0.99361
2.5	0.99378	0.99396	0.99412	0.99429	0.99445	0.99461	0.99476	0.99491	0.99505	0.99519
2.6	0.99533	0.99547	0.99560	0.99572	0.99585	0.99597	0.99609	0.99620	0.99631	0.99642
2.7	0.99653	0.99663	0.99673	0.99683	0.99692	0.99701	0.99710	0.99719	0.99727	0.99736
2.8	0.99744	0.99752	0.99759	0.99766	0.99774	0.99781	0.99787	0.99794	0.99800	0.99807
2.9	0.99813	0.99818	0.99824	0.99830	0.99835	0.99840	0.99845	0.99850	0.99855	0.99860
3.0	0.99864	0.99869	0.99873	0.99877	0.99881	0.99885	0.99889	0.99892	0.99896	0.99899
3.1	0.99902	0.99906	0.99909	0.99912	0.99915	0.99918	0.99920	0.99923	0.99926	0.99928
3.2	0.99930	0.99933	0.99935	0.99937	0.99939	0.99941	0.99943	0.99945	0.99947	0.99949
3.3	0.99951	0.99952	0.99954	0.99956	0.99957	0.99959	0.99960	0.99962	0.99963	0.99964
3.4	0.99965	0.99967	0.99968	0.99969	0.99970	0.99971	0.99972	0.99973	0.99974	0.99975

APPENDIX **4**

Percentage Points of the Student t_m Distribution

Percentage Points of the t_m Distribution*†

m \ α	.25	.1	.05	.025	.01	.005
1	1.000	3.078	6.314	12.706	31.821	63.657
2	0.816	1.886	2.920	4.303	6.965	9.925
3	0.765	1.638	2.353	3.182	4.541	5.841
4	0.741	1.533	2.132	2.776	3.747	4.604
5	0.727	1.476	2.015	2.571	3.365	4.032
6	0.718	1.440	1.943	2.447	3.143	3.707
7	0.711	1.415	1.895	2.365	2.998	3.499
8	0.706	1.397	1.860	2.306	2.896	3.355
9	0.703	1.383	1.833	2.262	2.821	3.250
10	0.700	1.372	1.812	2.228	2.764	3.169
11	0.697	1.363	1.796	2.201	2.718	3.106
12	0.695	1.356	1.782	2.179	2.681	3.055
13	0.694	1.350	1.771	2.160	2.650	3.012
14	0.692	1.345	1.761	2.145	2.624	2.977
15	0.691	1.341	1.753	2.131	2.602	2.947
16	0.690	1.337	1.746	2.120	2.583	2.921
17	0.689	1.333	1.740	2.110	2.567	2.898
18	0.688	1.330	1.734	2.101	2.552	2.878
19	0.688	1.328	1.729	2.093	2.539	2.861
20	0.687	1.325	1.725	2.086	2.528	2.845
21	0.686	1.323	1.721	2.080	2.518	2.831
22	0.686	1.321	1.717	2.074	2.508	2.819
23	0.685	1.319	1.714	2.069	2.500	2.807
24	0.685	1.318	1.711	2.064	2.492	2.797

PERCENTAGE POINTS OF THE t_m DISTRIBUTION*†

$m \backslash \alpha$	.25	.1	.05	.025	.01	.005
25	0.684	1.316	1.708	2.060	2.485	2.787
26	0.684	1.315	1.706	2.056	2.479	2.779
27	0.684	1.314	1.703	2.052	2.473	2.771
28	0.683	1.313	1.701	2.048	2.467	2.763
29	0.683	1.311	1.699	2.045	2.462	2.756
30	0.683	1.310	1.697	2.042	2.457	2.750
40	0.681	1.303	1.684	2.021	2.423	2.704
60	0.679	1.296	1.671	2.000	2.390	2.660
120	0.677	1.289	1.658	1.980	2.358	2.617
∞	0.674	1.282	1.645	1.960	2.326	2.576

*From E. S. Pearson and H. O. Hartley (Eds.), *Biometrika Tables for Statisticians*, Vol. 1, 3rd ed. Cambridge University Press, 1968; reproduced by permission of the publishers.

That is, values of $t_{m;\,\alpha}$, where m equals degrees of freedom and

$$\int_{-\infty}^{t_{m;\,\alpha}} \frac{\Gamma[(m+1)/2]}{\sqrt{\pi m}\,\Gamma(m/2)}\left(1+\frac{t^2}{m}\right)^{-(m+1)/2} dt = 1-\alpha.$$

†Where necessary, interpolation should be carried out using the reciprocals of the degrees of freedom, and for this the function $120/m$ is convenient.

APPENDIX **5**

Percentage Points of the Chi-Square χ^2_m Distribution

Percentage Points of the χ^2_m Distribution*

m \ α	.995	.990	.975	.950	.050	.025	.010	.005
1	392704×10^{-10}	157088×10^{-9}	982069×10^{-9}	393214×10^{-8}	3.84146	5.02389	6.63490	7.87944
2	0.0100251	0.0201007	0.0506356	0.102587	5.99147	7.37776	9.21034	10.5966
3	0.0717212	0.114832	0.215795	0.351846	7.81473	9.34840	11.3449	12.8381
4	0.206990	0.297110	0.484419	0.710721	9.48773	11.1433	13.2767	14.8602
5	0.411740	0.554300	0.831211	1.145476	11.0705	12.8325	15.0863	16.7496
6	0.675727	0.872085	1.237347	1.63539	12.5916	14.4494	16.8119	18.5476
7	0.989265	1.239043	1.68987	2.16735	14.0671	16.0128	18.4753	20.2777
8	1.344419	1.646482	2.17973	2.73264	15.5073	17.5346	20.0902	21.9550
9	1.734926	2.087912	2.70039	3.32511	16.9190	19.0228	21.6660	23.5893
10	2.15585	2.55821	3.24697	3.94030	18.3070	20.4831	23.2093	25.1882
11	2.60321	3.05347	3.81575	4.57481	19.6751	21.9200	24.7250	26.7569
12	3.07382	3.57056	4.40379	5.22603	21.0261	23.3367	26.2170	28.2995
13	3.56503	4.10691	5.00874	5.89186	22.3621	24.7356	27.6883	29.8194
14	4.07468	4.66043	5.62872	6.57063	23.6848	26.1190	29.1413	31.3193
15	4.60094	5.22935	6.26214	7.26094	24.9958	27.4884	30.5779	32.8013
16	5.14224	5.81221	6.90766	7.96164	26.2962	28.8454	31.9999	34.2672
17	5.69724	6.40776	7.56418	8.67176	27.5871	30.1910	33.4087	35.7185
18	6.26481	7.01491	8.23075	9.39046	28.8693	31.5264	34.8053	37.1564
19	6.84398	7.63273	8.90655	10.1170	30.1435	32.8523	36.1908	38.5822
20	7.43386	8.26040	9.59083	10.8508	31.4104	34.1696	37.5662	39.9968
21	8.03366	8.89720	10.28293	11.5913	32.6705	35.4789	38.9321	41.4010

22	8.64272	9.54249	10.9823	12.3380	33.9244	36.7807	40.2894	42.7956
23	9.26042	10.19567	11.6885	13.0905	35.1725	38.0757	41.6384	44.1813
24	9.88623	10.8564	12.4011	13.8484	36.4151	39.3641	42.9798	45.5585
25	10.5197	11.5240	13.1197	14.6114	37.6525	40.6465	44.3141	46.9278
26	11.1603	12.1981	13.8439	15.3791	38.8852	41.9232	45.6417	48.2899
27	11.8076	12.8786	14.5733	16.1513	40.1133	43.1944	46.9630	49.6449
28	12.4613	13.5648	15.3079	16.9279	41.3372	44.4607	48.2782	50.9933
29	13.1211	14.2565	16.0471	17.7083	42.5569	45.7222	49.5879	52.3356
30	13.7867	14.9535	16.7908	18.4926	43.7729	46.9792	50.8922	53.6720
40	20.7065	22.1643	24.4331	26.5093	55.7585	59.3417	63.6907	66.7659
50	27.9907	29.7067	32.3574	34.7642	67.5048	71.4202	76.1539	79.4900
60	35.5346	37.4848	40.4817	43.1879	79.0819	83.2976	88.3794	91.9517
70	43.2752	45.4418	48.7576	51.7393	90.5312	95.0231	100.425	104.215
80	51.1720	53.5400	57.1532	60.3915	101.879	106.629	112.329	116.321
90	59.1963	61.7541	65.6466	69.1260	113.145	118.136	124.116	128.299
100	67.3276	70.0648	74.2219	77.9295	124.342	129.561	135.807	140.169

*From E. S. Pearson and H. O. Hartley, (Eds.) *Biometrika Tables for Statisticians*, Vol. 1, 3rd ed., Cambridge University Press, 1968; reproduced by permission of the publishers.

That is, values of $\chi^2_{m;\,\alpha}$, where m represents degrees of freedom and

$$\int_0^{\chi^2_{m;\,\alpha}} \frac{1}{2\Gamma(m/2)} \left(\frac{\chi^2}{2}\right)^{(m/2)-1} e^{-\chi^2/2}\, d\chi^2 = 1 - \alpha.$$

For $m < 100$, linear interpolation is adequate. For $m > 100$, $\sqrt{2\chi^2_m}$ is approximately normally distributed with mean $\sqrt{2m-1}$ and unit variance, so that percentage points may be obtained from Appendix 5.

APPENDIX 6

Natural Logarithms

0.00	0.00000	-6.90775	-6.21461	-5.80914	-5.52146	-5.29832	-5.11600	-4.96185	-4.82831	-4.71053
0.01	-4.60517	-4.50986	-4.42285	-4.34281	-4.26870	-4.19971	-4.13517	-4.07454	-4.01738	-3.96332
0.02	-3.91202	-3.86323	-3.81671	-3.77226	-3.72970	-3.68888	-3.64966	-3.61192	-3.57555	-3.54046
0.03	-3.50656	-3.47377	-3.44202	-3.41125	-3.38140	-3.35241	-3.32424	-3.29684	-3.27017	-3.24419
0.04	-3.21888	-3.19418	-3.17009	-3.14656	-3.12357	-3.10109	-3.07911	-3.05761	-3.03656	-3.01594
0.05	-2.99573	-2.97593	-2.95651	-2.93746	-2.91877	-2.90042	-2.88240	-2.86471	-2.84731	-2.83022
0.06	-2.81341	-2.79688	-2.78062	-2.76462	-2.74887	-2.73337	-2.71810	-2.70306	-2.68825	-2.67365
0.07	-2.65926	-2.64508	-2.63109	-2.61730	-2.60369	-2.59027	-2.57703	-2.56395	-2.55105	-2.53831
0.08	-2.52573	-2.51331	-2.50104	-2.48892	-2.47694	-2.46511	-2.45341	-2.44185	-2.43042	-2.41912
0.09	-2.40795	-2.39690	-2.38597	-2.37516	-2.36447	-2.35388	-2.34341	-2.33305	-2.32279	-2.31264
0.10	-2.30259	-2.29264	-2.28279	-2.27303	-2.26337	-2.25380	-2.24432	-2.23493	-2.22563	-2.21641
0.11	-2.20728	-2.19823	-2.18926	-2.18037	-2.17156	-2.16283	-2.15417	-2.14559	-2.13708	-2.12864
0.12	-2.12027	-2.11197	-2.10374	-2.09558	-2.08748	-2.07945	-2.07148	-2.06358	-2.05573	-2.04795
0.13	-2.04023	-2.03257	-2.02496	-2.01741	-2.00992	-2.00249	-1.99511	-1.98778	-1.98051	-1.97329
0.14	-1.96612	-1.95900	-1.95194	-1.94492	-1.93795	-1.93103	-1.92416	-1.91733	-1.91055	-1.90382
0.15	-1.89713	-1.89048	-1.88388	-1.87733	-1.87081	-1.86434	-1.85791	-1.85152	-1.84517	-1.83886
0.16	-1.83259	-1.82636	-1.82017	-1.81401	-1.80790	-1.80182	-1.79578	-1.78977	-1.78380	-1.77787
0.17	-1.77197	-1.76610	-1.76027	-1.75447	-1.74871	-1.74298	-1.73728	-1.73161	-1.72598	-1.72038
0.18	-1.71481	-1.70927	-1.70376	-1.69828	-1.69283	-1.68741	-1.68202	-1.67666	-1.67132	-1.66602
0.19	-1.66074	-1.65549	-1.65027	-1.64507	-1.63991	-1.63476	-1.62965	-1.62456	-1.61950	-1.61446
0.20	-1.60945	-1.60446	-1.59950	-1.59456	-1.58964	-1.58475	-1.57989	-1.57505	-1.57023	-1.56543
0.21	-1.56066	-1.55591	-1.55118	-1.54647	-1.54179	-1.53713	-1.53249	-1.52787	-1.52327	-1.51869
0.22	-1.51414	-1.50960	-1.50509	-1.50059	-1.49612	-1.49166	-1.48723	-1.48281	-1.47842	-1.47404
0.23	-1.46969	-1.46535	-1.46103	-1.45673	-1.45244	-1.44818	-1.44393	-1.43970	-1.43549	-1.43130
0.24	-1.42713	-1.42297	-1.41883	-1.41470	-1.41060	-1.40651	-1.40243	-1.39838	-1.39434	-1.39031
0.25	-1.38630	-1.38231	-1.37834	-1.37438	-1.37043	-1.36650	-1.36259	-1.35869	-1.35481	-1.35094
0.26	-1.34708	-1.34324	-1.33942	-1.33561	-1.33182	-1.32804	-1.32427	-1.32052	-1.31678	-1.31305
0.27	-1.30934	-1.30565	-1.30196	-1.29829	-1.29464	-1.29099	-1.28736	-1.28375	-1.28014	-1.27655
0.28	-1.27298	-1.26941	-1.26586	-1.26232	-1.25879	-1.25528	-1.25177	-1.24828	-1.24481	-1.24134
0.29	-1.23788	-1.23444	-1.23101	-1.22759	-1.22419	-1.22079	-1.21741	-1.21403	-1.21067	-1.20732

0.30	-1.20398	-1.20065	-1.19734	-1.19403	-1.19074	-1.18745	-1.18418	-1.18092	-1.17767	-1.17442
0.31	-1.17119	-1.16797	-1.16476	-1.16156	-1.15837	-1.15519	-1.15202	-1.14886	-1.14571	-1.14257
0.32	-1.13944	-1.13632	-1.13321	-1.13011	-1.12702	-1.12394	-1.12087	-1.11781	-1.11475	-1.11171
0.33	-1.10867	-1.10565	-1.10263	-1.09962	-1.09662	-1.09364	-1.09065	-1.08768	-1.08472	-1.08177
0.34	-1.07882	-1.07588	-1.07296	-1.07003	-1.06712	-1.06422	-1.06133	-1.05844	-1.05556	-1.05269
0.35	-1.04983	-1.04698	-1.04414	-1.04130	-1.03847	-1.03565	-1.03284	-1.03003	-1.02723	-1.02444
0.36	-1.02166	-1.01889	-1.01612	-1.01336	-1.01061	-1.00787	-1.00513	-1.00240	-0.99968	-0.99697
0.37	-0.99426	-0.99156	-0.98887	-0.98619	-0.98351	-0.98084	-0.97818	-0.97552	-0.97287	-0.97023
0.38	-0.96760	-0.96497	-0.96235	-0.95973	-0.95712	-0.95452	-0.95193	-0.94934	-0.94676	-0.94419
0.39	-0.94162	-0.93906	-0.93650	-0.93396	-0.93142	-0.92888	-0.92635	-0.92383	-0.92131	-0.91881
0.40	-0.91630	-0.91381	-0.91131	-0.90883	-0.90635	-0.90388	-0.90141	-0.89895	-0.89650	-0.89405
0.41	-0.89161	-0.88917	-0.88674	-0.88432	-0.88190	-0.87949	-0.87708	-0.87468	-0.87229	-0.86990
0.42	-0.86751	-0.86513	-0.86276	-0.86039	-0.85803	-0.85568	-0.85333	-0.85098	-0.84864	-0.84631
0.43	-0.84398	-0.84166	-0.83934	-0.83703	-0.83472	-0.83242	-0.83012	-0.82783	-0.82555	-0.82327
0.44	-0.82099	-0.81872	-0.81646	-0.81420	-0.81194	-0.80969	-0.80745	-0.80521	-0.80297	-0.80074
0.45	-0.79852	-0.79630	-0.79408	-0.79187	-0.78967	-0.78747	-0.78527	-0.78308	-0.78090	-0.77872
0.46	-0.77654	-0.77437	-0.77220	-0.77004	-0.76788	-0.76573	-0.76358	-0.76144	-0.75930	-0.75716
0.47	-0.75503	-0.75291	-0.75079	-0.74867	-0.74656	-0.74445	-0.74235	-0.74025	-0.73816	-0.73607
0.48	-0.73398	-0.73190	-0.72982	-0.72775	-0.72568	-0.72362	-0.72156	-0.71950	-0.71745	-0.71540
0.49	-0.71336	-0.71132	-0.70929	-0.70726	-0.70523	-0.70321	-0.70119	-0.69918	-0.69717	-0.69516
0.50	-0.69316	-0.69116	-0.68917	-0.68718	-0.68519	-0.68321	-0.68123	-0.67926	-0.67729	-0.67532
0.51	-0.67336	-0.67140	-0.66944	-0.66749	-0.66554	-0.66360	-0.66166	-0.65972	-0.65779	-0.65586
0.52	-0.65394	-0.65202	-0.65010	-0.64819	-0.64628	-0.64437	-0.64247	-0.64057	-0.63867	-0.63678
0.53	-0.63489	-0.63300	-0.63112	-0.62925	-0.62737	-0.62550	-0.62363	-0.62177	-0.61991	-0.61805
0.54	-0.61620	-0.61435	-0.61250	-0.61066	-0.60882	-0.60698	-0.60515	-0.60332	-0.60149	-0.59967
0.55	-0.59785	-0.59603	-0.59422	-0.59241	-0.59060	-0.58880	-0.58700	-0.58520	-0.58341	-0.58162
0.56	-0.57983	-0.57805	-0.57627	-0.57449	-0.57271	-0.57094	-0.56917	-0.56741	-0.56565	-0.56389
0.57	-0.56213	-0.56038	-0.55863	-0.55688	-0.55514	-0.55340	-0.55166	-0.54992	-0.54819	-0.54646
0.58	-0.54474	-0.54302	-0.54130	-0.53958	-0.53787	-0.53616	-0.53445	-0.53274	-0.53104	-0.52934
0.59	-0.52764	-0.52595	-0.52426	-0.52257	-0.52089	-0.51921	-0.51753	-0.51585	-0.51418	-0.51251

0.60	-0.51084	-0.50917	-0.50751	-0.50585	-0.50419	-0.50254	-0.50089	-0.49924	-0.49759	-0.49595
0.61	-0.49431	-0.49267	-0.49103	-0.48940	-0.48777	-0.48614	-0.48452	-0.48290	-0.48128	-0.47966
0.62	-0.47805	-0.47644	-0.47483	-0.47322	-0.47162	-0.47002	-0.46842	-0.46682	-0.46523	-0.46364
0.63	-0.46205	-0.46046	-0.45888	-0.45730	-0.45572	-0.45414	-0.45257	-0.45100	-0.44943	-0.44786
0.64	-0.44630	-0.44474	-0.44318	-0.44162	-0.44007	-0.43852	-0.43697	-0.43542	-0.43388	-0.43233
0.65	-0.43079	-0.42926	-0.42772	-0.42619	-0.42466	-0.42313	-0.42161	-0.42008	-0.41856	-0.41704
0.66	-0.41553	-0.41401	-0.41250	-0.41099	-0.40948	-0.40798	-0.40648	-0.40498	-0.40348	-0.40198
0.67	-0.40049	-0.39900	-0.39751	-0.39602	-0.39454	-0.39305	-0.39157	-0.39010	-0.38862	-0.38715
0.68	-0.38567	-0.38420	-0.38274	-0.38127	-0.37981	-0.37835	-0.37689	-0.37543	-0.37398	-0.37253
0.69	-0.37108	-0.36963	-0.36818	-0.36674	-0.36530	-0.36386	-0.36242	-0.36098	-0.35955	-0.35812
0.70	-0.35669	-0.35526	-0.35383	-0.35241	-0.35099	-0.34957	-0.34815	-0.34674	-0.34532	-0.34391
0.71	-0.34250	-0.34109	-0.33969	-0.33829	-0.33688	-0.33548	-0.33409	-0.33269	-0.33130	-0.32991
0.72	-0.32852	-0.32713	-0.32574	-0.32436	-0.32298	-0.32160	-0.32022	-0.31884	-0.31747	-0.31609
0.73	-0.31472	-0.31335	-0.31199	-0.31062	-0.30926	-0.30790	-0.30654	-0.30518	-0.30382	-0.30247
0.74	-0.30112	-0.29977	-0.29842	-0.29707	-0.29573	-0.29438	-0.29304	-0.29170	-0.29036	-0.28903
0.75	-0.28769	-0.28636	-0.28503	-0.28370	-0.28237	-0.28105	-0.27973	-0.27840	-0.27708	-0.27577
0.76	-0.27445	-0.27313	-0.27182	-0.27051	-0.26920	-0.26789	-0.26659	-0.26528	-0.26398	-0.26268
0.77	-0.26138	-0.26008	-0.25878	-0.25749	-0.25620	-0.25490	-0.25361	-0.25233	-0.25104	-0.24976
0.78	-0.24847	-0.24719	-0.24591	-0.24463	-0.24336	-0.24208	-0.24081	-0.23954	-0.23827	-0.23700
0.79	-0.23573	-0.23447	-0.23321	-0.23194	-0.23068	-0.22943	-0.22817	-0.22691	-0.22566	-0.22441
0.80	-0.22316	-0.22191	-0.22066	-0.21941	-0.21817	-0.21693	-0.21568	-0.21444	-0.21321	-0.21197
0.81	-0.21073	-0.20950	-0.20827	-0.20704	-0.20581	-0.20458	-0.20335	-0.20213	-0.20090	-0.19968
0.82	-0.19846	-0.19724	-0.19603	-0.19481	-0.19360	-0.19238	-0.19117	-0.18996	-0.18875	-0.18755
0.83	-0.18634	-0.18514	-0.18393	-0.18273	-0.18153	-0.18034	-0.17914	-0.17794	-0.17675	-0.17556
0.84	-0.17437	-0.17318	-0.17199	-0.17080	-0.16961	-0.16843	-0.16725	-0.16607	-0.16489	-0.16371
0.85	-0.16253	-0.16136	-0.16018	-0.15901	-0.15784	-0.15667	-0.15550	-0.15433	-0.15316	-0.15200
0.86	-0.15083	-0.14967	-0.14851	-0.14735	-0.14619	-0.14504	-0.14388	-0.14273	-0.14158	-0.14042
0.87	-0.13927	-0.13813	-0.13698	-0.13583	-0.13469	-0.13354	-0.13240	-0.13126	-0.13012	-0.12898
0.88	-0.12785	-0.12671	-0.12558	-0.12444	-0.12331	-0.12218	-0.12105	-0.11992	-0.11880	-0.11767
0.89	-0.11655	-0.11542	-0.11430	-0.11318	-0.11206	-0.11094	-0.10983	-0.10871	-0.10760	-0.10648

0.90	-0.10537	-0.10426	-0.10315	-0.10204	-0.10094	-0.09983	-0.09873	-0.09762	-0.09652	-0.09542
0.91	-0.09432	-0.09322	-0.09213	-0.09103	-0.08994	-0.08884	-0.08775	-0.08666	-0.08557	-0.08448
0.92	-0.08339	-0.08231	-0.08122	-0.08014	-0.07906	-0.07797	-0.07689	-0.07581	-0.07474	-0.07366
0.93	-0.07258	-0.07151	-0.07043	-0.06936	-0.06829	-0.06722	-0.06615	-0.06508	-0.06402	-0.06295
0.94	-0.06189	-0.06082	-0.05976	-0.05870	-0.05764	-0.05658	-0.05552	-0.05447	-0.05341	-0.05236
0.95	-0.05131	-0.05025	-0.04920	-0.04815	-0.04710	-0.04606	-0.04501	-0.04396	-0.04292	-0.04188
0.96	-0.04083	-0.03979	-0.03875	-0.03771	-0.03668	-0.03564	-0.03460	-0.03357	-0.03254	-0.03150
0.97	-0.03047	-0.02944	-0.02841	-0.02738	-0.02636	-0.02533	-0.02430	-0.02328	-0.02226	-0.02124
0.98	-0.02021	-0.01920	-0.01818	-0.01716	-0.01614	-0.01513	-0.01411	-0.01310	-0.01208	-0.01107
0.99	-0.01006	-0.00905	-0.00804	-0.00704	-0.00603	-0.00502	-0.00402	-0.00302	-0.00201	-0.00101
1.0	0.00000	0.00995	0.01980	0.02956	0.03922	0.04879	0.05826	0.06765	0.07696	0.08617
1.1	0.09530	0.10435	0.11332	0.12221	0.13102	0.13975	0.14841	0.15699	0.16550	0.17394
1.2	0.18231	0.19061	0.19884	0.20700	0.21510	0.22313	0.23110	0.23900	0.24684	0.25463
1.3	0.26235	0.27001	0.27761	0.28516	0.29265	0.30009	0.30747	0.31479	0.32206	0.32928
1.4	0.33645	0.34357	0.35064	0.35765	0.36462	0.37154	0.37841	0.38524	0.39202	0.39875
1.5	0.40544	0.41209	0.41869	0.42524	0.43176	0.43823	0.44466	0.45105	0.45740	0.46371
1.6	0.46998	0.47621	0.48240	0.48855	0.49467	0.50075	0.50679	0.51279	0.51876	0.52470
1.7	0.53060	0.53646	0.54229	0.54809	0.55385	0.55958	0.56528	0.57095	0.57658	0.58218
1.8	0.58775	0.59329	0.59880	0.60428	0.60973	0.61515	0.62054	0.62590	0.63124	0.63654
1.9	0.64182	0.64707	0.65229	0.65749	0.66265	0.66779	0.67291	0.67800	0.68306	0.68810
2.0	0.69311	0.69810	0.70306	0.70800	0.71291	0.71780	0.72267	0.72751	0.73233	0.73713
2.1	0.74190	0.74665	0.75138	0.75608	0.76077	0.76543	0.77007	0.77469	0.77929	0.78386
2.2	0.78842	0.79295	0.79747	0.80196	0.80644	0.81089	0.81532	0.81974	0.82413	0.82851
2.3	0.83287	0.83721	0.84153	0.84583	0.85011	0.85437	0.85862	0.86285	0.86706	0.87125
2.4	0.87543	0.87958	0.88372	0.88785	0.89196	0.89605	0.90012	0.90417	0.90822	0.91224
2.5	0.91625	0.92024	0.92422	0.92818	0.93212	0.93605	0.93996	0.94386	0.94774	0.95161
2.6	0.95547	0.95931	0.96313	0.96694	0.97073	0.97451	0.97828	0.98203	0.98577	0.98950
2.7	0.99321	0.99690	1.00059	1.00426	1.00791	1.01155	1.01518	1.01880	1.02240	1.02599
2.8	1.02957	1.03314	1.03669	1.04023	1.04376	1.04727	1.05077	1.05426	1.05774	1.06121
2.9	1.06466	1.06810	1.07154	1.07495	1.07836	1.08176	1.08514	1.08851	1.09188	1.09522

3.0	1.09856	1.10189	1.10521	1.10851	1.11181	1.11509	1.11837	1.12163	1.12488	1.12812
3.1	1.13135	1.13457	1.13778	1.14098	1.14417	1.14735	1.15052	1.15368	1.15683	1.15997
3.2	1.16310	1.16622	1.16933	1.17243	1.17552	1.17860	1.18168	1.18474	1.18779	1.19084
3.3	1.19387	1.19690	1.19991	1.20292	1.20592	1.20891	1.21189	1.21486	1.21782	1.22078
3.4	1.22372	1.22666	1.22959	1.23251	1.23542	1.23832	1.24122	1.24410	1.24698	1.24985
3.5	1.25271	1.25556	1.25841	1.26125	1.26407	1.26690	1.26971	1.27251	1.27531	1.27810
3.6	1.28088	1.28366	1.28642	1.28918	1.29193	1.29467	1.29741	1.30014	1.30286	1.30557
3.7	1.30828	1.31098	1.31367	1.31635	1.31903	1.32170	1.32437	1.32702	1.32967	1.33231
3.8	1.33495	1.33757	1.34020	1.34281	1.34542	1.34802	1.35061	1.35320	1.35578	1.35835
3.9	1.36092	1.36348	1.36604	1.36858	1.37113	1.37366	1.37619	1.37871	1.38123	1.38374
4.0	1.38624	1.38874	1.39123	1.39371	1.39619	1.39866	1.40113	1.40359	1.40604	1.40849
4.1	1.41093	1.41337	1.41580	1.41822	1.42064	1.42305	1.42546	1.42786	1.43026	1.43264
4.2	1.43503	1.43741	1.43978	1.44215	1.44451	1.44686	1.44921	1.45156	1.45390	1.45623
4.3	1.45856	1.46088	1.46320	1.46551	1.46782	1.47012	1.47242	1.47471	1.47699	1.47927
4.4	1.48155	1.48382	1.48608	1.48834	1.49060	1.49285	1.49509	1.49733	1.49957	1.50180
4.5	1.50402	1.50624	1.50846	1.51066	1.51287	1.51507	1.51727	1.51946	1.52164	1.52388
4.6	1.52600	1.52817	1.53034	1.53250	1.53466	1.53681	1.53896	1.54110	1.54324	1.54543
4.7	1.54751	1.54963	1.55175	1.55387	1.55598	1.55809	1.56019	1.56229	1.56438	1.56653
4.8	1.56856	1.57064	1.57272	1.57479	1.57686	1.57892	1.58098	1.58304	1.58509	1.58719
4.9	1.58918	1.59122	1.59325	1.59528	1.59731	1.59933	1.60135	1.60336	1.60537	1.60744
5.0	1.60938	1.61138	1.61337	1.61536	1.61735	1.61933	1.62131	1.62328	1.62525	1.62728
5.1	1.62918	1.63114	1.63310	1.63505	1.63699	1.63894	1.64088	1.64281	1.64475	1.64673
5.2	1.64860	1.65052	1.65244	1.65435	1.65626	1.65817	1.66007	1.66197	1.66387	1.66582
5.3	1.66765	1.66953	1.67141	1.67329	1.67517	1.67704	1.67890	1.68077	1.68263	1.68455
5.4	1.68634	1.68819	1.69004	1.69188	1.69372	1.69556	1.69739	1.69922	1.70105	1.70293
5.5	1.70469	1.70650	1.70832	1.71013	1.71194	1.71374	1.71554	1.71733	1.71913	1.72092
5.6	1.72271	1.72449	1.72627	1.72805	1.72982	1.73160	1.73336	1.73513	1.73689	1.73865
5.7	1.74041	1.74216	1.74391	1.74566	1.74740	1.74914	1.75088	1.75261	1.75434	1.75607
5.8	1.75780	1.75952	1.76124	1.76296	1.76467	1.76638	1.76809	1.76979	1.77150	1.77320
5.9	1.77489	1.77659	1.77828	1.77996	1.78165	1.78333	1.78501	1.78669	1.78836	1.79003

6.0	1.79170	1.79336	1.79503	1.79669	1.79834	1.80000	1.80165	1.80330	1.80494	1.80659
6.1	1.80823	1.80987	1.81150	1.81313	1.81476	1.81639	1.81802	1.81964	1.82126	1.82287
6.2	1.82449	1.82610	1.82771	1.82932	1.83092	1.83252	1.83412	1.83572	1.83731	1.83890
6.3	1.84049	1.84207	1.84366	1.84524	1.84682	1.84839	1.84997	1.85154	1.85311	1.85467
6.4	1.85624	1.85780	1.85936	1.86091	1.86247	1.86402	1.86557	1.86711	1.86866	1.87020
6.5	1.87174	1.87328	1.87481	1.87634	1.87788	1.87940	1.88093	1.88245	1.88397	1.88549
6.6	1.88701	1.88852	1.89003	1.89154	1.89305	1.89456	1.89606	1.89756	1.89906	1.90055
6.7	1.90205	1.90354	1.90503	1.90651	1.90800	1.90948	1.91096	1.91244	1.91391	1.91539
6.8	1.91686	1.91833	1.91980	1.92126	1.92273	1.92419	1.92564	1.92710	1.92856	1.93001
6.9	1.93146	1.93291	1.93435	1.93580	1.93724	1.93868	1.94012	1.94155	1.94299	1.94442
7.0	1.94585	1.94728	1.94870	1.95012	1.95155	1.95296	1.95438	1.95580	1.95721	1.95862
7.1	1.96003	1.96144	1.96284	1.96425	1.96565	1.96705	1.96845	1.96984	1.97124	1.97263
7.2	1.97402	1.97541	1.97679	1.97818	1.97956	1.98094	1.98232	1.98369	1.98507	1.98644
7.3	1.98781	1.98918	1.99055	1.99191	1.99328	1.99464	1.99600	1.99735	1.99871	2.00006
7.4	2.00142	2.00277	2.00412	2.00546	2.00681	2.00815	2.00949	2.01083	2.01217	2.01351
7.5	2.01484	2.01617	2.01750	2.01883	2.02016	2.02148	2.02281	2.02413	2.02545	2.02677
7.6	2.02808	2.02940	2.03071	2.03202	2.03333	2.03464	2.03595	2.03725	2.03856	2.03986
7.7	2.04116	2.04245	2.04375	2.04504	2.04634	2.04763	2.04892	2.05021	2.05149	2.05278
7.8	2.05406	2.05534	2.05662	2.05790	2.05918	2.06045	2.06172	2.06299	2.06426	2.06553
7.9	2.06680	2.06806	2.06933	2.07059	2.07185	2.07311	2.07437	2.07562	2.07687	2.07813
8.0	2.07938	2.08063	2.08187	2.08312	2.08436	2.08561	2.08685	2.08809	2.08933	2.09056
8.1	2.09180	2.09303	2.09427	2.09550	2.09673	2.09795	2.09918	2.10040	2.10163	2.10285
8.2	2.10407	2.10529	2.10651	2.10772	2.10894	2.11015	2.11136	2.11257	2.11378	2.11499
8.3	2.11619	2.11740	2.11860	2.11980	2.12100	2.12220	2.12339	2.12459	2.12578	2.12698
8.4	2.12817	2.12936	2.13055	2.13173	2.13292	2.13410	2.13528	2.13647	2.13765	2.13882
8.5	2.14000	2.14118	2.14235	2.14353	2.14470	2.14587	2.14704	2.14820	2.14937	2.15053
8.6	2.15170	2.15286	2.15402	2.15518	2.15634	2.15749	2.15865	2.15980	2.16096	2.16211
8.7	2.16326	2.16441	2.16556	2.16670	2.16785	2.16899	2.17013	2.17127	2.17241	2.17355
8.8	2.17469	2.17582	2.17696	2.17809	2.17922	2.18035	2.18148	2.18261	2.18374	2.18486
8.9	2.18599	2.18711	2.18823	2.18935	2.19047	2.19159	2.19271	2.19382	2.19493	2.19605

9.0	2.19716	2.19827	2.19938	2.20049	2.20159	2.20270	2.20380	2.20491	2.20601	2.20711
9.1	2.20821	2.20931	2.21040	2.21150	2.21259	2.21369	2.21478	2.21587	2.21696	2.21805
9.2	2.21914	2.22022	2.22131	2.22239	2.22348	2.22456	2.22564	2.22672	2.22780	2.22887
9.3	2.22995	2.23102	2.23210	2.23317	2.23424	2.23531	2.23638	2.23745	2.23851	2.23958
9.4	2.24064	2.24171	2.24277	2.24383	2.24489	2.24595	2.24701	2.24806	2.24912	2.25017
9.5	2.25123	2.25228	2.25333	2.25438	2.25543	2.25648	2.25752	2.25857	2.25961	2.26066
9.6	2.26170	2.26274	2.26378	2.26482	2.26586	2.26689	2.26793	2.26896	2.27000	2.27103
9.7	2.27206	2.27309	2.27412	2.27515	2.27618	2.27720	2.27823	2.27925	2.28027	2.28130
9.8	2.28232	2.28334	2.28436	2.28537	2.28639	2.28741	2.28842	2.28943	2.29045	2.29146
9.9	2.29247	2.29348	2.29449	2.29550	2.29650	2.29751	2.29851	2.29951	2.30052	2.30152
10.	2.30258	2.31253	2.32239	2.33214	2.34181	2.35137	2.36085	2.37024	2.37955	2.38876
11.	2.39789	2.40694	2.41591	2.42480	2.43361	2.44235	2.45100	2.45959	2.46810	2.47654
12.	2.48491	2.49320	2.50143	2.50960	2.51769	2.52573	2.53370	2.54160	2.54944	2.55723
13.	2.56495	2.57261	2.58021	2.58776	2.59525	2.60269	2.61007	2.61739	2.62467	2.63189
14.	2.63906	2.64617	2.65324	2.66026	2.66723	2.67415	2.68102	2.68785	2.69462	2.70136
15.	2.70805	2.71469	2.72129	2.72785	2.73436	2.74084	2.74727	2.75366	2.76001	2.76632
16.	2.77259	2.77882	2.78501	2.79116	2.79728	2.80336	2.80940	2.81540	2.82137	2.82731
17.	2.83321	2.83907	2.84490	2.85070	2.85646	2.86219	2.86789	2.87355	2.87919	2.88479
18.	2.89036	2.89590	2.90141	2.90689	2.91234	2.91776	2.92315	2.92851	2.93384	2.93915
19.	2.94442	2.94967	2.95489	2.96009	2.96525	2.97040	2.97551	2.98060	2.98566	2.99070
20.	2.99571	3.00070	3.00566	3.01060	3.01551	3.02040	3.02527	3.03011	3.03493	3.03973
21.	3.04450	3.04925	3.05398	3.05868	3.06337	3.06803	3.07267	3.07729	3.08188	3.08646
22.	3.09102	3.09555	3.10007	3.10456	3.10903	3.11349	3.11792	3.12234	3.12673	3.13111
23.	3.13546	3.13980	3.14412	3.14842	3.15271	3.15697	3.16122	3.16544	3.16965	3.17385
24.	3.17802	3.18218	3.18632	3.19044	3.19455	3.19864	3.20271	3.20677	3.21081	3.21483
25.	3.21884	3.22283	3.22681	3.23077	3.23471	3.23864	3.24256	3.24646	3.25034	3.25421
26.	3.25806	3.26190	3.26572	3.26953	3.27333	3.27711	3.28087	3.28463	3.28836	3.29209
27.	3.29580	3.29949	3.30318	3.30685	3.31050	3.31415	3.31778	3.32139	3.32500	3.32859
28.	3.33216	3.33573	3.33928	3.34282	3.34635	3.34986	3.35336	3.35686	3.36033	3.36380
29.	3.36725	3.37070	3.37413	3.37754	3.38095	3.38435	3.38773	3.39110	3.39446	3.39781

30.	3.40115	3.40448	3.40780	3.41110	3.41440	3.41768	3.42095	3.42422	3.42747	3.43071
31.	3.43394	3.43716	3.44037	3.44357	3.44676	3.44994	3.45311	3.45627	3.45942	3.46256
32.	3.46569	3.46881	3.47192	3.47502	3.47811	3.48119	3.48426	3.48733	3.49038	3.49342
33.	3.49646	3.49949	3.50250	3.50551	3.50851	3.51150	3.51448	3.51745	3.52041	3.52337
34.	3.52631	3.52925	3.53218	3.53510	3.53801	3.54091	3.54380	3.54669	3.54957	3.55244
35.	3.55530	3.55815	3.56100	3.56383	3.56666	3.56948	3.57229	3.57510	3.57790	3.58069
36.	3.58347	3.58624	3.58901	3.59177	3.59452	3.59726	3.60000	3.60272	3.60544	3.60816
37.	3.61086	3.61356	3.61626	3.61894	3.62162	3.62429	3.62695	3.62961	3.63225	3.63490
38.	3.63753	3.64016	3.64278	3.64540	3.64800	3.65060	3.65320	3.65578	3.65837	3.66094
39.	3.66351	3.66607	3.66862	3.67117	3.67371	3.67624	3.67877	3.68130	3.68381	3.68632
40.	3.68882	3.69132	3.69381	3.69629	3.69877	3.70125	3.70371	3.70617	3.70862	3.71107
41.	3.71352	3.71595	3.71838	3.72081	3.72322	3.72564	3.72804	3.73044	3.73284	3.73523
42.	3.73761	3.73999	3.74236	3.74473	3.74709	3.74945	3.75180	3.75414	3.75648	3.75881
43.	3.76114	3.76346	3.76578	3.76809	3.77040	3.77270	3.77500	3.77729	3.77957	3.78185
44.	3.78413	3.78640	3.78866	3.79093	3.79318	3.79543	3.79767	3.79991	3.80215	3.80438
45.	3.80660	3.80882	3.81104	3.81325	3.81545	3.81765	3.81985	3.82204	3.82422	3.82640
46.	3.82858	3.83075	3.83292	3.83508	3.83724	3.83939	3.84154	3.84368	3.84582	3.84796
47.	3.85009	3.85221	3.85433	3.85645	3.85856	3.86067	3.86277	3.86487	3.86696	3.86905
48.	3.87114	3.87322	3.87530	3.87737	3.87944	3.88150	3.88356	3.88562	3.88767	3.88971
49.	3.89176	3.89380	3.89583	3.89786	3.89989	3.90191	3.90393	3.90594	3.90795	3.90996
50.	3.91196	3.91396	3.91595	3.91794	3.91993	3.92191	3.92389	3.92586	3.92783	3.92980
51.	3.93176	3.93372	3.93568	3.93763	3.93957	3.94152	3.94346	3.94539	3.94733	3.94925
52.	3.95118	3.95310	3.95502	3.95693	3.95884	3.96075	3.96265	3.96455	3.96645	3.96834
53.	3.97023	3.97211	3.97399	3.97587	3.97775	3.97962	3.98148	3.98335	3.98521	3.98707
54.	3.98892	3.99077	3.99262	3.99446	3.99630	3.99813	3.99997	4.00180	4.00362	4.00545
55.	4.00727	4.00908	4.01090	4.01271	4.01451	4.01632	4.01812	4.01991	4.02171	4.02350
56.	4.02529	4.02707	4.02885	4.03063	4.03240	4.03417	4.03594	4.03771	4.03947	4.04123
57.	4.04298	4.04474	4.04649	4.04823	4.04998	4.05172	4.05346	4.05519	4.05692	4.05865
58.	4.06038	4.06210	4.06382	4.06553	4.06725	4.06896	4.07067	4.07237	4.07407	4.07577
59.	4.07747	4.07916	4.08085	4.08254	4.08423	4.08591	4.08759	4.08926	4.09094	4.09261

60.	4.09428	4.09594	4.09760	4.09926	4.10092	4.10258	4.10423	4.10588	4.10752	4.10916
61.	4.11081	4.11244	4.11408	4.11571	4.11734	4.11897	4.12059	4.12222	4.12383	4.12545
62.	4.12707	4.12868	4.13029	4.13189	4.13350	4.13510	4.13670	4.13829	4.13989	4.14148
63.	4.14307	4.14465	4.14623	4.14782	4.14939	4.15097	4.15254	4.15411	4.15568	4.15725
64.	4.15881	4.16037	4.16193	4.16349	4.16504	4.16660	4.16814	4.16969	4.17124	4.17278
65.	4.17432	4.17585	4.17739	4.17892	4.18045	4.18198	4.18351	4.18503	4.18655	4.18807
66.	4.18958	4.19110	4.19261	4.19412	4.19563	4.19713	4.19863	4.20013	4.20163	4.20313
67.	4.20462	4.20611	4.20760	4.20909	4.21057	4.21206	4.21354	4.21502	4.21649	4.21797
68.	4.21944	4.22091	4.22237	4.22384	4.22530	4.22676	4.22822	4.22968	4.23113	4.23258
69.	4.23404	4.23548	4.23693	4.23837	4.23982	4.24126	4.24269	4.24413	4.24556	4.24699
70.	4.24842	4.24985	4.25128	4.25270	4.25412	4.25554	4.25696	4.25837	4.25979	4.26120
71.	4.26261	4.26402	4.26542	4.26682	4.26823	4.26963	4.27102	4.27242	4.27381	4.27520
72.	4.27659	4.27798	4.27937	4.28075	4.28213	4.28351	4.28489	4.28627	4.28764	4.28902
73.	4.29039	4.29176	4.29312	4.29449	4.29585	4.29721	4.29857	4.29993	4.30129	4.30264
74.	4.30399	4.30534	4.30669	4.30804	4.30938	4.31073	4.31207	4.31341	4.31474	4.31608
75.	4.31742	4.31875	4.32008	4.32141	4.32273	4.32406	4.32538	4.32670	4.32802	4.32934
76.	4.33066	4.33197	4.33329	4.33460	4.33591	4.33722	4.33852	4.33983	4.34113	4.34243
77.	4.34373	4.34503	4.34633	4.34762	4.34891	4.35020	4.35149	4.35278	4.35407	4.35535
78.	4.35664	4.35792	4.35920	4.36047	4.36175	4.36302	4.36430	4.36557	4.36684	4.36811
79.	4.36937	4.37064	4.37190	4.37316	4.37442	4.37568	4.37694	4.37820	4.37945	4.38070

80.	4.38195	4.38320	4.38445	4.38570	4.38694	4.38818	4.38942	4.39066	4.39190	4.39314
81.	4.39437	4.39561	4.39684	4.39807	4.39930	4.40053	4.40175	4.40298	4.40420	4.40542
82.	4.40664	4.40786	4.40908	4.41030	4.41151	4.41272	4.41393	4.41514	4.41635	4.41756
83.	4.41877	4.41997	4.42117	4.42237	4.42357	4.42477	4.42597	4.42716	4.42836	4.42955
84.	4.43074	4.43193	4.43312	4.43431	4.43549	4.43668	4.43786	4.43904	4.44022	4.44140
85.	4.44258	4.44375	4.44493	4.44610	4.44727	4.44844	4.44961	4.45078	4.45194	4.45311
86.	4.45427	4.45543	4.45659	4.45775	4.45891	4.46007	4.46122	4.46238	4.46353	4.46468
87.	4.46583	4.46698	4.46813	4.46927	4.47042	4.47156	4.47270	4.47385	4.47499	4.47612
88.	4.47726	4.47840	4.47953	4.48066	4.48180	4.48293	4.48406	4.48518	4.48631	4.48744
89.	4.48856	4.48968	4.49080	4.49193	4.49304	4.49416	4.49528	4.49640	4.49751	4.49862
90.	4.49973	4.50084	4.50195	4.50306	4.50417	4.50527	4.50638	4.50748	4.50858	4.50968
91.	4.51078	4.51188	4.51298	4.51407	4.51517	4.51626	4.51735	4.51845	4.51954	4.52062
92.	4.52171	4.52280	4.52388	4.52497	4.52605	4.52713	4.52821	4.52929	4.53037	4.53145
93.	4.53252	4.53360	4.53467	4.53574	4.53681	4.53788	4.53895	4.54002	4.54109	4.54215
94.	4.54322	4.54428	4.54534	4.54640	4.54746	4.54852	4.54958	4.55064	4.55169	4.55275
95.	4.55380	4.55485	4.55590	4.55695	4.55800	4.55905	4.56010	4.56114	4.56219	4.56323
96.	4.56427	4.56531	4.56635	4.56739	4.56843	4.56947	4.57050	4.57154	4.57257	4.57360
97.	4.57463	4.57566	4.57669	4.57772	4.57875	4.57977	4.58080	4.58182	4.58285	4.58387
98.	4.58489	4.58591	4.58693	4.58795	4.58896	4.58998	4.59099	4.59201	4.59302	4.59403
99.	4.59504	4.59605	4.59706	4.59807	4.59907	4.60008	4.60108	4.60209	4.60309	4.60409

APPENDIX 7

Exponential Function Values

0.0	1.00000	0.99005	0.98020	0.97045	0.96079	0.95123	0.94176	0.93239	0.92312	0.91393
0.1	0.90484	0.89583	0.88692	0.87810	0.86936	0.86071	0.85214	0.84366	0.83527	0.82696
0.2	0.81873	0.81058	0.80252	0.79453	0.78663	0.77880	0.77105	0.76338	0.75578	0.74826
0.3	0.74082	0.73345	0.72615	0.71892	0.71177	0.70469	0.69768	0.69073	0.68386	0.67706
0.4	0.67032	0.66365	0.65705	0.65051	0.64404	0.63763	0.63128	0.62500	0.61878	0.61263
0.5	0.60653	0.60050	0.59452	0.58861	0.58275	0.57695	0.57121	0.56553	0.55990	0.55433
0.6	0.54881	0.54335	0.53794	0.53259	0.52729	0.52205	0.51685	0.51171	0.50662	0.50158
0.7	0.49659	0.49164	0.48675	0.48191	0.47711	0.47237	0.46767	0.46301	0.45841	0.45385
0.8	0.44933	0.44486	0.44043	0.43605	0.43171	0.42742	0.42316	0.41895	0.41478	0.41066
0.9	0.40657	0.40252	0.39852	0.39455	0.39063	0.38674	0.38289	0.37908	0.37531	0.37158
1.0	0.36788	0.36422	0.36060	0.35701	0.35346	0.34994	0.34646	0.34301	0.33960	0.33622
1.1	0.33287	0.32956	0.32628	0.32304	0.31982	0.31664	0.31349	0.31037	0.30728	0.30423
1.2	0.30120	0.29820	0.29524	0.29230	0.28939	0.28651	0.28366	0.28084	0.27804	0.27528
1.3	0.27254	0.26983	0.26714	0.26448	0.26185	0.25925	0.25667	0.25411	0.25159	0.24908
1.4	0.24660	0.24415	0.24172	0.23932	0.23694	0.23458	0.23224	0.22993	0.22765	0.22538
1.5	0.22314	0.22092	0.21872	0.21654	0.21439	0.21226	0.21014	0.20805	0.20598	0.20393
1.6	0.20191	0.19990	0.19791	0.19594	0.19399	0.19206	0.19015	0.18826	0.18638	0.18453
1.7	0.18269	0.18088	0.17908	0.17729	0.17553	0.17378	0.17205	0.17034	0.16865	0.16697
1.8	0.16531	0.16366	0.16204	0.16042	0.15883	0.15725	0.15568	0.15413	0.15260	0.15108
1.9	0.14958	0.14809	0.14662	0.14516	0.14371	0.14228	0.14087	0.13947	0.13808	0.13671
2.0	0.13535	0.13400	0.13267	0.13135	0.13004	0.12874	0.12746	0.12620	0.12494	0.12370
2.1	0.12247	0.12125	0.12004	0.11885	0.11766	0.11649	0.11533	0.11419	0.11305	0.11193
2.2	0.11081	0.10971	0.10862	0.10754	0.10647	0.10541	0.10436	0.10332	0.10229	0.10128
2.3	0.10027	0.09927	0.09828	0.09731	0.09634	0.09538	0.09443	0.09349	0.09256	0.09164
2.4	0.09073	0.08982	0.08893	0.08805	0.08717	0.08630	0.08544	0.08459	0.08375	0.08292
2.5	0.08209	0.08128	0.08047	0.07967	0.07888	0.07809	0.07731	0.07654	0.07578	0.07503
2.6	0.07428	0.07354	0.07281	0.07209	0.07137	0.07066	0.06996	0.06926	0.06857	0.06789
2.7	0.06721	0.06655	0.06588	0.06523	0.06458	0.06394	0.06330	0.06267	0.06205	0.06143
2.8	0.06082	0.06021	0.05961	0.05902	0.05843	0.05785	0.05728	0.05671	0.05614	0.05558
2.9	0.05503	0.05448	0.05394	0.05340	0.05287	0.05235	0.05183	0.05131	0.05080	0.05029

3.0	0.04979	0.04930	0.04881	0.04832	0.04784	0.04737	0.04689	0.04643	0.04597	0.04551
3.1	0.04506	0.04461	0.04416	0.04372	0.04329	0.04286	0.04243	0.04201	0.04159	0.04118
3.2	0.04077	0.04036	0.03996	0.03956	0.03917	0.03878	0.03839	0.03801	0.03763	0.03726
3.3	0.03689	0.03652	0.03616	0.03580	0.03544	0.03509	0.03474	0.03440	0.03405	0.03371
3.4	0.03338	0.03305	0.03272	0.03239	0.03207	0.03175	0.03144	0.03112	0.03081	0.03051
3.5	0.03020	0.02990	0.02960	0.02931	0.02902	0.02873	0.02844	0.02816	0.02788	0.02760
3.6	0.02733	0.02706	0.02679	0.02652	0.02626	0.02600	0.02574	0.02548	0.02523	0.02498
3.7	0.02473	0.02448	0.02424	0.02400	0.02376	0.02352	0.02329	0.02306	0.02283	0.02260
3.8	0.02238	0.02215	0.02193	0.02171	0.02150	0.02128	0.02107	0.02086	0.02066	0.02045
3.9	0.02025	0.02004	0.01985	0.01965	0.01945	0.01926	0.01907	0.01888	0.01869	0.01850
4.0	0.01832	0.01814	0.01796	0.01778	0.01760	0.01743	0.01725	0.01708	0.01691	0.01674
4.1	0.01658	0.01641	0.01625	0.01609	0.01593	0.01577	0.01561	0.01546	0.01530	0.01515
4.2	0.01500	0.01485	0.01470	0.01456	0.01441	0.01427	0.01413	0.01399	0.01385	0.01371
4.3	0.01357	0.01344	0.01330	0.01317	0.01304	0.01291	0.01278	0.01265	0.01253	0.01240
4.4	0.01228	0.01216	0.01204	0.01192	0.01180	0.01168	0.01157	0.01145	0.01134	0.01122
4.5	0.01111	0.01100	0.01089	0.01078	0.01068	0.01057	0.01046	0.01036	0.01026	0.01016
4.6	0.01005	0.00995	0.00986	0.00976	0.00966	0.00956	0.00947	0.00937	0.00928	0.00919
4.7	0.00910	0.00901	0.00892	0.00883	0.00874	0.00865	0.00857	0.00848	0.00840	0.00831
4.8	0.00823	0.00815	0.00807	0.00799	0.00791	0.00783	0.00775	0.00768	0.00760	0.00752
4.9	0.00745	0.00737	0.00730	0.00723	0.00716	0.00709	0.00701	0.00695	0.00688	0.00681
5.0	0.00674	0.00667	0.00661	0.00654	0.00648	0.00641	0.00635	0.00628	0.00622	0.00616
5.1	0.00610	0.00604	0.00598	0.00592	0.00586	0.00580	0.00574	0.00569	0.00563	0.00557
5.2	0.00552	0.00546	0.00541	0.00536	0.00530	0.00525	0.00520	0.00515	0.00509	0.00504
5.3	0.00499	0.00494	0.00489	0.00485	0.00480	0.00475	0.00470	0.00466	0.00461	0.00456
5.4	0.00452	0.00447	0.00443	0.00438	0.00434	0.00430	0.00425	0.00421	0.00417	0.00413
5.5	0.00409	0.00405	0.00401	0.00397	0.00393	0.00389	0.00385	0.00381	0.00377	0.00374
5.6	0.00370	0.00366	0.00363	0.00359	0.00355	0.00352	0.00348	0.00345	0.00341	0.00338
5.7	0.00335	0.00331	0.00328	0.00325	0.00322	0.00318	0.00315	0.00312	0.00309	0.00306
5.8	0.00303	0.00300	0.00297	0.00294	0.00291	0.00288	0.00285	0.00282	0.00280	0.00277
5.9	0.00274	0.00271	0.00269	0.00266	0.00263	0.00261	0.00258	0.00256	0.00253	0.00250

6.0	0.00248	0.00245	0.00243	0.00241	0.00238	0.00236	0.00234	0.00231	0.00229	0.00227
6.1	0.00224	0.00222	0.00220	0.00218	0.00216	0.00213	0.00211	0.00209	0.00207	0.00205
6.2	0.00203	0.00201	0.00199	0.00197	0.00195	0.00193	0.00191	0.00189	0.00187	0.00186
6.3	0.00184	0.00182	0.00180	0.00178	0.00176	0.00175	0.00173	0.00171	0.00170	0.00168
6.4	0.00166	0.00165	0.00163	0.00161	0.00160	0.00158	0.00157	0.00155	0.00153	0.00152
6.5	0.00150	0.00149	0.00147	0.00146	0.00145	0.00143	0.00142	0.00140	0.00139	0.00137
6.6	0.00136	0.00135	0.00133	0.00132	0.00131	0.00129	0.00128	0.00127	0.00126	0.00124
6.7	0.00123	0.00122	0.00121	0.00120	0.00118	0.00117	0.00116	0.00115	0.00114	0.00113
6.8	0.00111	0.00110	0.00109	0.00108	0.00107	0.00106	0.00105	0.00104	0.00103	0.00102
6.9	0.00101	0.00100	0.00099	0.00098	0.00097	0.00096	0.00095	0.00094	0.00093	0.00092
7.0	0.00091	0.00090	0.00089	0.00089	0.00088	0.00087	0.00086	0.00085	0.00084	0.00083
7.1	0.00083	0.00082	0.00081	0.00080	0.00079	0.00079	0.00078	0.00077	0.00076	0.00075
7.2	0.00075	0.00074	0.00073	0.00072	0.00072	0.00071	0.00070	0.00070	0.00069	0.00068
7.3	0.00068	0.00067	0.00066	0.00066	0.00065	0.00064	0.00064	0.00063	0.00062	0.00062
7.4	0.00061	0.00061	0.00060	0.00059	0.00059	0.00058	0.00058	0.00057	0.00056	0.00056
7.5	0.00055	0.00055	0.00054	0.00054	0.00053	0.00053	0.00052	0.00052	0.00051	0.00051
7.6	0.00050	0.00050	0.00049	0.00049	0.00048	0.00048	0.00047	0.00047	0.00046	0.00046
7.7	0.00045	0.00045	0.00044	0.00044	0.00044	0.00043	0.00043	0.00042	0.00042	0.00041
7.8	0.00041	0.00041	0.00040	0.00040	0.00039	0.00039	0.00039	0.00038	0.00038	0.00037
7.9	0.00037	0.00037	0.00036	0.00036	0.00036	0.00035	0.00035	0.00035	0.00034	0.00034
8.0	0.00034	0.00033	0.00033	0.00033	0.00032	0.00032	0.00032	0.00031	0.00031	0.00031
8.1	0.00030	0.00030	0.00030	0.00029	0.00029	0.00029	0.00029	0.00028	0.00028	0.00028
8.2	0.00027	0.00027	0.00027	0.00027	0.00026	0.00026	0.00026	0.00026	0.00025	0.00025
8.3	0.00025	0.00025	0.00024	0.00024	0.00024	0.00024	0.00023	0.00023	0.00023	0.00023
8.4	0.00022	0.00022	0.00022	0.00022	0.00022	0.00021	0.00021	0.00021	0.00021	0.00021
8.5	0.00020	0.00020	0.00020	0.00020	0.00020	0.00019	0.00019	0.00019	0.00019	0.00019
8.6	0.00018	0.00018	0.00018	0.00018	0.00018	0.00018	0.00017	0.00017	0.00017	0.00017
8.7	0.00017	0.00017	0.00016	0.00016	0.00016	0.00016	0.00016	0.00016	0.00015	0.00015
8.8	0.00015	0.00015	0.00015	0.00015	0.00014	0.00014	0.00014	0.00014	0.00014	0.00014
8.9	0.00014	0.00014	0.00013	0.00013	0.00013	0.00013	0.00013	0.00013	0.00013	0.00012

9.0	0.00012	0.00012	0.00012	0.00012	0.00012	0.00012	0.00012	0.00012	0.00011	0.00011
9.1	0.00011	0.00011	0.00011	0.00011	0.00011	0.00011	0.00011	0.00010	0.00010	0.00010
9.2	0.00010	0.00010	0.00010	0.00010	0.00010	0.00010	0.00010	0.00009	0.00009	0.00009
9.3	0.00009	0.00009	0.00009	0.00009	0.00009	0.00009	0.00009	0.00009	0.00008	0.00008
9.4	0.00008	0.00008	0.00008	0.00008	0.00008	0.00008	0.00008	0.00008	0.00008	0.00008
9.5	0.00007	0.00007	0.00007	0.00007	0.00007	0.00007	0.00007	0.00007	0.00007	0.00007
9.6	0.00007	0.00007	0.00007	0.00007	0.00007	0.00006	0.00006	0.00006	0.00006	0.00006
9.7	0.00006	0.00006	0.00006	0.00006	0.00006	0.00006	0.00006	0.00006	0.00006	0.00006
9.8	0.00006	0.00005	0.00005	0.00005	0.00005	0.00005	0.00005	0.00005	0.00005	0.00005
9.9	0.00005	0.00005	0.00005	0.00005	0.00005	0.00005	0.00005	0.00005	0.00005	0.00005
10.0	0.00005	0.00004	0.00004	0.00004	0.00004	0.00004	0.00004	0.00004	0.00004	0.00004
10.1	0.00004	0.00004	0.00004	0.00004	0.00004	0.00004	0.00004	0.00004	0.00004	0.00004
10.2	0.00004	0.00004	0.00004	0.00004	0.00004	0.00004	0.00004	0.00003	0.00003	0.00003
10.3	0.00003	0.00003	0.00003	0.00003	0.00003	0.00003	0.00003	0.00003	0.00003	0.00003
10.4	0.00003	0.00003	0.00003	0.00003	0.00003	0.00003	0.00003	0.00003	0.00003	0.00003
10.5	0.00003	0.00003	0.00003	0.00003	0.00003	0.00003	0.00003	0.00003	0.00003	0.00003
10.6	0.00002	0.00002	0.00002	0.00002	0.00002	0.00002	0.00002	0.00002	0.00002	0.00002
10.7	0.00002	0.00002	0.00002	0.00002	0.00002	0.00002	0.00002	0.00002	0.00002	0.00002
10.8	0.00002	0.00002	0.00002	0.00002	0.00002	0.00002	0.00002	0.00002	0.00002	0.00002
10.9	0.00002	0.00002	0.00002	0.00002	0.00002	0.00002	0.00002	0.00002	0.00002	0.00002
11.0	0.00002	0.00002	0.00002	0.00002	0.00002	0.00002	0.00002	0.00002	0.00002	0.00002
11.1	0.00002	0.00001	0.00001	0.00001	0.00001	0.00001	0.00001	0.00001	0.00001	0.00001
11.2	0.00001	0.00001	0.00001	0.00001	0.00001	0.00001	0.00001	0.00001	0.00001	0.00001
11.3	0.00001	0.00001	0.00001	0.00001	0.00001	0.00001	0.00001	0.00001	0.00001	0.00001
11.4	0.00001	0.00001	0.00001	0.00001	0.00001	0.00001	0.00001	0.00001	0.00001	0.00001
11.5	0.00001	0.00001	0.00001	0.00001	0.00001	0.00001	0.00001	0.00001	0.00001	0.00001
11.6	0.00001	0.00001	0.00001	0.00001	0.00001	0.00001	0.00001	0.00001	0.00001	0.00001
11.7	0.00001	0.00001	0.00001	0.00001	0.00001	0.00001	0.00001	0.00001	0.00001	0.00001
11.8	0.00001	0.00001	0.00001	0.00001	0.00001	0.00001	0.00001	0.00001	0.00001	0.00001
11.9	0.00001	0.00001	0.00001	0.00001	0.00001	0.00001	0.00001	0.00001	0.00001	0.00001

Name Index

Subject Index